CW00350708

STREE

Derbyshire

st published in 1995 by

hilip's, a division of
topus Publishing Group Ltd
4 Heron Quays, London E14 4JP

econd colour edition 2002
econd impression with revisions 2003

BN 0-540-08116-7 (pocket)

Philip's 2003

Ordnance Survey®

his product includes mapping data licensed
om Ordnance Survey® with the permission
f the Controller of Her Majesty's Stationery
ffice. © Crown copyright 2003. All rights
eserved. Licence number 100011710

Printed and bound in Spain
by Cayfosa-Quebecor

Contents

III **Key to map symbols**

IV **Key to map pages**

VI **Route planning**

VIII **Administrative and Postcode boundaries**

1 **Street maps** at 2½ inches to 1 mile

266 **Street maps of centres of Chesterfield and Derby** at 5 inches to 1 mile

268 **Town maps** of Mansfield, Nottingham, Stafford and Stoke-on-Trent

270 **Index** of towns and villages

271 **Index** of streets, hospitals, industrial estates, railway stations, schools, shopping centres, universities and places of interest

Digital Data

The exceptionally high-quality mapping found in this atlas is available as digital data in TIFF format, which is easily convertible to other bitmapped (raster) image formats.

The index is also available in digital form as a standard database table. It contains all the details found in the printed index together with the National Grid reference for the map square in which each entry is named.

For further information and to discuss your requirements, please contact Philip's on 020 7644 6932 or james.mann@philips-maps.co.uk

Key to map symbols

III

Motorway with junction number	
Primary route – dual/single carriageway	
A road – dual/single carriageway	
B road – dual/single carriageway	
Minor road – dual/single carriageway	
Other minor road – dual/single carriageway	
Road under construction	
Pedestrianised area	
Postcode boundaries	
County and unitary authority boundaries	
Railway, railway under construction	
Tramway, tramway under construction	
Miniature railway	
Rural track, private road or narrow road in urban area	
Gate or obstruction to traffic (restrictions may not apply at all times or to all vehicles)	
Path, bridleway, byway open to all traffic, road used as a public path	

The representation in this atlas of a road, track or path is no evidence of the existence of a right of way

Adjoining page indicators

The map area within the pink band is shown at a larger scale on the page indicated by the red block and arrow

Abbr	Full	Abbr	Full
Acad	**Academy**	Mkt	**Market**
Allot Gdns	**Allotments**	Meml	**Memorial**
Cemy	**Cemetery**	Mon	**Monument**
C Ctr	**Civic Centre**	Mus	**Museum**
CH	**Club House**	Obsy	**Observatory**
Coll	**College**	Pal	**Royal Palace**
Crem	**Crematorium**	PH	**Public House**
Ent	**Enterprise**	Recn Gd	**Recreation Ground**
Ex H	**Exhibition Hall**	Resr	**Reservoir**
Ind Est	**Industrial Estate**	Ret Pk	**Retail Park**
IRB Sta	**Inshore Rescue Boat Station**	Sch	**School**
		Sh Ctr	**Shopping Centre**
Inst	**Institute**	TH	**Town Hall/House**
Ct	**Law Court**	Trad Est	**Trading Estate**
L Ctr	**Leisure Centre**	Univ	**University**
LC	**Level Crossing**	Wks	**Works**
Liby	**Library**	YH	**Youth Hostel**

The small numbers around the edges of the maps identify the 1 kilometre National Grid lines ■ The dark grey border on the inside edge of some pages indicates that the mapping does not continue onto the adjacent page

Walsall	**Railway station**
(W)	**Private railway station**
West Bromwich Central	**Metro station**
	Tram stop
	Bus, coach station
	Ambulance station
	Coastguard station
	Fire station
	Police station
+	**Accident and Emergency entrance to hospital**
H	**Hospital**
+	**Place of worship**
i	**Information Centre** (open all year)
P	**Parking**
P&R	**Park and Ride**
PO	**Post Office**
Ӿ	**Camping site**
	Caravan site
	Golf course
	Picnic site
Prim Sch	**Important buildings, schools, colleges, universities and hospitals**
River Medway	**Water name**
	River, stream
	Lock, weir
	Water
	Tidal water
	Woods
	Houses
Church	**Non-Roman antiquity**
ROMAN FORT	**Roman antiquity**

The scale of the maps on the pages numbered in blue
3.92 cm to 1 km • 2½ inches to 1 mile • 1: 25344

```
0        ¼          ½              ¾         1 mile
0    250m    500m      750m    1 kilometre
```

The scale of the maps on pages numbered in red
7.84 cm to 1 km • 5 inches to 1 mile • 1: 12672

```
0          220 yards      440 yards      660 yards    ½ mile
0      125m      250m      375m    ½ kilometre
```

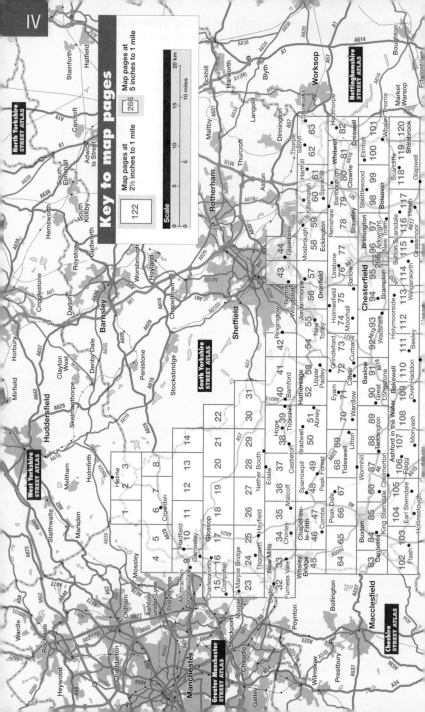

Route planning

Scale

0 1 2 3 4 5 6 7 8km

0 1 2 3 4 5 miles

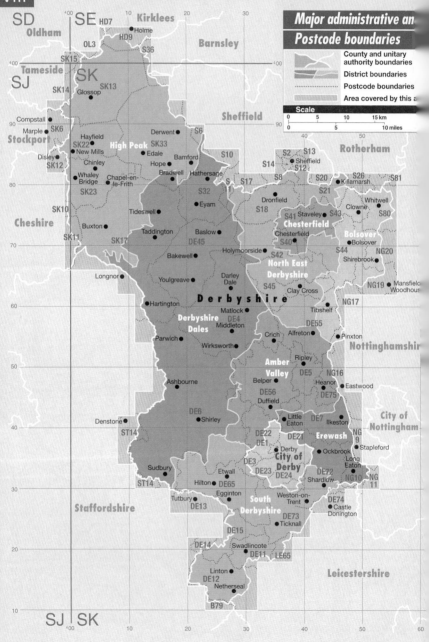

Major administrative an

Postcode boundaries

County and unitary authority boundaries
District boundaries
Postcode boundaries
Area covered by this a

Scale
0   5   10   15 km
0   5   10 miles

SD
Oldham
SE
HD7
Kirklees
Holme
Barnsley
OL3
HD9
S36
SK15
Tameside
SK14
SK
SK13
Sheffield
SJ
Glossop
Compstall
SK6
Marple
Stockport
Disley
SK12
Hayfield
SK22
New Mills
Chinley
Whaley
Bridge
SK23
Chapel-en-le-Frith
High Peak
SK33
Derwent
S6
Edale
Bamford
Hope
Bradwell
Hathersage
Rotherham
S2
S13
Sheffield
S14
S12
S20
S26
Killamarsh
S81
S8
S17
S21
S80
Whitwell
Clowne
SK10
Cheshire
Buxton
Tideswell
Taddington
SK11
SK17
Eyam
S32
S
1
S18
Dronfield
S41
Staveley
S43
Chesterfield
Chesterfield
S40
Bolsover
Bolsover
NG20
Baslow
DE45
Holymoorside
S42
North East
Derbyshire
Shirebrook
S44
Longnor
Bakewell
Youlgreave
Darley
Dale
S45
Clay Cross
NG19
Mansfield
Woodhous
Hartington
Derbyshire
Matlock
Tibshelf
NG17
Derbyshire
Dales
DE4
Middleton
DE55
Parwich
Wirksworth
Crich
Alfreton
Pinxton
Nottinghamshir
Ashbourne
Amber
Valley
Belper
Ripley
DE5
NG16
Heanor
DE75
Eastwood
Denstone
ST14
DE6
Shirley
DE56
Duffield
DE7
Ilkeston
City of
Nottingham
Little
Eaton
NG
9
Stapleford
DE22
DE1
DE21
Erewash
Sudbury
ST14
Etwall
DE3
Derby
City of
Derby
DE23
DE24
Ockbrook
DE72
Long
Eaton
NG10
NG
11
Hilton
DE65
Shardlow
Staffordshire
Tutbury
Egginton
DE13
Weston-on-Trent
South
Derbyshire
DE74
Castle
Donington
DE15
DE73
Ticknall
DE14
Swadlincote
DE11
LE65
Linton
DE12
Netherseal
Leicestershire
B79
SJ
SK

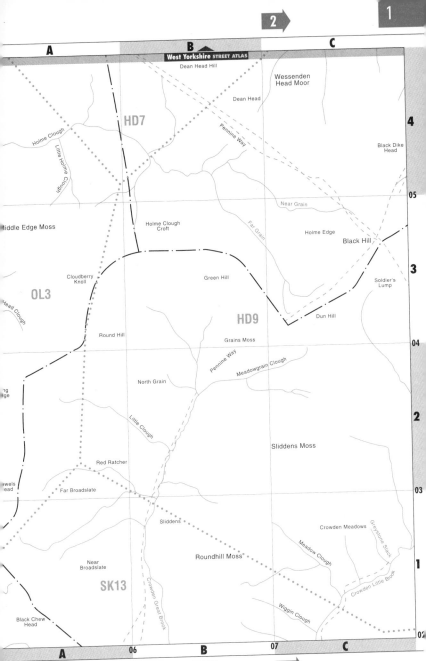

4

05

3

2

04

03

1

02

Dean Head Hill

Wessenden
Head Moor

HD7

Dean Head

Pennine Way

Black Dike
Head

Holme Clough

Little Holme Clough

Middle Edge Moss

Holme Clough
Croft

Near Grain

Far Grain

Holme Edge

Black Hill

Cloudberry
Knoll

OL3

Head Clough

Green Hill

Soldier's
Lump

HD9

Dun Hill

Round Hill

Grains Moss

Pennine Way

North Grain

Meadowgrain Clough

ng
ge

Little Clough

Sliddens Moss

Red Ratcher

awels
ead

Far Broadslate

Sliddens

Crowden Meadows

Greystone Slack

Meadow Clough

Near
Broadslate

Roundhill Moss

SK13

Crowden Great Brook

Crowden Little Brook

Black Chew
Head

Wiggin Clough

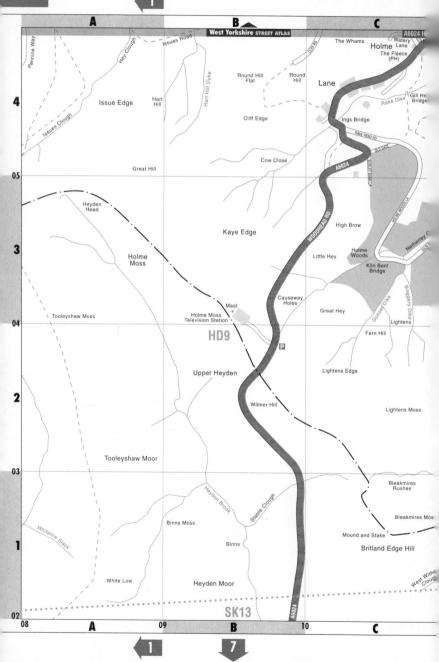

West Yorkshire STREET ATLAS

A   **B**   **C**

A6024 H

Pennine Way

Hey Clough

Issues Road

The Whams

Holme

Watery
Lane

The Fleece
(PH)

Issues Clough

Hart Hill

Hart Hill Dyke

Round Hill
Flat

Round
Hill

Lane

Gill He
Bridge

4

Issue Edge

Cliff Edge

Ings Bridge

Rake Dike

RAKE HEAD RD

OLD GATE

SHELLEY BANK LA

05

Great Hill

Cow Close

A6024

HOLME WOODS LA

Heyden
Head

Kaye Edge

High Brow

Netherley C

3

Holme
Moss

WOODHEAD RD

Little Hey

Holme
Woods

Kiln Bent
Bridge

Boggery Dike

Tooleyshaw Moss

Mast

Causeway
Holes

Great Hey

Gulsey Dike

Lightens

04

Holme Moss
Television Station

HD9

Fern Hill

P

Upper Heyden

Lightens Edge

Lightens Moss

2

Wilmer Hill

03

Tooleyshaw Moor

Heyden Brook

Stable Clough

Bleakmires
Rushes

Whitelow Slack

Binns Moss

Bleakmires Mos

Mound and Stake

1

Binns

Britland Edge Hill

White Low

Heyden Moor

West Wither
Clough

02

SK13

A6024

08   **A**   **09**   **B**   **10**   **C**

South Yorkshire STREET ATLAS

A   B   C

4

05

3

04

2

03

1

02

Brownhill Rear

Green House Lane

Moss Edge

Crow Hill

White Gate

Dobb Dike

WEATHER HILL LA

WEST GATE

Hollin Hill

Ramsden Rear

BROWNHILL LA

GREAT WHITE MOOR RD

RAMSDEN LA

Upper White Gate

Elysium

Kirklees Way

COPTHURST RD

Riding Wood Rear

Kirklees Way

HADES RD

COLDER HILL RD

WHITE CLOUGH RD

Copthurst Moor

Reynard Clough

Hades

Yateholme Cote

Crossley's Plantation

Ramsden Edge

Peat Pit Moss

Hades Green

Holme Valley Circular Walk

Lower Flat

Green House Hey Wood

Hades Peat Pits

HD9

Herbage Flat

The Rakes

Ruddle Clough Moss

Elbow End

Cook's Study Moss

LINSHAWS RD

Cook's Study Hill

Linshaws Scar

Herbage Edge

Ramsden Rocks

Ruddle Clough

Snailsden Resr

Herbage Hill

Ramsden Clough

Ruddle Clough Knoll

Upper Snailsden Moss

Little Twizle Clough

Lad Clough Knoll

Herbage Moss

Lad Clough

Reaps Moss

Reaps Dike

Snailsden Pike End

Snailsden Edge

Laund Moss

Great Twizle Hole

wizle

Head

Bailie Causeway Moss

Swiner Clough Top

Swiner Dike

Swiner Clough

S36

Don Well

Ford

Withens Clough

Swiner Clough Moss

Great Grains Clough

Great Grains

Grains Edge

River Don

Grains End

SK13

Grains Moss

Black Grough

Little Grain Clough

Dead Edge Flat

Withens Edge

A   12   B   13   C

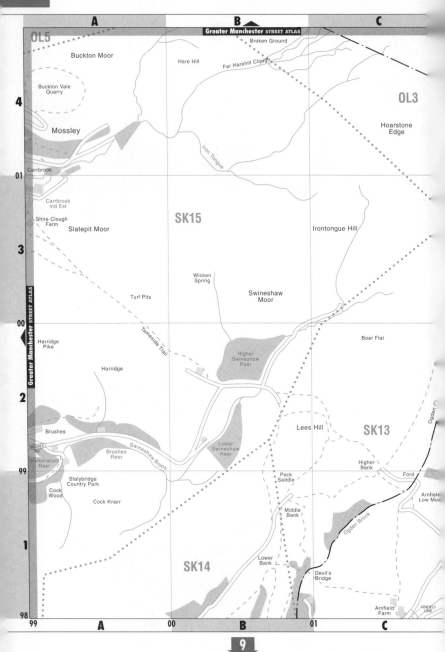

OL5

Buckton Moor

Hare Hill

Far Harehill Clough

Broken Ground

OL3

Buckton Vale
Quarry

4

Hoarstone
Edge

Mossley

Iron Tongue

Carrbrook

01

Carrbrook
Ind Est

SK15

Shire Clough
Farm

Slatepit Moor

Irontongue Hill

3

Wicken
Spring

Swineshaw
Moor

Turf Pits

00

Tameside Trail

Boar Flat

Harridge
Pike

Higher
Swineshaw
Resr

Harridge

2

Brushes

Lees Hill

SK13

BRUSHES
RD

Brushes
Resr

Swineshaw Brook

Lower
Swineshaw
Resr

Ogden Cl

Walkerwood
Resr

Higher
Bank

Ford

99

Pack
Saddle

Arnfield
Low Moor

Cock
Wood

Stalybridge
Country Park

Cock Knarr

Middle
Bank

Ogden Brook

1

Lower
Bank

Devil's
Bridge

SK14

Arnfield
Farm

ARNFIELD
LANE

98

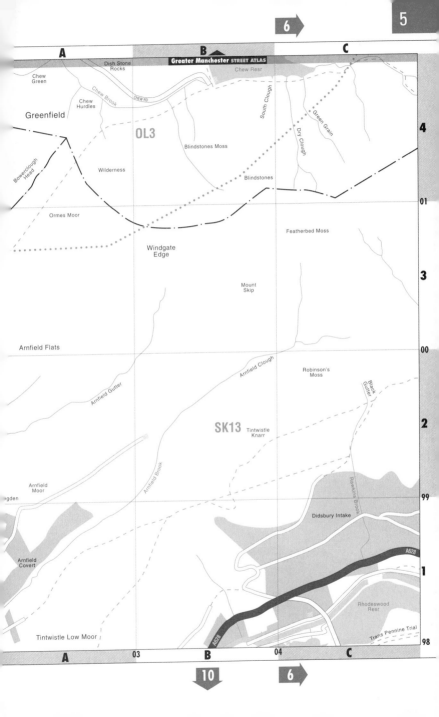

A
B
C

Chew
Green

Dish Stone
Rocks

Chew Resr

Chew Hurdles

CHEW RD

Chew Brook

South Clough

Green Grain

4

Greenfield

OL3

Blindstones Moss

Dry Clough

Bowerclough
Head

Wilderness

Blindstones

01

Ormes Moor

Windgate
Edge

Featherbed Moss

3

Mount
Skip

Arnfield Flats

00

Arnfield Clough

Robinson's
Moss

Black Gutter

Arnfield Gutter

SK13

Tintwistle
Knarr

2

Hawkins Brook

Arnfield Brook

Arnfield
Moor

gden

99

Didsbury Intake

A628

Arnfield
Covert

1

Rhodeswood
Resr

Tintwistle Low Moor

A628

Trans Pennine Trial

98

A
03
B
04
C

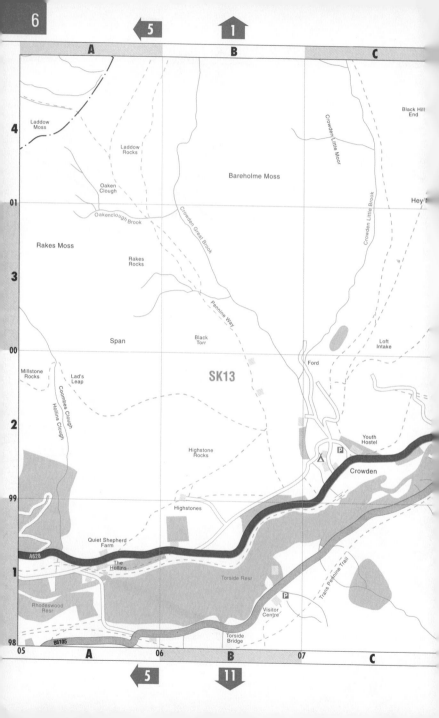

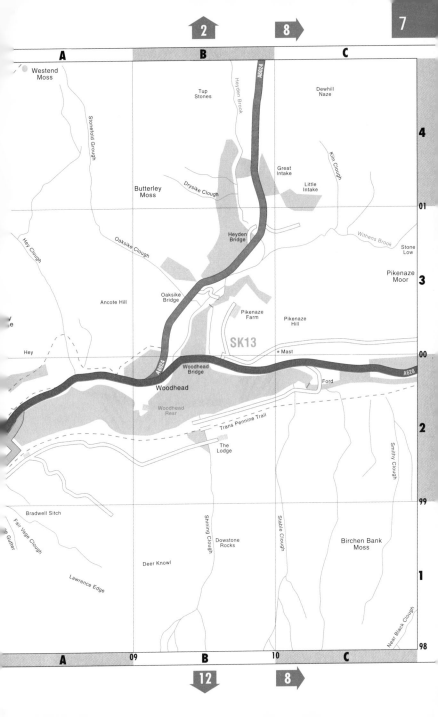

A   B   C

Westend
Moss

Stonefold Grough

Tup
Stones

Heyden Brook

A6024

Dewhill
Naze

4

Drysike Clough

Butterley
Moss

Great
Intake

Little
Intake

Kiln Clough

01

Oaksike Clough

Hey Clough

Heyden
Bridge

Withens Brook

Stone
Low

Pikenaze
Moor

3

Ancote Hill

Oaksike
Bridge

Pikenaze
Farm

Pikenaze
Hill

ve

Hey

SK13

• Mast

00

A6024

Woodhead
Bridge

Ford

A628

Woodhead

Woodhead
Resr

Trans Pennine Trail

2

The
Lodge

Smithy Clough

99

Bradwell Sitch

Fair Vage Clough

e Gutter

Shining Clough

Dowstone
Rocks

Stable Clough

Birchen Bank
Moss

1

Deer Knowl

Lawrence Edge

Near Black Clough

98

A   09   B   10   C

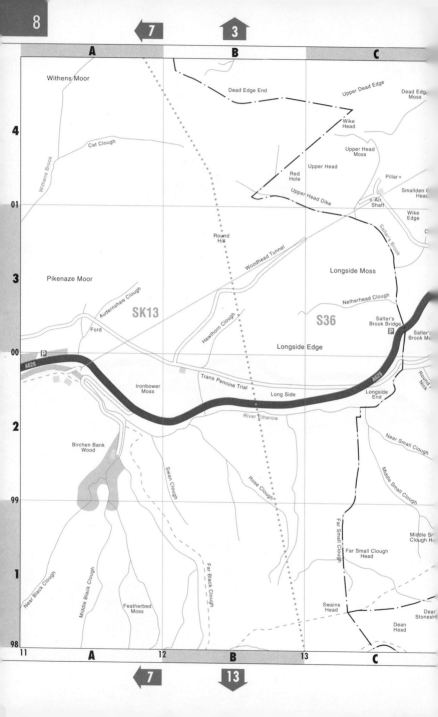

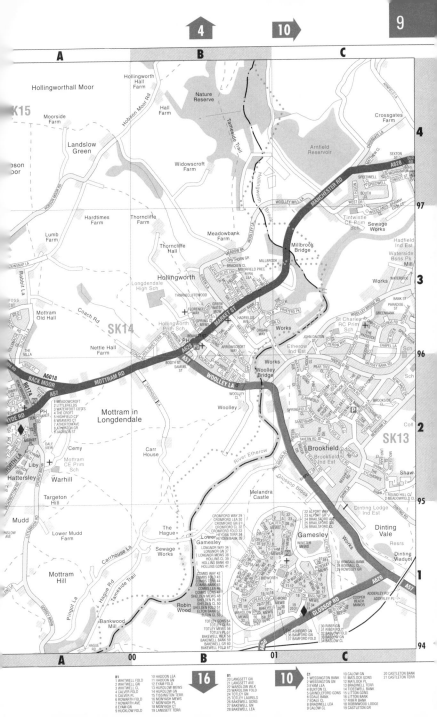

A   B   C

Reaps

Long Gutter Edge   White Mare

Bramah Edge   Torside Naze

4

Peaknaze Moor

Clough Edge   Toreside Clough

97

Pennine Way

Blackshaw Clough   Glossop Low   Torside Castle

3

Blake Moor   Cock Hill   Small Clough   Harrop Moss

96

SK13

Dog Rock

Blackemoor Plantation   Dowstone Clough   The Pike

2

Edge Plantation   Yellow Slacks   Ferny Hole

Shittern Clough   Lightside   Yellowslacks Brook   Wigan Clough

95

Shelf Benches

Mossy Lea Farm

-hire Hill   Resr   Lower Shelf   Little Clough

1

Wash Brow   Doctor's Gate
WOODCOCK RD   SNAKE PASS (S?)   Shelf Brook

Woodcock Farm

HURST RD

94

A   06   B   07   C

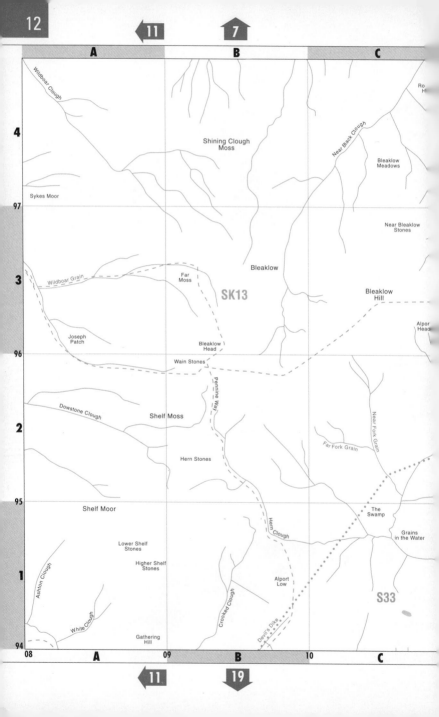

A　　　　B　　　　C

Wildboar Clough

Ro
H

4

Shining Clough
Moss

Near Back Clough

Bleaklow
Meadows

Sykes Moor

97

Near Bleaklow
Stones

Wildboar Grain

Far
Moss

3

SK13

Bleaklow

Bleaklow
Hill

Joseph
Patch

Bleaklow
Head

Alpor
Head

96

Wain Stones

Dowstone Clough

Shelf Moss

2

Pennine Way

Far Fork Grain

Near Fork Grain

Hern Stones

95

Shelf Moor

The
Swamp

Grains
in the Water

Lower Shelf
Stones

Hern Clough

Ashton Clough

Higher Shelf
Stones

1

Alport
Low

S33

White Clough

Crooked Clough

Devil's Dike

Gathering
Hill

08　　　　A　　　　09　　　　B　　　　10　　　　C

94

A B C

Middle Black Clough

Featherbed
Moss

4

White
Stones

Swains
Greave

S36

97

Barrow
Stones

Barrow Clough

SK13

Bleaklow
Stones

3

Grinah
Stones

Round
Hill

96

Westend
Head

Grinah Grain

2

The Ridge

Deep Grain

S33

Ridgewalk Moor

95

River Westend

1

Ravens Clough

Over Wood
Moss

94

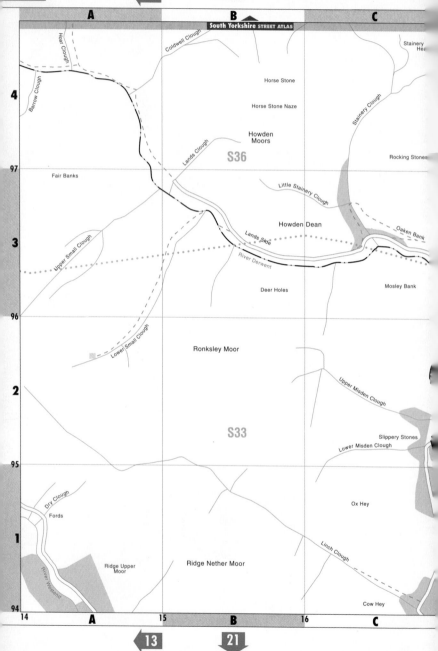

Hoar Clough

Coldwell Clough

Stainery Head

Barrow Clough

Horse Stone

4

Horse Stone Naze

Stainery Clough

Howden
Moors

Lands Clough

S36

Rocking Stones

97

Fair Banks

Little Stainery Clough

Howden Dean

Oaken Bank

Upper Small Clough

Lands Side

3

River Derwent

Mosley Bank

96

Lower Small Clough

Deer Holes

Ronksley Moor

Upper Misden Clough

2

S33

Slippery Stones

Lower Misden Clough

95

Dry Clough

Ox Hey

Fords

1

Linch Clough

River Westend

Ridge Upper
Moor

Ridge Nether Moor

Cow Hey

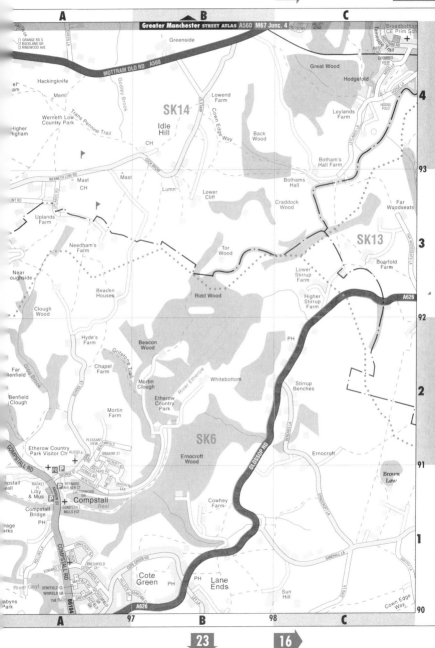

Greater Manchester STREET ATLAS A560 M67 Junc. 4

Broadbottom CE Prim Sch

1 GRANGE RD S
2 BUCKLAND GR
3 RINGWOOD AVE

Greenside

MOTTRAM OLD RD A560

Great Wood

Hodgfold

Hackingknife

Meml

Trans Pennine Trail

Werneth Low Country Park

Leylands Farm

Higher Higham

SK14

Idle Hill

CH

Lowend Farm

Cown Edge Way

Back Wood

Botham's Hall Farm

Bothams Hall

Mast CH

Mast

Lumn

Lower Cliff

Craddock Wood

SK13

Far Woodseats

Uplands Farm

Needham's Farm

Tor Wood

Lower Stirrup Farm

Boarfold Farm

Near oughside

Beacon Houses

Ridd Wood

Higher Stirrup Farm

A626

Clough Wood

Hyde's Farm

Beacon Wood

PH

Gritstone Trail

Chapel Farm

Mortin Clough

River Etherow

Whitebottom

Stirrup Benches

Far enfield

Benfield Clough

Mortin Farm

Etherow Country Park

SK6

Ernocroft Wood

Ernocroft

Etherow Country Park Visitor Ctr

Liby & Mus

Compstall

Compstall Bridge

PH

Cowhey Farm

Brown Low

GLOSSOP RD

Compstall Resr

Cote Green

PH

Lane Ends

Sun Hill

River Goyt

A626

Cown Edge Way

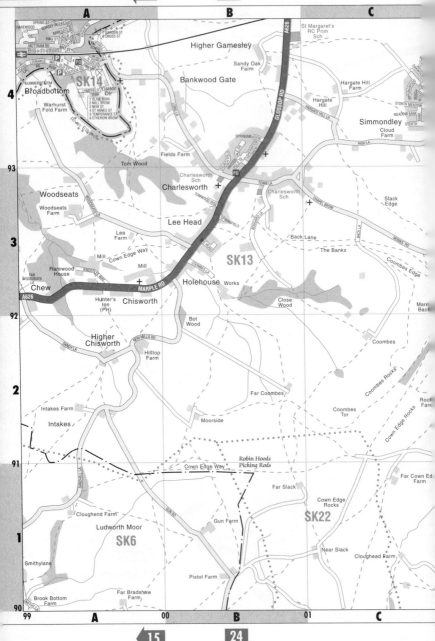

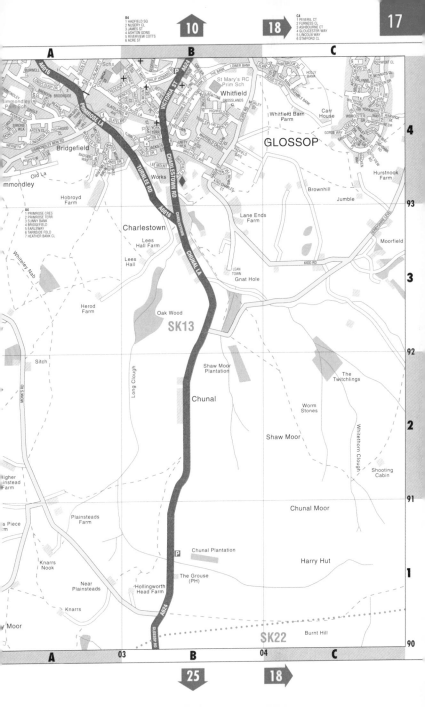

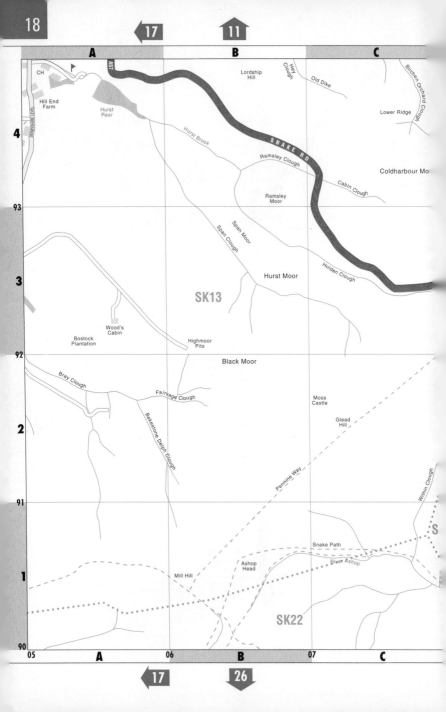

A

B

C

CH

Hill End
Farm

Hurst
Resr

Lordship
Hill

Hey
Clough

Old Dike

Birchen Orchard Clough

Lower Ridge

Hurst Brook

S N A K E   R D

Ramsley Clough

Cabin Clough

Coldharbour Mo

4

Ramsley
Moor

93

Span Moor

Span Clough

Holden Clough

3

Hurst Moor

SK13

Wood's
Cabin

Bostock
Plantation

Highmoor
Pits

92

Black Moor

Bray Clough

Fairvage Clough

Moss
Castle

Glead
Hill

2

Bakestone Delph Clough

Pennine Way

Within Clough

91

S

Snake Path

1

Mill Hill

Ashop
Head

River Ashop

SK22

90

05

A

06

B

07

C

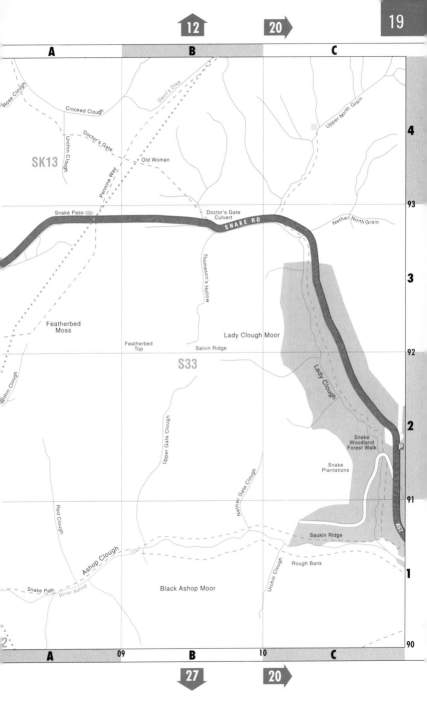

12
20

A   B   C

Rose Clough

Crooked Clough

Devil's Dike

Upper North Grain

Doctor's Gate

Urchin Clough

SK13

Pennine Way

Old Woman

4

Snake Pass

Doctor's Gate Culvert

93

SNAKE RD

Nether North Grain

Thomason's Hollow

3

Featherbed Moss

Lady Clough Moor

Featherbed Top

Salvin Ridge

92

Within Clough

S33

Lady Clough

Upper Gate Clough

2

Snake Woodland Forest Walk

P

Snake Plantations

91

Red Clough

Nether Gate Clough

A57

Saukin Ridge

Ashop Clough

Urchin Clough

Rough Bank

1

Snake Path

River Ashop

Black Ashop Moor

2

90

A   09   B   10   C

27
20

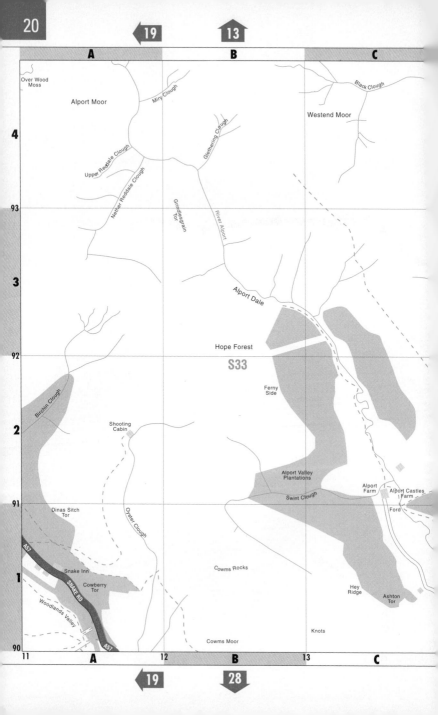

A   B   C

Over Wood Moss

Alport Moor

Miry Clough

Black Clough

Westend Moor

4

Upper Reddale Clough

Glethering Clough

Nether Reddale Clough

93

Grindlesgrain Tor

River Alport

3

Alport Dale

Hope Forest

S33

92

Ferny Side

Birchin Clough

2

Shooting Cabin

Alport Valley Plantations

Alport Farm

Alport Castles Farm

Swint Clough

Ford

91

Dinas Sitch Tor

Oyster Clough

A57

Snake Inn

SNAKE RD

Cowberry Tor

Cowms Rocks

Hey Ridge

Ashton Tor

1

Woodlands Valley

A57

Knots

90

Cowms Moor

11   A   12   B   13   C

A
B
C

Ridge Nether Moor

Upper Wood

Banktop Hey

Ronksley South Plantation

Ford

Ridge Clough

Nether Wood Plantation

4

River Westend

Ridge Wood

Banktop Plantation

Howden Resr

93

Fagney Plantation

Hern Side

West Cable Tip Plantation

Ditch Clough Plantation

Fox's Piece

Fagney Clough

Beaver's Croft

3

Ditch Clough

Green Clough

Chapel Plantation

Bank Clough

92

S33

Upper Derwent Valley

Birchinlee East Plantation

Derwent Resr

Birchinlee Pasture

Birchinlee

Calfhey Wood

2

Alport Castles

Little Moor

Cole Clough

...astles Wood

91

Ouzelden Clough

Gores Farm

...ucklow Lees Barn

Birchinlee New Piece

Gores Plantation

Whitefield Pits

Alport Grain

Gores Heights

1

Rowlee Pasture

Nabs Wood

90

A
15
B
16
C

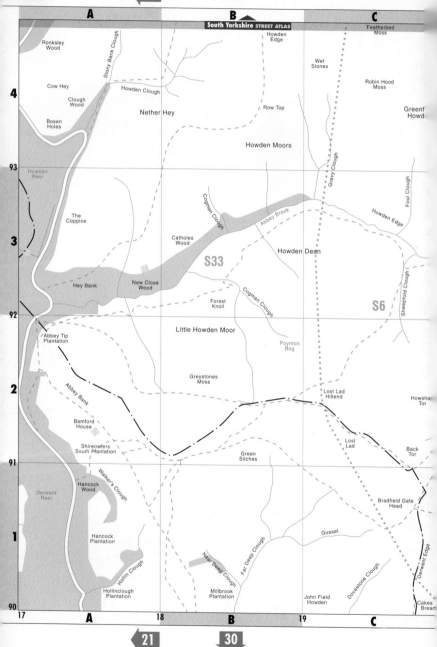

A

B

South Yorkshire STREET ATLAS

C

Ronksley
Wood

Stony Bank Clough

Featherbed
Moss

Howden
Edge

Wet
Stones

Cow Hey

Howden Clough

Robin Hood
Moss

Clough
Wood

4

Nether Hey

Row Top

Greenf
Howd

Bosen
Holes

Howden Moors

93

Gravy Clough

Foul Clough

Howden
Resr

Cogman Clough

Abbey Brook

Howden Edge

The
Coppice

Catholes
Wood

3

S33

Howden Dean

Sheepfold Clough

Hey Bank

New Close
Wood

Forest
Knoll

Cogman Clough

S6

92

Little Howden Moor

Poynton
Bog

Abbey Tip
Plantation

2

Abbey Bank

Greystones
Moss

Lost Lad
Hillend

Howsha
Tor

Bamford
House

Lost
Lad

Back
Tor

Shireowlers
South Plantation

91

Green
Sitches

Derwent
Resr

Walker's Clough

Hancock
Wood

Bradfield Gate
Head

1

Hancock
Plantation

Gusset

Derwent Edge

Hollin Clough

Near Deep Clough

Fat Deep Clough

Dovestone Clough

Hollinclough
Plantation

Millbrook
Plantation

John Field
Howden

Cakes
Breac

90

17

A

18

B

19

C

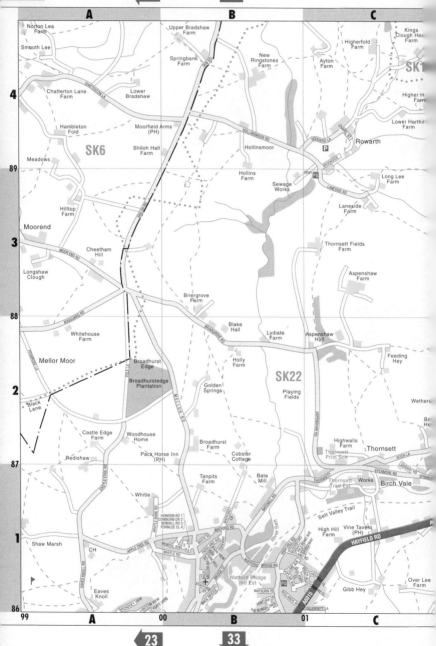

A B C

Norton Lea Farm
Smooth Lee

Upper Bradshaw Farm
Springbank Farm

New Ringstones Farm

Kings Clough Head Farm

Higherfold Farm

Ayton Farm

SK1

Chatterton Lane Farm
Lower Bradshaw

CHATTERTON LA

Higher H

Hambleton Fold

Moorfield Arms (PH)

HOLLINSMOOR RD

GODDARD LA

CHAPEL ST

Rowarth

Lower Harthill Farm

SK6
Meadows

Shiloh Hall Farm

Hollinsmoor

P

BROOKSIDE

Hollins Farm

Sewage Works

Inn
P

LANESIDE RD

Long Lee Farm

4

89

Hilltop Farm

Laneside Farm

Moorend

MOOR END RD

Cheetham Hill

Thornsett Fields Farm

3

Longshaw Clough

Aspenshaw Farm

88

Whitehouse Farm

Briergrove Farm

BRIARGROVE RD

Blake Hall

Lydiate Farm

Aspenshaw Hall

Feeding Hey

Mellor Moor

EDENSOR RD

Broadhurst Edge

Broadhurstedge Plantation

Holly Farm

SK22

2

Black Lane

Castle Edge Farm

Woodhouse Home

Pack Horse Inn (PH)

Golden Springs

MELLOR RD

Broadhurst Farm

Cobster Cottage

Playing Fields

ASPENSHAW RD

Highwalls Farm
Thornsett Prim Sch

Wethere

Ba
He

Thornsett

87

Redishaw

CASTLE EDGE RD

Whitle

Tanpits Farm

Bate Mill

THORNSETT

Thornsett Trad Est

Works

SYCAMORE RD

DERBYSHIRE RD

SETCH LA

SPINNER

Birch Vale

1

Shaw Marsh

CH

EAVES KNOLL RD

APPLE TREE RD

WHITLE RD

HOWDEN RD 1
COWBURN DR 2
WINHILL RD 3
FERNILEE CL 4

WATFORD RD

PEVERIL AVE

WHITLE RD

BEELEY RD

HAYFIELD RD

River Sett

Sett Valley Trail

High Hill Farm

Vine Tavern (PH)

P

Eaves Knoll

Watford Bridge Ind Est

WATBURN RD

WATFORD BRIDGE RD

PO

VENTURA

THE BUNGALOWS

BOGLANDS RD

A6015

COLLERSETT LA

Gibb Hey

Over Lee Farm

86

99 A 00 B 01 C

3

A
B
C

4

89

3

88

2

87

1

8

A
03
B
04
C

The Intakes

Hey Barn Farm

Matley Moor

Matleymoor Farm

Hey Brows

Tom Heys Farm

Hollingworth Clough

Lanehead Farm

Carr Meadow Farm

Stet Barn Farm

The Knott

Brookhouse Farm

Bullshaw Farm

Brookhouses

Spray House Wood

Blackshaw Farm

Spray House Farm

Marl House Farm

Middle Moor

Hey Wood

Park Hall

GLOSSOP RD

A624

Lantern Pike (PH)

Lantern Pike

Mon

Little Hayfield

Mill

SLACKS LA

Throstle

SK22

Oldpits Plantation

Sunny Side

Upper Cliffe Farm

Cliff

Mill

1 SHUDEHILL CL
2 SYCAMORE TERR
3 PRIMROSE CT
4 WAINHOUSE BROW
5 MILL ST
6 BARNSFOLD CT
7 BASINGWERKE CT
8 BROOKHOUSE CT
9 SWALLOW HOUSE CRES

Snake Path

Quarry (dis)

BANK HILL RD

SWALLOW HOUSE LA

Lower Cliff

Sewage Works

Hayfield Prim Sch

River Sett

Hayfield Vistor Ctr

FAIRY BANK

LUCAS TERR

FAIRY BANK RD

Cote Lane Farm

COTE LA

Kinder Bank

Bowden Bridge

P

Resr

PH

NEW MILLS RD

A6015

ST JOHN ST

A6015

BIRCH HALL CL

Birch Vale

Cemy

MEADOWS RD 1
CHAPEL ST 2
WALK MILL RD 3
STEEPLE END FOLD 4
FISHERS BRIDGE 5

CHAPEL RD

DIDSBURY TERR

SPRINGFIELD TERR

KINDER RD

The Sportsman (PH)

KINDER ROW

P

Elle Bank

Moorland House

MOORLAND RD

Little Ridge

Ridge Top

Meadows Farm

Hayfield

HIGHGATE RD

VALLEY RD

ROCKHALL TERR

Stubbs Farm

Quarry (dis)

Quarry

TV Mast

Barnsfold Farm

Highgate

Highgate Head

A624

Phoside Farm

Rowan Farm

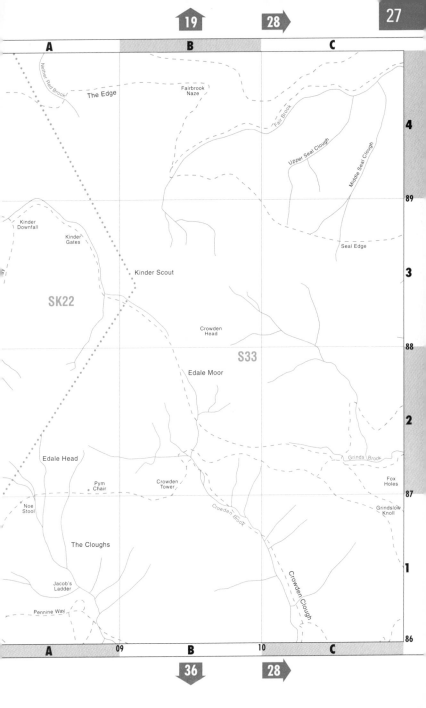

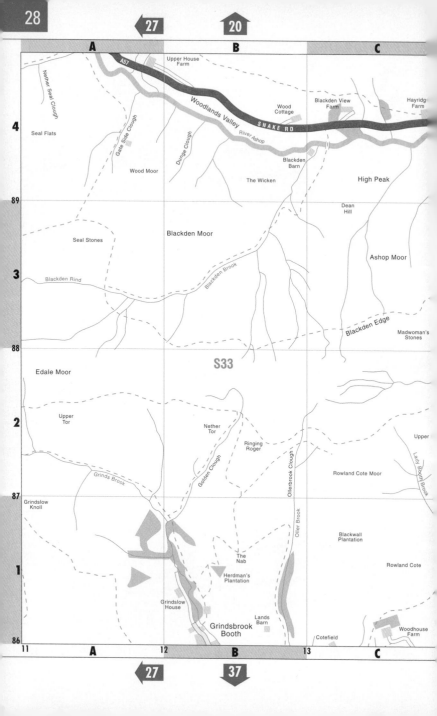

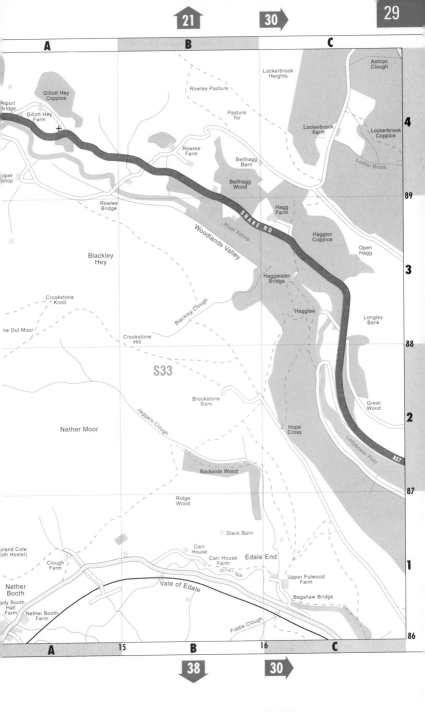

A
B
C

Alport Bridge
Gillott Hey Coppice
Gillott Hey Farm
Rowlee Pasture
Lockerbrook Heights
Ashton Clough

Pasture Tor
Lockerbrook Farm
Lockerbrook Coppice

Upper shop
Rowlee Farm
Bellhagg Barn
Locker Brook

4

Rowlee Bridge
Bellhagg Wood

89

Hagg Farm
SNAKE RD
River Ashop
Woodlands Valley
Haggtor Coppice
Open Hagg

Blackley Hey

3

Haggwater Bridge

Crookstone Knoll
Hagglee
Longley Bank

ne Out Moor
Blackley Clough

Crookstone Hill

88

S33

Brookstone Barn
Hope Cross
Great Wood

2

Nether Moor
Jaggars Clough
Ladybower Resr
A57

Backside Wood

87

Ridge Wood

Slack Barn

yland Cote (th Hostel)
Carr House
Carr House Farm
Edale End

1

Clough Farm
River Noe
Upper Fulwood Farm

Nether Booth
Vale of Edale
Bagshaw Bridge

dy Booth Hall Farm
Nether Booth Farm
Fiddle Clough

86

A
15
B
16
C

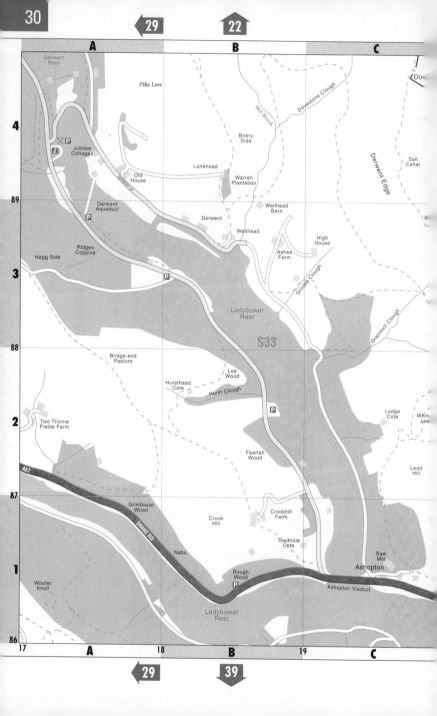

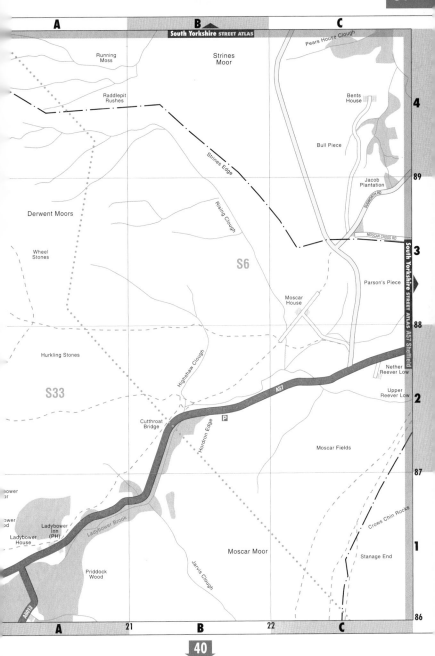

A · B · C

Pears House Clough

Running Moss

Strines Moor

Raddlepit Rushes

Bents House

4

Bull Piece

Strines Edge

Derwent Moors

Jacob Plantation

89

Rising Clough

Wheel Stones

S6

3

Parson's Piece

Moscar House

88

Hurkling Stones

Highshaw Clough

Nether Reever Low

S33

A57

Upper Reever Low

2

Cutthroat Bridge

Hordron Edge

P

Moscar Fields

87

ower or

Crows Chin Rocks

ower d

Ladybower Inn (PH)

Ladybower Brook

Ladybower House

Moscar Moor

1

Stanage End

Priddock Wood

Jarvis Clough

A6013

86

A · 21 · B · 22 · C

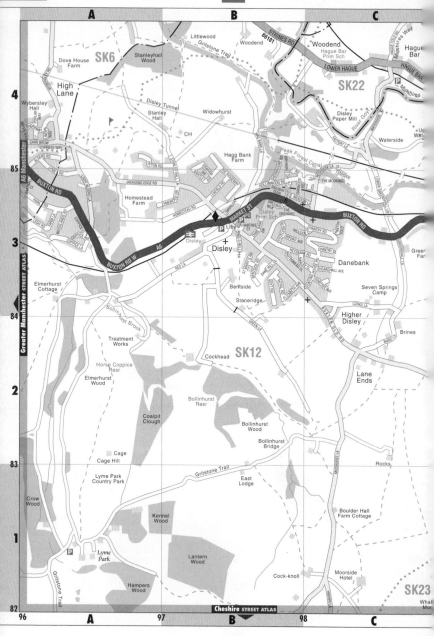

A   B   C

Littlewood
Woodend
B6101
Woodend
Hague Bar
Hague Bar Prim Sch
Hague Bar

Gritstone Trail
STRINES RD
LOWER HAGUE

Dove House Farm
SK6
Stanleyhall Wood
SK22

High Lane
Mushires

Wybersley Hall
Disley Tunnel
Stanley Hall
Widowhurst
Disley Paper Mill
River Goyt
Waterside
Up Wat

CARR BROW
CH
Hagg Bank Farm
Peak Forest Canal

A6 Manchester
BUXTON RD
JACKSONS EDGE RD
Homestead Farm
THE MOORINGS
BUXTON RD

85

Disley Prim Sch
THE ORCHARD

3
BUXTON RD W
A6
Disley
Liby
MARKET ST
CRABTREE CT
CHANTRY RD
Danebank
Greer Far

Disley
SHEARDHALL AVE
RED LA
Bertside
Stoneridge
Seven Springs Camp

Elmerhurst Cottage
Bollinhurst Brook
GREEN LA
Higher Disley
Brines

84

Treatment Works
Cockhead
SK12
Lane Ends

Horse Coppice Resr
Elmerhurst Wood

2
Bollinhurst Resr
Bollinhurst Wood

Coalpit Clough
Bollinhurst Bridge

Cage
Cage Hill
Rocks

83
Gritstone Trail
East Lodge

Lyme Park Country Park
Boulder Hall Farm Cottage

Crow Wood
Kennel Wood

1
Lyme Park
Lantern Wood
Cock-knoll
Moorside Hotel
SK23

Gritstone Trail
Hampers Wood
Whal Moo

82

96   A   97   B   98   C

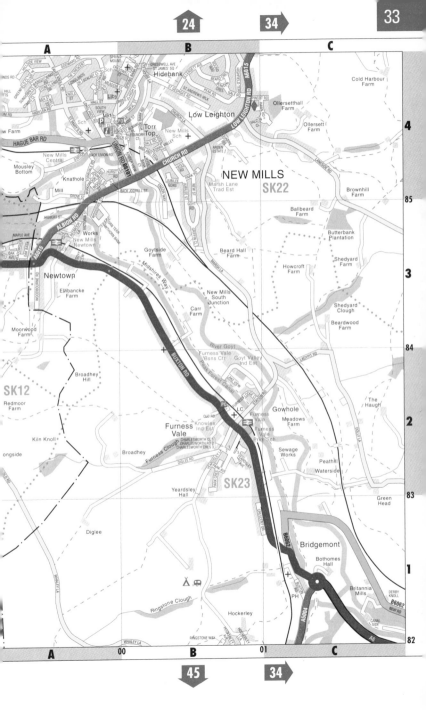

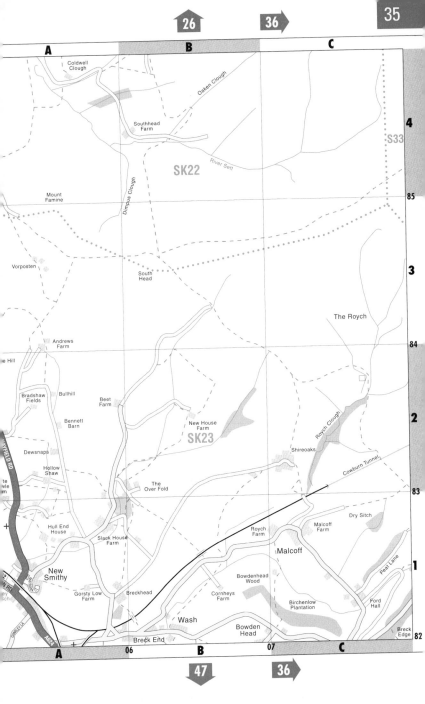

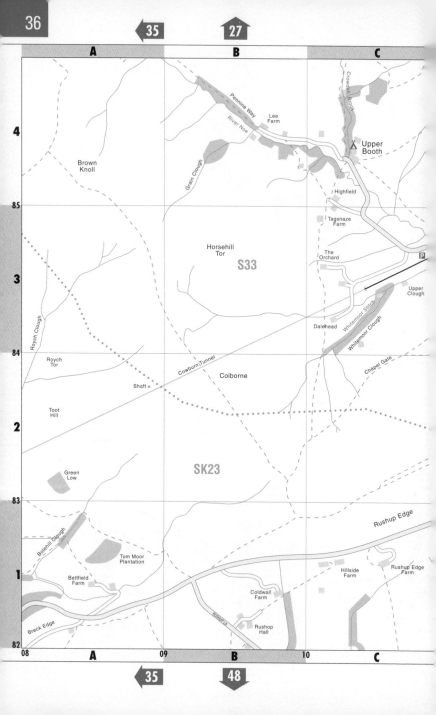

A
B
C

4

Pennine Way

River Noe

Lee Farm

Crowden Brook

△ Upper Booth

Brown Knoll

Grain Clough

Highfield

85

Tagsnaze Farm

Horsehill Tor

S33

The Orchard

3

Roych Clough

Upper Clough

Dalehead

Whitemoor Stitch

Whitemoor Clough

P

84

Roych Tor

Cowburn Tunnel

Colborne

Chapel Gate

Shaft

Toot Hill

2

Green Low

SK23

83

Rushup Edge

Bolehill Clough

Tom Moor Plantation

Hillside Farm

Rushup Edge Farm

1

Bettfield Farm

Coldwall Farm

RUSHUP LA

Rushop Hall

Breck Edge

82

08
A
09
B
10
C

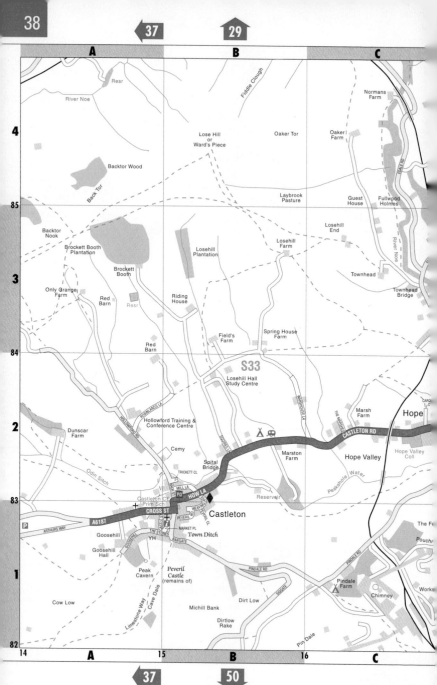

30 40

A B C

Hope Brink

Wiseman Hey Clough
Plantation

New
Barn
The
Springs

Winhill
Barn

4

Thornhill
Brink

Winhill
Pike

Parkin Clough

Win Hill
Winhill
Plantation

Yorkshire
Bridge

85

Fullwood Stile
Farm

Top
Plantation

Thornhill
Carrs

River Derwent

CAR LA

3

The
Homestead

Twitchill
Farm

Edge
Farm

Paddock
Wood

High Field Head
Farm

Birchfield

King's
Haigh

Dimings

S33

Cemy

Birchfield
Park

Farfield
Farm

Aston
Hall

84

Killhill
Bridge

Aston

Top
Croft

THORNHILL LA

Mill

ASTON LA

Ryecroft

Slack Lane

2

HAWTHORN CL

1 SHERWOOD AVE
2 THE CRESCENT

Thornhill

RD

STATION RD

Hope

Hallam
Barn

PARSONS LA

Netherhall
Bridge

Peakshole Water

Sewage
Works

STATION RD

83

Hardhurst
Farm

Glenbrook

WATER LA

eles House
Farm

Hope Valley

Inn

A6187

B6049

HOPE RD

River Noe

Lumbley
Pool

NAVIO
ROMAN
FORT

Mills

Wheat Hay
Farm

1

Brough
House

Brough

B6049 LA

TOWNFIELD LA

Shatton

STRETFIELD RD

Batham Gate

Upper
Shatton

YR HILL RD

B6049

Mill

Elmore Hill
Farm

82

A 18 B 19 C

51 40

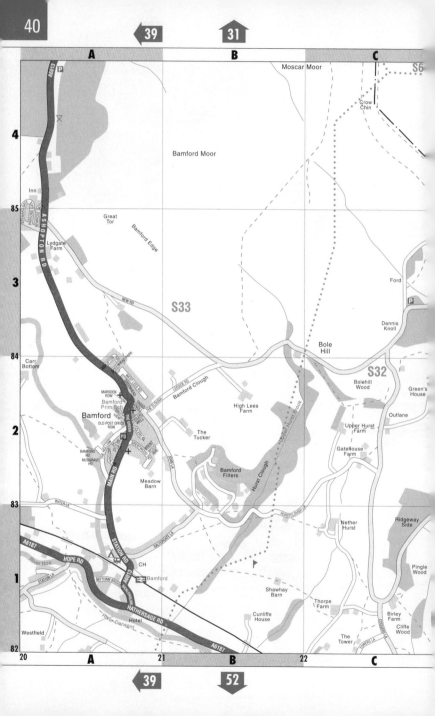

South Yorkshire STREET ATLAS

A   B   C

High Lad Ridge
Rape Piece

Hallam Moors

Broadshaw Plantation

Broadshaw

Redmires Reservoirs

Gin Piece

Fairthorn Lodge

Stanedge Lodge   S10

4

85

Buck stone

Stanage Edge

Spring Piece

Fairthorn Clough

3

Long Causeway   Stanedge Pole

wash nk

84

Friar's Ridge

Stanage Plantation

Robin Hood's Cave

S32

White Path Moss

2

North Lees

Hook's Car

Bronte Cottage

Cattis Side

Cattis-side Moor

Hookcar Stitch

Cowper Stone

Cam Height

83

Cowclose

Carhead Rocks

Overstones Farm

Brookfield Manor

Birchin Wood

Leveret Croft

Fidler's Elbow

1

Kimber Court Farm

Moorseats

Moorseats Wood   Carhead

Callow Bank

Toothill Farm

82

A   24   B   25   C

A   B   C

Lodge Moor

Reservoir
Cottages

Wyming
Brook
Farm

REDMIRES RD

Redmires
Plantaion

Works

Wyming
Brook
Farm

Soughley

Redmires Conduit

LODGE MOOR RD

BROWN HILLS LA

Peat
Farm

Fulwood
Grange
Farm

Brownhills
Farm

Birk's
Green
Farm

Redmires Reservoirs

4

Fulwood
Booth

FULWOOD HEAD RD

Knoll Top
Farm

Douse Croft
Farm

85

Fulwood
Head

Wagg Lane

Yarncliffe House
Farm

DOUSE CROFT LA

TOD

3   White
Stones

S10

BASSETT LA

MOORBELL LA

HAMPOLE LA

FULWOOD LA

Green
House
Farm

Bassett

Rud
Hill

Brown Edge
Farm

Clough Hollow

GREENHOUSE LA

Porter Clough

84

Hallam Moors

Clough Hollow

Moorfield
Farm

Brown Edge

Ringinglow

2

RINGINGLOW RD

Lady Canning's
Plantation

Upper Burbage
Bridge

S32

83

Ox Stones

S11

HOUNDKIRK RD

SHEEPHILL RD

JUMBLE RD

1

Burbage Moor

82   Ford

Houndkirk Moor

26   A   27   B   28   C

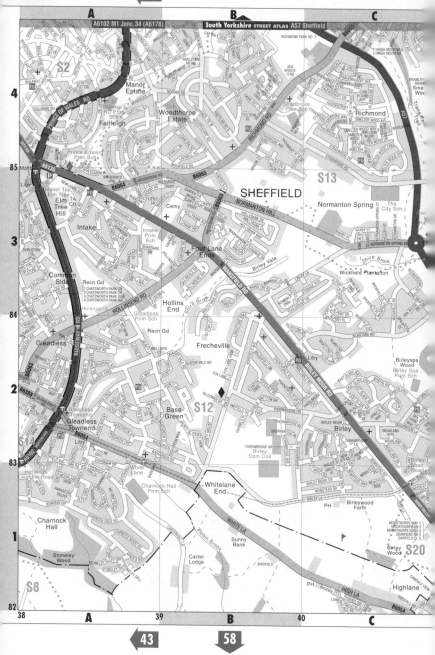

A **B** **C**

S2

4

Manor
Estate

Woodthorpe
Estate

RICHMOND PARK RD

SEA
BREEZE
TERR

Richmond

Stradbroke
Prim Sch

A57

Theresa
RC Prim Sch
Fairleigh

Prince Edward
Prim Sch

85

Matt

Liby

Manor Top
Elm Tree
Hill

Elm
Tree
Hill

TA
Ctr

A6135

P

PRINCE OF WALES RD

B6064

B6065

B6065

NORMANTON HILL

SHEFFIELD

S13

Normanton Spring

The
City Sch

NEWMAN RD

Cemy

Intake

Intake
Prim Sch

Hollicarrs

3

Four Lane
Ends

Birley Vale

Shire Brook

Wickfield Plantation

84

Common
Side

Hollinsend

Recn Gd
1 CHATSWORTH PARK GR
2 CHATSWORTH PARK DR
3 CHATSWORTH PARK RISE
4 CHATSWORTH PARK AVE

HOLLINSEND RD

Hollins
End

Gleadless
Prim Sch

Recn Gd

Frecheville

BIRLEY MOOR RD

Liby

Birleyspa
Wood
Birley Spa
Prim Sch

Gleadless

RIDGEWAY RD

2

B6063

B6388

S14

Gleadless
Townend

Gleadless
Townend

Liby

B6054

A6102

White
Lane

Base
Green

S12

Birley

Weakland
Way

Birley
Moor
Road

THORNBRIDGE GR
Birley
Com Coll

83

Herdings
Brighton Road

Charnock Hall
Prim Sch

Whitelane
End

BIRLEY MOOR DR

PH

Birleywood
Farm

MOORTHORPE WAY 1
MOORTHORPE DR 2
MOORTHORPE GDNS 3
DEANHEAD DR 4
DARFIELD CL 5

1

Charnock
Hall

Stoneley
Wood

WHITE LA

Robin Brook

Sunny
Bank

Carter
Lodge

Birdfield

Birley
Wood

S20

S8

PH

HIGH LA

PHOENIX CT

Highlane

B6054

82

38 **A** 39 **B** 40 **C**

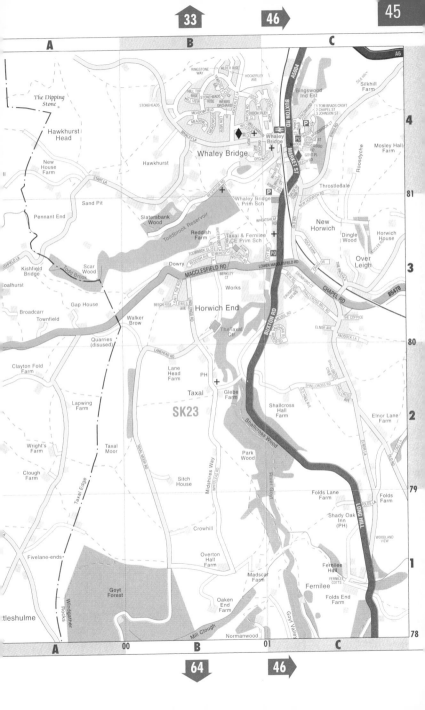

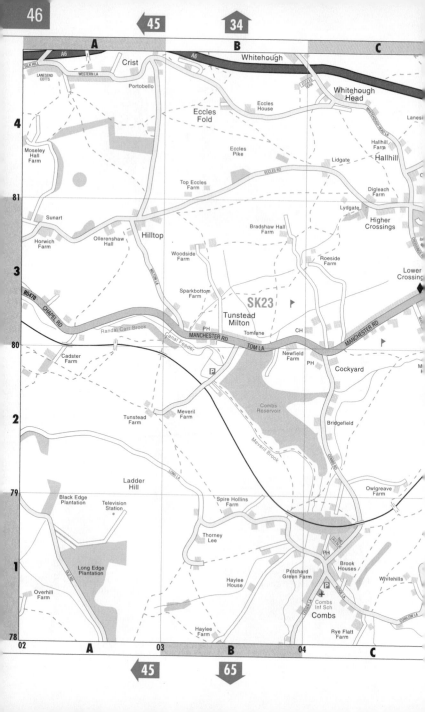

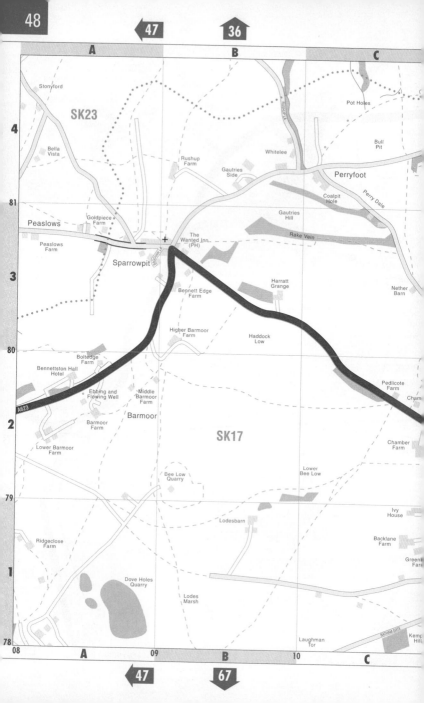

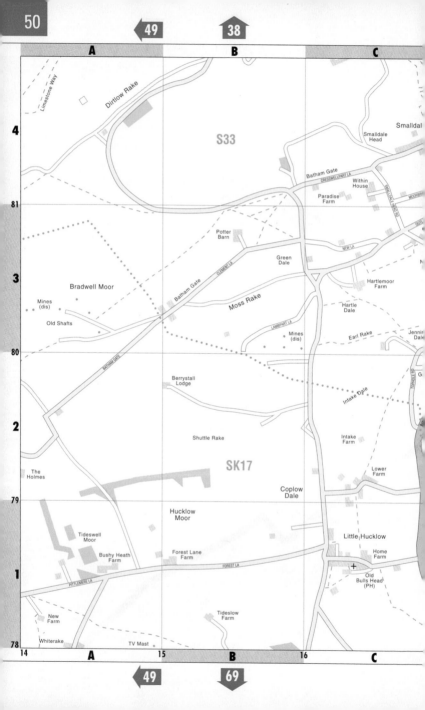

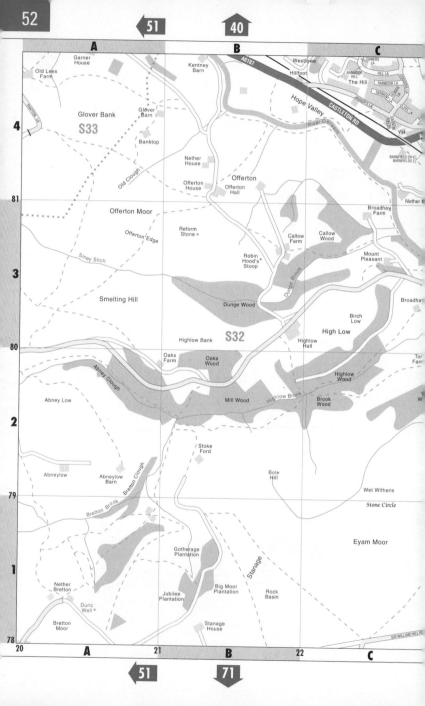

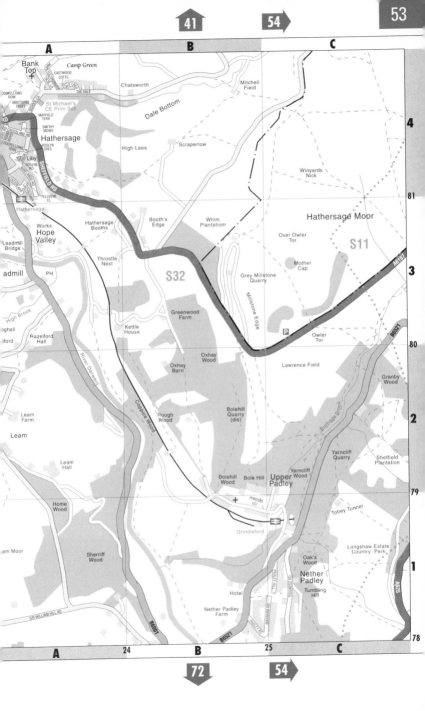

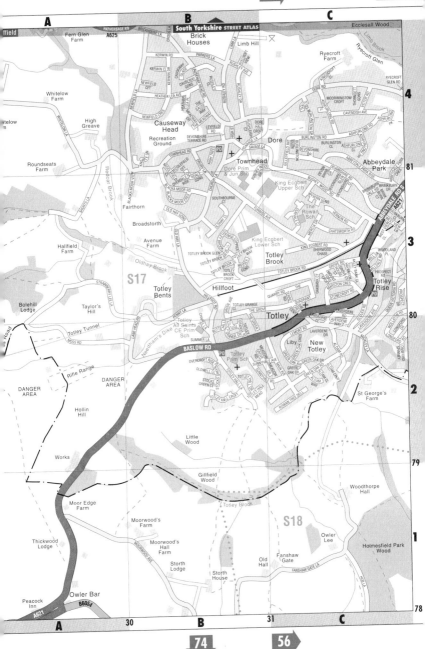

South Yorkshire STREET ATLAS

B1
1 STAFFORD CL
2 LONGCROFT CRES
3 REPTON PL
4 ROCKINGHAM CL
5 NEWSTEAD CL
6 MAPPERLEY RD
7 HAZELWOOD CL
8 BRADWELL CL
9 ASHFORD RD

10 ROSTON CL
11 GRASMERE RD
12 MONTROSE PL
13 BIRCHEN CL
14 GARDOM CL
15 SHERWOOD PL
16 INGLEBY CL
17 IVAN BROOK CL
18 ARUNDEL CL
19 LYNWOOD CL

20 HEATON CL
21 MILLSTONE CL
22 BUCKINGHAM CL
23 WELBECK CL
24 CHATSWORTH PL
25 BURBAGE CL
26 ORCHARD SQ

C1
1 KENTMERE CL
2 BOWNESS CL
3 PATTERDALE CL
4 TURNER CL
5 CASTLERIGG WAY
6 ULLSWATER PK
7 SHEARDS CL
8 SUMMERWOOD PL

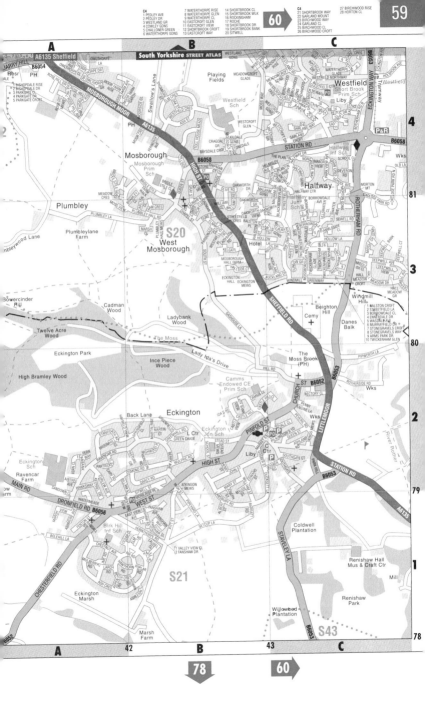

B South Yorkshire STREET ATLAS

A618 Rother

A

C

Angle

Int'l St

NEW ST
BUS LINK

LONG ACRE
VIEW

Holbrook

Cow
Lane

Short Brook

Works

Rother Valley
Country Park

Killamarsh
Meadows

Nether Green

Norw

Norwood
Ind Est

Barber's Lane

Canal (disused)

ELLISONS RD

ROTHERHAM RD

PRIMROSE

CROSS

4

Meadowbrook
Ind Est

STATION RD

B6058

S20

Sewage
Works

Nether Moor

1 SACKERVILLE TR
2 HAVERCROFT TR
NETHERTHORPE CL

NETHERGREEN GDNS 1
VALLEY DR 2
NETHERMOOR CL 3
NETHERMOOR AVE 4
NETHERGREEN CT 5

SHEFFIELD RD

Sh
Ctr

Liby

B6058

Ganno
Hill

Hi

81

Netherthorpe

Works

UPP AVE

METCALFE WAY

THE BUNGALOWS PO

POWELL

CANAL BR

KIRKCROFT LA

KIRKCROFT LA

LONG LA

The Crown
(PH)
Church
Town

Dale
Farm

Oxclose
Farm

GARTRICE
GDNS

GARTRICE
GR

River Rother

Sheepcote
Hill

BAKER DR

HARRISON DR

CHANDOS

ST Giles
CE Sch

ORCHARD
PL

SHEEPCOTE RD

RECTORY GDNS

CHERRY TREE DR

BIRCHLANDS DR

Killamarsh

3

RIETONY
CL

MULBERRY
WAY

MUNRO CL 1
GAUNT CL 2
SPOONER DR 3
KEMP CL 4
ROBINSON WAY 5
MUSARD WAY 6
MEWELL WAY 7
CYPRESS GL 8
SYCAMORE DR 9
YEW TREE DR 10
MAPLE DR 11

ASPEN

ELMWOOD AVE

HOLLY
DENE

SWALLOW
DR

PEARL
CL

OAK CL

ELM DR

HAWTHORNE

BEECH CL

SIMCRESS AVE

UPPERTHORPE
VILLAS

Upperthorpe

Traveller's Rest
(PH)

80

POPLAR

BIRCH CL

MAIN TREE

Hotel

Westthorpe
Green

CROFTON

BOILEY LA

Westthorpe

S21

MANOR RD

High Mo
Collier

2

Boiley
Farm

Park Brook

Trans Pennine Trail

Mine
(dis)

WESTTHORPE
FIELDS RD

Park Brook

Park
Brook

SPINKHILL RD

Comberwood
Farm

Chaplewheel
Dam

Birley
Farm

Spring
Wood

79

Mill
Farm

A6135

STATION RD

River Rother

Bridge
House

SPINKHILL LA

Sewage
Works

Smithy Brook

Mount St Mary's
RC Coll

COLLEGE RD

Spinkhill
Immaculate
Conception
Prim Sch

THE LANE

Top
Farm

Park
Farm

PARKHILL LA

Spinkhill

Parkhall
Farm

Park Hall
(Hotel)

Ingdale
Farm

Quarrydam
Cottages

1

Hotel

A6135 MAIN RD

STANIER
WAY

HAGUE
LA

Renishaw

Park
Farm

Quarrydam
Wood

S4

78

44

A

45

B

46

C

South Yorkshire STREET ATLAS

A B C

Devil's Hole
Bridge

Cuckoo Way

Manor Rd

Newton
Hill

Street Field

BURGESS HILL

Hawks
Wood

Chesterfield Canal
(disused)

Lady Field

4

Manor
Farm

Bull
Hill

THORPE RD

HARTHILL RD

Loscar Field

Thorpe
Hall

Parish
Oven
(PH)

Old Meadow
Wood

Pudding Dike

Hunger
Hill

Cuthbright
Wood

Church Field

WORKSOP RD

Thorpe
Salvin

81

Manor
Farm

COMMON RD

Loscar
Wood

ST APPLE LA

3

Crow
Wood

COMMON RD

Loscar Common
Plantations

PACKMAN LA

Little
Wood

S80

Moor
Fa

LITTLEWOODS LA

80

S26

Loscar Common

SOUTHARD'S LA

Thorpe Common

M

2

Loscar
Farm

Honeysyke

Honeysyke
Wood

Southard's
Bottoms

HARTHILL FIELD RD

Grange
Farm

Southard's
Plantation

79

Bondhay
Barn

CH

Bondhay
Farm

BONDHAY LA

Castle Hill

Bondhay
Plantation

Whitwell Wood

1

Mast

Castle Hill
Farm

Bondhay
Common

78

50 A 51 B 52 C

A B C

Browtop Farm

Hodgei Brook

4

Oldfield

Wks

River Goyt

LONG HILL

A5004

Ladbitch Wood

Hoo Moor

SK23

Fernilee Reservoir

Goyt Valley

77

Goyt Forest

P

Pymchair Farm

Pym Chair

Mishires Way

THE STREET

3

Oldgate Nick

Jep Clough

Cheshire STREET ATLAS

76

Cats Tor

Withinleach Moor

SK10

The Street Forest Walks

Sailing Club

2

Foxlow Edge

Errwood Reservoir

SK17

75

The Tors

Errwood Hall

Errwood Forest Walks

1

Shooter's Clough

SK11

River Goyt

Stake Side

74

99

A

00

B

01

C

A   B   C

4

SK23

77

3

Combs Moss

Pyegreave Brook

Hob Tor

Resrs

Blackedge Resr

Blackedge Farm

Field Farm

76

SK17

Tom Thorn Farm

Thorn Head Farm

Bat Ga

2

Hogshaw Brook

Television Station

Brownedge Plantation

Resr

Turner Lodge

High Peak Nurseries

Tomthorn

Breezemount Farm

75

Light Wood

Lightwood Resr

Frome Lodge

Brookhouse Farm

Brook House

Waterswallc Green

Works

Hogshaw Brook

Black Edge

Ashpiece Farm

Buxton Rd

PH

P

Bibbin

The Barms Farm

DAISYMERE

1

Corbar Hill

John Duncan Sch

Corbar Woods

Chestnut

St Anne's RC Prim Sch

Lascelles Rd

Nunsfield Farm

Fairfield Common

Waterswallows Mews Dakin Ct.

CH

Town End

Townend Farm

Fairfield Rd A6

4

05   A   06   B   07   C

A B C

BATHAM GATE

Dove Holes Quarry

Lodes La.

Smalldale

Heath Farm

4

DALE RD

Dovehole Dale

SMALLDALE COTTS

Works

SMALLDALE RD

Middle Hill

Gorsey Nook

77

PH

SMALL KNOWLE END

Higher Bibbington

BATHAM GATE RD

CHURCH RD

Peak Dale

Withered Low

3

Wormhill Moor

Peak Dale Prim Sch

SCHOOL RD

PO

Sewage Works

SK17

Ppg Sta

ayes

Upper End

NEW ST

76

SPRING BANK

FERNDALE RD

DALE RD

Broadlow Farm

LONGRIDGE LA

Buxton Bridge

Bole Hill

2

Great Rocks Lees

WATERSWALLOWS LA

IWS

Hardybarn

Taylor Farm

Water Swallows

75

Tunstead

terswallows Green

GREEN LA

Green La

Great Rocks Tunnel

1

aterswallows Quarry

Green La

Green Fairfield

Greenfairfield Farm

Tunstead Works

aisymere Farm

74

A 09 B 10 C

67

49

A523

A

B

C

4

77

Kempshill Farm

Lower Kempshill Farm

Stone Lea Farm

Dam Dale

Hay Dale

Dale Head Farm

Dale Head

Sitch House

WATER LA

Bottom Farm

Wheston

Hall

The Top Farm

3

76

Peter Dale

SK17

2

Hargatewall

Hayward Farm

Wind Low

Hargate Hall

Limestone Way

Cherryslack

Monks House

75

Hill Top Farm

Wormhill Hill

Monk's Dale

MONSAL DALE

1

Old Hall Farm

Wormhill

Nature Reserve

Wormhill Hall

74

11

A

12

B

13

C

67

87

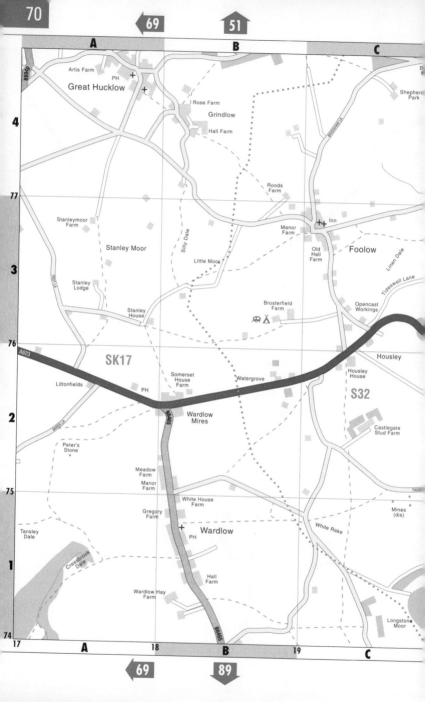

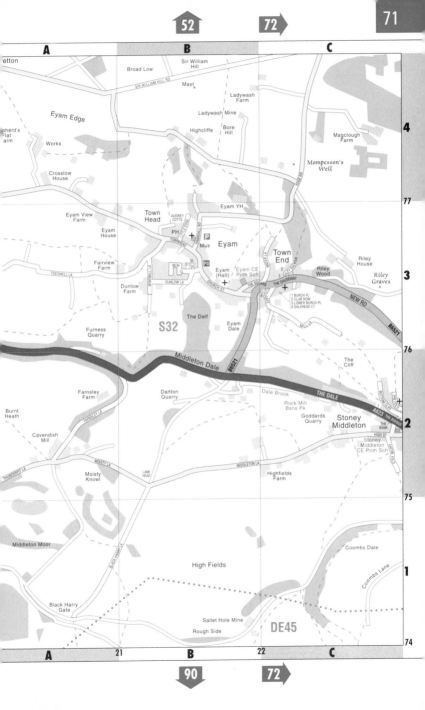

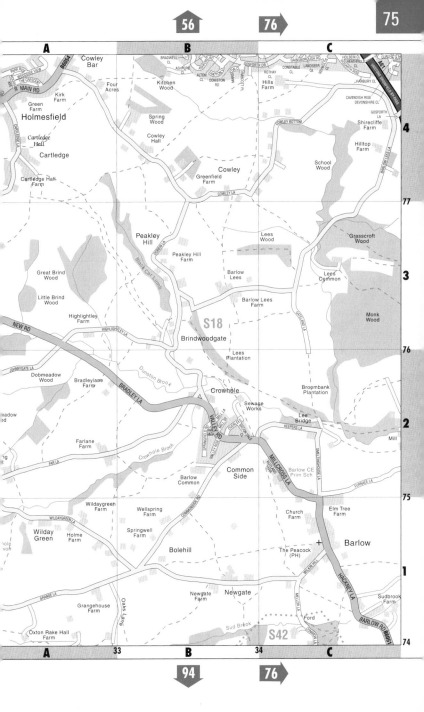

A
B
C

B6052

Whinnybank Wood
Red Lodge Cottages
Foxstone Wood
Renishaw Park
Milner Plantation
Thirbycliff Farm
Halfmoon Plantation

Red Lodge Farm
Little Foxstone Wood
Foxstone Dam
Mine (dis)

4

S21

Old Furnace Wood

STAVELEY LA

77

White Lodge
BRECK LA
Toadpool Farm
Slittingmill Farm

Hagge Farm
STAVELEY LA
HAWTHORN HILL

3

Breck Farm
S43
Hawthor Far

76

Barrow Hill
Breck Farm Cottages
Foxlowe Plantation

Clay Pit
Foxlow Junction

MIDLAND TERR 1
ALLPORT TERR 2
DUEWELL CT 3
PACIFIC TERR

HALL RD
BRECK RD
Hartington Ind Est
FARNDALE RD
ELKINGTON RD

2

WHITTINGTON RD
BRIDGWATER WAY
CROMWELL WAY
CAVENDISH WAY
HALL LA
DEEPDALE RD
FRANK

BELLHOUSE VIEW 1
VICTORIA AVE 2
Lowgates
Liby

Barrow Hill Prim Sch

75

Works
HAYFIELD
The Clock Tower Bsns Ctr
B6053
Works
CHURCH ST
A619 LOW
IRELAND ST

Chesterfield Canal (disused)

1

Works
River Rother
BARNFIELD WLK
MARKET
PORTER ST
DUKE ST
HUNTSMAN
Brindley Ind Est
Fan-Road Ind Est

Hollingwood
IMMINGHAM GR 1
WEST VIEW 2
DARLEY CL
LIME AVE

Pondhouse Farm
STAVELEY
Speedwell Inf Sch
STEPHENSON

Troughbrook Wood
CHESTERFIELD RD
A619
Staveley Jun Sch
Speedwell Ind Est
CEMETERY LA
MEADOWS DR
Ireland Trad Est

MOLINEUX AVE
Cemy

4
41
A
42
B
43
C

C1
1 BARNFIELD CL
2 DEVONSHIRE CL
3 DEVONSHIRE ST
4 KEDLESTON ST
5 HARDWICK CT
6 ARUNDEL CT
7 WELBECK CT
8 MELBOURNE CT
9 WATERINGBURY GR

10 TUDOR ST
11 NETHERTHORPE RD
12 WHITEHEAD ST
13 LEANDER CT
14 MALLARD CT

A **B** **C**

Arrow Farm

Half Moon Inn
(PH)

Finbeck La

Clinthill La

Worksop Rd Broad La

A619

4 Red Hill

Burnt Leys
Cottages

Burnt Leys

Darfoulds Dike

Ratcliffe
Grange

77

Ratcliffe
Cottages

A60 Mansfield Rd

Longcroft
View

Sunnyside

Mill La

Fox Rd

Mill Cres

Hangar

Birks
Farms

Hodthorpe

Sewage
Works

Birks
Cottages

Whitwell

St Martin's Wlk

Greenfield Ave

Rick Rd

Birks Cl

King Way

King St

Broad La

3

Queens Rd

Queens Cl

Hodthorpe
Prim Sch

Hall Leys
Farm

Walling Brook

Ox Pastures
Farm

Spring St
Longhurst View

Green La

Whitewell

Wallingbrook
Wood

76

Southfield
Ind Site

Southfield La

Tip
(disused)

S80

New Cottages

Penny
Green

Millash La

Belph

Belph
Grange

Millwood Brook

Bismark
Plantation

2

Chy
Works

Penny Green
Cottages

Springfield
Farm

Tip
(disused)

Millwood Lodge

Mill
Wood

75

B6042

Hennymoor La

Ladycroft
Wood

Henneymoor
Farm

Ganabrig
Wood

West Park

Fishpond
Lodge

Burial Ground
Plantation

1

Creswell
Crags
Visitor Ctr

Robin Hood Way

Oaksetts
Lodge

Caves

Cresswell Crags

Pin
Hole

Crags Rd

Works

Craggs
Cottages

Craft
Ctr

Cowcl
Woo

74

B6042

Crags Pond

Church Hole

53 **A** **54** **B** **55** **C**

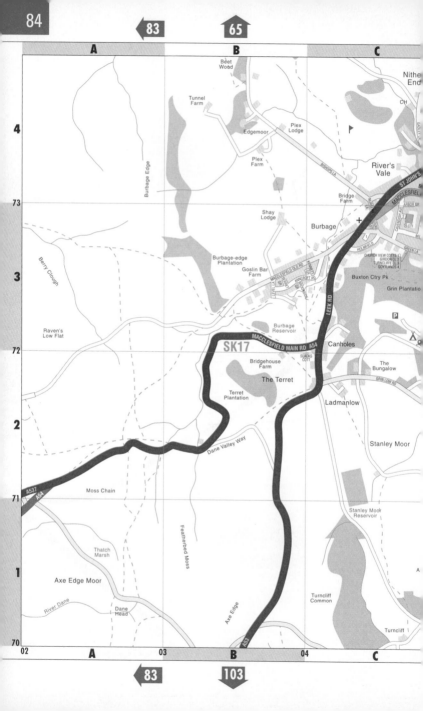

83
65

A   **B**   **C**

Nithe End

CH

4

Tunnel Farm

Beet Wood

Edgemoor

Plex Lodge

River's Vale

ST JOHN'S

MACCLESFIELD

Plex Farm

BISHOPS LA

Bridge Farm

73

Shay Lodge

Burbage

Sch

CHURCH VIEW COTTS 1
GIRIDONCLE 2
TURNCLIFFE CL 3
GOYTLANDS 4

HOLDFIELD

3

Burbage-edge Plantation

Goslin Bar Farm

MACCLESFIELD OLD RD

MINCROFT RD

Buxton Ctry Pk

Grin Plantatio

Berry Clough

LEEK RD

P

Raven's Low Flat

Burbage Reservoir

Burbage-edge Plantation

SLACKS COTT

Canholes

72

SK17   MACCLESFIELD MAIN RD **A54**

Bridgehouse Farm

The Terret

The Bungalow

GRIN LOW RD

Terret Plantation

Ladmanlow

2

Dane Valley Way

Stanley Moor

A537

A54

Moss Chain

71

Stanley Moor Reservoir

Featherbed Moss

1

Axe Edge Moor

Thatch Marsh

Turncliff Common

Axe Edge

River Dane

Dane Head

A53

Turncliff

70

02   **A**   **03**   **B**   **04**   **C**

83
103

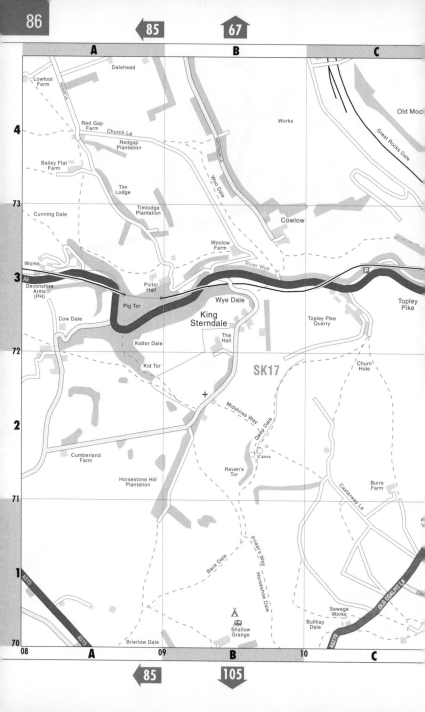

Lowfoot Farm

Dalehead

Red Gap Farm

Church La

Redgap Plantation

Bailey Flat Farm

Tim Lodge

4

Woo Dale

Works

Great Rocks Dale

Old Moo

73

Cunning Dale

Timlodge Plantation

Cowlow

Woolow Farm

Works

River Wye

3

A6

Devonshire Arms (PH)

Pictor Hall

P

Pig Tor

Wye Dale

Topley Pike

Cow Dale

King Sterndale

Topley Pike Quarry

Kidtor Dale

The Hall

72

Kid Tor

SK17

Churn Hole

+

Midshires Way

Deep Dale

2

Caves

Cumberland Farm

Raven's Tor

Burrs Farm

Horsestone Hill Plantation

Casterway La

71

Back Dale

Priest's Way

Horseshoe Dale

Old Coalpit La

1

A515

Sewage Works

Bullhay Dale

A5270

Shallow Grange

A515

Brierlow Dale

70

08

A

09

B

10

C

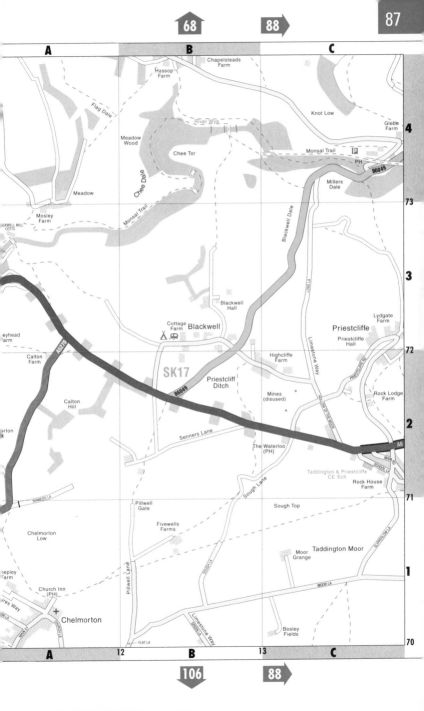

A
B
C

Chapelsteads Farm

Hassop Farm

Flag Dale

Meadow Wood

River Wye

Knot Low

Glebe Farm

4

Chee Tor

Monsal Trail

P

Millers Dale

PH

B6049

Meadow

Chee Dale

Monsal Trail

73

Mosley Farm

ORWELL MILL COTTS

Blackwell Dale

3

Blackwell Hall

Lydgate Farm

eyhead Farm

Cottage Farm

Blackwell

Priestcliffe

Priestcliffe Hall

72

Calton Farm

SK17

Highcliffe Farm

Limestone Way

A5270

B6049

Priestcliff Ditch

Rock Lodge Farm

orton

Calton Hill

Mines (disused)

SIDE OF THE WOOD

PRIESTCLIFFE RD

2

Senners Lane

The Waterloo (PH)

A6

MAIN RD

SENNERS LA

Taddington & Priestcliffe CE Sch

Rock House Farm

71

Pillwell Gate

Sough Lane

Sough Top

SLIPPERLOW LA

Chelmorton Low

Fivewells Farms

Moor Grange

Taddington Moor

1

hepley Farm

Pillwell Lane

SOUGH LA

MOOR LA

Church Inn (PH)

ures Way

Chelmorton

Limestone Way

GIBBS LA

Bosley Fields

MAIN ST

CHURCH LA

FLAT LA

70

A
12
B
13
C

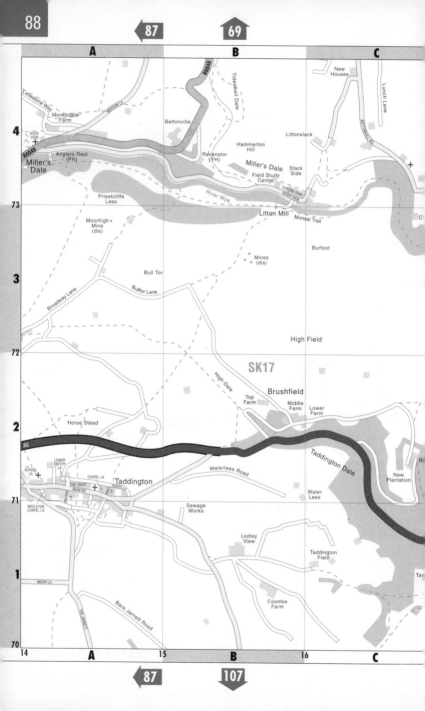

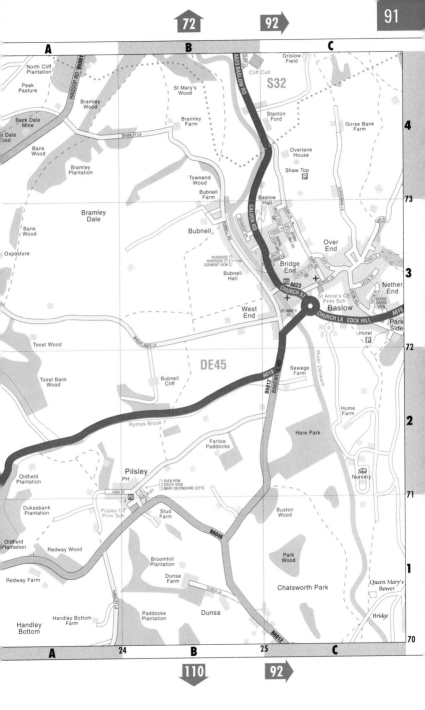

A **B** **C**

North Cliff
Plantation

Peak
Pasture

HASSOP RD B6001

Cliff Coll

Grislow
Field

S32

Back Dale
Mine

Bramley
Wood

St Mary's
Wood

Stanton
Ford

Gorse Bank
Farm

4

k Dale
od

Bank
Wood

BRAMLEY LA

Bramley
Farm

Overlane
House

Bramley
Plantation

Townend
Wood

CALVER RD

A623 BASLOW RD

Shaw Top
P

GORSE BANK LA

73

Bramley
Dale

Bubnell
Farm

Baslow
Hall

Bubnell

BUBNELL RD

WHITE EDGE
GORSE RIDGE DR

Over
End

Bank
Wood

Oxpasture

RIVERSIDE 1
RIVERSIDE CT 2
DERWENT VIEW 3

WHITE LODGE LA

Bridge
End

SCHOOL LA

EATON LA

GOOSE GREEN
VIEW

Nether
End

A619

3

Bubnell
Hall

PO A623
CHURCH ST

St Anne's CE
Prim Sch

West
End

ST ANNE'S
CL

Baslow

CHURCH LA COCK HILL

Park
Side

Hotel
P

72

BRIGHT LANDS LA

DE45

A619

BAKEWELL RD

River Derwent

Toost Wood

Sewage
Farm

Toost Bank
Wood

B6012

Bubnell
Cliff

Home
Farm

2

RYMAS BROOK

Farlow
Paddocks

Hare Park

Oldfield
Plantation

Pilsley
PH

HIGH ST

PO

DUCK ALLEY

1 DUCK ROW
2 SOUTH VIEW
3 MARY DEVONSHIRE COTTS

Nursery

71

Dukesbank
Plantation

Pilsley CE
Prim Sch

3

Stud
Farm

Buston
Wood

Oldfield
Plantation

Redway Wood

B6048

Broomhill
Plantation

Park
Wood

1

Redway Farm

Dunsa
Farm

DUNSA LA

Chatsworth Park

Queen Mary's
Bower

Handley
Bottom

HANDLEY LA

Handley Bottom
Farm

Paddocks
Plantation

Dunsa

B6012

Bridge

70

A **24** **B** **25** **C**

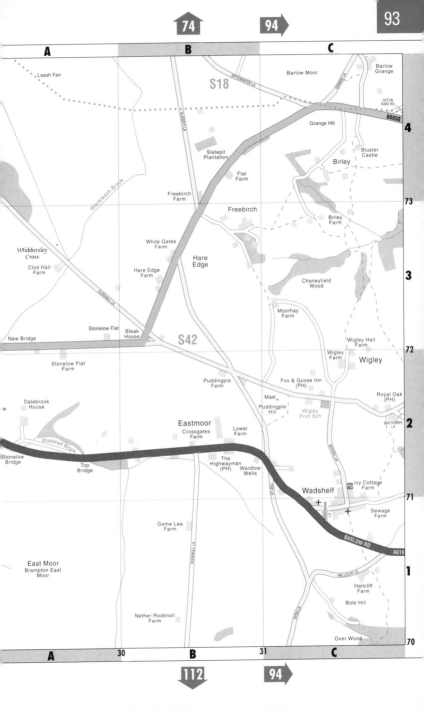

A
B
C

S18

Green Lane
Oaks Lane
DIXON BAKE RD

S18

Oxton Rakes

Jumble Hole

Salter Wood

Baines Wood

COMMON LA

Cutthorpe Common

Three Merry Lads (PH)

Overgreen

4

B6050

Gate Inn (PH)

Thorpe House

Ingmanthorpe

Cutthorpe Prim Sch

MAIN RD

Cutthorpe

HIGH CROFT PEAK CL

GREEN LA

Cow Close Farm

Pratthall

Pratthall Farm

The Cottages

Green Farm

Cutthorpe Green

Cutthorpe Hall

73

Birley Wood

Kitchenflat Wood

Hall Farm

Birley Brook

Linacre Wood

Water Works

P

BRIARDENE CL 1
WOODLEIGH CL 2
STANAGE WAY 3
WHEATFIELD WAY 4
FOXBROOK CL 5

WOODLAN

3

Dumble Wood

Priestfield Wood

Linacre Reservoirs

Linacre Resr Nature Trail

Ducksick Wood

Woodnook Farm

Sims Wood

Woodnook

Linacre Brook

ASHBURY CL

THORNHILL

WOODL

S42

The Grove

72

Hollins House

GROVE LA

Upper Ashgate Farm

Brampton Hall

NORTH LA

LOUNDSLEY CT
THORNE CL
WOODNOOK CL 1

MEA

Hollins

Hemmings Green

George & Dragon (PH)

Old Brampton

Ashgate

ASHGATE RD

2

BAGTHORPE LA

Bagthorpe Farm

Offley Place

Lady Wood

Nuttock Lane

Caushouse Farm

RIVELIN

Bramma Wood

The Birches

Frithhall Wood

Broomhall Farm

71

Horse Wood

Frith Hall

FRITHHALL LA

Westwick Farm

WESTWICK LA

Leadhill Farm

Brookside

Rufford Farm

Rufford House

A619

Ladywoods

BASLOW RD

Fairfield

CHATSWORTH

BROOKSIDE

1

Leagreave

Nether Chanderhill

HOLLYWOOD RD

Brookside Nurseries

S40

Hagg Wood

Cherry Trees

Chanderhill

CHANDER HILL LA

Old Barn Farm

MOORHALL

Foxbrook Farm

Belmont Park

70

32
33
34

A
B
C

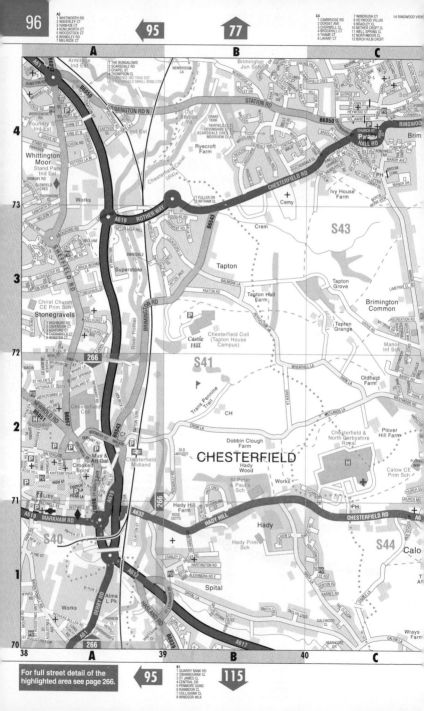

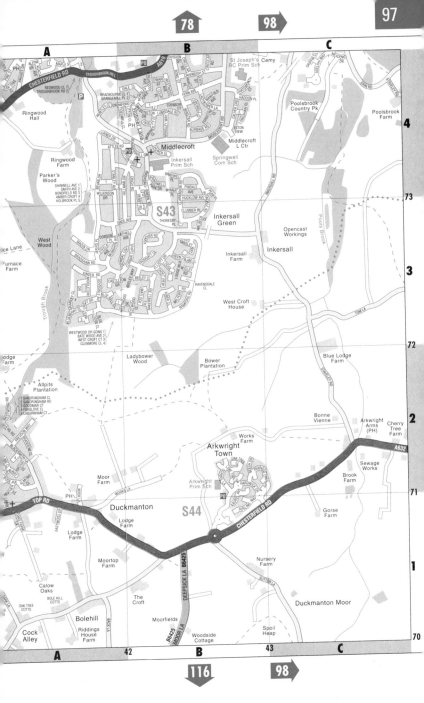

A
B
C

Seymour Junction

Poolsbrook Country Pk

B6419

MILL LA

Lodge Farm

STAVELEY RD
THE GROVE
POOLSBROOK VIEW
POOLSBROOK CRES
POOLSBROOK COTTAGES

S43

WOODTHORPE RD

BENTINCK RD

Poolsbrook
P

Poolsbrook Prim Sch
PH

Woodside

Shuttlewo Comm

Brock Prim Sch

4

73

Shuttlewood

WOODTHORPE
ACON RD
PH
PO

PRETORIA ST

Opencast Workings

CHESTERFIELD RD

The Nunnery

Wy

NORTH
EAST TREE
POOL BRICK RD
SOUTH CRES

Sch
The Oaks

PH
PO

3

MARKHAM RD

Duckmanton

Middle Farm

Nunnery Farm

Woodhouse Farm

Bolsover Woodhouse

TOM LA
RECTORY RD
DUCKMANTON RD

Poplar Farm

Resr

Sewage Works

Works

72

S44

Nether Woodhouse Farm

ROBERTSONS AVE
MARKHAM LA

M1 Commerce Pk

BUTTERMILK LA

WOODSIDE LA

NETHER SPRINGS RD 1
BRIAR BRIGGS RD 2
MANOR COURT RD 3
HARVEY CT 4
HASLAM CT 5
BOLSOVER HILL 6

CHERRY TREE DR
ST PETERS CL

2

Manor Farm

RECTORY LA
MENS LA

Works

River Doe Lea

Over Woodhouse

BLIND LA

A632

CHESTERFIELD RD

B6418

FARM RD

71

Long Duckmanton

LONGCOURSE LA

Railway Cottages

Lea-Holme

Mill Farm

Bsns Pk

Bsns Pk

STATION RD

Castle Ind Est

HOUGHTON
CREST

STAITH RD

MORRISON WAY

P

New Bolsover

VILLAS RD

1

Longcourse House

Longcourse Farm

Burton Barn

The Golf

RUTLAND AVE
KESWICK CL
AMBLESIDE DR
ESKDALE CL

New Bolsover Prim Sch

PO

NEW STAT

Sewage Works

NORTH VIEW ST

70

44
A
45
B
46
C

80
100

A   B   C   S43

Blackbanks
Stanfree
Oak House
B6419
DAMBROOK LA
MANSFIELD RD
B6417
BORDLE LA
OXCROFT LA

4

Oxcroft
ttlewood
mmon

Elmton Farm

Oxcroft Est

73

S80

CHURCH RD
OXCROFT LA

Fox Covert

Brockley Wood Farm

Elmton Park Farm

Elmton Lodge Farm

SPRING LA

3

Brockley Wood

72

 odge arm

S44

Ovencroft Lane

Moor Farm

Petticoat Lane

Bolsover Moor Quarry

SHUTTLEWOOD RD

FEATHERBED LA

Sutherland Farm

Works

2

Cemy
Wks
MILL WK

Keepers Hollow

Farnsworth Farm

Nook Villa

Limekiln Field

Pond House

71

QUARRY RD

Bolsover Moor

LANDEMERE CT

Bolsover Com

Sycamore Farm

Pondfield Bungalow

ROTHERHAM RD

1

P
TOWN END
P
BOLSOVER

B6419

STEEL LA
THE VILLAS
LONGLANDS

School

Sch

CEDAR ST
ELSWORTH
PARK
DR
HIGH ST
MEADOWS RD
HORSE
BECK CL
RD
OWLANDS

Tree
SYCAMORE

HILL

MOORACRE LA

Scarcliffe Grange

Langwith Rd
SANDHILLS RD
MOOR LA
AVE
LANGSTONE AVE

Bolsover Sch

Bolsover Moor Farm

ST LAWRENCE AVE

70

A   48   B   49   C

118
100

A   B   C

Huncecroft

Adventure Park

The Winnings

Norton

Hunters Lea

Robin Hood Way

4

S80

Holbeck

Woodhouse Hall

Main Gates Lodge

Tile Kiln Wood

High Holbeck

PO

Holbeck Woodhouse

73

Bonbusk

Woodhouse Hill

A60

A60 Mansfield

Little Remise

Hill Top Remise

Kennels

3

Hilltop House

South Carr Farm

Collingthwaite Farm

72

Woodend

Woodend Farm

NG20

BUCKLEYFIELD LA

Nottinghamshire STREET ATLAS A616 Newark-on-Trent

Graves Wood

Gorse Covert

A616

2

Cemy

Whaley Thorns Prim Sch

Blue Barn Farm

Shireoaks Hill Farm

NEW COTTS

WOODLAND VIEW

Whaley Thorns Heritage Ctr

Cuckney

71

Cuckney Dam

Whaley Thorns

Mill Hill

A632 Newark-on-Trent (A616)

Langwith Lodge

Pasture Hill Farm

1

PH

The Lake

MAIN RD

Nether Langwith

Sewage Works

Langwith Mill House

A632

Park House Cottages

BROOKHOUSE CT

QUEEN'S WLK

Park House Plantation

Park House Farm

Boon Hills Farm

A   54   B   55   C

A · B · C

4

Cumberland Cottage

Cumberland Brook

A54

Chy

Wood Moss

Sparbent

Holt

Dane Valley Way

69

Blackclough

A54

Three Shire Heads

Panniers Pool

Kno Com

3

Leech Wood

Cut-thorn Hill

SK11

Cut-thorn

Knotbury Farm

Knotbury

68

Birchenough Hill

Robins Clough

River Dane

Dane Valley Way

Knotbury Lee Farm

Knar

Turn Edge

SK17

2

Far Hole-edge

Hawk's Nest

Axe E Green

Parks

Wicken Walls

Far E Fa

67

Hole-edge

Bennettshitch

Spring Head

1

Higher Bangs

Lower Bangs

New Cottage

Burntcliff Top

Midgleygate

Greens

Wilds Roe

Goosetree

The Wash

66

Gradbach Mill (YH)

Greenstitch

Manor Farm

99 · A · 00 · B · 01 · C

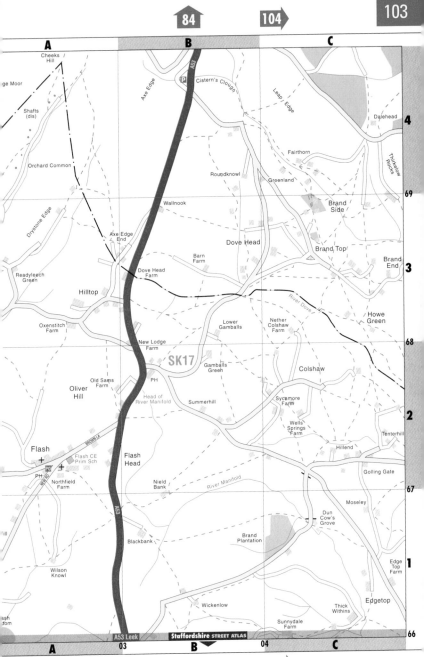

A B C

Cheeks
Hill

ge Moor

Shafts
(dis)

Orchard Common

Drystone Edge

Readyleech
Green

Hilltop

Oxenstitch
Farm

Oliver
Hill

Old Sams
Farm

Flash

Northfield
Farm

PH

Wilson
Knowl

ash
tom

Axe Edge

P

Cistern's Clough

Leap Edge

Dalehead

Thirkelow
Rocks

4

Fairthorn

Roundknowl

Greenland

Wallnook

Brand
Side

69

Axe Edge
End

Dove Head

Brand Top

Barn
Farm

Dove Head
Farm

Brand
End

3

River Dove

Howe
Green

Lower
Gamballs

Nether
Colshaw
Farm

68

New Lodge
Farm

SK17

Gamballs
Green

Colshaw

PH

Head of
River Manifold

Summerhill

Sycamore
Farm

2

Wells
Springs
Farm

Tenterhill

BROWN LA

Hillend

Flash
Head

Golling Gate

Flash CE
Prim Sch

Nield
Bank

River Manifold

67

A53

Moseley

Dun
Cow's
Grove

Blackbank

Brand
Plantation

Edge
Top
Farm

1

Wickenlow

Thick
Withins

Edgetop

Sunnydale
Farm

66

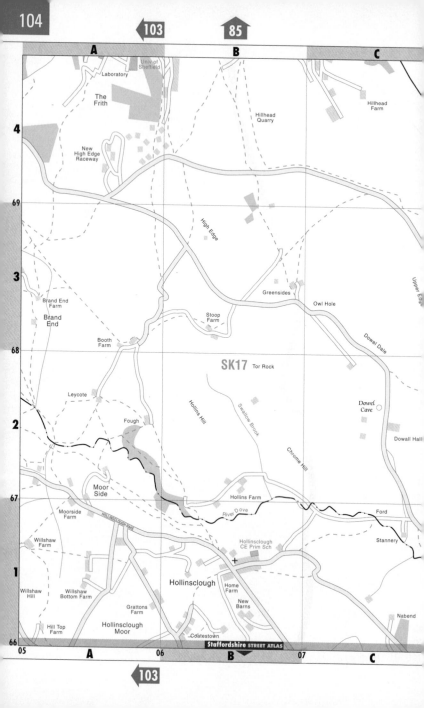

A B C

Laboratory

Univ of Sheffield

The Frith

Hillhead Farm

Hillhead Quarry

4

New High Edge Raceway

69

High Edge

3

Brand End Farm

Greensides

Owl Hole

Brand End

Stoop Farm

Upper Edge

Booth Farm

Dowel Dale

68

SK17 Tor Rock

Leycote

Hollins Hill

Swallow Brook

Dowel Cave

2

Fough

Chrome Hill

Dowall Hall

Moor Side

67

Hollins Farm

Moorside Farm

HOLLINSCLOUGH ROAD

River Dove

Ford

Willshaw Farm

Hollinsclough CE Prim Sch

Stannery

1

Willshaw Hill

Willshaw Bottom Farm

Hollinsclough

Home Farm

New Barns

Nabend

Grattons Farm

Hill Top Farm

Hollinsclough Moor

Coatestown

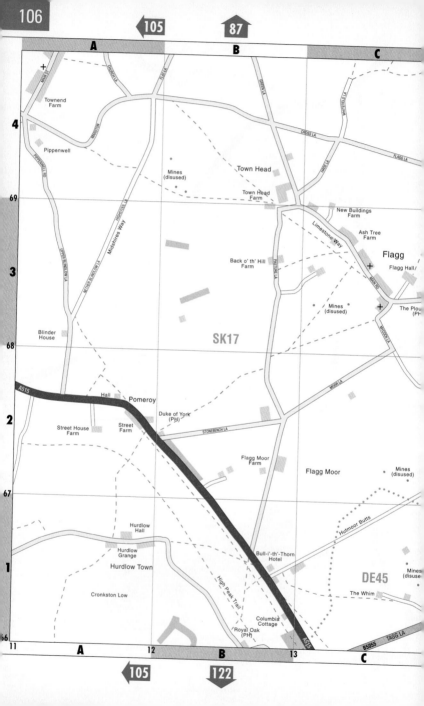

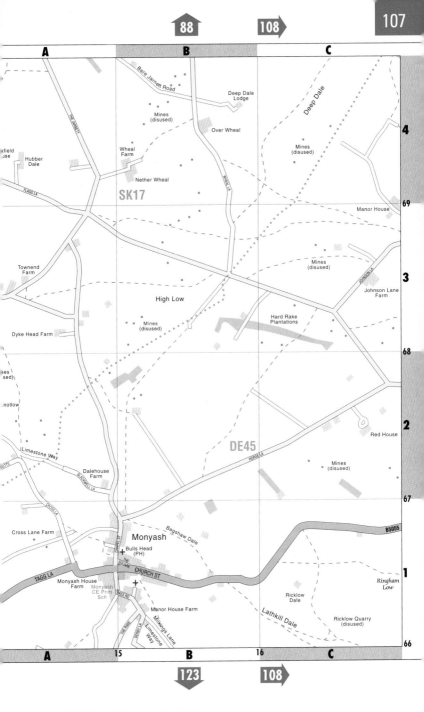

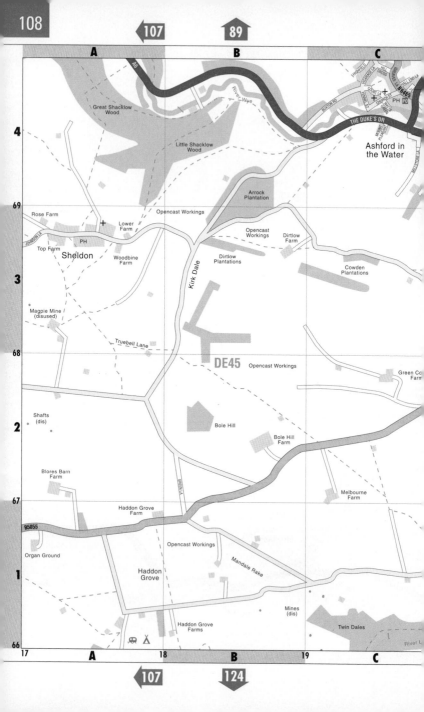

107
89

A   **B**   **C**

A6

River Wye

Great Shacklow
Wood

Little Shacklow
Wood

THORNELL
CRAGG LA
HILL
CROSS
BRIDGE ST B6465
CHURCH LA
GREAVES LA
CLAYTON LA
BUXTON RD
FENNEL ST
VICARAGE LA
COURT
PH
PO

THE DUKE'S DR

4

Ashford in
the Water

MONSAL
DALE
FACKLESS
MILLSTONE LA

Arrock
Plantation

69

Rose Farm

Opencast Workings

Opencast
Workings

Dirtlow
Farm

JOHNSON LA

Lower
Farm

PH

Top Farm

Sheldon

Woodbine
Farm

Dirtlow
Plantations

Cowden
Plantations

3

Kirk Dale

Magpie Mine
(disused)

Truebell Lane

68

DE45

Opencast Workings

Green Co
Farm

2

Shafts
(dis)

Bole Hill

Bole Hill
Farm

Melbourne
Farm

67

Blores Barn
Farm

GREEN LA

Haddon Grove
Farm

B5055

Organ Ground

Opencast Workings

Mandale Rake

1

Haddon
Grove

Mines
(dis)

Twin Dales

Haddon Grove
Farms

River L

66

17   **A**   **18**   **B**   **19**   **C**

107
124

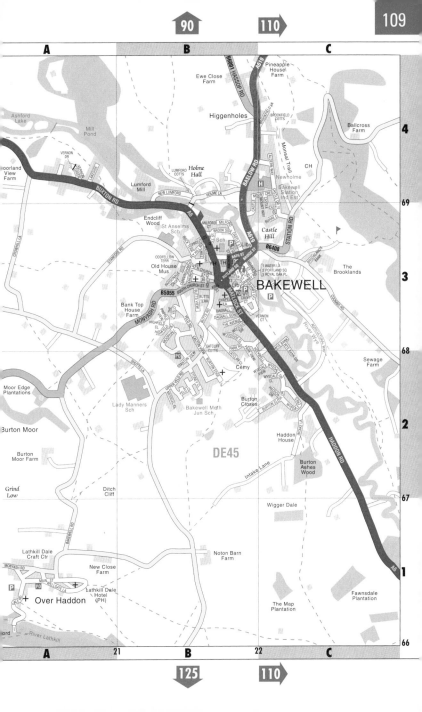

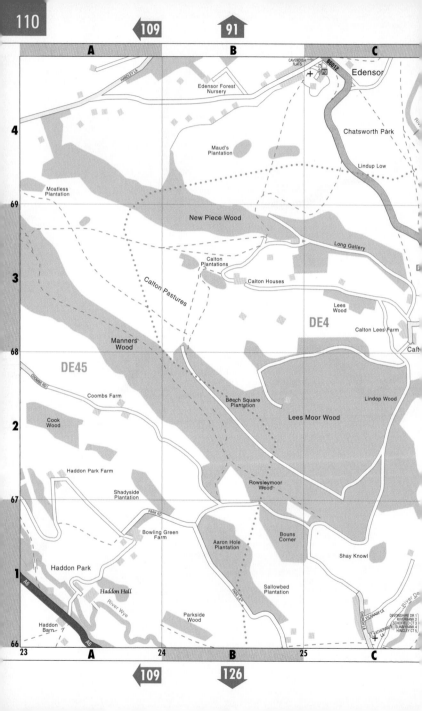

109
91

A   B   C

HANDLEY LA

CAVENDISH FLATS

B6012

Edensor

Edensor Forest Nursery

4

Maud's Plantation

Chatsworth Park

Lindup Low

Moatless Plantation

69

New Piece Wood

Long Gallery

Calton Plantations

3

Calton Pastures

Calton Houses

Lees Wood

DE4

Calton Lees Farm

Manners Wood

68

Calt

DE45

COOMBS RD

Coombs Farm

Beech Square Plantation

Lindop Wood

2

Cook Wood

Lees Moor Wood

Haddon Park Farm

Shadyside Plantation

67

Rowsleymoor Wood

PARK RD

Bowling Green Farm

Aaron Hole Plantation

Bouns Corner

Shay Knowl

1

Haddon Park

A6

Haddon Hall

River Wye

Parkside Wood

Sallowbed Plantation

River De

CHURCH LA

VICARAGE LA

ST CATHERINE'S LA

DEVONSHIRE DR 1
RIVERBANK 2
SCHOFIELD CT 3
SUNNYBANK 4
HINCKLEY CT 5

Haddon Barn

A6

66

23   A   24   B   25   C

109
126

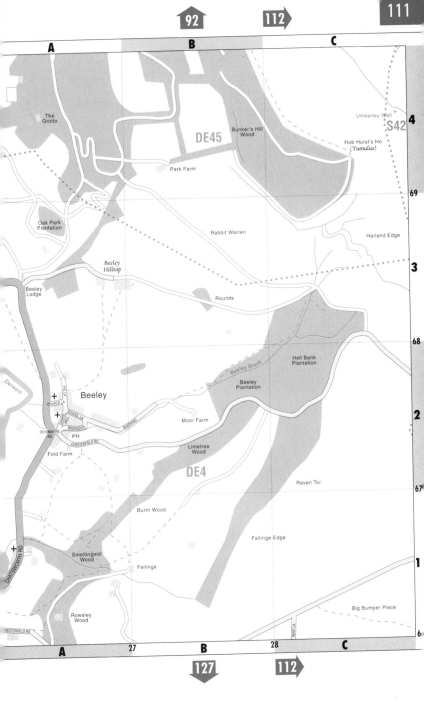

A   B   C

The Grotto

Umberley Well

S42

DE45

Bunker's Hill Wood

Hob Hurst's Ho (Tumulus)

4

Park Farm

69

Oak Park Plantation

Rabbit Warren

Harland Edge

Beeley Hilltop

3

Beeley Lodge

Rounds

68

Hell Bank Plantation

Beeley Brook

Beeley Plantation

Derwent

Beeley

School La

Moor Farm

2

PH

Chesterfield Rd

Limetree Wood

Fold Farm

DE4

Raven Tor

67

Burnt Wood

Fallinge Edge

1

Chatsworth Rd

Smeltingmill Wood

Fallinge

Rowsley Wood

Big Bumper Piece

Brent La

Chesterfield Rd

6

A   27   B   28   C

A　　　**B**　　　**C**

Rodknoll Farm

Mast

Loads Head Farm

Loads Fa

LOADSHEAD LA

ROCKNOLL LA

SYDA LA

CLAYPIT LA

4

Umberley Sick

Upper Loads

Well Lane Farm

Syda Farm

69

S42

LONGSIDE RD

Hipper Sick

Longside Moor

DE45

3

Beeley Moor

Slagmill Plantation

Harland Sick

Arkwright Plantation

DE4

Lamb Pasture

Harewood Grange

68

Harewood Grange Farm

Ha

2

Millstone Sick

Harewood Moor

67

S45

KELBY LA

1

DE4

Sitchs Plantation

Screetham House Farm

Moor Hall Farm

Gladwin's Mark

Gladwin's Mark Wood

SCREETHAM LA

Al

Roac Woc

Peasunhurst

Sitchs

Upper Dogkennel Plantation

Roach Farm

B5057

66

29　　**A**　　**30**　　**B**　　**31**　　**C**

A   B   C

Somersall Hall

Horse Wood

Walton

A632 WALTON RD

S40
Walton

HAREHILL CT 3
BIRCHWOOD CT 5
GRANGEWOOD CT 5
LONGCROFT CT 6
THORNTREE CT 7
STOCKWELL CT 8

CHESTERFIELD

Spring House Farm

Park Hall Cl

Allison Farm

Walton House

MATLOCK RD

Birdholme Brook

Walton Lodge

PH

Walton Wood

Widdowson Spring Wood

Walton Lodge Farm

A632

Broadgorse Farm

Emmet Field Wood

Clayton Upper Wood

Well Close Wood

Nether Spr Wood

Harperhill Farm

S42

Green Wood

Swathwick Farm

CHARTWELL AVE

FLORENCE RD
WELBECK DR
FRANCES DR
BRADBURY DR
RECTORY DR

Winge

Harper Hill

SWATHWICK LA

Swathwick

SWATHWICK CL

Harehill Plantation

Up Spe Wo

The Great Pond of Stubbing

Bradbury Wood

Hill Houses

Deer Park Prim Sch

Stubbing Court

PEARCE LA

Pearce Lane Farm

BALLHOUSES LA

Tricket Brook

Nether House Farm

Stubbing Court Home Farm

Bolehill Farm

Cowley Wood

Belfit Hill

Silbigh Wood

Ivyspring Wood

S45

Black Wood

Works

Hardwick Wood

A   B   C

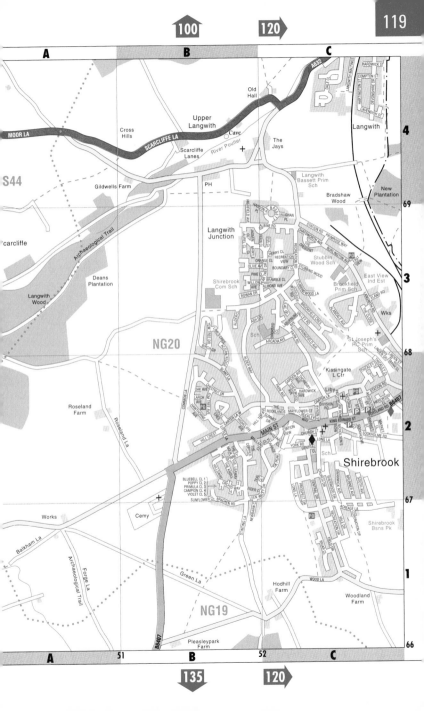

A   B   C

4

Boon Hills Wood

Top Farm

Cuckney Hay Wood

Lady's Grove

Warsop Wood

Minster Wood

Collier Spring

WOOD LA

69

Lord Stubbins Wood

NG20

William Wood Lane

Spring Lane

Spoil Heap

3

Warsop Cottage Farm

William Wood Farm

Parson's Wood

68

1 MUSTERS ST
2 NEW LINDEN ST
3 MANVERS ST
4 MANVERS CT

NORTH ST

MURDELL LA

KING ST

Hills and Holes

WEST ST

MAR

STATION RD

VERNON

Sookholme Lodge Farm

PH

Warsop Vale

Sookholme Moor

WAR

HARDWICK ST

Shirebrook

William Wood Bridge

MERCHANT ST

2

Works

CARTER LA

B6031

B6407

Bully Lane

Hammerwater Bridge

SOOKHOLME RD

Spring Lane

SOOKHOLME LA

River Meden

Spoil Heap

67

Colliery

Spoil Heap

LONGSTER LA

Mill Farm

Spring Farm

Sookholme

Mosscar L

Spion Kop

BATH LA

Bath Lane Farm

1

WOOD LA

Sookholme Bath

NG19

Rough Wood

SOOKHOLME RD

A60

MAN

Ox Pasture Wood

66

Spring Wood

Nettleworth Farm

B6407

53   A   54   B   55   C

Yewtree Grange

Under the Hill

Green Lane

Beggar's Bridge

4

Underhill Farm

Meadow Farm

Crowdecote

Bank Top Farm

Daisy Knowl

Sewage Works

River Dove

PH

St Bartholomew's CE Prim Sch

Top o'th' Edge

Stiff Close

Craft Centre

Gauledge

CARDER GREEN

CHURCH ST

MARKET PL

HIGH ST

65

Longnor

Longnor Bridge

QUEEN ST

CHAPEL ST

RIVER VIEW

WINDYRIDGE

Folds End

Gosslecroft

Bridge End Farm

Longnor Saw Mill

Windy Arbour Bridge

Crofts Farm

Edgetop

Upper Whitle

3

The Cottage

Boothlow Hayes

Knowsley Cross

64

SK17

Under Whitle

Waterhouse Farm

Over Boothlow

Brownspit

Sheen Moor

Top Farm

2

Lower Boothlow

Pumping Station

Ball Ridge Farm

Race House

63

Frog Hole

Fernyknowle

Ridge Farm

Bridge End

The Low

Ridge End Farm

Ludburn

1

Park House

Hill End

Blake Brook

Broadham

The Holmes

Pool

Flat Head

Sheen Lane Farm

Slate House Farm

62

121
106

A

B

C

Sparklow

Needham Grange

Cronkston Grange

High Needham

Mines (dis)

TAGG LA

Endmoor

B5055

A515

Monyash

D

Cronkston Lodge

Clemonseats Plantation

Mi

4

Waggon Low

65

Midshires Way

Mine (dis)

Cotesfield

3

Mosey Low

SK17

Custare Fa

64

Pilsbury Castle Hills

Pilsbury Lodge

Sand Pit

2

Broadmeadow Hall

Pilsbury

River Dove

Parks Barn

Vin Hol

63

Mines (dis)

Sheen Hill

Carder Low

Long

1

High Sheen Farm

Ludwell Farm

Mines (dis)

Harris Close

HIGH LA

62

11

A

12

B

13

C

121
137

A B C

Palmerston Wood

River Lathkill

Lathkill Dale

Low Wood

Meadow Place
Wood

4

Calling Low Dale

Nature
Reserve

Mines
(dis)

Bee Low Wood

65

Cales Dale

Calling Low

Limestone Way

Bee Low

BACK LA

3

Low Moor
Plantation

MOOR LA

P

Mines
(dis)

Mine

LONG RAKE

64

Works

Lomberdale
Hall

DE45

Crossflat
Plantation

2

Greenseats
Plantation

Castle
Farm

Bushey
Wood

Flax Dale

Middleton

Castle
(remains of)

Middleton Common

Thorntree

RAKE LA

Rake
Wood

63

Mere Farm

THE PINFOLD

Middleton
Hall

Green Lane

WHITFIELD LA

1

MIDDLETON WAY

Woodside
Farm

Kenslow
Farm

62

Little Rookery
Plantation

Kenslow
Wood

17 A 18 B 19 C

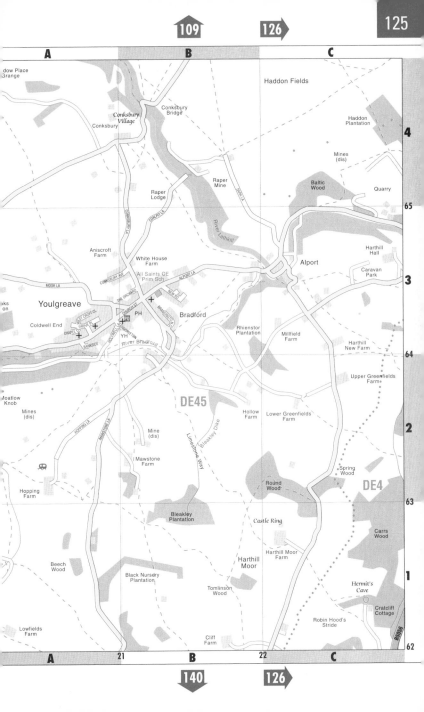

125
110

A   **B**   **C**

A6

Nutseats Quarry
(dis)

B5056

Wye
Farm

WYE TERR

Mill
WOODHOUSE LA

CHURCH LA

PO

CHATSWORTH

SCHOOL LA

Rowsley
CE P
Sc

Shafts
(dis)

Pickering
Wood

River Wye

River Lathkill

Dove House
Farm

Peak
Tor

Rowsley

4

Oxclose
Wood

Sewage
Farm

Congreave
Farm

The
Plantation

The
Plantation

PEAR TREE LA

DE45

Congreave

Pilhough

65

Bowers
Hall

Pilhough
Farm

Stanton in Peak

Smithy
Wood

Beighton
Houses

PILHOUGH LA

Holly
Wood

Tolls
Wood

3

Stanton-in-Peak
CE Prim Sch

Sheepwalk
Wood

PILHOUGH RD

Stanton
Woodhouse
Farm

Park
Farm

SCHOOL LA

*Stanton
Woodhouse*

The
Lodge

PH
MAIN
ST

THE GREEN

PARK
LA

THE LANE

*Stanton
Hall*

64

DE4

Stoney Ley
Wood

Mast

The
Scraggs

Stanton Moor
Quarries
(dis)

*King
Stone*

Nine Ladies
Stone Circle

Tower

Hillcarr Wood

2

Stanton Lee

Stoney Ley
Lodge

BIRCHOVER RD

Cow Close
Farm

Stanton Moor
Plantation

LEES RD

Bee Hill

63

Black Knowle
Plantation

Eagle Tor

Mires
Farm

Stanton Park
Quarry

Hill
Wood

War

Hi
F

Warrencarr
Farm

1

Dungeon
Plantation

Birchover
Quarry

BARTON HILL

B5056

Birchover

EAGLE TERR

CLOUGH LANE

Barn Farm

PH
THE GREEN

P

Brookfield
Farm

UPPER TOWN LA

BRADLEY CT

62

23   **A**   **24**   **B**   **25**   **C**

125
141

A

B

C

CHESTERFIELD RD
Rowsley
Wood

Falling
Edge

Little Bumper
Piece

Whitesprings
Plantation

4

Copy
Wood

Copywood

Bumper
Castle

Wayne
Piece

Tinkersley

Tinkersley
Farm

Black Hill

Wayne Corner
Plantation

65

Northwood
Carr

BENT LA

Halldale Brook

Woodside
Farm

Sitch
Plantation

NORTHWOOD LA
THE AVENUE

Northwood

Burley Fields
Farm

Halldale Wood

Hall Dale

3

DALE RD N

PARK
COTTS
PARK
TERR

Stancliffe
Hall Sch

Newtonlot
Plantation

DE4

Peak Railway

Stancliffe
Quarries

Playing
Field

VINEYARD
TERR

Darley Hillside

Hallmoor
Wood

DALE HILL LA

Cock's Head
Wood

BUTCHER S LA

B5057

64

STANCLIFFE VIEW

STRATHALLAN CL
HAWKSLEY

MOOR LA

DERWENT AVE

1 PEVERIL CL
2 ARKWRIGHT CL
3 OLD HALL CL
4 NEWELL WAY
5 JOHN TURNER RD
6 BOWLER RD

Hazel
Farm

SYDNOPE HILL

Potter
Dam

2

STANCLIFFE VIEW
STANTON
CL

Molyneaux
Bsns Pk
PEARLAND
VIEW

WHITWORTH RD

STANCLIFFE RD

Fancy
Dam

Abbey
Farm

ST HELEN'S CL 1
CROWSTONES RD 2
OKER DR 3

LIME GR

THE PARKWAY

PARK VIEW

LADY GROVE RD

Two
Dales

63

BUTTS RD
LC

DALE RD

OKER AVE

OKER RISE

ROMAN RD

HALL DALE LA

WHITWORTH RD

BLACKSMITHS YD

Darley
Churchtown CE
Prim Sch

Rectory
Farm

BROADMEADOW

UNDERHALL

CHESTERFIELD RD

Holt
Farm

Churchtown

River Derwent

STATION RD

Darley
Dale

B5057

RYECROFT

Warney Brook

Darley Dale
Prim Sch

Holt
Wood

Darley Dale

LC

GREENAWAY LA

HOLT RD

1

FOUR LANE
ENDS

OLD RD

DALE RD S

GRANGE RD

JUDY HILL

Redhouse Stables
Working Carriage Mus

St Elphins
Sch

Bridge
Farm

MAIN RD

River Derwent

NORMANHURST
PK

DAKEYNE

rks

OLDFIELD LA

Flatts
Farm

27

B5057

B

28

C

62

127
112

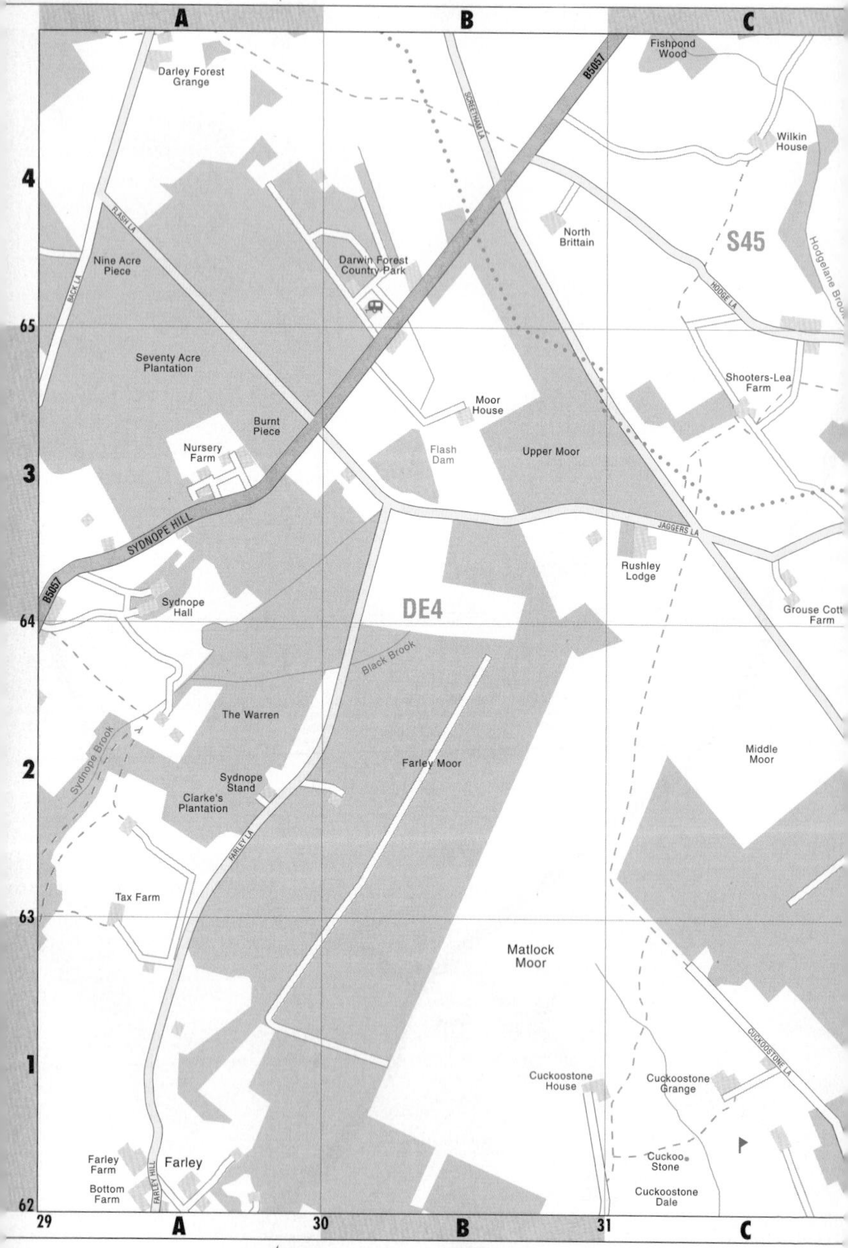

A   **B**   **C**

Fishpond Wood

Darley Forest Grange

Wilkin House

4

Nine Acre Piece

North Brittain

S45

Hodgelane Brook

Darwin Forest Country Park

65

Seventy Acre Plantation

Shooters-Lea Farm

Moor House

Burnt Piece

Nursery Farm

3

Flash Dam

Upper Moor

SYDNOPE HILL

JAGGERS LA

Rushley Lodge

B5057

Grouse Cott Farm

64

Sydnope Hall

DE4

Black Brook

The Warren

Sydnope Brook

Middle Moor

2

Farley Moor

Sydnope Stand

Clarke's Plantation

FARLEY LA

63

Tax Farm

Matlock Moor

CUCKOOSTONE LA

1

Cuckoostone House

Cuckoostone Grange

Farley Farm

FARLEY HILL

Farley

Cuckoo Stone

Bottom Farm

Cuckoostone Dale

62

29   **A**   **30**   **B**   **31**   **C**

127
143

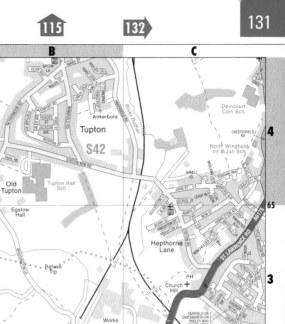

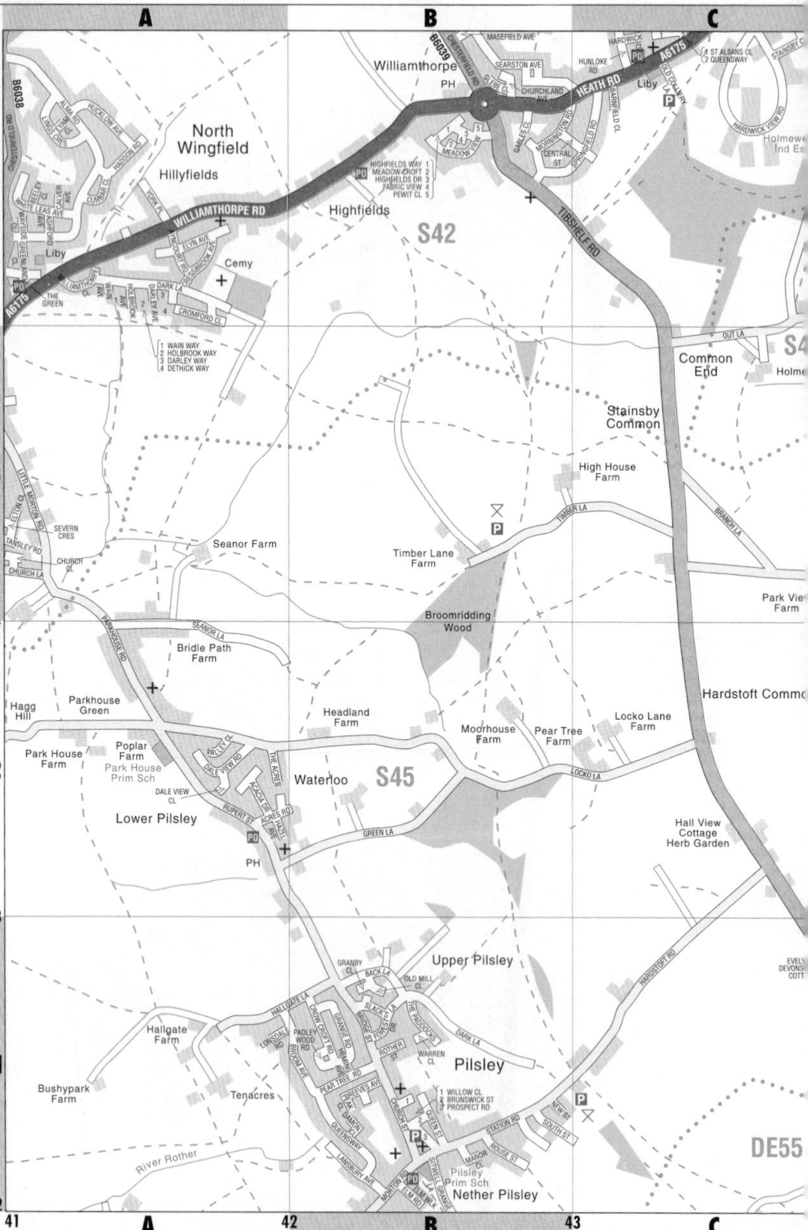

A
B
C
4
3
2
1
65
64
63
62
41
42
43
North Wingfield
Hillyfields
Williamthorpe
PH
Highfields
S42
Liby
Cemy
B6038
B6039
A6175
CHESTERFIELD RD
WILLIAMTHORPE RD
HEATH RD
TIBSHELF RD
ALMA RD
HUCKLOW AVE
LINGS CRES
ELYAM CL
HADDON RD
CLARBAR CL
YORK PL
BEELEY CL
CALVER AVE
WHITE LEAS AVE
ASHFORD AVE
WAYSIDE GREENLAND
THE GREEN
WILLIAMTHORPE AVE
WAIN AVE
HOLBROOK AVE
DARLEY AVE
DARK LA
CROMFORD CL
ELVIN AVE
SYNCOURT RD
CRESSBROOK AVE
1 WAIN WAY
2 HOLBROOK WAY
3 DARLEY WAY
4 DETHICK WAY
HIGHFIELDS WAY 1
MEADOW CROFT 2
HIGHFIELDS DR 3
FABRIC VIEW 4
PEWIT CL 5
MEADOW VIEW
MASEFIELD AVE
SEARSTON AVE
GLEBE CL
CHURCHLAND AVE
GABLES CL
MORNINGTON RD
CENTRAL ST
SPRINGFIELD RD
BARNFIELD CL
HUNLOKE RD
HARDWICK CL
OLD COLLIERY LA
1 ST ALBANS CL
2 QUEENSWAY
STAINSBY CL
HARDWICK VIEW RD
Holmewood Ind Est
OUT LA
Common End
Holme
Stainsby Common
High House Farm
TIMBER LA
BRANCH LA
Timber Lane Farm
Seanor Farm
Broomridding Wood
Park View Farm
LITTLE MORTON RD
ELTON CL
SEVERN CRES
TANSLEY RD
CHURCH CL
CHURCH LA
PARKHOUSE RD
SEANOR LA
Bridle Path Farm
Hagg Hill
Parkhouse Green
Headland Farm
Moorhouse Farm
Pear Tree Farm
Locko Lane Farm
Hardstoft Commo
Park House Farm
Poplar Farm
Park House Prim Sch
VALLEY CL
DALE VIEW RD
DALE VIEW CL
THE ACRES
ACACIA DR
Waterloo
S45
LOCKO LA
Lower Pilsley
RUPERT ST
ACRES RD
HAZEL AVE
GREEN LA
PH
Hall View Cottage Herb Garden
HARDSTOFT RD
Upper Pilsley
GRANBY CL
BACK LA
OLD MILL CL
HALLGATE LA
CROW CROFT RD
GRANGE RD
SLACK'S LA
FOREST DR
THE PADDOCKS
DARK LA
BRIDGE ST
LONSDALE RD
PADLEY WOOD RD
BROOM AVE
HEMING AVE
ROTHER ST
WARREN CL
Pilsley
Hallgate Farm
Bushypark Farm
Tenacres
PEAR TREE RD
BREEVES AVE
PEAK CL
DAMON CL
QUEENSWAY
CHURCH ST
QUEEN ST
1 WILLOW CL
2 BRUNSWICK ST
3 PROSPECT RD
STATION RD
NEW ST
SOUTH ST
ROUSE ST
MANOR CL
LANSBURY AVE
MORTON RD
ELM WLK
ELM RD
STITWELL GRANGE
Pilsley Prim Sch
Nether Pilsley
River Rother
DE55
EVELY
DEVONS
COTT

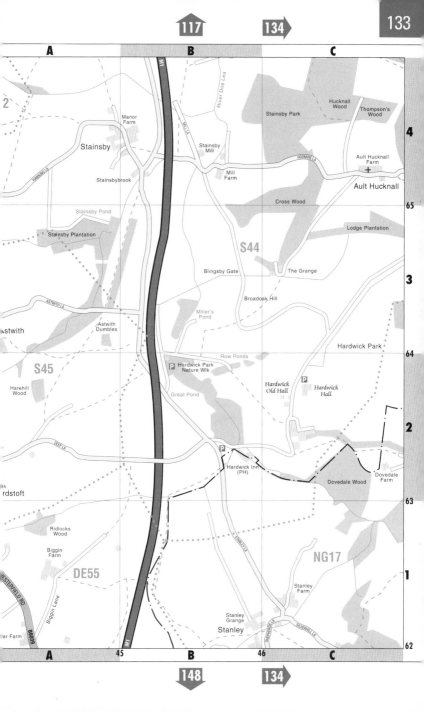

A

B

C

Strickle Brook

BEECH CRES

MAPLE GR

POPLAR GR

LIME TREE AVE

SYCAMORE AVE

LILAC GR

THE GREEN

ORCHARD CLOSE

HAWTHORN AVE

HARDWICK AVE

A617

Glapwell

MANSFIELD RD

GREEN LA

B6417

ROTHERHAM RD

Hill Top Farm

Longman Nook

New Houghton

CHESTERFIELD RD

GARDEN CRES

PINFOLD

4

Griff Wood

AULT HUCKNALL LA

S44

Top Farm

ROWTHORNE LA

GILL LA

65

BESTWOOD LA

Hall Farm

Rowthorne

FIELD LA

Anthony Bek Com Prim Sc

3

Car Plantation

P

Farfield Lane

Norcliff Wood

NG19

Batley Farm

Car Ponds

Merril Sick

LONGEDGE LA

Park Piece

64

Loneedge Lane

2

Hardwick Park Farm

Norwood

Norwood Lodge

NG17

Newbound Farm

BATLEY LA

Newboundmill Farm

MOOR

63

Crossley Plantation

NEWBOUND LA

Baxterhill

1

Hare Plantation

PLEATTLE LA

Hill Farm

River Meden

Little Dawgates Wood

62

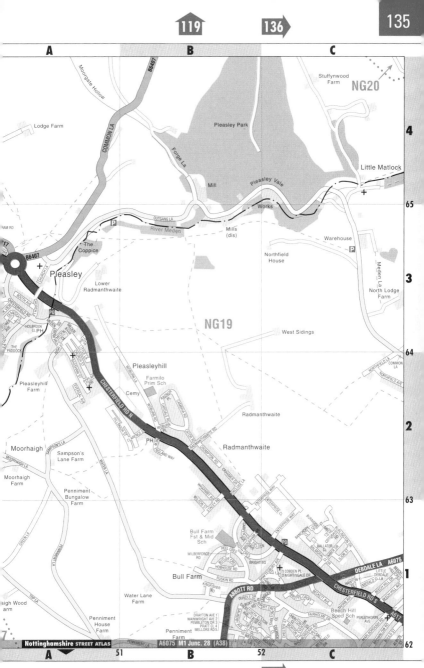

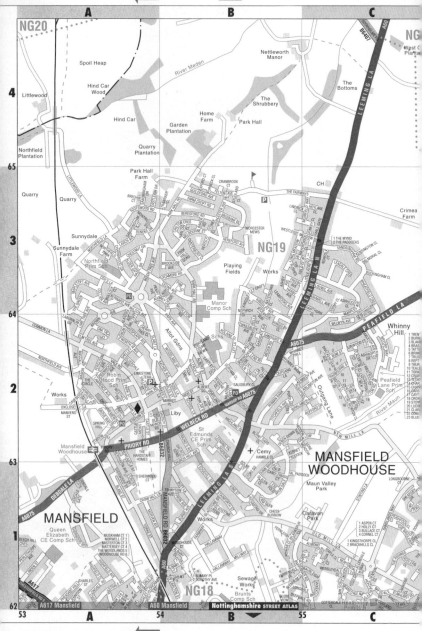

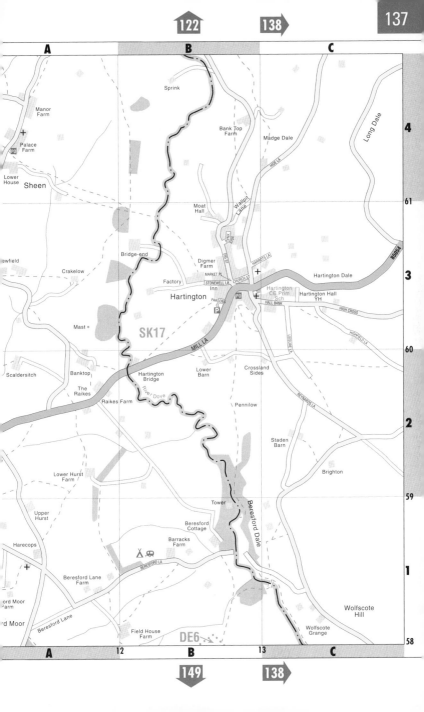

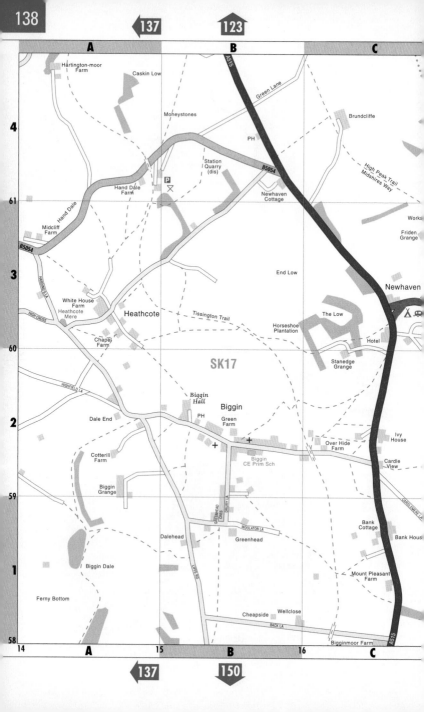

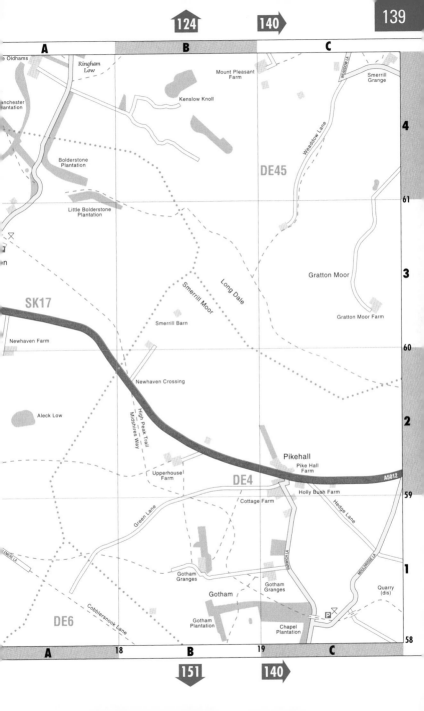

124
140

A
B
C

e Oldhams

Ringham Low

anchester lantation

Mount Pleasant Farm

Smerrill Grange

Kenslow Knoll

Weddlow Lane

4

Bolderstone Plantation

DE45

Little Bolderstone Plantation

61

Gratton Moor

3

Smerrill Moor

Long Dale

SK17

Smerrill Barn

Gratton Moor Farm

Newhaven Farm

60

Newhaven Crossing

Aleck Low

High Peak Trail Midshires Way

2

Pikehall

Pike Hall Farm

A5012

Upperhouse Farm

DE4

Holly Bush Farm

59

Cottage Farm

Hedge Lane

Green Lane

Gotham Granges

Gotham Granges

1

Quarry (dis)

Gotham

MOUSELOWE LA

DE6

Cobblersnook Lane

Gotham Plantation

Chapel Plantation

P

58

A
18
B
19
C

151
140

139

125

A

B

C

Fishpond Wood

Gratton Grange Farm

Rock Farm

Dud Wood

Dudwood Farm

Anthony Hill

Dale End House

Dale End

DE45

Dale End Farm

Woodbine Farm

Bury Cliff Farm

Well Street Farm

4

61

Oddo House Farm

Dark Lane

Elton House Farm

Elton CE Prim Sch

WEST END

EAST END

BACK LA

WINSTER

EAST END

Gratton Moor

Hungerhill Lane

Elton

Gratton Dale

Leadmines Farm

3

Blake Low

Shafts (dis)

60

Barker Barn

MOOR LA

P

2

Elton Common

DE4

Mouldridge Grange

Allsop Barn

Sacheveral Farm

A5012

MOULDRIDGE LA

Little Wisels Wood

59

Grange Barn

Astonhill

1

New Barn

High Peak Trail
Midshires Way

Rockhurst Farm

Greenlow Farm

58

20

A

21

B

22

C

139

152

141
127

A **B** **C**

OLDFIELD LE

River Derwent

B5057

PO

IVONBROOK CL

GOLD CL

EVERSLEIGH RISE

NORMANHURST DR
A6 DALE END S
GROVE RD
GREENAWAY LA
HILL CREST COTTS

DARLEY LODGE DR 1
OAKWOOD DR 2
ORCHARD RD 2

Upper
Hackney

Darley Bridge

DARLEY
HOUSE
EST

Wenslees
Farm

Cross
Green

Normanhurst
Farm

Whitworth

DARLEY
HACKNEY LA

4

Cambridge
Wood

South Darley
CE Prim Sch

OKER RD

HILL LA

Darley
Dale

H

PEAK RAILWAY

BAKEWELL RD

Oker
Farm

MOOR VIEW
MEADOW
VIEW
ALTON RISE

Mi

Wensley

Field
Farm

Oker

CHATSWORTH AVE
ELM AVE 2
LONSDALE GR 3
DEVONSHIRE AVE 4
CLEVE AVE 5

WOODS LA

PH

OKER LA

BR DALE

COURT RISE

61 B5057

Lobby
Farm

WILL
SHORE'S
LA

LOCKO LA

EATON LA

Ashton
Farm

River Derwent

ASKER LA

Big
Dungeon

OKER TERR
EAGLE TERR

Wensley Dale

Dalefields
Barn

Northern
Dale

Manor
Farm

Quarry
(dis)

SNITTERTON

3

Mines
(dis)

Snitterton

DE4

Snitterton
Hall

Hall
Qu

Leawood
Farm

60

Tearsall
Farm

Lea
Cottage

Masson

Brightgate
Farm

Brightgate

BONSALL LA

Jughole
Wood

SALTERS LA

2

Cottage
Farm

Bright Gate
Farm

NAILOR LA

Tower
Lane
Shafts
(dis)

BLAKELOW LA

MOORLANDS LA

POUND LANE

59

Opencast
Workings

Manor
Barn

Low
Farm

BLAKELOW LA

Wellmead Lane

Limestone
Way

Croft
Farm

Town
Head

Masson
Hill

MOOR LA

Brumlea
Farm

ABEL LA

UPPER TOWN LA

HIGH ST

Low
Mine

1

Horse Dale

Upper Town

THE DALE

YEOMAN ST

Bonsall

Ember
Farm

Horsedale
Farm

THE DALE

Bonsall
Dale

ABEL LA

CLATTERWAY

EMBER LA

Bonsall
CE Prim
Sch

58

26 **A** 27 **B** 28 **C**

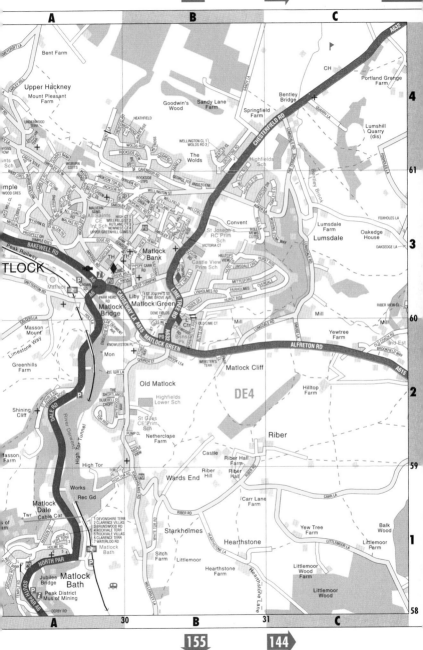

A   B   C

Bent Farm

Upper Hackney

Mount Pleasant
Farm

Goodwin's
Wood

Sandy Lane
Farm

Springfield
Farm

Bentley
Bridge

CH

Portland Grange
Farm

Lumshill
Quarry
(dis)

4

HEATHFIELD

WELLINGTON CL 1
WOLDS RD 2

The
Wolds

Highfields
Sch

ROCKSIDE
STPS

CHESTERFIELD RD

Bentley Brook

FOXHOLES LA

61

WOLDS RISE

ROCKSIDE

CAVENDISH RD

GEORGE RD   AMBERDENE

Lumsdale
Farm

Oakedge
House

OAKSEDGE LA

Convent

St Joseph's
RC Prim
Sch

VICTORIA CT

Lumsdale

All Saints
CE
Int Sch

HIGH CT 1
WELLFIELD ST 2
RUTLAND CT 3
NEWNES CT 4
UPPER GREENHILL GDNS 5

EDGE RD

Matlock
Bank

HILLTOPS
VIEW

Castle View
Prim Sch

Mill

RIBER VIEW CL

3

BAKEWELL RD

Peak Railway

TLOCK

Matlock

P

CROWN
SQ

PO

TH

Matlock
Bridge

CAUDWELL LA A615

PARK HEAD
RD

Liby

Matlock Green

1 ST JOSEPH'S ST
2 LIME GROVE AVE

DENE FIELDS
CT

OLD LIME CT

LIME TREE RD

VINHOLMES RD

METTEFORD

FAIRHOLMES

HURST RISE

LUMSDALE RD

Mill

Mill

Yewtree
Farm

Ind Est

BROOKFIELD WAY

OLD COACH RD

60

BALERS LA

Masson
Mount

Limestone
Way

Greenhills
Farm

Mon

KNOWLESTON PL

MATLOCK GREEN

CHURCH ST   BROOK LEA

WEBSTER'S
TERR

ALFRETON RD   A615

Matlock Cliff

DE4

Hilltop
Farm

2

Shining
Cliff

Old Matlock

Highfields
Lower Sch

St Giles
CE Prim
Sch

Netherclose
Farm

Riber

Castle

Riber Hall
Farm

Riber
Hill

Riber
Hall

59

Masson
Farm

High Tor

Works

Wards End

Carr Lane
Farm

CARR LA

Yew Tree
Farm

LITTLEMOOR LA

Balk
Wood

Littlemoor
Farm

1

Matlock
Dale

Twr   Cable Car

1 DEVONSHIRE TERR
2 CLARENCE VILLAS
3 BRUNSWOOD RD
4 ROCKVALE TERR
5 ROCKVALE VILLAS
6 CLARENCE TERR
7 WATERLOO RD

River Derwent

High Tor or Tunnel

Rec Gd

RIBER RD

Starkholmes

Hearthstone

Littlemoor
Wood
Farm

Littlemoor
Wood

Matlock
Bath

HOLME RD

NORTH PAR

P

Sitch
Farm

Littlemoor

Hearthstone
Farm

Jubilee
Bridge

Matlock
Bath

SOUTH PAR RD

P

Peak District
Mus of Mining

DERBY RD

Hearthstone Lane

58

A   30   B   31   C

143
129

A
B
C

Wayside Farm
Lant Lodge Farm
Packhorse Farm
Old Engine Farm
Cocking Tor
Ra

4

Holestone
North Carolina
Ravensnest

Silver Ridge
Sandyford Farm
South Carolina Farm
Ravensnest Wood

Tansley Moor

61

Foxholes
Blakelow Farm
ALLEN LA
Red House Farm
Ravensnest Tor

FOXHOLES LA
WHITELEA LA
White Lea Farm
Sunnyside
Blakelow Hill
S45

3

Mooredge Farm
KNABB LA
Butterley Top Farm
Butterle

Tansley Knoll
Mooredge
BUTTERLEY LA
Butterle

PO
Moorside Farm
Scotland Nursery
Butterley Hill
COLUMBINE LA
Reservoir

60

Tansley Prim Sch
DE4
SPOW LA
GOLDHILL
OLD COACH RD
CHURCH ST

TAWNEY CROFT
OAK TREE GDNS
Tansley
Yewtree Farm
RED HILL
LADYCROFT LA

Jackhill Farm
B6014
JETTING ST
Slag Hills

A615 ALFRETON RD
NOTTINGHAM RD

2

MOORLAND TERR
THATCHERS LA
Heathylea Farm
Redhill Farm
DOEHOLE LA
Moo

Yew Tree Farm
GREEN LA
STITCH LA

CABIN LA
Cunnery
CUNNERY LA
Dethick Common
Moor Wood
Dewey L Farm

59

Cookhill Plantation
Nursery
D

Balk Wood
WOOD LANE
HIGH LA
Canada Farm

1

WOOD LA
Well Wood
DETHICK LA
ST MARYS

Dethick
CROSS LANES

58
Babbington Farm
MILL LA

32
A
33
B
34
C

143
156

145 131

A B C

Ménel Farm
S45
Stretton House
PH
A61 STRETTON RD
Top Farm
STRAW LA
Ain Moor
S45

Opencast Workings

4
Cemy
B6036
B6014
Sidness Farm
Smithy Moor
Stretton
Stretton Farm
Averill Farm

PH
Hillside Farm
61
Hilltop Farm
MORTON ROAD

South Hill
South Hill Farm
Smithy Brook
Stretton Plantation
MAIN RD
Fold House Farm
BURNSHAW ST
DE55
STRETTON RD
3

Stretton Hillside
CEDAR ST
Northedge Farm
Morton

Reservoir Houses
Mickley Est
Yew Tree Farm
60
Ogston
SHAKESPEARE AVE
FIR TREE AVE
Mickley Inf Sch
HIGHAM LA

Ogston Bridge
OGSTON LA
SYCAMORE CL
Mickley Farm
Stonebroom
The Double Six (PH)
2
Pingle Farm
PH
WELL LA
Goosegreen

River Amber
B6013
CHESTERFIELD RD
59
Higham
Higham Farm Hotel
STRETTEA LA
NEW ST
THE CROFT
SCHOOL LA
Shirland Prim Sch
New Higham
PH
WELLINGTON MEWS

1
BELPER RD
Shirland Prim Sch
BOWAN DR
ASPEN RISE
MAIN RD
WELLINGTON LA
CHURCH ST
Shirland
Higham Dairy Farm
BUMPMILL LA
HALLGATE LA
HALLFIELDGATE LA
PIT LA
BEVAN ST
PO
PARK LA

58
BACK LA
Carr Hill Farm
Hallfield Gate
Hallfield Hall
A61
CROSS LA
38 A 39 B 40 C

A   **B**   **C**

The Hurst

Shepherd's
Lane Farm

Dunsil
Farm

4

Lane
End

Inn

MANSFIELD RD

Tibshelf Wharf
Farm

Silve
Fa

Tibshelf
Schs

Overmoor
Farm

Tibshelf
Wharf

WILD HILL

61

Saw Pit
Ind Est

Tibshelf

Marlpits
Farm

Whiteborough
Farm

City of
Whiteborou
Farm

Manor
Farm

DE55

Works

3

Service
Area

NEWTONWOOD LA

Newtonwood
Lodge Farm

NG17

Herro
Hil

PH

60

Service
Area

SUNNY
BANK

Bridge House
Farm

Woodland
Cottage

CHESTERFIELD RD

PENNINE

Johr
Pri

New
Newton
Green

MAIN ST

Littlemoor

Red Barn
Farm

Longside
Farm

STRAWBERRY BANK

CROFT
CT

MARKET PL 1
OLD FALL ST 2
NEW FALL ST 3
SAMPSONS YD 4
SWANN YD 5

Huthwaite

2

Newton Prim
Sch

PH

Sunnyside
Farm

59

Newton
Top
Farm

Pipes
Farm

HUTHWAITE LA

BLACKWELL RD

All Saints
CE Inf Sch

The County
Est

Robin Hood
Inn

Commonside

Depot

1

Church
Hill

Blackwell

NEW LA

Twinyards
Farm

B6406

BURN BROOK RD

PROSPECT PL

SUTTON IN
ASHFIELD

Hilcote
Hall

HILCOTE LA

PASTURE LA COKEFIELD
TERR

PH

Hilcote

FULWOOD RD

58

44   **A**   45   **B**   46   **C**

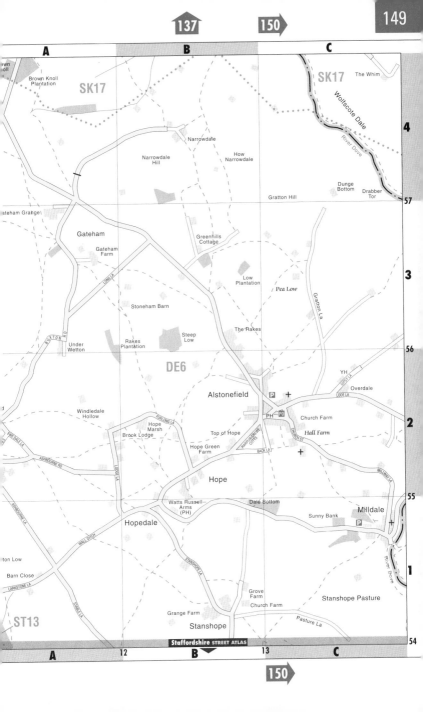

A   B   C

Brown Knoll
Plantation

SK17

SK17   The Whim

Wolfscote Dale

Narrowdale

River Dove

4

Narrowdale
Hill

How
Narrowdale

Gateham Grange

Gratton Hill

Dunge
Bottom

Drabber
Tor

57

Gateham

Greenhills
Cottage

Gateham
Farm

LONG LA

Low
Plantation

Pea Low

Gratton La

3

Stoneham Barn

BUXTON

Under
Wetton

Rakes
Plantation

Steep
Low

The Rakes

56

DE6

YH

Overdale

GIPSY LA

Alstonefield

P

+

LODE LA

Windledale
Hollow

FURLONG LA

Hope
Marsh

PH

Church Farm

Brook Lodge

Top of Hope

Hall Farm

MAJOR'S LANE

Hope Green
Farm

BACK LA

CHAPEL ST

+

ASHBOURNE RD

LODE LA

Hope

MILLWAY LA

55

ASHBOURNE LA

Watts Russell
Arms
(PH)

Dale Bottom

Sunny Bank

Milldale

P

+

Hopedale

HALL DITCH

STANSHOPE LA

River Dove

LARKSTONE LA

ton Low

Barn Close

1

LARKSTONE LA

Grove
Farm

Stanshope Pasture

Church Farm

ST13

TIDESWELL LA

Grange Farm

Stanshope

Pasture La

54

A   12   B   13   C

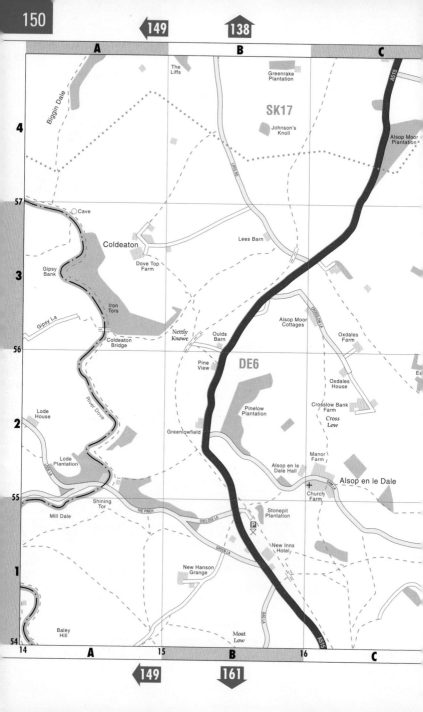

149
138

A B C

Biggin Dale

The Liffs

Greenrake Plantation

SK17

Johnson's Knoll

Alsop Moor Plantation

4

57

Cave

Coldeaton

Lees Barn

Dove Top Farm

Gipsy Bank

3

Iron Tors

Gipsy La

Coldeaton Bridge

Nettly Knowe

Ouds Barn

Alsop Moor Cottages

Oxdales Farm

56

Pine View

DE6

Oxdales House

Crosslow Bank Farm

Cross Low

River Dove

Lode House

Pinelow Plantation

Greenlowfield

Manor Farm

2

Lode Plantation

Alsop en le Dale Hall

Alsop en le Dale

Church Farm

55

Shining Tor

THE PINCH

Mill Dale

OXCLOSE LA

Stonepit Plantation

P

New Inns Hotel

GREEN LA

New Hanson Grange

1

Baley Hill

Moat Low

A515

54

14 A 15 B 16 C

149
161

139 **152**

SK17

A **B** **C**

Uppermoor
Farm

Cobblersnook
Plantation

Cobblersnook Lane

Minninglow Lane

The
Nook

4

White Cliffe
Farm

Mountain
Ash
Farm

Roystone
Cottages

The
Bungalow

Middlemoor
Farm

57

Lowmoor
Plantation

DE4

Lowmoor
Farm

3

Lowmoor
Cottages

Hawkslow
Farm

Twodale
Barn

56

DE6

Ballidon
Quarry

2

Lombard's
Green

Dale End
Farm

Hilltop
Farm

Middlehill
Farm

Foufinside

Parwich
Hill

55

Peakway

Middlehill
Barn

MONSDALE LA

Close
Farm

ROTHBOURNE
CROFT

Littlewood
Farm

Parwich
Prim Sch

DAM LA

KILN LA

Parwich
Lees

Flaxdale
Holding

1

Parwich

Sycamore
Inn
(PH)

SMITH
LA

SYCAMORE
COTTS

Pits
Lane

54

A 18 **B** 19 **C**

162 **152**

151
140

A

B

C

4

Minninglow
Grange

Works

Minninglow Lane

Longedge
Plantation

Rockhurst
Farm

Green
Farm

Aldwark

Minning
Low

Minninglow
Hill

Tithe
Farm

Hilltop
Farm

Shafts
(dis)

57

Roystone
Grange

*Slipper
Low*

Slipper Low
Farm

3

Daisy
Bank

DE4

Gallowlow Lane

Haven Hoe
Farm

56

High Peak Trail
Midshires Way

Hoe
Grange

Longcliffe
Farm

Lo

2

Ballidon
Quarry

*Blackstone's
Low*

Ballidonmoor

Pinder's
Rock

Works

Beardsley's
Plantation

Nut
Wood

55

Oldfields
Farm

White
Edge

Black
Rocks

Black
Plantation

Rainster
Rocks

Ballidonhall
Farm

Ballidon

Cow Close
Farm

DE6

PASTURE LA

Lots Lane

1

Overfields
Barn

Works

Hipley
Farm

Caves

Hipley
Barn

Hipley
Works

Middle
Lane

WEST END

Hipley
Hill

B5056

54

20

A

21

B

22

C

151
163

A
B
C

A5012

B5056

Tophill
Farm

Whitelow
Farm

Mill
Farm

Grangemill

GRANGE DALE

TOPHILL LA

GREEN LA

LEYS LA

PH

Middle Hills
Farm

Hollybush
Inn

Grange Mill
Quarry

Prospect
Quarry

GRANGE LA

The
Beeches
Farm

Home
Farm

Ible

WHITECLIFFE LA

CROSS LA

Leys
Farm

Whitecliffe
Farm

4

57

WOOD LA

Griffe Grange Valley

Ible
Wood

Limestone Way

Bruns Wood

Griffe
Grange
Farm

Hopton
Wood

A5012

3

n Lodge

Griffe Walk
Farm

56

DE4

Griffe Grange

New Harboro'
Farm

Pearsons
Farm

2

Dale

Harboro'
Rocks

Cave

Works

55

MANYSTONES LA

Works

Midshires Way
High Peak Trail

Works

Mine
(dis)

1

1 BOWLING GN
2 MADDOCK LA
3 RED LION HILL

Carsington Pasture

Brassington

Round Low
Brassington
Prim Sch

Wester Lane

Eniscloud Barn

Sycamore
Farm

WASH HILLS
CL

Shafts
(dis)

Old Knoll

54

A
24
B
25
C

153
142

A　　　　　B　　　　　C

THE DALE

Town End
Farm

Byeway Lane

Fairy Lane

CHURCH ST

CLATTERWAY

Study
Farm

Slaley
Farm

Black
Tor

PH

Via Gellia
Mill

Bailey
Quarry

4

Leys

*Bonsall
Mines*
(dis)

BLACK TOR RD

Sunnyside
Farm

Slaley

Bonsall Wood

Works

Mill
Pond

Bonsall
Hollow

Slinter
Wood

LEYS LA

Sunnyside
Farm

VIA GELLIA RD

Groaning
Tor

57

Via Gellia

Middleton
Wood

Griffe
Grange
Valley

Dean
Hollow

3

A5012

B5023

NEW RD

Cemy

BLUNDSTONE LA

LONGLOAD LA

DUKE ST

CHAPEL LA

KING ST

WELL ST

WATER LA

THE GREEN

Hopton
Wood

Steeple
Grange
Light Rly

56

DE4

THE MEER

FERN AVE

HOPTONWOOD
CL

Willowdene
Farm

Middleton

NEW RD

THE MOOR

DOSSAL LA

RAIKE'S LA

MAIN ST

THE ALLEY

THE BELFRY

Middleton
Prim Sch

Works

Hopton
Quarries

Middleton Moor

Rise End

PORTER LA

2

Arm Lees
Farm

PH

B5035

Middleton
Top
Visitor's
Centre

Ireland
Farm

National
Stone Ctr

High Peak Trail
Midshires Way

Intake
Quarry

**Middle
Peak**

Middlepeak

Wirksworth
Ind Ctr

55

Moor
Farm

Middle
Peak
Quarry

ECCLESBOURNE
COTTS
CAVENDISH
COTTS
VERNON
COTTS

1

Broxendale
Farm

THE DALE

HARRISON DR 1
BARMOTE CROFT 2
COLDWELL ST 3
CHURCH ST 4
MARKET PL 5
DALE END 6

Mus

TH

Mines
(dis)

B5035

Norbreck
Farm

WEST END

GREEN HILL

B5023

B5503

54

26　　　　　A　　　　　27　　　　　B　　　　　28　　　　　C

153
165

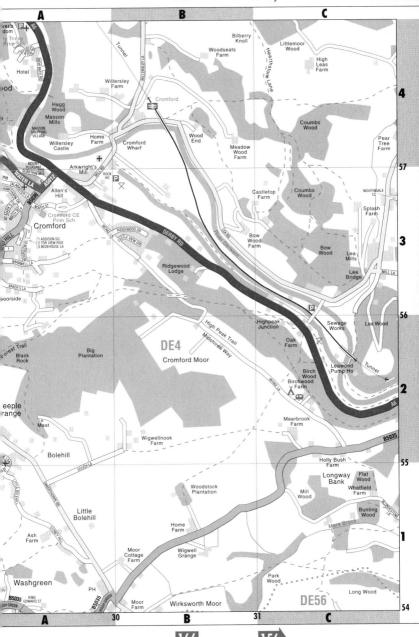

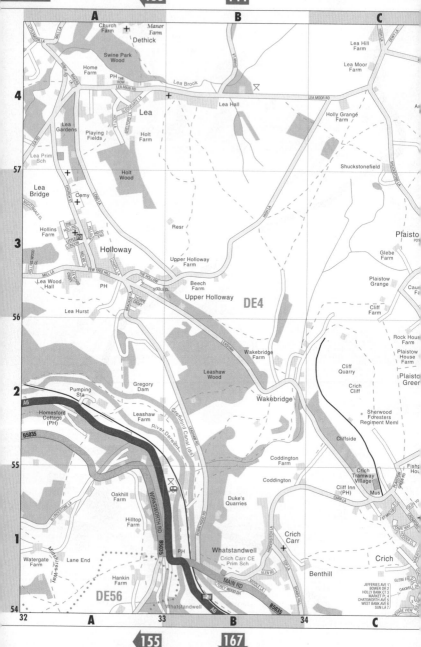

A   B   C

Church Farm
Manor Farm
Dethick

Lea Hill Farm

Swine Park Wood

Home Farm
PH THE ROW
LEA MAIN RD
Lea Brook

Lea Moor Farm

4
LEA MOOR RD

Lea Hall

Holly Grange Farm

Lea
Lea Gardens
Playing Fields
Holt Farm

57
Shuckstonefield

Holt Wood

Lea Bridge
Cemy
Plaisto

Hollins Farm
THE HOLLINS
LITTLE ?
LONGDEN
Resr
Glebe Farm

3
Holloway

Upper Holloway Farm
Plaistow Grange

Lea Wood Hall
YEW TREE HILL
PH
THE HOLLOW
STABLE CL
Beech Farm
Caus Fa

Lea Hurst
BRICKFILL
Upper Holloway
DE4
Cliff Farm

56
Leashaw Wood
Wakebridge Farm
Rock House Farm

Plaistow House Farm

Cliff Quarry

Pumping Sta
Gregory Dam
Wakebridge
Crich Cliff
Plaisto Greer

2
A6
Homesford Cottage (PH)
Leashaw Farm
River Derwent
Cromford Canal (dis)
Sherwood Foresters Regiment Meml

B5035
Cliffside

55
Coddington Farm
Crich Tramway Village
Fishp Ho

Oakhill Farm
WIRKSWORTH RD
Coddington
Cliff Inn (PH)
Mus

Hilltop Farm
Duke's Quarries

1
Watergate Farm
Lane End
B5035
PH
Whatstandwell
Crich Carr CE Prim Sch
Crich Carr
Benthill
Crich

Hankin Farm
DE56
MAIN RD
NICCOL LA
A6
GLEN RD

54
Whatstandwell

JEFFERIES AVE 1
BOWER DR 2
HOLLY BANK CT 3
MARKET PL 4
CHATSWORTH AVE 5
WEST BANK AVE 6
SUN LA 7

32   A   33   B   34   C

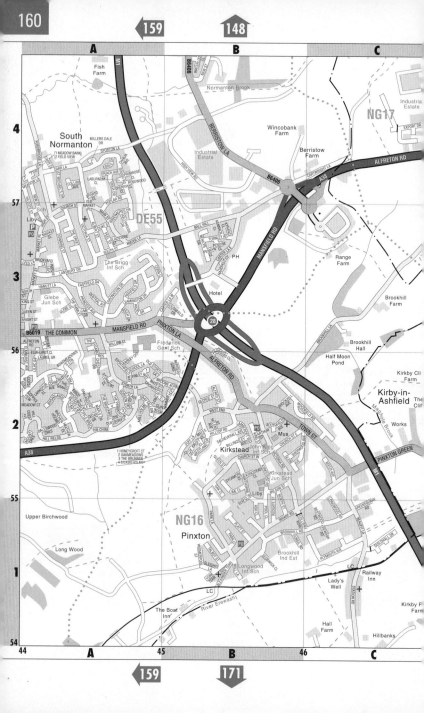

159
148

A **B** **C**

4

Fish
Farm

M1

B6406

Normanton Brook

Wincobank
Farm

NG17

Industria
Estate

EXPORT DR

South
Normanton

MILLERS DALE
DR

1 MEADOW BANK
2 FIELD VIEW

BERRISTOW LA

Industrial
Estate

Berristow
Farm

ALFRETON RD

A38

B6406

CARTWRIGHT LA

57

LibY
P
PO

DE55

MARKET ST

BALL HILL
TURNEY LA
PINDINE

PH

Range
Farm

The Brigg
Inf Sch

MANSFIELD RD

3

Glebe
Jun Sch

NORTH
ST
KING ST
QUEEN ST
BRIGHT ST
PO

HAMLET LA

EASTFIELD DR

LANGBURY DR

LIME GR

LAMINGTON DR

BLACKSTONE

Hotel

Brookhill
Farm

28

Brookhill
Hall

Half Moon
Pond

Kirkby Cli
Farm

56

B6019

ALFRETON
RD

THE COMMON

ELMHURST CL
LAUREL GR

MANSFIELD RD

PINXTON LA

WILLOW CL

Frederick
Gent Sch

BROOKS CL

ALFRETON RD

BROOKHILL LA

Kirby-in-
Ashfield

The
Clif

Works

Magdale Brook

2

MEADOW CT

A38

NILL FIELDS

THE CHINE

1 HONEYCROFT CT
2 OAKMEADOWS
3 THE BRUNNEN
4 SILKEN HOLME

WEST END

SAGGARVALE AVE

HILLTOP RD

BILLINGS

Kirkstead

John King
Inf Sch

CHURCH ST W

Mus

CHURCH ST E

TOWN ST

PINXTON GREEN

M1

55

Upper Birchwood

Long Wood

NG16

Pinxton

WHARF

WHARF

Kirkstead
Jun Sch

LibY

BROOKHILL RD

Brookhill
Ind Est

PLYMOUTH AVE

GREENSQUARE
RD

GRETNA CL

1

A

The Boat
Inn

SLEIGHTS LN

LC

Longwood
Inf Sch

LC

River Erewash

STATION RD

LC

Lady's
Well

Railway
Inn

Hall
Farm

Kirkby F
Farm

Hillbanks

54

44 **A** 45 **B** 46 **C**

159
171

161
151

A

B

C

The Thorns

4

Crakelow
Farm

Crake
Low

Shaw's
Farm

Bleich Brook

Sitterlow
Farm

Rushycliffe
Barn

White
Meadow

53

Hunger
Hill

High
Flats

Tissington Trail

Gorsehill
Farm

RAKES LA

3

Town Head
Farm

CHAPEL LA

Tissington

Wibben Hill

Tissington
Hall

Bent
Farm

BENT LA

THE GREENE

THE GREEN

Keepers
Cottage

52

DARFIELD LA

Lea Cottage
Farm

Lea Hall

A515

WASHBROOK
LA

Square
Plantation

DE6

Bluebell
Inn
(PH)

Mill Pond
Plantation

2

Darfield
Plantation

Bradbourne Brook

Bassett Wood
Farm

Choughriddins

Tissington Wood
Farm

51

Brookwood
Farm

Woodeaves
Farm

Woodside

Bentley
Hall

1

Lees Farm

The
Priory

Woodeaves
Mill

Firs Farm

Fenny
Bentley

Fitzherbert CE
Prim. Sch.

Cherry Orchard
Farm

Bentley Brook

Ravenscliffe

A515

Bentley Old Hall

Coach and Horses
(PH)

B5056

Riddings
Park

50

17

A

18

B

19

C

161
173

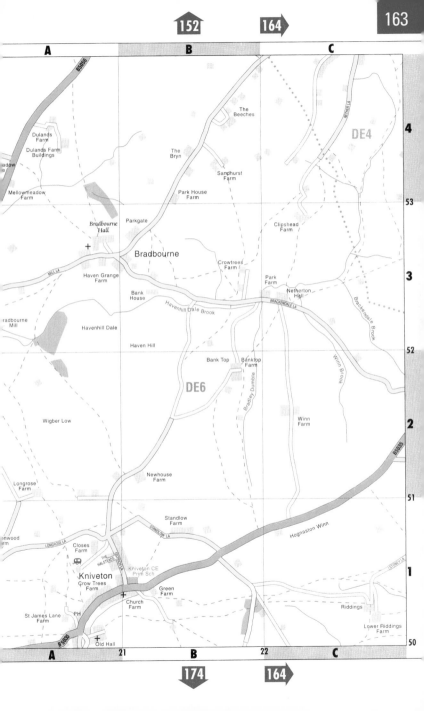

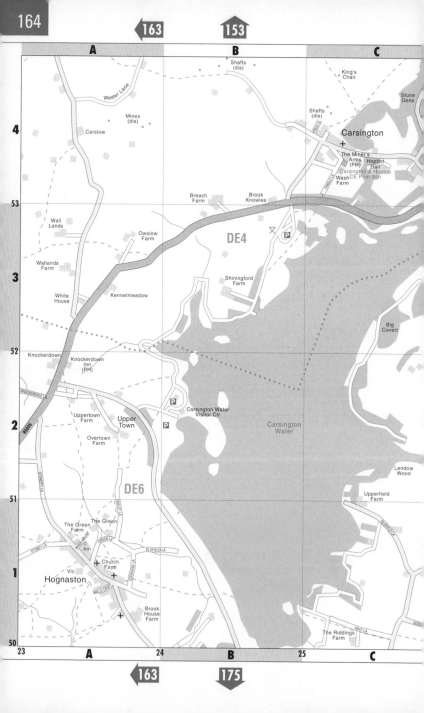

163
153

A
B
C

Shafts
(dis)

King's
Chair

Stone
Dene

Wester Lane

Mines
(dis)

Carslow

Shafts
(dis)

4

Carsington
+

The Miner's
Arms
(PH)

Hopton
Hall

Carsington & Hopton
CE Prim Sch

Wash
Farm

53

Breach
Farm

Brook
Knowles

Wall
Lands

Owslow
Farm

DE4

P

Wallands
Farm

Shiningford
Farm

3

White
House

Kennelmeadow

Big
Covert

52

Knockerdown

Knockerdown
Inn
(PH)

BRACKENDALE LA

Carsington
Water

Uppertown
Farm

Upper
Town

P

Carsington Water
Visitor Ctr

P

2

Overtown
Farm

Lendow
Wood

Upperfield
Farm

51

STONEYLA

The Green
Farm

The Green

DE6

GREEN LA

OLDFIELD LA

OLDFIELD LA

Inn

COCKAYNE LA

1

Vic

Church
Farm

+

Hognaston

+

WELL CROFT

Brook
House
Farm

The Riddings
Farm

HAYD LA

50

23
A
24
B
25
C

163
175

Yokecliffe

WIRKSWORTH

Godfreyhole

Godfreyhole Farm

Warmbrook

Mines (dis)

Sycamore Farm

Yokecliffe Rake Mines (dis)

BARNES CROFT

1 BLIND LA
2 CHURCH ST
3 ST MARY'S GATE

Anthony Gell Sch

Summer Lane

LC

Gorseybank

Stainsbro' Hall

Soldiers' Knoll

Sprink Wood

Pittywood Farm

Recn Gd
Kingsfield Ind Est
CORN MILL CL

Hob Hall

DE4

Round Meadow Farm

Millers Green

Rough Pitty Side

Hob Wood

Cathole Wood

Sewage Works

LC

Upper House Farm

Callow Carr Farm

Stonebridge Farm

Callow

(dis)

Callow Hall

Sunnybank Wood

Carr Bank

The Kennels

Callow Park Farm

Beighton Hill Farm

Parkhill Wood

Millbank Wood

Alton Manor Farm

Callow Moor Farm

DE6

Topshill Brook

Alton Manor

Windmill Farm

Moorside Spring Farm

Topshill Farm

Moorside

Moorside Farm

DE56

Alton Brook

Quarry Wood

Pearl Well Farm

Barley Hill

Ivy Cottage

Kirk Ireton CE Prim Sch

PH

Kirk Ireton

Alton Hall

Town End Farm

Alton Farm

Alton Mill Farm

A   B   C

WASH GREEN B5035

B5035

WASH GR

KING EDWARD ST

The Gilkin

Alderwasley

Moor Farm

Wigwell Cottage Farm

Knob Farm

4

Boggart's Inn Farm

Breamfield

Breamfields Farm

Lanehead

Ford

Willetts Farm

Gorsebank

53

Notonsteer

Hardhurst Farm

Nook Farm

Bear Inn (PH)

The Fishpools

The Bent

Colebrook Farm

3

Doves Wood

DE4

Sycamore Farm

Sandhail Farm

Doveswood Farm

Broadgates

Clearsprings Farm

Holehouse Farm

Coldaston

52

New Buildings Farm

Roughpiece Farm

DE56

Hillside Farm

Nethercommon Farm

Masts

Spencer Barn

2

Beighton Hill

P

Alport Height

Topias Farm

Spout

Coneygreave Farm

Coneygrave Hillock

Storer Farm

Lane End

51

Lane End Farm

Bowmerlane

Palerow Farm

PALEROW LA

Brownhouse Farm

1

Brownhouse Wood

Palace Cottage

Norman Hill Farm

Hilltop

Gibbet Wood

Dannah Farm

Lawn Farm

50

29   A   30   B   31   C

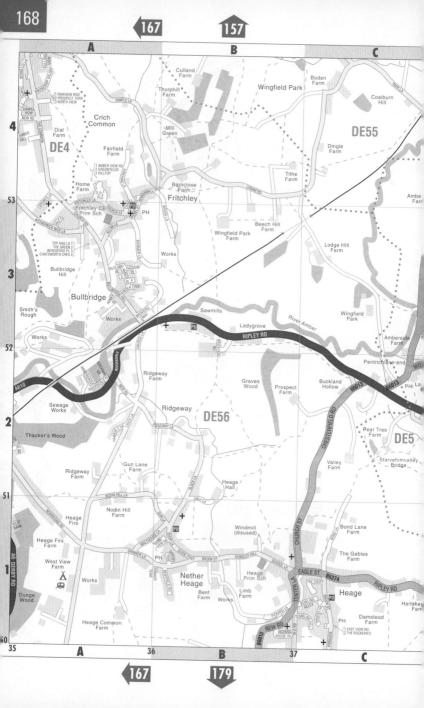

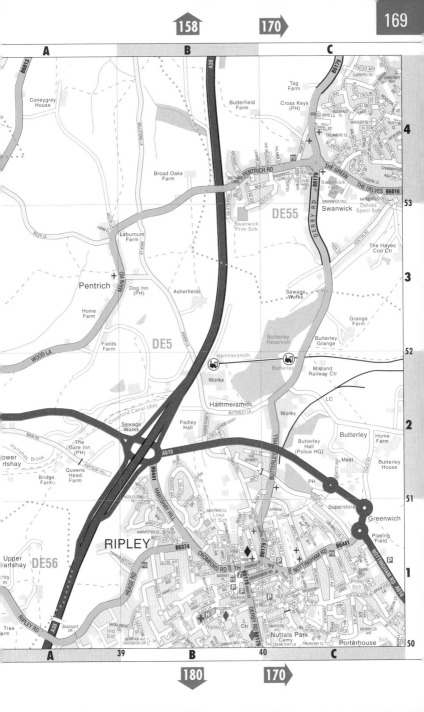

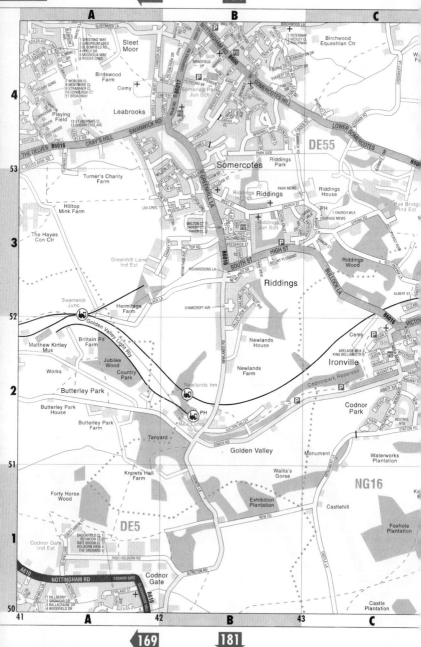

B   C

Sewage Works

Hobsic Farm

PH

Hall Green

Hillbank Farm

Commonside

Hobsic La

Hall Green Farm

Rosemaryhill

ALBERTA AVE 1
CHESTNUT DR 2
CEDAR DR 3
FOSSETT'S AVE 4

4

Pye Bridge Junction

mea rm

DE55

Pinfold Farm

Selston Green

Church La

HOMECROFT DR

Stoney La

Selston

L Ctr

Liby

Matthew Holland Comp Sch

HOOLEY ST

53

Pye Bridge

ALFRETON RD

Home Farm Ct

Green Farm Ct

Crescent Rd

Sleepy Hole

Selston CE Inf Sch

PH

Nottingham Rd

B6016

B600

Jubilee

Toadhole

CH

P

Dove Green

Ashes Farm

Allen's Green

Hanstubbin

B6018

3

Barrows Green

Selston Rd

Langton Hollow B6016

Barrows Hill

Home Farm

Lea Farm

St Michaels View

Pye Hill

NG16

Bagthorpe Hill La

New Row

Pye Hill Rd

Liby

PH

Jacksdale

THE ORCHARDS

Jacksdale Prim Sch

Wagstaff La

Melton La

Barker Ave

Shropshire Ave

Wiltshire Ave

Hampshire Ct

Kent Ave

Westmorland

Albert Ave St

Dixie St

Rutland Rd

Cornwall

Somerset Cl

Westwood Inf Sch

New Westwood

Gate Inn (PH)

Flatts La

Bagthorpe Brook

Manor Farm

Bagthorpe Shepherds Rest (PH)

Brookside Farm

52

2

Westwood

Westwood Farm

Yewtree Farm

Lower Bagthorpe

Wansley Hall

Cromford Canal (disused)

Main Rd

Brinsley Hill

Plain Spot Farm

Frances St

Plain Spot

Underwood Hill

Hole in the Wall (PH)

Underwood Green

BLUEBELL

PRIMROSE AVE

Underwood CE Prim Sch

51

1

PH

Main St

Clumber Ave

High St

Bagot La

Pollington House

New Brinsley

Oaktree Farm

A608

50

A   45   B   46   C

Nottinghamshire STREET ATLAS

A608 M1 Junc 27

A B C

4

49

3

48

2

47

1

46

Staffordshire STREET ATLAS

A523 Leek

14 A 15 B 16 C

Caldwall Bridge

Limestone Way

Coldwall

Little Peg's Wood

Tissington Trail

Spendlane Farm

SPEND LA

Littlepark

Lees House Farm

Yerley Farm

TIRLEY HILL

Kendar Wood

Hinchley Wood

Hinchley

Cowclose Wood

Okeover Hall

Mill Okeover Bridge

Bank Farm

DE6

Martin Hill

Okeover Park

Okeover Arms (PH)

Maple

Marten Hill

Limestone Way

Lower Grounds Farm

Smythe's Plantation

River Dove

PICCADILLY LA

The Orchards

Manor House

Callowend Farm

Cornpark

Snelsdale

Snelsdale Wood

SWINSCOE HILL

A52

Ca

Throstle Nest

Birdsgrove Farm

Butler's Holme

Lordspiece

STANTON LA

The Cliffs

Bentley Brook

Limestone Way

Harlow Farm

Big Quarry Wood

Upper Mayfield

PICCADILLY LA

HOLLOW LA

SLACK LA

Birdsgrove House

A52

Ashbourne

Sewage Wks

Buckholme

C

WATERY

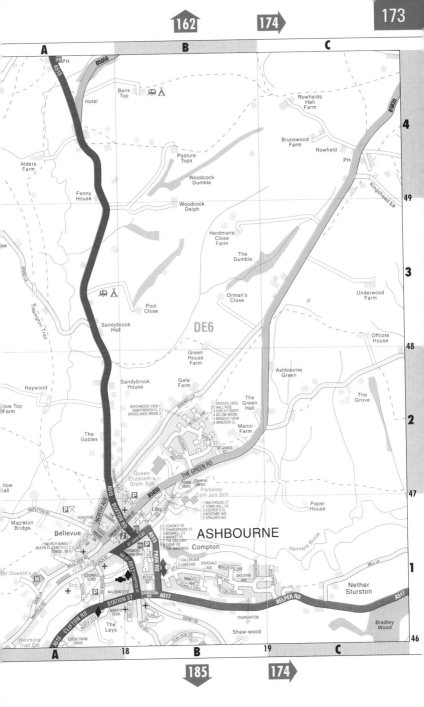

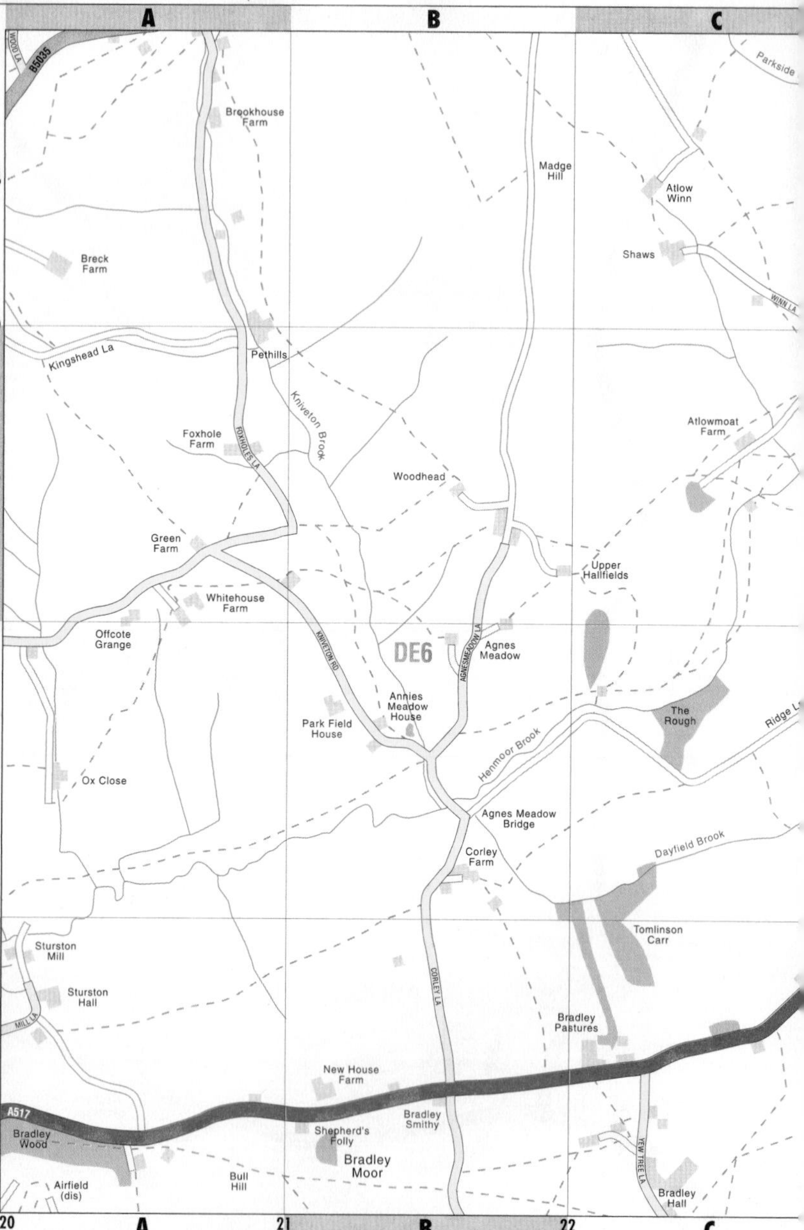

A   B   C

Parkside

Brookhouse Farm

Madge Hill

Atlow Winn

4

Breck Farm

Shaws

WINN LA

49

Kingshead La

Pethills

Knivston Brook

Atlowmoat Farm

Foxhole Farm

Woodhead

3

KNIVETON LA

Green Farm

Upper Hallfields

Whitehouse Farm

48

Offcote Grange

DE6

Agnes Meadow

ASHBOURNE LA

PRESTON RD

Annies Meadow House

Park Field House

Hanmoor Brook

The Rough

Ridge La

2

Ox Close

Agnes Meadow Bridge

Corley Farm

Dayfield Brook

47

Sturston Mill

Tomlinson Carr

Sturston Hall

MILL LA

CHURCH LA

Bradley Pastures

1

New House Farm

A517

Bradley Wood

Bradley Smithy

Bradley Moor

YEW TREE LA

Bradley Hall

Shepherd's Folly

Airfield (dis)

Bull Hill

46

20   A   21   B   22   C

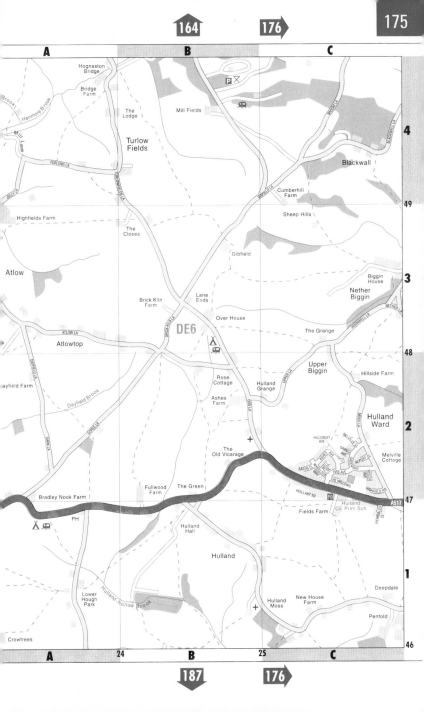

A   **B**   **C**

BLACKWALL LA
FIELD LA
BROOK SIDE
FP TOR LA
ROTTEN LA

Addcrofts

HOB LA
WOOD LA

TIMBERLEY

B5023

JEBB

Winneyhill

Holm Brook

Field Farm

4

Bennywall
Wood

The Mountain

Bullhill

Idridgehay
Green

FP NORBRIGG

Bennywall Brook

49

Biggin
Head
Farm

Rakestones
Farm

CLIFFASH LA

WIRKSWORTH

Hays Farm

FOSSE

Idridgehay

Southside
House

3

Biggin

HOONWELL LA

Carr Wood

DE6

Ford

Cherry Orchard

CLIFFASH LA

WINDLEY LA

Nether Biggin

Mill

MAG LA

DE56

48

Millington
Green

NETHER LA

Hillside
Farm

Ireton Wood

Redhouse
Farm

Hall

NEW RD

Brook
Farm

Lanehead Farm

Iretonwood
Farm

INTAKE LA

2

Sherbourne Brook

Mount Pleasant

Biggin Old
Hall

Toad Holes
Farm

Bull Hill

BIGGIN LA

Stock-a-Sitch

Lumber Lane
Farm

OLD LA

HILLSIDE LA

Springhill
Farm

47 A517

PH

Massey's
Barn

LUMBS LA

CROSSWAYS LA

Crossways
Farm

1

Cross o' th' hands

Magfield

MONEYHILLS LA

Beech-hill Farm

Waterlagg
Cottage

Derbyhill Farm

46

Moneyhills

26   **A**   **27**   **B**   **28**   **C**

177
167

A   B   C

4

Wilderbrook La

Coppice Wood

Narrow Lane

Hillside

Handley Farm

Wyver Farm

Wyver Wood

PH

JESSES LA

Handleywood Farm

Lane End Farm

Belper Lane End

49

Mount Pleasant

Wyver

Scotches

Hollyseat

Handley Wood

The Dalley

Bridgehill

3

Newbuildings Farm

Black Brook

Midshires Way

BRADSHAW

MOUNT PLEASANT DR

QUEEN'S

DERWENT VIEW

DALE LA

DE56

Holly House

Dalley Farm

BRIDGE HILL

A517

BRIDGE ST

A6

48

Chapel House Farm

Crossroads Farm

Belper Bridge

Mills

Liby

PLAINS LA

ASHBOURNE RD

River Derwent

P

BRIDGE ST

MEADOW

DERWENT ST

CHAPEL ST

Ford

Blackbrook

C2
1 ST GEORGE'S PL
2 CROWN TERR
3 CLUSTER CT
4 SHORT ROW
5 FIELD ROW
6 THE ORCHARD
7 INGLE'S CHANNEL
8 CHURCH LA
9 WELLINGTON CT
10 CHEAPSIDE
11 BELLE ACRE CL

2

Shottlegate Farm

PH

LUMB LA

FARNAH GREEN RD

Superstore

A6

A517

Cow-Ways

Shottlegate

Lumb Brook

Chevin Green Farm

MEADOW VIEW

47

Farnah Green

HAZELDENE COTTS

Chevin Mount

H

Babington

Sch

Lumb Grange

PH

DERWENT VALE 1
SUNNY BANK GDNS 2
THREE GATES 3
GLEN VIEW 4

LUMB LA

GREEN LA

CHEVIN RD

FIRESTONE LA

NORTH LA

1

Overlane Farm

Goodwin's Lumbs

Chevinside

Sewage Works

Chevin House Farm

Ireton's Farm

Mast

Firestone Hill

Hazelwood

HOB HILL

GOODWIN'S LA

46

32   33   34

A   B   C

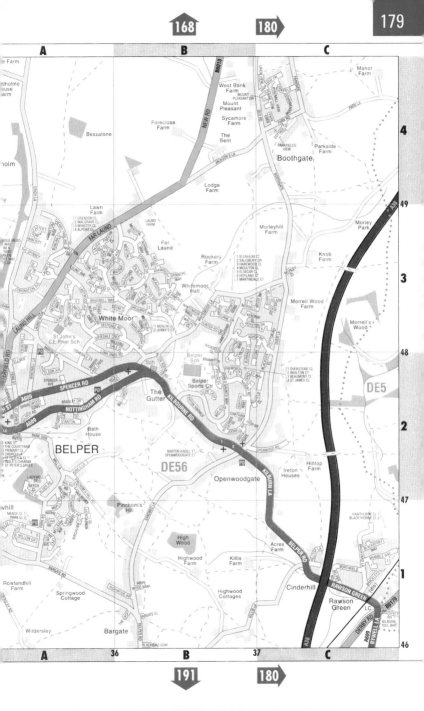

179
169

A B C

Sandham Farm

Morleypark Farm

Strelley Court Farm

STRELLEY AVE
LAWRENCE AVE
FORD CT
HIGH MEADOW CL

PEAR TREE AVE
ASH CRES
OAK AVS
BROOK LA

POPLAR AVE
RIPLEY AVE

Ripley Jun & Inf Schs

LIME AVE
NORMAN AVE
HOLLY AVE
SYCAMORE AVE

The Elms

1 WEAVERS CROFT
2 PROVIDENCE ST

STEAM MILL LA 1
WAINGROVES RD 2
GROVE CT 3

Mill H Sch

Iron Works Farm

BIRCH CL 1
BRIARS WAY 2
CHERRY TREE AVE 4
LAUREL AVE 5
CEDAR AVE 6
SAMUEL CT 7
WOODSIDE AVE 8
WESTON SPOT CL 9

Old Farm

DRIVE
LANE

ALLISSA AVE

PEASEHILL RD

Rope Wlk

GREENHILL RD

Coppice Farm

Butterley Croft Bsns Ctr

WHITE LEAD RD

SHEEPYARD LA

Benjamin Outram Bsns Ctr

Coppice Farm

Morley Park

Norman Court Farm

BOWLER ST
THE GARDENS
BAMFORD ST

Greenhillocks

Works

49

Marehay Hall

WANROVES RD

DOVE DALE CL

Marehay

1 MILLDALE CL
2 PEAKDALE CL

Clay Pit

Street Lane Farm

Durham Ox (PH)

BELLE VUE AVE 3
MULBERRY MEWS 4

UPPER MAREHAY RD

Border Bank

WESTERLY CL

Lumb Farm (PH)

3

Street Lane Prim Sch

DE5

Salter Wood

Opencast Mine

Sewage Works

Primrose Farm

48

Mount Pleasant

Opencast Mine

Denby Comn Farm

DENBY RD

Park Hall

Works

Bull's (P

2

Denby Pottery Visitor Ctr

WESTERLY CL

PARK HALL DR
SEATON RD

John Flamsted Com Sch

(dis)
SEAL RD
SHIRE DR

RYKNELD HALL

Opencast Mine

47

Rykneld Hill Farm

Ticknall Hill

Denby Free CE Prim Sch

Hill Farm

Lady La

Denby

PH

Church Farm

POTERS BANK

LIME TREE

1

B6179

PRIESTCLIFF
PRESTWICH RISE
SPENCER RISE

DANESBY RISE
DANESBY CRES

Denby Bottles

DE56

PROSPECT RD

RYKNELD RD

PASSINGS

Bottom Dumbles

Prospect House

Bottlebrook Houses

Bottle Brook

DERBY LA
OAKS

FLAMSTEAD LA

Flamsteadlane Farm

Flamstead House Farm

B6179

38 A 39 B 40 C

46

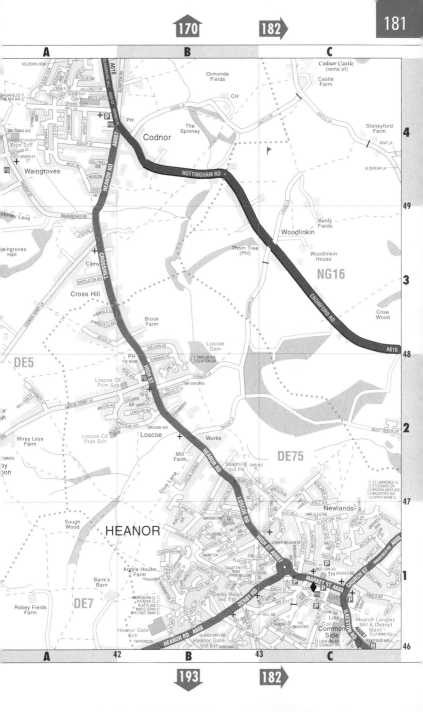

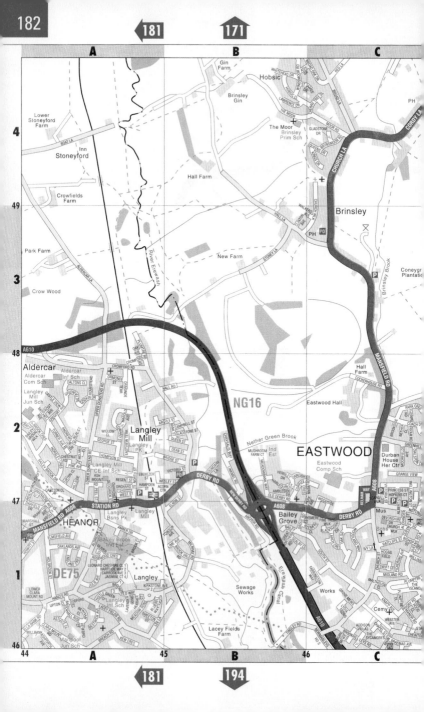

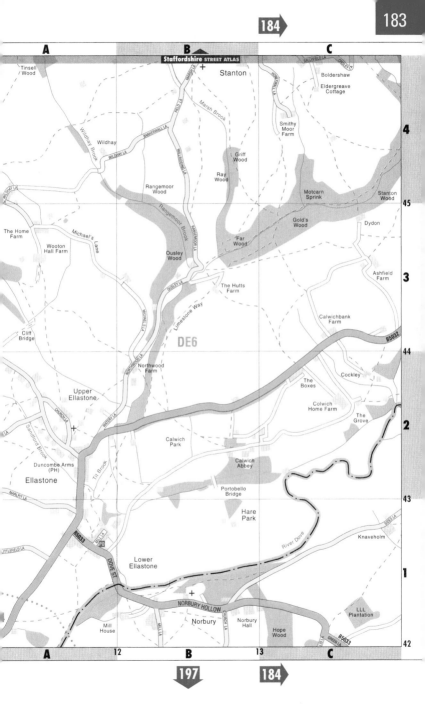

Staffordshire STREET ATLAS

A **B** **C**

4

Tinsell Wood

Stanton

Boldershaw

Eldergreave Cottage

Smithy Moor Farm

Wildhay

Griff Wood

Ray Wood

Rangemoor Wood

Motcarn Sprink

Stanton Wood

45

The Home Farm

Michael's Lane

Ousley Wood

Far Wood

Gold's Wood

Dydon

Wooton Hall Farm

Ashfield Farm

3

The Hutts Farm

Calwichbank Farm

Limestone Way

B5032

Cliff Bridge

DE6

44

Northwood Farm

Cockley

The Boxes

Upper Ellastone

Colwich Home Farm

The Grove

2

Calwich Park

Duncombe Arms (PH)

Calwich Abbey

Ellastone

Portobello Bridge

43

Hare Park

Knaveholm

B5033

River Dove

1

Lower Ellastone

LLL Plantation

Mill House

NORBURY HOLLOW

Norbury

Norbury Hall

Hope Wood

B5033

42

A 12 **B** 13 **C**

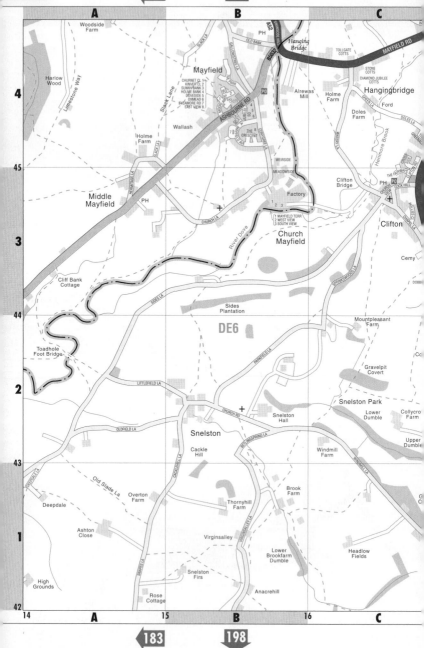

183
172

A
B
C

Woodside
Farm

PH

A52
OLD BANK
Hanging
Bridge

Tollgate
Cotts

MAYFIELD RD

STONE
COTTS

Harlow
Wood

Mayfield

CHURNET CL 1
KINVER CL 2
SUNNYBANK 3
HOLME BANK 4
DOVESIDE 5
OXMEAD 6
SYCAMORE RD 7
EAST VIEW 8

PO

Alrewas
Mill

Holme
Farm

DIAMOND JUBILEE
COTTS

Hangingbridge

4

Slack Lane
Limestone Way

ASHBOURNE RD

Doles
Farm

Ford

DOLES LA

Wallash

THE
CRESCENT

Henmore Brook

GREENHILL

Holme
Farm

PH

WEIRSIDE

MEADOWSIDE

THE FOOTPATHS

PH

PO

45

Middle
Mayfield

Factory

Clifton
Bridge

COCK HILL

Clifton

1 MAYFIELD TERR
2 WEST VIEW
3 SOUTH VIEW

1 2 3

HOLLIES LA

River Dove

Church
Mayfield

Cemy

DOBBI

3

Cliff Bank
Cottage

OGES LA

Sides
Plantation

SPRINKSWOOD LA

Mountpleasant
Farm

Cc

44

DE6

Gravelpit
Covert

Toadhole
Foot Bridge

LITTLEFIELD LA

PARKFIELD LA

Snelston Park

Lower
Dumble

Collycro
Farm

2

OLDFIELD LA

CHURCH RD

Snelston
Hall

Windmill
Farm

Upper
Dumble

Snelston

Cackle
Hill

WET WITHIN SPRING LA

BROOKHILL LA

43

Old Slade La

CHOCKERHILL LA

Brook
Farm

Deepdale

Overton
Farm

Thornyhill
Farm

Ashton
Close

Virginsalley

1

Lower
Brookfarm
Dumble

Headlow
Fields

C
G

High
Grounds

Snelston
Firs

Anacrehill

Rose
Cottage

42

14
A
15
B
16
C

183
198

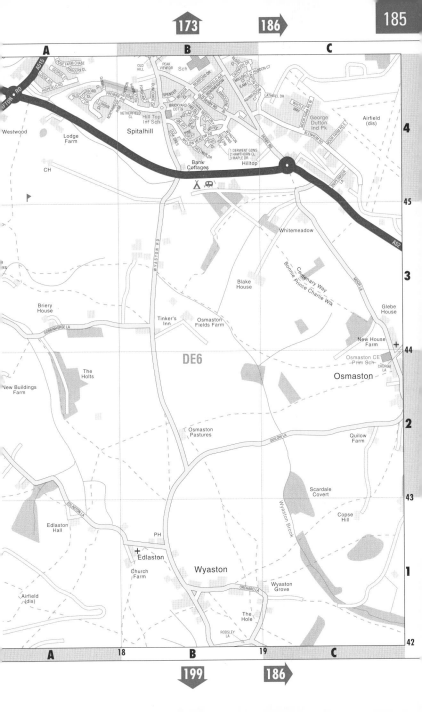

A   B   C

Smith Hall Farm

Carrhall Farm

Waterlagg Brook

Works

The Carr

Hollinghurst

4

Blackbrook Farm

Mast

Common Farm

Pit (disused)

Herbalshaw M Farm

Blackbrook Farm

DE56

The Clives

45

Redmiregap

Mansellpark

Humblebee Hill

Parkhill Farm

Muggintonlane End

SMITH HILL LA

The Hollies

Black Brook

3

Sand Pit

Sand Pit

Park Farm

Old Covert Farm

High F

DE6

Old Covert

44

Coc Inn (PH

Shuckton Manor Farm

MERCASTON LA

2

Hill Top Farm

Brook Farm

Ling Hill

Mill House

BULLHURST LA

Mercaston Green

Hunger Hill

Hungerhill Brook

HUNGER LA

Mercaston

Schoolhouse Farm

43

Brailsford Common

Ford

Mercaston Brook

TADNOLE LA

Mugginton CE Prim Sch

Mugginton

Malkin Lane

Hazlehurst

Wood Lane

The Gables

CHURCH LA

GREEN LA

Greenhil

1

Top House Farm

NEW RD

Sewage Works

ALLEN LA

New House Farm

Trent Trout Farm

42

26   A   27   B   28   C

189
178

A   B   C

Swainsley Farm

Hillside Farm

The
Knowle

Hazelwood

The Firs Farm

Mount
Farm

Quarry
(dis)

Wallstones
Farm
House

Hazelwood
Hall
Farm

North Lane

Chevinend

River Derwent

BANK
BLDGS

Milford C
Prim Se

CHEVIN ALLE

SUNNY

4

Bradshaw House

Courthouse
Farm

Milford Tunnel

DERBY RD

45

Milford
House

Lapwing
Farm

The
Oaks

Spring
Hill

Moscow
Farm

3   B5023

River
Ecclesbourne

(dis)

DE56

ASH TREE CL

CH

CHEESE LA

CHURCH ST

CHURCHWALK

Cemy

River Derwent

Windley
Meadows

Brookhouse
Farm

Centenary Way

WIRKSWORTH RD

Meadows
Farm

ST ALKMUNDS
WAY

44

Duffield Meadows

Works

HOLLOWAY RD

Sch

Duffield

TAMWORTH
TERR

2   Spring
Carr

Farnah House
Farm

Broom
Park

SNAKE LA

SPRINGFIELD DR 1
HAZEL GR 2
MEADOWS CROFT 3
BROOM CL 4
OLD MILL CL 5

ORCHARD
COTTS

PARK RD

MEADOW VW

The
Park

The
Ecclesbourne
Sch

EYES CT
CURZON CT

ECCLESBOURNE
AVE

VILLAGE CT

Duffi

DUFFIELD
CT

TOWN ST

Centenary
Way

MAKENEY RD

Champion Farm

HILL VIEW

WIRKSWORTH RD

CANTERBURY CL

MARSDEN CL
SCARSDALE RD

Liby

43

Cumberhills
Farm

CAVENDISH

BROADWAY

CHURCH
VIEW

1   Centenary Way

DE22

Park
Leys

CUMBERHILLS RD

Celadon

B5023

DERBY RD

Cumberhill
Farm

BEECH AVE

Flaxholme

FLAXHOLME
AVE

32   A   33   B   34   C

189
204

A   **B**   **C**

Kilburn
Kilburn Jun Sch
DE56
CHAPEL ST
BROADFIELDS DR
KING'S DR
ST EDWARDS CRES
ROWAN DR

Broadfields Farm

Carr Farm

Rosy Lee Farm

DE5

Flamstead Plantation

4 A609 WOODHOUSE RD

Spring Cottage

Crab House

Barden Farm

1 DALE VIEW GDNS
2 ST JOHN'S DR
3 DOVE CL
4 SITWELL DR
5 BOWLER DR
6 VINCENT CL

ARBEYDALE

PH MAIN ST

CHESTNUT CL
CLEMENT RD
FAIRDALE DR
CARR FIELDS
MEADOW CL
THE ORCHARD

PO

Hirst Farm

45

Works

Cemy

Dobholes

A609

A608

Slackfields Farm

Horsley Woodhouse Prim Sch

CHURCH LA

DOBHOLES LA

VICARAGE CL
WILMOT DR
GLEBE AVE
ST CRES
ST JOHN'S DR

STA

S

Coach and Horses Inn (PH)

LADY LEA RD

DERBY RD

Golden Valley

Horsley Woodhouse

Gypsy Brook

HORSETON RD

GOLDEN VALLEY

3 CHURCH ST

Horsley

COXBENCH RD

Parkgate Farm

Hilltop Farm

Sitwell Arms (PH)

WOOD LA

Stainsby House

Widdowson's Plantation

44

CH

Horsley Lodge

Park Brook

SMALLEY MILL RD

Woodside

Barn Farm

DE7

Smalley Hall

New Plantation

2

DE21

Abbott's Rough Plantation

MAIN RD

Small Gree

Smalley G Farm

Horsley Park Farm

Marks Hill

WOODSIDE

Yew Tree Farm

43

Brackley Gate Farm

Rose and Crown (PH)

A609 ILKESTON RD

BEL

BRACKLEY GATE

Dobb's Hill Plantation

CLOVES HILL

THE CROFT

Cloves Wood

Morley Manor

Small Comm

1

Moor Plantation

Quarry Farm

QUARRY RD

Quarry Cottages

CH

Hayes Farm

Morley Wo

42 Midshires Way

The Sycamores

Morleymoor Farm

A608

38 A   **39** B   **40** C

Kidsleypark Farm

HEANOR RD

A608

Heanor Gate

THE GRANGE

BEXFORD MANS

HEANOR GATE RD

THORPE RD

SLACK LA

Heanor Gate Ind Est

STANSBY AVE

DELVES CT

LOCKTON AVE

WESTFIELD AVE

ILKESTON RD

ABBOT

Cemy

Marlpool

Coppice Prim Sch

THE HOPEWALK

WESTERN DR

BIRCHELL CL

CANDLE CL

P

SUNNINGDALE AVE

GREEN AVE

PO

AVIS AVE

BUXTON DR

CORFIELD AVE

THE COPPICE CT

BEECHFIELD

RIDGEWAY

4

Holly Mount Farm

n's

Visitor Centre

Cinderhill Coppice

45

Office Coppice

Whiteley's Plantation

Flatmeadow Farm

DE75

Shipley Country Park

Manchester Wood

Prospect Farm

Derby Lodge

Home Farm

SHIPLEY LA

Shipley Hill

3

The Bungalow

John Wood

44

Whitehouse Farm

Abbot's Rough

P

DE7

Mapperley Reservoir

Mapperley Park

Mapperley Pond

Mapperley Wood

2

Mapperley

Mapperley CE Prim Sch

PH

COACHWAYS

SYCAMORE CL

SLACK RD

THE LIMES

Park Hall Farm

MAIN ST

PO

CORONATION RD

43

Opencast Workings

MAPPERLEY LA

Simonfield

Club Room Farm

SW

Mapperley Park Wood

Stanley Common

BELPER RD

PH

OAKFIELD CT

PO

Smalley Common

Stanley Com Prim Sch

HAYES WOOD RD

THE BOWALK

Coppice Farm

Brook Farm

1

Oakfield Farm

HIGH LA CENTRAL

A609

A609

HIGH LA W

A609

41

193 182

A B C

4

45

DE75

3

44

2

43

1

42

Marlpool Inf Sch

ILKESTON RD

A6007 HARDY BARN

1 SUNNINGDALE AVE
2 HUFTON'S DR

NG16

Factory

Canal (disused)

The Shipley Boat (PH)

Ship Ga

Erewash Canal

Hufton's Coppice

HASSOCK LA N

Algrave Hall Farm

Purdy House Farm

Poplars Farm

The Coppice Inn

THE FIELD

Shipley

HASSOCK LA S

Cotmanhay Wood

Michael House - Rudolf Steiner Sch

Shipley Lake

The American Adventure Theme Park

Chapel Hill Farm

HARTINGTON PL 1
MILLERSDALE AVE 2
BIRCHOVER PL 3
CASTLETON AVE 4
DEVONSHIRE CL 5

Cotmanhay Inf & Jun Sch

HOPEWELL WLK

Lodge Farm

Shipley Wood

Ilkeston Com

Cotmanhay

DE7

MOUNT PLEASANT

RICHMOND AVE

BENNERLEY AVE

VERNON ST

Shipley Country Park

Shipley Common

Shipley Common La

HEANOR RD

Head House Farm

The Brook

Mapperley Brook

ILKESTON

Allotment Gardens

Charlotte Inf Sch

BOATMANS CL

SPRINGFIELD GDNS

West Hallam

PH

HIGH LA CENTRAL A609

HIGH LA E

Manners Ind Est

Orchard Bsns Pk

VICTORIA ST

L Ctr

B6007

MANNERS RD

BRISTOL RD

A6096

C1
1 BRUSSELS TERR
2 BURLEIGH ST
3 STAMFORD ST
4 ESSEX ST
5 DURHAM ST
6 NORTHGATE ST
7 WILTON ST
8 WEST TERR
9 NORTH ST
10 STATION CT
11 FULLWOOD AVE
12 PROVIDENCE PL
13 FULLWOOD ST
14 WHARNCLIFFE RD
15 JACKSON AVE
16 GREGORY ST
17 CHAPEL ST
18 LOWER CHAPEL ST
19 RIGLEY AVE

ST10

Holbrook Farm

Saltersford Lane

Folly Farm

Alverton Hall Farm

Quixhill La

Quixhill La

4

Quixhill

Denstone La

Quixhill Bridge

Staffordshire Way

41

Windyharbour

Little Park Farm

Oliver's Green

THE WEAVERS

MILL PIT LA

THE WESTLANDS

Denstone Hall

B5031

Denstone Hall

GREENFIELDS 1
ST CHAD'S CL 2
CROFTSTEAD AVE 3

COLLEGE RD

The Tavern (PH)

Manor Farm

HOLLIS LA

Nabb Farm

COLLEGE RD

BIRCH CL

ELM VIEW

Denstone
All Saints
CE Fst Sch

PO

Harper Meadow

3

Denstone Coll

ST14

STUBWOOD HOLLOW

Stubwood Farm

B5031

40

Hallriddings

Smalley

Nabb Brook

Riddings

RYLOFT LA

Stubwood

Rycroft CE Mid Sch

River Churnet

2

Armitage

JARDINE LA

STUBWOOD LA

Works

Woodhouse Farm

Churnet Bridge

HIGH ST

MILL ST 1
WESTGATE CL 2
ABBEY RD 3
CHURCH LA 4
WHITAKER MEWS 5
NORTHFIELD AVE 6

39

Woodhouse Field Farm

Woodhouse Fields

Banks Farm

1

Wottons Farm

Alders

Alders Brook

New Plantation

Pit Holes Plantation

Woodseat

Ford

Cornhill Farm

Nothill Brook

Field Head Farm

B5030

DE6

38

08 | 09 | 10

A | B | C

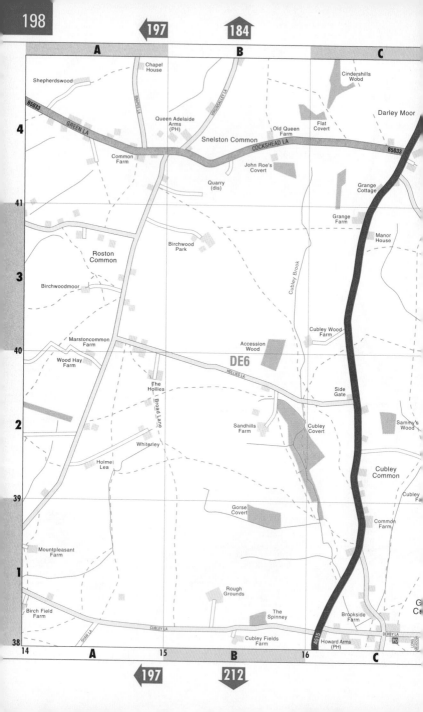

A   B   C

Shepherdswood

Chapel House

Cindershills Wood

B5033

GREEN LA

Darley Moor

4

Queen Adelaide Arms (PH)

Old Queen Farm

Flat Covert

Snelston Common

COCKSHEAD LA

B5033

Common Farm

John Roe's Covert

Quarry (dis)

Grange Cottage

41

Grange Farm

Manor House

Birchwood Park

Roston Common

3

Cubley Brook

Birchwoodmoor

Cubley Wood Farm

Marstoncommon Farm

Accession Wood

40

DE6

Wood Hay Farm

HOLLIES LA

Side Gate

The Hollies

Broad Lane

Sammy's Wood

2

Sandhills Farm

Cubley Covert

Whiterley

Holme Lea

Cubley Common

39

Cubley Fa

Gorse Covert

Common Farm

Mountpleasant Farm

1

Rough Grounds

G Ce

Birch Field Farm

The Spinney

Brookside Farm

38

SWAN LA

CUBLEY LA

Cubley Fields Farm

A515

Howard Arms (PH)

DERBY LA

LONG MOOR

14   A   15   B   16   C

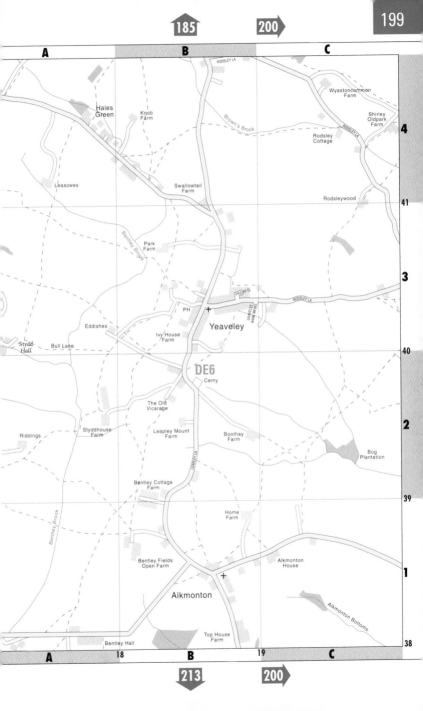

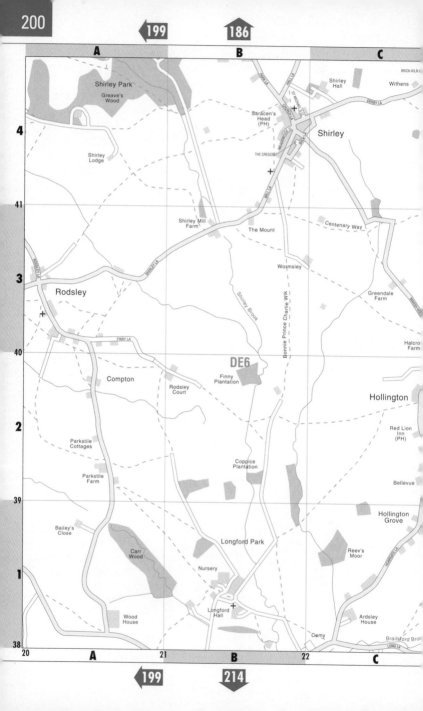

A **A52** DERBY LA

Brailsford Mill BACK LA

B

C

Yew Tree Inn (PH)

THE SPINNEY

CORNER FARM

LUKE LA

THE PLAIN

CHESTER WEST WAY

4

Ednaston Hall

Ednaston

EDNASTON HALL FARM MEWS

Ednaston House

Ednaston Hall Farm

Centenary Way

Brailsford Green

Hall Farm

CHURCH LA

THE GREEN

+

Brailsford CE Prim Sch

MAIN RD

Brailsford

PH

A52

MILL LA

The Spinney

41

CH

ollington Cottage

Mossnip Cottage

Churchfields Farm

Pools Head

3

Brailsford Brook

Peatmoss Plantation

40

DE6

Upper Burrows Farm

Slade Hollow

PICKLING LA

Culland Hall

Culland Mount

Culland Cottage

Cullandmanor Farm

2

The Burrows

39

BURROWS LA

Water Tower

1

Nunsfield

GLEBE CL

Stoop Farm

The Stoop

PH

Glebe Farm

Longlane

Long Lane CE Prim Sch

+

A 24 B LONG LA 25 C **38**

201
188

A **B** **C**

Centenary Way

Mercaston Hall Farm

Netherfield Farm

Whiteleys Plantation

Top Wild Park Farm

4

Wood Lane

Wildpark Brook

EAGLE LA

Wildpark

A52

Middle Wild Park

Lower Wild Park Farm

41

Brailsford Hall

Home Farm

Buck Haze

WILDPARK LA

Carr Wood

Windy Arbour

HALL LA

3

Meynell Lang

Mast

Coppice Ponds

Snapes Farm

40

Hilltop Farm

DE6

ASHBOURNE RD

FLAGSHAW LA

The Burma Road

Hill Side Farm

Hall Farm

Over Burrows

Burrows Hall Farm

BURROWS LA

Brooklands Farm

Langley Hall

2

Nether Burrows

Works

Gate House Farm

Nether Burrows Farm

Nether Burrows

New House Farm

Town E Farm

39

Close Farm

CHURCH LA

LONGFO

+

Kirk Langle CE Prim Sch

Langley Green

Green Farm

Green Foot Farm

Kirk Langle

1

Riddings Lane

Twenty Acres

BELPER LANE

THE GREEN

Parson's Gorse

The Pastures

38

LONG LA

26 **A** 27 **B** 28 **C**

201
216

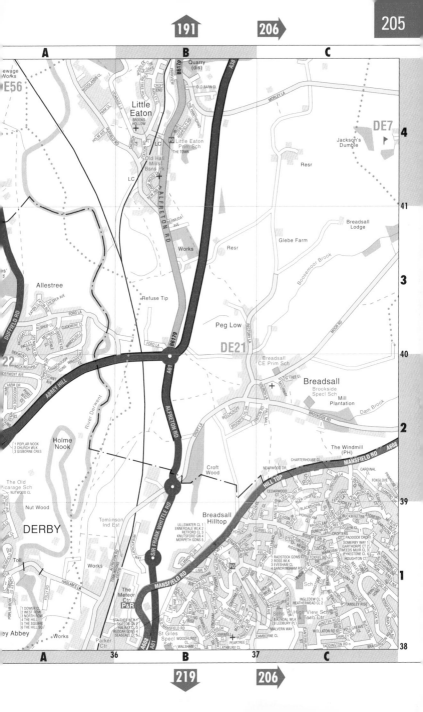

205
192

A B C

Priory
Cottages

MORLEY LA

QUARRY RD

BRICKKILN LA

Morley
Smithy

Little
Wood

Breadsall
Priory
Hotel

Almshouses

Smithy
Farm

PH

Morley
Prim Sch

Park
Farm

MOSES LA

4

MORK RD

MORLEY ALMSHOUSES

Lodge
Farm

Morleymoor

PENNINE DR

Morley
House
Farm

Morley
Hall

41

The
Mound

Midshires Way

CHURCH LA

Spring
Oak
Farm

Morley

DE7

Jesse
Farm

3

Top
Farm

A608

Derby Coll
(Broomfield Campus)

Broomfield
Cottages

LIME LA

40

Broomfield
Farm

Lime
Farm

The
Limes

Kings
Corner

Ferriby Brook

North
Lodge

DERBY RD

BROOKSIDE
RD

A608

Chaddesden
Common

1 GLENORCHY CT
2 APPLEGATE CL
3 BRAMBLEBERRY CT
4 TISSINGTON DR
5 CRESSBROOK WAY

1 HEDGEROW GDNS
2 HEDGEBANK CT

PH

2

MANSFIELD
RD

DERBY

Chaddesden
Wood

MEADOW VIEW

LIME LA

CONSORT
GDNS

SOVEREIGN WAY

BARON

PRIMROSE
CL

1 COLUMBINE CL
2 CELANDINE CL
3 DUNKERY CT
4 SELWORTHY CL
5 PORLOCK CT
6 BUNNYRIGG DR
7 HAREBELL CL

DE21

DIAMOND
DR

39

Parkview
Prim Sch

1 ELKSTONE CL
8 CHURCHDOWN CL
10 ADAMSCOTE CL
11 BARCHESTON CL
12 CULWORTH CT
13 MOUNTFORD CL
14 LAMPETER CL
15 OXWICH CT
16 BRIDGEND CT
17 SHREWSBURY CL

Birch
Wood

Oakwood
L Ctr

Birchwood
House

Locko
Park

1

8 SWANWICK GDNS
9 ANSTEY CT
10 THURLOW CT
11 DELAMERE CL

1 THORESBY CL
2 BASSINGHAM CL
3 ROSEBERRY CT
4 FIRTREE GR
5 WHYTELEAFE GR
6 BICKLEY MOSS
7 SAMANTHA CT

Crow
Wood
Farm

OAKWOOD
DR

The Lake

Hill
Farm

GAINSBOROUGH

38

38 A 39 B 40 C

A   B   C

A609 BELPER RD
HIGH LA W
PARK HALL LA

The Tinklers

West Hallam Common

1 DERBYSHIRE CL
2 ECKINGTON CL
3 DARLEY DR
4 BRASSINGTON CL

West Hallam

4

Briggswood Farm

Hilltop Farm

White Hart (PH)

Scargill CE Prim Sch

Scargill Rd

Holme Croft

BURNCROFT

BEECH LA

TWYFORD CL 1
ELIZABETH CL 2
WEYBRIDGE CL 3
FARNHAM WLK 4

THE VILLAGE

ORCHARD CT

Glebe Farm

41

The Grange

QUEENS AVE
HURST RD
STATION RD

Depot

Moat Wood

Stanley Grange

3

tehouse Farm

MORLEY

Stanley Farm

GLEBE CL

NEW ST

Stanley

Stanley Brook

St Andrew's CE Prim Sch

The Bridge Inn (PH)

DALE RD

DERBY RD

CAT AND FIDDLE LA

Cat and Fiddle

Cat and Fiddle Farm

DE7

40

r Farm

Quarry Farm

Lower Hagg Farm

Upper Hagg Farm

Ashtree Farm

Windmill (dis)

LADYWOOD RD A6096

2

Hill Farm

Farm

Midshires Way

HAGG LA

ARBOUR HILL

Carpenters' Arms (PH)

Gateway Christian Sch

39

Locko Grange Farm

Flourish Farm

Arbour Hill

MIXER LA

Dale Abbey (rems of)

Hollies Farm

Closes Farm

TATTLE HILL

DE21

The Flourish

Waterlog Farm

Dale Abbey

The Hermitage

1

Columbine Farm

Lodge Farm

Dunnshill

A6096

DE72

Dale Hills

Ockbrook Wood

Crow Wood

Burnwood

38

A   42   B   43   C

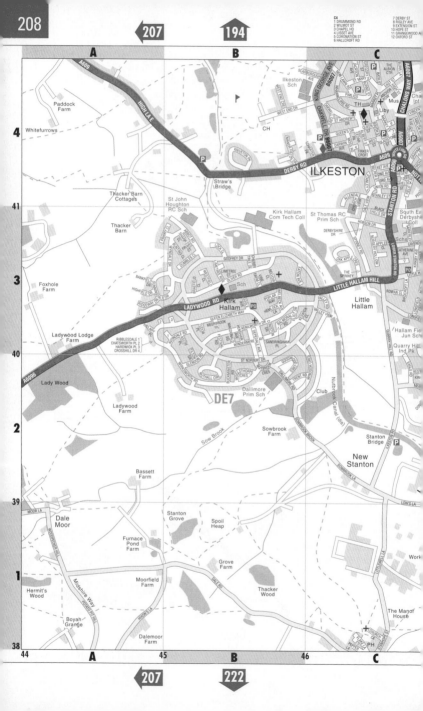

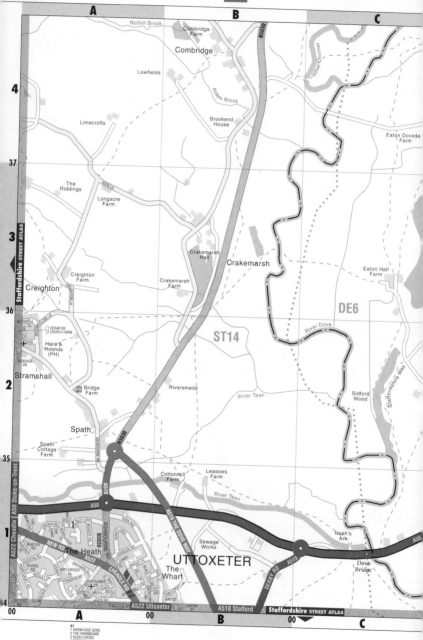

A1
1 HERMITAGE GDNS
2 THE HORNBEAMS
3 HEATH CROSS
4 WINDMILL CL

197
212

A   **B**   **C**

Morry House Farm

ST14

Sch PO
Manor House
1 WESTON BANK
2 THURVASTON RD
Marston Montgomery
PH

Eaton Barn

Havenhouse Farm

4

Beggarsbutts

The Beeches

Banktop

37

Waldley

Waldley Farm

Marston Brook

Marston Woodhouse

3

Upper Eaton Farm

Old Woodhouse Farm

36

Upwoods Farm

DE6

Lady Coppice

Hill Farm

2

Holmlea Farm

Somersal Farm

Victory Farm

Woodhouse Farm

Somersal Herbert

Mount Pleasant

The Hall

35

North Lodge

Brocksford Brook

Grove Cottages

Eaton Lodge

Field Farm

Oaklea

1

Mill Cottage

PH

veridge

OAK LA
WEST DR
HAWTHORN
EAST DR
LAKE DR
MAPLE CL
HARRIS LA
DERBY RD
UPWOODS RD
ORCHARD CT
GATEHOUSE DR
FLORENCE DR
HIGH ST
LAKE LODGE
SCH
PH
ALMS RD
CHURCH LA
HALL LA
MILL LA

Mill Farm

A50

34

A   **B**   **C**
12   13

224
212

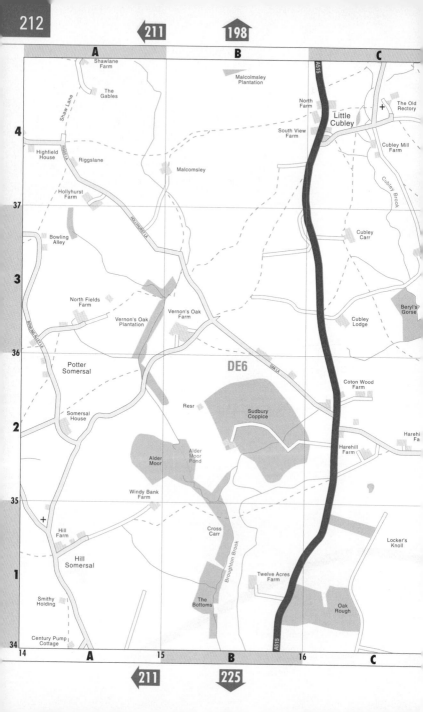

211
198

A

B

C

Shawlane
Farm

Malcolmsley
Plantation

The Gables

North
Farm

Little
Cubley

The Old
Rectory

4

Shaw Lane

South View
Farm

Cubley Mill
Farm

Highfield
House

Riggslane

Malcomsley

Cubley Brook

37

Hollyhurst
Farm

HOLLYHURST LA

Cubley
Carr

Bowling
Alley

3

North Fields
Farm

Vernon's Oak
Farm

Cubley
Lodge

Beryl's
Gorse

BOWLING ALLEY LA

Vernon's Oak
Plantation

36

DE6

OAK LA

Potter
Somersal

Coton Wood
Farm

Resr

Sudbury
Coppice

Somersal
House

2

Harehi
Fa

Alder
Moor
Pond

Harehill
Farm

Alder
Moor

35

Windy Bank
Farm

Hill
Farm

Cross
Carr

Locker's
Knoll

Broughton Brook

Hill
Somersal

1

Twelve Acres
Farm

Smithy
Holding

The
Bottoms

Oak
Rough

Century Pump
Cottage

A515

34

14

A

15

B

16

C

211

211
225

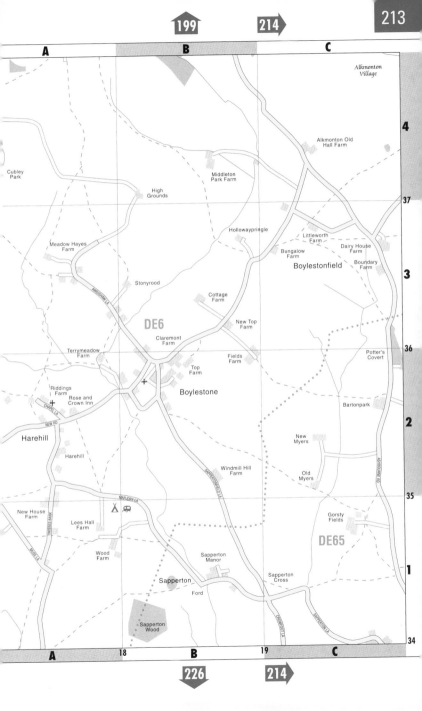

199
214

A B C

4

37

3

36

2

35

1

34

Alkmonton Village

Alkmonton Old Hall Farm

Cubley Park

Middleton Park Farm

High Grounds

Hollowaypringle

Littleworth Farm

Dairy House Farm

Meadow Hayes Farm

Bungalow Farm

Boylestonfield

Boundary Farm

Stonyrood

Cottage Farm

DE6

New Top Farm

Claremont Farm

Terrymeadow Farm

Fields Farm

Potter's Covert

Top Farm

Riddings Farm

Rose and Crown Inn

Boylestone

Bartonpark

Harehill

Harehill

New Myers

Old Myers

Windmill Hill Farm

New House Farm

MARJORY LA

Lees Hall Farm

Gorsty Fields

DE65

Wood Farm

Sapperton Manor

Sapperton Cross

Sapperton

Ford

Sapperton Wood

AMBUSHAW LA

SAPPERTON LA

CROSS LA

ASHBOURNE RD

NEW RD

CHAPEL LA

TWOSS PK

MUSE LA

A B C

18
19

226
214

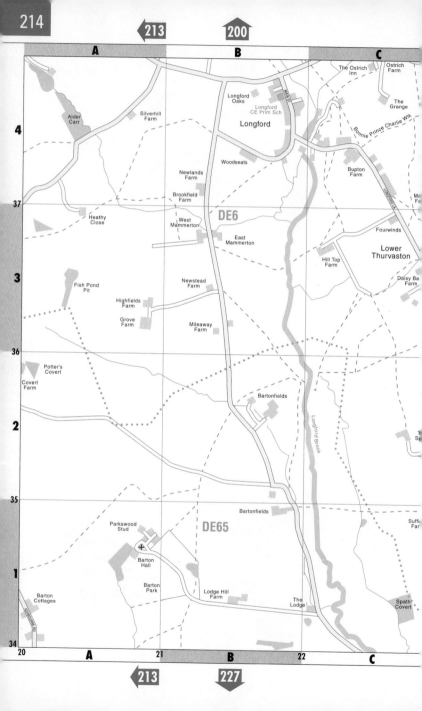

A   B   C

The Ostrich Inn
Ostrich Farm

Longford Oaks
Longford CE Prim Sch
Longford

The Grange

Bonnie Prince Charlie Wlk

4

Alder Carr

Silverhill Farm

Woodseats

Bupton Farm

Newlands Farm

Brookfield Farm

37

Heathy Close

DE6

West Mammerton

East Mammerton

Fourwinds

Lower Thurvaston

Hill Top Farm

3

Fish Pond Pit

Newstead Farm

Daisy Ba Farm

Highfields Farm

Grove Farm

Mileaway Farm

36

Potter's Covert

Covert Farm

2

Bartonfields

Longford Brook

35

Bartonfields

Suffi Far

DE65

Parkswood Stud

Barton Hall

1

Barton Park

Lodge Hill Farm

The Lodge

Spath Covert

Barton Cottages

34

20   A   21   B   22   C

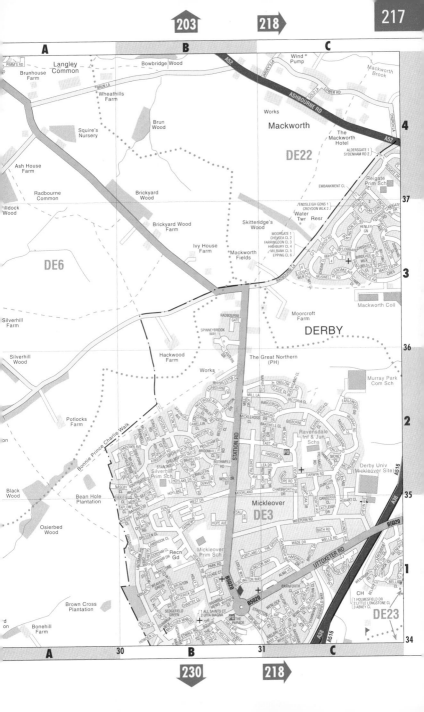

Langley Common

Bowbridge Wood

PIMM'S RD

Brunhouse Farm

Wheathills Farm

Squire's Nursery

Brun Wood

Ash House Farm

Radbourne Common

Brickyard Wood

Brickyard Wood Farm

illock Wood

DE6

Ivy House Farm

Skitteridge's Wood

Mackworth Fields

Silverhill Farm

Silverhill Wood

Black Wood

Potlocks Farm

Osierbed Wood

Bonnie Prince Charlie Walk

Bean Hole Plantation

Hackwood Farm

Radbourne Gate

SPINNEYBROOK WAY

The Great Northern (PH)

Works

Whistlestop Cl

Silverhill Prim Sch

STATION RD

Mickleover Prim Sch

Recn Gd

Mickleover DE3

Brown Cross Plantation

Bonehill Farm

Sedgefield Green

ALL SAINTS CT
BUFFA MAGNA

THE PARADE

ASHBOURNE RD

A52

Wind Pump

Mackworth Brook

Works

Mackworth

The Mackworth Hotel

DE22

ALDERSGATE 1
SYDENHAM RD 2

EMBANKMENT CL

Reigate Prim Sch

ENDSLEIGH GDNS 1
CROYDON WLK 2

Water Twr   Resr

MOORGATE 1
CHELSEA CL 2
FARRINGDON CL 3
HIGHBURY CL 4
MILBANK CL 5
EPPING CL 6

HENLEY GN

Mackworth Coll

Moorcroft Farm

DERBY

Murray Park Com Sch

Ravensdale Inf & Jun Schs

Derby Univ (Mickleover Site)

A516

A38

UTTOXETER RD

B5020

CH
1 HOLMESFIELD DR
2 LITTLE LONGSTONE CL
3 ABNEY CL

DE23

A516

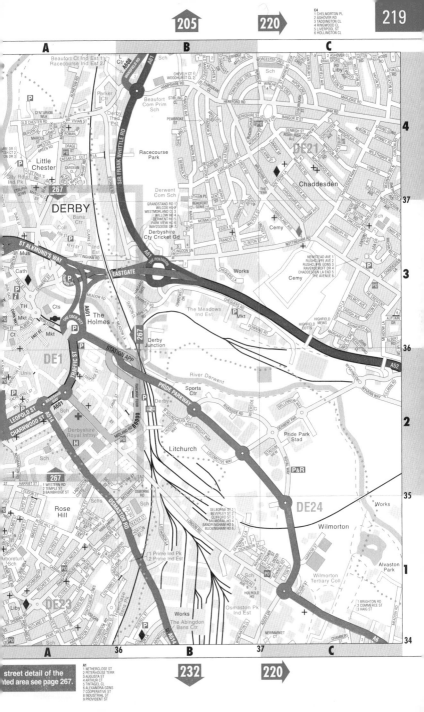

C4
1 CHELMORTON PL
2 ASHOVER RD
3 TADDINGTON CL
4 RINGWOOD CL
5 LIVERPOOL ST
6 HOLLINGTON CL

A4
1 NETHERCLOSE ST
2 PETERHOUSE TERR
3 AUGUSTA ST
4 ARTHUR CT
5 TINTAGEL CL
6 ALEXANDRA GDNS
7 COOPERATIVE ST
8 INDUSTRIAL ST
9 PROVIDENT ST

street detail of the
ted area see page 267.

219
206

A   B   C

South Lodge

Brunswood Farm

4

Cavendish Close Inf & Jun Schs

1 SANDFIELD CL
2 GLEADMOSS LA
3 LATHKILL RD
4 HASSOP RD

Lees Brook Com Sch

Chaddesden Park Inf & Jun Schs

4 JOHN KENNEDY GDNS
5 ATCHISON GDNS

Lees Brook

DERBY

37

Mossey Yard Plantation

Liby

Chaddesden Park

GOLDCREST DR 1
LINNET CL 2
GREENFINCH CL 3

DEER PARK VIEW

REDSTART CL

TRENTON GREEN DR 1
HOUSTON CL 2
DENISON GDNS 3

Chaddesden Brook

3

Cherry Tree Hill Inf & Jun Schs

Cherrytree Hill

Springfield Farm

Springfield Prim Sch

MILL ROW

Spondon

Borrow Wood Inf & Jun Schs

Cemy

West Park Com Sch

DE21

Meadow Farm Com Prim Sch

36

1 ENOCH STONE DR
2 CYPRESS WLK

MERCIAN MEWS 1
PRIESTLAND AVE 2
GILBERT CL 3
CHURCH HILL 4
BAMBURGH CL 5
SILVEY GR 6
GREENBANK 7

Church Mews

Liby

SITWELL ST

GOLDSTONE CT 1
TRIVERS CT 2
BERESFORD DR 3
VERNON DR 4

DERBY RD

Aspen Bsns Ctr

A6005

A5111

BORROWASH BY-PASS

2

Wyvern Bsns Pk

The Wyvern

STANIER WAY

STEVENSONS WAY

DERBY RD

MICAH OUGHTON LA

LC

DERBY RD

DERWENT

A6096

WILLOWCROFT RD

NOTTINGHAM RD

A52

HADDON DR

RACEWAY

PRIDE PARK

WILT PRIDE RD

CELANESE RD

LC

STONEY GATE RD

Spondon

35

Water Reclamation Works

P

HOLME

BELPAR HO 5
HEANOR HO 6
MATLOCK HO 7
MELBOURNE HO 8
RIPLEY HO 9
SILVERHILL RD 10

A6005

BURROWF MEWS

Works

Sewage Works

Works

River Derwent

Electricity Generating Station

Chy

River Derwent

1

P

Nature Reserve

DE24

Mast

A5111

RACEWAY LA

DE24

DE72

34

38   A   39   B   40   C

219
233

207
222

A
B
C

DE7

The
Spots

PH   Mast

Bartlewood
Farm

The Spots
Plantation

4

Spondon Wood
Farm

Little Hay
Grange

Little
London

don Wood

Moor Lane
Farm

Piggin
Wood

37

Pheasant
Field House

DALE RD

Waterworks
Plantation

Poplars
Farm

Fields
Farm

1 PHEASANT FIELD DR
2 LANCASTER WLK

3

1 WINDMILL CL
2 ANNE POTTER CL
3 HARGRAVE AVE

Toot
Hills

DE21

PH

Scotland
Farm

Hopwell
Hall

Ockbrook
Grange

Redhill
Prim Sch

Ockbrook

Ockbrook
Sch

DE72

36

Moravian
Settlement

Hopwell
Nook

Windmill
Farm

PO

Castle
Hill

COLLER LA

2

Birchfield

Carr Hill
Farm

Manor
Farm

Hopwell
House

B5010

A52

BORROWASH BY-PASS

35

FIELD CL

GREENWAY

BEECH AVE

CHESTNUT AVE

DERWENT ROW

TEESDALE CL

Draycott
House

orrowash
House

FAIRFIELD
AVE

DEANS DR

VICTORIA AVE

WOODLAND AVE

SHERWOOD
GROVE

KNIGHTSBRIDGE

Ashbrook
Inf & Jun
Sch

AVE RUTLAND AVE

DEVONSHIRE AVE

Liby

LADYSMITH RD

KIMBERLEY RD

Borrowash

HARRINGTON AVE

CHARNWOOD AVE

DERBY RD

ELM ST

NURSERY

PRIORSBARN CL

1

DOVECOTE DR

PO

NOTTINGHAM RD

MANOR RD

STATION RD

B5010

BALMORAL RD

DRAYCOTT RD

B5010

1 PRIORWAY GDNS
2 WINDSOR CL
3 BRADBURY CL
4 COOPERS CL
5 FAIRES CL

PRINCESS DR

CENTRAL

SHACKLECROSS
CL

BRIDS WAY

OAK TREE

Shacklecross

DERBY RD

The
ryne

TREVACRES

MEADOW

MEAR DR

A6005

Harris
Grange
Farm

Hotel

WASHINGTON
COTTS

34

A
42
B
43
C

234
222

A   B   C

Boyah
Grange
Farm

POTATO
PIT
LA

Sandiacre
Lodge
Farm

DALE RD

BURR LA

MAIN ST

STANHOPE
ST

PARK RD

High
Lodge
Farm

Manor
Farm

DE7   Stanton-by-Dale

Mast

ST MARY'S LA

Wards
Farm

Park
Farm

Risley
Park

Wisteria
Farm

The
Hewarths

4

37

Keys
Farm

Maywood
Farm

The
Hewarths
Farm

NG10

CH

RISLEY LA

Risley
Lodge
Farm

Constitution
Hill

Risley
Coppice

Willow
Lodge

Friesla
Sch

Sports
Ctr

3

Hopwell
Hall
Farm

Midshires Way

The
Nook

Hopwell
Hall

Peatmeadow
Farm

Risley
Lodge

SECOND AV

CHERRY

PHELPS AV

36

Hopwell
Park

Lindley
House

Manor
Farm

Risley Lower Gram
CE Prim Sch

DE72

Pastures
Farm

DERBY RD

BRASSINGTON LA

Risley

2

Golden
Valley
Farm

PH

WILLOUGHBY CT 1
PRIMROSE COTTS 2

YEW TREE
COTTS

Sandboro'
Fields

B5010 NOTTINGHAM RD

Hill Top
Farm

Risleyhall
Farm

A52

BORROWASH BY-PASS

Willowbrook
Farm

THE
CRESCENT

35

Near
Meadow
Farm

Lane

Mill Hill

1

Golden Brook

RISLEY LA

Sun Close
Farm

Draycott
Fields
Farm

Cottage
Farm

Bridge
Farm

Ryehill
Farm

Breaston

LONGMOOR LA

34

44   A   45   B   46   C

221   235

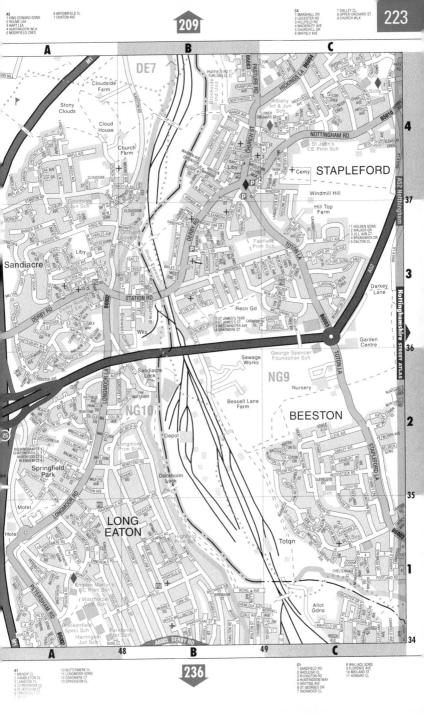

A3
1 KING EDWARD GDNS
2 HOLME LEA
3 HART LEA
4 HUNTINGDON WLK
5 MOORFIELD CRES
6 BROOMFIELD CL
7 DENTON AVE

C4
1 MARSHALL DR
2 LEICESTER RD
3 HILLFIELD RD
4 MACKINLEY AVE
5 CHURCHILL DR
6 WHITELY AVE
7 DALLEY CL
8 UPPER ORCHARD ST
9 CHURCH WLK

A1
1 MENDIP CL
2 HAMBLETON CL
3 LANGDON CL
4 CAIRNSMORE CL
5 PETERSHAM CT
6 ENNERDALE CT
10 BUTTERMERE CL
11 LONGMOOR GDNS
12 GRASMERE CT
13 SPRIDGEON CL

C1
1 SANDFIELD RD
2 HADLEIGH CL
3 RIVINGTON RD
4 HUNTINGDON WAY
5 WHITING AVE
6 ST GEORGES DR
7 INCHWOOD CL
8 WALLACE GDNS
9 FLORENCE AVE
10 MIDLAND ST
11 HOWARD CL

A   **B**   **C**

A50

Old Hall

Sewage Works

Manor House

Doveridge Prim Sch

Bell Cotts

Ley-Hill Farm

Palmer Moor Farm

4

BLACKPIT LA

Deepmoor Farm

Doveridge

Yelt Farm

Brocksford Bridge

Palmer Moor

Brocksford Hall School

BROCKSFORD CT

33

DE6

Brocksford Brook

Brocksford Gorse

3

Holtwood Cottages

Herepark

Holtwood

32

Woodford Rough

Woodford

River Dove

Railway Cottages

2

Riddings Farm

Slade's Farm

Green Acres

MOISTY LA

ST14

Hall Croft

31

Pear Tree Farm

Field Farm

St Peter's CE Fst Sch

PH

THE SQUARE

Marchington

Upper Brook House

Birch Cross

GREEN LA

CHURCH LA

1

Brookside Farm

PH

Brickhill Hill

Field House Stables

Small Silve Green

Lower Brook House

The Vicarage

B5017

Carrig

30

Marchington Ind Est

11   **A**   **12**   **B**   **13**   **C**

227
215

A	B	C

The Hall Farm

MAIN PIT LA

The Hall

COMMON LA

BROOK LA

Sutton on the Hill

DE6

Fieldgate Farm

Dishfields Farm

Acre La

DISH LA

Dizzybeard Plantation

Gamekeepers Cottage

Fields Farm

Baldfie Farm

A

Arbourfield Covert

Ash Farm

Ash Co

Ash Co

ASH LA

4

33

Ivy House Farm

Park Farm

Hilton Fields

Holly Bush Farm

WILLOWPIT LA

3

32

Hoon Mount

Roystone House

Hoon Ridge

Sutton Brook

SEETON LA

DE65

Hilton Gorse

Burntheath

Blakelow Farm

2

A50

Lodge Farm

DERBY RD

Hilto

Hallcroft

Hoon Villa Farm

Ind Est

A5132

31

1 MONTGOMERY CL
2 CHURCHILL DR
3 SHAEF CL
4 SHERMAN CL

Moorend

DERBY RD

UTTOXETER RD

PH

Elm Tree Farm

Hilton Com

EGGINTON RD

Hargate Lodge

1

P

Hilton Prim Sch

Peacroft

Harg

Hilton Brook

Hilton

BACK LA

ORCHARD

1 MARSTON BROOK
2 DALE BROOK
3 SANDFORD BROOK

Depot

Hargate Manor

NENE WAY

A51

30

23	A	24	B	25	C

A B C

DE6

Highfield

Highwall
Lodge

Bannell's Farm

DE3

Bannell's Lane Farm

A516

Bearwardcote
Farm

Highfields Farm

4

Hepnalls

Marsh Farm

33

Ashe
Hall

Oakdene

The Marsh

The
Lawns

ETWALL LA
TINDERBOX LA

3

Marsh
Cottage
Farm

BURNASTON LA

Greenacres

DEE LA
MARSH FARM MEWS

Burnaston

SUTTON LA

ALMSHOUSES

SLADE CL

SANDYPITS LA

32

Etwall Brook

John Port
Sch

Liby

Etwall
Prim
Sch

Sandypits Farm

DE65

RIDGEWAY

DERBY RD

Friary Farm

OLD STATION
HILTON RD

Lodge Farm

2

Etwall

WELLINGTON RD

New Close Farm

New Gorse
Fox Covert

BELFIELD CT 1
BELFIELD TERR 2

Sewage
Works

Marlpit
Plantation

COMMON END

31

DE1

JACKSONS LA

TYNEFIELD
MEWS

BLAKELEY LA

Broomhill
Cottages

TYNEFIELD CT

Etwall Common

Works

Blakeley Lodge

1

Egginton
Common

A50

A B C

30

A B C

4 A516 Field House GRASSY CT The Grange Hotel A516 WOODSIDE SQ HEDINGHAM WAY LINGHAM LA VALLEY WALK ROUGHTON CL 1 ARDLEIGH CL 2 WRETHAM CL 3 KIPLING DR Sch BLENHEIM DR BRIERFIELD WAY A38 Bunkers W

33 DE3 Staker Flats Latimer CL WATERLOO LA 1 MALCOLM GR 2 GREGORY WLK 3 RODNEY WLK ATWORTH CHESTERTON Midlandscr Nuffield DE23 PH

3 Bushy Cottage Micklemeadow WITCHILL WAY BURNLEY WAY RYKNELD RD Hotel Highfield's Farm COMFRE CRANBERR MEADOW BROO

Millway House

Burnaston Hill Farm New Buildings Farm GREEN LA DERVEN LA MINES LA

32 Nursery Blakemere Farm BARE ACRE LA

2 Depot Fields Farm Park House Nursery Landown Farm GREEN LA DERVEN LA

DE65

31 CARDALES CL MEADOW CL BAGNALL DOLES LA Findern Mill Farm EAST LAWN WILLOW FARM CT Doles Brook DE1 GREEN WAY PH HD

1 Works Rumenco Farm THE HALVES ALDAMS LA LOVEGREAVE LA BRIDGE GREEN PRIORY LA DOMINIE PIECE LA Se W

30 A38 A50

29 A 30 B 31 C

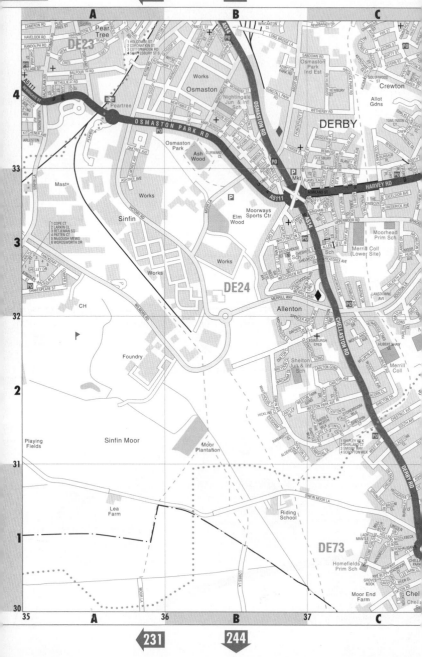

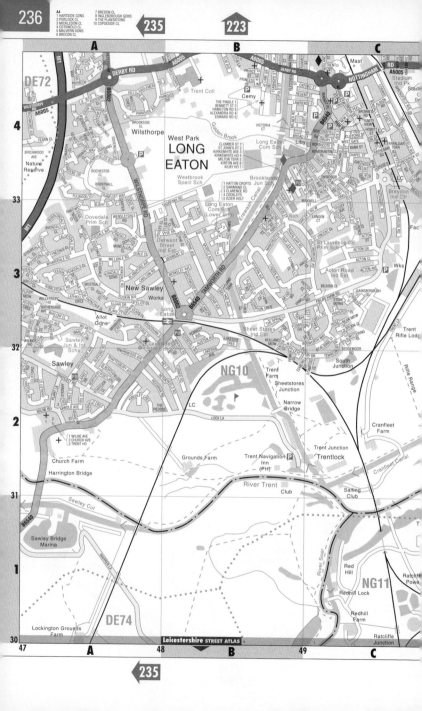

6005 Nottingham

HARLAXTON DR

Sewage Works

SOMERSET CL

Attenborough Junction

Golden Brook

WARWICK RD
2 LITCHFIELD CL
3 RUGELEY AVE

River Erewash

Attenborough Sailing Club

Attenborough Nature Reserve

NG9

Barton Island

River Trent

Grange Farm

Brandshill Wood

Old Farm

THE LIMES

Manor Farm

Barton in Fabis

LC

1 THRUMPTON AVE
2 CHATSWORTH AVE

P

Home Farm

RD

NG10

PASTURE LA

Trent Valley Way

LITTLE LANNON

MANOR RD

A453 Nottingham

Nottinghamshire STREET ATLAS

NG11

Glebe Farm

Ferry Farm

Thrumpton

Fields Farm

Thrumpton Hall

Thrumpton Park

PO

CHURCH LA

Manor Farm

A453 GREEN ST

Church Farm

Wood Farm

Old Wood

Twenty Lands Plantation

Wright's Hill

Wright's Hill Plantation

Hillside Cottage

Gotham Hill

Gotham Hill Wood

Cottagers Hill

LC

Power Station

LC

Cottagers Hill Spinney

Stonepit Wood

Morley's Barn Farm

4

33

3

32

2

31

1

30

A   51   B   52   C

226

A   B   C

River Dove

Riverside Farm

DE65

Old Dove Plantation

4

DE6

River Dove

Fauld Fe

Coton Farm

Row Hill

Coton in the Clay

FAULD LA

Boundary House

29

Coton Hall Farm

Fauld Hall

SPINNEY LODGE

Fauld Ind Pk

Fauld House

Fauld

3

Fauld Manor

Stonepit Hills

HANBURY HILL

P

Sewage Works

Mill & Mine

Queen's Purse Wood

Hanbury

Hanbury Hill

Brown's Coppice

28

MARTIN LA

DE13

CHURCH LA

OAKFIELDS

The Cottages

PO

PH St Werburgh's CE Prim Sch

WOOD LA

CAST

Hanbury House Farm

Hall

2

Castle Hayes Park Farm

Croft Farm

Hare Holes Rough

Hare Holes Farm

The Farm

27

Capertition Wood

ASHBROOK LA

The Villa

1

Moat Farm

Top Farm

Woodend

Blackbrook Spinney

Lower Castle Hayes Farm

Hanbury Park Farm

Belmot Bridge

BELMOT RD

Blackbrook Farm

Hanbury Park Dingle

Blackbrook

26

17   A   18   B   19   C

Staffordshire STREET ATLAS

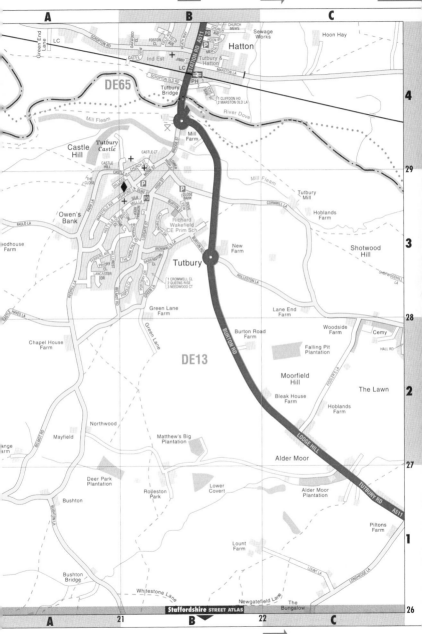

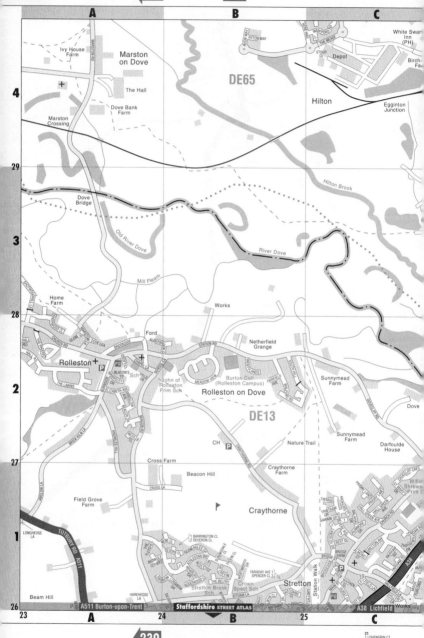

A B C

4

29

3

28

2

27

1

26

DE65

Hilton

White Swan
Inn (PH)

Depot

Birch Fa

Eggington
Junction

Ivy House
Farm

Marston
on Dove

The Hall

Dove Bank
Farm

Marston
Crossing

Dove
Bridge

Old River Dove

Hilton Brook

River Dove

Mill Fleam

Works

Home
Farm

Ford

Netherfield
Grange

Rolleston

Bladon's
Yd

John of
Rolleston
Prim Sch

Burton Coll
(Rolleston Campus)

Rolleston on Dove

DE13

Sunnymead
Farm

Dove

Sunnymead
Farm

Darfoulde
House

CH

Nature Trail

Cross Farm

Beacon Hill

Craythorne
Farm

Field Grove
Farm

CROSS LA

Craythorne

Willi
Shrews
Prim

Longhedge
LA

TUTBURY RD A511

1 BARRINGTON CL
2 DEVERON CL

1 FARADAY AVE
2 SPENCER CL

Station Walk

BRIDGE
FARM

Beam Hill

HAREHEDGE
LA

Crown
Speel Sch

Stretton Brook
Sch

THE BELFRY

Stretton

Works

A511 Burton-upon-Trent **Staffordshire STREET ATLAS** A38 Lichfield

C1
1 LOHENGRIN CT
2 CAMELOT CL
3 KNIGHTS CT
4 PRINCESS WAY
5 CARISBROOKE DR
6 ALDERHOLME DR
7 MANTON CL

A B C

Gorse Farm
Gravel Pit
Round House
Boundary Rd
Standpipe Cottages
Elvall Brook
EGGINTON RD
LC
Egginton Common
4
Park Hill
RAILWAY COTTS
Sewage Farm
RAILWAY COTTS
A38
HILTON RD
Saltersford Bridge
ELVALL RD
Marlpit Plantation
BURTON RD
29
Gravel Pit Plantation
South Boundary Cottages
CARRIERS RD
Ash Grove
The Bungalow
ASH GROVE LA
DE65
Egginton Bridge
Willington
3
Egginton
A5132
THE CASTLE WAY
OLD FORGE
DUCK ST
WELLINGTON CL
BUTTON CL
DOVE CLOSE
POSSETTER LA
MAIN ST
Brunt's Lane
MILL
Egginton Brook
Grange Farm
POUND LA
VICARAGE CY
Green Plantation
Egginton Prim Sch
SWADLEY CY
PO
Egginton Cottage
28
Every Arms Farm
+
CHURCH RD
Every Arms (PH)
RECTORY MEWS
DERBY RD
2
Trent and Mersey Canal
Pumping Station
High Bridge
Forge Poultry Farm
Egginton Bridge
27
Clay Mills
A5121
DE13
Mill Stream
River Dove
River Trent
1
Sewage Works
DE15
Repton
TRENT LA
B5008
BURTON RD
26
FIELD

A 27 B 28 C

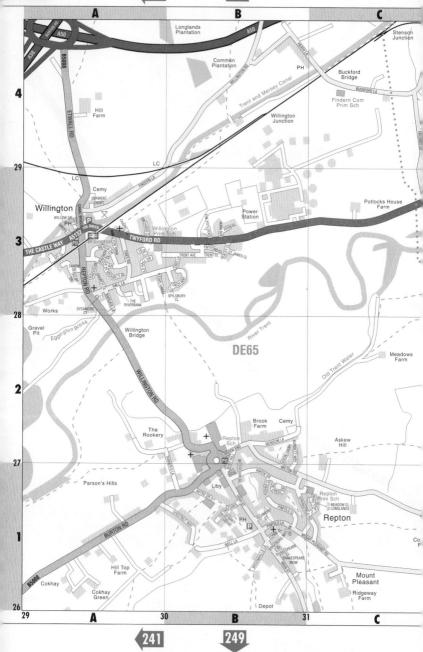

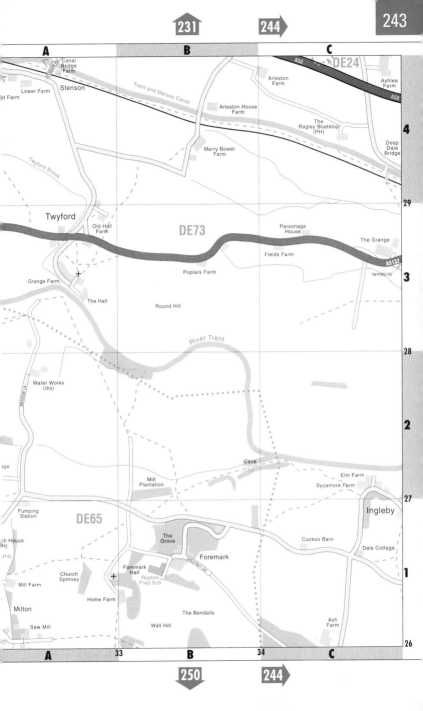

A
B
C

4

29

3

28

2

27

1

26

A
33
B
34
C

Canal
Bridge
Farm
Stenson
Lower Farm
st Farm
AY S
STENSON RD

Trent and Mersey Canal

A50
DE24
Arleston
Farm
Ashlea
Farm
A50

Arleston House
Farm

The
Ragley Boatstop
(PH)

Deep
Dale
Bridge

Merry Bower
Farm

Twyford Brook

Twyford

Old Hall
Farm

DE73

Parsonage
House

The Grange

Fields Farm

A5132
TWYFORD RD

Grange Farm

Poplars Farm

The Hall

Round Hill

River Trent

Water Works
(dis)

MEADOW LA

Cave

Elm Farm

Sycamore Farm

Ingleby

Mill
Plantation

Pumping
Station

DE65

Cuckoo Barn

Dale Cottage

ch House
PH)

UT CL

The
Grove

Foremark

Foremark
Hall

Mill Farm

Church
Spinney

CHESTNUT DR

Repton Prep Sch

Home Farm

The Bendalls

Ash
Farm

Milton

Saw Mill

Wall Hill

243
232

A   **B**   **C**

A50

4

Barrow-hill

The Lowes
Farm

Swarkestone
Lows

Chellaston
Sch

Cuttle
Brook

KINGSDALE
GR

Hill
Farm

DEEPDALE LA

MOOR LA

LOWES LA

Lowes
Bridge

Trent and Mersey Canal

Barrow
Bridge

29

Cuttle
Bridge

WALNUT
CL

FERNELEY
CL

SWARKESTONE RD

Swarkestone

BARROW LA

A5132

A5132

A514

PH

Old Hall
(rems of)

Old Hall
Farm

TWYFORD RD

SWARKESTONE RD

3

Sale & Davys
CE Sch

CHAPEL

MANOR
CT

THE WICKET

CHURCH LA

CLUB LA

WOODCOCK
CL

THE
ARBOUR

Meadow
Farm

River Trent

Barrow upon
Trent

Sand and
Gravel Pit

GREEN LA

28

DE73

Swarkestone Bridge

2

Sailing
Club

Poplars
Farm

Hollies
Farm

Hollow
Farm

Stanton
Barn

HOLLIES
FARM
CL

CHURCH
CL

Stanton by
Bridge

Manor
Farm

ACRES RD

27

Ash Farm

The
Hills

B587

WISE LA

Ingleby
Toft

1

West
Wood

Woodend
Cottage

BREACH LA

T

Warsick La

The Moor

Breach
Close

PH

A514

26

35   **A**   **36**   **B**   **37**   **C**

243
251

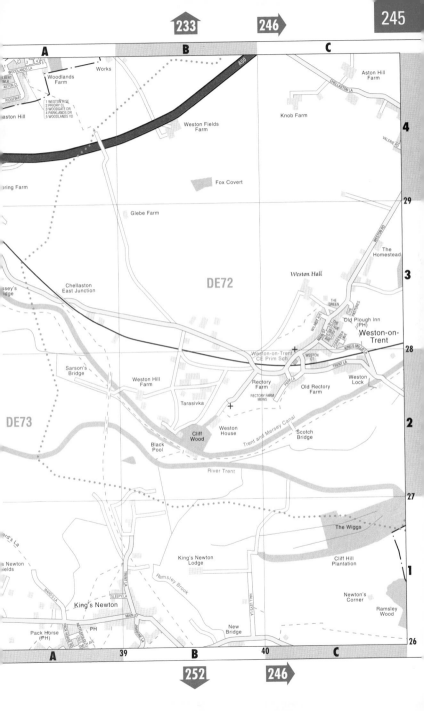

A   B   C

Roydon Hall Farm

Aston-on-Trent Prim Sch

HANGER BANK

Cemy

Big Moorside

Hicken's Bridge

A50

THE LAWNS

DERBY RD

LONG CROFT

GREEN LEYS

HOLDEN AVE

CHELLASTON LA

LITTLE MOORSIDE

ACRE LA

Acrelane Bridge

BARLEY CROFT

Aston-on-Trent

1 OLD SCHOOL MEWS
2 MANOR FARM MEWS
3 LODGE EST
4 PARK VIEW

3 4

LODGE MEWS

RECTORY RD

THE BONDS

SHIRLEY

SHARDLOW RD

Aston Lock

4

THE SIDINGS

YATES AVE

LAURIE

Aston Hall

DE72

Middle Wood

29

Weston Grange

Trent and Mersey Canal

3

River Trent

28

KING'S MILL LA

King's Mills

Mill Stream

Quarry Hill Plantation

The Priest House (Hotel)

DE74

Highfields

RENO

ROBY LEA

MINTO

2

Home Farm

PARK LA

Innisfree

STARKIE AVE

Boathouse Walk Plantation

The Shrubbery

Captain's Gorse

Studbrook Hollow

REDOCK LA

BONYTH RD

27

Stud Brook

Donington Hall

Dalby's Covert

All Hooks

1

Donington Park (Deer Park)

DE73

Thirteen Acre Plantation

Holly Wood

Donington Park Motor Racing Circuit

Starkey's Bridge

Coppice Wood

Gallows Flesh Wood

Leicestershire STREET ATLAS

26

41   A   42   B   43   C

A   B   C

Cavendish Bridge

R. Trent

LONDON RD

DONINGTON LA
PH

TAMWORTH RD
B6540

B6540

DE72

Sand and Gravel Pit

NETHERFIELD LA

M1

M1 Leicester

4

A50

A50 M1 Junc. 24

29

JOHNSON LA

BLACK LA

Willow Farm Bsns Pk

RYDROFT RD

LC

Trent Farm

Sewage Works

SYCAMORE RD

OAKLE AVE

NEWBOLD DR

STATION RD

New Delight Cottages

3

Trent Lane Ind Est

Works

TRENT LA

VICTORIA ST

GRANGE STREET

Hemington

HEMINGTON LA

Lockington

MAIN ST

Lockington Park

CARNIVAL WAY

GEORGINA CT

LOCKINGTON RD

HEMINGTON CT

PO

Hemington Sch

DE74

PALL MALL
KINGS GATE

PO

Lockington Hall

28

CAMPION HILL

SPITTAL

THE HORSE SHOES

Daleacre Hill

CHURCH RD

MAIN ST

HASCROFT

War Meml

2 LIONS

HEMINGTON HILL

Orchard Com Prim Sch

P
PO

Cemy

CHARNWOOD AVE

CHURCH LA

The Dumps

2

MARKET

Sch

Castle Donington

1 CHURCH LA
2 ST ANNE'S LA
3 GRAYS CL

EASTWAY

Liby

HALL FARM CL

King Street Plantation

27

Castle Donington Com Coll

ST EDWARD'S

Field Farm

1

East Midlands International Airport

Mast

26

A   45   B   46   C

A   B   C

Staffordshire STREET ATLAS

MEADOW LA
LC
Sewage
Works

DE13

A5121 Burton-upon-Trent

4

DE14

25

River Trent

River Trent

NEWTON RD

3

Meadows
Farm

Burton
Mill

Dale Brook

24

A511 Burton-upon-Trent

2

Abbot Beyne
Sch

Abbot Beyne
Sch

Holy
Rosary
RC Prim Sch

Winshill

23

ASHBY RD

Water
Tower

Cemy

1

1 HOPMEADOW WAY
2 HERITAGE WAY
3 BARLEYCORN CL

22

26   A   27   B   28   C

Castle
Wood

Bladon
Castle

Bladon
Hill

Bladon House
Sch

Bladon
Paddocks

Bladon
Farm
Cotts

Newton
Park

Hotel

Home
Wood

Newton
Park Farm

Wranglands
Plantation

Victory
Plantation

Bladon
Farm

DE15

Winshill Inf Sch

Bend
Oak
Jun Sch

Greensmiths

Canterbury Rd

Tower
View
Prim
Sch

Blenheim

Brizlincote
Hall Farm

Stockings
Plantation

Main St

Newton
Solney
CE Inf Sch

Trent
Farm

Grange
Farm

Newton
Solney

The Hill
Farm

Beaconhill
Plantation

REPTON RD

B501

DE

Grafton
Smallholdings

Nursery

Common
Farm

HARTFIELD LA

Oldicote
Farm

Bretby

Geary
House

Stanhope
Bretby

CH

ASHBY RD E

A511

249

243

A

B

C

Bendalls
Clump

Heath
Wood

4

Sever
F

ROBIN'S CROSS
LA

DE65

Orangehill
Bridge

The Bendalls
Farmhouse

Knowle Hill
Farm

25

Orange Hill

Brookdale Farm

Spur's Bottom

Dove Cote
Hill

3

Tower

P

Repton
Common

P

24

Foremark Reservoir

The Gra

DE73

2

Fairview Farm

DE15

SCADDOWS LA

The Scaddows

Repton
Shrubs

Repton
Bog

Bondwood
Farm

Foremark Park
Farm

Basfords H
Farm

23

Carver's
Rocks

The
Scaddows

Pottery
House

Hartshorn
Bog

P

1

DE11

Top Farm
House

DERBY RD

B5069

Gravelpit Hill

THE BUILDINGS
FARM

A514

COAL
LA

Smith's
Gorse

22

32

A

33

B

34

C

249

257

A **B** **C**

Coppy Hill

Lady Acre Wood

Robin Wood

Mount Pleasant

4

BOURNE CT 1
HOPE ST 2

B587

DROMORE LA

Fox Hole Wood

Melbourne Ride

Ingerholmes Wood

Highfields

The Roundlet

Gorsey Leys

St Bride's

25

Woodside

RIGBY LANE

Shaw House

Stanton's Wood

ROBINSON'S HILL

B587

Melbourne Common

Bleak House

Tower

Brickyard Cottage

STANTON'S LA

Hemsley's Barn

BOG LA

Visitor Ctr

P

3

Derby Hills House Farm

Sailing Club

MELBOURNE LA

STANTON HILL

Broadstone Lane End

DERBY HILLS HOUSE CT

MAIN ST

Ticknall

CHAPEL ST

STANTON'S LA

HAYES FARM CT

HARPUR AVE

PO

ROW LA

BROADSTONE LA

24

DE73

Works

Staunton Harold Resr

Walker's La

Lodge Plantation

Shaw's Plantation

White Leys

2

Derby Hills Farm

Serpentine Wood

Middle Lodge

Kennel Cottages

Clay Pit Plantation

The Rookery

Mere Pond

23

Jubilee Plantation

Betty's Pond

Calke Park

Calke Abbey

P

Spring Wood

1

Gorsey Covert

Poker's Leys

Home Farm

LE65

Calke

The Gables

Ivanhoe Way

White Hollows Farm

Dark Plantation

A 36 **B** 37 **C**

22

Map labels

A B C

4

Cemy
Melbourne Jun & Inf Schs
Melbourne
Lilypool
THE LILYPOOLS
New York
CASTLE LA
THE MEWS
CHANTRY
Liby L Ctr.
SALISBURY LA
PENN LA
BLACKWELL LA
PENISTON
Melbourne Hall & Gardens
DRUID

Melbourne View

Ramsley Brook

Carr Brook

PH

Forty Foot La

25

The Pool

Nurseries
SHORT HILL
MAIN ST
Wilson
PH

3

The Intake

Woodhouse Farm
Pool Farm

Chestnut Park

DE73

Park Farm
CH

Woodhouses

Staunton Harold Reservoir

Works

The Common Farm

Melbourne Parks

24

High Wood

Quarry Wood

Square Plantation

Paddock Pool

Hobbes' Hole

The Bulwarks Fort

SIR HENRY'S LA

2

Gorse Covert

Breedon Hill

Breedon on the Hill St Hardulph's CE Prim Sch

Melbourne Plantation

The Coppice

23

Coppice Nook

Green

La

Studfarm Cl

Hastings

Breedon on the Hill

Spring Wood

1

Scotland

Cha Fa

Springwood Farm
Scotlands Farm

LE65

B587

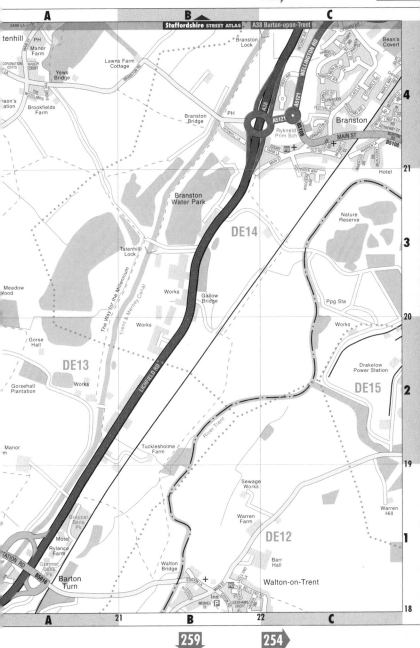

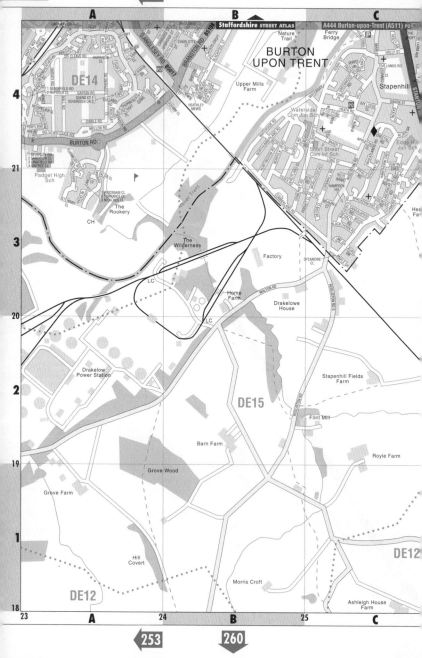

BURTON
UPON TRENT

DE14

Stapenhill

Nature
Trail

Ferry
Bridge

Five Lands Rd

Upper Mills
Farm

Waterside
Com Jun Sch

Short Street
Com Inf Sch

Edge Hill
Jun Sch

Padget High
Sch

The Rookery

CH

The
Wilderness

Factory

SYCAMORE
CL

Home
Farm

Drakelowe
House

LC

LC

Drakelow
Power Station

DE15

Stapenhill Fields
Farm

Flint Mill

Barn Farm

Royle Farm

Grove Wood

Grove Farm

DE12

Hill
Covert

Morris Croft

DE12

Ashleigh House
Farm

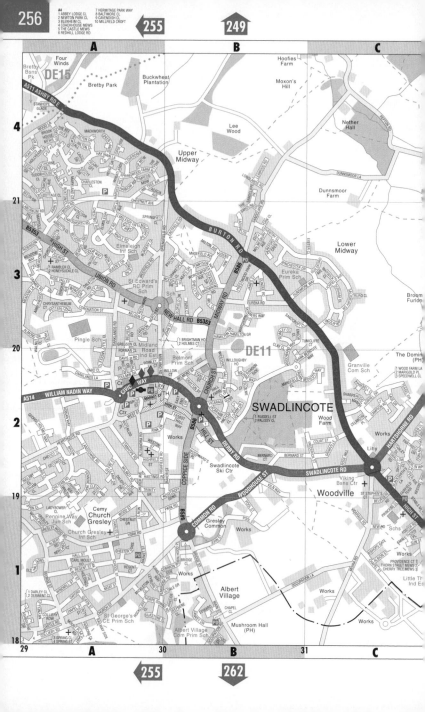

A   B   C

Henson's
Coppice

Spring
Farm

COAL LA

White Hollows
Farm

DE73

4

Coppice House
Farm

Coppice
Farm

TICKNALL LA

A514

BS006

DERBY RD

Tadsor
Farm

Shaw's
Alders

Manor
Farm

Ladyfields
Plantation

MEASHAM LA

Pisternhill
Plantation

21

Hartshorne
CE Prim Sch

MAIN ST

Hartshorne

Limehouse
Dam

Daniel Hayes
Farm

Long
Alders

P

The
Elms

PH

BLACK LA

Horn
Hill

Sharp's
Bottom

Pistern
Hill

3

WOODVILLE RD

TOWER RD

Goseley
Dale

DE11

BS006

Several
Wood

20

MANCHESTER LA

Heath
Farm

Hartshorne
Heath

Short Hazels
Farm

HEATH LA

The
Forties

2

FORTIES LA

NELSON
PL

1 BELL LA
2 BENTLEY DALE
3 LIMESTONE CL

Hilltop
Farm

EDWARD
ST

Stonehouse
Farm

Manor
Farm

CHAPEL ST

MAIN ST

PH

PH

Tithe
Farm

Myrtle Lodge
Farm

19

ASHBY RD

Boundary

LE65

1 THE SHRUBBERY
2 HOLLY CT
3 CANNER CL
4 THORN ST

Gardens

Tournament
Field

HEATH ST

FIELDS LA

ANNWELL LA

1

Blackfordby
House

Scam-Hazel
Farm

A511

Blackfordby
St Margaret's
CE Prim Sch

PH

Annwell
Place

BUTTS LA

STRAWBERRY LA 1
CHURCH CL 2
PARKERS CL 3

WELD LA

Works

Hall

Holywell
Farm

Blackfordby

Leicestershire STREET ATLAS

18

A   33   B   34   C

A   B   C

LEEDHAMS CROFT
← BELLS END RD
Walton Hall
Old Hall
Walton-on-Trent CE Prim Sch
STANDING BUTTS CL
Fairfield
ROSLISTON RD
The Dumps
Marlpit Spinney
Old Barn Farm
4
Borough Hill
Walton Hill Farm
Coppershill Spinney
17
Ryelands Lodge
Walton Wood
COTON RD
River Trent
Oaklands Farm
3
Borough Fields Farm
16
DE12
Donkhill Cottages
The Rough
Catton Farm Cottages
2
Catton Hall
Cherry Holme
Summerfields
King's Covert
Donkhill Plantation
Donkhill Farm
15
Mansditch Farm
Catton Park
Catton Wood
1
Croxall Wood
Pessall Brook
Pessall La
B79
Homestall Wood
WS13

259
254

A **B** **C**

DE15

Nursery

ROSLISTON RD

Corner
Farm

Rosliston
Forestry
Ctr

Walton Lane
Farm

Fox
Covert

The
Royal Oak
(PH)

Priory
Farm

Caldwell

Calves Croft
Farm

Pegasus
Sch

Manor
Farm

4

Moonraker

17

THE CROSS

The
Bull's Head
(PH)

Rosliston

BURTON RD

HOLDON CROFT

Rosliston CE
Prim Sch

Caldwell
Covert

CHURCH LA

THE GLEBE

VICARAGE WLK

YEW TREE RD

NEW ST

VIEW TREE
GDNS

MAIN ST

TURNBURY LA

LINTON RD

CALDWELL

Blakenh
Farm

3

CATON LA

COTON RD

Field House
Farm

Beehive
Farm

DE12

16

Lads Grave

Longfurlong
Farm

BURTON RD

COTON LA

Pessall Brook

P

Coton in the Elms

2

Overfields
Farm

Church
Farm

CHURCH CROFT

ELMS RD

CHANDLERS

PO

Coton in the
Elms CE Prim
Sch

Queen's Head
Inn (PH)

LITTLE LA

CHURCH ST

GREENACRE
PK

VICARAGE

GLEBE

RD

OLD RECTORY CL

MILL ST

MAIN ST

CHAPEL ST

COURT LA

15

Pessall Brook

MALT GREEN CL

Malt House
Farm

P

Garland's
Wood

Pessall Brook

1

The Crosses

Little
Liverpool

Church Flatts
Farm

Grafton
House

B79

14

A **24** **B** **25** **C**

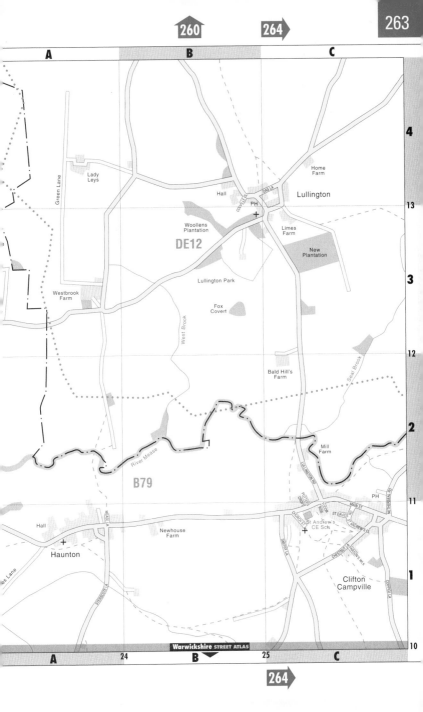

A
B
C

4

13

3

12

2

11

1

10

Home
Farm

Lullington

Lady
Leys

Green Lane

Hall

DRIVE LA

QUARELL LA

PH

Woollens
Plantation

Limes
Farm

DE12

New
Plantation

Westbrook
Farm

Lullington Park

Fox
Covert

West Brook

Bald Hill's
Farm

Seal Brook

River Mease

Mill
Farm

LULLINGTON RD

B79

PH

POTTERS
DRIVE

VICTORIA
TERR

MAIN ST

NETHERSEAL RD

ST DAVID'S

St Andrew's
CE Sch

ST ANDREW'S CL

Hall

Newhouse
Farm

MEASE LA

CHESTNUT LA

CLIFTON ST

BARTON LA

CHURCH LA

Haunton

MAIN'S WK

Clifton
Campville

OFFICE LA

os Lane

PETERSFIELD LA

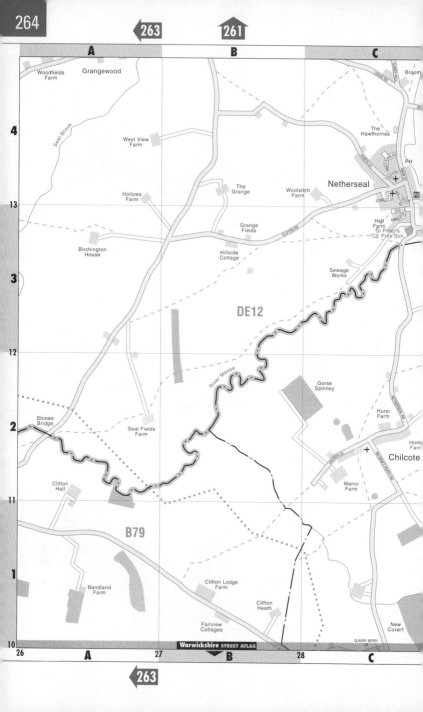

A   B   C

4

13

3

12

2

11

1

10

A   B   C

30   31

Seale
Pastures

PH
Acresford

Eastfield

BORSEY LA

A444

ACRESFORD RD

Hoborough Brook

STANLEIGH GDNS 1
IVY CL 2
NARROW LA
CHAPEL ST
DELPH RD
NEW ST
TALBOT PL
HALL LA
RANG ST
PH

Hall
Farm

Ivanhoe Way

STRETTON
VIEW

CORINGTON LA

Mine
(dis)

CHAPEL LA

Moneyhill
Farm

MEASHAM RD

Saltersford
Cottages

Saltersford
Farm

Saltersford Brook

Saltersford
Bridge

Oak
Villa

River Mease

Stretton
Bridge

Mill
House

DE12

Hall
Farm

Stretton en le Field

Park
Farm

Manor House
Farm

A42

A42

A42 M1 Junc 23A

Leicestershire STREET ATLAS

Heath
Lodge

TAMWORTH RD

MEASHAM RD

Hill
Farm

A444

M42

B5493

The Old
Rectory

RECTORY LA

CHURCH ST

PARKFIELD CRES

SIDNEY RD

ST MICHAEL'S DR

Warwickshire STREET ATLAS M42 Birmingham A444 Nuneaton

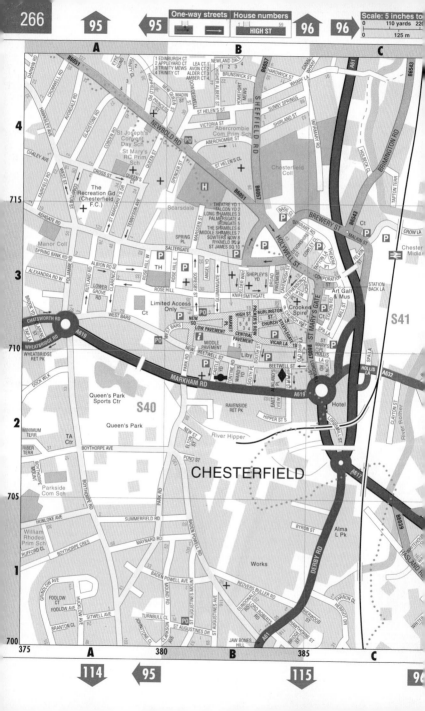

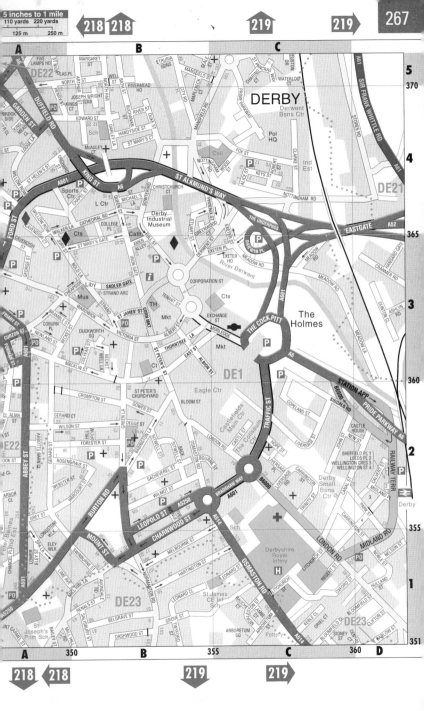

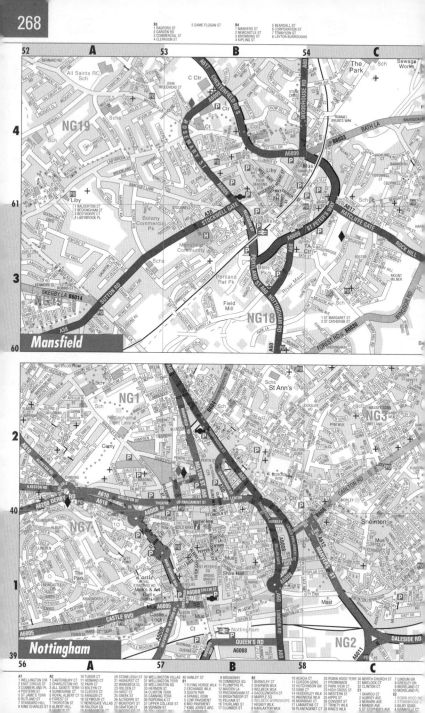

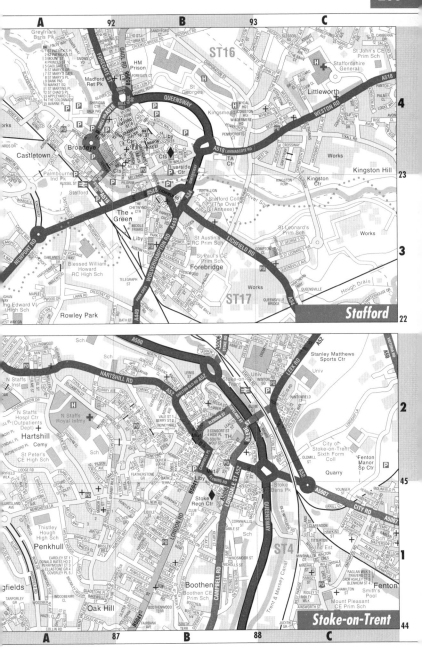

Stafford

Stoke-on-Trent

Index

Church Rd **6** Beckenham BR2..........**53** C6

Place name
May be abbreviated on the map

Location number
Present when a number indicates the place's position in a crowded area of mapping

Locality, town or village
Shown when more than one place has the same name

Postcode district
District for the indexed place

Page and grid square
Page number and gr reference for the sta mapping

Public and commercial buildings are highlighted in magenta. Places of interest are highlighted in blue with a star★

Abbreviations used in the index

Acad	**Academy**	Comm	**Common**	Gd	**Ground**	L	**Leisure**	Prom	**Prom**
App	**Approach**	Cott	**Cottage**	Gdn	**Garden**	La	**Lane**	Rd	**Road**
Arc	**Arcade**	Cres	**Crescent**	Gn	**Green**	Liby	**Library**	Recn	**Recreat**
Ave	**Avenue**	Cswy	**Causeway**	Gr	**Grove**	Mdw	**Meadow**	Ret	**Retail**
Bglw	**Bungalow**	Ct	**Court**	H	**Hall**	Meml	**Memorial**	Sh	**Shoppin**
Bldg	**Building**	Ctr	**Centre**	Ho	**House**	Mkt	**Market**	Sq	**Square**
Bsns, Bus	**Business**	Ctry	**Country**	Hospl	**Hospital**	Mus	**Museum**	St	**Street**
Bvd	**Boulevard**	Cty	**County**	HQ	**Headquarters**	Orch	**Orchard**	Sta	**Station**
Cath	**Cathedral**	Dr	**Drive**	Hts	**Heights**	Pal	**Palace**	Terr	**Terrace**
Cir	**Circus**	Dro	**Drove**	Ind	**Industrial**	Par	**Parade**	TH	**Town Ha**
Cl	**Close**	Ed	**Education**	Inst	**Institute**	Pas	**Passage**	Univ	**Universi**
Cnr	**Corner**	Emb	**Embankment**	Int	**International**	Pk	**Park**	Wk, Wlk	**Walk**
Coll	**College**	Est	**Estate**	Intc	**Interchange**	Pl	**Place**	Wr	**Water**
Com	**Community**	Ex	**Exhibition**	Junc	**Junction**	Prec	**Precinct**	Yd	**Yard**

Index of localities, towns and villages

Abney ... 51 C2
Aldercar ... 182 A2
Alderwasley ... 166 C4
Alfreton ... 159 B2
Alkmonton ... 199 B1
Alsop en le Dale ... 150 C2
Alstonefield ... 149 B2
Alton ... 130 B3
Ambergate ... 167 C2
Apperknowle ... 58 A1
Ashbourne ... 173 B2
Ashby-de-la-Zouch ... 258 B1
Ashford in the Water ... 108 C4
Ashover ... 129 C2
Aston-on-Trent ... 246 A4
Atlow ... 175 A3
Ault Hucknall ... 133 C4
Awsworth ... 195 B2
Bakewell ... 109 C3
Bamford ... 40 A2
Barlborough ... 80 A4
Barlow ... 75 C1
Barrow Hill ... 78 A2
Barrow upon Trent ... 244 A3
Barton in Fabis ... 237 C3
Barton Turn ... 253 A1
Baslow ... 91 C3
Beeley ... 111 A2
Beeston ... 223 C2
Belper ... 179 A2
Biggin ... 138 B2
Birchover ... 126 A1
Blackfordby ... 257 B1
Blackwell ... 147 C1
Bolsover ... 99 A1
Bonsall ... 142 C1
Borrowash ... 221 B1
Boylestone ... 213 B2
Brackenfield ... 145 B1
Bradbourne ... 163 B3
Bradley ... 186 C4
Bradwell ... 51 A4
Brailsford ... 201 C4
Bramley-Vale ... 117 C1
Branston ... 253 C4
Brassington ... 153 A1
Breadsall ... 205 C2
Breaston ... 235 B4
Breedon on the Hill ... 252 C1
Bretby ... 249 A2
Brimington ... 96 C4
Brinsley ... 182 C3
Broadbottom ... 16 A4
Bullbridge ... 168 A3
Burnaston ... 229 C3
Burton upon Trent ... 254 B2
Buxton ... 85 A4
Caldwell ... 260 C4
Calow ... 96 C1
Calver ... 72 B1
Carsington ... 164 C4
Castle Donington ... 247 B2
Castleton ... 38 B1
Chapel-en-le-Frith ... 47 A3
Chelmorton ... 87 A1
Chesterfield ... 96 B2
Chinley ... 34 C1
Church Broughton ... 227 A4
Clay Cross ... 131 A2
Clifton ... 184 C3
Clifton Campville ... 263 C1
Clowne ... 80 B2
Codnor ... 181 B4
Compstall ... 15 A1
Cossall ... 195 B1
Coton in the Elms ... 260 B2
Creswell ... 81 C1
Crich ... 156 C1
Cromford ... 155 A3
Curbar ... 72 C1
Dale Abbey ... 207 C1
Darley Dale ... 127 B1
Denby ... 180 B1
Denstone ... 196 B3
Derby ... 219 A3
Derwent ... 30 B3
Disley ... 32 B3
Donisthorpe ... 262 C1
Dore ... 55 C4
Dove Holes ... 47 C1
Doveridge ... 211 A1
Draycott ... 234 C4
Dronfield ... 56 C1
Duffield ... 190 C2
Earl Sterndale ... 105 B2
Eastwood ... 182 C2
Eckington ... 59 B2
Edale ... 37 B4
Egginton ... 241 A3
Ellastone ... 183 A2
Elmton ... 100 A4
Elton ... 140 C3
Elvaston ... 234 A3
Etwall ... 229 B2
Eyam ... 71 B3
Fenny Bentley ... 162 A1
Fenton ... 269 C1
Findern ... 230 B1
Flagg ... 106 C3
Flash ... 103 A2
Fritchley ... 168 B4
Gamesley ... 9 C1
Glapwell ... 134 B4
Glossop ... 10 A1
Grassmoor ... 115 C2
Great Cubley ... 198 C1
Great Hucklow ... 70 A4
Great Longstone ... 90 A2
Grindleford ... 72 B4
Hanbury ... 238 A3
Harthill ... 61 C3
Hartington ... 137 B3
Hartshorne ... 257 A3
Hassop ... 90 C3
Hathersage ... 53 A4
Hatton ... 239 B4
Hayfield ... 25 B1
Hazelwood ... 190 A4
Heage ... 168 C1
Heanor ... 181 B1
Heath ... 117 A1
High Lane ... 32 A4
High Peak ... 28 C4
Hilcote ... 148 B1
Hilton ... 228 B1
Hognaston ... 164 A1
Holbeck ... 101 B4
Holbrook ... 191 B3
Hollington ... 200 C2
Hollingworth ... 9 B3
Hollinsclough ... 104 B1
Holloway ... 156 A3
Holme ... 2 C4
Holmesfield ... 75 A4
Holmewood ... 116 C1
Holymoorside ... 113 B4
Hope ... 38 C2
Horsley ... 191 C3
Hulland Ward ... 175 C2
Ible ... 153 C4
Idridgehay ... 176 C3
Ilkeston ... 208 C4
Ironville ... 170 C2
Kettleshulme ... 45 A1
Kilburn ... 192 A4
Killamarsh ... 60 C3
Kimberley ... 195 C4
King's Newton ... 245 A1
Kirby-in-Ashfield ... 160 C2
Kirk Ireton ... 165 B1
Kirk Langley ... 202 C1
Kniveton ... 163 A1
Langley Mill ... 182 A2
Langwith ... 119 C4
Linton ... 261 B3
Little Eaton ... 205 B4
Lockington ... 247 C3
Long Duckmanton ... 98 A2
Long Eaton ... 236 B4
Longford ... 214 B4
Longnor ... 121 A3
Lount ... 258 C3
Lullington ... 263 C4
Mackworth ... 217 C4
Mansfield ... 136 A1
Mansfield ... 268
Mansfield Woodhouse ... 136 C1
Mapperley ... 193 C2
Marchington ... 224 C1
Market Warsop ... 120 C2
Marple ... 23 A3
Marston Montgomery ... 211 C4
Mastin Moor ... 79 B2
Matlock ... 143 A3
Matlock Bath ... 143 A1
Mayfield ... 184 B4
Melbourne ... 252 A4
Middleton ... 124 C2
Middleton (Nr Wirksworth) ... 154 B2
Moira ... 262 C2
Monyash ... 107 B1
Morley ... 206 B3
Mosborough ... 59 B4
Mossley ... 4 A4
Mottram in Longdendale ... 9 A2
Nether Heage ... 168 B1
Nether Padley ... 53 C1
Netherseal ... 264 C4
New Houghton ... 134 C4
New Mills ... 33 B4
Newton ... 148 A2
Newton Solney ... 248 C4
North Wingfield ... 132 A4
Northedge ... 130 B3
Northwood ... 127 A3
Nottingham ... 268
Ockbrook ... 221 B3
Old Brampton ... 94 B2
Osmaston ... 185 C2
Over Haddon ... 109 A1
Overseal ... 262 A2
Palterton ... 118 A3
Parwich ... 151 C1
Peak Forest ... 49 A2
Pikehall ... 139 C2
Pilsley (Nr Baslow) ... 91 B2
Pilsley (Nr Clay Cross) ... 132 B1
Pinxton ... 160 B1
Pleasley ... 135 A3
Poolsbrook ... 98 A4
Quarndon ... 204 B3
Renishaw ... 79 A4
Repton ... 242 C1
Ridgeway ... 168 B2
Ringinglow ... 42 A3
Ripley ... 169 B1
Risley ... 222 C2
Rocester ... 197 A2
Rodsley ... 200 A3
Rolleston ... 240 A2
Rosliston ... 260 B3
Roston ... 197 C4
Sandiacre ... 223 A3
Scarcliffe ... 118 C3
Scropton ... 226 C1
Selston ... 171 C4
Shardlow ... 234 C1
Sheffield ... 44 B3
Shipley ... 194 A3
Shirebrook ... 119 C2
Shireoaks ... 63 C3
Shirland ... 146 B1
Shirley ... 200 C4
Shottle ... 177 C4
Smalley ... 192 C3
Smisby ... 258 A2
Snelston ... 184 B2
Somercotes ...
Somersal Herbert ...
South Normanton ...
South Wingfield ...
Spout ...
Stafford ...
Stanley ...
Stanton-by-Dale ...
Stapleford ...
Staveley ...
Stoke-on-Trent ...
Stonebroom ...
Stoney Middleton ...
Stretton en le Field ...
Strines Moor ...
Sudbury ...
Sutton in Ashfield ...
Sutton on the Hill ...
Swadlincote ...
Swanwick ...
Taddington ...
Tansley ...
Thornhill ...
Thorpe ...
Thorpe Salvin ...
Thrumpton ...
Thurvaston ...
Tibshelf ...
Ticknall ...
Tideswell ...
Tissington ...
Toadmoor ...
Totley ...
Trowell ...
Trusley ...
Tupton ...
Turnditch ...
Tutbury ...
Underwood Green ...
Unstone ...
Uttoxeter ...
Walton-on-Trent ...
Wensley ...
Wessington ...
West Hallam ...
Weston Underwood ...
Weston-on-Trent ...
Westwood ...
Whaley Bridge ...
Whaley Thorns ...
Whitwell ...
Willington ...
Windley ...
Wingerworth ...
Winster ...
Wirksworth ...
Woodville ...
Worksop ...
Wyaston ...
Yeaveley ...
Youlgreave ...

e DE7 .....208 C4

e DE7 .....208 C4

e DE7 .....208 C4

CI NG16 .....195 C4
Brook Dr S8 .....56 C4
CI ST14 .....197 A2
Croft
field S40 .....95 A4
aw S21 .....79 B4
Gdns SK14 .....9 A2
Hill DE21,DE22 .....205 A2
Rd DE22 .....204 B1
La DE22 .....205 A1
Lodge CI **1**
.....256 A4
St
DE1,DE21 .....267 A2
on DE7 .....194 C1
View Dr S8 .....43 A2
View Rd S8 .....43 A2
Yd DE22 .....205 A1
dale CI DE56 .....192 A4
dale Park Cres
.....55 C3
dale Park Rise S17 .....55 C3
dale Rd S S17 .....56 A4
Beyne Sch DE15 .....248 A2
nill CI S42 .....95 A2
CI DE21 .....205 C3
Rd DE7 .....208 B3
St NG16 .....195 B2
s Dr DE56 .....179 A3
sford Dr NG3 .....268 B2
sford Mews De7 .....194 B2
sholme Sch ST14 .....197 A1
t Rd DE55 .....159 A2
t St Heanor De75 .....181 C1
Eaton NG10 .....236 B3
s Barn CI DE22 .....267 A2
ts CI DE11 .....256 A3
ts Croft NG19 .....135 C1
ts Rd DE11 .....256 A3
...a DE4 .....142 B1
...DE5 .....180 B1
rombie Com Prim Sch
.....266 B4
rombie St S41 .....266 B4
are CI DE21 .....206 A1
een St NG3 .....268 C2
don Bsns Ctr The
.....219 B1
don St DE24 .....232 B4
CI Chesterfield S40 .....95 B3
I DE3 .....217 C1
eld S14 .....43 B3
Dr S14 .....43 B3
Rd S14 .....43 B3
s Ave Brimington S43 .....97 A4
r DE3 .....217 C1
lincote DE11 .....256 A4
a Cres S21 .....60 A3
a Ct
field NG19 .....136 C1
ttingham NG3 .....268 B2
a Dr
ourne DE7 .....208 C4
y S45 .....132 A2
Ave NG16 .....195 C4
CI Kilamarsh S21 .....60 B3
m NG16 .....160 B2
Croft DE21 .....205 C2
right's Mill* DE4 .....155 A4
Ave NG16 .....195 B4
s Bsns Pk NG18 .....268 B3
CI DE24 .....232 C2
a Ctr NG16 .....182 B2
r Dr DE56 .....179 A3
Ridge
field S40 .....114 A4
ck DE4 .....143 A3
on NG16 .....119 B3
a Terr SK22 .....33 A3
a Way Belper DE56 .....179 A3
a DE22 .....246 B4
St **6** S13 .....17 B4
age La NG20 .....119 C1
ield Way DE73 .....233 A1
s Rd S45 .....132 A2
The S45 .....132 A2
a View CI S41 .....95 C4
sford Rd
thorpe DE12 .....265 B4
erseal DE12 .....262 A1
seal DE12 .....262 A1
a Ave NG10 .....236 C3
a CI NG10 .....236 C3
a Gr NG10 .....236 C3
a Rd Derby DE22 .....217 C3
Eaton NG10 .....236 C3

Acton Road Ind Est
NG10 .....236 C3
Acton St NG10 .....236 C3
Adale Rd DE7 .....193 A4
Adam Bede Cres DE4 .....165 C3
Adam St DE7 .....209 A3
Adam's Rd DE6 .....217 A4
Adams CI DE75 .....193 B4
Adams Ct DE7 .....194 C2
Adastral Ave S12 .....44 A1
Adderley PI SK13 .....9 C1
Adderley Rd SK13 .....9 C1
Addison Dr DE55 .....159 A2
Addison Rd Derby DE24 .....232 B4
Stonebroom DE55 .....146 C2
Addison Sq DE4 .....155 A3
Addison St
Nottingham NG1 .....268 A2
Tibshelf DE55 .....148 A4
Addison Villas NG16 .....182 C1
Adelaide CI Derby DE3 .....217 C2
Stapleford NG9 .....223 B3
Adelaide Cres DE15 .....248 B1
Adelaide Wlk NG16 .....170 C2
Adelphi CI DE23 .....231 A3
Adelphi Way S42 .....97 C4
Adin Ave S44 .....118 B2
Adlington Ave S42 .....115 B1
Adlington La S22 .....72 B4
Admiral CI DE75 .....181 B1
Adrian CI NG9 .....223 C1
Adrian St DE24 .....232 B3
Adwick CI DE3 .....217 B1
Agard St DE1 .....218 C3
Agnesmeadow La DE6 .....174 B2
Agricultural Way DE45 .....109 C3
Aimploy Ct DE23 .....219 A1
Ainley CI DE24 .....232 C4
Ainsworth Dr DE23 .....231 C4
Ainsworth St ST4 .....269 C1
Aintree Ave S21 .....59 C4
Aintree CI
Burton u T DE14 .....254 A4
Kimberley NG16 .....195 C4
Airedale CI NG10 .....236 A3
Airedale Wlk **3** DE24 .....233 B3
Akley Bank CI S17 .....55 C3
Alabaster La DE4 .....155 A3
Alandale Ave NG20 .....119 C2
Albany CI NG19 .....136 B1
Albany Rd NG9 .....209 C1
Albany St NG19 .....136 B1
Albany Inf & Jun Schs
NG9 .....223 C4
Albany Inf Sch NG9 .....209 C1
Albany PI NG19 .....136 B1
Albany St DE22 .....218 B2
Stoke-on-T ST4 .....269 A2
Albemarle Rd DE7 .....209 A3
Albemarle Rd DE24 .....220 A4
Albert Ave
Chesterfield S43 .....77 B2
Stapleford NG9 .....223 B4
Westwood NG16 .....171 A2
Albert Cres DE21 .....220 A2
Albert Hill **1** NG7 .....268 A1
Albert Rd Breaston DE72 .....235 A4
Chesterfield S43 .....77 B2
Derby DE21 .....220 A2
Long Eaton NG10 .....236 B4
Ripley DE5 .....169 B1
Sandiacre NG10 .....223 A3
Sheffield S8 .....43 A3
Swadlincote DE11 .....256 A1
Albert St Belper DE56 .....178 C2
Derby DE1 .....267 B2
Eastwood NG16 .....182 C2
Eckington S21 .....59 B1
Glossop SK13 .....10 A3
Ilkeston DE7 .....208 C4
Ironville NG16 .....170 C3
Mansfield NG18 .....268 B3
Mansfield Woodhouse
NG19 .....136 B2
Nottingham NG1 .....268 B1
Ripley DE5 .....169 C1
Somercotes DE55 .....170 A4
South Normanton DE55 .....160 A3
Stapleford NG9 .....223 B4
Albert St S41 .....76 C1
Albert Village Com Prim Sch
DE11 .....256 B1
Alberta Ave NG16 .....171 C4
Albine Rd NG20 .....119 C3
Albion Ctr The DE7 .....208 C4
Albion Rd
Chesterfield S40 .....266 A3
Long Eaton NG10 .....236 C4
New Mills SK22 .....33 A3
Albion St Derby DE1 .....267 B3
Ilkeston DE7 .....194 C1
Mansfield NG19 .....135 C1
Nottingham NG1 .....268 B1
Ripley DE5 .....169 C1
Woodville DE11 .....256 C1
Albrighton Ave DE24 .....231 B1
Albury Sq NG7 .....268 A1
Alcock Ave NG18 .....268 C4
Aldam CI S17 .....55 C2
Aldam Croft S17 .....55 C2
Aldam Way S17 .....55 C2
Alder Brook SK23 .....34 C1
Alder CI Derby DE22 .....205 C2
Mansfield NG19 .....136 C1
Shirebrook NG20 .....119 B3
Alder Cl Chesterfield S41 .....266 B4
Derby DE21 .....219 A4

Alder Gr Burton u T DE15 .....254 C4
Buxton SK17 .....85 A4
Mansfield Woodhouse
NG19 .....136 A3
Alder Rd DE56 .....179 A2
Alder Rise SK23 .....45 B4
Alder Way NG19 .....136 B2
Alderbrook CI DE13 .....240 A2
Aldercar Com Sch
NG16 .....182 A2
Aldercar Inf Sch NG16 .....182 A2
Aldercar La NG16 .....182 A3
Alderd CI S21 .....60 C4
Alderfen Ct DE24 .....232 B2
Alderholme Dr **6** DE13 .....240 C1
Alderley Ct DE21 .....206 A1
Aldern Way DE45 .....109 C4
Alderney Rd S2 .....43 A4
Alders Ave SK23 .....34 C1
Alders Brook DE65 .....228 B1
Alders La Chinley SK23 .....34 C1
Tansley DE4 .....144 A2
Aiders Rd SK12 .....32 A4
Alders The S42 .....113 B4
Aldersgate Derby DE22 .....217 C4
New Mills SK22 .....33 A4
Alderslade CI DE7 .....234 A1
Aldersley CI DE65 .....230 B1
Alderson Dr S2 .....43 A4
Alderson PI S2 .....43 A4
Alderson Rd S2 .....43 A4
Alderson Rd N **3** S2 .....43 A4
Alderwashley Hall Sch
DE56 .....167 A4
Aldred's La DE75, NG16 .....182 A1
Aldridge CI NG9 .....223 C1
Aldwark Rd SK17 .....85 B3
Aldwych DE22 .....218 A3
Alexander Ave NG16 .....171 B4
Alexander Rd
Dove Holes SK17 .....47 C1
Nottingham NG7 .....268 A1
Alexander St NG16 .....182 C1
Alexander Terr NG16 .....160 B1
Alexandra Ave NG19 .....136 A3
Alexandra Ct DE15 .....248 A2
Alexandra Gdns **6**
.....219 A1
Alexandra Rd
Burton u T DE15 .....248 A2
Buxton SK17 .....85 B3
Dronfield S18 .....57 A1
Long Eaton NG10 .....236 B4
Overseal DE12 .....262 A2
Sheffield S2 .....43 A4
Stafford ST17 .....269 B3
Swadlincote DE11 .....256 A1
Alexandra Rd E S41 .....96 B1
Alexandra Rd W S40 .....266 A3
Alexandra St NG9 .....223 B3
Alexandra Ct DE23 .....231 B3
Alford CI S40 .....95 B2
Alfred CI NG3 .....268 B2
Alfred Ct NG18 .....268 B4
Alfred Rd DE56 .....192 A4
Alfred St Alfreton DE55 .....158 C2
Pinxton NG16 .....160 B2
Ripley DE5 .....169 C1
Somercotes DE55 .....170 B3
South Normanton DE55 .....159 C3
Alfred St Central NG3 .....268 B2
Alfred St N NG1,NG3 .....268 B2
Alfred St S NG3 .....268 C2
Alfreton & Mansfield
Parkway Sta DE55 .....158 C3
Alfreton L Ctr DE55 .....158 C2
Alfreton Motorway Link Ind
Est DE55 .....159 A1
Alfreton Rd
Blackwell DE55 .....147 C1
Breadsall DE21 .....205 B3
Codnor DE5 .....170 B1
Holbrook DE21 .....191 B1
Little Eaton DE21 .....205 B3
Matlock DE4 .....143 C2
Nottingham NG7 .....268 A2
Pinxton NG16 .....160 B2
Selston DE55, NG16 .....171 B3
Tibshelf DE55 .....148 A3
Alfreton Trad Est DE55 .....159 A1
Algar CI S2 .....43 C4
Algar Cres S2 .....43 C4
Algar Rd S2 .....43 C4
Algar PI S2 .....43 C4
Algar Sheffield S2 .....43 C4
Alice St DE1 .....267 A4
Alice Way S18 .....76 C3
Alicehead Rd S45 .....113 A1
Alison CI DE21 .....219 C4
All Saints CE Inf Sch
S18 .....196 C3
All Saints CE Inf Sch
Matlock DE4 .....143 A3
Sutton in A NG17 .....148 C1
All Saints CE Jun Sch
DE4 .....143 A4
All Saints CE Prim Sch
DE45 .....125 B3
All Saints Croft DE14 .....254 B4
All Saints Ct DE3 .....217 B1
All Saints Prim Sch SK6 .....23 A3
All Saints Rd NG19 .....268 A4
All Saints RC Prim Sch
SK13 .....10 B1

All Saints' Rd DE4 .....143 A3
All Saints' St NG7 .....268 A2
All Saints' Terr **3** NG7 .....268 A2
Allan Ave DE23 .....230 C4
Allan La DE56 .....168 A3
Allandale Rd DE75 .....181 B1
Allcroft St NG19 .....136 B2
Allen Hill DE4 .....143 A3
Allen La Ashover DE4 .....144 B3
Weston Underwood DE6 .....188 B1
Allen St Derby DE24 .....232 C3
Stoke-on-T ST4 .....269 A2
Allen's Green Ave NG16 .....171 C1
Allen's La S17 .....224 C1
Allenby CI S8 .....56 C4
Allenby Dr S8 .....56 C4
Allendale DE7 .....208 C4
Allendale Rd S42 .....114 C2
Allendale Way NG19 .....136 C1
Allens La S17 .....224 C1
Allenpark Inf Sch DE24 .....232 C3
Allenton Com Prim Sch
DE24 .....232 C3
Allestree CI DE24 .....232 C4
Allestree Dr S18 .....56 B1
Allestree La DE22 .....204 B2
Allestree Park* DE22 .....204 C3
Allestree St DE24 .....232 C4
Alley Wlk De6 .....201 C4
Allison Ave DE11 .....256 A2
Allison Gdns DE7 .....195 A1
Alissa Ave DE5 .....180 C4
Allpits Rd S44 .....96 C2
Allport Terr
Barrow Hill S43 .....78 A2
Blackwell DE55 .....147 B1
Allsops PI S41 .....95 C4
Allstone Lee DE56 .....178 C3
Alma CI NG1 .....268 B2
Alma Cres S18 .....57 A2
Alma Hill NG16 .....195 C4
Alma Hts DE3 .....217 C1
Alma Rd
North Wingfield S42 .....132 A4
Nottingham NG3 .....268 C2
Selston NG16 .....171 C3
Swadlincote DE11 .....255 C3
Tideswell SK17 .....69 B3
Alma St Alfreton DE55 .....159 A2
Buxton SK17 .....85 A4
Derby DE22 .....218 C2
Fenton ST4 .....269 C1
Melbourne DE73 .....252 A4
North Wingfield S42 .....131 C3
Ripley DE5 .....169 B2
Alma St W S40 .....266 A4
Almond Ave Ripley DE5 .....180 B4
Shirebrook NG20 .....119 C3
Almond CI Calow S44 .....97 A2
Kimberley NG16 .....195 C4
Almond Cres S43 .....97 A4
Almond Ct DE13 .....240 C1
Almond Dr S21 .....59 B2
Almond Gr
Swadlincote DE11 .....256 A3
Swanwick DE55 .....170 A4
Almond Rise NG19 .....136 C2
Almshouses Etwall DE65 .....229 C4
Newton Solney DE15 .....248 C4
Alnwick Dr S12 .....44 A3
Alnwick Rd S12 .....44 A3
Alpha St SK23 .....34 C1
Alpha Terr NG11 .....192 A2
Alpine Gr S43 .....97 A4
Alport Ave Buxton SK17 .....85 B4
Sheffield S12 .....44 C3
Alport Belper DE56 .....179 A3
Alport Dr S12 .....44 C3
Alport La Spout DE4,DE56 .....166 C4
Youlgreave DE45 .....125 B3
Alport PI S12 .....44 C3
Alport Rd S12 .....44 C3
Alport Rise S18 .....56 B1
Alport Way S12 .....44 C3
Alsager CI DE21 .....206 A1
Alsfield Way SK22 .....33 A4
Alsop CI SK17 .....85 C4
Alsop PI SK17 .....85 C4
Alsop Way SK17 .....85 C4
Alston Rd SK23 .....47 A3
Alstonefield YH* DE6 .....149 C2
Alstonfield Dr DE22 .....204 C1
Alum CI DE24 .....233 B4
Alvaston Inf Sch DE24 .....233 B4
Alvaston Jun Com Sch
DE24 .....233 B4
Alvaston St DE24 .....233 B4
Alvenor St DE7 .....194 C1
Alverton CI DE7 .....208 C3
Alward's CI DE24 .....233 A3

Ambaston La
Elvaston DE72 .....234 A3
Shardlow DE72 .....234 C2
Amber Bldgs DE55 .....159 A3
Amber CI DE56 .....168 A3
Amber Cres S40 .....95 B1
Amber Croft S43 .....97 B4
Amber Ct Belper DE56 .....179 A3
Chesterfield S41 .....266 B4
Heanor DE75 .....181 C1
Amber Dr NG16 .....182 A1
Amber Gr DE55 .....158 C1
Amber Hill DE4 .....168 A4
Amber Hts DE5 .....169 B1
Amber La S45 .....129 B2
Amber PI S45 .....131 A2
Amber Rd
Bullbridge DE56 .....168 A3
Derby DE22 .....204 B1
Amber St DE24 .....232 B4
Amber Trad Est NG16 .....195 B4
Amber View Rd DE56 .....168 A4
Amberdene DE4 .....143 B3
Ambergate Prim Sch
DE56 .....167 C2
Ambergate Sta DE56 .....167 C2
Ambergrove DE56 .....168 A4
Amberlands DE55 .....240 C1
Amberley CI DE7 .....208 C4
Amberley Dr Buxton SK17 .....85 B3
Derby DE22 .....204 C1
Amberley St DE24 .....232 C3
Ambervale CI DE23 .....231 A3
Amberwood DE11 .....256 A3
Ambleside CI
Chesterfield S41 .....95 B4
Dronfield S18 .....56 C3
Ambleside Dr
Bolsover S44 .....98 C1
Eastwood NG16 .....182 B2
Ambrose Terr DE1 .....218 C3
Amen Alley DE1 .....267 B3
American Adventure Theme
Pk The* DE75 .....194 A3
Amesbury CI S41 .....95 C4
Amesbury La DE21 .....205 C1
Ameycroft La DE4 .....143 A4
Amilda Ave DE7 .....208 C4
Amy St **SE** DE22 .....218 C2
Anchor Ave SK23 .....47 B3
Anchor CI DE11 .....256 B2
Anchor Rd NG16 .....182 B1
Anchor Row DE7 .....208 C4
Anchor Sq DE45 .....109 B4
Ancient High House Mus*
ST16 .....269 B4
Anderby Gdns DE11 .....255 C1
Anderson CI S43 .....77 C2
Anderson Sch The SK17 .....85 A4
Anderson St DE24 .....232 C4
Andrew Ave DE7 .....209 A4
Andrew CI DE23 .....230 C4
Andrew St S45 .....131 C2
Andrews Dr
Langley Mill NG16 .....182 A2
Stanley DE7 .....193 A1
Andwell La S10 .....42 C3
Angel Row NG1 .....268 B1
Angel Yd S40 .....266 B3
Angerford Ave S8 .....43 A2
Anglers' La DE21 .....220 C2
Anglesey Rd
Burton u T DE14 .....254 A4
Dronfield S18 .....57 A1
Anglesey St DE21 .....219 B4
Angleton Ave S2 .....44 B4
Angleton CI S2 .....44 B4
Angleton Gdns S2 .....44 B4
Angleton Gn S2 .....44 B4
Angleton Mews S2 .....44 B4
Ankerbold Rd S42 .....131 B4
Ann St S80 .....81 C1
Anncroft Rd SK17 .....84 B4
Anne Potter CI DE72 .....221 B3
Annesley CI
Chesterfield S41 .....115 B4
Sheffield S8 .....56 C4
Annesley Rd S8 .....56 C4
Anns Grove Prim Sch S2 .....43 A4
Anns Rd S2 .....43 A4
Anns Rd N S2 .....43 A4
Annwell La LE65 .....257 C1
Anslow La DE13 .....240 A1
Anslow Rd DE13 .....238 A1
Anson Wlk DE7 .....194 C2
Anstee Rd NG10 .....236 B3
Anstey Ct DE21 .....206 A1
Anstey Rise NG3 .....268 C2
Anthony Bek Com Prim Sch
NG19 .....136 C3
Anthony Cres DE24 .....232 C3
Anthony Dr DE24 .....232 C3
Anthony Gell Sch DE4 .....165 C4
Antill St NG9 .....223 B3
Apiary Gate DE74 .....247 A2
Apperknowle Jun Sch
S18 .....58 A1
Appian CI DE7 .....221 B1
Appian Way
Clay Cross S45 .....131 B1
Derby DE21 .....233 B3
Apple St S14 .....15 A4
Apple Tree Rd SK22 .....24 A1
Appleby CI DE7 .....208 C3

Appleby Ct DE22 ....218 C2
Appleby Glade DE11 .....255 B1
Appleby Rd NG19 ....134 C3
Applecross Ct DE24 ......206 A1
Appledown Way DE23 ....231 A3
Applegarth Cl S12 ....44 A3
Applegarth Dr S12 ....44 A3
Applegate Cl DE21 ....206 A2
Applemead Cl DE21 ......205 C1
Appleton Cl
  Burton u T DE15 ....254 C4
  Derby DE21 ....220 A4
  Swadlincote DE11 ....255 C3
Appleton Dr Belper DE56 179 C4
  Glossop SK13 ....17 C4
Appletree Cl DE72 ....221 B1
Appletree Dr S17 ....57 A1
Appletree Rd
  Bolsover S44 ....80 A1
  Hatton DE65 ....239 B2
Appletree Wlk S18 ....57 A1
Applewood Cl
  Belper DE56 ....179 A3
  Uttoxeter ST14 ....210 A1
Appleyard Ct
  Chesterfield S41 ....266 A4
  ⑮ Stafford ST16 ....269 B4
Aquinas St DE24 ....269 B2
Aragon Ct ⑱ NG7 ....268 A2
Arbor Cl DE22 ....267 A2
Arbor Gr SK17 ....84 C4
Arbor Low (Henge)★
  DE45 ....123 C2
Arboretum Prim Sch
  DE23 ....219 A1
Arboretum Sq DE23 ......267 C1
Arboretum St
  Derby DE23 ....267 C1
  Nottingham NG1,NG7 ....268 A2
Arbour Hill DE7 ....207 C1
Arbourthorne Cotts S2 ..43 B4
Arbourthorne Jun Sch
  S2 ....43 B3
Arbourthorne Rd
  Sheffield S2 ....43 A3
  Sheffield S2 ....43 C3
Arcadia Ave NG20 ....119 C3
Archdale Cl S2 ....44 A4
Archdale Pl S2 ....44 A4
Archdale Rd S2 ....44 A4
Archer Rd NG9 ....223 C3
Archer St Derby DE24 ...219 C1
  Ilkeston DE7 ....194 C2
Arden Cl Chesterfield S40 95 B3
  Derby DE23 ....218 C1
  Glossop SK13 ....17 A4
Arden Est SK22 ....33 B4
Arden St SK22 ....33 B4
Ardleigh Cl DE3 ....230 B4
Ardmore Cl NG2 ....268 C1
Ardsley Cl Heanor DE75 .182 A1
  Sheffield S20 ....44 C1
Ardsley Dr S20 ....44 C1
Ardsley Gr S20 ....44 C1
Ardsley Rd S40 ....95 A2
Argyle Cl
  Market Warsop NG20 ....120 C2
  Sheffield S8 ....43 A3
Argyle St Derby DE22 ....218 C2
  Langley Mill NG16 ....182 B2
Argyll Ct DE21 ....220 C3
Argyll Rd DE5 ....169 C1
Arkendale Wlk ④ DE24 ..233 B3
Arklow Cl S41 ....115 A4
Arkwright Ave DE56 .....179 B3
Arkwright Cl DE4 ....127 B2
Arkwright Dr SK6 ....23 A3
Arkwright Rd SK6 ....23 A3
Arkwright St Derby DE24 .219 C1
  Wirksworth DE4 ....154 C4
Arleston La DE24 ....231 B1
Arleston St DE23 ....231 C4
Arlington Ave
  ⑧ Nottingham NG19 ....136 C2
Arlington Dr Derby DE24 232 C3
  Swanwick DE55 ....169 C4
Arlington Rd DE23 ....218 B1
Armitage Dr NG10 ....237 A4
Arms Park Dr S20 ....59 C3
Armscote Cl DE21 ....206 A1
Armstrong Ave ST16 .....269 C4
Armstrong Rd NG6 ....268 A4
Armytage Ind Est S41 ....77 A1
Arnfield La SK13 ....13 A3
Arnhem Terr DE22 ....220 C2
Arnold & Carlton Coll of F Ed
  NG1 ....268 B2
Arnold Ave
  Long Eaton NG10 ....236 A2
  Sheffield S12 ....44 A1
Arnold Cl DE11 ....261 C4
Arnold Cres S41 ....236 A2
Arnold St DE22 ....218 B3
Arnot Rd DE14 ....254 A4
Arnside DE7 ....223 C3
Arnside Cl
  Chesterfield S41 ....76 B1
  Swadlincote DE11 ....256 B1
Arran Cl Derby DE24 ....231 C2
  Stapleford NG9 ....209 C1
Arran Ct DE55 ....147 C3
Arridge Rd DE21 ....220 C3

Arrowscroft Way SK14 ....9 B3
Arthington St S8 ....43 A3
Arthur Ave NG9 ....223 C4
Arthur Cl ④ DE23 ......219 A1
Arthur Hind Cl DE22 ....218 C4
Arthur Mee Ctr (Coll of F Ed)
  The NG9 ....223 B4
Arthur Mee Rd NG9 .....223 C3
Arthur Short Cl S80 ......82 A3
Arthur St Alfreton DE55 .159 A3
  Derby DE1 ....267 B5
  Draycott DE72 ....234 C4
  Linton DE11 ....261 C4
  Mansfield NG18 ....268 C3
  Nottingham NG7 ....268 A2
  Pinxton NG16 ....160 B2
Arthur St DE13 ....240 C1
Arthurs View NG16 .....170 C2
Arthurs Way S33 ....38 A1
Artic Way NG16 ....195 B4
Artisan View S8 ....43 A3
Arun Dale NG19 ....136 B1
Arundel Ave DE3 ....217 C1
Arundel Ct
  Chesterfield S41 ....95 C4
  ⑯ Dronfield S18 ....56 B1
  Sandiacre NG10 ....223 A2
Arundel Dr Derby ② DE21 220 C3
  Mansfield NG18 ....268 A4
Arundel St Derby DE22 .218 B2
  Glossop SK13 ....17 C4
  Nottingham NG7 ....268 A2
Ascot Ave NG16 ....195 C4
Ascot Cl Burton u T DE15 248 A2
  West Hallam DE7 ....207 B4
Ascot Ct DE24 ....232 B4
Ascot Park Est NG10 ...223 B2
Ascot Pl DE7 ....208 B3
Ascott Dr DE11 ....256 A4
Ashcroft Ct S41 ....77 A2
Ash Acre DE56 ....179 B2
Ash Cl Ashton-on-T DE72 246 A4
  Derby DE22 ....204 B2
  Killamarsh S21 ....60 B3
  Mottram in L SK14 ....9 A2
  Pinxton NG16 ....160 B1
Ash Cres Eckington S21 ..59 A4
  Ripley DE5 ....180 B4
Ash Croft Prim Sch
  DE24 ....231 C1
Ash Ct DE55 ....159 B2
Ash Gr Brinsley NG16 ...182 B4
  Chinley SK23 ....34 C1
  Long Eaton NG10 ....236 B3
  Mastin Moor S43 ....79 A2
  Sandiacre NG10 ....223 A4
  Selston NG16 ....171 C4
  Shirebrook NG20 ....119 C3
  Stapleford NG9 ....223 B3
Ash La Chesterfield S21 ..77 B4
  Eckington S18 ....57 C2
  Sutton on t H DE6,DE65 228 C4
Ash Mount Rd NG16 ...182 A2
Ash St Buxton SK17 ......85 A3
  Ilkeston DE7 ....194 C2
  Mosborough S20 ....59 B4
Ash Terr SK17 ....85 B4
Ash Tree Ave NG16 .....136 B3
Ash Tree Cl
  Breadsall DE21 ....205 C2
  Chesterfield S40 ....95 B2
  Duffield DE56 ....190 C3
Ash Vale DE56 ....80 C1
Ash Vale Rd S43 ....80 C1
Ash Vale 95 A2
Ash View Cl DE65 ......229 C2
Ashbourne Ave S45 ....131 A3
Ashbourne Cl ④ S40 ....95 A3
Ashbourne Ct
  Derby DE22 ....218 C3
  ③ Glossop SK13 ....17 C4
  Ilkeston DE7 ....194 B1
Ashbourne Dr DE11 ....256 C4
Ashbourne La
  Alstonefield DE6 ....149 A1
  Chapel-en-le-f SK23 .....47 B3
Ashbourne Rd
  Alstonefield DE6 ....149 A2
  Belper DE56 ....178 B2
  Buxton SK17 ....85 B2
  Church Broughton DE65 .217 C2
  Derby DE22 ....218 B4
  Kirk Langley DE6 ....202 B2
  Mackworth DE22 ....217 C4
  Mayfield DE6 ....184 B4
  Rocester ST14 ....196 C2
  Shottle DE56 ....177 B2
  Turnditch DE56 ....177 B2
Ashbourne St
  Nottingham NG7 ....268 A2
  Scarcliffe NG20 ....119 C2
Ashbrook DE15 ....248 A1
Ashbrook Ave DE72 ....221 B1
Ashbrook Cl DE22 .....204 B2
Ashbrook Inf & Jun Sch
  DE72 ....221 A1
Ashbury Dr S8 ....43 B1
Ashbury La S8 ....43 B1
Ashby Ave NG19 ....136 B3
Ashby La DE11 ....255 C2
Ashby Rd
  Blackfordby DE11,LE65 ..257 B1
  Breedon on t H DE73 ...252 C1
  Burton u T DE15 ....248 A1
  Melbourne DE73 ....252 A3

Ashby Rd continued
  Moira DE12 ....262 C2
Ashby Rd E DE15 ......248 C1
Ashby St DE24 ....232 C3
Ashcombe Gdns DE21 ..206 A1
Ashcroft Cl DE24 ......232 C4
Ashcroft Dr S41 ....77 A1
Ashdale Cl DE15 ....255 A4
Ashdale Rd DE7 ....209 A3
Ashdene Gdns DE56 ...179 B3
Ashdown Dr S40 ....95 B1
Ashe Pl DE23 ....218 C1
Asher La DE5 ....169 B3
Ashes Ave DE6 ....175 C2
Ashes La
  Fenny Bentley DE6 .....162 A1
  Glossop SK13 ....10 A1
Ashfield Ave Derby DE21 219 C4
  Mansfield NG18 ....268 B4
  Somercotes DE55 ....159 B1
Ashfield Cl S12 ....43 C2
Ashfield Dr S43 ....80 C2
Ashfield Gr SK6 ....15 A1
Ashfield Rd
  Chapel-en-le-f SK23 ....47 B3
  Chesterfield S41 ....115 B4
  Glossop SK13 ....9 C2
  Nottingham NG2 ....268 C1
Ashford Ave S42 ....132 A4
Ashford Cl S18 ....75 B4
Ashford Ct
  West Hallam DE7 ....207 B4
  Chesterfield S41 ....96 A3
Ashford La SK13 ....9 B1
Ashford Mews S43 ......9 B1
Ashford Pl DE7 ....194 C3
Ashford Rise S18 ....75 B4
Ashford Rise DE56 .....179 B3
Ashford St S44 ....269 C2
Ashforth Ave DE75 ....194 A4
Ashforth St NG3 ....268 B2
Ashfurlong Cl S17 .....55 C4
Ashfurlong Dr S17 ......55 C4
Ashfurlong Rd S17 .....55 C4
Ashgate Ave S40 ....95 B2
Ashgate Croft Sch S40 .95 B2
Ashgate Prim Sch DE22 218 B3
Ashgate Rd S40 ....95 B2
Ashgate Valley Rd S40 .95 B3
Ashgrove Cl DE21 ......206 A1
Ashland Rd S21 ....59 C2
Ashlands Ave ST4 ......269 A4
Ashlands Cl ST4 ....269 A4
Ashlands Gr ST4 ......269 A4
Ashlands Rd ST4 ......269 A4
Ashlar Dr DE12 ....262 C1
Ashlea Dr DE6 ....184 B4
Ashlea Wlk S41 ....81 A3
Ashleigh Ave
  Glossop SK13 ....10 A1
  Sheffield S12 ....43 C3
  Swadlincote DE11 ......255 C3
Ashleigh Cl S21 ....59 B1
Ashleigh Croft S21 .....43 C3
Ashleigh Ct S21 ....59 B1
Ashleigh Dr Derby DE73 232 C2
  Sheffield S12 ....43 C3
Ashleigh Pl S12 ....43 C3
Ashleigh Rd S43 ....80 A4
Ashley Cl Killamarsh S21 60 B3
  Overseal DE12 ....262 A2
  Tansley DE4 ....144 A2
Ashley La DE21 ....248 A2
Ashley St Derby DE22 ..218 B3
  Nottingham NG3 ....268 B2
Ashlyn Rd DE21 ....267 D3
Ashmead Dr DE72 ......221 A1
Ashmeadow DE6 ......185 B4
Ashmore Ave S21 ....59 A1
Ashop Rd DE56 ....179 B3
Ashopton Ave DE23 ...231 C4
Ashopton Dr S33 ......40 A2
Ashopton Rd Bamford S33 40 A3
  Chesterfield S41 ....95 B3
Ashover Cl DE21 ......219 C4
Ashover New Rd DE55,
  S45 ....145 C4
Ashover Prim Sch S45 .129 C2
Ashover Rd Alton S45 ..130 C2
  Ashover S45 ....129 C2
  Derby DE22 ....204 B1
  ② Derby, Chaddesden
  DE21 ....219 C4
Ashover View DE55 ....147 B1
Ashton Cl
  Chesterfield S40 ....114 B4
  Derby DE3 ....217 B2
  Killamarsh S21 ....60 B3
  Swanwick DE55 ....170 A4
Ashton Gdns
  Clay Cross S42 ....131 A3
  ④ Chesterfield S41 ....96 B2
Ashton St SK13 ....17 B4
Ashton Way SK16 .....179 B2
Ashtree Ave DE24 .....232 A3
Ashurlong Pk S17 .....55 C4
Ashview Cl NG10 ......236 A4
Ashwater Cl DE24 .....231 C1
Ashwell Ave NG19 ....136 C3
Ashwood S43 ....80 C4
Ashwood Cl Buxton SK17 85 B4

Ashwood Cl continued
  Mansfield Woodhouse
  NG19 ....136 C3
Ashwood Rd Buxton SK17 66 C1
  Disley SK12 ....32 B3
Ashworth Ave
  Burton u T DE15 ....248 B1
  Derby DE21 ....219 C3
Ashworth Dr NG19 ....136 C2
Ashworth La NG14 .....9 A2
Ashworth St ST4 ......269 C1
Asker La DE4 ....143 B3
Askerfield Ave DE21 ...204 B2
Askew Gr DE65 ....242 B1
Asline Rd S2 ....43 A4
Aspen Bsns Ctr DE21 ..220 A2
Aspen Cl Buxton SK17 ..66 C1
  Killamarsh S21 ....60 B3
Aspen Ct NG19 ....136 C1
Aspen Dr DE21 ....220 B2
Aspen Rd S21 ....59 A1
Aspen Rise DE55 ......146 B1
Aspenshaw Rd SK22 ...24 C2
Aspley Cl S40 ....95 C3
Astcote Cl DE75 ......182 A1
Asterdale Prim Sch
  DE21 ....220 C2
Asterdale View DE21 ..220 C2
Astlow Dr DE56 ....179 A3
Aston Cl Derby DE3 ...245 A4
  Dronfield S18 ....57 B2
Aston Ct Ilkeston DE7 .194 C1
  Staveley S43 ....78 C1
Aston Dr DE13 ....256 A4
Aston Gn NG9 ....223 C2
Aston Hall Dr DE72 ...246 A4
Aston Hall Hospl DE72 .246 A3
Aston La Derby DE72 ..233 A1
  Hope S33 ....39 B2
  Shardlow DE72 ....234 C1
  Sudbury DE6 ....226 A3
  Wensley DE4 ....142 B3
Aston Rd DE23 ....231 B3
Aston-on-Trent Prim Sch
  DE72 ....234 C1
Astorville Park Rd DE73 232 C1
Astwith Cl S44 ....116 C1
Astwith La S44,S45 ....133 A3
Atchison Gdns DE21 ...220 A4
Atherfield Gdns NG16 .182 C2
Atherton Ave SK14 .....9 A2
Atherton Cl S2 ....43 C3
Atherton Gr SK14 ......9 A2
Atherton Rd
  Ilkeston DE7 ....194 B2
  Sheffield S2 ....43 C3
Athlestan Way DE21 ..240 B1
Athlone Cl DE21 ......219 B4
Athol Cl Chesterfield S40 114 A4
  Derby DE24 ....231 C2
Atkin Pl ⑦ S2 ....43 A4
Atkins Way ST14 ......196 C2
Atkinson Mews S21 ....59 B2
Atlantic Cres S8 ....56 C3
Atlantic Dr S8 ....56 C3
Atlantic Rd S8 ....56 B3
Atlantic Way S8 ....56 C3
Atlantic Wlk S8 ......56 C3
Atlow Brow DE6 ......173 B2
Atlow Cl S40 ....95 A3
Atlow La DE6 ....175 A3
Atlow Rd DE21 ....219 C4
Attenborough Nature
  Reserve★ NG9 ....237 B4
Attewell Cl DE72 .....235 A4
Attewell Rd NG16 ....195 A3
Attlebridge Cl DE21 ..219 B4
Attlee Rd S43 ....97 A4
Atworth Gr DE23 .....230 C4
Aubrey Ave ⑥ NG2 ..268 C1
Auburn Cl DE7 ....207 A4
Auckland Cl DE3 .....217 C2
Auckland Dr S20 ....59 C3
Auckland Rd S20 ......59 C3
Auckland Way S20 ....59 C3
Auction Cl DE6 ....173 B1
Auden Cl DE65 ....227 A4
Audens Way DE11 ....256 B3
Audley Cl DE7 ....194 B2
Audrey Cotts S32 .....71 B3
Audrey Cres NG19 ...136 B3
Audrey Dr DE21 ......220 A4
Audrey Rd S13 ....44 B4
Aughton Cl S13 ......44 B4
Aughton Cres S13 ....44 B4
Aughton Dr S13 ......44 B4
Augusta St ③ DE23 ..219 A1
Aukland's Pl S40 .....266 B2
Ault Hucknall La S44 ..134 A4
Aults Cl DE65 ....230 B1
Austen Ave Derby DE23 231 A4
  Long Eaton NG10 .....236 B3
Austin Friars ST17 ....269 B3
Austin Sq DE23 ......231 C4
Austin St NG20 ......120 A2
Austwick Gr DE4 .....143 B1
Austwick Gr ST4 .....269 A1
Autumn Gr DE21 .....219 C3
Avarne Pl ⑱ ST16 ...269 B4
Avenue 1 S41 ....115 A4
Avenue 2 S41 ....115 A4
Avenue 3 S41 ....115 A4
Avenue 4 S41 ....115 A4
Avenue 5 S41 ....115 A4
Avenue 6 S41 ....115 A4
Avenue 7 S41 ....115 A4

Avenue 8 S41 ....115 A4
Avenue Cl S32 ....72 A2
Avenue E NG3 ....118 C3
Avenue Rd
  Chesterfield S41 ....115 A4
  Duffield DE56 ....190 C2
Avenue The
  Bakewell DE45 ....109 A4
  Belper DE56 ....179 A3
  Chapel-en-le-f SK23 ...47 B3
  Derby DE1 ....267 B3
  Derby, Chaddesden DE21 220 A4
  Dronfield S18 ....57 A2
  Glossop SK13 ....10 A1
  Killamarsh S21 ....60 B3
  Northwood DE4 ....127 A3
  Stoney Middleton S32 ..72 A2
  Tissington DE6 ....162 A4
  Sutton-on-t DE72 ......245 A2
Averham Ct Derby DE21 205 C1
  Swadlincote DE11 .....255 C2
Aviemore Cl S43 ....97 C4
Aviemore Way DE24 ...231 C2
Avis Ave DE75 ....181 B1
Avocet Ct ⑧ DE24 ....219 A1
Avon Cl Derby DE24 ...231 C2
  Dronfield S18 ....57 B2
  Stafford ST16 ....269 B4
  Swadlincote DE11 .....256 A3
Avon Ct S41 ....115 A4
Avon Rise ST16 ....269 A4
Avon St DE24 ....232 C4
Avon Way
  Burton u T DE15 ......248 A2
  Hilton DE65 ....228 B1
  Mansfield NG18 ......268 A3
Avondale Cl NG10 ....236 A4
Avondale Rd
  Bolsover S44 ....118 C4
  Chesterfield S40 ....266 A4
  Derby DE23 ....219 A1
  Derby, Spondon DE21 ..220 C3
  Ilkeston DE7 ....208 B3
  Staveley S43 ....78 C1
Avonlea Cl DE7 ....208 B3
Avonmouth Dr DE24 ..219 C1
Awdishaw La DE6 ....211 B4
Awsworth Inf Sch NG16 195 B3
Awsworth Jun Sch
  NG16 ....195 B3
Awsworth La NG16 ...195 A4
Awsworth Rd DE7 ....194 C2
Aycliffe Gdns DE24 ...231 C1
Aylesbury Ave DE21 ..205 C1
Aylward Cl S2 ....43 C4
Aylward Rd S2 ....43 C4
Ayncourt Rd S42 .....131 C3
Ayr Cl DE21 ....220 C3
Ayr St NG7 ....268 A3
Azalea Cl DE55 ....146 C4
Azalea Ct DE55 ......146 C4
Azalea Ct NG16 ......146 C4

B

Babbacombe Cl DE24 ..233 A3
Babbington Cl DE24 ...219 A1
Babbington La NG16 ..182 B2
Babbington St DE55 ..147 C2
Babbs La DE6 ....151 C2
Babington Ct S2 ......43 C3
Babington Hospl DE56 .178 C2
Babington La DE1 ...267 B2
Babworth Ct NG18 ...268 A3
Bacchus Way S23 ....95 C4
Back Bridge St S43 ...78 C2
Back Browning St ST16 .269 B4
Back Croft S45 ....132 A3
Back Jodrell St SK22 ..33 B4
Back La
  Alderwasley DE56 ......166 C1
  Alstonefield DE6 ....149 A1
  Biggin SK17 ....138 B2
  Brackenfield DE55 .....145 A1
  Calow S44 ....96 C2
  Castle Donington DE74 ..247 A2
  Darley Dale DE4 ......127 B3
  Derby DE73 ....244 C4
  Ellastone DE6 ....183 A2
  Elton DE4 ....140 B3
  Glapwell S44 ....134 A4
  Glossop SK13 ....10 A1
  Hathersage S32 ......53 A1
  Hilton DE65 ....228 B2
  Ilkeston DE7 ....194 C1
  Mottram in L SK14 ....9 A1
  Palterton S44 ....118 A3
  Pilsley S45 ....132 B3
  Ripley DE5 ....169 A2
  Shirley DE6 ....200 B4
  Spout DE4 ....166 A2
  Stonebroom DE55 .....147 A3
  Sutton in A NG17 .....148 C1
  Thorpe Salvin S80 .....63 A1
  Tibshelf DE55 ....148 A2
  Unstone S18 ....76 B4
  Wessington DE55 .....157 C3
  Youlgreave DE45 ......125 A4
Back Mellor Rd SK22 ..24 B4
Back Moor SK14 ....9 A3
Back Rd S18 ....57 A2
Back Sitwell St DE1 ...267 B2
Back South St S43 ....77 C1
Back St S33 ....51 A4
Back Union Rd SK22 ..33 C4

Belle View Rd DE6 ....173 A1
Belle Vue Ave DE5 ....180 B3
Belle Vue St S43 ....96 B4
Belledere Cl DE55 ....169 C4
Bellevue Ct NG3 ....268 C2
Bellhouse La S43 ....78 C2
Bellhouse View S43 ....78 C2
Bellingham Ct DE22 ....204 B1
Bells End Rd DE12 ....253 B1
Bellsfield Cl S80 ....82 A3
Belmont Ave DE72 ....221 A1
Belmont Dr
  Borrowash DE72 ....221 A1
  Marple SK6 ....15 A1
  Staveley S43 ....78 C1
Belmont Prim Sch DE11 .....256 B2
Belmont St DE11 ....256 B2
Belmont Terr 2 SK17 ....85 A4
Belond La S45 ....113 B1
Belpar Ho DE21 ....220 C2
Belper La DE56 ....178 C3
Belper Rd
  Ashbourne DE6 ....173 C1
  Derby DE1 ....218 C4
  Holbrook DE56 ....191 B4
  Kilburn DE56 ....179 C1
  Morley DE7 ....192 C1
  Shirland DE55 ....146 B1
  Stanley DE7 ....193 A1
  West Hallam DE7 ....207 B4
Belper Sch DE56 ....178 C2
Belper Sports Ctr DE56 .....179 B2
Belper St Ilkeston DE7 ....208 C4
  Mansfield NG18 ....268 C2
Belper Way NG18 ....268 C4
Belsize Cl DE22 ....217 C3
Belton Cl Dronfield S18 ....56 B3
  Sandiacre NG10 ....223 A2
Belton Dr DE5 ....169 C1
Belvedere Ave S40 ....114 C4
Belvedere Cl
  Chesterfield S40 ....114 A4
  Derby DE3 ....217 B2
Belvedere Rd DE11 ....256 C1
Belvedere St NG18 ....268 B3
Belvedere Terr SK17 ....85 A3
Belvoir Cl Breaston DE72 ...235 B4
  Ilkeston DE7 ....208 B3
  Long Eaton NG10 ....236 A3
Belvoir Cres DE11 ....256 A3
Belvoir Hill NG2 ....268 C2
Belvoir St DE23 ....218 C1
Belvoir Way DE55 ....159 B1
Bembridge Dr DE24 ....233 B3
Bemrose Com Sch
  DE22 ....218 B2
Bemrose Gate S33 ....40 A3
Bemrose Mews DE1 ....218 B2
Bemrose Rd DE24 ....232 C4
Benbow Ave DE72 ....232 A4
Bench Rd SK17 ....85 B4
Benches La SK6 ....15 C2
Bend Oak Dr DE15 ....248 B2
Bend Oak Jun Sch DE15 .....248 B2
Bendall Gn DE23 ....231 A3
Beninmoor Way NG10 ....114 C4
Benjamin Outram Bsns Ctr
  DE5 ....180 C2
Benmore Ct DE21 ....206 A2
Benner Ave DE7 ....209 A3
Bennerley Ave DE7 ....194 C2
Bennerley Fields Sch
  DE7 ....194 C2
Bennerley Sch DE7 ....194 C2
Bennett St Buxton SK17 ......85 B3
  Derby DE24 ....232 B3
  Hollingworth SK14 ....9 B3
  Long Eaton NG10 ....223 B1
  Sandiacre NG10 ....223 A3
Bennetts La DE4 ....143 A4
Bennington Wlk NG19 ....136 C2
Bennion Gr S17 ....196 C3
Bennison Gdns S45 ....131 B2
Bentley Cl DE73 ....233 A1
Benson St DE24 ....232 C4
Bent La
  Church Broughton DE65 ......227 B3
  Darley Dale DE4 ....127 B3
  Matlock DE4 ....143 A4
  Spout DE4,DE56 ....166 B3
  Staveley S43 ....79 A2
  Tissington DE6 ....162 B3
Bent The S32 ....72 C2
Bent's La S18 ....57 B1
Bentfield Rd DE6 ....168 B1
Bentham Rd S40 ....95 C3
Bentinck St NG18 ....268 C4
Bentinck Dr S43 ....81 A2
Bentinck Rd S44 ....98 C4
Bentinck St S43 ....81 B1
Bentley Brook DE65 ....228 C1
Bentley Cl Alfreton DE55 ....159 A2
  Matlock DE4 ....143 B4
Bentley Dale DE7 ....257 A2
Bentley Fields Open Farm *
  DE6 ....199 B1
Bentley Rd
  Castle Donington DE74 ....246 C2
  Uttoxeter ST14 ....210 A1
Bentley St DE24 ....232 C3
Benton Dr S44 ....23 B4
Bents Cres S18 ....57 B2
Bents La S18 ....57 B2

Bentside Rd SK12 ....32 B3
Beowulf Covert DE13 ....240 A1
Beresford Ave
  Ashbourne DE6 ....173 B1
  Chapel-en-le-F SK23 ....47 B3
Beresford Cl S41 ....131 B1
Beresford Dale DE11 ....255 C1
Beresford Dr
  Derby DE21 ....220 C2
  Ilkeston DE7 ....194 C3
Beresford La SK17 ....137 B1
Beresford Pl DE56 ....168 A3
Beresford Rd
  Chapel-en-le-F SK23 ....47 B3
  Long Eaton NG10 ....236 A3
  Mansfield Woodhouse
  NG19 ....136 B3
Berkeley Ave NG10 ....236 B3
Berkeley Cl DE23 ....231 B4
Berkshire St DE21 ....219 B4
Berle Ave DE75 ....181 C1
Bermuda Ave DE21 ....205 B3
Bernard Ave NG19 ....136 A3
Bernard Cl S43 ....96 C4
Bernard Ct DE11 ....256 B2
Bernard Rd NG19 ....136 A4
Bernard St Glossop SK13 .....10 B1
  Swadlincote DE11 ....256 B2
Bernard Walker Ct SK6 ......15 B1
Berners Cl S2 ....43 C3
Berners Pl S2 ....43 C3
Berners Rd S2 ....43 C3
Berridge La S45 ....145 A2
Berrisford La S45 ....145 B4
Berristow La DE55 ....160 B4
Berry Ave S21 ....60 B3
Berry Gdns DE15 ....248 B2
Berry Hedge La DE15 ....248 B2
Berry Hill Rd NG18 ....268 C3
Berry Park Cl DE22 ....204 C1
Berry St
  North Wingfield S42 ....131 C3
  Stoke-on-T ST4 ....269 B2
Bertrand Ave S45 ....131 B2
Berwick Ave
  Chesterfield S40 ....114 A4
  Derby DE21 ....219 B4
Berwick Cl DE24 ....233 A3
Berwick Dr DE24 ....231 B2
Berwick Rd SK17 ....85 B2
Berwin Cl NG10 ....223 A2
Berwyn Cl S40 ....95 B3
Bessaline Dr DE56 ....179 A3
Bessell La S9 ....51 A3
Best Ave DE15 ....248 A4
Besthill Cotts SK14 ....16 A4
Besthorpe Cl DE21 ....206 A1
Besthorpe Ct NG19 ....268 A4
Bestwick Ave DE75 ....182 A1
Bestwick Cl DE7 ....209 A2
Bestwood Dr S45 ....131 B2
Bestwood Pk S45 ....131 B2
Bethel Terr S80 ....63 C4
Bethulie Rd DE23 ....232 A4
Betjeman Sq DE24 ....232 A3
Betlingspring La DE6 ....184 B2
Betony St S21 ....60 A3
Bevan Ct S43 ....97 A4
Bevan St S43 ....131 B1
Bevan St DE55 ....146 C1
Beverley Dr NG16 ....195 C4
Beverley Rd DE14 ....254 A4
Beverley St DE24 ....219 B1
Beverleys Rd S8 ....43 A2
Bewdley Cl DE73 ....233 A2
Bexley Cl SK13 ....10 B2
Bicester Ave DE24 ....231 B1
Bickley Moss DE21 ....206 A1
Bideford Cl DE5 ....169 B1
Bideford Dr DE23 ....231 B3
Bidston Cl DE4 ....143 B4
Bidworth La SK13 ....9 B1
Biggin CE Prim Sch
  SK17 ....138 B2
Biggin Cl S45 ....131 B2
Biggin La DE6 ....176 A2
Biggin The DE74 ....247 A2
Bigginmill La DE6 ....176 B3
Bilberry Cl DE21 ....205 C1
Bilberry Wlk NG3 ....268 C2
Bilby Gdns 3 NG3 ....268 C2
Bilby La S43 ....77 C1
Billam St DE21 ....59 A2
Billingsley Ave NG16 ....160 B2
Bilton St ST4 ....269 B1
Bingham St DE24 ....269 B1
Bings Rd SK23 ....45 C4
Bingswood Ave S43 ....45 A4
Bingswood Ind Est SK23 ....45 C4
Bingswood Rd SK23 ....45 C4
Binscombe La DE21 ....205 C2
Birch Ave Ilkeston DE7 ......209 A4
  Swadlincote DE11 ....256 A4
  Toadmoor DE56 ....167 C2
Birch Cl DE55 ....159 A3
  Burton u T DE14 ....254 A4
  Burton SK17 ....66 A1
  Denstone ST14 ....196 B3
  Derby DE21 ....221 A3
  Grassmoor S42 ....115 C2
  Killamarsh S21 ....60 B3
  Ripley DE5 ....180 B4

Birch Cl continued
  Wessington DE55 ....157 C4
Birch Farm Ave S8 ....57 A4
Birch Gn SK13 ....10 C1
Birch Gr Hatton DE65 ....227 B1
  Shirebrook NG20 ....119 B3
Birch Holt Gr S18 ....76 C3
Birch Kiln Croft 18 S43 .....76 C4
Birch La S43 ....78 A1
Birch Rd S80 ....82 B3
Birch Row DE4 ....218 C4
Birch St DE6 ....173 A1
Birch Vale Ind Est SK22 .....25 A1
Birch's Terr DE6 ....173 A1
Birches Cl
  Chesterfield S40 ....95 B3
  18 Dronfield S18 ....56 B1
Birchen Holme DE55 ....160 A2
Birches Ave DE55 ....157 C3
Birches Fold S18 ....57 B2
Birches La Dronfield S18 ......57 B2
  South Wingfield DE55 ....158 A3
Birches The SK22 ....25 B1
Birchfield Cl DE73 ....232 C1
Birchfield Pk DE75 ....193 C4
Birchfield Rd DE55 ....254 C3
Birchills The S80 ....81 B1
Birchitt Cl S17 ....56 B3
Birchitt Pl S17 ....56 B3
Birchitt Rd S17 ....56 B3
Birchitt View S18 ....57 A2
Birchlands NG19 ....136 C1
Birchlands Dr S21 ....60 B3
Birchover Edge DE4 ....141 A4
Birchover Ho DE22 ....204 C2
Birchover La DE4 ....141 A4
Birchover Rd
  Birchover DE4 ....126 B2
  Youlgreave DE4 ....126 B2
Birchover Rise DE21 ....205 C1
Birchover Way DE22 ....204 C1
Birchside Ave SK13 ....10 A1
Birchvale Rd S12 ....44 A2
Birchview Cl S40 ....179 A1
Birchwood Cl DE75 ....181 B2
Birchwood Ave
  Derby DE23 ....231 B3
  Long Eaton, Breaston
  NG10 ....236 A4
  Long Eaton, New Sawley
  NG10 ....236 B3
Birchwood Cl
  18 Mosborough S20 ....59 C4
  South Normanton DE55 .....160 A2
Birchwood Cres
  Chesterfield S40 ....114 C4
  Somercotes DE55 ....170 B4
Birchwood Croft 18 S20 .....59 C4
Birchwood Ct S40 ....114 C4
Birchwood Dr DE56 ....168 A2
Birchwood Gdns S20 ....59 C4
Birchwood Gr S20 ....59 C4
Birchwood La
  Pinxton DE55 ....159 C2
  Somercotes DE55 ....159 C2
  South Normanton DE55 .....159 B2
  Wood DE55 ....159 B2
Birchwood Rise 27 S20 ....59 C4
Birchwood View
  Ashbourne DE6 ....173 B2
  Mosborough S20 ....59 C4
Birchwood Way
  18 Mosborough S20 ....59 C4
  Somercotes DE55 ....159 C4
Bircumshaw's Rd DE75 ......181 C1
Bird St S43 ....78 C1
Birdcage Wlk DE22 ....217 C3
Birdcroft La DE7 ....208 C3
Birdfield S12 ....44 A4
Birdholme Cres S40 ....115 A4
Birdholme Inf Sch S40 ....115 A4
Birding St NG19 ....136 A1
Birdsgrove La
  Ashbourne DE6 ....172 B2
  Mayfield DE6 ....172 B2
Birdwood St DE23 ....218 C1
Birk Hill Inf Sch S21 ....59 A1
Birkdale Ave DE14 ....254 A3
Birkdale Cl Derby DE3 ....218 A1
  Ilkeston DE7 ....194 B4
Birkdale Dr S40 ....114 B4
Birkin La Grassmoor S42 ....115 C1
  Wingerworth S40,S42 ....114 A2
Birkin La W S42 ....115 C1
Birkinstyle La S45 ....146 C2
Birkinstyle La DE55 ....146 C2
Birkland Ave
  Mansfield Woodhouse
  NG19 ....136 B2
  Nottingham NG1 ....268 B2
Birkland St NG18 ....268 C4
Birks Cl S80 ....82 B3
Birks Rd S17 ....56 A3
Birley Brook Dr S40 ....95 A4
Birley Com Coll S12 ....44 B2
Birley Croft S41 ....95 A4
Birley La S12 ....44 C1
Birley Moor Ave S12 ....44 C2
Birley Moor Cl S12 ....44 C2
Birley Moor Cres S12 ....44 C1
Birley Moor Dr S12 ....44 C1
Birley Moor Pl S12 ....44 C1

Birley Moor Rd
  Sheffield S12 ....44 C2
  Sheffield S13 ....44 C1
Birley Moor Way S12 ....44 C2
Birley Spa La S12 ....44 C2
Birley Spa Prim Sch S12 .....44 C2
Birley St NG9 ....223 B3
Birley Vale Ave S12 ....44 B3
Birley Vale Cl S12 ....44 B3
Birstall Cl S41 ....95 B4
Biscay Ct DE21 ....206 B1
Bishop Lonsdale CE Prim Sch
  DE22 ....218 C2
Bishop Pursglove CE Prim
  Sch SK17 ....269 B1
Bishop St Alfreton DE55 .....159 A3
  Eastwood NG16 ....182 C1
  Mansfield NG18 ....268 B3
Bishop Stamer CE Prim Sch
  ST4 ....269 B1
Bishop's Ct DE73 ....252 A4
Bishop's Dr DE21 ....205 C1
Bishopdale Cl NG10 ....236 A3
Bishopdale Dr S20 ....59 A4
Bishops Ct S8 ....43 A3
Bishops Gate DE11 ....256 C1
Bishops House Mus * S8 .....43 A2
Bishops La SK17 ....84 C4
Bishopscourt Rd S8 ....43 A3
Bispham Dr NG9 ....223 C1
Bitham Ct DE13 ....240 B1
Bitham La DE13 ....240 B1
Blaby Cl DE23 ....231 C3
Black Harry La S32 ....71 A1
Black Hills Dr DE7 ....208 C3
Black Rock * DE4 ....155 A2
Black Tor Rd DE4 ....154 B4
Blacka Moor Cres S17 ....55 B3
Blacka Moor Rd S17 ....55 B3
Blacka Moor View S17 ....55 B3
Blackberry Flats S20 ....59 C4
Blackberry La S16 ....54 A4
Blackberry La NG14 ....269 A4
Blackbird Row DE56 ....179 B1
Blackbrook La SK23 ....47 C3
Blackburn Pl DE7 ....194 C2
Blackcliff Field Cl S80 ....82 A3
Blackden Cl DE56 ....179 C2
Blackdown Ave S40 ....95 A3
Blackfordby St Margaret's CE
  Prim Sch DE11 ....257 B1
Blackmore St S12 ....231 C4
Blackmount Cl 7 DE24 ....231 B2
Blackpit La DE6 ....224 A4
Blackpool St DE14 ....254 B4
Blackrocks Ave DE4 ....142 C4
Blacks La S42 ....131 C4
Blackshaw Rd S13 ....44 C1
Blacksmith La S44 ....97 A2
Blacksmith's La
  Egginton DE65 ....241 A3
  Newton Solney DE15 ....248 C4
  Woodville DE11 ....256 C2
Blacksmiths Yd DE4 ....127 C1
Blackstock Cl S14 ....43 B1
Blackstock Cres S14 ....43 B1
Blackstock Dr S14 ....43 B1
Blackstock Rd S14 ....43 B2
Blackstone Cl DE55 ....170 B4
Blackthorn Cl
  Chesterfield S41 ....115 B4
  Derby DE21 ....205 C1
  Melbourne DE73 ....252 A4
Blackthorn Rd DE15 ....254 C3
Blackthorn Cl DE6 ....179 C1
Blackwall La DE6 ....176 A4
Blackwell La
  Melbourne DE73 ....252 A4
  Monyash DE45 ....107 A2
Blackwell Mill Cotts
  SK17 ....87 A3
Blackwell Prim Sch
  DE55 ....147 C1
Blackwell Rd NG17 ....148 C2
Bladon House Sch
  DE15 ....248 A3
Bladon Cl DE56 ....248 B2
Bladon View S13 ....241 A2
Bladon's Yd DE13 ....240 A2
Blagdon Cl DE4 ....127 B2
Blagreaves Ave DE23 ....231 B3
Blagreaves La DE23 ....231 B3
Blair Gr NG10 ....223 B3
Blair Ho DE23 ....231 B3
Blake Cres NG18 ....268 C4
Blake Rd NG10 ....236 A3
Blake St NG9 ....223 C3
Blake St Ilkeston DE7 ....194 C1
Blakebrook Cl DE73 ....233 A2
Blakebrook Dr DE73 ....252 A4
Blakeley La DE65 ....229 A1
Blakelow Dr DE65 ....229 A3
Blakelow La S45 ....142 A2
Blakemere La DE4 ....141 C1
Blakemore Ave DE73 ....252 A4
Blakeney Ct Derby DE21 .....206 B1
  Mansfield Woodhouse
  NG19 ....136 C2
Blakiston St S14 ....268 B4
Blanch Croft DE73 ....252 A4
Blandford Ave NG10 ....236 A3
Blandford Cl DE24 ....232 B3
Blandford Dr S41 ....95 C4
Blankney Cl DE24 ....231 B1
Bleasby St NG2 ....268 C1
Blencathra Dr DE3 ....230 C4

Blenheim Ave DE55 ....159 A3
Blenheim Cl
  Burton u T DE15 ....255 ..
  4 Glossop SK13 ....
  Mansfield NG19 ....
Blenheim Ct DE22 ....
4 Swadlincote DE11 ....
Blenheim Dr DE22 ....
Blenheim Mews DE65 ....
Blenheim Par DE22 ....
Blenheim Pl NG17 ....
Blenheim Rd DE6 ....
Blenheim Cl Belper DE56 ...
  Sandiacre NG10 ....
Blessed William Howard
  High Sch ST17 ....
Blind La Bolsover S44 ....
  Breaston DE72 ....
  Darley Dale DE4 ....
  Kirk Ireton DE6 ....
Blissworth Way DE55 ....
Blithe Cl DE1 ....
Bloomfield Cl Derby DE1 ...
Bloomfield Rd DE55 ....
Bloomfield St DE1 ....
Bloomgrove Rd DE7 ....
Blore Cl DE6 ....
Blossom Cres S12 ....
Blue Bell S43 ....
Blue Bell Hill Jun & Inf Sch
  NG3 ....
Blue Bell Hill Rd NG3 ....
Blue John Cavern * S33 .....
Blue Lodge Cl S43 ....
Bluebank View S43 ....
Bluebell Cl
  Barlborough S43 ....
  Derby DE4 ....
  Donisthorpe DE12 ....
  Hayfield SK22 ....
  Shirebrook NG20 ....
  Somercotes DE55 ....
  Underwood Green NG16 ...
Bluebell Hill DE55 ....
Bluebell Pl NG19 ....
Bluebell Way DE75 ....
Blueberry Cl S43 ....
Bluebird Ct S43 ....
Bluecoat Cl NG1 ....
Bluecoat St NG1 ....
Bluestone La DE4 ....
Bluestone Prim Sch S2 .....
Bluestone La DE4 ....
Blunt Ave S43 ....
Blunt St DE7 ....
Blyth Cl Chesterfield S40 ....
  Mansfield NG19 ....
Blyth Pl DE21 ....
Boadmeadows S Ctr
  DE55 ....
Boam La DE4 ....
Boardman Cres ST16 ....
Boardman Ind Est DE11 ....
Boardman Rd DE11 ....
Boarslack La SK17 ....
Boarstones La SK17 ....
Boat La NG16 ....
Boatmans Cl DE7 ....
Bobbin Mill La S40 ....
Bobbinmill Hill DE56 ....
Bochum Parkway S8 ....
Bocking La S8 ....
Bocking Rise S8 ....
Boden St DE23 ....
Bodmin Cl DE24 ....
Bodmin Way 3 S40 ....
Bog La DE73 ....
Boggard La SK6 ....
Bogguard Rd SK6 ....
Boggy La Bramwell S33 .....
  Church Broughton DE65 ...
Bohem Rd NG10 ....
Boiley La S21 ....
Boland Rd S8 ....
Bold La DE1 ....
Bole Hill S8 ....
Bole Hill Cotts S44 ....
Bolehill La Eckington S21 ..
  Eckington, Marsh Lane S21
  Northedge S42 ....
  Wingerworth S42 ....
Bolehill Rd DE4 ....
Boleyn Ct 18 NG1 ....
Bolsover Castle * S44 ....
Bolsover CE Jun Sch
  S44 ....
Bolsover Ct DE55 ....
Bolsover Com Hospl S44 ...
Bolsover Hill S44 ....
Bolsover Inf Sch S44 ....
Bolsover Rd Bolsover S44 ...
  Mastin Moor S43 ....
Bolsover St NG18 ....
Bolton St DE55 ....
Boman's La DE56 ....
Bonchurch Cl DE24 ....
Bond La DE56 ....
Bond St Nottingham NG2 ...
  Staveley S43 ....
Bondfield Rd S43 ....
Bondgate DE74 ....
Bondhay La S80 ....

on Rd NG19 . . . . . .268 A3
Bank SK13 . . . . .9 C1
CE Prim Sch
. . . . .142 C1
Ct S41 . . . . .95 B4
Ct 2 S41 . . . . .95 B4
Dr Derby DE3 . . . . .217 C2
es DE55 . . . . .170 B4
La Alfreton DE55 . .158 C2
DE4 . . . . .141 B2
DE4 . . . . .141 B2
St NG10 . . . . .236 C4
moor La DE4 . . . . . .141 C1
Dr DE55 . . . . .170 B4
Cres NG17 . . . . .148 C1
ne ST4 . . . . .269 B2
ll DE65 . . . . .242 B2
ve NG19 . . . . .135 A3
13 NG3 . . . . .268 B2
Cres NG19 . . . . .135 A3
st Derby DE24 . . . . .232 C4
worth SK14 . . . . .9 B3
d Woodhouse
. . . . .136 A2
DE5 . . . . .169 C1
St ST4 . . . . .269 B1
Ct SK13 . . . . .10 B1
y Ave DE6 . . . . .173 B1
n CE Prim Sch
. . . . .269 B1
n Ct S41 . . . . .269 B1
n Gn S41 . . . . .269 B1
n Old Rd ST4 . . . . . .269 B1
n Rd S41 . . . . .269 B1
nwood Terr ST4 . . .269 B1
y S43 . . . . .95 C4
d NG17 . . . . .148 C2
Ct S43 . . . . .80 C2
Cres NG9 . . . . .223 C3
sh St DE74 . . . . .247 A2
. Wood Inf & Jun Schs
. . . . .220 C3
rash By-pass
. . . . .221 B2
ash Rd DE21 . . . . . .220 C2
dale Ave S20 . . . . . .59 C3
dale Cl S20 . . . . . . .59 C3
dale Dr
S20 . . . . .236 A3
rough S20 . . . . .59 C3
field Rd DE22 . . . . .219 C4
fields DE72 . . . . . . .221 A1
stle Rd DE47 . . . . . .194 C2
wan Ct DE7 . . . . . . .194 C2
Mews DE56 . . . . . . .178 C3
t Ave DE23 . . . . .231 B4
Rd SK14 . . . . .16 A4
ck's La
NG10,DE72 . . . . . .222 C2
acre NG10 . . . . .223 A4
n Cl DE21 . . . . .220 B3
n St NG1 . . . . .268 B2
n Ct DE6 . . . . .173 A1
ll Sq DE23 . . . . .231 C4
rth Ave DE73 . . . . . .231 C3
rth Rd DE74 . . . . . . .246 C2
rth Way NG10 . . . . .223 A3
y Ave NG18 . . . . . . .268 A3
n Commercial Pk
. . . . .268 A3
n Dr DE7 . . . . .194 C3
Ct NG10 . . . . .236 B3
La NG1 . . . . .268 B2
n Cliff S32 . . . . .71 C1
n Lons DE6 . . . . . . .176 A4
ne S42 . . . . .114 C1
nhill Rd SK17 . . . . . .69 C1
La S32 . . . . .72 A1
ey Rd ST4 . . . . .269 C2
ey St ST4 . . . . .269 B1
ton Dr DE55 . . . . . .169 C4
ton La S43 . . . . .80 B2
st NG19 . . . . .135 C1
yard The SK14 . . . . . .9 B2
n Cl S40 . . . . .95 B4
on DE24 . . . . .233 A3
n La
. Allenton DE24 . . . .232 C3
. Boulton DE24 . . . .233 A3
lary Cl
brook NG20 . . . . . . .119 C3
y S43 . . . . .79 A2
lary Gdns DE55 . . . .147 C3
lary La NG16 . . . . . .182 C2
lary Rd
DE22 . . . . .218 C2
DE56 . . . . .241 B4
lary Wlk NG20 . . . . .100 C1
re Cl Brimington S43 .96 B4
y DE13 . . . . .239 A3
re DE13 . . . . .251 C4
e Mill Cl S43 . . . . . . .80 A4
ne Sq DE72 . . . . . . .235 C4
e St DE1 . . . . .267 B2
ne Way DE11 . . . . . .256 B2
nebrook Ave DE11 .165 C4
St NG19 . . . . .136 C2
ank Cl DE23 . . . . . . .231 B3

Bowbridge Ave DE23 . . .231 B3
Bowden Cl Hayfield SK22 . .25 B2
. Swadlincote DE11 . . . . . .256 A3
Bowden Cres SK22 . . . . . .33 A4
Bowden La SK23 . . . . .47 B4
Bowden Rd S13 . . . . .80 A2
Bowdon Ave S43 . . . . .80 A3
Bower Dr DE4 . . . . .156 C1
Bower Farm Rd S41 . . . . . .77 A1
Bower St DE24 . . . . .232 C4
Bowes Well Rd DE7 . . . . .194 C1
Bowland Cl DE3 . . . . .217 C1
Bowland Dr S41 . . . . .114 A4
Bowland Rd SK13 . . . . .17 A4
Bowlees Ct DE23 . . . . . . .230 C4
Bowler Dr DE56 . . . . .178 C4
Bowler Rd DE4 . . . . .127 B2
Bowler St DE5 . . . . .180 B4
Bowling Alley DE56 . . . . .168 C1
Bowling Alley La DE6 . . . .212 C2
Bowling Cl DE7 . . . . .222 C4
Bowling Gn La DE4 . . . . . .143 C1
Bowling Green La DE4 . .154 C2
Bowling St NG18 . . . . . . .268 C3
Bowman Cl S12 . . . . .43 C1
Bowman Dr S12 . . . . .44 A1
Bowmer La DE56 . . . . . . .168 A2
Bowmer Rd DE24 . . . . . . .219 C1
Bown Cl DE56 . . . . .192 A4
Bowness Cl
. Chesterfield S41 . . . . . . .95 B4
. 2 Dronfield S18 . . . . . . .56 C1
Bowness Rd S41 . . . . .95 B4
Bowns Hill S42 . . . . .157 A1
Bowshaw Ave S8 . . . . .57 A3
Bowshaw Cl S8 . . . . .57 A3
Bowshaw View S8 . . . . . . .57 A3
Bowstead St S8 . . . . .269 B2
Boxmoor Cl DE23 . . . . . . .230 C4
Boyd Gr DE73 . . . . .245 A4
Boyer St DE22 . . . . .267 A1
Boyer Wlk DE22 . . . . .267 A1
Boylestone Rd DE23 . . . . .231 B3
Boythorpe Ave S40 . . . . . .266 A2
Boythorpe Cres S40 . . . . .266 A1
Boythorpe Mount S40 . . .266 A2
Boythorpe Rd S40 . . . . . .266 A2
Boythorpe Rise S40 . . . . .266 A2
Brabyns Brow SK6 . . . . . . .23 A4
Bracken Ave S44 . . . . . . .116 C1
Bracken Cl
. Hollingworth SK14 . . . . . .9 B3
. Long Eaton NG10 . . . . .223 A4
. Marple SK6 . . . . .23 B4
Bracken La
. Barlborough S43 . . . . . . .80 A3
. Holloway DE4 . . . . .156 A3
Bracken Rd
. Long Eaton NG10 . . . . .223 A4
. Shirebrook NG20 . . . . . .119 B2
Bracken Way SK13 . . . . . .17 C4
Bracken's La DE24 . . . . . .232 C3
Brackendale Cl
. Brimington S43 . . . . .96 B4
. Clay Cross S45 . . . . .131 C1
Brackendale La DE56 . . . .163 C3
Brackenfield Ave NG16 .182 C1
Brackenfield Dr NG16 . . .195 A4
Brackenfield Gr S12 . . . . . .44 B2
Brackenfield La
. Brackenfield DE55 . . . . . .145 A1
. Wessington DE55 . . . . .157 B4
Brackens Ave S44 . . . . . . .232 C3
Brackensdale Inf Sch
. . . . .218 A3
Brackensdale Jun Sch
. . . . .218 A3
Brackenwood Rd DE15 .254 C3
Brackhills Cl NG19 . . . . . .136 C1
Brackley DE56 . . . . .179 C1
Brackley Dr DE21 . . . . . . .206 A2
Brackley Gate DE7 . . . . . .192 A1
Bracknell Dr DE24 . . . . . .232 C3
Bracton Dr NG3 . . . . .268 C2
Bradbourne Cl S43 . . . . . . .97 B4
Bradbourne Ct DE22 . . . .204 C1
Bradbury Cl
. Borrowash DE72 . . . . . .221 B1
. Chesterfield S42 . . . . . . .114 C2
Bradbury Dr S42 . . . . .43 A3
Bradbury St S8 . . . . .43 A3
Bradden Ave NG9 . . . . . . .209 C1
Bradder Way NG18 . . . . . .268 A3
Bradgate Cl NG10 . . . . . .223 A2
Bradgate Croft S41 . . . . .115 B4
Bradgate Dr DE5 . . . . . . .169 A1
Brading Cl DE24 . . . . .233 B3
Bradley CE Prim Sch
. DE6 . . . . .186 C4
Bradley Cl Birchover DE4 .126 A1
. 3 Brimington S43 . . . . . .96 C4
Bradley Dr DE56 . . . . .179 A2
Bradley Gr S43 . . . . .80 A4
Bradley St
. Burton u T DE15 . . . . . .254 C4
. Derby DE22 . . . . .218 C4
. Sandiacre NG10 . . . . . .223 B3
Bradley View DE6 . . . . . . .173 B2
Bradley Way S43 . . . . .96 C4
Bradmoor Gr DE73 . . . . . .233 A1
Bradshaw Ave DE55 . . . . .170 C3

Bradshaw Cres 23 A4
Bradshaw Croft DE56 . .178 C3
Bradshaw Dr DE56 . . . . .191 B3
Bradshaw La
. Old Brampton S42 . . . . . .93 C1
. Stoney Middleton S32 . . .70 C4
Bradshaw Mdw DE65 . . .227 B1
Bradshaw Rd Marple SK6 . .23 A4
. Staveley S43 . . . . .97 A3
Bradshaw St NG10 . . . . .236 A3
Bradshaw Way DE1 . . . .267 C2
Bradway Cl S17 . . . . .56 A3
Bradway Dr S17 . . . . .56 A3
Bradway Grange Rd S17 . .56 B3
Bradway Rd S17 . . . . .56 B3
Bradwell CE Inf Sch S33 . .51 A4
Bradwell Cl Derby DE3 . .217 C1
. 8 Dronfield S18 . . . . . . .56 B1
. Eastwood NG16 . . . . . . .195 B4
Bradwell Gr S45 . . . . . . .131 A1
Bradwell Head Rd S33 . . .51 A4
Bradwell Jun Sch S33 . . . .51 A4
Bradwell Lea 8 SK13 . . . . .9 C2
Bradwell St S2 . . . . .97 B4
Bradwell St S2 . . . . .43 A3
Bradwell Terr 13 SK13 . . . .9 C2
Bradwell Way DE56 . . . . .179 A3
Braefield Ct DE7 . . . . . . .208 B3
Braemar Ave NG16 . . . . .182 C1
Braemar Cl
. Chesterfield S41 . . . . . . .76 C1
. 6 Derby DE21 . . . . .231 B2
Brafield Cl DE56 . . . . . . .179 B2
Brailsford Ave
. Gamesley SK13 . . . . .9 C1
. Swadlincote DE11 . . . . . . .256 A3
Brailsford CE Prim Sch
. . . . .201 C4
Brailsford Cl SK13 . . . . .9 C1
Brailsford Gn SK13 . . . . . . .9 C1
Brailsford Rd DE21 . . . . .219 C4
Braintree Cl DE21 . . . . . .205 B1
Braithwell Cl DE22 . . . . .204 C1
Bramah Edge Ct SK13 . . . .9 C4
Bramall Cl 2 S2 . . . . .43 A4
Bramall La S2 . . . . .43 A4
Bramble Bank S17 . . . . . .17 C4
Bramble Cl
. Holmewood S44 . . . . . . .116 C1
. Long Eaton NG10 . . . . .223 A1
. South Normanton DE55 . .160 A3
Bramble Mews DE56 . . . .217 B1
Bramble St DE1 . . . . .267 A3
Bramble Way DE56 . . . . .179 C1
Bramble Wlk SK13 . . . . .9 C2
Bramblebury Ct DE21 . . .206 A2
Brambleberry Ct DE72 . . .231 A3
Brambling Ct S41 . . . . .96 C1
Bramell Cl DE14 . . . . . . .253 C4
Bramfield Ave DE22 . . . .218 C2
Bramfield Ct DE22 . . . . . .218 C2
Bramham Rd S42 . . . . . . .114 C4
Bramley Ave S13 . . . . .44 C4
Bramley Cl Hatton DE65 . .227 B1
. Kimberley NG16 . . . . . .195 C3
Bramley Dale DE11 . . . . .255 C1
Bramley Hall Rd S13 . . . . . .44 C4
Bramley La Baslow DE45 . .44 C4
. Sheffield S13 . . . . .44 C4
Bramley Park Cl S13 . . . . .44 C4
Bramley Park Rd S13 . . . .44 C4
Bramley Pk Caravan Site
. S21 . . . . .58 C2
Bramley Rd
. Bramley-Vale S44 . . . . . .117 C1
. Eckington S21 . . . . .58 C1
Bramley Vale Prim Sch
. . . . .117 C1
Bramleymoor La S21 . . . . .58 C1
Bramlyn Cl S43 . . . . .80 C3
Bramlyn Cl S43 . . . . .80 C3
Brampton Ave DE75 . . . .182 C1
Brampton Cl DE3 . . . . . . .217 B2
Brampton Dr NG9 . . . . . .209 C2
Brampton Prim Sch S40 . .95 A2
Bramshill Rise S40 . . . . . . .95 B2
Branch La S45 . . . . .132 C3
Brancliffe La S81 . . . . .63 C4
Brandelhow Ct DE21 . . . .206 B2
Brandene Cl S44 . . . . .97 A2
Brandreth Dr NG16 . . . . .195 A4
Branklene Cl NG16 . . . . .195 A4
Bransdale Ave NG19 . . . .136 C1
Branston Rd
. Branston DE13,DE14 . . . .253 B4
. Burton u T DE14 . . . . . .254 B4
Branston Water Pk
. DE14 . . . . .253 B3
Branton Cl S40 . . . . .266 A1
Brassington Cl
. Mansfield NG16 . . . . .195 A4
. West Hallam DE7 . . . . . .207 C4
. Youlgreave DE45 . . . . . . .125 B3
Brassington Cres NG19 . .136 C2
Brassington La S42,S45 . .131 B3

Brassington Prim Sch
. DE4 . . . . .153 A2
Brassington Rd DE21 . . .205 C1
Brassington St S45 . . . . .131 B2
Braybrook Cl DE55 . . . . .169 C4
Brayfield Ave DE23 . . . . .231 B4
Brayfield Rd DE23 . . . . . .231 B4
Breach La
. Barrow-u-T DE73 . . . . . .244 C1
. Hatton DE65 . . . . .226 B3
. Scropton DE6 . . . . .226 B3
Breach Rd Derby DE5 . . .181 A2
. Heanor DE75 . . . . .194 A4
Breadsall CE Prim Sch
. DE21 . . . . .205 C2
Breadsall Cl DE11 . . . . . .256 A4
Breadsall Ct DE7 . . . . . . .194 C2
Breadsall Hill Top Inf Sch
. . . . .205 C2
Breadsall Hill Top Jun Sch
. DE21 . . . . .205 C2
Breamfield La DE4 . . . . . .166 A4
Brearley Ave S43 . . . . .77 B2
Brearley St S41 . . . . .77 A2
Brearley Hall S41 . . . . . . .77 A2
Brearley St S41 . . . . .77 A2
Breaston Ind Est DE72 . .235 B4
Breaston La DE72 . . . . . .222 B2
Brechin Ct NG19 . . . . . . .136 A3
Breck La S43 . . . . .79 C3
Breckbank NG19 . . . . . . .136 C1
Breckland Rd S40,S42 . .114 A4
Brecon Cl Chesterfield S40 . .95 B3
. Derby DE21 . . . . .220 C3
. 6 Long Eaton NG10 . . . .236 A4
Bredon Ave DE23 . . . . . .231 B3
Breedon on the Hill St
. Hardulph's CE Prim Sch
. DE73 . . . . .252 C1
Breedon St NG10 . . . . . .223 B1
Bren Way DE65 . . . . .228 C1
Brenden Ave DE55 . . . . . .170 B4
Brenden Cl DE55 . . . . . . .170 B4
Brendon Cl S40 . . . . .95 B3
Brendon Dr NG16 . . . . . .195 C4
Brendon Dr NG16 . . . . . .195 C4
Brendon Way NG10 . . . . .223 A3
Brent Cl S40 . . . . .95 B3
Brentford Dr DE22 . . . . . .218 A3
Brentnall Cl NG10 . . . . . .236 A4
Brentwood Ave S33 . . . . . .40 A2
Brentwood Rd S33 . . . . . . .40 A2
Bretby Bsns Pk DE15 . . .255 C4
Bretby Hollow DE11 . . . . .255 C4
Bretby La
. Burton u T DE15 . . . . . .248 B1
. Burton u T DE15 . . . . . .248 B1
Bretby Mews DE15 . . . . . .249 A1
Bretby Rd Chesterfield S40 . .95 A3
. Swadlincote DE11 . . . . . .255 C4
Bretby St S40 . . . . .95 A3
Bretton Gr S12 . . . . .44 B2
Bretton Rd DE56 . . . . . . .179 C3
Brewash St NG10 . . . . . .223 B2
Brewery St
. Chesterfield S41 . . . . . . .266 C3
. Kimberley NG16 . . . . . .195 C3
Brewhouse Yd (Mus of
. Nottingham Life)*
. NG7 . . . . .268 A3
Breydon Dr DE22 . . . . . .232 B2
Breydon Ind Ctr NG10 . .236 C4
Briar Ave NG17 . . . . .160 B3
Briar Briggs Rd S44 . . . . .98 C3
Briar Cl Alfreton DE55 . . .159 B2
. Borrowash DE72 . . . . . .221 B1
. Chesterfield S41 . . . . . . .266 C3
. Derby DE21 . . . . .220 A3
. Swadlincote DE11 . . . . . .255 C3
Briar Gate NG10 . . . . . . .223 A1
Briar Lea Cl DE24 . . . . . .231 C2
Briar Rd NG16 . . . . .195 A4
Briar View S43 . . . . .96 C1
Briar's La DE4 . . . . .168 A4
Briardene Cl S40 . . . . .94 C3
Briargrove Rd SK22 . . . . . .24 A2
Briars Way S45 . . . . .180 B4
Briarsgate DE22 . . . . . . .204 B1
Briarwood Cres SK6 . . . . .23 A3
Briarwood Way DE23 . . . .231 B3
Brick Kiln La
. Mansfield NG19 . . . . .268 A4
. Rolleston DE13 . . . . .240 A2
Brick Row DE22 . . . . .205 A1
Brick St DE1 . . . . .218 C3
Brick-kiln La
. Brailsford DE6 . . . . .186 C1
. Hulland Ward DE6 . . . . . .175 B3
Brickbridge Rd SK6 . . . . . .23 A2
Brickfield St SK13 . . . . .10 A3
Brickfields Cl DE7 . . . . . .207 B2
Brickhouse La S17 . . . . . . .55 B4
Brickhouse Yd S43 . . . . . . .96 C1
Brickkiln La DE7 . . . . . . .206 B4
Bricky Cl S43 . . . . .97 A4
Brickyard Cotts DE6 . . . .185 B4
Brickyard La
. Kilburn DE56 . . . . .179 C1
. Ripley DE5 . . . . .169 C1
. South Normanton DE55 . .160 A3
Brickyard Rd DE56 . . . . .168 B3

Bon – Bri **275**

Brickyard The DE7 . . . . . .193 A1
Bridge Bank Cl 1 S40 . . . .95 B3
Bridge Cl
. Swadlincote DE11 . . . . .256 B1
. Whitwell S80 . . . . .82 A3
Bridge End Ave NG16 . . .171 C4
Bridge Farm NG13 . . . . . .240 C1
Bridge Field DE72 . . . . . .235 B4
Bridge Foot DE56 . . . . . .178 C3
Bridge Hill DE56 . . . . . . .178 C3
Bridge St Bakewell DE45 .109 B3
. Belper DE56 . . . . .178 C4
. Bradwell S33 . . . . .51 A4
. Burton u L, Stretton DE13 .240 C1
. Buxton SK17 . . . . .85 B4
. Chesterfield S40 . . . . . . .266 B3
. Clay Cross S45 . . . . .131 B2
. Derby DE1 . . . . .218 C3
. Ilkeston DE7 . . . . .194 C2
. Killamarsh S21 . . . . .60 B4
. Langley Mill NG16 . . . . .182 B2
. Linton DE11 . . . . .261 C4
. Long Eaton NG10 . . . . .223 B1
. Mansfield NG18 . . . . . . .268 C4
. New Mills SK22 . . . . .24 B1
. Pilsley S45 . . . . .132 B1
. Sandiacre NG10 . . . . . .223 B3
. Stafford ST16 . . . . .269 B3
. Swadlincote DE11 . . . . . .256 B1
. Tupton S42 . . . . .115 B1
. Tutbury DE13 . . . . .239 B4
. Whaley Bridge SK23 . . . .45 C4
Bridge View S6 . . . . .191 A4
Bridge Way S41 . . . . .76 B2
Bridgefield 4 S43 . . . . .17 A4
Bridgend Cl NG9 . . . . . . .223 B3
Bridgeness Rd DE23 . . . .230 C3
Bridgeport Rd DE21 . . . .220 B3
Bridgeside DE13 . . . . . . .240 C1
Bridgett Cl ST4 . . . . .269 A1
Bridgewater St S42 . . . . .115 B1
Bridgeway S2 . . . . .47 A2
Bridgford Ave DE14 . . . . .223 C2
Bridgnorth Way NG9 . . . .223 C2
Bridgwater Cl DE23 . . . . .233 A1
Bridle Cl S43 . . . . .233 A1
Bridle La
. Ripley, Greenwich DE5 . . .169 C1
. Ripley, Lower Hartshay
. DE5, DE56 . . . . .169 A1
. Somercotes DE55 . . . . . .170 A4
. Swadlincote DE15 . . . . . .255 A3
Bridle Rd Bolsover S44 . . .80 A1
. Staveley S43 . . . . .79 A1
Bridle Stile S21 . . . . .59 A4
Bridle Stile Cl S21 . . . . . . .59 A4
Bridle Stile Gdns S20 . . . .59 A4
Bridlesmith Gate NG1 . . .268 B1
Bridleway SK22 . . . . .24 B1
Bridleway The NG16 . . . .136 C1
Brierfield Ave S12 . . . . . . .44 A2
Brierfield Rd S12 . . . . .44 A2
Brierfield Way DE23 . . . .230 C4
Brierley Cl S43 . . . . .82 A3
Brierley Pk SK23 . . . . .34 A1
Brierley Rd
. Stonebroom DE55 . . . . . .146 C2
. Unstone S18 . . . . .76 C3
Brierlow Bar SK17 . . . . . .105 A4
Brigden Ave DE24 . . . . . .232 C4
Brigg Inf Sch The The
. . . . .268 A3
Bright Mdw S20 . . . . .60 A3
Bright Side NG16 . . . . . . .195 C3
Bright Sq NG19 . . . . .135 B1
Bright St Derby DE22 . . . .218 B2
. Ilkeston DE7 . . . . .194 C2
. North Wingfield S42 . . . . .131 C3
. South Normanton DE55 . .159 C3
Brightman Ho DE11 . . . . .256 A3
Brightmoor St 14 NG1 . .268 B1
Brighton Rd DE24 . . . . . .232 C4
Brighton St S13 . . . . .44 C4
Brightstone Cl DE24 . . . .233 B3
Brigmor Wlk DE22 . . . . . .218 B3
Brimington Ct NG19 . . . . .96 B4
Brimington Jun Sch
. Brimington S43 . . . . .96 B4
. Brimington S43 . . . . .96 B4
Brimington Rd S41 . . . . . . .96 B4
Brimington Rd N S41 . . . . .96 C4
Brimmesfield Cl S2 . . . . . .43 C4
Brimmesfield Dr S2 . . . . . .43 C4
Brimmesfield Rd S2 . . . . . .43 C4
Brincliffe Cl S40 . . . . .95 A1
Brindle Way DE23 . . . . . .231 A3
Brindley Cl S8 . . . . .43 A2
Brindley Cres S8 . . . . .43 A2
Brindley Ct S21 . . . . .60 B3
Brindley Rd 6 S41 . . . . . . .96 A3
Brindley Wlk DE24 . . . . . .231 C1
Brinkburn Cl S17 . . . . .55 C3
Brinkburn Ct S17 . . . . .55 C3
Brinkburn Dr S17 . . . . .55 C3
Brinkburn Vale Rd S17 . . .55 C3
Brinks Rd S33 . . . . .39 A4
Brinsley Hill NG16 . . . . . .171 B1
Brinsley Prim Sch NG16 .182 B4
Brisbane Cl NG19 . . . . . .136 B3
Brisbane Dr NG9 . . . . . . .209 C1
Brisbane Rd DE3 . . . . . . .217 C2

Briset Cl DE24 .... 231 C1
Brisley Hill ST4 .... 269 A1
Bristol Dr DE3 .... 217 C1
Bristol Rd DE7 .... 194 C1
Britannia Ave DE5 ...... 181 A4
Britannia Dr DE13 .... 240 B1
Britannia Rd
Chesterfield S40 .... 115 A4
Long Eaton NG10 .... 223 B1
Briton Lodge Cl DE12 ... 262 C2
Brittain Dr DE5 .... 170 A1
Brittain Pit Farm* DE5 .. 170 A2
Britten Gdns NG3 .... 268 C2
Brizlincote La DE15 ..... 248 B1
Broad Bank DE22 .... 218 C4
Broad Eye ST16 .... 269 A4
Broad La Brinsley NG16 .. 182 C4
Creswell S80 .... 82 B3
Elvaston DE72 .... 233 C2
Broad Marsh Ctr NG1 ... 268 B1
Broad Oak Dr
Brinsley NG16 .... 182 C4
Stapleford NG9 .... 223 B3
Broad Pavement S40 .... 266 B3
Broad Pl S80 .... 82 B3
Broad St
Long Eaton NG10 .... 236 B4
Nottingham NG1 .... 268 B1
Stafford ST16 .... 269 A4
Broad Way DE6 .... 176 A4
Broad Wlk Buxton SK17 ... 85 A4
Darley Dale DE4 .... 127 B2
Broadbottom CE Prim Sch
SK14 .... 15 C4
Broadbottom Rd SK14 ..... 9 A2
Broadbottom Sta SK14 ... 16 A4
Broadfield Rd S8 .... 43 A4
Broadfields Cl DE22 ..... 218 C4
Broadgorse Cl S40 ...... 114 C4
Broadhey View SK22 ..... 24 A1
Broadholme La DE56 .... 179 A4
Broadlands
Sandiacre NG10 .... 223 A2
South Normanton DE55 ... 160 A2
Broadleaf Cl DE21 ...... 205 C1
Broadleys S45 .... 131 B2
Broadmeadow DE4 .... 127 B2
Broadoaks Cl S41 .... 266 C3
Broadstairs Rd NG9 ..... 223 C1
Broadstone Cl DE21 ..... 206 A1
Broadstone La DE73 ..... 251 B2
Broadway Derby DE22 .... 218 C4
Duffield DE56 .... 190 C1
Heanor DE75 .... 181 C1
Ilkeston DE7 .... 194 C2
9 Nottingham NG1 ...... 268 B1
Ripley DE5 .... 169 C1
Swanwick DE55 .... 169 C4
Broadway Ave DE5 ...... 169 C1
Broadway Park Cl DE22 . 218 C4
Broadway St DE14 ...... 254 B4
Broadway The NG18 ..... 268 C3
Brockhall Rise DE75 .... 182 A1
Brockhill Ct 4 S43 .... 96 C4
Brockholes SK13 .... 16 C4
Brockhurst Gdns NG3 ... 268 C2
Brockhurst La S45 ...... 129 B3
Brocklehurst Ave S8 ...... 57 B4
Brocklehurst Ct S40 ...... 95 B1
Brocklehurst Piece S40 .. 95 B1
Brockley DE21 .... 220 C3
Brockley Ave S44 .... 98 C3
Brockley Prim Sch S44 ... 98 C4
Brocksford Ct DE6 ...... 224 C4
Brocksford Hall Sch
DE6 .... 224 C4
Brockway Cl S45 .... 131 B1
Brockwell Ct 13 S41 ...... 95 B3
Brockwell Inf & Jun Sch
S40 .... 95 B2
Brockwell La Barlow S42 .. 94 C4
Chesterfield S40 .... 95 B2
Brockwell Pl S40 .... 95 C2
Brockwell Terr S40 .... 95 C2
Brockwell The DE55 .... 160 A2
Bromehead Way S41 ..... 95 B4
Bromley Hough ST4 ..... 269 A1
Bromley Pl NG1 .... 268 A1
Bromley St DE22 .... 218 C4
Brompton Rd DE22 ...... 217 C3
Bromyard Dr DE73 ...... 233 A2
Bronte Cl NG10 .... 236 A4
Bronte Pl DE23 .... 231 A4
Bronte St DE55 .... 146 B3
Brook Ave DE55 .... 159 A2
Brook Bottom Rd SK22 .... 33 A4
Brook Cl Alfreton DE55 ... 159 A2
Doveridge DE6 .... 224 B4
Findern DE65 .... 230 B1
Hatton DE65 .... 227 B1
Holymoorside S42 .... 113 B4
Long Eaton NG10 .... 236 C3
Quarndon DE22 .... 204 B2
Brook Cotts DE7 .... 194 C2
Brook Ct NG16 .... 182 A1
Brook End DE65 .... 242 B2
Brook House Mews
DE11 .... 256 A4
Brook La Alfreton DE55 .. 159 A2
Clowne S43 .... 80 C2
Crich DE56 .... 168 B3
Hatton DE65 .... 227 B2
Ripley DE5 .... 180 B4
Sutton on t H DE6 .... 228 A4
Brook Lea DE4 .... 143 B2
Brook Mdw SK13 .... 10 C1
Brook Rd
Borrowash DE72 .... 221 A1
Elvaston DE72 .... 233 C2
Sheffield S8 .... 43 A3
Brook Side DE45 .... 109 B3
Brook St Clay Cross S45 .. 131 A2
Derby DE1 .... 267 A4
Glossop SK13 .... 10 B1
Hartshorne DE11 .... 257 A4
Heage DE56 .... 168 C1
Heanor DE75 .... 181 A3
Nether Heage DE56 ...... 168 B1
Nottingham NG1 .... 268 B2
Renishaw S21 .... 79 B4
Stoke-on-T ST4 .... 269 B2
Swadlincote DE11 .... 256 A2
Swadlincote, Newhall
DE11 .... 255 C3
Tibshelf DE55 .... 148 A3
Brook Vale Cl S18 .... 75 B2
Brook Vale Rd NG16 ..... 182 B1
Brook Wlk DE1 .... 267 A4
Brook Yd S40 .... 266 A3
Brookbank Ave S40 .... 95 B2
Brookbank Rd S43 .... 80 C2
Brookdale Ave SK6 .... 23 A2
Brookdale Dr DE23 ...... 231 A3
Brookdale Rd DE11 ..... 257 A2
Brooke Dr S43 .... 96 C3
Brooke St Ilkeston DE7 ... 209 A3
Sandiacre NG10 .... 223 A3
Brookfield DE73 .... 244 A3
Brookfield Ave
Chesterfield S40 .... 95 A1
Derby, Chaddesden DE21 .. 220 A4
Derby, Littleover DE23 ... 231 B3
Brookfield Cl DE5 .... 170 A1
Brookfield Com Sch S40 . 95 A1
Brookfield Cres NG20 ... 119 C3
Brookfield Ind Est SK13 ... 9 C2
Brookfield La DE45 ..... 109 C4
Brookfield Park Ind Est
DE4 .... 143 C2
Brookfield Prim Sch
Derby DE3 .... 230 B4
Shirebrook NG20 .... 119 C3
Brookfield Rd S44 ...... 118 A4
Brookfield Way
Heanor DE75 .... 182 A1
Tansley DE4 .... 143 C2
Brookfields Calver S32 .... 72 B1
Horsley DE56 .... 191 C4
Brookfields Dr DE21 .... 205 B2
Brookhill S43 .... 80 C2
Brookhill Ave NG16 ..... 160 B2
Brookhill Ind Est NG16 .. 160 B1
Brookhill La NG16 ...... 160 C3
Brookhill Leys Rd NG16 . 182 C1
Brookhill Rd NG16 ...... 160 B1
Brookhill St NG9 .... 223 B3
Brookhouse Ct
Hayfield SK22 .... 25 B2
Whaley Thorns NG20 ..... 101 A1
Brookhouse St DE24 .... 232 B3
Brookland Ave NG18 .... 268 A4
Brooklands SK17 .... 85 B4
Brooklands Ave
Chapel-en-le-F SK23 .... 47 B3
Heanor DE75 .... 181 C1
Wirksworth DE4 .... 165 C4
Brooklands Bank DE45 .. 109 C3
Brooklands Dr
Derby DE23 .... 231 B4
Glossop SK13 .... 17 A4
Brooklands Inf Sch
NG10 .... 236 B3
Brooklands Jun Sch
NG10 .... 236 B4
Brooklands Rd SK23 ...... 47 B3
Brookleton DE45 .... 125 B3
Brooklyn Dr S40 .... 95 B2
Brooklyn Pl S8 .... 43 A3
Brooklyn Rd S8 .... 43 A3
Brooks Hollow DE21 .... 205 B4
Brooks Rd S43 .... 78 A2
Brookside
Ashbourne DE6 .... 173 B1
Beeley DE4 .... 111 A2
Belper DE56 .... 178 C2
Bradwell S33 .... 51 A4
Burton u T DE15 .... 248 A3
Chapel-en-le-Frith SK23 .... 34 A1
Derby DE1 .... 267 A4
Eastwood NG16 .... 182 C2
Glossop SK13 .... 17 A4
New Mills SK22 .... 24 C4
Rolleston DE13 .... 240 A2
Brookside Ave NG19 .... 136 B3
Brookside Bar S40 .... 94 C1
Brookside Cl Derby DE1 . 218 C4
Glossop SK13 .... 9 C2
Long Eaton NG10 .... 236 A4
Repton DE65 .... 242 B1
Brookside Glen S40 .... 94 C1
Brookside Gr SK17 .... 84 B3
Brookside Ind Unit NG9 . 223 B3
Brookside Rd
Breadsall DE21 .... 205 C2
Chapel-en-le-F SK23 .... 47 A3
Brookside Specl Sch
DE21 .... 205 C2
Brookside Way NG17 .... 148 C1
Brookvale Ave
Codnor DE5 .... 181 A4
Denby DE5 .... 180 A1
Brookvale Rd DE5 .... 180 A1
Brookvale Rise DE5 ..... 180 A1
Brookview Ct S18 .... 57 A2
Broom Ave Pilsley S45 ... 132 B1
Swanwick DE55 .... 169 C4
Broom Cl Belper DE56 ... 178 C3
Chesterfield S41 .... 95 B4
Derby, Chellaston DE73 ... 232 C1
Derby, Sinfin DE73 ...... 231 C1
Duffield DE56 .... 190 B2
Broom Dr S42 .... 115 C1
Broom Gdns S43 .... 96 C4
Broom La DE6 .... 175 C4
Broom's La DE6 .... 226 A1
Broombank Pk S41 .... 76 B2
Broombank Rd S41 .... 76 B2
Broome Acre DE55 ...... 160 B2
Broomfield Ave S41 ..... 115 B4
Broomfield Cl 6 NG10 ... 223 A3
Broomhill Ave DE7 ...... 209 A3
Broomhill Cl Derby DE3 .. 217 B2
Eckington S21 .... 59 A2
Broomhill Fst Sch NG19 . 268 A4
Broomhill La NG19 ...... 268 A4
Broomhill Rd S41 .... 76 C1
Broomhills La DE65 ..... 242 B1
Broomyclose La ST14 ... 210 A2
Brosscroft SK13 .... 10 A3
Brosscroft Village SK13 ... 10 A3
Brough La S33 .... 51 B4
Brough Rd DE15 .... 248 B2
Brough St DE22 .... 218 B3
Brougham Ave NG19 .... 135 B1
Broughton Ave DE23 .... 218 B1
Broughton Cl
Church Broughton DE65 ... 227 A4
Ilkeston DE7 .... 194 B1
Broughton Rd S41 .... 95 B4
Brow Cres S20 .... 59 C4
Brown Ave NG19 .... 136 A2
Brown Edge Rd SK17 ..... 66 B1
Brown Hills La S10 .... 42 B4
Brown La Ashover S45 ... 145 A4
Barton in F NG11 .... 237 C3
Dronfield S18 .... 57 B2
Flash SK17 .... 103 A2
Brown St NG19 .... 268 A4
Brown's Flats NG16 ..... 195 C3
Brown's La DE56 .... 191 B4
Brown's Rd NG10 .... 236 C4
Brown's Yd DE55 .... 170 B4
Brownhill La HD9 .... 3 A4
Brownhills La S42 .... 130 B2
Browning Cir DE23 ...... 231 C4
Browning Rd DE11 ...... 256 B3
Browning St Derby DE23 . 231 C4
3 Mansfield NG18 .... 268 B4
Stafford ST16 .... 269 A4
Brownlow Rd NG19 ..... 135 C1
Broxtowe Ave NG16 ..... 195 B3
Broxtowe Dr NG18 ...... 268 C3
Brun La DE6,DE22 .... 217 A4
Brunnen The DE55 ...... 160 A2
Brunner Ave NG20 ...... 119 C2
Brunswick Dr NG9 ...... 223 C3
Brunswick St
Chesterfield S41 .... 266 B4
Derby DE23 .... 231 C4
Pilsley S45 .... 132 B1
Brunswick Terr ST16 .... 269 A3
Brunswood Cl DE21 ..... 220 C3
Brunswood La DE6 ...... 187 B4
Brunswood Rd DE4 ..... 143 A1
Brunt St NG18 .... 268 C3
Brunton Cl DE3 .... 217 B1
Brunts Comp Sch NG19 . 136 B1
Brushes Rd SK15 .... 4 A2
Brushfield Gr S12 .... 44 B2
Brushfield Rd S40,S42 .... 94 C3
Brussels Terr 1 DE7 .... 194 C1
Bryant La DE55 .... 160 A2
Bryn Lea S41 .... 96 B1
Brynsmoor Rd NG16 .... 182 C4
Bryony DE14 .... 254 A4
Bryony Cl Derby DE21 ... 206 A1
Killamarsh S21 .... 60 A3
Bryony Way NG19 ...... 136 C2
Bubnell Rd DE45 .... 91 B3
Buchan St DE24 .... 232 B4
Buchanan St DE1 .... 267 B4
Buck Wood View S12 ..... 43 B3
Buckden Cl S40 .... 95 B2
Buckfast Cl DE55 .... 169 C4
Buckford La DE65,DE73 . 242 C4
Buckhazels La DE6,DE22 . 203 A4
Buckingham Ave DE21 .. 219 B4
Buckingham Cl
22 Dronfield S18 .... 56 B1
Mansfield Woodhouse
NG19 .... 136 C3
Swanwick DE55 .... 170 A4
Buckingham Ct
Burton u T DE15 .... 248 B2
Sandiacre NG10 .... 223 A2
Buckingham Dr DE75 ... 181 B1
Buckingham Ho DE24 ... 219 B1
Buckingham Rd NG10 ... 223 A2
Buckland Cl DE1 .... 218 C3
Buckland Gr SK14 .... 15 A4
Buckleather La S18 .... 74 B1
Buckley Cl DE11 .... 256 C1
Buckminster Cl DE21 ... 205 C1
Buckminster Rd DE7 .... 208 B2
Bull Farm Fst & Mid Sch
NG19 .... 135 B1
Bull Hill ST16 .... 269 B4
Bull La DE4 .... 143 B3
Bull Mews Cotts DE4 ... 143 B3
Bullace Ct NG19 .... 136 C1
Bullbridge Hill DE56 .... 168 A3
Buller St Derby DE23 .... 218 C1
Ilkeston DE7 .... 209 A3
Bullhill La DE56 .... 176 C2
Bullhurst La DE6 .... 188 C2
Bulling La DE4 .... 156 C1
Bullivant Ave S80 .... 100 B4
Bullivant St NG3 .... 268 B2
Bullock Cl NG19 .... 136 A3
Bullock La Brailsford DE6 . 201 C4
Ironville NG16, DE55 ..... 170 C3
Bullpit La DE56 .... 205 A4
Bulls Mews Cotts DE4 ... 143 B3
Bullsmoor DE56 .... 179 B2
Bumpmill La DE55 .... 146 A1
Bun Alley DE45 .... 91 B2
Bungalows The
Chesterfield, Brampton S40 . 95 B2
Chesterfield, Hady S41 ... 266 C2
1 Chesterfield, Newbold
S41 .... 95 C4
Chesterfield, Whittington Moor
S41 .... 96 A4
Killamarsh S21 .... 60 B3
New Mills SK22 .... 24 B1
Stonebroom DE55 .... 146 C2
Bunker S Hill S21 .... 60 C3
Bunker's Hill S80 .... 62 B4
Bunting Cl
Chesterfield S42 .... 95 A1
Ilkeston DE7 .... 208 B3
Sheffield S8 .... 43 A1
Bunting Ho S41 .... 77 A2
Bunting Nook S8 .... 43 A1
Buntingbank Cl DE55 ... 159 C2
Buntingfield La S45 ..... 129 A4
Buntings Cl DE3 .... 218 A2
Bunyan Cres DE55 ...... 146 C2
Bunyan Green Rd NG16 . 171 B4
Burbage Cl Belper DE56 . 179 B3
25 Dronfield S18 .... 56 B1
Burbage Gr S12 .... 44 B3
Burbage Pl DE24 .... 232 C4
Burbage Prim Sch SK17 .. 84 C3
Burbage Rd S43 .... 97 B4
Burch Pl S32 .... 71 C3
Burcot Cl DE7 .... 207 C4
Burdekin Cl SK23 .... 47 B3
Burdett Way DE65 .... 242 B2
Burdock Cl DE21 .... 205 C1
Burgess Cl S41 .... 115 B4
Burghley Cl DE73 .... 232 C1
Burghley Way DE23 ..... 230 C3
Burke Dr DE55 .... 170 B4
Burkitt Dr S43 .... 79 A2
Burland Green La DE6 .. 189 A2
Burleigh Cres DE55 ..... 169 C4
Burleigh Dr DE22 .... 218 C4
Burleigh St 2 DE7 .... 194 C1
Burley Bank La HD7 .... 2 C4
Burley Cl S40 .... 115 A4
Burley Dr DE22 .... 204 C4
Burley Hill DE22, DE56 ... 205 A4
Burley La DE22 .... 204 C4
Burlington Ave NG20 .... 119 C3
Burlington Cl
Breaston DE72 .... 235 B4
Dore S17 .... 55 C4
Burlington Dr NG19 ..... 135 C1
Burlington Glen S17 ...... 55 C4
Burlington Gr S17 .... 55 C4
Burlington Rd
Buxton SK17 .... 85 A4
Derby DE22 .... 217 C3
Dore S17 .... 55 C4
Burlington St S40 .... 266 B3
Burlington Way DE3 .... 217 B1
Burlow Ave SK17 .... 85 B2
Burlow Rd SK17 .... 85 B1
Burnaby St DE24 .... 232 C4
Burnage Ct DE22 .... 218 C2
Burnaston Cl S18 .... 56 B1
Burnaston Ct NG19 ...... 136 C2
Burnaston La DE65 ...... 229 B3
Burnbridge Rd S41 .... 77 B2
Burncroft DE7 .... 207 C4
Burnell St S43 .... 96 C4
Burnett La DE4 .... 143 A4
Burney La DE73 .... 252 B1
Burnham Cl DE7 .... 207 B4
Burnham Dr DE3 .... 217 B1
Burnham Way NG2 ...... 268 B1
Burns Ave
Mansfield Woodhouse
NG19 .... 136 B1
Nottingham NG7 .... 268 A2
Burns Cl Chesterfield S40 . 114 C4
Derby DE23 .... 231 A4
Burns Dr Dronfield S18 .... 76 B4
Grassmoor S42 .... 115 C2
Burns St Ilkeston DE7 .... 208 C4
Mansfield NG18 .... 268 B4
Nottingham NG7 .... 268 A2
Burnshaw St DE55 .... 146 B3
Burnside Glossop SK13 ...... 9 C2
Rolleston DE13 .... 240 A2
Burnside Ave Sheffield S8 . 43 A3
Shirland DE55 .... 146 B1
Burnside Cl DE24 .... 231 B2
Burnside Dr Derby DE21 . 220 C2
Mansfield NG19 .... 135 C1
Burnside St DE24 .... 233 A4
Burnt House Rd DE75 ... 181 B1
Burnt Oaks Cl NG19 ..... 136 B2
Burr La DE7 .... 194 C1
Burre Cl DE45 .... 109 C3
Burrfields Rd SK23 .... 47 A3
Burrowfield Mews
DE21 .... 220 C1
Burrows Ct NG3 .....
Burrows La
Brailsford DE6 ....
Middleton (Nr Wirksworth)
DE4 ...
Burrows The DE11 .....
Burrs Wood Croft S41 ..
Bursdon Cl S41 .....
Burton Close Dr DE45 ..
Burton Edge DE45 .....
Burton Rd
Burton u T DE14 ....
Coton in t E DE12 ....
Derby DE23 ....
Findern DE65 ....
Linton DE11 ....
Overseal DE12 ....
Repton DE15,DE65 ....
Rosliston DE12 ....
Swadlincote DE11 ....
Tutbury DE13 ....
Willington DE65 ....
Burton St Heanor DE75 ..
Nottingham NG1 ....
Tutbury DE13 ....
Burton Tech Coll (Rolles
Campus) DE13 ....
Burwell Cl SK13 ....
Burwell Ct NG19 ....
Buscott Dr DE6 ....
Bush Vale DE56 ....
Bushey Wood Gr S17 ..
Bushey Wood Rd S17 ..
Bushton La DE13 ....
Bushy Cl NG10 ....
Buskeyfield La NG20 ...
Butcher's La DE4 ....
Bute St SK13 ....
Butler Cres NG19 ....
Butler St ST4 ....
Butler Way S21 ....
Butt Hill S80 ....
Butt Hill Cl S80 ....
Butt La Blackfordby DE11
Mansfield Woodhouse
NG19 ....
Butt St NG10 ....
Buttercup Ave DE12 ...
Butterfield Cres DE55 ..
Butterfield La DE55 ...
Butterhall Cl S80 ....
Butterley Croft Bsns Ctr
DE5 ....
Butterley Ct NG16 .....
Butterley Hill DE5 .....
Butterley La
Ashover DE4,S45 ....
Ripley DE5 ....
Butterley Sta DE5 ....
Buttermead Cl NG9 .....
Buttermere Cl
Chesterfield S41 ....
10 Long Eaton NG10 .....
Buttermere Dr
Derby DE22 ....
Dronfield S18 ....
Buttermilk La S44 .....
Butterpot La DE6 ....
Butterton Cl DE7 ....
Butterton Dr 6 S40 ....
Butterwick Cl DE23 .....
Buttonoak Dr DE73 .....
Butts Cl DE7 ....
Butts Dr DE4 ....
Butts Hill S17 ....
Butts Rd Ashover S45 ....
Bakewell DE45 ....
Darley Dale DE4 ....
Butts Terr DE45 ....
Butts The DE56 ....
Butts View DE45 ....
Buxton Ave DE75 ....
Buxton Cl
4 Gamesley SK13 ....
Swadlincote DE11 ....
Buxton Com Sch SK17 ...
Buxton Ct DE7 ....
Buxton Ctry Pk* SK17 ...
Buxton Dr Derby DE3 ....
Little Eaton DE21 ....
Buxton Gn DE75 ....
Buxton Hospl SK17 ....
Buxton Inf Sch SK17 .....
Buxton Jun Sch SK17 ....
Buxton Mews SK13 .....
Buxton Mus & Art Gal*
SK17 ....
Buxton New Rd SK11 ....
Buxton Old Rd SK12 .....
Buxton Rd
Alstonefield DE6 ....
Ashbourne DE6 ....
Ashford in t W DE45 .....
Bakewell DE45 ....
Chapel-en-le-F SK17,SK23
Chinley SK23 ....
Derby DE21 ....
Disley SK12 ....
Dove Holes SK17 ....
High Lane SK12 ....
Longnor SK17 ....
Mansfield NG19 ....
New Mills SK22,SK23 .....
Tideswell SK17 ....
Whaley Bridge SK23 .....
Whaley Bridge, New Horwich
SK23 ....
Buxton Rd W SK12 .....

...n Sta SK17 .....85 A4
...n Terr SK14 .....9 B3
...orth Prim Sch SK13 34 A1
...La NG1 .....268 B1
...ell CI DE21 .....206 A1
...burn Ave DE23 .....231 C4
...t Ave Alfreton DE55 .159 A2
...d W DE15 .....254 C4
...Eaton NG10 .....223 A3
...field Woodhouse
..... .136 B1
...CI Dronfield S18 ..76 B4
...ead Rd S42 .....115 C2
...Cres NG16 .....195 B2
...Ct NG9 .....209 C1
...dle Gr DE55 .....146 C2
...a Rd
...field S40 .....115 A4
...llincote DE11 .....256 A4
...t Buxton SK17 .....85 B3
...erfield S40 .....95 B3
...r DE23 .....218 C1
...del CI DE7 .....194 C1
...field NG18 .....268 B4
...brook NG20 .....119 C2
...and DE55 .....146 B1
...l La DE56 .....179 C1

...ehill La DE6 .....184 B1
...by Ct DE55 .....170 B3
...with Dr DE22 .....204 C2
...y Hill Rd DE11 ...255 C1
...an CI S20 .....59 B3
...an Rd S12 .....44 B3
...an St S20 .....59 B3
...ell CI DE24 .....233 B3
...hays Ct DE24 .....231 B2
...narton CI DE55 ...170 A4
...narvon CI
...chesterfield S40 .....95 B1
...t DE21 .....220 C3
...narvon Rd S18 ....76 A4
...ar St DE1 .....219 A4
...l S3 .....77 B2
...gorm CI S43 .....77 B2
...agorm Dr DE24 ...231 B2
...as CI Burton u T DE15
...ch S21 .....217 C2
...as St NG1 .....268 B2
...ismore CI ⑩ NG10 ..223 A1
...ne Terr SK23 .....45 C4
...er CI Derby DE22 ...204 C2
...t DE55 .....160 A3
...erdale Dr NG10 ...236 A3
...ermill Dr DE21 ....206 A1
...er Rd S18 .....76 A4
...sdale CI SK17 .....85 A3
...Croft S80 .....82 A3
...ary Cres DE15 ....248 B2
...ornia Gdns DE22 .218 B2
...ornia La S43 .....80 A4
...e Abbey* LE65 ...251 B1
...la Ave NG17 .....148 C1
...ia Rise DE55 .....169 C1
...dline La
...sley Woodhouse DE7 .192 B3
...B56 .....177 B3
...adine Rd DE75 ...257 A1
...an's La LE65 .....258 B4
...ew Dr S14 .....43 B3
...ew Hill Way DE23 .231 A4
...ow La DE46 .....165 B3
...ow Mount S14 ....43 B3
...ow S14 .....43 B3
...ow Rd S14 .....43 B3
...white La S18 .....57 B1
...ew Brook Dr S41 ..115 C4
...w CE Prim Sch S44 ..96 C2
...ow S13 .....9 C1
...ow Gn ⑩ SK13 .....9 C1
...ow La Calow S41,S44 ..96 C1
...sterfield S41 .....115 C4
...ow La Ind Est S41 .115 C4
...ow DE45 .....109 B3
...er Ave S42 .....132 A4
...er CI Belper DE56 ..179 A3
...by DE21 .....205 C2
...er Cres S43 .....97 B4
...er Fold ❹ SK13 .....9 B1
...er Mews S43 .....97 B4
...er Mill S32 .....72 B1
...er PI ❺ SK13 .....9 B1
...ter St DE7 .....194 C1
...ter St NG19 .....136 C2
...ter St DE7 .....267 C2
...erton CI DE24 ....232 C2
...rn CI DE24 .....233 A3
...berwell Ave DE22 .218 A3
...borne CI DE21 ....205 C1
...bria Rd NG17 .....135 B2
...brian CI ❼ S40 .....95 B3
...brian Way DE11 ...256 A2
...bridge Cres
...miley-Vale S44 ....117 C1
...pleford NG9 .....209 B1
...bridge Rd
...Brimington S43 .....96 C4
...ffield S18 .....43 A3
...bridge St
...ckwell DE55 .....147 C1
... Rose Hill DE23 .219 A1
...by, Sandiacre NG10 ..223 C2
...gham NG18 .....268 B3

Cambridge St continued
Stafford ST16 .....269 C4
Camdale Rise S12 .....44 C1
Camdale View S12 .....44 C1
Camden CI NG2 .....268 C1
Camden St DE22 .....218 B2
Camellia CI DE3 .....217 B2
Camellia CI ❷ DE13 .240 C1
Cameron Rd DE23 ...248 A1
Cameron CI S21 .....248 A1
Camerory Way S43 ...77 B3
Camms CI S21 .....59 B2
Camms Endowed CE Prim
Sch S21 .....59 B2
Camp St DE1 .....219 A4
Camp Wood CI DE21 ..205 B4
Campbell CI S43 .....77 B2
Campbell Dr S43 .....78 A2
Campbell Dr DE24 ...268 B2
Campbell Rd ❿ NG3 .268 B2
Campbell Rd DE7 .....269 B2
Campbell St ST4 .....269 B2
Campbell Rd Belper DE56 178 C2
Derby DE21 .....232 B4
Langley Mill NG16 .....182 B2
Campion NG18 .....268 B2
Campion CI NG20 .....119 B2
Campion Hill DE74 ...247 A2
Campion Rd DE11 ....256 C2
Campion St DE22 .....218 B3
Campsie Ct ❻ DE24 .231 B2
Canada St
Canal Bank DE72 .....235 A1
Canal Br S21 .....60 B3
Canal Bridge DE65 ...242 A3
Canal Mus NG1 .....268 B1
Canal Side SK23 .....33 C1
Canal St Derby DE1 ..267 B2
Ilkeston DE7 .....195 A1
Long Eaton NG10 ....223 B1
Marple SK6 .....23 A3
Nottingham NG1 .....268 B1
Sandiacre NG10 .....223 B3
Whaley Bridge SK23 ....45 C4
Canal Wharf S41 .....96 A3
Canberra CI Derby DE3 .217 C1
Stapleford NG9 .....209 C1
Canberra Dr ST16 ...269 C4
Candlemass CI S41 ..136 B1
Cannell CI S45 .....131 A2
Canner CI DE21 .....257 A1
Canning Cir NG7 .....268 A2
Canning Terr ⓯ NG7 ..268 A2
Cannock Way NG10 ...237 A4
Cannon Fields S32 ....52 C4
Cannon St SK14 .....9 B3
Canon CI DE7 .....194 C3
Canon's Wlk DE22 ...204 C1
Cantelupe Rd DE7 ...209 A4
Canterbury CI
Duffield DE56 .....190 C2
Mansfield Woodhouse
..... .136 B3
Canterbury CI ❶ NG1 .268 A2
Canterbury Rd
Burton u T DE15 .....248 B2
Sheffield S8 .....43 A3
Wirksworth DE4 .....165 C4
Canterbury Terr DE21 .219 C4
Cantley CI DE24 .....232 B2
Cantley CI DE24 .....170 B3
Cape St NG18 .....268 A4
Capel Rise S43 .....96 B4
Capthorne CI S40 .....94 C3
Car Rd S18 .....74 A3
Car Vale Dr S13 .....44 B4
Car Vale View S13 ....44 B4
Caraway Dr DE14 ....254 A4
Cardale Rd NG19 .....135 B2
Cardales CI DE65 ....230 B1
Cardean CI DE1 .....219 A4
Carder Dr S43 .....121 A3
Cardiff St NG3 .....268 B4
Cardigan St DE21 ...205 C1
Cardinal CI Derby DE21 ..205 C1
Nottingham NG3 .....268 C2
Cardlemere La SK17 .138 C1
Cardrona Ct DE21 ...205 C1
Cardwell Ave S13 ....44 C4
Cardwell Dr S13 .....44 C4
Carfield Ave S8 .....43 A3
Carfield La S8 .....43 B3
Carfield PI S8 .....43 A3
Carfield Prim Sch S8 ..43 A3
Carisbrooke Dr ⓭ DE24 .231 C1
Carisbrooke Gdns DE23 231 B3
Carl Moult Ho DE11 ..256 A1
Carlin CI DE7 .....235 C4
Carlin St S13 .....44 C3
Carlisle Ave DE23 ...231 A4
Carlisle CI S41 .....76 C2
Carlisle Gr SK17 .....85 A4
Carlisle Rd SK17 .....84 C4
Northwood DE4 .....127 A3
Carlton CI Clay Cross S45 .131 B1
Heanor DE75 .....182 A2
Mosborough S20 .....59 B3
Carlton Dr DE24 .....232 C2
Carlton Gdns DE24 ..232 C2
Carlton Mews S2 .....43 C4
Carlton Rd
Chesterfield S40 .....115 A3
Derby DE23 .....218 C3
Long Eaton NG10 ....236 A3
Nottingham NG3,NG3 .268 C2
Stoke-on-T ST4 .....269 C2

Carlton St
Mansfield Woodhouse
..... .136 B1
Nottingham NG1 .....268 B1
Carlyle Inf Sch DE23 ..231 A4
Carlyle PI DE75 .....181 B2
Carlyle Rd DE75 .....146 C2
Carlyle St Derby DE24 ..231 C3
Heanor DE75 .....181 B2
Carlyon Gdns S40 ...114 C4
Carnarvon Rd NG17 .148 C1
Carnegie St DE23 ....232 A4
Carnfield Hall* DE55 .159 B3
Carnfield Hill DE55 ..159 B3
Carnforth CI Derby DE24 160 B4
Stapleford NG9 .....223 B3
Carnival Way DE74 ..247 A2
Carnoustie Ave S40 ..114 B4
Carnoustie CI DE3 ...217 C1
Carol Cres DE21 .....206 A1
Caroline CI DE24 .....233 B4
Caroline Ct Hope S33 ..38 C2
Ilkeston DE7 .....209 A3
Carpenter Ave
Mansfield Woodhouse
..... .135 B1
Mastin Moor S43 .....79 A2
Carpenter CI DE15 ...248 B1
Carpenter Croft S12 ..44 B3
Carpenter Gdns S12 ..44 B3
Carpenter Mews S12 ..44 B3
Carper La DE6 .....187 C1
Carr Bank SK13 .....17 C4
Carr Brow S16 .....32 A4
Carr CI DE55 .....160 A4
Carr Fields DE7 .....192 B4
Carr La Brackenfield DE55 158 C3
Dronfield S18 .....56 B1
Matlock DE4 .....143 C1
Scarcliffe S44 .....117 C4
South Normanton DE55 .160 A4
Thornhill S33 .....39 C3
Carr Lane Mews S18 ..56 B1
Carr Vale Rd S44 .....98 C1
Carrbrook Ind Est SK15 ..4 A3
Carrfield Ave S8 .....43 A3
Carrfield CI ⓭ S8 .....43 A3
Carrfield Dr S8 .....43 A3
Carrfield PI S8 .....43 A3
Carrfield Rd S8 .....43 A3
Carrfield St S8 .....43 A3
Carrhouse La S14 .....9 B2
Carriage Dr The S43 ..9 C3
Carriers Mdw S23 .....47 A4
Carriers Rd DE65 ....241 B3
Carrington Ct Ind Est
DE1 .....218 C3
Carrington St Derby DE1 267 C2
Nottingham NG1 .....268 B1
Carrock Ave DE75 ...182 A1
Carr La DE24 .....231 C2
Carsington & Hopton CE
Prim Sch DE4 .....164 C4
Carsington CI S40 .....95 A3
Carsington Cres DE22 204 B3
Carsington CI NG19 ..136 C2
Carsington Mews DE22 204 C1
Carsington Water Visitor
Ctr* DE6 .....164 B2
Carson Croft DE4 ....143 B3
Carson Mount S12 ....44 A2
Carson Rd S12 .....220 A3
Carson Way ST16 ....269 A4
Cart Rd DE55 .....157 C2
Carter CI DE24 .....170 A3
Carter La
Market Warsop NG20 .120 B2
Shirebrook NG20 .....119 C2
Carter La E DE55 .....160 B3
Carter La W
Shirebrook NG20 .....119 B2
South Normanton DE55 .160 B3
Carter PI S8 .....43 A3
Carter St S8 .....43 A3
Carterhall La S12 .....44 B1
Carterhall Rd S12 ....44 A1
Cartledge La S18 .....75 A4
Cartmel CI S18 .....56 C1
Cartmel Cres S41 .....95 C4
Cartworth Moor Rd HD9 ..3 A1
Cartwright La DE55 ..160 C4
Cartwright St S81 ....63 C4
Carver CI S20 .....59 C2
Carver Way S16 .....61 C3
Cary Rd Eckington S21 ..59 A2
Sheffield S12 .....44 B3
Cascade Gr DE23 ....231 A4
Cascon CI DE23 .....230 A3
Casson Dr S26 .....61 C4
Casson St NG16 .....170 C2
Castings Rd DE23 ....232 A4
Castle Bvd NG7 .....268 A1
Castle CI Bakewell DE45 109 C2
Borrowash DE72 .....221 B1
Castle Croft DE4 .....233 B3
Castle Ct Elvaston DE72 .234 A3
Tutbury DE13 .....239 B4
Castle Donington Com Coll
DE74 .....247 A2
Castle Dr Bakewell DE45 109 C4
Codnor NG16 .....181 C4
Somercotes DE55 ....170 B4

Castle Edge Rd SK22 ..24 A1
Castle Gate NG1 .....268 B1
Castle Gn S44 .....118 A4
Castle Gr NG7 .....268 A1
Castle Gresley Inf Sch
DE11 .....261 C4
Castle Hayes La DE13 .239 A3
Castle Hill
Castle Donington DE74
Duffield DE56 .....190 C2
Eckington S21 .....59 B2
Findern DE65 .....230 B1
Glossop SK13 .....10 C1
Tutbury DE13 .....239 A4
Castle Hill CI S21 .....59 B2
Castle Ho DE1 .....267 D2
Castle Ind Est S44 .....98 C1
Castle La Bolsover S44 ..99 A1
Ironville NG16 .....170 C1
Melbourne DE73 .....252 A4
Castle Meadow Rd NG2 .268 A1
Castle Mews
Mansfield Woodhouse
..... .136 A2
Castle Mews The ❺
DE11 .....256 A4
Castle Mills DE73 ...252 A4
Castle Mount Cres
DE45 .....109 B4
Castle Mount Way DE45 .109 C4
Castle Mus & Art Gall
NG1 .....268 A1
Castle Orch DE56 ...190 C2
Castle Pk NG1 .....268 A1
Castle Quay NG1 ....268 A1
Castle Rd
Nottingham NG1 .....268 B1
Swadlincote DE11 ...255 C1
Castle Row S17 .....56 A3
Castle St Bakewell DE45 109 C2
Bolsover S44 .....99 A1
Castleton S33 .....38 A1
Derby DE1 .....267 C2
Glossop SK13 .....10 C1
Mansfield NG18 .....268 B4
Mansfield Woodhouse
..... .136 A2
Melbourne DE73 .....252 A4
Nottingham NG2 .....268 B1
Stafford ST16 .....269 A4
Tutbury DE13 .....239 B3
Castle View
Aldercar NG16 .....182 A2
Duffield DE56 .....190 C2
Eckington S21 .....59 B2
Mansfield NG18 .....268 B4
Castle View Dr DE4 ..155 B3
Castle View Prim Sch
DE4 .....143 B3
Castle Way S20 .....59 B3
Castle Way The DE65 .241 C3
Castlebeck Ave S2 ...44 B4
Castlebeck Dr S2 .....44 B4
Castlecraig Croft S2 ..44 B4
Castledale Croft S2 ..44 A4
Castledale Gr S2 .....44 A4
Castledale PI S2 .....44 A4
Castledene Dr ST16 ..269 A3
Castlefields
Ironville NG16 .....170 C2
Stafford ST16 .....269 A3
Castlefields Main Ctr
..... .267 C2
Castlegate La S17 ....89 B3
Castlerigg Way ❽ S18 ..56 C1
Castlerow CI S17 .....56 A3
Castlerow Dr S17 ....56 A3
Castleton Ave
Derby DE23 .....231 C4
Ilkeston DE7 .....194 C3
Somercotes DE55 ....170 B3
Castleton Bank ❿ SK13 ..9 C1
Castleton CE Prim Sch
S33 .....38 B1
Castleton CI Derby DE21 .136 B2
Castleton Cres SK13 ..9 C1
Castleton Gr
❿ Gamesley SK13 .....9 C1
Staveley S43 .....97 A3
Castleton Terr ㉑ SK13 ..9 C1
Castleton Tourist Information
Ctr* S33 .....38 A1
Castleton YH* S33 ....38 A1
Cat & Fiddle La DE7 .207 C3
Cat La S14 .....43 B3
Catchford View S40 ..95 A4
Catcliff CI DE45 .....109 B2
Catcliff Cotts DE45 ..109 B3
Cathedral of All Saints*
DE1 .....267 B4
Cathedral Rd DE22 ..218 B4
Cathedral View DE22 .218 B1
Catherine Ave
Ilkeston DE7 .....208 C3
Mansfield Woodhouse
..... .136 B2
Catherine CI
Ashbourne DE6 .....173 A1
Chesterfield S40 .....95 C2
Catherine McAuley Ho
DE22 .....204 C1

Catherine St
Alfreton DE55 .....159 B2
Chesterfield S40 .....95 C2
Derby DE23 .....219 A1
Catkin Dr NG16 .....195 B4
Cator Rd NG19 .....135 B2
Catterick Dr DE3 .....217 B1
Catterwood Dr S46 ....15 A1
Catton La DE12 .....260 A3
Caudwell's Mill & Working
Craft Ctr* DE4 .....126 C4
Cauldwell CI S42 .....131 B4
Cauldon Dr S40 .....95 A3
Cauldwell Rd DE12 ..261 A3
Caunton CI NG18 ....268 A3
Causeway DE22 .....204 C1
Causeway Gdns S17 ..55 B4
Causeway Glade S17 ..55 B4
Causeway Head Rd S17 .55 B4
Causeway La DE4 ....143 B3
Causeway The
Ashover S45 .....129 B2
Eyam S32 .....55 B4
Eyam S32 .....71 C3
Wirksworth DE4 .....165 C4
Cavan Dr DE21 .....220 A2
Cavell Dr S45 .....131 C1
Cavendish Ave
Buxton SK17 .....84 C3
Derby DE22 .....204 C4
Dore S17 .....55 C4
Cavendish Cir SK17 ..85 A4
Cavendish CI
Castle Donington DE74 .247 A1
Creswell S80 .....81 B1
Doveridge DE6 .....211 B1
Duffield DE56 .....190 B1
Holmewood S42 .....116 C1
Shardlow DE72 .....235 A1
⓭ Swadlincote DE11 ..255 C1
Cavendish Close Inf & Jun
Schs DE21 .....220 A4
Cavendish Cotts DE4 .154 C1
Cavendish Cres NG9 .209 B1
Cavendish Cres N NG7 .268 A1
Cavendish Cres S NG7 .268 A1
Cavendish Ct
Chesterfield S41 .....96 A3
Derby DE1 .....267 A4
Shardlow DE72 .....235 A1
Cavendish Dr
Ashbourne DE6 .....185 B4
Clowne S44 .....81 A2
Ripley DE5 .....169 B1
Cavendish Flats S45 .110 C3
Cavendish Hospl The
SK17 .....85 C4
Cavendish Jun Sch S41 .95 C4
Cavendish PI S43 .....78 A2
Cavendish Rd
Bolsover S44 .....99 A1
Ilkeston DE7 .....208 C3
Long Eaton NG10 ....223 B1
Matlock DE4 .....143 B4
Cavendish Rd E ❷ NG1 .268 A1
Cavendish Rd W NG7 .268 A1
Cavendish Rise S18 ..75 C4
Cavendish Sq S21 ...77 B4
Cavendish St
Chesterfield S40 .....266 B3
Derby DE1 .....267 A3
Langwith NG18 .....119 C3
Mansfield NG18 .....268 C2
Mansfield Woodhouse
..... .136 A2
Staveley S43 .....97 B4
Cavendish St N S41 ...77 A1
Cavendish Way DE23 .217 C1
Caversfield CI DE23 .231 A4
Caversham Way DE7 .207 B4
Cavill Rd S8 .....43 A2
Cawdor Rd S2 .....43 C3
Caxton CI S43 .....77 B2
Caxton St
Derby, Littleover DE23 .231 C3
Derby, Normanton DE23 .231 C4
Caythorpe Ct NG19 ..136 C2
Ceal The SK6 .....15 A1
Cecil Ave S18 .....57 A1
Cecil Rd Dronfield S18 ..57 A1
Swadlincote DE11 ....255 C3
Cedar Ave Alfreton DE55 .159 A2
Chesterfield S40 .....95 B3
Long Eaton NG10 ....236 B3
Mansfield Woodhouse
..... .136 B3
Ripley DE5 .....169 B1
Cedar CI Ashbourne DE6 .185 B4
Derby DE22 .....218 A4
Glapwell S44 .....118 A1
Glossop SK13 .....10 A1
Killamarsh S21 .....60 B3
Sandiacre NG10 .....223 A4
Cedar Croft
Aston-on-T DE72 .....246 A4
Kilburn DE56 .....192 A4
Cedar Dr Ockbrook DE72 221 B2
Selston NG16 .....171 C4
Uttoxeter ST14 .....210 A2
Cedar Gr Belper DE56 .179 A1
Linton DE12 .....261 B3
South Normanton DE55 .160 A2
Swadlincote DE11 ....256 A4
Cedar Park Dr S44 ....99 B3

Cedar Pk DE7 ....208 C4
Cedar Rd
Castle Donington DE74 .247 A1
Linton DE11 ....261 C4
Cedar St Brimington S43 ..78 A1
Derby DE22 ....218 C4
Mansfield NG18 ....268 C3
Shirland DE55 ....146 B3
Cedarwood Ct DE21 ...205 C1
Celandine Cl DE21 .....206 A1
Celandine Ct 11 S17 ....56 A3
Celandine Gdns S17 .....56 A3
Celandine Pl DE11 .....256 C2
Celanese Rd DE21 .....220 B2
Cemetery La Ripley DE5 .169 C1
Staveley S43 ....78 C1
Wirksworth DE4 ....154 C1
Cemetery Rd
Belper DE56 ....179 A3
Chesterfield S41 ....96 B1
Clay Cross S45 ....131 C1
Dronfield S18 ....76 A4
Glossop SK13 ....10 B2
Somercotes DE55 ....170 B4
Stapleford NG9 ....223 C4
Cemetery Terr S43 ......96 C4
Central Ave
Borrowash DE72 ....221 A1
Chesterfield S40 ....95 C1
Creswell S80 ....100 B4
Mansfield NG18 ....268 C3
Sandiacre NG10 ....223 A3
South Normanton DE55 .160 A3
Stapleford NG9 ....223 C4
Central Cl
Shirebrook NG20 ....119 C2
Unstone S18 ....76 C3
Central Dr
Blackwell DE55 ....147 C1
Buxton SK17 ....85 B3
Calow S44 ....96 C2
Chesterfield S41 ....96 B1
Shirebrook NG20 ....119 C2
Wingerworth S42 ....96 C2
Central Pavement S40 .266 B3
Central Rd S25 ....159 A2
Central St Chesterfield S41 ..96 B1
Holmewood S42 ....132 C4
Nottingham NG3 ....268 C2
Central Wlk S43 ....96 B4
Centre Cl DE7 ....267 C1
Centre St S44 ....117 B1
Centurion Wlk DE7 .....219 A4
Chaddesden La S21 ....220 A3
Chaddesden La Inf DE21 ..220 A3
Chaddesden Lane End
DE21 ....219 C3
Chaddesden Park Inf & Jun
Schs DE21 ....219 C4
Chaddesden Park Rd
DE21 ....219 C4
Chadfield Rd DE56 .....190 C3
Chadwick Ave DE24 ....232 C3
Chadwick Hill DE4 ......141 A3
Chadwick Nick La DE4 ..167 C4
Chadwick Rd S13 ....44 B4
Chadwick St SK13 ....17 A4
Chaffinch Cl DE21 .....220 C3
Chain La DE3 ....218 A1
Chalfont Sq DE21 ......206 A1
Chalkley Cl DE24 ......232 C2
Challands Cl S41 ....115 B4
Challands Way S41 .....115 B4
Challis Ave DE21 ....220 A4
Challoner Gn 11 S20 ....59 C4
Challoner Way S20 ......59 C4
Chalons Cl DE7 ....194 C1
Chalons Way DE7 ......208 C4
Chamberlain Ave ST4 ..269 B1
Chambers Dr DE7 ....209 A4
Chambers Ct SK14 ......9 A2
Chambers St DE24 ......219 C1
Champion Ave DE7 .....194 B2
Champion Cres NG19 ...268 A4
Champion Dr S21 ....60 B3
Champion Hill DE56 ....190 C2
Chancel Pl DE22 ....267 A1
Chancery La DE22 ......218 A3
Chancet Wood Cl S8 ...56 C4
Chancet Wood Dr S8 ...56 C4
Chancet Wood Rise S8 .56 C4
Chancet Wood View S8 .56 C4
Chander Hill La S42 ....113 B4
Chandlers Ford DE21 ...205 C1
Chandos Cres S21 ......60 B3
Chandos Pole St DE22 .218 B3
Chandres Ct DE22 ......204 C2
Chaneyfield Way S40 ...95 A4
Channel The DE4 ....173 A1
Chantrey Ave S41 ......96 A3
Chantrey Rd S8 ....43 A2
Chantry Cl Derby DE3 ..217 B1
Disley SK12 ....32 C3
Long Eaton NG10 ....236 A2
Chantry Fold SK12 .....32 C2
Chantry La SK12 ....32 C2
Chantry Rd SK12 ....32 C3
Chapel Bar NG1 ....268 A1
Chapel Brow
Broadbottom SK13 ....16 C3
Glossop SK13 ....10 A4
Chapel Cl Clowne S43 ..80 C2

Chapel Cl continued
Moira DE11 ....256 B1
Willington DE65 ....242 A3
Youlgreave DE45 ....125 A3
Chapel Croft Elton DE4 .140 C3
Middleton (Nr Wirksworth)
DE4 ....154 B3
Chapel Ct DE7 ....194 C1
Chapel Gn DE6 ....224 B4
Chapel Hill Ashover S45 .129 C2
Beeley DE4 ....111 A2
Cromford DE4 ....155 A4
Chapel Ho 3 DE7 ....194 C1
Chapel Houses SK6 .....23 A3
Chapel Inf Sch SK23 ....47 A3
Chapel La
Apperknowle S18 ....58 A1
Bakewell DE45 ....109 B3
Barrow u T DE73 ....244 A3
Boylestone DE6 ....213 A2
Church Broughton DE65 .227 A4
Clifton DE6 ....184 C3
Crich DE4 ....168 A4
Derby DE73 ....233 A1
Derby, Chaddesden DE21 .220 A4
Derby, Spondon DE21 ...220 C3
Glossop SK13 ....9 C2
Hanbury DE13 ....238 A1
Holloway DE4 ....156 A3
Middleton (Nr Wirksworth)
DE4 ....154 B3
Rolleston DE13 ....240 A2
Taddington SK17 ....88 A2
Tissington DE6 ....162 A3
Totley S17 ....55 B2
Wirksworth DE4 ....154 C1
Chapel La E S41 ....115 B4
Chapel La W S40 ....95 B1
Chapel Pl NG16 ....195 C3
Chapel Rd Bolsover S44 ..98 C1
Grassmoor S42 ....115 C2
Hayfield SK22 ....25 B1
Selston NG16 ....171 C3
Whaley Bridge SK23 .....45 C3
Chapel Row
Borrowash DE72 ....221 A1
Crich DE4 ....168 A4
Chapel Side DE21 ......220 C3
Chapel St Alfreton DE55 .159 A2
Belper DE56 ....178 C2
Brimington S43 ....96 C4
Buxton SK17 ....85 A4
Chesterfield S41 ....96 A4
Coton in t E DE12 ....260 B2
Derby DE1 ....267 B4
Derby, Spondon DE21 ...220 C3
Donisthorpe DE12 ......265 C4
Duffield DE56 ....190 C2
Eastwood NG16 ....182 C1
Fritchley DE56 ....168 A3
Glossop SK13 ....10 B1
Hayfield SK22 ....25 A1
Heanor DE75 ....194 A4
Holbrook DE56 ....191 B4
17 Ilkeston DE7 ....194 C1
Kilburn DE56 ....192 A4
Kimberley NG16 ....195 C3
Linton DE11 ....261 C4
Long Eaton NG10 ....236 C4
Longnor SK17 ....121 A3
Melbourne DE73 ....252 A4
Monyash DE45 ....107 A1
Mosborough S20 ....59 B3
New Mills SK22 ....33 A3
New Mills, Rowarth SK22 .24 C4
Ripley DE5 ....169 B1
Smisby LE65 ....257 C2
Somercotes DE55 ....170 B4
Stafford ST16 ....269 B4
Stonebroom DE55 ......147 A2
Stretton en le F DE12 ...265 C3
Swadlincote, Church Gresley
DE11 ....256 A1
Swadlincote, Newhall
DE11 ....255 C3
Swanwick DE55 ....169 C4
Ticknall DE73 ....251 A3
Whaley Bridge SK23 .....45 C4
Whaley Thorns NG20 ...101 A2
Woodville DE11 ....256 C1
Chapel Terr ST16 ......269 B4
Chapel Way S42 ....115 B1
Chapel Wlk
Alfreton DE55 ....159 A2
Curbar S32 ....72 C2
Chapel Yd Dronfield S18 .57 A1
Harthill S26 ....61 C3
South Wingfield DE55 ...157 C2
Chapel-en-le-Frith CE Inf
Sch SK23 ....47 B3
Chapel-en-le-Frith High Sch
SK23 ....47 A3
Chapel-en-le-Frith Sta
SK23 ....47 A2
Chapman Ave DE24 ....233 A3
Chapman La S42 ....115 C2
Chapmans Croft DE12 .260 B2
Chapter Cl DE21 ....205 B1
Chardin Ave SK6 ....23 B4
Charing Ct DE1 ....267 C5
Charingworth Rd DE21 .206 A2
Chariot Cl DE24 ....233 B3
Charity Rd DE55 ....170 B3
Charlbury Cl DE23 .....231 A4
Charles Ashmore Rd S8 .57 A4
Charles Ave Derby DE21 .220 B3
Sandiacre NG10 ....223 A3
Stapleford NG9 ....223 C4

Charles Cl DE7 ....209 A3
Charles La SK13 ....10 C2
Charles St Alfreton DE55 .159 A3
4 Buxton SK17 ....85 B4
Chesterfield S40 ....95 C2
Glossop SK13 ....10 B1
Long Eaton NG10 ....236 B3
Mansfield NG19 ....136 A1
Mansfield Woodhouse
NG19 ....136 B2
Somercotes DE55 ....170 B4
Swadlincote DE11 ....256 A1
Charleston Cl DE11 .....256 A4
Charleston Ho 2 NG1 ...268 A2
Charleston Rd DE11 .....220 B3
Charlestown SK13 ....17 B3
Charlestown Dr DE22 ...204 B2
Charlestown Rd SK13 ...17 B4
Charlesworth Cl SK23 ...33 B2
Charlesworth Cres SK23 .33 B2
Charlesworth Ct NG19 ..136 C2
Charlesworth Rd SK23 ...33 B2
Charlesworth Sch SK13 ..16 B3
Charlesworth St S44 ....117 C4
Charley La SK23 ....47 A4
Charlotte Ct DE14 .....254 B4
Charlotte Inf Sch DE7 ..194 C2
Charlotte La S33 ....51 A4
Charlotte Rd S2 ....43 A4
Charlotte St Derby DE23 .219 A1
Ilkeston DE7 ....194 C2
Charlton Ave NG10 .....223 C1
Charlton Cl DE12 ....261 B3
Charlton St S14 ....269 B2
Charnock Ave S12 ....44 A2
Charnock Cres S12 ......44 A2
Charnock Dale Rd S12 ..44 A2
Charnock Dr S12 ....44 A2
Charnock Gr S12 ....44 A2
Charnock Hall Prim Sch
S12 ....44 A1
Charnock Hall Rd S12 ...44 A1
Charnock View Rd S12 ..44 A1
Charnock Wood Rd S12 ..44 A1
Charnwood Ave
Belper DE56 ....179 A2
Borrowash DE72 ....221 B1
Castle Donington DE74 .247 A2
Derby DE23 ....231 B3
Long Eaton NG10 ....236 A2
Sandiacre NG10 ....223 A2
Charnwood Cl DE55 ....169 C4
Charnwood Cres DE55 ..169 B1
Charnwood Dr DE11 ....256 A3
Charnwood Gr NG19 ....136 A3
Charnwood St DE1 ......267 B1
Charter Pk DE7 ....208 C4
Charterhouse Cl DE21 ..205 C2
Charterhouse Dr ST17 .269 C3
Charterstone La DE22 ..204 C2
Chartwell Ave S42 ......114 B3
Chartwell Dr DE21 .....219 B3
Chase Cl DE73 ....233 A1
Chase Rd DE55 ....167 C2
Chase The Derby DE24 .231 C2
Kilburn DE56 ....192 A4
Little Eaton DE21 ....191 B1
Rosliston DE12 ....260 B3
Chase View DE4 ....156 C1
Chasecliff Cl S40 ....95 B3
Chatfield Cl DE15 ......248 B1
Chatham Ave DE55 .....159 B2
Chatham Ct DE56 ......179 B2
Chatham St Derby DE23 .232 A4
Nottingham NG1 ....268 B2
Chatsworth Cl
Chesterfield S40 ....95 A1
Clowne S43 ....80 C2
Crich DE4 ....168 A4
Darley Dale DE4 ....142 C4
Long Eaton NG10 ....237 A3
Shirebrook NG20 ....119 C3
Chatsworth Cres
Bullbridge DE56 ....168 A3
Derby DE22 ....204 C2
Chatsworth Ct
Derby DE24 ....231 C2
Staveley S43 ....97 B4
West Hallam DE7 ....207 C4
Chatsworth Dr
Derby DE3 ....217 C2
Little Eaton DE21 ....191 B1
North Wingfield S42 ....131 C3
Tutbury DE13 ....239 B3
Chatsworth Ho* DE45 ...92 A1
Chatsworth Lodge SK7 .85 A4
Chatsworth Park Ave
S12 ....44 A3
Chatsworth Park Dr S12 .44 A3
Chatsworth Park Gr S12 .44 A3
Chatsworth Park Rd S12 .44 A3
Chatsworth Park Rise
S12 ....44 A3
Chatsworth Pl
20 Dronfield S18 ....56 B1
Ilkeston DE7 ....208 A3
Chatsworth Rd
Buxton SK17 ....85 C4
Chesterfield S40 ....95 B1
Creswell S80 ....81 B1
Darley Dale DE4 ....111 A1
Dore S17 ....55 C3
Swadlincote DE11 ....256 A3

Chatsworth St
Derby DE23 ....218 C1
Tibshelf DE55 ....148 A3
Chatteris Dr DE21 .....205 B1
Chatterton La S33 ......36 A4
Chaucer Dr S18 ....76 B4
Chaucer Inf Sch DE7 ...208 C4
Chaucer Jun Sch DE7 ..194 C1
Chaucer Rd S41 ....95 C4
Chaucer St Ilkeston DE7 .194 C1
Mansfield NG18 ....268 B4
Nottingham NG1 ....268 A2
Chavery Rd S45 ....131 C2
Cheadle Cl DE23 ....218 A1
Cheadle Rd ST14 ......210 A1
Cheam Cl DE22 ....217 C3
Cheapside
10 Belper DE56 ....178 C2
Derby DE1 ....267 B3
Nottingham NG1 ....268 B1
Chedworth Cl NG3 .....268 C2
Chedworth Dr DE24 ....233 B3
Cheedale Cl
Burton u T DE15 ....248 A3
Chesterfield S40 ....95 B3
Cheetham Ave S18 ......76 C3
Chell Rd ST16 ....269 A4
Cheedale Cl
Chellaston Inf Sch
DE73 ....233 A1
Chellaston Jun Sch
DE73 ....232 C1
Chellaston La
DE73 ....232 C1
Chellaston Park Ct
DE73 ....232 C1
Chellaston Rd DE24 ....232 C2
Chellaston Sch DE73 ...232 C1
Chelmarsh Cl DE73 ....233 A2
Chelmorton Cl NG19 ...136 C2
Chelmorton Pl 1 DE21 .219 C4
Chelmsford Cl DE3 .....217 B2
Chelmsford Way S41 ....78 A2
Chelsea Cl DE22 ....217 C3
Chelsea Way ST16 .....269 A3
Cheltenham Cl NG9 ....223 C1
Chelwood Rd DE73 .....232 C1
Chendre Cl SK22 ....25 B2
Chepstow Cl S40 ......114 C4
Chepstow Gdns S40 ...114 C4
Chequer La DE56 ......166 B1
Chequers La DE21 ......219 B3
Chequers Rd DE21 .....219 B3
Cheribough Rd DE74 ...247 A2
Cheriton Cl NG19 ......135 C1
Cheriton Dr DE7 ....194 B2
Cheriton Gdns DE23 ...230 C4
Cherry Bank Rd S8 .....56 C4
Cherry Cl Breaston DE72 .235 C4
Shirebrook NG20 ....119 C3
South Normanton DE55 .160 A4
Cherry Ct DE14 ....253 C4
Cherry Garth DE65 .....228 B1
Cherry Gr NG18 ....268 A3
Cherry Leys DE15 ......248 B2
Cherry St S2 ....43 A4
Cherry Tree Ave
Belper DE56 ....179 A3
Ripley DE5 ....180 B4
Shireoaks S81 ....63 C4
Cherry Tree Cl
Barlborough S43 ....80 A4
Bolsover S44 ....99 B1
Brinsley NG16 ....182 C4
Derby DE22 ....218 A2
Hilton DE65 ....228 B1
Ilkeston DE7 ....208 B3
Mansfield Woodhouse
NG19 ....136 A2
Risley DE72 ....222 C2
Swadlincote DE11 ....255 C3
Cherry Tree Dr
Buxton SK17 ....66 B1
Killamarsh S21 ....60 B3
Long Duckmanton S44 ..98 A2
Cherry Tree Gr
Mastin Moor S43 ....79 B2
North Wingfield S42 ....131 C3
Cherry Tree Hill Inf & Jun
Schs DE21 ....220 A3
Cherry Tree Mews
Derby DE21 ....220 A2
Woodville DE11 ....256 C1
Cherry Tree Sq SK17 ...66 B2
Cherrybrook Dr DE21 ..206 A2
Cherrydale Ct DE23 ....233 A3
Cherrytree Ave DE55 ..170 A4
Cherrytree Rd DE15 ...254 C4
Chertpit La SK17,DE45 .89 B3
Chertsey Cl S40 ....114 C4
Chertsey Ct DE7 ....207 B4
Chertsey Rd DE3 ....217 B1
Cherwell Cl 3 S43 ......96 C4
Chesapeake Rd DE21 ..220 A3
Chesham Cl SK13 ....10 A3
Cheshire St DE24 ......232 C3
Cheshire Way NG16 ....171 B2
Chess Burrow NG19 ....136 B1
Chessel Cl S8 ....43 A2
Chester Ave DE22 ......205 A3
Chester Cl DE21 ....220 C2
Chester Gdns DE11 ....256 A1
Chester Gn NG9 ....223 C1
Chester Green Rd DE1 .219 A4
Chester Ho S40 ....95 C2
Chester St
Chesterfield S40 ....95 C2

Chester St continued
Mansfield NG19 1
Chesterfield & North
Derbyshire Royal Hospl
S44 2
Chesterfield Art Gall & M
S41 2
Chesterfield Ave
Long Eaton NG10 1
Swadlincote DE11 2
Chesterfield Coll S41 2
Chesterfield Coll (Tapton
House Campus) S41
Chesterfield Dr DE12 1
Chesterfield Midland Sta
S41 2
Chesterfield Rd
Alfreton DE55 1
Barlborough S43 1
Beeley DE4 1
Belper DE56 1
Bolsover S44
Brimington, Middlecroft S41,
S43
Brimington, Tapton S41,
S43
Calow S41,S44
Darley Dale DE4 1
Dronfield S18
Eckington S21
Grassmoor S42 1
Heage DE56 1
Holmewood S42 1
Long Duckmanton S44 1
Matlock DE4
New Houghton NG19 1
North Wingfield S42 1
Pilsley DE55 1
Pleasley NG19
1 Sheffield S8 ....
Shirland DE55 1
Sutton in a NG17 1
Chesterfield Rd N NG19 .1
Chesterfield Rd S
Mansfield NG18,NG19 1
Sheffield S8 ....
Chesterfield Small Bsns Ct
S41
Chesterfield Trad Est
S41
Chesterfield Ct DE23 2
Chesterman Cl NG16 1
Chesterton Ave DE23 2
Chesterton Cl S43 ....
Chesterton Rd DE21 2
Chestnut Ave
Belper DE56 1
Derby DE3 2
Derby, Chaddesden DE21 .2
Derby, Rose Hill DE23 2
Eckington S21
Holbrook DE56 1
Killamarsh S21 ....
Ripley DE5 1
Somercotes DE55 1
Swadlincote DE11 2
Chestnut Bank DE75 1
Chestnut Centre
Conservatory Pk* SK23 ..
Chestnut Cl Buxton SK17 ..
Dronfield S18 ....
Duffield DE56 1
Horsley Woodhouse DE7 ..1
New Mills SK22 ....
Chestnut Ctr* SK23 ....
Chestnut Dr
Ashbourne DE6 1
Clowne S43 ....
Creswell S80 ....
Repton DE65 2
Selston NG16 1
Shirebrook NG20 1
South Normanton DE55 ...1
Chestnut Gn DE11 2
Chestnut Gr
Borrowash DE72 2
Etwall DE65 2
Mansfield Woodhouse
NG19 1
Sandiacre NG10 2
Tibshelf DE55 1
Chestnut La
Barton in F NG11 2
Clifton Campville B79 2
Chestnut Rd
Burton u T DE15 2
Langley Mill NG16 1
Chestnut Way
Repton DE65 2
Swanwick DE55 1
Chestnuts The NG10 2
Chetwynd Ctr The ST17 ..2
Chevely Ct DE21 2
Cheverton Cl DE24 2
Chevin Alley DE56 1
Chevin Ave
Borrowash DE72 2
Derby DE3 2
Chevin Bank DE56 1
Derby DE1 2
Chevin Pl
Belper, Chevinside DE56 ..1
Belper, Milford DE56 1
Derby DE1 2
Duffield DE56 1
Chevin The DE13 2
Chevin Vale DE56 1

View DE56 .....178 C2
Ave NG16 .....170 C2
CI DE11 .....256 A2
Rd NG10 .....223 A1
St DE22 .....218 B3
Way 1 S40 .....95 B3
ol DE3 .....5 B4
n St NG16 .....182 C2
ne Gdns DE21 .....220 B3
Wlk DE22 .....218 B3
ster CI DE7 .....209 A4
II Way S43 .....78 A2
Dr DE3 .....217 B2
n CI
field S40 .....95 B2
Dr DE7 .....207 C4
n Gdns NG10 .....223 A1
n Rd DE11 .....256 A2
Cres NG19 .....136 B3
CI DE21 .....205 C1
St DE65 .....160 A2
ard Ct DE22 .....218 A3
r Prim Sch SK23 .....35 A1
s Rd DE21 .....206 A1
s Sta SK23 .....34 B1
ghouse St S8 .....43 A4
k CI DE22 .....217 C3
rth Ct NG19 .....136 C2
on CI S18 .....57 A1
n Terr ST14 .....210 B1
Church RC Prim Sch 96 A3
the King RC Prim Sch 159 A3
hurch Ct DE1 .....267 B4
e Ave ST16 .....269 A4
pher Terr ST17 .....269 C2
es Way NG16 .....182 B2
nthemum Ct 256 A3
La SK13 .....17 B3
Alley DE45 .....109 B3
e Ave Buxton SK17 .....67 A3
oss S45 .....131 C2
DE65 .....239 B4
on NG10 .....236 A2
ncote DE11 .....256 A2
ell SK17 .....69 B2
Bank S32 .....53 A4
Banks DE6 .....173 A1
e Banks S45 .....45 B4
Broughton CE Prim 227 B2
n Brow
-en-le-f SK23 .....47 A3
n I SK14 .....9 A2
n CI
u-T DE73 .....244 B2
rdby DE11 .....257 A1
ell DE55 .....147 B1
u-T DE11 .....248 A2
S43 .....80 C2
DE73 .....233 A1
SK13 .....10 C1
ington ST14 .....224 C1
Wingfield S45 .....132 A3
gham NG3 .....268 B2
orest SK17 .....49 A2
aw S21 .....79 A4
y S43 .....97 B4
S21 .....209 B2
worth S40 .....242 A3
rworth S42 .....115 A2
n Cnr DE6 .....165 A1
n Croft
t CI DE12 .....260 B2
DE5 .....169 B1
t CI NG20 .....119 C2
n Dr Ilkeston DE7 .....194 B2
acre NG10 .....223 A4
rook NG20 .....119 C2
n Farm ST14 .....210 A2
n Fold SK13 .....16 B4
n Gdns NG19 .....136 B2
n Gresley Inf Sch 256 A1
n Hill Derby DE21 .....220 B3
DE65 .....229 A3
iely NG16 .....195 C3
ield Woodhouse 136 B2
DE55 .....148 A1
n Hill Ave NG19 .....136 B2
n Hill Ctr Broxtowe Coll 195 C3
n Hill St DE15 .....248 A2
n La Bakewell DE45 .....109 B3
in r DE73 .....244 A3
in F NG11 .....237 C3
DE45 .....91 C3
t DE4 .....111 A2
DE56 .....179 A2
onfield DE55 .....145 B1
sall DE21 .....201 C4
ID55 .....205 C2
ey NG10 .....182 C4
ell DE11 .....260 C4
S44 .....97 A2
e Donington DE74 .....247 A2
Donington, Hemington 247 A2
-len-le-f SK23 .....47 A3
eton SK17 .....106 A4
erfield S40 .....266 B3
e S43 .....80 C2

Church La continued
Cossall NG16 .....195 B3
Darley Dale DE4 .....110 C1
Derby, Chaddesden DE21 .....220 A3
Derby, Darley Abbey DE22 .....205 A1
Dore S17 .....55 B3
Doveridge DE6 .....211 A1
Ellastone DE6 .....183 A2
Fritchley DE56 .....168 A3
Great Longstone DE45 .....90 A2
Hanbury DE13 .....238 A4
Heath S44 .....117 A2
Heath, Stockley S44 .....117 B2
Holmewood S42 .....116 A2
Horsley Woodhouse DE7 .....192 C3
Killamarsh S21 .....60 C2
Kirk Langley DE6 .....202 C1
Little Eaton DE21 .....205 B4
Mackworth DE22 .....217 C4
Mansfield NG18 .....268 C3
Marchington ST14 .....224 C1
Maple SK6 .....23 A3
Mayfield DE6 .....184 B3
Morley DE7 .....206 C3
Nethersale DE12 .....264 C2
New Mills SK22 .....33 B4
Newton Solney DE15 .....248 B4
North Wingfield S42 .....131 C3
Osmaston DE6 .....186 A3
Peak Forest SK17 .....49 A2
Pleasley NG19 .....135 A3
Rocester ST14 .....197 A2
Roston DE6 .....197 B4
Selston NG16 .....171 B4
Shirley DE6 .....200 B4
South Wingfield S55 .....157 C2
Stafford ST16 .....269 A4
Stanton-by-D DE7 .....208 C1
Stapleford NG9 .....223 B4
Stonebroom DE55 .....146 C3
Sutton on t H DE6 .....215 A1
Thorpe DE6 .....161 B1
Thrumpton NG11 .....237 B2
Tibshelf DE55 .....147 C3
Ticknall DE73 .....251 A2
Tideswell SK17 .....69 B2
Weston Underwood DE6 .....188 C1
Church La N
Chesterfield S40 .....77 A2
Derby DE22 .....204 C2
Church Level DE6 .....165 A1
Church Mdws Calow S44 .....96 C2
North Wingfield S42 .....131 C3
Church Mews
Derby DE22 .....220 B2
Hatton DE65 .....227 B1
Killamarsh S21 .....60 C4
Mosborough S20 .....59 B4
Church Rd Bolsover S44 .....99 A4
Branston DE14 .....253 C4
Burton u T DE13 .....240 C1
Church Broughton DE65 .....227 A4
Darley Dale DE4 .....127 A1
Egginton DE65 .....241 A2
Fritchley DE56 .....168 A3
Hollingworth SK14 .....9 B2
Marple SK6 .....23 B4
New Mills SK22 .....33 B4
Nottingham NG3 .....268 B2
Quarndon DE22 .....204 B3
Rocester DE13 .....240 A2
Snelston DE6 .....184 A3
Swadlincote DE11 .....256 A3
Church Rise DE55 .....158 B3
Church Side Calow S44 .....96 C2
Mansfield NG18 .....268 C3
Sutton in A NG17 .....148 C2
Church Sq Heanor DE75 .....181 C1
Melbourne DE73 .....252 A3
Church St Alfreton DE55 .....158 C2
Alstonefield DE6 .....149 C2
Ashbourne DE6 .....173 A1
Ashford in t W DE45 .....108 C4
Ashover S45 .....129 C2
Barlborough S43 .....80 A4
Baslow DE45 .....91 C3
Belper DE56 .....179 A2
Bolsover S44 .....99 A1
Bonsall DE4 .....142 B1
Bradwell S33 .....51 A4
Brassington DE4 .....153 A1
Brimington S43 .....96 C4
Buxton SK17 .....85 B4
Calow S44 .....96 C2
Clifton Campville B79 .....263 C1
Coton in t DE12 .....260 B2
Creswell S80 .....100 A1
Cresswell DE6 .....180 B1
Derby DE23 .....218 B1
Derby, Alvaston DE24 .....219 A3
Derby, Spondon DE21 .....220 B3
Donisthorpe DE12 .....262 C1
Dronfield S18 .....57 A1
Eastwood NG16 .....182 C1
Eckington S21 .....59 C2
Eyam S32 .....71 B3
Fritchley DE56 .....168 A3
Glossop SK13 .....10 B1
Glossop, Hadfield SK13 .....10 A2
Glossop, Tintwistle SK13 .....10 A4
Hartington SK17 .....137 B3
Hartshorne DE11 .....257 A3
Hayfield SK22 .....25 B1
Heage DE56 .....168 C1
Heanor DE75 .....181 C1

Church St continued
Holbrook DE56 .....191 B3
Holloway DE4 .....156 A3
Horsley DE21 .....191 C3
Ilkeston DE7 .....194 C1
Kilburn DE56 .....191 C4
Lockington DE74 .....247 C2
Longnor SK17 .....121 A3
Mansfield NG18, NG19 .....268 B4
Mansfield Woodhouse
NG19 .....136 B2
Marple SK6 .....23 A3
Matlock DE4 .....143 B2
Melbourne DE73 .....252 A4
Monyash DE45 .....107 B1
Nethersale DE12 .....264 C2
Ockbrook DE72 .....221 B2
Pilsley S45 .....132 B1
Pleasley NG19 .....135 A2
Ripley DE5 .....169 B1
Ripley, Waingroves DE5 .....170 A3
Sandiacre NG10 .....223 A4
Shirland DE55 .....146 B1
Somercotes DE55 .....170 B3
South Normanton DE55 .....160 A3
Stapleford NG9 .....223 B4
Staveley S43 .....78 C1
Stoke-on-T ST4 .....269 B2
Stretton en le F DE12 .....265 C1
Swadlincote DE11 .....256 A3
Swadlincote, Lower Midway
DE11 .....256 B2
Swadlincote, Newhall
DE11 .....256 A3
Tansley DE4 .....144 A2
Tideswell SK17 .....69 B2
Tintwistle S33 .....239 B4
Unstone S18 .....76 C4
Whaley Thorns NG20 .....101 A1
Wirksworth DE4 .....165 C4
Youlgreave SK45 .....125 B3
Church St N S41 .....160 B2
Church St S
Chesterfield S40 .....115 A4
Glossop SK13 .....10 C1
Church St W
Chesterfield S40 .....95 B1
Pinxton NG16 .....160 B2
Church View
Barlborough S43 .....80 A4
Branston DE72 .....253 B4
Chesterfield S40 .....95 B1
Clifton DE6 .....184 C3
Clowne S43 .....80 C2
Duffield S56 .....190 C1
Glapwell S44 .....118 A3
Heanor DE75 .....181 A2
Ilkeston DE7 .....208 C4
Killamarsh S21 .....60 C4
Mottram in t SK14 .....9 A2
New Houghton NG19 .....134 C4
Church View Cotts SK17 .....84 C3
Church View Dr DE45 .....91 C3
Church Wlk S40 .....266 B3
Church Wlk
Brinsley NG16 .....182 C4
Chesterfield S40 .....266 B3
Derby DE22 .....205 A2
Duffield DE56 .....190 C1
Eastwood NG16 .....182 C1
Glossop SK13 .....10 C1
Somercotes DE55 .....170 B3
2 Stapleford NG9 .....223 C4
Churchdale Rd S12 .....44 A2
Churchdown CI DE21 .....206 A1
Churchill CI DE72 .....235 A4
Churchill Dr Hilton DE65 .....228 C1
2 Stapleford NG9 .....223 C4
Churchland Ave S42 .....132 B4
Churchside
Barlborough S43 .....115 A3
Willington DE65 .....242 A3
Churchside La S43 .....115 B3
Churchside Wlk DE22 .....217 C2
Churchward Dr DE13 .....240 C1
Churnet CI DE6 .....184 B4
Churston Rd S40 .....95 B2
Cinder Bank NG16 .....170 C2
Cinder La Killamarsh S21 .....60 C4
Wirksworth DE4 .....165 C4
Cinder Rd DE55 .....170 B4
Cinderhill La S8 .....57 B4
Circle The Derby DE24 .....231 C3
Mansfield Woodhouse
NG19 .....136 A2
Circular Dr S21 .....79 A4
Circular Rd
Chesterfield S40 .....115 A4
Staveley S43 .....78 B1
City Link NG2 .....268 C1
City of Stoke-on-Trent Sixth
Form Coll ST4 .....269 C2
City Point ST4 .....268 A1
City Rd Derby DE1 .....219 A4
Fenton ST4 .....269 C2
Sheffield S2 .....43 C4
City Rd Ind Pk DE1 .....219 A4
City Sch The S13 .....44 A4
City The Woodville DE11 .....256 C1
Woodville, Blackfordby
DE11 .....257 A1
Civic Ctr S18 .....57 A1
Civic Way DE11 .....256 A2
Clamp Dr DE11 .....256 A2

Clapgun St DE74 .....247 A2
Clara Mount Rd DE75 .....182 A1
Clare Valley NG7 .....268 A1
Clarehaven NG9 .....223 C3
Claremont CI NG19 .....136 C2
Clarence Ind Trad Est
S41 .....96 A4
Clarence Rd
Chesterfield S40 .....266 A3
Derby DE23 .....218 C1
Long Eaton NG10 .....236 B3
Clarence St
Chesterfield S40 .....266 A3
Mansfield NG18 .....268 B3
Mansfield, Moorhaigh
NG19 .....268 C2
Nottingham NG3 .....268 C2
Stonebroom DE55 .....147 A2
Clarence Terr DE4 .....143 A1
Clarence Villas DE4 .....143 A1
Clarendon Rd
Mansfield NG18 .....268 A4
Staveley S43 .....78 C1
Clarendon St Fenton ST4 .....269 C1
Nottingham NG1 .....268 A2
Clark St S16 .....259 B4
Clarke Ave S43 .....181 B1
Clarke Dr NG10 .....236 A2
Clarke St DE1 .....267 C4
Clarkes CI ST14 .....210 A1
Clarkes La DE72 .....246 A4
Clarkson Ave S40 .....266 B1
Clatterway DE4 .....154 C4
Claverhouse Rd DE15 .....248 A1
Claxton St DE75 .....181 B1
Claxton Terr DE75 .....181 B1
Clay CI DE11 .....256 C3
Clay Cross Com Hospl
S45 .....131 B2
Clay Cross Inf & Jun Sch
S45 .....131 B2
Clay La Clay Cross S45 .....131 A1
Heanor DE75 .....181 C1
Clay Pit Way S43 .....80 B3
Clay St Burton u T DE15 .....248 A1
Draycott DE72 .....235 A4
Shirland DE55 .....146 C1
Claye St Long Eaton NG10 .....236 C4
Claylands CI SK14 .....9 B2
Claylands Gr S80 .....81 C3
Claylands PI S80 .....81 C3
Claylands Rd S80 .....81 C3
Claymar Dr DE11 .....256 A4
Claymills Rd DE13 .....241 A1
Claypit La S42 .....111 C2
Clays CI DE14 .....253 C4
Clays La DE14 .....253 C4
Clayton Gr DE75 .....181 B2
Clayton St S41 .....266 C2
Cleave Rd DE14 .....254 A4
Cleeves Ct 7 NG7 .....268 A2
Clegg Hill Dr NG17 .....148 C2
Clematis Cres S44 .....96 C4
Clement La S33 .....50 B3
Clement Rd
Horsley Woodhouse DE7 .....192 B4
Marple SK6 .....23 B4
Clerkson St 2 NG18 .....268 B3
Clerkson's Alley NG18 .....268 B3
Cleve Ave Beeston NG9 .....223 C3
Darley Dale DE42 .....142 C4
Cleveland Ave
Derby DE21 .....220 A3
Draycott DE72 .....235 A4
Long Eaton NG10 .....223 C1
Cleveland CI DE11 .....256 A2
Cleveland Rd DE55 .....146 C2
Cleveland Way S40 .....95 B3
Cleveleys Rd NG9 .....223 C2
Clewley Dr DE14 .....253 C4
Cliff Bvd NG16 .....195 C4
Cliff CI S80 .....81 C3
Cliff La Curbar S32 .....72 C1
Elton DE4 .....140 B4
Kirby-in-A NG16 .....160 C2
Tideswell SK17 .....69 B2
Cliff Nook DE55 .....160 A4
Cliff Rd Buxton SK17 .....85 B4
Holme HD7 .....2 C4
Nottingham NG3 .....268 B1
Cliff St NG18 .....268 C4
Cliffash La DE56 .....178 A3
Cliffe Bank ST16 .....269 A4
Cliffe Fall Rd S8 .....43 A2 (?)
Cliffe Field Rd S8 .....43 A2
Cliffe Hill Ave NG9 .....223 B4
Cliffe La S32 .....52 C4
Cliffe Rd SK13 .....17 A4
Cliffe View Rd S8 .....43 A2
Clifford CI
Chesterfield S40 .....95 A1
Long Eaton NG10 .....236 A2
Clifford St Derby DE24 .....219 B1
Long Eaton NG10 .....236 A2
Clifton Ave
Barlborough S43 .....80 A4
Long Eaton NG10 .....236 A2
Clifton CE Prim Sch
DE6 .....184 C3
Clifton CI Chesterfield DE72 .....262 A2 (?)
Stafford ST16 .....269 C4
Swadlincote DE11 .....256 A2
Clifton Dr Buxton SK17 .....85 B2
Derby DE22 .....217 C2
Stafford ST16 .....269 C4
Clifton PI NG18 .....268 B4
Clifton Rd
Ashbourne DE6 .....185 A4

Clifton Rd continued
Buxton SK17 .....85 B4
Derby DE22 .....204 B2
Matlock Bath DE4 .....155 A4
Nethersale DE12 .....264 B3
Clifton St Chesterfield S40 .....95 C2
Derby DE1 .....267 D1
Clifton Terr NG2 .....268 A1
Clifton Thorn Mdws
LE65 .....258 A1
Clifton Way DE15 .....248 A1
Clinthill La S80 .....81 C4
Clinton Ave NG16 .....182 B3
Clinton Ct 12 NG1 .....268 B2
Clinton St DE21 .....219 B3
Clinton St E NG1 .....268 B2
Clinton St W NG1 .....268 B2
Clinton Terr 14 NG2 .....268 A1
Clipstone Ave
Mansfield NG18 .....268 C4
Nottingham NG1 .....268 B2
Clipstone Gdns DE21 .....206 A1
Clive Ho DE15 .....248 A1
Clock Tower Bsns Ctr The
S43 .....79 A2
Clodhall La Curbar S32 .....72 C1
Old Brampton S42 .....93 A3
Cloisters Ct DE21 .....205 C1
Cloonmore Croft S8 .....43 B1
Cloonmore Dr S8 .....43 B1
Close Bank DE13 .....239 B3
Close Jun Sch The ST4 .....269 A2
Close The
Derby, Allestree DE22 .....204 C1
Derby, Normanton Park
DE23 .....218 B1
Great Longstone DE45 .....89 C2
Linton DE12 .....261 B3
Marple SK6 .....15 A1
Matlock DE4 .....143 A3
Moira DE11 .....262 B4
Shirebrook NG20 .....119 B4
Stafford, Rowley Park
ST16 .....269 A3
Tutbury DE13 .....239 A3
Cloud Ave NG9 .....223 C4
Cloudside Ct NG10 .....223 A4
Cloudside Jun Sch
NG10 .....223 A4
Cloudside Rd NG10 .....223 A4
Cloudwood CI DE21 .....218 A1
Clough Ave SK6 .....23 B4
Clough Bank S43 .....43 A4
Clough La Hayfield SK22 .....25 B3
Birchover DE4 .....141 B4
Ringinglow S10 .....42 C3
Wensley DE4 .....141 B4
Clough Side SK6 .....23 B4 (?)
Clough St SK17 .....85 A4
Clough The Bamford S33 .....40 A2
Chesterfield S41 .....96 C1
Cloughside SK17 .....32 C3
Clover CI DE21 .....220 C3
Clover Ct Shardlow DE72 .....234 C1
Sheffield S8 .....43 C1
Tibshelf DE55 .....148 A4
Clover Nook Ind Est
DE55 .....159 C2
Clover Nook Rd
Pinxton DE55 .....159 C2
Somercotes DE55 .....159 C2
South Normanton DE55 .....159 C2
Clover Rise NG16 .....195 A4
Cloverdale DE11 .....256 A4
Cloverdale Dr DE21 .....206 C3
Coverdale DE11 .....231 C1 (?)
Cloverslade DE65 .....230 B1
Cloves Hill DE7 .....192 B1
Clowne Rd
Barlborough S43 .....80 B3
Bolsover S44 .....99 A4
Club La DE7 .....244 A3
Club Row S10 .....71 C3
Club St ST4 .....269 B1
Clubmill Terr S40 .....95 C2
Clumber Ave NG16 .....171 C1
Clumber CI
Ashbourne DE6 .....185 A4
Clowne S43 .....80 C2
Clumber Cres N NG7 .....268 A1
Clumber Cres S NG7 .....268 A1
Clumber Ct Ilkeston DE7 .....194 C3
Mansfield NG19 .....135 C1
Nottingham NG7 .....268 A1
Clumber Dr NG19 .....135 C1
Clumber PI S43 .....97 B3
Clumber Rd E NG7 .....268 A1
Clumber Rd W NG7 .....268 A1
Clumber St
Long Eaton NG10 .....236 B4
Mansfield NG18 .....268 B4
17 Nottingham NG1 .....268 B2
Clun CI NG19 .....136 B1
Clune St S43 .....81 A3
Cluster Ct 8 DE56 .....178 C2
Cluster Rd DE56 .....178 C2
Co-operative St
Derby DE23 .....218 C1
Long Eaton NG10 .....236 B4
Coach Dr Selston NG16 .....182 C2 (?)
Nottingham DE21 .....204 B4 (?)
Coach Rd Hollingworth SK14 .....9 B3
Ironville DE55 .....170 B2
Ripley DE5 .....169 C2

Coach Way DE65 ....242 B3
Coachhouse Mews 4
DE11 ....256 A4
Coachways DE7 ....193 C2
Coal La DE11,DE73 ....257 B4
Coalpit La
  Coton in t DE12 ....260 C2
  Youlgreave DE45 ....125 B3
Coarses View SK23 ....47 B4
Coasthill DE4 ....156 C1
Coatsby Rd NG16 ....195 C4
Cobden Pl NG19 ....135 C1
Cobden Rd
  Chesterfield S40 ....266 A4
  Matlock DE4 ....143 B3
Cobden St Derby DE22 ....218 B3
  Long Eaton NG10 ....236 C4
  Ripley DE5 ....169 B1
Cobham Cl DE24 ....231 B2
Cobnar Ave S8 ....43 A1
Cobnar Dr
  Chesterfield S41 ....95 B4
  Sheffield S8 ....43 A1
Cobnar Rd S8 ....43 A1
Cobnar Wood Cl S18 ....76 A2
Cobthorn Dr DE22 ....204 B2
Coburn Pl DE1 ....267 A3
Cock Ayne Cl NG10 ....223 A2
Cock Brow SK14 ....15 B4
Cock Hill Baslow DE45 ....91 C3
  Clifton DE6 ....184 C3
Cock Pitt The DE1 ....267 C3
Cockayne La DE6 ....164 A1
Cockayne St N DE24 ....232 C3
Cockayne St S DE24 ....232 C3
Cockerhouse Rd NG16 ....182 C2
Cockleys NG10 ....236 B3
Cockshead La DE6 ....198 B4
Cockshut La
  Holbeck SK22 ....101 A2
  Melbourne DE73 ....251 A2
  Whaley Thorns NG20 ....101 A2
Cockshutt Ave S8 ....56 B4
Cockshutt Dr S8 ....56 B4
Cockshutt La DE55 ....170 C4
Cockshutt Rd S8 ....56 B4
Cod Beck Cl DE24 ....233 B3
Codnor Com Prim Sch
  DE5 ....181 A4
Codnor Denby La DE5 ....181 A3
Codnor Gate DE5 ....170 A1
Codnor Gate Ind Est
  DE5 ....170 A1
Codnor La DE55 ....170 B1
Coffin La DE6 ....165 A1
Coggers La S32 ....52 C4
Coisley Hill S13 ....44 C3
Cokayne Ave DE6 ....173 B1
Cokayne Mews DE6 ....173 B2
Coke St DE22 ....218 B3
Cokefield Terr DE55 ....148 B1
Coldharbour La S45 ....145 A2
Coldstream Wlk DE24 ....231 C2
Coldwell St DE4 ....154 C1
Cole Dr ST16 ....269 A3
Cole La DE72 ....221 B2
Coleman St DE24 ....232 C4
Coleraine Cl DE21 ....220 A2
Coleridge St
  Derby, Littleover DE23 ....231 C1
  Derby, Normanton DE23 .....231 C4
Colin Ave S41 ....181 A4
Colin St DE55 ....159 A2
Colindene Gr ST14 ....269 B1
Coliseum Ctr The DE1 ....267 C2
Colledge St DE55 ....170 B3
College Ave S43 ....78 B1
College Mews DE1 ....218 C3
College Pl DE1 ....267 B4
College Rd Buxton SK17 ....85 A3
  Denstone SK14 ....196 B3
  Killamarsh S21 ....60 B1
  Stoke-on-T ST4 ....269 B2
College St
  Long Eaton NG10 ....223 B1
  Nottingham NG1 ....268 A1
College Way SK17 ....85 A3
Collier La DE72 ....221 B2
Collier St S43 ....17 B4
Colliers Trek S43 ....80 B3
Colliers Way S45 ....131 A2
Colliery Cl S43 ....78 C1
Colliery La DE12 ....261 B2
Colliery Rd
  Blackwell DE55 ....147 C1
  Swadlincote DE11 ....256 A1
Colliery Row
  Alfreton DE55 ....159 A3
  Pinxton NG16 ....160 B1
  Swadlincote DE11 ....256 A1
Collin Ave NG10 ....223 A2
Collin Rd ST4 ....269 A1
Collin St NG1 ....268 B1
Collingham Gdns DE22 ....218 A3
Collingham St NG19 ....135 B1
Collingwood Cres DE4 ....143 A3
Collingwood Gr ST4 ....269 A2
Collingwood Rd NG10 ....236 C3
Collins Ave DE55 ....160 A4
Collis Cl DE24 ....232 C4
Collishaw Cl S41 ....96 B1
Collumbell Ave DE72 ....221 B3
Colne Ct NG19 ....136 B1
Colombo St DE23 ....219 A1
Colonnade The 14 ST16 .....269 B4
Colonsay Cl NG9 ....209 B2
Colton Cl S41 ....76 C1
Coltsfoot Dr DE24 ....231 C1
Coltsworth La S43 ....80 C4
Columbell Way DE4 ....127 B1
Columbia St NG17 ....148 C2
Columbine Cl DE21 ....206 A1
Colver Rd 8 S2 ....43 A4
Colvile St DE22 ....218 B3
Colville Cl DE12 ....263 B4
Colville St NG1 ....268 A2
Colwell Dr DE24 ....233 B3
Colwick Cl NG19 ....135 C1
Colwick Rd NG2 ....268 C1
Colwyn Ave DE23 ....218 B1
Colyear St DE1 ....267 B3
Combs Bank SK13 ....9 B1
Combs Cl SK22 ....33 A4
Combs Fold SK13 ....9 B1
Combs Gdns SK13 ....9 B1
Combs Inf Sch SK23 ....46 C1
Combs Lea SK13 ....9 B1
Combs Mews SK13 ....9 B1
Combs Rd SK24 ....46 C2
Combs Terr SK13 ....9 B1
Combs Way SK13 ....9 B1
Comfrey Cl DE23 ....230 C3
Commerce Sq 10 NG1 ....268 B1
Commerce St
  Derby DE1 ....232 C4
  Melbourne DE73 ....252 A4
Commercial Gate NG18 ......268 B3
Commercial Rd SK17 ....69 B2
Commercial Row S32 ....72 B4
Commercial St 8 NG18 ....268 B3
Common End DE65 ....229 A2
Common La
  Chelmorton SK17 ....87 A1
  Mansfield Woodhouse
    NG19 ....136 A2
  Old Brampton S42 ....94 C4
  Pleasley NG20 ....119 B2
  Scarcliffe NG20 ....119 B2
  Shirebrook NG20 ....119 B2
  Shirley DE7 ....207 A4
  Sutton on t In DE6 ....228 A4
Common Piece La DE65 ....230 C1
Sutton in A NG17 ....148 C1
Swadlincote DE11 ....256 B1
Thorpe Salvin S80 ....62 C3
Common Side
  Selston NG16 ....171 C4
  Swadlincote DE11 ....256 B1
Common The Crich DE4 ......168 A4
  Quarndon DE22 ....204 B4
  South Normanton DE55 ....160 A3
Common Wood DE4 ....143 A2
Commonpiece La DE6 ....215 A1
Commonpiece Rd S45 ....131 B2
Commons Cl NG16 ....195 A4
Commonside Rd S18 ....75 B1
Comms Cres S41 ....77 B2
Compass Cres S41 ....77 B2
Compstall Mills Est SK6 ....15 A1
Compstall Rd
  Compstall SK6 ....15 A2
  Marple SK6 ....15 A3
Compton Cl DE72 ....246 A4
Compton Cl
  10 Derby DE24 ....233 B3
  Stafford ST17 ....269 C3
Compton Dr S80 ....81 B1
Compton Gr SK17 ....85 A3
Compton Rd SK17 ....85 A3
Compton St
  Ashbourne DE6 ....173 B1
  Chesterfield S40 ....266 A4
  Holmewood S42 ....116 C1
  Langwith NG20 ....119 C4
Comyn Gdns NG3 ....268 B2
Conalan Ave S17 ....56 A3
Concert Pl 8 SK17 ....85 A4
Condiff Rd SK17 ....119 A4
Conduit St S43 ....96 A3
Coney Green Bsns Ctr
  S45 ....131 C2
Coney Green Rd S45 ....131 C2
Coniston Ave DE21 ....220 C3
Coniston Cl DE21 ....205 B3
Coniston Cres DE21 ....205 B3
Coniston Dr
  Clay Cross S45 ....131 A1
  Ilkeston DE7 ....208 B3
Coniston Rd
  Chesterfield S41 ....95 C4
  Dronfield S18 ....56 C1
  Long Eaton NG10 ....223 A1
Coniston Way S41 ....95 C4
Conkers Discovery*
  DE12 ....262 B2
Conkers Waterside*
  DE12 ....262 B2
Conksbury Ave DE45 ....125 B3
Conksbury La DE45 ....125 B3
Connaught Ct DE55 ....159 A2
Connaught Rd DE22 ....204 C1
Connelly Ct S40 ....95 C2
Consett Cl DE21 ....205 B1
Consort Gdns DE21 ....206 B2
Constable Ave DE23 ....218 B1
Constable Cl
  Dronfield S18 ....56 C1
  Sheffield S14 ....43 C1
Constable Dr
  Derby DE23 ....218 A1
Constable Dr continued
  Marple SK6 ....23 A4
  Sheffield S14 ....43 B1
Constable La DE23 ....218 B2
Constable Pl S14 ....43 C1
Constable Rd S14 ....43 B1
Constable Way S14 ....43 C1
Convent Ct
  Burton u T DE15 ....254 C4
  Stoke-on-T ST4 ....269 B2
Convent Ct S14 ....269 B2
Convent Dr 26 NG1 ....268 A2
Conway Ave DE72 ....221 B1
Conway St
  Long Eaton NG10 ....236 C4
  Stoke-on-T ST4 ....269 C2
Conygree La DE4 ....184 B4
Conygre La DE4 ....184 B4
  Clay Cross S45 ....131 B3
Cook Dr DE7 ....209 A3
Cook La DE6 ....211 A1
Cooke Cl NG10 ....236 A3
Cookfield DE56 ....179 C4
Cookham Cl DE3 ....217 B1
Cooks Ave DE7 ....247 A2
Coombes La SK13 ....16 B3
Coombes View SK14 ....15 C4
Coombs Rd DE45 ....126 C4
Cooper St Derby DE22 ....218 B3
Cope St DE24 ....232 A3
Cope St ST16 ....269 B4
Copeland Ave NG9 ....223 C4
Copeland St Derby DE1 ....267 C2
Copenhagen Rd S45 ....131 C2
Copes Way Derby DE21 ....220 A4
  Ilkeston DE7 ....194 C3
Copley Croft DE6 ....173 B2
Coplow La DE65 ....226 B3
Copper Beech Manor
  SK13 ....9 C1
Copper Beech Dr SK13 ....9 C1
Copper Beeches DE55 ....169 B1
Copper Glade ST16 ....269 C4
Copper Yd DE5 ....180 C1
Copperas Rd DE11 ....255 B3
Copperleaf Cl DE24 ....267 A2
Coppice Ave
  High Lane SK12 ....32 A3
  Ilkeston DE7 ....194 B3
Coppice Cl
  Chesterfield S41 ....115 B3
  Derby DE24 ....204 C1
  High Lane SK12 ....32 A3
  Kilburn DE56 ....192 A4
Coppice Dr
  Eastwood NG16 ....182 B2
  Heanor DE75 ....193 C4
Coppice La
  Clifton Campville B79 ....263 C1
  High Lane SK12 ....32 A3
Coppice Prim Sch DE75 ......193 C4
Coppice Side DE11 ....256 B2
Coppice The
  Shirebrook NG20 ....119 B2
  Whaley Bridge SK23 ....45 C3
Coppice View DE21 ....160 A2
Coppicewood Dr DE23 ....218 A1
Copse Cl DE4 ....165 C4
Copse La DE24 ....231 A4
Copse Rise DE21 ....255 B4
Copse The Ilkeston DE7 ......194 B3
  Marple SK6 ....23 A4
Copseside Cl 10 NG10 ....236 A4
Copsewood DE55 ....160 A2
Copsey Croft Ct NG10 ....236 C4
Copthorne Com Inf Sch
  DE55 ....159 A3
Copthurst Rd HD9 ....3 A3
Coral Way S45 ....131 C2
Corbar Rd SK17 ....66 A4
Corbarwoods La SK17 ....66 A1
Corbel Cl DE21 ....205 C1
Corbridge Gr DE21 ....231 A4
Corden Ave DE3 ....218 A1
Corden St DE23 ....219 A1
Cordville Cl DE21 ....220 A3
Cordwell Ave S41 ....115 A4
Cordwell Cl
  Castle Donington DE74 ......246 C2
  Staveley S43 ....97 B4
Cordwell La S18 ....74 C3
Cordy La Brinsley NG16 ....182 C2
  Selston NG16 ....182 C4
Corfe Cl DE21 ....205 B1
Corfield Ave DE75 ....193 C4
Corfield CI 1 S42 ....95 A3
Corfield Rd NG16 ....195 C4
Cornflower Dr DE21 ....206 A2
Cornhill DE22 ....204 C2
Cornhill Dr DE55 ....159 A2
Cornmill Cl Bolsover S44 ......99 A1
  Calver S32 ....72 B1
  10 Derby DE72 ....233 B3
Cornmill La DE13 ....239 C3
Cornwall Ave
  Brimington S43 ....96 C4
  Buxton SK17 ....85 C4
Cornwall Cl
  Brimington S43 ....96 C4
  Westwood NG16 ....171 B2
Cornwall Dr
  Brimington S43 ....96 C4
  Grassmoor S42 ....115 C2
Cornwall Rd
  Burton u T DE15 ....254 C3
  Derby DE21 ....219 B3
  Shireoaks S81 ....63 C4
Cornwallis Cl NG10 ....236 B3
Cornwallis St 4 DE45 ....269 B1
Coronation Ave
  Belper DE56 ....179 A3
  Derby DE24 ....233 B3
  New Houghton NG19 ....134 C4
  Sandiacre NG10 ....223 A4
Coronation Cl DE73 ....252 A4
Coronation Cotts DE13 ....253 A4
Coronation Cres ST14 ....197 A2
Coronation La
  Shirebrook NG20 ....119 C1
  South Normanton DE55 .....160 B3
Coronation La DE55 ....265 C3
Coronation Rd
  Brimington S43 ....96 C4
  Cossall DE7, NG16 ....195 A1
  Mapperley DE7 ....193 C2
  Stanley DE7 ....207 B3
  Stoke-on-T, Hartshill ST4 ...269 A2
Coronation St
  Derby DE23 ....232 A4
  8 Ilkeston DE7 ....208 C4
  Mansfield NG18 ....268 C3
  Overseal DE12 ....262 A2
  Swadlincote DE11 ....256 A3
  Whitwell S80 ....82 A3
Coronet Ct DE21 ....206 B2
Corporation Rd DE7 ....209 A3
Corporation St
  Chesterfield S41 ....266 C3
  Derby DE1 ....267 B3
  8 Mansfield NG18 ....268 B4
  Stafford ST16 ....269 B4
  Stoke-on-T ST4 ....269 B1
Corve Way S40 ....94 C3
Cosby Rd NG2 ....268 C1
Cossall Rd NG9 ....209 B3
Cote Bottom La DE11 ....227 A4
Cote Green La S6 ....15 A1
Cote Green Rd S6 ....15 A1
Cote Hilloc DE4 ....127 A3
Cote La S22 ....25 B2
Cotes Park Ind Est
  DE55 ....159 B1
Cotes Park La DE55 ....159 B1
Cotgrave Rd NG19 ....136 B2
Cotman Dr S66 ....23 B4
Cotmanhay Inf & Jun Sch
  DE7 ....194 C3
Cotmanhay Rd DE7 ....194 C2
Coton Ave S40 ....94 C3
Coton Cl NG19 ....136 A2
Coton in the Elms CE Prim
  Sch DE12 ....260 B2
Coton La DE12 ....260 B3
Coton Pk DE12 ....255 B1
Coton Rd Derby DE22 ....219 A1
  Walton-on-T DE12 ....260 C2
Cotswold Cl
  2 Chesterfield S40 ....95 B3
  Derby DE23 ....231 B4
  Glossop SK13 ....17 A4
  4 Long Eaton NG10 ....236 A4
  Swadlincote DE11 ....256 A2
Cotswold Dr S42 ....115 C2
Cotswold Rd DE14 ....253 C4
Cottage Cl Heage DE56 ......179 C4
  Ilkeston DE7 ....194 B2
  Poolsbrook S43 ....98 A4
  Swadlincote DE11 ....256 A4
Cottage Garden La
  DE75 ....181 B3
Cottage La SK13 ....9 B1
Cottam Cres SK6 ....23 A4
Cottam Dr S43 ....80 B3
Cotterdale Cl NG19 ....136 C1
Cotterhill La S43 ....96 C4
Cottesmore Rd DE15 ....248 A1
Cottisford Cl DE21 ....231 A4
Cotton La DE24 ....219 B1
Cotton Mill Hill S42 ....113 C4
Cotton St S44 ....99 A1
Coundult Rd S44 ....118 A4
Counting House Rd SK12 ....32 C2
Countisbury Dr DE21 ....206 A1
County Est The NG17 ....148 C1
County Rd ST16 ....269 B4
Coupe La S42, S45 ....131 A3
Coupe St DE5 ....169 A2
Coupland Cl DE21 ....77 B2
Coupland Pl DE55 ....159 B1
Court Farm La DE14 ....253 C4
Court Cl DE45 ....108 C4
Court Pl S43 ....97 B4
Court St DE11 ....256 C2
Court The DE24 ....233 A3
Court View S43 ....80 C2
Courtland Dr DE24 ....
Courtland Gdns DE24 ....
Courtland Rd DE65 ....
Courtney Way DE56 ....
Courtyard Mews DE24 ....
Courtyard The
  Belper DE56 ....
  Darley Dale DE4 ....
  Hollingworth SK14 ....
Coventry Cl DE11 ....
Coventry La NG9 ....
Coverdale Wlk DE24 ....
Covert Pl DE11 ....
Covert The DE21 ....
Cow La S43 ....
Cowan Dr ST16 ....
Cowan St NG1 ....
Cowbrook Ave SK13 ....
Cowburn Dr SK22 ....
Cowdray Cl DE24 ....
Cowham St DE55 ....
Cowley Bottom S18 ....
Cowley Cl S41 ....
Cowley Gdns 4 S20 ....
Cowley La S18 ....
Cowlishaw Cl DE72 ....
Cowlow La SK17,SK23 ....
Cowper Rd NG16 ....
Cowper St DE24 ....
Cowringle La S43 ....
Cowsell Dr S45 ....
Cowslip La DE4 ....
Cox Green Ct DE23 ....
Cox's La NG19 ....
Coxbench Rd DE21 ....
Coxon St DE21 ....
Coxon's Yd DE4 ....
Coyt Rd SK23 ....
Crab Tree Hill DE21 ....
Crabbery St S14 ....
Crabtree Ave SK12 ....
Crabtree Cl
  Castle Donington DE74 ......
  Wirksworth DE4 ....
Crabtree Ct SK12 ....
Crabtree Hill DE22 ....
Cracken Cl SK23 ....
Craddock Ave S41 ....
Craddock Mews S2 ....
Craddock Rd S43 ....
Cragdale Gr S20 ....
Cragg La DE55 ....
Craggon Dr S43 ....
Craggs Dr S43 ....
Craggs Rd S44 ....
Craglands Gr S40 ....
Crags Bsns Pk S80 ....
Crags Rd S80 ....
Crags View S80 ....
Craig Dr SK23 ....
Craig St NG10 ....
Craiglee Ct DE24 ....
Craigs Gn NG18 ....
Cramer St S17 ....
Cranberry Gr DE21 ....
Cranbourne Rd S41 ....
Cranbourne Cl NG9 ....
Cranbrook Ct NG19 ....
Cranbrook St NG1 ....
Cranfleet Way NG10 ....
Cranhill Cl DE23 ....
Cranleigh Rd S43 ....
Cranmer Gr NG19 ....
Cranmer Rd DE21 ....
Cranmer St Ilkeston DE7 .....
  Long Eaton NG10 ....
  Stoke-on-T ST4 ....
Craven Rd S41 ....
Crawford Ave NG9 ....
Crawford St ST4 ....
Crawley Rd DE24 ....
Crawshaw Ave S8 ....
Crawshaw Gr S8 ....
Cray's Hill DE55 ....
Crayford Rd DE24 ....
Craythorne Cl DE11 ....
Craythorne Rd DE13 ....
Creamery La DE6 ....
Crecy Cl DE22 ....
Creighton La ST14 ....
Crescent S26 ....
Crescent Dr SK23 ....
Crescent Rd Ashover S42 ....
  Selston NG16 ....
  Stafford ST17 ....
Crescent The
  Alfreton DE55 ....
  Barlborough S43 ....
  Bradwell S33 ....
  Breaston DE72 ....
  Breedon on t H DE73 ....
  Brimington S43 ....
  Buxton SK17 ....
  Chapel-en-le-F SK23 ....
  Clay Cross S45 ....
  Derby, Boulton DE24 ....
  Derby, Chaddesden DE21 ...
  Hayfield SK22 ....
  Holmesfield S18 ....
  Holymoorside S42 ....
  Hope S33 ....
  Horsley Woodhouse DE7 ...
  Mayfield DE6 ....
  New Mills SK22 ....

De Sutton Pl S26 61 C3
De Warren Pl S26 61 C3
Deacon Cl Derby DE21 205 C1
Swanwick DE55 169 C4
Dead La NG16 195 B1
Deadman's La DE24 219 B1
Deamon St DE55 147 C1
Dean Cl DE23 218 A1
Dean Ct DE23 218 C1
Dean Rd DE56 167 C1
Dean St Derby DE22 218 C2
Langley Mill NG16 182 B2
Nottingham NG1 268 B1
Deanhead Dr S20 44 C1
Deans Dr DE72 221 A1
Deansgate NG19 135 A3
Deanshill Cl ST16 269 A3
Debdale Gate NG19 136 A1
Debdale La NG19 136 A1
Deben Cl S40 114 B4
Deben Down NG19 136 B2
Deborah Dr DE21 220 A4
Dee Cl DE24 231 C2
Dee La DE65 229 C3
Deep Dale La
Barrow u T DE73 244 A4
Derby DE24, DE73 231 C1
Deep La S45 133 A2
Deepdale NG16 170 C2
Deepdale Ave
Borrowash DE72 221 B1
Stapleford NG9 223 B3
Deepdale Cl
Burton u T DE15 248 A3
Staveley S43 78 C2
Deepdale Ct DE75 181 C1
Deepdale La DE6 184 A1
Deepdale Rd
Belper DE56 179 A3
Bolsover S44 98 C2
Derby DE21 220 C2
Long Eaton NG10 236 A3
Mansfield NG19 136 C1
Deepdene Cl DE11 256 B1
Deepsick La S44 97 B1
Deepwell Ave
Killamarsh S20 60 A3
Mosborough S20 59 C3
Deepwell Bank S20 59 C3
Deepwell Ct S20 59 C3
Deepwell View S20 59 C3
Deer Park Prim Sch S42 114 C2
Deer Park View DE21 220 C3
Deerlands Rd
Chesterfield S40 95 A2
Wingerworth S42 114 C1
Deerleap La S42 130 B2
Deerpark Cres S42 114 C2
Degge St DE1 267 B2
Deincourt Cl DE21 221 A3
Deincourt Com Sch S42 131 C4
Deincourt Cres S42 131 C4
Delamere Cl
Breaston DE72 235 B4
Derby DE21 206 A1
Swanwick DE55 169 C4
Delamere Dr NG18 268 C3
Delhi Cl DE15 248 B2
Dell The S40 95 A2
Delph Bank S40 114 C4
Delph Cl S32 71 B3
Delph St S2 43 A4
Delph The DE73 252 C1
Delta Ct NG1 268 A2
Delven La DE74 247 A2
Delves Bank Rd DE55 170 A4
Delves Cl S40 95 B1
Delves Ct DE75 193 C4
Delves Rd DE75 193 B4
Delves Specl Sch DE55 169 C4
Delves The DE55 169 C4
Denacre Ave NG10 223 C1
Denacre La DE4 127 C2
Denarth Ave DE24 232 C2
Denbigh St DE21 219 C4
Denby Comm DE5 180 C2
Denby Free CE Prim Sch DE5 180 B1
Denby La DE5,DE56 180 B1
Denby Pottery Visitor Ctr* DE5 180 B2
Denby Rd S43 97 B4
Dene Fields Ct DE4 143 B3
Denefield Cl SK6 15 A1
Denham St S45 131 B2
Denison Cl 7 S2 43 A3
Denison Gdns DE21 220 A3
Denman Cres S32 72 A2
Denmark Rd S2 43 A3
Dennett Cl NG3 268 C2
Dennis Barsby Cl DE11 255 C2
Dennis Cl DE23 230 C4
Dennor Dr NG19 136 C3
Denstone Coll ST14 196 A3
Denstone Dr DE24 233 A2
Denstone La ST14 196 B4
Denstone Rd NG3 268 C2
Dent La S20,S12 44 C1
Dentdale Ct DE24 233 B4
Denton Ave 7 NG10 223 A3
Denton Cl NG19 136 C1
Denton Way DE55 169 C4
Denver Ct NG9 209 C1
Denver Rd DE3 217 B2
Depedale Ave DE7 208 B3
Depot St DE23 219 A1
Derby Cath DE1 267 B4
Derby City Hospl DE23 218 A1
Derby Coll (Broomfield Campus) DE7 206 A3
Derby High Sch DE23 218 A1
Derby Hills House Ct DE73 251 C3
Derby Ind Gram Sch for Boys DE23 230 C4
Derby Industrial Mus* DE1 267 B3
Derby Knoll SK23 33 C1
Derby La Brailsford DE6 201 A4
Derby DE23 231 C4
Great Cubley DE6 198 C1
Monyash DE45 123 B4
Shirley DE6 200 C4
Derby Moor Com Sch DE23 231 A4
Derby Mus & Art Gallery* DE1 267 B3
Derby Pl S2 43 B3
Derby Rd
Alderwasley DE56 167 C1
Alfreton DE55 158 C2
Ambergate DE56 167 C2
Ashbourne DE6 185 C4
Aston-on-T DE72 234 A1
Belper DE56 190 C4
Borrowash DE21,DE72 221 A1
Burton u T DE13 241 A1
Clay Cross S45,S42 131 B3
Cromford DE4 155 B3
Dale Abbey DE7,DE21 206 C2
Derby, Chellaston DE73 232 C1
Derby, Spondon DE21 220 B2
Doveridge DE6 211 A1
Draycott DE72 234 C4
Duffield DE56 190 C1
Eastwood NG16 182 C1
Egginton DE65 241 B2
Hatton DE65 227 C1
Heanor DE75 181 B1
Hilton DE65 228 C2
Horsley DE21,DE56 191 B3
Ilkeston DE7 208 B4
Kilburn DE56 179 C1
Langley Mill NG16 182 B2
Long Eaton NG10 236 A4
Marston on D DE65 228 A1
Melbourne DE73 252 A4
New Mills SK22 24 B1
Nottingham NG7 268 A2
Ripley DE5 180 B2
Risley DE72 222 B2
Sandiacre NG10 223 A3
Smisby LE65 258 A2
Stanley DE7 207 A2
Stapleford NG9 223 B3
Swadlincote DE11 256 B2
Swanwick DE5, DE55 169 C3
Ticknall DE11,DE73 257 C4
Uttoxeter ST14 210 B1
Wingerworth S42 115 A3
Wirksworth DE4 165 C3
Derby Road Ind Est
Heanor DE75 181 B1
Sandiacre NG10 223 A3
Derby Small Bsns Ctr DE1 267 C2
Derby St Glossop SK13 17 B4
7 Ilkeston DE7 208 C4
Mansfield NG18 268 C3
Nottingham NG1 268 A2
Sheffield S2 43 B3
Stafford ST16 269 A4
Derby Sta DE1 219 B2
Derby Terr S2 43 B3
Derby Trad Est DE21 219 A4
Derby Univ (Mickleover Site) DE3 217 C2
Derbyshire Ave
Trowell NG9 209 B2
West Hallam DE7 207 C4
Derbyshire Cl DE7 207 C4
Derbyshire Cty Cricket Gd DE21 219 B3
Derbyshire Dr
Ilkeston DE7 208 C3
Westwood NG16 171 B2
Derbyshire La S8 43 A2
Derbyshire Level SK13 17 C3
Derbyshire Royal Infmy DE1 267 C1
Derrington Leys DE24 233 B3
Derventio Cl DE1 219 A4
Derwent Ave
Belper DE56 179 A1
Borrowash DE72 221 B2
Darley Dale DE4 127 B2
Derby DE72 205 A2
Grindleford S32 72 B4
Ilkeston DE7 194 B1
West Hallam DE7 207 C4
Derwent Bsns Ctr DE1 267 C4
Derwent Cl Derby DE22 205 A2
Dronfield S18 57 A2
Glossop SK13 17 C4
Grindleford S32 72 B4
Swadlincote DE11 256 A1
Derwent Com Sch DE21 219 B4
Derwent Cres S41 95 B4
Derwent Croft DE65 242 A3
Derwent Ct 10 S17 56 A3
Derwent Dr Baslow DE45 91 B3
Derwent Dr *continued*
Chinley SK23 34 C1
Derby DE24 231 B1
Tibshelf DE55 147 C3
Derwent Gdns DE6 185 B4
Derwent Gr DE55 158 C1
Derwent Ho DE21 219 B3
Derwent La Derwent S33 30 A4
Hathersage S32 52 C4
Northwood DE4 127 A3
Derwent Par DE21,DE24 219 C2
Derwent Pl S45 131 A3
Derwent Rd
Burton u T DE15 248 A1
Buxton SK17 85 B3
Derby DE21 220 B2
Dronfield S18 57 A2
Ripley DE5 169 B1
Derwent Rise DE21 220 C2
Derwent Sq SK23 34 C1
Derwent St Belper DE56 178 C2
Derby DE1 267 B3
Draycott DE72 235 A4
Long Eaton NG10 236 B3
Derwent Street Ind Est NG10 236 B3
Derwent Terr DE4 143 A4
Derwent Vale DE56 178 C1
Derwent View
Baslow DE45 91 C3
Belper, Milford DE56 191 A4
Belper, Mount Pleasant DE56 178 C3
Mastin Moor S43 79 B2
Desborough Rd NG16 171 B4
Dethick La DE4 144 B1
Dethick Way S42 132 A4
Devas Gdns DE21 220 B3
Deveron Cl DE13 240 B1
Deveron Rd S20 59 C4
Devizes Cl S40 114 C4
Devon Cl Burton u T DE15 254 C3
Derby DE21 219 B4
Grassmoor S42 115 C1
Sandiacre NG10 223 A3
Devon Dr Brimington S43 96 C4
Mansfield NG19 268 A4
Devon Park View S43 96 C4
Devon St Ilkeston DE7 209 A3
Nottingham NG3 268 C2
Devonish Royal Hospl The SK17 85 A4
Devonshire Ave
Borrowash DE72 221 B1
Darley Dale DE4 142 C4
Derby DE22 204 C2
Long Eaton NG10 237 A4
Devonshire Ave E S41 115 B4
Devonshire Ave N S43 77 C2
Devonshire Cl
Chesterfield S41 95 C4
Dore S17 55 C3
Dronfield S18 75 C4
Ilkeston DE7 194 C3
2 Staveley S43 78 C1
Devonshire Ct S43 96 B4
Devonshire Dr
Chinley SK23 34 B1
Creswell S80 81 B1
Darley Dale DE4 110 C1
Derby DE3 217 C2
Dore S17 55 C4
Duffield DE56 190 B2
Eastwood NG16 182 C1
Langwith NG20 119 C4
Somercotes DE55 170 A4
Stapleford NG9 209 B1
Devonshire Glen S17 55 C3
Devonshire Gr S17 55 C3
Devonshire Rd
Buxton SK17 85 A4
Dore S17 55 C3
Devonshire Rd E S41 115 B4
Devonshire Rd N S43 77 B2
Devonshire Sq DE4 111 A2
Devonshire St
Brimington S43 96 C4
Chesterfield S41 266 B3
New Houghton NG19 135 A4
3 Staveley S43 78 C1
Toadmoor DE56 167 C2
Devonshire Terr
Holmewood S42 116 C1
Matlock Bath DE4 143 A1
Devonshire Terrace Rd S17 55 B4
Devonshire Villas 8 S41 95 C4
Devonshire Way S43 81 A2
Dew Pond La SK17 85 B4
Dewchurch Dr DE23 231 C3
Dewint Ave SK6 23 A4
Dewsnap La SK14 9 A3
Dewy La DE4,DE55 144 C1
Dexter St DE23 219 B1
Dialstone S33 51 A4
Diamond Dr DE21 205 C2
Diamond Jubilee Cotts DE6 184 C4
Dibble Rd DE14 254 A4
Dickens Dr
Holmewood S42 116 B1
Swadlincote DE11 256 B3
Dickens Sq DE23 231 C4
Dickenson Rd S41 266 C1
Dickinson St DE24 219 B1
Dickinson's La DE6 215 A1
Dicklant La S45 145 A4
Didcot Cl S40 114 C4
Didsbury Terr SK22 25 C1
Dig St Ashbourne DE6 173 B1
Hartington SK17 137 B3
Digby St Cossall DE7 195 A1
Kimberley NG16 195 B4
Diglands Ave SK22 24 B1
Diglands Cl SK22 24 B1
Diglee Rd SK23 33 B2
Digmire La DE6 161 B1
Dimple Cres DE4 143 A3
Dimple La DE56 168 A4
Dimple Rd DE4 143 A3
Dingle Cl SK13 17 A4
Dingle La S41,S44 96 C1
Dingle The DE15 254 C4
Dingley Cl NG19 136 C3
Dinmore Grange DE11 257 A3
Dinting CE Prim Sch SK13 10 A1
Dinting La SK13 10 A1
Dinting Lane Trad Est SK13 10 A1
Dinting Lodge Ind Est SK13 9 C1
Dinting Rd SK13 10 A1
Dinting Sta SK13 10 A1
Dinting Vale SK13 10 A1
Discovery Way S41 77 A1
Diseworth Rd DE74 247 A1
Dish La DE6,DE65 228 A3
Dishwell La S26 61 C3
Disley Prim Sch SK12 32 B3
Disley Sta SK12 32 B3
Ditch Cotts SK17 105 C4
Ditch The SK17 105 C4
Division Rd NG20 119 C2
Division St S43 97 B4
Dix Ave DE7 192 C3
Dixie St NG16 171 A2
Dixon Croft S43 77 B2
Dixon Ct S41 77 A2
Dixon's Rd S41 266 C2
Dobbin La S18 75 B3
Dobbinhorse La DE6 185 A3
Dobholes La DE7 192 C3
Dobson Pl S43 97 A3
Dock Wlk S40 266 A2
Dockholm Rd NG10 223 B1
Doctor La S26 61 C3
Doctor's La DE73 252 C1
Dodburn Ct DE24 231 B2
Dodford Ct DE75 182 A1
Dodslow Ave DE13 240 A2
Doe Hill La DE55 147 B3
Doehole La
Ashover DE4,DE55 144 C2
Brackenfield DE55 145 A1
Dog La
Breedon on t H DE73 252 C3
Hulland Ward DE6 175 B2
Netherseal DE12 264 C3
Stonebroom DE55 146 C1
Doghole La DE4 154 B2
Dogkennel La DE6 186 C4
Dolby Rd SK17 85 B1
Doles La Clifton DE6 184 C4
Findern DE65 230 B2
Whitwell S80 82 A4
Dolly La Chinley SK23 34 A1
Whaley Bridge SK23 33 C2
Dolly Wood Cl SK23 34 A1
Dolphin Cl DE21 221 A3
Dominic St ST4 269 B2
Dominion Rd DE11 256 A3
Dominoe Gr S12 44 B3
Donald Bates Ho ST4 269 A1
Donald Hawley Way DE56 190 C2
Doncaster Ave NG10 223 A3
Doncaster Gr NG10 223 C1
Doncaster La ST4 269 A2
Donegal Wlk DE21 220 A2
Donington La DE72,DE74 247 B4
Donisthorpe La DE12 262 C1
Donkey La S32 72 B1
Donner Cres DE7 194 C3
Donnington Cl DE23 231 C3
Donnington Dr DE23 231 C3
Dorchester Ave DE21 219 C4
Dorchester Rd NG16 195 C4
Dore Cl S17 56 A4
Dore Hall Croft S17 55 B4
Dore La S32 53 A4
Dore Prim & Jun Sch S17 55 B3
Dore Rd S17 55 C4
Dore Sta S17 56 A4
Doris Rd DE7 209 A4
Dorking Rd DE22 218 A3
Dormy Cl NG19 136 C3
Dorothy Ave
Mansfield Woodhouse NG19 136 B1
Sandiacre NG10 223 A3
Dorothy Dr NG19 136 C1
Dorothy Vale S40 95 B2
Dorrien Ave DE23 232 A4
Dorset Ave 2 S43 96 C4
Dorset Cl Brimington S43 77 C1
Burton u T DE15 254 C3
Buxton SK17 85 B2
Dorset Dr S43 96 C4
Dorset St DE21 219 B3
Dorterry Cres DE7 209 A3
Douglas Ave
Awsworth NG16 195 B3
Heanor DE75 181 B1
Stoke-on-T ST4 269 A1
Douglas Rd
Chesterfield S41
Long Eaton NG10
Somercotes DE55
Douglas St DE23
Douse Croft La S10
Dove Bk SK6
Dove Cl Derby DE3
Kilburn DE56
Woodville DE11
Dove Fst Sch ST14
Dove Gr DE65
Dove Holes CE Prim Sc[h] SK17
Dove Holes Sta SK17
Dove House Gn DE6
Dove La Long Eaton NG10
Rocester ST14
Dove Lea DE13
Dove Rd DE5
Dove Ridge SK17
Dove Rise DE65
Dove Side DE65
Dove St DE6
Dove Valley Pk DE65
Dove View DE13
Dove Way The ST14
Dovecliff Cres DE13
Dovecliff Rd DE13
Dovecote DE74
Dovecote Dr DE72
Dovecote The
Breedon on t H DE73
Horsley DE21
Dovecotes S45
Dovedale Ave
Ashbourne DE6
Derby DE24
Long Eaton NG10
Staveley S43
Dovedale Cir DE7
Dovedale Cl
Burton u T DE15
Ripley DE5
Dovedale Cres
Belper DE56
Buxton SK17
Dovedale Ct Belper DE56
4 Chesterfield S41
Glossop SK13
Long Eaton NG10
Dovedale Prim Sch NG10
Dovedale Rd DE21
Dovedale Rise DE22
Dovefields ST14
Dover Ct DE23
Dover St Creswell S80
Derby DE23
Doveridge Cl S41
Doveridge Gr SK17
Doveridge Prim Sch
Doveridge DE6
Doveridge, Manor House DE6
Doveridge Rd DE15
Doveridge Wlk DE23
Doveside DE6
Dovewood Ct DE23
Dowcarr La S26
Dowdeswell St S41
Dower Cl DE22
Dowie Way DE4
Downham Cl DE3
Downing Cl DE22
Downing Rd Derby DE21
Sheffield S8
Downing St DE55
Downings The S26
Downlands S43
Downlee Cl SK23
Downmeadow DE56
Downs The NG19
Dowson St NG3
Doxey Rd ST16
Dr John Bingham Prim S[ch] S8
Drabbles Rd DE4
Drage St DE1
Drake Terr S43
Draycott Cl DE75
Draycott Com Prim Sch DE72
Draycott Ct DE7
Draycott Dr DE3
Draycott Pl S18
Draycott Rd
Borrowash DE72
Breaston DE72
Long Eaton NG10
North Wingfield S42
Drayton Ave Derby DE22
Mansfield NG19
Drayton St DE11
Dresden Cl DE3
Drewry Ct DE1
Drewry La DE22
Dreyfus Cl DE21
Drive The DE56
Dronfield Holmesdale Inf S18
Dronfield Inf & Jun Sch S18
Dronfield Pl DE7
Dronfield Rd S21
Dronfield Sch (Gosforth [Sch]) The S18
Dronfield Sch The S18

ield Sta S18 ....57 A1
rs Way
urne DE6 ....173 A2
idge DE56 ....168 A3
rs Wlk SK13 ....10 B1
mond Rd DE7 ....194 C1
ne DE21 ....220 B2
La Biggin SK17 .....138 B1
S17 ....55 B4
ield S18 ....57 B2
ne Ave S40 ....115 A4
an Cres ST17 ....269 A3
en St NG9 ....209 C1
en St Derby DE23 ..231 C4
ngham NG1 ....268 A2
lrst Dr SK12 ....32 B3
lrst La SK12 ....32 B3
ale Rd DE3 ....217 B2
Row DE45 ....91 B2
d St DE56 ....241 A3
manton Prim Sch
................................98 A3
manton Rd S44 ......98 A3
sett La S21 ....59 B2
worth Sq DE1 ....267 B3
ood La DE4 ....140 C4
oury Cl DE24 ....232 C4
oury The DE55 ......160 A2
ell Ct S43 ....74 B2
eld Bank DE56 ......191 A2
eld Cl NG10 ....236 A3
eld Rd DE56 ....190 C2
eld Rd DE24 ....205 A3
eld Sta S18 ....57 B2
Field DE4 ....154 B3
r Norfolk's CE Prim
SK13 ....10 B1
r Norfolk's CE Prim
(Annexe) SK13 ....10 C1
St Buxton SK17 ....84 C3
erfield S41 ....96 A4
ne S43 ....81 A2
well S80 ....81 C1
eld DE7 ....267 B4
ton DE7 ....194 C2
ileton (in Wirksworth)
................................154 B3
orough S20 ....59 B3
h Normanton DE55 .160 A3
ey S43 ....78 C1
ory DE13 ....239 B3
well S80 ....82 A3
William Mount
................................268 A1
's Dr
Hucknall S44 ....134 A4
on SK17 ....85 B3
rs Dr The DE45 .....108 C4
rs Pl NG1 ....268 B1
ries Ct S43 ....99 B2
ries La DE21 ....206 A1
s Cl S42 ....116 C1
s Dr Chesterfield S41 .95 C3
ar S32 ....72 B1
s Fold SK13 ....17 A4
s Pl DE7 ....194 C2
s St SK13 ....17 B4
th Ave DE21 ....220 A4
erton Ave DE24 .....231 B1
ich Rd DE22 ....217 C3
ble Wood Grange
................................95 B4
bles Cl DE7 ....208 B3
bles La DE55 ....180 C1
bles Rd S44 ....98 A3
bleton Rd S21 ....60 C3
bar Cl DE21 ....231 C1
zan Cl DE56 ....179 A3
zcan Rd DE24 ....231 C4
cliffe La DE73 ....252 A4
ombe Dr DE6 ....185 B4
las Ct NG1 ....268 B2
lee Dr NG19 ....136 A3
lee Rd DE11 ....256 B3
onald Rd S40 ....266 B3
edin Cl DE3 ....217 C2
edin Cres DE11 .....248 B1
edin Glen S20 ....59 C3
edin Gr S20 ....59 C3
gley Hill DE56 ......168 B1
greave Ave DE4 ....127 A3
very Ct DE21 ....206 A1
kirk DE22 ....267 A2
ow La S32 ....71 B3
n Brigg NG19 ....136 B1
ne La SS13 ....10 C1
nett Rd NG18 ....268 A3
nsmoor La DE11 ...256 C4
ion DE24 ....231 C2
rard Rd NG18 ....268 A3
sa La DE45 ....91 B3
sford Rd DE55 ......159 A3
shill Wlk S45 ....131 C2
sil Rd NG16 ....160 B1
smore Dr DE21 .....205 C1
smore Way DE11 ...256 B3
Brook DE15 ....248 A1
stall Park Rd DE24 .232 B4
stall Rd S41 ....76 C1
ston Cl S41 ....76 C1
ston La S41 ....95 B4
ston Pl S41 ....95 B4
ston Prim Sch S41 ..95 B4
ston Rd S41 ....76 B1

Dunston Tech Pk S41 ....76 C1
Dunston Trad Est S41 ...76 C1
Dunton Cl DE21 ....267 D3
Dunvegan Ave S45 ....131 C1
Dunvegan Cl DE24 ....231 B1
Duper La S32 ....51 C3
Durban Cl DE15 ....248 C3
Durban House Her Ctr*
....................................182 C2
Durham Ave
Chesterfield S43 ....77 B2
Derby DE21 ....219 C3
Grassmoor S42 ....115 C1
Nottingham NG2 ....268 C1
Durham Cl
Chesterfield S43 ....77 B2
Mansfield Woodhouse ....
NG19 ....136 B2
Nottingham NG2 ....268 C1
Swadlincote DE11 ....256 C3
Durham St **5** DE7 ......194 C2
Durley Chine Dr S41 ....115 B4
Durley Cl DE24 ....233 B4
Durlstone Cl S12 ....44 A3
Durlstone Cres S12 ....44 A3
Durlstone Dr S12 ....44 A3
Durrant Rd S41 ....266 B3
Durvale Ct S17 ....55 C3
Durward Rd DE24 ....232 B4
Dyche Cl S8 ....57 A3
Dyche Dr S8 ....57 A3
Dyche La S8,S18 ....57 A3
Dyche Pl S8 ....57 A3
Dyche Rd S8 ....57 A3
Dye House La SK22 ......33 B4
Dyke Vale Rd S12 ....44 C3
Dykes Cl S44 ....99 A1
Dymond Gr S42 ....115 C2
Dystelegh Rd SK12 ....32 B3

E

Each Well La DE55 ....158 C2
Eagle Cl DE56 ....178 C1
Eagle Ctr DE1 ....267 B2
Eagle Hts DE55 ....248 B2
Eagle Par **4** SK17 ....85 A4
Eagle St **3** Buxton SK17 ..85 A4
Heage DE56 ....91 A3
Eagle Terr Birchover DE4 ..126 A1
Wensley DE4 ....142 A4
Ealing Cl DE22 ....218 A3
Eardley Cl DE21 ....220 A3
Eardley St S14 ....269 A1
Earl St ST16 ....269 A1
Earl Sterndale CE Prim Sch
SK17 ....105 B2
Earls Cres DE21 ....206 A1
Earlsway **5** SK13 ....17 A4
Earlswood Ct DE72 ......235 B4
Earlswood Dr S12 ....217 C2
Earnshaw St SK14 ....9 B2
Easedale Cl S40 ....94 C3
East Ave Bolsover S44 ..80 A1
Derby DE3 ....72 B1
East Bank Cl S44 ....80 A1
East Bank Dr S44 ....141 B3
East Bank Pl S2 ....43 B3
East Bank Rd S2 ....43 B3
East Bank View S2 ....43 B3
East Bank Way S2 ....43 B3
East Circus St **2** NG1 ..268 A1
East Cl DE22 ....204 C1
East Cres Holbrook DE56 ..191 B4
Long Duckmanton S44 ..98 A3
East Croft Ave DE23 ....231 B3
East Dr DE6 ....211 A1
East End Dr DE11 ....256 B2
East Glade Ave S12 .....44 C2
East Glade Cl S12 ....44 C2
East Glade Cres S12 .....44 C2
East Glade Pl S12 ....44 C2
East Glade Rd S12 ....44 C2
East Glade Sq S12 ....44 C2
East Glade Way S12 .....44 C2
East Hill Prim Sch S2 ...43 B4
East Lawn DE65 ....230 B1
East Midlands International
Airport S74 ....247 B1
East Midlands Nuffield Hospl
DE23 ....231 A4
East Nelson St DE75 ....181 C1
East Rd S2 ....43 A4
East Service Rd DE21 ..220 A2
East St Bramley-Vale S44 ..117 B1
Burton u T DE15 ....248 A1
Clay Cross S45 ....131 B2
Clowne S43 ....81 A3
Creswell S80 ....81 B1
Derby S80 ....267 B3
Heanor DE75 ....208 C4
Ilkeston DE7 ....208 C4
Long Eaton NG10 ....236 C4
Nottingham NG1 ....268 B2
Renishaw S43 ....79 A4
Scarcliffe S44 ....118 C3
Shirland S14 ....46 B3
East View
Chesterfield S40 ....266 B2
Mayfield DE6 ....184 B4
Shirebrook NG20 ....119 C3
Whaley Thorns NG20 ...101 A2
East View Ave S21 ....59 B1
East View Ind Est NG20 ..119 C3
East View Rd DE56 ......168 C1

Eastbrae Rd DE23 ....231 B4
Eastbrook Cl SK23 ....47 B3
Eastcliffe Ct S2 ....43 B4
Eastcliffe Rd S20 ....59 C4
Eastcroft Cl S20 ....59 C4
Eastcroft Dr S20 ....59 C4
Eastcroft Glen **10** S20 ..59 C4
Eastcroft View **11** S20 ..59 C4
Eastcroft Way **13** S20 ..59 C4
Eastdale Rd
Bolsover S44 ....118 A4
Sheffield S2 ....43 C4
Eastern Ave S43 ....43 B3
Eastern Cres S2 ....43 B3
Eastern Dr S2 ....43 B3
Eastern Wlk S2 ....43 B4
Eastfield Dr DE55 ....160 A3
Eastfield Rd Dronfield S18 ..76 B4
Ripley DE5 ....170 A1
Swadlincote DE11 ....256 B3
Eastgate DE1,DE21 ....267 D4
Eastgate St ST16 ....269 B4
Eastlake Cl NG3 ....268 C2
Eastleigh Dr DE23 ....231 A4
Eastleigh Dr Derby DE3 ..217 C1
Mansfield Woodhouse ....
NG19 ....136 A3
Eastmoor Rd S43 ....96 C2
Eastside Cl S41 ....96 A4
Eastside Rd S41 ....96 A4
Eastview Terr NG16 .....182 A2
Eastway DE74 ....247 A2
Eastwood Ave DE23 .....218 B1
Eastwood Cl S41 ....115 B4
Eastwood Comp Sch
NG16 ....182 C2
Eastwood Cotts S32 .....53 A4
Eastwood Dr Calow S44 ..97 A1
Derby DE23 ....231 A4
Eastwood Jun & Inf Schs
NG16 ....182 C1
Eastwood La S45 ....130 A1
Eastwood Park Dr S41 ..115 B4
Eastwood Rd NG16 ......195 C3
Easy Par S80 ....63 A4
Eather Ave NG19 ....136 B2
Eaton Ave Derby DE22 ..205 B2
Ilkeston DE7 ....208 B3
Eaton Bank DE6 ....191 A1
Eaton Cl Derby DE22 ...205 B2
Hatton DE65 ....227 B1
Hulland Ward DE6 ....175 C2
Eaton Ct Derby DE1 .....218 C3
Duffield DE56 ....190 C1
Eaton Dr DE45 ....91 C3
Eaton Grange Dr NG10 ..236 A4
Eaton Hill DE45 ....91 C3
Eaton La DE45 ....91 C3
Eaton Rd
Castle Donington DE74 ..247 A2
Rocester ST14 ....196 C2
Sheffield S11 ....210 B1
Eatons Rd NG9 ....223 B3
Eaves La S43 ....47 B3
Eaves Knoll Rd SK22 ...33 A4
Ebenezer St Glossop SK13 ..17 B4
Ilkeston DE7 ....194 C2
Langley Mill NG16 ....182 A2
Eccles Cl Hope S33 ....39 A2
Whaley Bridge SK23 ....45 B4
Eccles Fold S33 ....47 A3
Eccles Rd
Chapel-en-le-F, Higher Crossings ..
SK23 ....46 A3
Chapel-en-le-F, Hilltop SK23 ..46 B4
Eccles Terr SK23 ....46 B4
Ecclesbourne Ave DE56 ..190 C2
Ecclesbourne Cl
SK13 ....190 C2
Wirksworth DE4 ....165 C4
Ecclesbourne Cotts
DE4 ....154 C1
Ecclesbourne Dr SK17 ..85 A3
Ecclesbourne La DE56 ..176 C3
Ecclesbourne Pk DE55 ..159 B1
Ecclesbourne Sch The
DE56 ....190 C2
Eckington Cl DE7 ....207 C4
Eckington Hall S20 ....59 B3
Eckington Jun Sch S21 ..59 A2
Eckington Mews S20 ....59 B3
Eckington Rd
Dronfield S18 ....57 B2
Mosborough S20 ....59 C4
Staveley S43 ....78 C2
Unstone S43 ....77 B3
Eckington Sch S21 ....59 A2
Eckington Way S20 ......59 C4
Eclipse Yd NG18 ....268 B3
Edale Ave DE7 ....218 C1
Derby, Alvaston DE24 ..233 A4
Derby, Mickleover DE3 ..217 B1
Edale Bank **6** SK13 ....9 C1
Edale Cl Derby DE22 ...204 B1
Glossop SK13 ....9 C1
Long Eaton NG10 ....236 A3
Edale Cres SK13 ....9 C1
Edale Ct **1** S41 ....95 C4
Edale Dr Derby DE21 ....220 C2
South Normanton DE55 ..160 A4
Edale Gr SK17 ....85 C4
Edale Rd Hayfield SK22 ..26 A1
Hope S33 ....39 A2
Mastin Moor S43 ....79 B2
Edale Rise NG2 ....223 C2
Edale Sq DE7 ....194 C3
Edale St S33 ....37 B4

Edale Way DE56 ....179 A3
Edale YH* S33 ....29 A1
Eden Bank DE56 ....167 C1
Eden Low NG19 ....136 C2
Eden Rd DE21 ....220 A2
Eden St Derby DE24 ....233 A4
Wingerworth S42 ....114 C2
Edenhall Rd S2 ....43 C4
Edensor Ave SK17 ....85 C4
Edensor Cl S42 ....131 C3
Edensor Ct **3** S43 ....97 B4
Edensor Dr DE56 ....179 B3
Edensor Sq DE22 ....218 C2
Edes Farm Dr ST14 ......196 C2
Edgar Ave NG18 ....268 C4
Edgbaston Ct DE23 ......231 B4
Edge Hill DE73 ....232 C2
Edge Hill Ave NG3 ......268 B2
Edge Hill Jun Sch DE15 ..254 C4
Edge La S33 ....39 A2
Edge Mount View S32 ..72 C1
Edge Rd Eyam S32 ....71 C4
Matlock DE4 ....143 A3
Edge View S32 ....72 A2
Edge View Ct S32 ....72 B4
Edge View Dr DE45 ......90 A2
Edgecote Dr DE11 ....256 A4
Edgefold Rd DE4 ....143 A3
Edgehill Gr NG19 ....136 B1
Edgelaw Ct **10** DE24 ..231 B2
Edgewood Rd NG16 .....195 C3
Edginton St NG3 ....268 B2
Edinboro Row NG16 .....195 C4
Edinburgh Cres DE24 ...232 C2
Edinburgh Ct
Chesterfield S41 ....266 A4
Swanwick DE55 ....170 A4
Edinburgh Rd
Chesterfield S41 ....95 C3
Wingerworth S42 ....114 C2
Edison St ST4 ....269 C1
Edison Way DE24 ....233 A3
Edlaston La S16 ....185 A1
Edmonton Pl DE15 ......248 B1
Edmund Ave S17 ....56 B3
Edmund Cl S17 ....56 B3
Edmund Rd Derby DE22 ..220 C2
Sheffield S2 ....43 B4
Edmund St S43 ....230 A4
Edmund's Sq DE7 ....230 A4
Ednaston Ave DE23 .....231 B3
Ednaston Hall Farm Mews
DE6 ....201 A4
Edward Ave Derby DE21 ..220 A3
Westwood NG16 ....171 A3
Edward Rd NG10 ....236 C4
Edward St Aldercar NG16 ..182 A2
Belper DE56 ....179 A2
Derby DE1 ....267 A2
Eckington S21 ....59 B2
Glossop SK13 ....10 B1
Hartshorne DE11 ....257 A2
Marple SK6 ....15 A1
Moira DE11 ....256 B1
Overseal DE12 ....262 A2
Stapleford NG9 ....223 B4
Staveley S43 ....97 B4
Edwards Ct DE56 ....179 B4
Edwards Cres DE56 .....190 A2
Edwards Dr ST16 ....269 A4
Edwin Ave S40 ....114 B4
Edwin Rd S2 ....43 B3
Edwinstowe Rd DE21 ..206 A1
Egerton Dr NG9 ....209 B1
Egerton Rd Dronfield S18 ..57 A1
Stoke-on-T ST4 ....269 A2
Eggesford Rd DE24 .....231 B1
Egginton Prim Sch
DE65 ....241 A3
Egginton Rd Etwall DE65 ..229 A1
Hilton DE65 ....228 C1
Egmanton Cl DE21 ......206 A1
Egreaves Ave DE75 .....181 B2
Egstow Pl S45 ....131 B2
Egstow St S45 ....131 B2
Ehlinger Ave SK13 ....10 A3
Eider Cl NG20 ....119 C3
Eighth Ave DE24 ....232 C1
Eland Cl DE21 ....223 A3
Eland Rd NG20 ....119 C3
Elder Cl DE21 ....170 A4
Elder Ct S21 ....60 B3
Elder Way S40 ....266 B3
Eldon Cl SK23 ....47 B3
Eldon Ct SK17 ....49 A3
Eldon La SK17 ....49 A3
Eldon St Burton u T DE15 ..248 A2
Clay Cross S45 ....131 B2
Eleanor Ave DE7 ....209 A3
Eleanor Cres NG9 ....223 C4
Elenora St ST4 ....269 B2
Eley Cl DE7 ....194 B1
Eley Wlk DE22 ....267 A1
Elgar Dr NG10 ....236 A3
Elgin Ave DE23 ....218 A1
Elgin Cl S40 ....114 B4
Eliot Cl NG20 ....101 A1
Eliot Dr DE7 ....208 B3
Eliot Rd DE23 ....231 A4
Eliot Way ST17 ....269 A3
Elizabeth Ave
Buxton SK17 ....85 B4
Disley SK12 ....32 B3
Rolleston DE13 ....240 A2
Elizabeth Cl DE21 ....220 A3

Elizabeth Cl continued
West Hallam DE7 ....207 B4
Elizabeth Ct Ilkeston DE7 ..194 B1
Stoke-on-T ST4 ....269 A2
Elizabeth Pk NG16 ....170 C3
Elkstone Cl DE21 ....206 A1
Elkstone Rd S40 ....95 A3
Ella Bank Rd DE75 ......181 C1
Ellastone Gdns DE24 ...233 A4
Ellastone Gr ST4 ....269 A1
Ellendale Rd DE21 ....220 A4
Ellerslie Gr NG10 ....223 A3
Ellesmere Ave
Alfreton DE55 ....159 A2
Derby DE6 ....219 B1
Ellesmere Dr NG9 ....209 B3
Ellington Ave ST16 ......269 C4
Elliot Ave S33 ....51 A4
Elliott Dr S43 ....97 B3
Elliott St NG7 ....268 A2
Ellis Cl NG10 ....236 B3
Ellis Cl S41 ....268 B2
Ellison Ave DE72 ....246 A4
Ellison Cl S14 ....9 B3
Ellison St S43 ....10 B1
Elm Ave Belper DE56 ...179 A1
Darley Dale DE4 ....142 C4
Long Eaton NG10 ....236 B4
Sandiacre NG10 ....223 A4
Elm Cl Bolsover S44 .....99 B1
Branston DE14 ....253 C4
Chesterfield S41 ....95 C4
Doveridge DE6 ....224 B4
Killamarsh S21 ....60 B3
Mottram in Lxdd S 9 A2
Pinxton NG16 ....160 B2
Elm Cres S20 ....59 B4
Killamarsh S21 ....60 B3
Elm Gr Clay Cross S45 ..131 B2
Derby DE24 ....204 B3
Derby, Cherrytree Hill ....
DE21 ....220 A3
Elm St S41 ....10 B1
Elm Lodge Farm Cl S41 ..267 A5
Elm Park Ct S41 ....267 A5
Elm Rd Eckington S21 ..59 B1
Pilsley S45 ....132 B1
Elm St E Borrowash DE72 ..221 A1
Brimington S43 ....97 A4
Holmewood S42 ....116 A2
Elm Tree Ave
Kilburn DE56 ....192 A4
Mansfield Woodhouse ....
NG19 ....119 A2
Shirebrook NG20 ....119 B2
Shirland DE55 ....146 B1
Elm Tree Cres S18 ....57 A2
Elm Tree Dr S42 ....116 A2
Elm Tree St NG18 ....268 C4
Elm View S31 ....196 C3
Elm Wlk S45 ....132 B1
Elma La S80 ....101 B3
Elmfield SK23 ....47 B3
Elmhurst Ave DE55 .....241 A3
Elmhurst Cl DE11 ....160 A2
Elmhurst Cl DE55 ....160 B2
Elmhurst Rd NG19 ....136 C1
Elmore Ct NG7 ....268 A2
Elms Ave Alfreton DE55 ..159 A2
Derby DE23 ....218 A1
Elms Cl DE55 ....159 A2
Elms Farm Way DE23 ..218 A1
Elms Gr DE55 ....229 B2
Elms Rd Burton u T DE15 ..248 A1
Coton in t E DE12 ....260 B2
Elms St DE1 ....218 C4
Elms The NG16 ....195 C4
Elmsdale Rd DE11 ....257 A2
Elmsfield Ave DE75 .....182 A1
Elmslea Ave DE12 ....260 B2
Elmsleigh Cl DE11 ....256 A3
Elmsleigh Dr DE11 ......256 A3
Elmsleigh Inf Sch DE11 ..256 A3
Elmton Cl Clowne S43 ..80 C2
Creswell S80 ....100 B4
Elmton La S44 ....81 C1
Elmton Rd S80 ....81 C1
Elmtree Ave DE24 ....232 A4
Selston NG16 ....171 C4
Elmtree Cl S81 ....63 C4
Elmwood Dr DE21 ....205 B1
Mosborough S20 ....59 B2
Elnor Ave S43 ....45 C3
Elnor La SK23 ....45 C3
Elnor St NG16 ....182 B2
Elsecar Cl DE56 ....179 B3
Elstead La DE11 ....257 A1
Elston Cl NG19 ....135 B1
Elstree Dr S12 ....44 A2
Elstree Rd S12 ....44 A2
Elton Bank SK13 ....9 B1
North Wingfield S42 .....132 A3
Stapleford NG9 ....223 A4
Elton Cl Gamesley SK13 ..9 B1
Derby DE22 ....218 A1
Elton Rd Derby DE24 ...232 A4
Winster DE4 ....141 A3
Elton St S40 ....266 B2
Elton View S43 ....97 A4

Elvaston Castle* DE21 233 C4
Elvaston Castle Ctry Pk DE21 233 C3
Elvaston Cl S18 56 A1
Elvaston Dr NG10 236 A2
Elvaston Estate Mus* DE72 233 C4
Elvaston La DE24 233 B4
Elvaston Rd S42 131 C3
Elvaston St DE72 235 A4
Elveden Dr DE7 194 B2
Elvin Way S42 131 B4
Elwood Rd S17 56 B3
Elwyn Cl DE13 240 B1
Ely Cl
Mansfield Woodhouse NG19 136 B2
Swadlincote DE11 256 B3
Elyn Ave S42 132 A4
Elysee Gdns SK17 85 B2
Embankment Cl DE22 217 C4
Ember La DE4 142 C1
Embridge Cswy SK10, SK17 64 A3
Emerald Cl Derby DE21 206 A1
Mansfield NG19 135 C1
Emerson Sq DE23 231 C3
Emery Cl DE12 261 B3
Emmas Williams Ct DE5 169 B1
Emmet Field Cl S40 114 C4
Emmett Carr Cl S21 79 B4
Emmett Carr Dr S21 79 B4
Emmett Carr La S21 79 B4
Empire Pas ST4 269 B1
Empire Rd DE15 248 B2
Empire St
Mansfield NG18 268 C3
Stoke-on-T ST4 269 B1
Empress Rd DE23 267 A1
Emsworth Cl DE7 194 B2
Ena Ave NG2 268 C2
End The DE15 248 C4
Endland Ind Est DE1 218 B3
Endowood Rd S40 114 A4
Endsleigh Gdns DE22 217 C3
Enfield Cl DE65 228 C1
Enfield Rd
Chesterfield S41 96 A3
Derby DE22 218 A3
England Cres DE75 182 A1
English Martyrs RC Prim Sch NG10 223 A1
Englishe Rd DE4 143 A2
Ennerdale Ave S20 59 C3
Ennerdale Cl S18 56 C1
Ennerdale Cres S41 95 B4
Ennerdale Ct 6 NG10 223 A1
Ennerdale Dr S20 59 C3
Ennerdale Rd NG10 223 A1
Ennerdale Wlk DE21 205 B1
Ennis Cl DE21 220 B4
Enoch Stone Dr DE21 220 A2
Enslet La DE6 164 A2
Ensor Cl DE11 256 B3
Ensor Way SK22 33 B4
Enterprise Cl NG19 135 C1
Enterprise Ct S80 81 C1
Enterprise Dr S42 116 B1
Enterprise Way NG19 135 C2
Epping Cl DE22 217 C3
Epsley's Yd ST16 269 B3
Epsom Cl DE14 253 C4
Epsom Rd NG9 223 C2
Epworth Dr DE24 233 A2
Epworth Ho DE15 248 B2
Epworth St ST4 269 B2
Erdington Way NG9 223 C2
Erewash Ct DE7 194 B1
Erewash Dr DE7 209 A3
Erewash Gr NG9 223 C1
Erewash Mus* DE7 208 C4
Erewash Rd NG16 160 C1
Erewash Sq DE7 209 A3
Erewash St DE55 171 A3
Erica Dr DE55 160 A4
Erin Rd S43,S44 98 A4
Ernest Hall Way DE11 256 B2
Ernocroft La SK6 15 C1
Ernocroft Rd SK6 15 A1
Errill Cl ST4 269 C1
Errington Ave S2 43 C3
Errington Cl S2 43 C3
Errington Cres S2 43 C3
Errington Rd
Chesterfield S40 114 B4
Sheffield S2 43 C3
Errington Way S2 43 C4
Errwood Ave SK17 85 A3
Errwood Forest Walks* SK17 64 C1
Erskine Cres S2 43 B4
Erskine Rd S2 43 B4
Erskine St SK6 15 A2
Erskine View S2 43 B4
Escolme Cl DE11 256 B2
Eskdale Cl Bolsover S44 98 C1
Dronfield S18 56 C1
Long Eaton NG10 236 A3
Eskdale Wlk 8 DE24 233 B3
Essendine Cres S8 43 A2
Essex Rd DE15 254 B3
Essex St Derby DE21 219 B3
4 Ilkeston DE7 194 C1
Estwic Ave NG16 182 C2
Ethel Wainwright Fst & Mid Schs NG19 268 A4
Etherow Brow SK14 16 A4
Etherow Ctry Pk SK6 15 B2
Etherow Ctry Pk Visitor Ctr SK6 15 A2
Etherow Ind Est SK13 9 C3
Etherow Way SK13 9 C3
Eton Ct DE7 207 B4
Eton St DE24 219 C1
Etruria Gdns DE1 267 B5
Etta's Way DE65 229 A2
Ettrick Cl 4 S40 95 B3
Ettrick Dr DE24 231 C1
Etwall Cl S40 95 A3
Etwall La DE65 229 C3
Etwall Prim Sch DE65 229 A2
Etwall Rd Derby DE3 217 B1
Egginton DE65 241 A4
Willington DE65 242 A4
Etwall St DE22 218 C3
Eugene St NG2 268 B1
Eureka Prim Sch DE11 256 B3
Eureka Rd DE11 256 B3
Euston Dr DE1 267 C5
Evans Ave DE22 205 A3
Evans St DE24 232 C3
Evanston Gdns DE21 220 A3
Evelyn Devonshire Cotts S45 132 C1
Evelyn Gr DE21 220 A3
Evelyn St NG1 268 C1
Everard Ave S17 56 A3
Everard Dr S17 56 A3
Everard Glade 6 S17 56 A3
Everest Dr DE55 170 B4
Everett Cl S43 96 C4
Evergreen Cl DE21 206 A2
Evershill Cl DE55 146 C3
Evershill La DE55 146 C3
Eversleigh Rise DE4 142 A4
Everton St NG19 135 C1
Evesham Ave SK13 10 A3
Evesham Cl DE21 205 C1
Ewart La DE55 158 C2
Ewe Dale La DE6 149 A2
Ewe Lamb Cl NG9 209 C1
Ewe Lamb La NG9 209 C1
Excelsior Ave DE24 232 C3
Exchange St DE1 267 B3
Exchange Wlk 2 NG1 268 B1
Exe Fold NG19 136 B1
Exeter Cl DE11 256 C3
Exeter Ho DE1 267 C3
Exeter Pl DE1 267 C3
Exeter St DE1 267 C4
Exford Ct NG19 136 B3
Exlowmere La DE4 140 C3
Export Dr NG17 160 C4
Extension St 9 DE7 208 C4
Eyam CE Prim Sch S32 71 B3
Eyam Cl Burton u T DE15 248 A1
North Wingfield S42 132 A4
Eyam Fold 12 SK13 9 B1
Eyam Gn 8 SK13 9 B1
Eyam Hall* S32 71 B3
Eyam La SK13 9 B1
Eyam Lea 3 SK13 9 C1
Eyam Mews SK13 9 C1
Eyam Mus* S32 71 B3
Eyam Wlk DE56 179 A3
Eyam YH* S32 71 B3
Eyes Ct DE56 190 C2
Eyre Gdns S40 266 A4
Eyre St Clay Cross S45 131 B2
Creswell S80 81 B1
Nottingham NG2 268 C1
Eyre St E S41 115 B4
Eyre's Gdns DE7 194 C1
Eyrie The
Burton u T DE15 248 B2
Derby DE24 231 C1

F

Fabis Cl DE11 256 A2
Fabric View S42 132 B4
Factory La Disley SK12 32 C4
Ilkeston DE7 194 C1
Factory St S40 95 B1
Fair Lea Cl NG10 236 B3
Fair View S40 95 C2
Fairbank Ave ST4 269 B1
Fairbourne Dr DE3 217 B2
Fairburn Croft Cres S43 80 A3
Faircroft Ave NG10 223 A3
Fairdene DE23 218 C1
Faire St DE22 218 C2
Faires Cl DE72 221 B1
Fairfax Dr S2 44 A4
Fairfax Rd Derby DE23 218 C1
Sheffield S2 44 A4
Fairfield Ave
Borrowash DE72 221 B2
Hilcote DE55 148 B1
Rolleston DE13 240 B2
Stonebroom DE55 147 A2
Fairfield Cl Brimington S43 96 B4
Whaley Thorns NG20 101 A1
Fairfield Cres
Long Eaton NG10 236 A2
Swadlincote DE11 255 C3
Fairfield Ct S42 94 C2
Fairfield Dr S42 94 C2
Fairfield Endowed CE Jun Sch SK17 85 C4
Fairfield Inf Sch SK17 85 B4
Fairfield Prim Sch NG9 223 B3
Fairfield Rd
Bolsover S44 118 A4
Buxton SK17 85 B4
Chesterfield S40 266 A4
Derby DE23 218 C1
Horsley Woodhouse DE7 192 B4
Fairfield Terr DE11 256 C2
Fairford Cl S40 114 C4
Fairford Gdns DE23 231 A3
Fairham Rd DE13 240 C1
Fairholme Dr NG19 135 C1
Fairholmes DE4 143 B3
Fairisle Cl DE21 206 B2
Fairlawns DE56 190 B2
Fairleigh S2 44 A4
Fairmeadows Prim Sch DE11 255 C3
Fairview Ave NG16 171 C1
Fairview Cl Derby DE23 231 A4
Kilburn DE56 192 A4
Fairview Grange DE56 192 A4
Fairview Rd S18 57 A2
Fairview Rise DE4 168 A4
Fairway Burton u T DE14 254 A3
Stafford ST16,ST17 269 C3
Fairway Cl DE22 204 B1
Fairway Cres DE22 204 B1
Fairway The Clifton DE6 184 C3
Swadlincote DE11 255 C3
Fairways Cl SK13 10 C1
Fairways The
Clay Cross S45 131 C2
Mansfield Woodhouse NG19 136 B3
Fairwinds Cl S18 57 A1
Fairwood Dr DE24 233 B3
Fairy Bank Cres SK22 25 B2
Fairy Bank Rd SK22 25 B2
Fal Paddock NG19 136 B1
Falaise Way DE65 228 C1
Falcon Cl SK22 33 B4
Falcon Ct DE7 194 B1
Falcon Rd S18 57 B2
Falcon Rise S18 57 B2
Falcon Way Derby DE24 231 C1
Woodville DE11 256 C2
Falcon Yd S40 266 B3
Falcons Rise DE56 179 B3
Faldo Cl DE14 254 A3
Falkland Rise S18 76 A4
Fall Rd DE75 181 C2
Fallow Rd DE21 220 C3
Fallowfield Rd S43 77 B2
Falmouth Rd DE24 233 B3
Fan Rd S43 78 C1
Fan Road Ind Est S43 78 C1
Fanny Ave S21 60 C3
Fanshaw Ave S21 59 B1
Fanshaw Bank S18 57 A1
Fanshaw Cl S21 59 B1
Fanshaw Dr S21 59 B1
Fanshaw Gate La S18 55 C1
Fanshaw Rd Dronfield S18 57 A1
Eckington S21 59 B1
Fanshaw Way S21 59 B1
Far Croft DE72 235 B4
Far Cross DE4 143 B4
Far Gn DE4 143 A3
Far Hill S33 51 A4
Far La Barlow S18 75 A2
Ockbrook DE72 221 B3
Far Laund DE56 179 A3
Far New Cl NG10 223 A3
Far Woodseats La SK13 15 C3
Faraday Ave DE13 240 B1
Faraday Ct NG9 209 C1
Faraday Pl ST4 269 A2
Farfield Rd DE7 209 A4
Farish Pl 8 S2 43 A3
Farley Hill DE4 143 A4
Farley La DE4 128 A2
Farley Rd DE23 218 B1
Farm Cl Belper DE56 179 B2
Chesterfield S40 114 C3
Dronfield S18 57 A2
Hilton DE65 228 B1
Ilkeston DE7 209 A4
Kilburn DE56 192 A4
Long Eaton NG10 236 C3
Ripley DE5 169 A3
Sheffield S12 44 A1
Somercotes DE55 170 B4
Farm Cres S20 59 B3
Farm Croft Rd NG19 136 B3
Farm Dr DE24 233 A3
Farm La High Lane SK12 32 A3
Matlock DE4 143 B4
Newton Solney DE15 248 C4
Farm Side DE11 255 C3
Farm St DE22 218 C2
Farm View S42 131 B4
Farm Wlk S20 59 B4
Farmfields Cl S44 98 C2
Farmhouse Rd DE24 231 C1
Farmilo Cres NG19 135 C1
Farmilo Prim Sch NG19 135 B2
Farmlands La DE23 231 A3
Farmstead Cl S14 43 B3
Farmway NG19 136 B1
Farnah Green Rd DE56 178 B2
Farnborough Gdns DE22 205 A2
Farncombe La DE21 205 C2
Farndale Ave S40 114 A4
Farndale Cl NG10 236 A3
Farndale Ct 5 DE24 233 B3
Farndale Rd S43 78 C2
Farndon Dr NG9 223 C2
Farndon Way NG19 268 A4
Farneworth Rd DE3 217 B1
Farnham Cl DE3 217 B1
Farnham Wlk DE7 207 B4
Farningham Cl DE21 220 C3
Farnon Cl S40 266 C1
Farnsley La S32 71 A2
Farnsworth Gr NG17 148 C2
Farnsworth St S41 115 B4
Farnway DE22 204 C1
Farrendale Cl NG19 136 B1
Farrier Gdns DE23 231 A4
Farriers Croft DE7 194 B2
Farringdon Cl DE22 217 C3
Farrington Way NG16 182 C1
Farthing Ct NG10 236 A4
Farwater Cl S18 76 A4
Farwater La S18 56 C1
Fauld Ind Pk DE13 238 C3
Fauld La Tutbury DE13 239 A3
Tutbury, Fauld DE13 238 B4
Fauvel Pl SK13 10 B1
Fauvel Rd SK13 10 B1
Faversham Cl DE24 232 C3
Fawn Cl S42 114 C2
Fay Gdns SK13 9 C2
Faywood Dr SK6 23 A3
Fearn Ave DE5 169 C1
Fearn Cl
Church Broughton DE65 227 A4
Long Eaton DE72 236 A4
Featherbed La
Bolsover S44 99 A3
Whitwell S80 63 C1
Featherstone Gr ST4 269 B2
Felkin St S41 266 C3
Fellbrigg Rd S2 43 B4
Fellowlands Way DE73 233 A1
Fellside Belper DE56 179 A2
Derby DE21 220 C3
Fellview Cl S32 53 A4
Felton Ave NG19 136 B3
Fenchurch Wlk DE22 218 A4
Fenland Way S40 114 C4
Fennel St DE45 108 C4
Fenton Ave DE11 257 A1
Fenton Rd DE3 217 B1
Fenton St S21 59 A1
Fenwick St DE24 232 B4
Ferguson Ave NG19 136 A2
Fern Ave Staveley S43 97 B4
Willington DE65 242 B3
Fern Bank Ave DE55 147 C1
Fern Cl Eckington S21 59 A2
Holmewood S44 116 C1
Shirebrook NG20 119 C3
Willington DE65 242 B3
Fern Cres NG16 182 B2
Fern Lea Hollingworth SK14 9 B3
Shirland DE55 146 B2
Fern Rd SK17 85 A3
Fern Royd S32 53 A4
Fern Way S21 59 A2
Fernbank S33 51 A4
Fernbank Dr S21 59 A2
Ferncroft Ave S20 59 B4
Ferndale Ave SK17 67 B2
Ferndale Cl S18 57 B2
Ferndale Rd Buxton SK17 67 B2
Dronfield S18 57 B2
Ferndale Rise S18 57 B2
Ferndene Dr NG10 236 A4
Fernello Cl DE73 244 A3
Ferneydale Ave SK17 85 B2
Fernhill SK6 23 A3
Fernhill Cl SK13 10 B2
Fernhill Ct DE73 233 A2
Fernilee Cl New Mills SK22 24 B1
West Hallam DE7 207 C4
Fernilee Cotts SK23 45 C1
Fernlea Cl SK13 9 C2
Fernleigh Rise NG19 136 B1
Fernway SK17 85 B2
Fernwood SK6 23 B4
Fernwood Cl
Chesterfield S41 115 C4
Derby DE23 231 B4
Shirland DE55 146 B2
Ferrers Ave DE13 239 A3
Ferrers Cl DE74 247 A2
Ferrers Cres DE56 190 B2
Ferrers Ctr for Arts & Crafts* LE65 258 C4
Ferrers Way Derby DE22 204 C1
Ripley DE5 169 B2
Ferrers Wlk NG3 268 C2
Ferry Gn DE65 242 A3
Ferry St DE15 254 C4
Ferry Vale Cl DE15 254 C4
Festival Ave DE72 235 B4
Festival Rd
Branston DE14 253 C4
Ilkeston DE7 208 B3
Festus Cl NG3 268 B2
Fiddle St SK17 85 B2
Fiddler's La DE13 239 C2
Fidlers Cl S33 40 A2
Fidlers Well S33 40 A2
Field Ave Hatton DE65 239 B4
Renishaw S21 79 A4
Field Cl Borrowash DE72 221 A2
Breaston DE72 235 C4
Dronfield S18 56 B1
Hilton DE65 228 B1
Mansfield Woodhouse NG19 136 B3
Field Cres DE24 233 A3
Field Ct Chesterfield S43 ..
Kilburn DE56 1
Field Dr Derby DE24 2
Rolleston DE13 2
Shirebrook NG20 1
Field End DE4 1
Field Head Way DE21 2
Field House Inf Sch DE7 2
Field House La SK6
Field La
Ault Hucknall NG19,S44 1
Belper DE56 1
Blackfordby DE11 2
Derby, Boulton DE24 2
Derby, Chaddesden DE21 2
Kirk Ireton DE6 1
Mayfield DE6 1
Field Rd DE7 2
Field Rise DE23 2
Field Row 5 DE56 1
Field St DE5 1
Field Terr DE5 1
Field The DE75 1
Field View
Chesterfield S40 1
Clowne S43
South Normanton DE55 1
Field View Cl DE24 2
Field Way DE11 2
Fielden Ave NG19 1
Fieldfare Ct DE23 2
Fieldfare Ho S41
Fieldgate Dr DE21 2
Fieldhead Rd S8
Fieldhead Way S41
Fielding St ST4 2
Fieldings Rd S80
Fieldon Cl DE6 2
Fields Cres SK14
Fields Farm Rd NG10 2
Fields Gr SK14
Fields La Killamarsh S21
Linton DE11 2
Fields The DE4 1
Fieldsway Dr DE21 2
Fieldview Pl S41
Fiennes Cres NG7 2
Fife St DE24 2
Filbert Wlk DE73 2
Finch Cl DE11 2
Finch Cres DE3 2
Fincham Cl DE21 2
Finchley Ave DE22 2
Findern Cl Belper DE56 1
Derby DE22 2
Findern Com Prim Sch DE65 2
Findern La
Burnaston DE65 2
Willington DE65 2
Findern St DE22 2
Finley Way DE55 1
Finmere Cl DE23 2
Finney Cl DE12 2
Finningley Dr DE22 2
Finny La DE6 2
Finsbury Ave
Derby DE22 2
Nottingham NG2 2
Finsley Wlk DE23 2
Fir Cl NG20 1
Fir Pl S21
Fir Rd S21
Fir St S43
Fir Tree Ave DE55 1
Firestone DE56 1
Firfield Ave DE72 23
Firfield Prim Sch DE72 23
Firs Ave Alfreton DE55 15
Hulland Ward DE6 17
Ripley DE5 16
Firs Cres DE22 20
Firs Estate Prim Sch DE22 21
Firs Gdns DE55 15
Firs Par DE4 14
Firs St NG10 23
Firs The DE6 17
First Ave Branston DE14 25
Risley NG10 22
Firth Ct S43 7
Firthwood Ave S18 5
Firthwood Cl S18 5
Firthwood Rd S18 5
Firtree Gr DE21 20
Firvale S26 6
Firvale Rd S40 11
Fish Pond Dr NG7 26
Fisher Cl
Chesterfield S40 11
Repton DE65 24
Fisher Ct DE7 19
Fisher Gate NG1 26
Fisher La Duffield DE56 19
Mansfield NG18 26
Fisher St DE24 23
Fishers Bridge SK22 2
Fishpond La
Egginton DE65 24
Tutbury DE13 23
Fishponds Cl S42 11
Fishponds Rd S13 4
Fishponds Rd W S13 4
Fiskerton Way DE21 20
Fitzalan St SK13 1
Fitzherbert CE Prim Sch DE6 16

...bert Rd S2 ....44 A4
...y Rd S2 ....43 A3
...illiam Dr NG19 ....136 C1
Lamps Cl DE1 ....218 C3
Lamps Ho DE1 ....267 A5
Lands Rd DE15 ....254 C4
...Trees Ave 1 S17 ....56 A3
...Trees Cl 3 S17 ....56 A3
...Trees Dr 2 S17 ....56 A3
...cets La DE6 ....225 A4
...a La SK17 ....106 C4
...shaw La DE7 ....202 C2
...La DE7 ....208 C1
...stead Ave DE75 ....181 B2
...stead La S18 ....180 C1
...stead Rd DE7 ....194 C1
...stead Cres S41 ....96 A3
...CE Prim Sch
.... 103 A2
...a La DE4 ....128 A4
...La SK17 ....106 B4
...DE56 ....191 C4
...s La NG16 ....171 B2
...Croft DE85 ....227 B1
...st S14 ....269 B1
...holme Ave DE56 ....190 C1
...piece Rd S45 ....131 B2
...t Cres DE56 ....178 C2
...t dun Sch DE56 ....178 C1
...t Pk DE56 ....179 A2
...t St DE24 ....219 A1
...t St DE56 ....178 C1
...ning Rd S14 ....269 B2
...cher La S18 ....57 A1
...cher Gate NG1 ....268 B1
...cher St Heanor DE75 ....181 C1
...ning Eaton NG10
...ley DE5 ....169 C1
...cher's Row DE55 ....169 C1
...ches The DE13 ....240 A1
...wilt Gdns NG3 ....268 C2
...t Ave NG19 ....136 C1
...e La S43 ....142 A4
...st St DE24 ....232 B3
...ntson Ave S43 ....77 B2
...ton Rd NG16 ....195 C4
...rence Dr DE72 ....221 B2
...rence Ave 9 NG10 ....223 C1
...esterfield S40 ....114 C3
...easley NG19 ....134 C2
...rence Ct DE7 ....194 C1
...rence Dr DE6 ....224 B4
...rence Gladwin Cl
.... 141 B3

...rence Rd
...ay Cross S45 ....131 C2
...DE7 ....114 C2
...rence Way SK14 ....9 B3
...wren Gdns NG10 ....236 A4
...wery Leys La DE55 ....159 B2
...yd St ST4 ....269 B2
...ery Cl S14 ....43 C2
...ery Cres S14 ....43 C2
...ery Rd S14 ....43 C2
...ery Rd S14 ....43 C2
...ery Rise S14 ....43 C2
...er Hill 109 B3
...ering Horse Wlk 1
...den St ST4 ....269 B1
...ngs Entry DE14 ....165 C4
...ld The S32 ....71 C2
...lds La S43 ....45 C2
...lds Yd DE4 ....156 C1
...jambe Ave S40 ....114 B4
...jambe Rd
...jambe S43 ....96 C4
...chesterfield S40 ....266 A3
...alkstone Dr S40 ....233 A3
...ally Rd DE72 ....205 A1
...ontwell Rd DE14 ....253 C4
...owlow La S40 ....266 A1
...oolow Ct S40 ....266 A1
...rbes Cl NG10 ....236 C3
...ord Ave DE70 ....181 B4
...rd Cl Dronfield S18 ....56 C1
...Ripley DE5 ....180 B4
...ord Gr S14 ....43 C2
...La at Breadsall DE21 ....205 B3
...Derby DE22 ....205 A3
...Ridgeway S12 ....58 C3
...Willington DE65 ....242 B3
...ord Rd S21 ....58 C2
...ord St Belper DE56 ....178 C2
...Burton u T DE15 ....254 C4
...Derby DE1 ....218 C3
...Tupton S42 ....131 B4
...ordbridge La DE55 ....160 A4
...ordcliffe Cl DE23 ....231 A4
...oregate Ct ST16 ....269 A4
...oregate St ST16 ....269 A4
Foremark Ave DE23 ....231 C4
Forest Ave Buxton SK17 ....85 B3
...Mansfield NG18 ....268 C3
Forest Cl DE56 ....179 A3
Forest Ct Barlborough S43 ....80 A3
6 Nottingham NG7 ....268 A2
Forest Dr S45 ....132 B2
Forest La NG7 ....268 A2
Forest La S17 ....50 B1
Forest Lea DE12 ....262 C2
Forest Rd NG18 ....268 A2
Forest Rd NG1,NG7 ....268 A2
Forest Rd W NG1 ....268 A2

Forest View DE12 ....262 A2
Forester St DE1 ....267 A3
Foresters Way DE1 ....169 B1
Forge Cl DE65 ....242 B1
Forge La Burton u T DE13 ....241 A1
...Killamarsh S21 ....60 A4
Forge Rd SK23 ....45 C4
Forge The NG9 ....34 C1
Forman Cl DE11 ....209 A3
Forman St 256 A2
...Derby DE1,DE21 ....267 A3
...Nottingham NG3 ....268 B2
Forrester Ave DE72 ....245 C3
Forrester's La S18 ....57 B2
Forshaw Cl DE56 ....185 B4
Forth Ave S18 ....57 A4
Forties La LE65 ....257 C2
Forty Horse Cl DE55 ....170 A1
Forum Cl 16 DE24 ....233 B3
Fosbrook Dr DE74 ....246 C2
Fosbrooke Dr NG10 ....236 B3
Fosse Cl DE7 ....194 C3
Fossett's Ave NG16 ....171 C4
Foster Rd DE11 ....256 C1
Foster St NG18 ....268 C3
Foston Cl DE65 ....239 B4
Foston Dr S40 ....95 A3
Foundry Cl SK22 ....33 B4
Foundry La DE56 ....190 C4
Foundry St S40 ....96 A4
Foundry Street Ind Est
...S41 ....96 A4
Fountain Sq SK17 ....69 B2
Fountain St SK17 ....85 A4
Fountains Cl DE22 ....205 A2
Four Lanes Ends DE7 ....207 C2
Four Lanes SK14 ....9 A2
Four Seasons Ctr NG18 ....268 B4
Fowler Ave DE21 ....220 B2
Fowler St Chesterfield S41 ....76 C1
...Derby DE22 ....218 C3
...Draycott DE72 ....235 A4
Fox Cl Burton u T DE14 ....254 A4
...Derby DE24 ....231 B1
...Long Eaton NG10 ....236 B3
Fox Croft DE55 ....147 C3
Fox Hill S44 ....118 C4
Fox La Holmesfield S18 ....74 A3
...Sheffield S8,S17 ....56 B3
...Sheffield, Frecheville S12 ....44 B2
Fox Lane Cl S12 ....44 B2
Fox Lane View S12 ....44 B2
Fox Rd
...Castle Donington DE74 ....246 C2
...Whitwell S80 ....82 A3
Fox St S41 ....267 C4
Foxbrook Cl
...Chesterfield S40 ....94 C3
...Derby DE23 ....231 A4
Foxbrook Dr S40 ....95 A1
Foxcote Way S40 ....114 A4
Foxcroft Chase S21 ....60 B3
Foxcroft Dr S21 ....60 B3
Foxcroft Gr S21 ....60 B3
Foxdale Ave S12 ....44 A3
Foxdell Way DE73 ....233 A1
Foxes Cl NG7 ....268 A1
Foxes Wlk DE22 ....204 C2
Foxfield Dr S17 ....66 B1
Foxfields Dr DE21 ....205 C1
Foxglove Ave
...Burton u T DE15 ....255 A4
...Donisthorpe DE12 ....262 C1
Foxglove Cl S44 ....97 A2
Foxglove Rd NG16 ....195 A4
Foxhall La S10 ....42 C3
Foxholes La
...Kniveton DE6 ....174 A3
...Tansley DE4 ....204 C1
Foxlands Ave DE22 ....204 C1
Foxlea SK13 ....16 C4
Foxley Ct DE21 ....206 A1
Foxley Oaks S41 ....77 A1
Foxlow Ave S44 ....118 A1
Foxpark View DE55 ....147 C3
Foxstone Cl S43 ....97 B4
Foxton Cl DE7 ....194 B2
Foxwood Ave S12 ....44 A3
Foxwood Cl
...Chesterfield S41 ....115 B3
...Chesterfield, Sheepbridge
...S41 ....76 C1
Foxwood Ct S40 ....114 A4
Foxwood Dr
...Chesterfield S41 ....114 A4
...Sheffield S12 ....44 A3
Foxwood Gr S12 ....44 A3
Foxwood Ind Pk S41 ....76 C1
Foxwood Rd
...Chesterfield S41 ....76 C1
...Sheffield S12 ....44 A3
Foxwood Way S41 ....76 C1
Foyle Ave DE21 ....220 C3
Framlingham Pl S2 ....43 B4
Framlingham Rd S2 ....43 B4
Frampton Gdns DE23 ....230 C3
Frances Dr S42 ....114 C2
Frances St NG16 ....171 B1
Franchise St DE22 ....218 C2
Francis Cl S43 ....96 A4
Francis St Derby DE21 ....219 B3
8 Nottingham NG7 ....268 A2
Frank Bedicote Way
...DE11 ....256 B2
Frank Foley Way S16 ....269 A4
Frank St ST4 ....269 B1

Franklin Ave S80 ....81 C3
Franklin Cl DE15 ....248 A1
Franklin Cres S80 ....81 C3
Franklin Rd
...Stoke-on-T ST4 ....269 A2
...Westwood NG16 ....171 A2
Franklyn Dr Derby DE24 ....233 A3
...Staveley S43 ....78 C2
Franklyn Rd S40 ....95 C2
Frazer Cl DE21 ....220 C3
Frecheville St S43 ....78 B2
Freckingham St 16 NG1 ....268 B1
Frederic Ave DE75 ....193 C4
Frederick Ave
...Derby DE24 ....232 C3
...Ilkeston DE7 ....209 A3
...Stoke-on-T ST4 ....269 B2
Frederick Gent Sch
...DE55 ....160 A3
Frederick Harrison Inf Sch
...NG9 ....223 C4
Frederick Rd NG9 ....223 B4
Frederick St
...Alfreton DE55 ....159 A3
...Burton u T DE15 ....254 C4
...Derby DE22 ....218 B3
...Grassmoor S42 ....115 C2
...Long Eaton NG10 ....236 C4
...Mansfield NG18 ....268 C3
...Somercotes DE55 ....170 B3
...Swadlincote DE11 ....256 C2
Freebirch View S40 ....95 A4
Freeby Ave NG19 ....136 B3
Freehold St DE22 ....218 C2
Freeland Cl NG9 ....223 C2
Freeman Ave DE23 ....231 C3
Freemantle Rd DE3 ....217 C2
Freesia Cl DE7 ....217 C1
Freetown S13 ....17 B4
French La DE21 ....191 C3
French St DE7 ....218 C1
...Ilkeston DE7 ....209 A3
French Terr NG20 ....101 A1
Fresco Dr DE23 ....230 C4
Fresh Ct S43 ....16 C4
Freshfield Cl SK6 ....15 A1
Freshwaters S42 ....116 B1
Fretson Cl S2 ....44 A4
Fretson Gn S2 ....44 A4
Fretson Rd S2 ....44 A4
Frew Cl ST16 ....269 C4
Freydon Way S44 ....97 A2
Friar Gate DE1 ....218 C3
Friar Gate Ct DE1 ....218 C3
Friar Gate House Sch
...DE1 ....218 C3
Friar La NG1 ....268 B1
Friar St Long Eaton NG10 ....236 B4
...Stafford ST16 ....269 A4
Friars Cl DE22 ....205 A1
Friars Ct Ilkeston DE7 ....208 B3
...Nottingham NG7 ....268 A1
Friars' Rd ST17 ....269 C3
Friars' Terr ST17 ....269 C3
Friars' Wlk ST17 ....269 C3
Friary Ave DE24 ....232 C3
Friary Croft DE11 ....256 A4
Friary St DE1 ....267 A2
Friesland Dr NG10 ....223 C3
Friesland Sch NG10 ....222 C3
Frinton Cl S40 ....114 C4
Frisby Ave NG10 ....236 C3
Fritchley CE Prim Sch
...DE56 ....168 A3
Fritchley Cl DE21 ....206 A1
Fritchley La DE56 ....168 A4
Frith Cl S12 ....44 A3
Frith Gr NG19 ....268 A4
Frith Knoll Rd SK23 ....47 A3
Frith Rd S12 ....44 A3
Frith View S42 ....94 B1
Frithall La S42 ....94 B1
Frithwood La S80 ....100 B4
Frizams La DE73 ....252 C4
Froggatt Cl Derby DE23 ....205 A3
...Staveley S43 ....97 B3
Froggett Cl DE55 ....170 B4
Frogmore St NG1 ....268 B2
Front St DE56 ....168 C2
Frood Cl S43 ....78 B4
Frost Ave NG16 ....182 A2
Fryar Rd NG16 ....182 C2
Fulbrook Rd DE23 ....231 A4
Fulford Cl S40 ....114 A4
Fulforth St NG1 ....268 B2
Fulham Rd DE22 ....218 A3
Full St DE1 ....267 B3
Fuller Dr S41 ....96 B3
Fullwood Ave 11 DE7 ....194 C1
Fullwood St 11 DE7 ....194 C1
Fulmar Cl DE3 ....217 C1
Fulwood Dr NG10 ....236 A4
Fulwood Head Rd S10 ....42 B4
Fulwood La S10 ....54 A1
Fulwood Rd N NG17 ....148 C1
Fulwood Rd S NG17 ....160 C4
Furlong Cl NG9 ....223 B3
Furlong La
...Alstonefield DE6 ....149 B2
...Atlow DE6 ....175 A4
Furnace Cl S41 ....115 C1
Furnace La Barlow S18 ....75 C2
...Heanor DE75 ....181 B2
...Moira DE12 ....262 C2
Furnace Lane Ind Est
...DE12 ....262 C2

Furnace Row DE55 ....170 C4
Furnall Ave DE45 ....90 A2
Furness Cl 2 SK13 ....17 C4
Furness Lodge Cl SK23 ....33 B2
Furness Vale Bsns Ctr
...SK23 ....33 B2
Furness Vale Prim Sch
...SK23 ....33 B2
Furness Vale Sta SK23 ....33 B2
Furness Ave S17 ....55 B3
Furrows Cl DE21 ....206 B2
Fyfield Rd DE15 ....254 C3
Fylde Cl NG9 ....223 C1

G

Gable Ct DE3 ....230 C4
Gable St ST4 ....269 C4
Gables Cl S42 ....132 B4
Gables The DE11 ....255 C3
Gadley Cl SK17 ....84 C4
Gadley La SK17 ....84 C4
Gadsby Cl DE7 ....209 A2
Gadsby Rise DE56 ....168 B1
Gag La DE6 ....161 A3
Gainborough Cl DE21 ....206 A1
Gainsborough Ave SK6 ....23 A4
Gainsborough Cl
...Long Eaton NG10 ....236 C3
...Stapleford NG9 ....223 C3
Gainsborough Rd S18 ....75 C4
Gainsborough Way
...DE15 ....248 A2
Gairloch Cl DE24 ....231 B1
Galahad Dr S14 ....33 B4
Gale Rd SK22 ....33 B4
Gallery La S42 ....113 B4
Gallery The DE41 ....173 B1
Gallows Inn Cl DE7 ....209 A3
Gallowstree La DE6 ....186 A4
Galway Ave DE7 ....220 A2
Gamble St NG7 ....268 A2
Gamesley Com Prim Sch
...SK13 ....9 C1
Gang La S44 ....118 C3
Gannow Cl S21 ....60 C4
Gaol Rd ST16 ....269 B4
Gaol Sq ST16 ....269 B4
Goalgate St 5 DE55 ....269 B4
Gapsick La S43,S80 ....81 A3
Garden Ave Ilkeston DE7 ....208 C3
...New Houghton NG19 ....134 C4
...Renishaw S21 ....79 A4
...Shirebrook NG20 ....119 C2
Garden Cl S43 ....77 B2
Garden Cr DE55 ....159 C2
Garden Cres DE74 ....247 A2
Garden Pl Stafford ST17 ....269 B3
...Stoke-on-T ST4 ....269 A2
Garden Rd
...Eastwood NG16 ....182 C2
...8 Mansfield NG18 ....268 B3
Garden Row S44 ....117 B1
Garden St
...Broadbottom SK14 ....16 A4
...Derby DE1 ....267 A4
...Stafford ST17 ....269 B3
...Stoke-on-T ST4 ....269 A1
Gardeners Ct S44 ....99 A1
Gardens The
...Heanor DE75 ....181 B2
...Ripley DE5 ....180 B4
Gardom Cl S18 ....56 B1
Gardom Pl S14 ....210 A1
Gardom Cl 14 S18 ....56 B1
Garfield Ave DE72 ....235 A4
Garfield Cl Derby DE23 ....231 B3
...Stapleford NG9 ....209 C1
Garland Cl 20 S20 ....59 C4
Garland Croft S20 ....59 C4
Garland Mount 22 S20 ....59 C4
Garland Way S20 ....59 C4
Garner La DE4,DE55 ....157 C2
Garnet Cl NG3 ....268 B2
Garnett Ave DE75 ....181 C1
Garnham Cl DE55 ....159 B1
Garnon St NG18 ....268 A3
Garratt Ave NG18 ....131 B3
Garrett La S45 ....131 B4
Garrick St DE24 ....233 A4
Garry Cl DE24 ....231 B1
Garsdale Ct 9 DE24 ....233 B3
Gartan Rd DE14 ....254 A4
Garth Cres DE24 ....233 A3
Garth Rd SK6 ....23 A4
Garth Way S18 ....56 C1
Garth Cres DE24 ....233 A3
Garthorpe Cl DE21 ....205 C1
Gartrice Gdns S20 ....60 A3
Gartrice Gr S21 ....60 A3
Gary Cl DE23 ....231 B3
Gas St Hollingworth SK14 ....9 B3
...Sandiacre NG10 ....223 B3
...Uttoxeter ST14 ....210 B1
Gascoine Dr DE21 ....220 B2
Gashouse La S20 ....59 B3
Gaskell Ave DE23 ....231 C4
Gasny Ave DE74 ....247 A3
Gatcombe Cl
...Burton u T DE13 ....240 B1
...Derby DE21 ....206 A1
Gatcombe Gr NG10 ....223 B3
Gate Brook Cl DE55 ....170 A1
Gate Ho The S32 ....72 B1
Gatefield Cl S41 ....95 B4
Gateland La S18 ....75 A1
Gateway Christian Sch
...DE7 ....207 C1

Gauledge La SK17 ....121 A3
Gaunt Cl Killamarsh S21 ....60 B3
Sheffield S14 ....43 B2
Gaunt Dr S14 ....43 B2
Gaunt Pl S14 ....43 B2
Gaunt Rd S14 ....43 B2
Gaunt Way S14 ....43 B2
Gawain Gr DE13 ....240 C1
Gawsworth Cl SK13 ....10 A3
Gayton Ave DE23 ....231 B3
Gayton Com Jun Sch
.... 231 B3
Gayton Thorpe Cl DE23 ....230 C4
Geary La DE11 ....248 C1
Gedling Gr NG7 ....268 A2
Gedling St NG1 ....268 B1
Geen St S14 ....43 B2
Geer La S12 ....58 B3
Gelderd Pl LE18 ....76 A4
Gema Cl DE22 ....205 A2
Genista Cl DE15 ....255 A4
Gentshill Ave S45 ....131 C1
George Ave NG10 ....223 C1
George Bailly Cl ST17 ....269 B3
George Cres DE55 ....170 C4
George Dutton Ind Pk
...DE6 ....185 C4
George Holmes Way
...DE11 ....256 A2
George Percival Pl S45 ....131 A2
George Rd DE4 ....143 B3
George Spencer Foundation
...Sch NG9 ....223 C3
George St Alfreton DE55 ....159 A2
...Alfreton, Riddings DE55 ....170 B3
...Ashbourne DE6 ....185 A4
...Belper DE56 ....178 C2
...Brimington S43 ....96 C4
...Buxton SK17 ....85 A4
...Chesterfield S41 ....76 C1
...Compstall SK6 ....15 A1
...Derby DE1 ....267 A3
...Glossop SK13 ....10 A2
...Langley Mill NG16 ....182 A2
...Mansfield NG18 ....268 A4
...Mansfield Woodhouse
...NG19 ....136 B2
...Melbourne DE73 ....252 A4
...North Wingfield S42 ....131 C4
...Nottingham NG1 ....268 B2
...Pinxton NG16 ....160 B2
...Somercotes DE55 ....170 B4
...South Normanton DE55 ....159 C3
...Swadlincote DE11 ....256 A1
...Whaley Bridge SK23 ....45 C4
...Whaley Thorns NG20 ....101 A1
Georgina Cl DE74 ....247 A2
Gerard Cl
...4 Chesterfield S40 ....95 B1
Derby DE21 ....220 C3
...9 Sheffield S8 ....43 A3
Gerard Ct DE1 ....267 A2
Gerard Gr DE65 ....229 B2
Gerard St Derby DE1 ....267 A2
...Sheffield S8 ....43 A3
Gerrard St S14 ....269 B2
Gertrude Rd Derby DE21 ....220 A4
...Draycott DE72 ....235 A4
Gervase Ave S8 ....56 C3
Gervase Dr S8 ....56 C3
Gervase Pl S8 ....56 C3
Gervase Rd S8 ....56 C3
Gervase Wlk S8 ....56 C3
Gibb La Marsh SK6 ....23 C3
...Sudbury DE6 ....225 C3
Gibb St NG10 ....236 C4
Gibbons Ave NG9 ....223 B3
Gibbons Dr S14 ....43 C1
Gibbons Rd NG18 ....268 A3
Gibbons Way S14 ....43 C1
Gibfield La Belper DE56 ....178 C1
...Kirk Ireton DE6 ....175 C4
Gifford Rd S14 ....269 A1
Gifford Rd 12 S8 ....43 A4
Gilbert Ave S40 ....114 B4
Gilbert Cl DE21 ....220 B2
Gilbert Cres DE56 ....190 C1
Gilbert Heathcote Inf Sch
...S41 ....96 A4
Gilbert St S18 ....233 A3
Gilcroft St NG18 ....268 B4
Gilderdale Way DE21 ....206 A2
Gill La DE4 ....127 B2
Gill St NG1 ....268 A2
Gill's La S42 ....115 C1
Gillamoor Cl DE24 ....233 B3
Gilleyfield Ave S17 ....55 C4
Gillies The NG19 ....144 C4
Gilliver Gdns DE72 ....235 A4
Gillot St DE75 ....195 B4
Gill Hill NG16 ....195 B4
Gillthbrook Cres NG16 ....195 B4
Gilthill Prim Sch NG16 ....195 B4
Giltway NG16 ....195 B4
Gimson Cl S14 ....195 B3
Gin Close Way NG16 ....195 B3
Gin La S45 ....144 C4
Gipsy La Alstonefield DE6 ....149 C2
...Apperknowle S18 ....58 A1
...Chesterfield S41 ....77 B1
Gipyshill La S80 ....81 A4
Gird La S6 ....15 C1
Girdon Cl SK17 ....84 C3
Gisborne Cl DE21 ....217 C2
Gisborne Cres DE22 ....204 C2

Gisborne Gn DE1 . . . . .218 C3
Gisbourne Dr S43 . . . . .47 A3
Glade Cl S40 . . . . .95 C3
Glade Croft S12 . . . . .44 A2
Glade Lands Dr DE73 . . . . .233 C3
Glade Lea S12 . . . . .44 A2
Glade The Buxton SK17 . . . . .85 A4
Chesterfield S40 . . . . .95 B2
Gladstone Ave
Blackwell DE55 . . . . .147 C1
Heanor DE75 . . . . .181 C1
Gladstone Cl Derby DE73 .232 D7
Glossop SK13 . . . . .17 B4
Gladstone Dr NG16 . . . . . . .182 C4
Gladstone Pl ST14 . . . . .269 A1
Gladstone Rd
Alfreton DE55 . . . . .158 C2
Chesterfield S40 . . . . .266 A4
Derby DE21 . . . . .220 C3
Gladstone St Derby DE23 . .218 A1
Glossop SK13 . . . . .17 B4
Glossop, Hadfield SK13 . . . . .10 A2
Heanor DE75 . . . . .181 C1
Ilkeston DE7 . . . . .208 C4
Langley Mill NG16 . . . . .182 B2
Long Eaton NG10 . . . . .236 B3
Mansfield NG18 . . . . .268 C4
Mansfield Woodhouse
NG19 . . . . .136 B1
South Normanton DE55 . . . .160 A3
Gladstone St E DE7 . . . . . . .208 C4
Gladstone Terr NG19 . . . . . .136 B1
Gladwin Gdns S40 . . . . .114 B4
Glaisdale Nook 6 DE24 . . .233 D3
Glamis Cl DE21 . . . . .206 A1
Glapwell La S44 . . . . .118 A1
Glasshouse Hill DE55 . . . . .181 A4
Glasshouse La S41 . . . . .77 B2
Glasshouse St NG1 . . . . .268 B2
Glastonbury La NG19 . . . . . .136 B2
Glastonbury Rd DE24 . . . . . .233 B4
Glaven Cl NG19 . . . . .136 B1
Gleadless Ave S12 . . . . .44 A2
Gleadless Bank S12 . . . . .44 A3
Gleadless Comm S12 . . . . . . .44 A3
Gleadless Ct S12 . . . . .43 C3
Gleadless Ct 6 S12 . . . . .43 C3
Gleadless Dr S12 . . . . .43 C2
Gleadless Mount S12 . . . . . . .44 A2
Gleadless Prim Sch S12 . . . .44 A3
Gleadless Rd S2 . . . . .43 A3
Gleadless Townend S12 . . . .44 A2
Glebe Ave
Great Longstone DE45 . . . . . .90 A2
Harthill S26 . . . . .61 C4
Pinxton NG16 . . . . .160 B2
Ripley DE5 . . . . .169 B1
Smalley DE7 . . . . .192 C3
Glebe Cl
Coton in t E DE12 . . . . .260 B2
Doveridge DE6 . . . . .224 A4
Holmewood S42 . . . . .132 B4
Rolleston DE13 . . . . .240 A2
South Normanton DE55 . . . .160 A3
Thurvaston DE6 . . . . .201 C1
Glebe Cres Ilkeston DE7 . . .209 A4
Stanley DE7 . . . . .207 A3
Glebe Ct
Great Longstone DE45 . . . . . .89 C2
Stoke-on-T ST4 . . . . .269 C2
Glebe Farm Cl S26 . . . . .61 C4
Glebe Field Cl DE4 . . . . .156 C1
Glebe Gdns S42 . . . . .131 C3
Glebe Jun Sch DE55 . . . . . .160 A3
Glebe Rd SK17 . . . . .85 B4
Glebe Rise DE21 . . . . .218 B1
Glebe St Stoke-on-T ST4 . . .269 B2
Swadlincote DE11 . . . . .256 A2
Glebe The
Awsworth NG16 . . . . .195 A4
Chesterfield S41 . . . . .77 A1
Rosliston DE12 . . . . .260 B3
Glebe Way The S41 . . . . .77 A1
Gledhill Cl S18 . . . . .57 A1
Glen Ave DE56 . . . . .191 B4
Glen Cl DE55 . . . . .148 A2
Glen Park Cl DE73 . . . . .244 C4
Glen Rd DE4 . . . . .156 B1
Glen View DE56 . . . . .178 C1
Glen View Rd S8 . . . . .56 C4
Glen Vine S8 . . . . .170 A1
Glenavon Cl S43 . . . . .77 B3
Glenbrook Hill SK13 . . . . .10 B1
Glencoe Way S40 . . . . .95 C4
Glencroft Cl DE24 . . . . .254 A4
Glencroft Dr DE24 . . . . .231 B2
Glendon St DE7 . . . . .220 C3
Glendon Rd Derby DE24 . . .231 B2
Ilkeston DE7 . . . . .208 B2
Glendon St DE7 . . . . .193 A1
Gleneagles Cl
Chesterfield S40 . . . . .114 B4
Derby DE3 . . . . .217 C1
Gleneagles Dr DE13 . . . . . . .240 B1
Glenfield Ave NG16 . . . . . . .195 B4
Glenfield Cres
Chesterfield S41 . . . . .96 A4
Derby DE3 . . . . .217 B1
Glenfield Rd NG10 . . . . .236 B3
Glengarry Way DE24 . . . . . .231 C2
Glenholme Dr S13 . . . . .44 C4
Glenholme Pl S13 . . . . .44 C4
Glenholme Way S13 . . . . . . .44 C4
Glenmoor Rd SK17 . . . . .66 B1

Glenmore Cl S43 . . . . .97 A3
Glenmore Croft S12 . . . . . . .44 B3
Glenmore Dr DE24 . . . . .231 B4
Glenmore Cl DE22 . . . . .231 B4
Glenn Way DE21 . . . . .234 C1
Glenorchy Ct DE21 . . . . .206 A2
Glenthorn Cl S81 . . . . .63 C4
Glenthorne Cl S40 . . . . .95 B1
Glenwood Rd DE73 . . . . .245 A4
Glinton Ave DE55 . . . . .147 C1
Glossop Brook Rd SK13 . . .10 A1
Glossop Central Sta
SK13 . . . . .10 B1
Glossop Heritage Ctr* 10 B1
Glossop Rd Hayfield SK22 . .25 B3
Broadbottom SK13 . . . . .16 B4
Gamesley SK13 . . . . .9 A1
Marsh SK6 . . . . .15 B2
Glossop St DE24 . . . . .232 A4
Glossop's Croft S41 . . . . .77 A1
Glossopdale Comm Coll
SK13 . . . . .10 B1
Glossopdale Comm Coll
(Annexe) SK13 . . . . .10 A2
Gloster St DE24 . . . . .219 C1
Gloucester Ave
Chesterfield S41 . . . . .95 C3
Sandiacre NG10 . . . . .223 A2
Gloucester Rd S41 . . . . .95 C3
Gloucester Way
Burton u T DE15 . . . . .248 A1
4 Glossop SK13 . . . . .17 C4
Glover Rd Sheffield S8 . . . . .43 A4
Totley S17 . . . . .55 C3
Glover St S18 . . . . .269 A4
Gloves La DE55 . . . . .147 B1
Glumangate S40 . . . . .266 B3
Goathland Rd DE24 . . . . . . .231 B1
Goatscliffe Cotts S32 . . . . . .72 B4
Goddard La Glossop SK13 . .10 A2
New Mills SK22 . . . . .24 C4
Goddard Rd SK13 . . . . .10 A2
Godfrey Dr DE7 . . . . .208 B3
Godfrey St DE75 . . . . .181 C1
Godkin Dr NG16 . . . . .182 A2
Godward Rd SK22 . . . . .33 A4
Gold Cl DE4 . . . . .142 A4
Gold La DE22 . . . . .217 C4
Goldcrest Dr DE21 . . . . .220 C3
Goldcrest Ho S41 . . . . .77 C2
Golden Valley
Horsley Woodhouse DE7 . . .192 A3
Somercotes DE55 . . . . .170 B2
Golders Green Wlk
DE22 .218 A3
Goldhill DE4 . . . . .144 A2
Goldsmith St
Mansfield NG18 . . . . .268 B4
Nottingham NG1 . . . . .268 A1
Goldstone Ct DE21 . . . . .220 C2
Golf Cl DE23 . . . . .218 A1
Golf Club Rd DE7 . . . . .209 A1
Golf La DE56 . . . . .190 C3
Gomersal La S18 . . . . .57 A1
Goodacre St NG18 . . . . .268 C4
Goodale St DE23 . . . . .219 A1
Goodhand Cres DE21 . . . . . .268 A3
Goodman Cl NG16 . . . . .195 B4
Goodman Ct S44 . . . . .97 A2
Goodrington Rd DE21 . . . . .206 B2
Goods Rd DE56 . . . . .178 C1
Goods Yd DE56 . . . . .178 C1
Goodsmoor Rd DE23,
DE24 .231 C1
Goodwin Cl NG10 . . . . .223 A3
Goodwin Dr NG16 . . . . .195 C3
Goodwin Rd 2 S8 . . . . .43 A3
Goodwin's La DE56 . . . . . . .178 B1
Goodwood Cl DE13 . . . . . . .240 B1
Goodwood Cres DE7 . . . . . .208 B2
Goodwood Dr
Beeston NG9 . . . . .223 C1
Derby DE23 . . . . .233 B3
Gooker La DE55 . . . . .159 C1
Goole Ave DE7 . . . . .208 B3
Goose Gate NG1 . . . . .268 B1
Goose Green La DE45 . . . . .146 B2
Goose Green View S45 . . . . .91 C3
Goosehill S33 . . . . .38 A3
Gordon Ave S8 . . . . .43 A1
Gordon Cres DE55 . . . . .160 A2
Gordon Rd
Borrowash DE72 . . . . .221 A1
Derby DE23 . . . . .218 C2
Nottingham NG3 . . . . .268 C2
Swanwick DE55 . . . . .169 C4
Tideswell SK17 . . . . .69 B2
Gordon St DE7 . . . . .195 A1
Gordondale Rd NG19 . . . . . .136 A1
Gore La S33 . . . . .41 A4
Gorman Cl S41 . . . . .95 C4
Gorse Bank S44 . . . . .116 C1
Gorse Cl Derby DE23 . . . . . .231 B3
Eastwood NG16 . . . . .195 A4
Long Eaton NG10 . . . . .223 A1
Gorse Dr S21 . . . . .60 B3
Gorse Ridge Dr DE45 . . . . . .91 B3
Gorse Valley Rd S41 . . . . . . .115 C4
Gorse Valley Way S41 . . . . .115 C4
Gorse Way SK13 . . . . .17 C4
Gorsebank La DE45 . . . . .91 C4
Gorsehill Gr DE23 . . . . .231 A4
Gorses Alderwasley DE56 . .178 B4

Gorses continued
Idridgehay DE56 . . . . .176 B3
Gorsey Bank DE4 . . . . .165 C4
Gorsey Brigg S18 . . . . .56 B1
Gorsey Brow SK14 . . . . .9 A1
Gorsey Cl DE56 . . . . .178 C3
Gorsey Intakes SK14 . . . . . . .16 A4
Gorsey La
Kirk Ireton DE6 . . . . .165 A1
Netherseal DE12 . . . . .265 A3
Gorseybrigg Inf Sch S18 . .56 B1
Gorseybrigg Jun Sch
S18 . . . . .56 B1
Gorsty Leys DE65 . . . . .230 B1
Gosber Rd S21 . . . . .59 C2
Gosber St S21 . . . . .59 B2
Goseley Ave DE11 . . . . .257 A2
Goseley Cres DE11 . . . . .257 A2
Gosforth Cl S18 . . . . .56 C1
Gosforth Cres S18 . . . . .56 C1
Gosforth Dr S18 . . . . .56 C1
Gosforth Gn S18 . . . . .56 C1
Gosforth La DE24 . . . . .232 C4
Goshawk Rd DE7 . . . . .209 A2
Gower Cres S40 . . . . .95 B3
Gower St S21 . . . . .267 B2
Goyt Pl SK23 . . . . .45 C4
Goyt Rd Disley SK12 . . . . . . .32 B3
New Mills SK22 . . . . .32 B3
Goyt Side Rd S40 . . . . .95 C1
Goyt Valley Ind Est SK23 . .33 B2
Goyt View SK22 . . . . .33 A3
Goyt's La S17 . . . . .65 A4
Goytlands S17 . . . . .84 C3
Grace Cres DE75 . . . . .181 C1
Gradbach Mill* SK17 . . . . .102 A1
Grafham Cl DE73 . . . . .233 A2
Grafton Ct 20 NG7 . . . . .268 A2
Grafton Rd DE15 . . . . .248 A3
Grafton St DE23 . . . . .218 C1
Graham Cl DE14 . . . . .254 B4
Graham Dr SK12 . . . . .32 B3
Graham St DE7 . . . . .208 C4
Grammer St DE5 . . . . .181 A2
Grampian Cres S40 . . . . .95 A2
Grampian Prim Sch
DE24 .231 B2
Grampian Way
Derby DE24 . . . . .231 C2
Long Eaton NG10 . . . . .236 A4
Granary Cl S40 . . . . .95 A4
Granby Ave Chinley SK23 . . .34 C1
Mansfield NG18 . . . . .268 B4
Granby Cres DE55 . . . . .132 B1
Granby Croft DE45 . . . . .109 B3
Granby Jun Sch DE7 . . . . . .194 C2
Granby Rd
Bakewell DE45 . . . . .109 B3
Bradwell S33 . . . . .50 C4
Buxton SK17 . . . . .85 A3
Granby St DE7 . . . . .194 C1
Granby Wlk ST4 . . . . .269 A1
Grandfield St DE75 . . . . . . .181 B2
Grandstand Rd DE21 . . . . . .219 B3
Grange Ave
Breaston DE72 . . . . .235 B4
Chapel-en-le-F SK23 . . . . . . .47 A3
Derby DE23 . . . . .231 C4
Dronfield S18 . . . . .56 C1
Hulland Ward DE6 . . . . .175 C2
Mansfield NG18 . . . . .268 A3
Grange Cl
Melbourne DE73 . . . . .252 A4
Somercotes DE55 . . . . .159 C1
Ticknall DE73 . . . . .251 A2
Grange Cl DE65 . . . . .241 A3
Grange Dale DE4 . . . . .153 B4
Grange Dr
Castle Donington DE74 . . . .247 A2
Long Eaton NG10 . . . . .236 C4
Grange La Barlow S18 . . . . . .75 A1
Darley Dale DE4 . . . . .127 C1
Ible DE4 . . . . .153 B4
Grange Park
Calow S42 . . . . .96 C2
Chapel-en-le-F SK23 . . . . . . .47 A3
Grange Prim Sch NG10 . . .236 C4
Grange Rd Buxton SK17 . . . .85 A2
Derby DE24 . . . . .233 A3
Long Eaton NG10 . . . . .236 C4
Pilsley S45 . . . . .132 B1
Swadlincote DE11 . . . . .255 C3
Uttoxeter ST14 . . . . .210 A1
Grange Rd S S45 . . . . .132 B1
Grange St 5 Alfreton DE55 .159 A2
Derby DE23 . . . . .219 A1
Grange The
Old Brampton S42 . . . . .94 C2
Smalley DE75 . . . . .193 B4
Swadlincote DE11 . . . . .260 A2
Grange View NG16 . . . . .182 C2
Grangemill Pl S43 . . . . .97 B4
Grangemill PI DE7 . . . . . . .208 C4
Grangewood Cl S40 . . . . . . .114 C4
Grangewood Dr DE56 . . . . .191 A4
Grangewood Rd S40 . . . . . .114 C4
Gransden Way S40 . . . . .114 B4
Grant Ave DE21 . . . . .220 A3
Grant St ST4 . . . . .269 C2
Grantham Ave DE21 . . . . . . .205 C1
Grantham Cl NG16 . . . . .195 B4
Granville Ave NG10 . . . . . . .223 B3

Granville Cl
Chesterfield S41 . . . . .115 B4
Duffield DE56 . . . . .190 C2
Hatton DE65 . . . . .227 B1
Granville Com Sch
DE11 .256 C2
Granville Ct 4 NG3 . . . . . . .268 C2
Granville St Derby DE1 . . . .218 C3
Swadlincote DE11 . . . . .256 C2
Grasmere Ave
Clay Cross S45 . . . . .131 A2
Derby DE21 . . . . .220 C3
Grasmere Cl
Burton u T DE15 . . . . .248 A1
Chesterfield S41 . . . . .95 B4
Grasmere Cres DE24 . . . . . .231 C2
Grasmere Ct 12 NG10 . . . . .223 A3
Grasmere Rd
11 Dronfield S18 . . . . .56 B1
Long Eaton NG10 . . . . .223 A1
Mansfield NG10 . . . . .223 B3
Grass St DE7 . . . . .194 C2
Grasscroft Cl 12 S40 . . . . . .95 A4
Grassdale View S12 . . . . .44 C2
Grassmoor Cl S12 . . . . .43 C3
Grassmoor Cres SK13 . . . . . .9 B2
Grassmoor Ctry Pk*
S42,S41 . . . . .116 A2
Grassmoor Prim Sch
S42 . . . . .115 C1
Grassthorpe Cl DE21 . . . . . .206 A1
Grassthorpe Rd S12 . . . . . . .44 A2
Grassy St S33 . . . . .230 A4
Gratton Cl S45 . . . . .78 C2
Gratton La DE45 . . . . .144 C1
Gravel Pit Hill DE65 . . . . . .249 C4
Gravel Pit La DE22 . . . . .220 C2
Gravelly Bank Mews
DE6 . . . . .199 B3
Graves Park Animal Farm*
S8 . . . . .57 A4
Graves Tennis & L Ctr
S8 . . . . .57 A4
Gray Fallow DE55 . . . . .160 A2
Gray St Clowne S43 . . . . .80 C3
Mosborough S20 . . . . .58 C3
Graycar Bsns Pk DE13 . . . .253 A1
Grayling St DE23 . . . . .219 A1
Grays Cl DE74 . . . . .247 A2
Grayswood Cl DE55 . . . . . . .170 B4
Great Central Rd NG18 . . .268 C3
Great Common Cl S43 . . . . .80 A3
Great Croft S18 . . . . .56 B1
Great Freeman St NG1,
NG3 .268 B2
Great Hucklow CE Prim Sch
SK17 .51 A1
Great Longstone Ind Est
DE45 . . . . .90 A2
Great Northern Cl The
NG2 .268 B1
Great Northern Cotts
NG19 . . . . .135 A3
Great Northern Rd
Derby DE1 . . . . .218 C3
Eastwood NG16 . . . . .182 B1
Greatbatch Ave DE7 . . . . . .269 A2
Greatorex Rd DE24 . . . . . . .232 C3
Greaves La DE45 . . . . .108 C4
Greaves St Ripley DE5 . . . . .169 C1
Shirland DE55 . . . . .146 C1
Greek St 8 NG7 . . . . .268 A2
Green Ave DE73 . . . . .233 A1
Green Bank SK13 . . . . .16 C4
Green Chase S21 . . . . .59 A1
Green Cl Curbar S32 . . . . . . .72 C1
Matlock DE4 . . . . .143 A3
Newton DE55 . . . . .148 A2
Staveley S43 . . . . .97 B3
Unstone S18 . . . . .76 C3
Willington DE65 . . . . .242 A3
Green Cres NG16 . . . . .171 C3
Green Cross S18 . . . . .57 A1
Green Farm Cl S40 . . . . .95 B3
Green Farm Rd NG16 . . . . . .171 B3
Green Glen S40 . . . . .95 B3
Green Hill DE4 . . . . .154 C1
Green Inf Sch The DE55 . . .160 A3
Green La
Alsop en le D DE6 . . . . .150 B1
Bakewell DE45 . . . . .108 B2
Barrow u T DE73 . . . . .244 A3
Belper DE56 . . . . .178 C2
Bonsall DE4 . . . . .153 C4
Breedon on t H DE73 . . . . . .252 C3
Burnaston DE65 . . . . .230 A2
Buxton SK17 . . . . .85 A3
Buxton, Water Swallows
SK17 .67 B1
Chelmorton SK17 . . . . .106 B4
Chesterfield S41 . . . . .96 B2
Chinley SK23 . . . . .34 C1
Clifton DE6 . . . . .184 C4
Compstall SK14 . . . . .15 A4
Creswell S80 . . . . .82 B3
Darley Dale DE4 . . . . .127 B2
Derby DE1 . . . . .267 B2
Derby, Alvaston DE24 . . . . .233 B4
Disley SK12 . . . . .32 B2
Dronfield S18 . . . . .57 A1
Glossop SK13 . . . . .9 C2
Glossop, Brookfield SK14 . . .16 B4
Hognaston DE6 . . . . .164 A1
Hollingworth SK14 . . . . .9 B3
Ilkeston DE7 . . . . .209 A4
Killamarsh S21 . . . . .60 B2
Mansfield NG19 . . . . .135 A1

Green La continued
Marchington ST14 2
Ockbrook DE72 2
Old Brampton S42 . . . .
Overseal DE12 2
Pilsley S45 1
Pleasley S44 1
Roston DE6 1
Tansley DE4 1
Tupton S42 1
Tutbury DE13 2
Weston underwood DE6 1
Green Lands DE11 2
Green Lea S18 . . . .
Green Leas DE72 2
Green Oak Ave S17 . . . .
Green Oak Cres S17 . . . .
Green Oak Dr S17 . . . .
Green Oak Rd S17 . . . .
Green Oak Rd S17 . . . .
Green Park Ave SK23 . . . .
Green Pk DE22 2
Green Rd The DE6 2
Green St
Barton in F NG11 2
Chesterfield S41 . . . .
Green The Alfreton DE55 . . .1
Aston-on-T DE72 2
Bamford S33 . . . .
Belper DE56 . . . .
Birchover DE4 1
Bradwell S33 . . . .
Brailsford DE6 2
Breaston DE72 2
Breedon on t H DE73 2
Burton u T DE13 2
Castle Donington DE74 2
Chesterfield S41 . . . .
Clowne S43 . . . .
Curbar S32 . . . .
Derby DE72 2
Derby, Mickleover DE3 2
Draycott DE72 2
Findern DE65 2
Fritchley DE56 1
Glapwell S44 1
Glossop SK13 . . . .
Kirk Langley DE6 2
Mansfield Woodhouse
NG19 1
Marple SK6 . . . .
Middleton (Nr Wirksworth)
DE4 1
North Wingfield S42 1
Pilsley S45 1
Stoke-on-T ST4 2
Stoney Middleton S32 . . . . . .
Sutton in A NG17 1
Swanwick DE55 1
Tissington DE6 1
Totley S17 . . . .
Weston-on-T DE72 2
Willington DE65 2
Youlgreave DE4 1
Green Water Mdw SK14 . . . .
Green Way Findern DE65 . . .2
Wingerworth S42 1
Greenacre Ave DE75 1
Greenacre Pk DE12 2
Greenacre The DE6 1
Greenacres DE23 2
Greenacres Cl S18 . . . .
Greenacres Dr
South Normanton DE55 1
Uttoxeter ST14 1
Greenaway La DE4 1
Greenbank Derby DE21 2
Hollingworth SK13 . . . .
Greenbank Dr S40 . . . .
Greenbank Rd SK6 . . . .
Greendale Ave S42 1
Greendale Ct S18 . . . .
Greendale Sh Ctr S18 . . . . . .
Greenfell Ave DE23 2
Greenfield Ave S80 . . . .
Greenfield Cl
New Mills SK22 . . . .
Sheffield S8 . . . .
Greenfield Dr
Linton DE12 2
Sheffield S8 . . . .
Greenfield Rd S8 . . . .
Greenfield St SK13 . . . .
Greenfields
Aldercar NG16 18
Denstone ST14 1
Eckington S21 . . . .
Fritchley DE56 1
Greenfields Ave DE23 2
Greenfinch Cl DE21 22
Greengate Cl S40 . . . .
Greengate St ST16 2
Greenhall Rd S21 . . . .
Greenhead . . . .
Greenhead Cres SK17 13
Greenhead Pk S33 . . . .
Greenhill Ave Ripley DE5 . . .
Sheffield S8 . . . .
Greenhill La DE55 1
Greenhill Lane Ind Est
DE55 17
Greenhill Main Rd S8 . . . . . .
Greenhill Parkway S8 . . . . . .
Greenhill Prim Sch S8 . . . . .
Greenhill Wlk SK12 . . . .
Greenhills Rd NG16 18
Greenhouse La S10 . . . .

and Ave DE22 ....218 A3
aton CI ST4 ....132 A4
mount CI DE23 ....231 A3
s Ct DE7 ....194 B1
e La NG16 ....195 C3
hall La SK12 ....23 C4
side Ave S41 ....96 A4

Grosvenor Ave continued
Long Eaton NG10 ....236 A2
Grosvenor Dr DE23 ....231 B3
Grosvenor Rd
Eastwood NG16 ....182 C1
Marple SK6 ....23 A4
Ripley DE5 ....169 B1
Grosvenor St DE24 ....232 B4

Grove Ave
Nottingham NG7 ....268 A2
Totley S17 ....55 B3
Grove CI DE72 ....233 C2
Grove Ct DE5 ....180 C4
Grove Farm CI S43 ....96 C4
Grove Gdns S43 ....96 C3
Grove Hospl The DE72 ....234 B1
Grove House Ct S17 ....55 C3
Grove La Buxton SK17 ......85 B3
Darley Dale DE4 ....127 C1
Old Brampton S42 ....94 A2
Somersal Herbert DE6 .....211 C1
Grove Mews NG16 ....182 C1
Grove Pk DE65 ....229 A1
Grove Pl DE55 ....125 A3
Grove Rd Calow S43 ....96 C3
Chesterfield S41 ....96 A4
Totley S17 ....55 C3
Grove St Chesterfield S41 .115 B4
Derby DE23 ....267 A4
Mansfield Woodhouse
NG19 ....136 C3
New Mills SK22 ....33 A4
Swadlincote DE11 ....256 A4
Grove The
Branston DE13 ....253 A4
Breaston DE72 ....235 C4
Derby DE21 ....217 C1
Glossop SK13 ....98 A4
Poolsbrook S43 ....98 C1
Totley S17 ....55 B3
Grove Way Calow S43 ......96 C3
Mansfield Woodhouse
NG19 ....136 A2
Grovebury Dr DE23 ....231 B3
Groves Nook DE73 ....232 C1
Grundy Ave S43 ....171 B4
Grundy Nook S80 ....82 A3
Grundy Rd S45 ....131 B2
Grunmore Dr DE13 ....240 C1
Guendolen Dr S42 ....43 A4
Guide Post S18 ....168 B1
Guildford Ave
Chesterfield S40 ....114 B4
Mansfield Woodhouse
NG19 ....136 B3
Sheffield S2 ....43 B4
Swadlincote DE11 ....256 C3
Guildford CI S2 ....43 B4
Guildford Dr S2 ....43 B4
Guildford Rise S2 ....43 C4
Guildford St S4 ....269 C2
Guildford View S2 ....43 C4
Guildhall Dr NG16 ....160 C1
Guildford CI S45 ....131 C2
Guildford La S45 ....131 C2
Guinea CI NG16 ....236 A4
Guinevere Ave DE13 ......240 C1
Gun La DE56 ....191 A1
Gun Rd SK6 ....16 B1
Gurney Hill DE12 ....261 C1
Gunhills La DE56 ....189 C3
Gunnel CI ST16 ....269 A3
Gurney Ave DE21 ....223 C4
Guteridsh Ct NG9 ....223 C4
Guy CI NG9 ....223 C3
Gypsy La Creswell S80 .....81 C1
Draycott DE72 ....221 C1

H

Hackney La S18 ....75 C1
Hackney Rd S18 ....143 A4
Hackthorne Rd S8 ....81 A2
Haddon Ave S42 ....81 A2
Haddon CI Alfreton DE55 .158 C2
Bullbridge DE56 ....168 A3
Chesterfield S40 ....95 B1
Derby DE22 ....204 C1
Dronfield S18 ....57 A1
West Hallam DE7 ....207 C4
Haddon Ct DE6 ....185 B4
Haddon Dr
Bakewell DE45 ....109 C2
Derby DE23 ....204 B2
Derby, Mickleover DE3 ....217 C2
Derby, Spondon DE21 ....220 C2
Little Eaton DE21 ....191 B1
Haddon Gn S13 ....9 B1
Haddon Hall* DE45 ......110 A1
Haddon La SK13 ....9 B3
Haddon Nurseries
DE7 ....194 C2
Haddon Pl
Shirebrook NG20 ....119 B3
Staveley S43 ....97 B4
Haddon Rd
Bakewell DE45 ....109 C2
Buxton SK17 ....85 B4
Mansfield NG18 ....268 B4
North Wingfield S42 ......132 A4
Haddon St Derby DE24 ...232 B4
Ilkeston DE7 ....194 C2
Tibshelf DE55 ....148 A3
Haddon Way NG10 ....235 C2
Hade La SK17 ....106 C4
Hades La SK17 ....88 A2
Hadfield CE Jun Sch SK13 .9 C2

Hadfield Ind Est SK13 ....9 C3
Hadfield Inf Sch SK13 ....9 C3
Hadfield Pl SK13 ....17 B4
Hadfield Rd SK13 ....17 B4
Hadfield Sq **1** SK13 ......17 B4
Hadfield Sq **1** SK13 ......17 B4
Hadfield St SK13 ....10 A3
Hadfields Ave S14 ....9 B3
Hadleigh CI **2** NG9 ......223 C1
Hadley La DE6 ....186 C4
Hadley St DE7 ....209 A3
Hady's Ct DE12 ....262 B2
Hadlington Dr DE75 ....181 B1
Hadmoor Rd DE4 ....127 B2
Hallowes Ct S18 ....57 A1
Hallowes Dr S18 ....76 B4
Hallowes La S18 ....76 B4
Hallowes Rise S18 ....76 B4
Hady Cres S41 ....96 B2
Hady Hill S41 ....96 B1
Hady La S41 ....96 B1
Hady Prim Sch S41 ....96 B1
Hag Bank La S12 ....32 B4
Hagg La Dale Abbey DE7 .207 B2
Hague Ave S2 ....79 A4
Hague Bar Prim Sch
SK22 ....32 C4
Hague Bar Rd SK22 ....33 A4
Hague Fold Rd SK22 ....32 A4
Hague La S21, S43 ....79 A3
Hague Rd SK14 ....17 A4
Haig Meml Homes S8 ......57 A4
Haig St DE24 ....232 B4
Haigh Moor Rd S13 ....44 C4
Haigh Moor Wlk S13 ....44 C4
Hailsham CI DE7 ....217 B2
Haines CI DE21 ....221 C2
Halcyon App S42 ....115 B1
Halcyon CI S12 ....44 C2
Haldane CI S80 ....81 C1
Haldane Cres S44 ....98 C1
Halesworth CI S40 ....114 A4
Haley CI NG16 ....195 B3
Half Acre La S18 ....76 B4
Half Croft S43 ....96 C4
Halfmoon La DE4 ....163 A2
Halfway Ctr S20 ....59 C4
Halfway Dr S20 ....59 C4
Halfway Gdns S20 ....59 C4
Halfway Inf Sch S20 ....59 C4
Halfway Jun Sch S20 ....59 C3
Halifax CI Derby DE21 ....205 B1
Hilton DE65 ....228 C1
Halifax Pl NG1 ....268 B1
Hall Bank Buxton SK17 ....85 A4
Hartington SK17 ....137 C3
Hall Cl Barlow S42 ....94 C4
Dronfield S18 ....56 B1
Mottram in L SK14 ....9 A3
Hall Ct DE7 ....207 C4
Hall Dale View DE4 ....127 B2
Hall Dr For Doveridge DE6 .211 A1
Sandiacre NG10 ....223 A3
Hall Dyke DE21 ....220 B3
Hall End La DE45 ....108 C4
Hall Farm CI
Castle Donington DE74 ...247 A2
Swadlincote DE11 ....256 B2
Hall Farm Rd
Duffield DE56 ....190 C1
Swadlincote DE11 ....256 B2
Hall Gate View S33 ....51 A4
Hall Gdns
Castle Donington DE74 ...247 B2
Marchington ST14 ....224 C1
Hall Green Ave DE13 ......173 B1
Hall La Ashbourne DE6 ....202 A3
Brailsford DE6 ....202 A3
Brinsley NG16 ....182 B3
Donisthorpe DE12 ....265 C4
Doveridge DE6 ....224 A4
Mayfield DE6 ....183 A4
Nether Heage DE56 ....168 B2
Newton DE55 ....148 A2
Shirley DE6 ....200 B4
Staveley DE6 ....88 A2
Taddington SK17 ....69 C2
Willington DE65 ....242 A3
Hall Leys La DE55 ....145 A4
Hall Meadow Croft S20 ....59 C3
Hall Meadow Dr S20 ....59 C3
Hall Meadow Gr S20 ....59 C3
Hall Meadow Rd SK13 .....10 B1
Hall Pk DE73 ....244 A3
Hall Rd Aldercar NG16 ...182 B2
Brimington S43 ....96 B4
Marchington ST14 ....224 C1
Rolleston DE13 ....239 C2
Hall Rise Aldercar NG16 ..182 B2
Darley Dale DE4 ....127 B2
Hall St Alfreton DE55 .....159 B2
Derby DE24 ....233 A4
New Mills SK22 ....33 A4
Swadlincote DE11 ....256 A1
Hall Terr S45 ....131 B2
Hall The DE4 ....156 C3
Hall View S45 ....95 C3
Hall View Cottage Herb
Gdn* S45 ....132 C2
Hall Wlk S42 ....115 B1
Hall's Ct S43 ....80 C3
Hall's Row **8** S40 ....95 B1
Halladale Ct S40 ....269 B2
Hallahan Gr ST4 ....76 A4
Hallam Ct S18 ....76 B4
Hallam Fields DE74 ....247 A1
Hallam Fields Jun Sch
DE7 ....208 C3
Hallam Fields Rd DE7 ....209 A2
Hallam Way DE7 ....207 B4
Hallamway NG19 ....136 B1

Hallcliff La S42 ....93 C1
Hallcroft Ave DE12 ....262 A2
Hallcroft Rd **6** DE7 ....208 C4
Halldale CI S42 ....115 A2
Hallfield CI DE55 ....148 C3
Hallfield Rd DE55 ....148 C3
Hallfieldgate La DE55 .....146 B1
Hallfields Rd DE55 ....146 B1
Hallfields Rise DE55 ....146 B1
Halflash La S44 ....116 A4
Hallgarth CI DE21 ....206 B2
Hallgate La S45 ....132 A1
Hallington Dr DE75 ....181 B1
Hallmoor Rd DE4 ....127 B2
Hallam Cl S40 ....95 B3
Hallamble CI S40 ....95 B3
Hambleton CI S40 ....95 B3
Hambleton Dr DE24 ......231 C1
Hambleton Ave S42 ....131 C1
Hambleton CI
Ashbourne DE6 ....185 B4
3 Long Eaton NG10 ....223 A1
Hamblin Cres DE24 ....231 C2
Hamill CI S42 ....131 C4
Hamilton CI
Beeston NG9 ....223 C1
Derby DE3 ....217 C2
Hamilton Dr
Nottingham NG7 ....268 A1
Swadlincote DE11 ....256 B3
Hamilton Gdns DE15 .....248 A1
Hamilton Gr DE11 ....256 B3
Hamilton Rd
Burton u T DE15 ....248 A1
Derby DE21 ....218 C1
Derby, Spondon DE21 ....220 C3
Long Eaton NG10 ....223 B1
Hamilton St S3 ....160 A1
Hamlet La DE55 ....170 A3
Hamlet The Heanor DE75 .181 C2
South Normanton DE55 ..160 A3
Hammer Leys DE55 ....160 B2
Hammersmith DE5 ....169 B2
Hammersmith Sta*
DE5 ....169 B2
Hammonds Dr DE7 ....165 C4
Hampden Ho DE55 ....254 C3
Hampden St Derby DE23 .232 A4
Eastwood NG16 ....195 B4
Heanor NG16 ....182 A2
Nottingham NG1 ....268 A2
Hampshire CI NG16 ....17 C4
Hampshire Dr NG10 ......223 A3
Hampshire Rd DE21 ......219 B4
Hampstead Dr DE22 ......204 B4
Hampton CI
Beeston NG9 ....223 C2
Derby DE21 ....205 B4
West Hallam DE7 ....207 B4
Hampton Dr DE75 ....181 B1
Hampton St S41 ....115 B4
Hanbury Ave DE65 ....227 B1
Hanbury CI
Chesterfield S40 ....95 A3
Dronfield S18 ....56 C1
Hanbury Hill DE13 ....238 A3
Hanbury Rd DE21 ....219 C3
Hanchurch Ct DE15 ......248 A2
Hancock St S41 ....76 B4
Handby St S45 ....132 A1
Handel CI DE15 ....248 B4
Handel St
Nottingham NG1,NG3 ....268 C2
Handford CI DE21 ....218 B3
Handford St DE22 ....218 B3
Handley Arc NG18 ....268 B4
Handley CI S42 ....77 B2
Handley La
Clay Cross S45 ....131 A1
Shirland S45 ....145 C4
Handley Rd S43 ....77 B3
Handsacre CI DE11 ....255 C2
Handyside St DE1 ....267 B4
Hangar Hill S80 ....82 A3
Hanger Bank DE7 ....246 A4
Hanley CI S42 ....32 B3
Hanley St NG1 ....268 A2
Hannage Way DE4 ....165 B4
Hanover Sq DE22 ....218 A3
Hansard Gate DE7 ....267 B3
Hanslyn DE72 ....233 C2
Hanstubbin Rd NG16 .....171 C3
Hanwell Way DE22 ....218 A3
Harbin Rd DE12 ....265 C1
Harborck CI DE7 ....165 A4
Harborough Ave S2 ....44 A4
Harby Ave NG19 ....136 B3
Harcourt CI S41 ....115 B4

Harcourt Pl DE74 ....247 A2
Harcourt Rd DE14 ....253 C4
Harcourt St DE7 ....267 B2
Mansfield NG18 ....268 C3
Hard La S26 ....61 C4
Hardacre CI DE73 ....252 A4
Hardhurst Rd
Derby DE4 ....233 A3
Unstone S18 ....76 C3
Hardie Ave DE55 ....160 A3
Hardie Pl S43 ....97 B4
Harding Terr ST4 ....269 B1
Harding's CI DE6 ....165 A1
Harding's La SK17 ....138 A3
Hardinge St ST4 ....269 A1
Hardmeadow La S45 .....130 A1
Hardstaff Homes The
NG19 ....136 A2
Hardstoft Rd S45 ....132 C1
Hardwick Ave
Chesterfield S43 ....77 B2
Derby DE22 ....204 B2
Glapwell S44 ....134 A4
Shirebrook NG20 ....119 C3
West Hallam DE7 ....207 C4
Hardwick CI
Blackwell DE55 ....81 A2
Clowne S18 ....57 B1
Dronfield S18 ....57 B1
Holmewood S42 ....132 C4
Ripley DE5 ....169 B2
Hardwick CI
Long Eaton NG10 ....235 C2
8 Staveley S43 ....78 C1
Hardwick Ct Derby DE3 ..217 C1
Long Duckmanton S44 ....97 B2
Hardwick Hall* S44 ....133 C2
Hardwick Inf & Jun Schs
DE23 ....219 A1
Hardwick La S45 ....129 B3
Hardwick Mount S17 ......55 A4
Hardwick Old Hall*
S44 ....133 C2
Hardwick Park Nature Wlk*
NG17 ....133 C2
Hardwick Pk* S44,
NG17 ....133 C2
Hardwick Pl DE7 ....208 B3
Hardwick Rd NG17 ....268 A1
Hardwick Sq E SK17 ....85 B4
Hardwick Sq N SK17 ....85 B4
Hardwick Sq S SK17 ....85 A4
Hardwick Sq W SK17 ......85 A4
Hardwick St Buxton SK17 .85 A4
Chesterfield S41 ....266 B4
Derby DE24 ....232 B4
Langwith NG20 ....119 C4
Mansfield NG18 ....268 C4
Shirebrook NG20 ....120 A2
Tibshelf DE55 ....148 A4
Hardwick's Yd S40 ....132 C4
Hardwick's Yd S40 ....77 B2
Hardy Barn DE75 ....194 C4
Hardy CI Kimberley NG16 .195 C4
Long Eaton NG10 ....236 B3
Hardy Cres S42 ....181 A4
Hardy PI NG19 ....268 A4
Hardy St Alfreton DE55 ..158 C3
Kimberley NG16 ....195 C4
Hardybarn La S17 ....86 B4
Harebell CI DE21 ....206 A2
Swadlincote DE11 ....256 C2
Harehedge La DE13 ......240 A1
Harehill Cres S42 ....114 B2
Harehill Ct S40 ....114 C4
Harehill Rd S40 ....114 C4
Hareholme St NG19 ......268 B4
Harepit CI DE22 ....203 A3
Harewood CI DE56 ....179 B3
Harewood Cres S42 ......131 A3
Harewood Rd NG10 ......223 A2
Harewood Rd SK14 ....16 A4
Harewood Rd
Derby DE22 ....204 B2
Holymoorside S42 ....113 B3
Hargate Hill La SK13 ......16 C4
Hargate Rd
Burton u T DE15 ....248 B1
Buxton SK17 ....84 C3
Hargrave Ave DE22 ....221 B3
Hargreaves CI DE23 .....231 A3
Hargreaves La ST17 ......269 A3
Harlaxton Dr
Long Eaton NG10 ....237 A4
Nottingham NG7 ....268 A1
Harlaxton Wlk **8** NG3 .268 B2
Harlech CI DE21 ....221 A3
Ilkeston DE7 ....194 B3
Harlequin Ct NG16 ....182 B2
Harlesden Ave DE22 ......218 A4
Harlesthorpe Ave S43 ....80 C3
Harlesthorpe La S43 ....80 C3
Harlow CI Derby DE24 ...232 C2
Mansfield Woodhouse
NG19 ....136 B3
Harlow Ct DE7 ....207 B4
Harnett CI NG1 ....268 B1
Harold Ave NG16 ....182 A2
Harold St NG2 ....268 C1
Harperhill CI S40 ....114 C4
Harpfield Rd ST4 ....269 A1
Harpole CI DE55 ....169 C4
Harport Dr S41 ....131 C1
Harpswell CI DE22 ....204 C3

Harpur Ave Derby DE23 . . . . . **231** A4
Ticknall DE73 . . . . **251** A2
Harpur Hill Prim Sch
SK17 . . . . **85** B2
Harpur Hill Rd SK17 . . . . **85** B2
Harpur-Crewe Cotts
DE6 . . . . **149** B2
Harrier Rd DE55 . . . . **179** B3
Harrier Way DE24 . . . . **231** C2
Harriet St DE23 . . . . **219** A2
Harriett St NG9 . . . . **223** B4
Harrimans Dr DE72 . . . . **235** C4
Harringay Gdns DE22 . . . . . . **218** B3
Harrington Ave DE72 . . . . . . **221** B1
Harrington Jun Sch
NG10 . . . . **223** A1
Harrington Rd
Derby DE23 . . . . **218** B1
Sheffield S2 . . . . **43** A4
Harrington St
Derby, Allenton DE24 . . . . . . **232** C3
Derby, Normanton DE23 . . . . **232** A4
Draycott DE72 . . . . **235** A4
Long Eaton NG10 . . . . **236** A3
Mansfield NG18 . . . . **268** B3
Harris Ave DE5 . . . . **169** B1
Harris Cl DE5 . . . . **169** B1
Harris Rd Buxton SK17 . . . . . . **85** B2
Stafford ST16 . . . . **269** C4
Harris St ST4 . . . . **269** B2
Harrison Dr DE4 . . . . **254** A4
Harrison Dr DE4 . . . . **154** C1
Harrison La
Ringinglow S10 . . . . **42** C4
Tibshelf DE55 . . . . **147** C3
Harrison Rd
Mansfield NG18 . . . . **268** A3
Stapleford NG9 . . . . **223** B4
Harrison St DE22 . . . . **218** C2
Harrison Way DE4 . . . . **127** A3
Harrogate Cres DE21 . . . . . . **205** B1
Harrop La S10 . . . . **42** C3
Harrop White Rd NG18,
NG19 . . . . **268** A4
Harrots La SK17 . . . . **137** B3
Harrow Dr
Burton u T DE14 . . . . **254** B4
Ilkeston DE7 . . . . **209** A2
Harrow Rd DE11 . . . . **256** A4
Harrow St DE24 . . . . **219** C1
Harrowby St ST16 . . . . **269** C4
Hart Ave NG10 . . . . **223** A3
Hart Lea **3** NG10 . . . . **223** A3
Hartfield Cl S41 . . . . **115** A4
Hartford Rd S8 . . . . **43** A2
Hartford Rd S8 . . . . **43** A2
Harthill Field Rd S26 . . . . **62** A2
Harthill Prim Sch S26 . . . . **61** C3
Harthill Rd Sheffield S13 . . . . **44** A4
Thorpe Salvin S80 . . . . **63** A3
Hartill St ST4 . . . . **269** C2
Hartington CE Prim Sch
SK17 . . . . **137** B3
Hartington Cl DE7 . . . . **207** C4
Hartington Ct Clowne S43 . . . **81** A2
Dronfield S18 . . . . **57** A1
Hartington Dr
Chinley SK23 . . . . **34** C1
Creswell S80 . . . . **81** B1
Hartington Hall YH*
SK17 . . . . **137** C3
Hartington Ind Est S43 . . . . . . **78** C2
Hartington Pl DE7 . . . . **194** C3
Hartington Rd
Buxton SK17 . . . . **85** A4
Chesterfield S41 . . . . **96** B1
Dronfield S18 . . . . **57** A1
Hartington St
Derby DE1, DE23 . . . . **267** B1
Langwith NG20 . . . . **119** C4
Hartington View S43 . . . . **78** C2
Hartington Way DE75 . . . . . . **217** B1
Hartland Dr DE23 . . . . **231** C3
Hartland Way S41 . . . . **77** A1
Hartley St S2 . . . . **43** A4
Hartopp Ave S2 . . . . **43** B3
Hartopp Cl S2 . . . . **43** B3
Hartopp Dr S2 . . . . **43** B3
Hartopp Rd S2 . . . . **43** B3
Hartshay Hill DE5 . . . . **169** B1
Hartshill Rd
Hartshorne DE11 . . . . **257** A2
Stoke-on-T ST4 . . . . **269** A2
Hartshorne CE Prim Sch
DE11 . . . . **257** A3
Hartshorne Rd
Derby DE23 . . . . **231** B3
Repton DE65 . . . . **249** C4
Woodville DE11 . . . . **256** C2
Hartside Cl **9** S40 . . . . **95** B3
Hartside Gdns **1** NG10 . . . . **236** A4
Hartside Way DE75 . . . . **182** A1
Hartwell St NG3 . . . . **268** B2
Hartwood Dr NG9 . . . . **209** B1
Harvest Hill DE11 . . . . **256** A4
Harvest Way Derby DE24 . . **206** B2
2 Old Brampton S42 . . . . **95** A3
Harvester Cl DE5 . . . . **169** B1
Harvey Clough Mews S8 . . . . **43** A2
Harvey Clough Rd S8 . . . . **43** A2
Harvey Croft NG9 . . . . **209** B2
Harvey Ct S44 . . . . **98** C1
Harvey Pl ST14 . . . . **210** A1

Harvey Rd
Burton u T DE14 . . . . **254** A4
Castle Donington DE74 . . . . . **247** A1
Chesterfield S41 . . . . **96** C1
Derby DE24 . . . . **232** C3
Harwood Ave DE14 . . . . **253** C4
Harwood Cl S2 . . . . **43** A4
Hasgill Ct DE21 . . . . **206** B2
Haslam Cres S8 . . . . **56** C3
Haslam Ct S44 . . . . **98** C1
Haslam St NG7 . . . . **268** A1
Haslam's La DE21,DE22 . . . **205** A1
Hasland Hall Com Sch
S41 . . . . **115** B4
Hasland Inf Sch S41 . . . . **115** B4
Hasland Jun Sch S41 . . . . **115** B4
Hasland Rd S41 . . . . **115** B4
Haslemere Ct DE23 . . . . **219** A1
Haslemere Rd NG10 . . . . **236** A3
Haslin Rd SK17 . . . . **85** B1
Hassall Rd DE65 . . . . **227** B1
Hassock La N DE75 . . . . **194** A4
Hassock La S DE7,DE75 . . . . **194** B3
Hassocky La S44,S42 . . . . **116** A3
Hassop Cl Chesterfield S41 . . . **95** B3
Dronfield S18 . . . . **57** B1
Hassop Rd Calver S32 . . . . **72** A1
Derby DE21 . . . . **220** A4
Hassop DE45 . . . . **90** B1
Staveley S43 . . . . **78** C2
Hastilar Cl S2 . . . . **44** A4
Hastilar Rd S2 . . . . **44** A4
Hastilar Rd S S13 . . . . **44** A4
Hasting St DE74 . . . . **247** A1
Hastings Cl
Breedon on t H DE73 . . . . **252** C1
Chesterfield S41 . . . . **95** B3
Hastings Rd Buxton SK17 . . . . **85** B2
Hastings St DE23 . . . . **219** A1
Haston Dr DE55 . . . . **170** B4
Hatchmere Cl DE21 . . . . **206** A1
Hatfield Ave NG10 . . . . **223** A2
Hatfield Rd DE24 . . . . **232** C3
Hathaway Cl S42 . . . . **131** A3
Hathern Cl Calow S42 . . . . **96** C2
Chesterfield S41 . . . . **95** B3
Long Eaton NG10 . . . . **236** B3
Hathersage Ave
Derby DE23 . . . . **231** C4
Long Eaton NG10 . . . . **235** C3
Hathersage Cres SK13 . . . . **9** C1
Hathersage Dr
Glossop SK13 . . . . **17** C4
Somercotes DE55 . . . . **170** A4
Hathersage Rd
Bamford S33 . . . . **40** A1
Totley S11 . . . . **54** B3
Hathersage Sta S32 . . . . **53** A4
Hathersage St CI S18 . . . . **269** C4
Hatton Cl S18 . . . . **75** B4
Hatton Crofts NG10 . . . . **236** B3
Hatton Ct DE73 . . . . **252** A4
Hatton Dr S40 . . . . **95** A3
Haulton Dr DE74 . . . . **247** A2
Havelock Gdns NG3 . . . . **268** B2
Havelock Rd DE23 . . . . **232** A4
Havelock St Ilkeston DE7 . . . **208** C4
Ripley DE5 . . . . **169** C1
Haven Baulk Ave DE23 . . . . . **230** C4
Haven Baulk La DE23 . . . . . . **230** C4
Haven Cl DE24 . . . . **232** B3
Havenwood Gr DE23 . . . . **231** B3
Havercroft Tr S21 . . . . **60** A4
Hawfield La
Burton u T DE15 . . . . **248** B2
Newton Solney DE15 . . . . **248** C2
Hawk Green Rd SK6 . . . . **23** A2
Hawk Rd SK22 . . . . **33** C4
Hawk's Dr DE15 . . . . **248** B2
Hawke St DE22 . . . . **218** B3
Hawkeshead Ave S18 . . . . **56** C1
Hawkhill Rd S32 . . . . **71** B3
Hawking La S44 . . . . **133** A4
Hawkinge Ho **6** S41 . . . . **95** B3
Hawkins Cl DE7 . . . . **194** C2
Hawkins Dr DE56 . . . . **168** A2
Hawkins St ST4 . . . . **269** C1
Hawksdale Cl DE73 . . . . **233** A1
Hawkshead Ave DE21 . . . . . . **205** B1
Hawkshead Rd SK13 . . . . **10** C2
Hawksley Ave S40 . . . . **95** C2
Hawksley Dr
Darley Dale DE4 . . . . **127** A2
Rolleston DE13 . . . . **240** A2
Hawksway S21 . . . . **60** A4
Hawksworth St NG3 . . . . **268** B2
Hawley St S18 . . . . **58** A1
Hawleys Cl DE4 . . . . **143** C3
Hawthorn Ave
Breaston DE72 . . . . **235** C4
Creswell S80 . . . . **81** C1
Derby DE24 . . . . **233** A4
Glapwell S44 . . . . **134** A4
Mastin Moor S43 . . . . **79** B2
Netherthal DE12 . . . . **264** C4
Ripley DE5 . . . . **180** B4
Stapleford NG9 . . . . **223** B3
Hawthorn Bank
Glossop SK13 . . . . **9** C2
New Mills SK22 . . . . **33** A3
Hawthorn Cl
Ashbourne DE6 . . . . **185** B4
Chinley SK23 . . . . **34** C1
Clowne S43 . . . . **80** B2
Denstone ST14 . . . . **196** C3
Doveridge DE6 . . . . **211** A1
Hilton DE65 . . . . **228** B1

Hawthorn Cl *continued*
Hope u T DE14 . . . . **39** A2
Mansfield Woodhouse
NG19 . . . . **136** C3
Hawthorn Cres DE15 . . . . . . **254** C4
Hawthorn Dr DE4 . . . . **155** A3
Hawthorn Gr SK14 . . . . **9** B3
Hawthorn Hill S43 . . . . **78** C2
Hawthorn Rd
Castle Donington DE74 . . . . . **247** A3
Eckington S21 . . . . **59** A1
Hawthorn Rise DE11 . . . . **255** C4
Hawthorn St DE24 . . . . **232** B4
Hawthorn Way ST17 . . . . **269** C3
Hawthorne Ave
Borrowash DE72 . . . . **221** B1
Dronfield S18 . . . . **57** A2
Long Eaton NG10 . . . . **236** B3
Shirebrook NG20 . . . . **119** B2
Shirland DE55 . . . . **146** B3
Stoke-on-T ST4 . . . . **269** A1
Tibshelf DE55 . . . . **148** A4
Hawthorne Cl
Barlborough S43 . . . . **80** A3
Kilburn DE56 . . . . **179** C1
Killamarsh S21 . . . . **60** B3
Shirland DE55 . . . . **145** B4
Hawthorne Rd NG16 . . . . **160** B2
Headingley Ct DE23 . . . . **231** B4
Hawthorne St S40 . . . . **266** B1
Hawthornes Ave DE55 . . . . . **159** C3
Hawthorns The
Belper DE56 . . . . **179** B3
Chapel-en-le-f SK23 . . . . **47** A2
Little Eaton DE21 . . . . **205** B4
Hawton Cl NG19 . . . . **135** C1
Hawtrey Gdns DE24 . . . . **233** A3
Haxby Cl S13 . . . . **44** C3
Haxby Pl S13 . . . . **44** C3
Haxby St S13 . . . . **44** C3
Hay La Ashover S45 . . . . **145** A4
Scropton DE65 . . . . **226** C3
Spout DE4 . . . . **166** A2
Hay Wain La DE11 . . . . **256** A4
Haybrook Ct S17 . . . . **55** C3
Haycroft Cl NG19 . . . . **136** C3
Haycroft Ct DE23 . . . . **231** A4
Hayden Ct S13 . . . . **10** B1
Hayden Fold S42 . . . . **16** B4
Haydn Rd DE21 . . . . **219** C4
Haydock Cl
Burton u T DE14 . . . . **254** A4
Kimberley NG16 . . . . **195** C4
Haydock Park Rd DE24 . . . . **232** C4
Hayes Ave
Breaston DE72 . . . . **235** A4
Derby DE23 . . . . **231** B4
Hayes Cl Pinxton NG16 . . . . . **160** B2
West Hallam DE7 . . . . **207** C4
Hayes Cottage Cl
DE55 . . . . **170** A3
Hayes Cres S20 . . . . **59** C4
Hayes Ct S20 . . . . **59** C3
Hayes Dr S20 . . . . **59** C3
Hayes Farm Ct DE73 . . . . **251** A2
Hayes La DE55 . . . . **169** C4
Hayes The DE65 . . . . **230** B1
Hayes Wood Rd DE7 . . . . **193** A1
Hayfield Cl Belper DE56 . . . . **179** A3
Dronfield S18 . . . . **56** B1
Staveley S43 . . . . **78** C2
Wingerworth S42 . . . . **114** C2
Hayfield Cres S12 . . . . **44** B2
Hayfield Dr S12 . . . . **44** B2
Hayfield Gdns DE23 . . . . **231** A3
Hayfield Pl S12 . . . . **44** B2
Hayfield Prim Sch SK22 . . . . . **25** B2
Hayfield Rd
Chapel-en-le-f SK23 . . . . **47** A4
Chinley SK23 . . . . **35** A2
New Mills SK22 . . . . **24** C1
Hayfield View S21 . . . . **59** B2
Hayfield Vistor Ctr*
SK22 . . . . **25** C1
Hayford Way S43 . . . . **78** C1
Hayley Croft DE56 . . . . **190** C1
Hayling Cl DE7 . . . . **194** B2
Haynes Ave NG9 . . . . **209** B3
Hays Cl DE7 . . . . **194** B3
Hays La DE6 . . . . **164** C1
Hays The DE65 . . . . **227** B1
Haywards Cl SK13 . . . . **10** B2
Haywood Cl DE24 . . . . **233** A3
Haywood St NG2 . . . . **268** C3
Hayworth Rd NG10 . . . . **223** A3
Hazel Ave Derby DE23 . . . . . . **231** B3
Killamarsh S21 . . . . **60** B3
Pilsley S45 . . . . **132** A2
Hazel Cl Ashbourne DE6 . . . . **185** B4
Dronfield S18 . . . . **76** A4
Findern DE65 . . . . **230** C1
Heanor DE75 . . . . **181** B1
Stoke-on-T ST4 . . . . **269** A1
Swadlincote DE11 . . . . **256** A3
Hazel Cres NG20 . . . . **119** B2
Hazel Ct S18 . . . . **76** A4
Hazel Dr Chesterfield S40 . . . **114** C4
Derby DE21 . . . . **221** A3
Wingerworth S42 . . . . **115** A2
Hazel Gr Calver S32 . . . . **72** B1
Duffield DE56 . . . . **190** C2
Mansfield Woodhouse
NG19 . . . . **136** A3
Mastin Moor S43 . . . . **79** B2
Matlock DE4 . . . . **143** B3

Hazel Gr *continued*
South Normanton DE55 . . . . **160** A3
Hazel Rd S21 . . . . **59** B1
Hazelbadge Cres S12 . . . . **44** C2
Hazelby Rd S80 . . . . **100** C4
Hazeldene DE56 . . . . **190** C3
Hazeldene Cotts DE56 . . . . . **178** B1
Hazelhurst S41 . . . . **115** B3
Hazelhurst Ave S41 . . . . **96** B3
Hazelhurst La S41 . . . . **96** A3
Hazelmere Rd S80 . . . . **81** B2
Hazelrigg Cl DE74 . . . . **246** C2
Hazeltree Cl DE5 . . . . **180** B4
Hazelwood Cl **3** S18 . . . . **56** B1
Hazelwood Hill DE56 . . . . . . **190** B4
Hazelwood Rd
Burton u T DE15 . . . . **254** C3
Derby DE21 . . . . **219** C4
Duffield DE56 . . . . **190** B3
Hazlebarrow Cl S8 . . . . **57** B3
Hazlebarrow Cres S8 . . . . **57** B4
Hazlebarrow Ct S8 . . . . **57** A4
Hazlebarrow Dr S8 . . . . **57** A4
Hazlebarrow Rd S8 . . . . **57** A4
Hazlehurst La S8 . . . . **57** C4
Hazletarrow Prim Schs
S8 . . . . **57** B3
Hazlewood Dr S43 . . . . **80** A3
Headingley Ct DE23 . . . . **231** B4
Headland Cl S43 . . . . **96** C4
Headland Rd S43 . . . . **96** C4
Heage La DE65 . . . . **229** B4
Heage Prim Sch DE56 . . . . . . **168** B1
Heage Rd DE5 . . . . **169** B2
Healaugh Way S40 . . . . **115** A4
Heale St S43 . . . . **80** C2
Heanor Gate Ind Est
DE75 . . . . **193** B4
Heanor Gate Rd DE75 . . . . . **193** B4
Heanor Gate Sch DE75 . . . . . **181** B1
Heanor Ho DE21 . . . . **220** C2
Heanor Langley Mill &
District Meml Hosp
DE75 . . . . **181** C2
Heanor Rd Codnor DE55 . . . . **181** A4
Denby DE5 . . . . **181** A4
Heanor, Loscoe DE75 . . . . **181** B2
Ilkeston DE7 . . . . **194** B2
Smalley DE7,DE75 . . . . **193** B3
Heanor Rd, DE75 . . . . **181** B1
Hearthcote Rd DE11 . . . . **256** A2
Hearthstone La DE4 . . . . **143** B1
Heath Ave Derby DE23 . . . . . **218** B1
Killamarsh S21 . . . . **60** B2
Heath Cross ST14 . . . . **210** A1
Heath Ct Chesterfield S40 . . . **115** A4
Derby DE24 . . . . **231** C2
Heath Fields Prim Sch
DE65 . . . . **227** B1
Heath Gdns DE72 . . . . **236** A4
Heath Gr SK17 . . . . **85** B3
Heath La
Blackfordby DE11 . . . . **257** B1
Findern DE65 . . . . **242** B4
Hartshorne DE11 . . . . **257** C2
Smisby LE65 . . . . **258** A3
Ticknall LE65 . . . . **258** A3
Heath Park Rd SK17 . . . . **85** B3
Heath Prim Sch S44 . . . . **116** C1
Heath Rd
Burton u T DE15 . . . . **254** C4
Glossop SK13 . . . . **10** B1
Holmewood S44 . . . . **116** C1
Holmewood, Williamthorpe
S42 . . . . **132** C4
Ripley DE5 . . . . **169** C1
Uttoxeter ST14 . . . . **210** A1
Heath St S41 . . . . **85** A3
Heath The NG16 . . . . **195** A4
Heath View S17 . . . . **55** C1
Heath Way DE65 . . . . **227** B1
Heathcoat St NG1 . . . . **268** B2
Heathcote Cl DE24 . . . . **233** B3
Heathcote Dr S41 . . . . **115** C4
Heather Ave S44 . . . . **116** B1
Heather Bank Cl **7** SK13 . . . **17** A4
Heather Cl
Burton u T DE14 . . . . **254** A4
Calow S44 . . . . **97** A2
Derby DE24 . . . . **231** B1
Mansfield NG18 . . . . **268** A4
South Normanton DE55 . . . . **160** A2
Swanwick DE55 . . . . **170** A4
Heather Cres
Breaston DE72 . . . . **235** C4
Derby DE23 . . . . **231** B3
Heather Ct DE75 . . . . **182** A1
Heather Gdns S44 . . . . **115** C4
Heather Gr SK14 . . . . **9** B3
Heather Lea Ave S17 . . . . **55** B4
Heather Lea Pl S17 . . . . **55** B4
Heather Vale S41 . . . . **115** C4
Heather Vale Cl S41 . . . . **115** C4
Heather Way S42 . . . . **113** B4
Heatherdene Dr NG19 . . . . . **136** C1
Heatherley Prim Sch
NG19 . . . . **136** C1
Heathermead Cl DE21 . . . . . **205** C1
Heathervale Rd S41 . . . . **57** A2
Heathfield Ave S41 . . . . **143** B4
Heathfield Ave
Chesterfield S40 . . . . **95** B2
Ilkeston DE7 . . . . **209** A4
Heathfield Cl
Dronfield S18 . . . . **75** C4
Wingerworth S42 . . . . **115** A2

Heathfield Gdns
Buxton SK17 . . . . **85** A3
Tibshelf DE55 . . . . **148** A4
Heathfield Nook Rd
SK17 . . . . **86** A1
Heathfield Rd S12 . . . . **44** A3
Heathlands Dr ST14 . . . . **210** A1
Heathley Mews DE14 . . . . . . **253** A4
Heaton Cl **12** S18 . . . . **56** B1
Heaton St S40 . . . . **266** A4
Heavygate La S10 . . . . **42** C4
Hebden Cl DE23 . . . . **231** A4
Hebden Dr SK13 . . . . **9** C2
Hebrides Cl DE24 . . . . **231** C2
Hedderley WR **4** NG3 . . . . . . **268** B2
Heddon Bar NG19 . . . . **136** B1
Hedge Gr DE11 . . . . **256** A3
Hedgebank Ct DE21 . . . . **206** A1
Hedgerow Gdns DE21 . . . . . **205** C1
Hedges Dr DE7 . . . . **209** A4
Hedingham Way DE3 . . . . . . **230** C4
Hedley Cl DE55 . . . . **170** C3
Hedley Dr S43 . . . . **80** A3
Heeley Arches S2 . . . . **43** A4
Heeley Bank Rd S2 . . . . **43** A4
Heeley City Farm* S2 . . . . **43** A4
Heeley Gn S2 . . . . **43** A4
Heigham Cl DE24 . . . . **233** A3
Heights of Abraham*
DE4 . . . . **156** C4
Heights of Abraham Cabl
Car* DE4 . . . . **155** C3
Helmsdale Cl NG18 . . . . **268** A4
Helmsley Ave S20 . . . . **59** C4
Helmsley Cl S41 . . . . **95** C1
Helmton Dr S8 . . . . **56** C3
Helmton Rd S8 . . . . **56** C3
Helpston Cl DE55 . . . . **170** C3
Helston Cl
Chesterfield S41 . . . . **95** B3
Derby DE24 . . . . **233** A3
Linton DE12 . . . . **261** C3
Helvellyn Way **7** NG10 . . . . . **223** A3
Heming Ave S45 . . . . **131** C3
Hemington Ct DE74 . . . . **247** C3
Hemington Hill DE74 . . . . . . **247** C3
Hemington La DE74 . . . . **247** B3
Hemington St DE74 . . . . **247** C3
Hemlock Ave
Long Eaton NG10 . . . . **223** C2
Stapleford NG9 . . . . **223** C4
Hemlock Cl DE21 . . . . **205** C1
Hemlock La DE7 . . . . **208** A3
Hemp Yd DE6 . . . . **224** C4
Hemper Gr S8 . . . . **56** B3
Hemper La S8 . . . . **56** B3
Hemsley Dr NG16 . . . . **171** C3
Hemsworth Prim Sch
S14 . . . . **43** C1
Hemsworth Rd S8 . . . . **43** C1
Henly Ave DE22 . . . . **204** B2
Henley Ave S8 . . . . **57** A3
Henley Gdns NG9 . . . . **209** B2
Henley Gn DE22 . . . . **204** B2
Henley Way DE7 . . . . **207** C2
Henmore Pl DE6 . . . . **173** B1
Henmore Trad Est DE6 . . . . . **185** B4
Hennymoor Cl S80 . . . . **82** A3
Hennymoor La S80 . . . . **82** B3
Henry Ave
Mansfield Woodhouse
NG19 . . . . **136** B2
Matlock DE4 . . . . **143** A3
Henry Bradley Inf Sch
S43 . . . . **78** C1
Henry Cres DE55 . . . . **170** C4
Henry Prince CE Fst Sch
DE6 . . . . **151** B1
Henry St Chesterfield S41 . . . . **77** A1
Derby DE1 . . . . **267** C4
Eckington S21 . . . . **59** B1
Glossop SK13 . . . . **10** B2
Grassmoor S42 . . . . **115** C2
Nottingham NG2 . . . . **268** C4
Ripley DE5 . . . . **169** C1
Henshaw Ave DE7 . . . . **208** A1
Henshaw Pl DE7 . . . . **194** C3
Herbert Rd ST17 . . . . **269** C4
Herbert St
Burton u T DE15 . . . . **248** A2
Fenton ST4 . . . . **269** C2
Mansfield NG18 . . . . **268** B3
Herbert Strutt Prim Sch
DE56 . . . . **179** A3
Herdings Ct S12 . . . . **43** C2
Herdings Leighton Rd
S12 . . . . **43** C1
Herdings Pk S14 . . . . **43** C2
Herdings Prim Sch S14 . . . . . **43** C1
Herdings Rd S12 . . . . **43** C1
Herdings View S12 . . . . **43** C1
Hereford Ave NG19 . . . . **136** B1
Hereford Cl SK17 . . . . **85** B2
Hereford Cres DE11 . . . . **256** B1
Hereford Dr S43 . . . . **96** C4
Hereford Rd Buxton SK17 . . . . **85** B2
Derby DE21 . . . . **219** C4
Hereward's Rd S14 . . . . **43** C1
Herewood Cl NG20 . . . . **119** C3
Heritage Com Sch S43 . . . . . . **80** B4
Heritage Dr S43 . . . . **80** B4
Heritage Way DE15 . . . . **248** B2
Hermitage Ave
Borrowash DE72 . . . . **221** B1
Mansfield NG18 . . . . **268** A4
Somercotes DE55 . . . . **170** B4
Hermitage Ct DE21 . . . . **219** B2

Her – Hol 289

itage Gdns 1
210 A1
itage La
sfield NG18 268 A3
ield DE6 184 A3
itage Park Way 7
256 A4
itage Sq 6 NG2 268 C1
itage Wlk
ston DE7 208 C3
ingham NG7 268 A1
on St 33 NG7 268 A2
stone La SK17 49 A1
n Dr DE11 256 C2
n Way DE3 218 A1
nswood Dr DE21 220 B3
ot Dr S40 266 C1
ey Cl NG3 268 B2
ey Wlk 7 NG3 268 B2
ey St S13 44 C3
ers Holt S43 80 A3
ett St NG20 120 B3
tt Pl S26 61 C3
am Ave DE7 209 A2
am Wlk DE21 205 C1
St NG10 236 B2
en Bank SK13 9 B1
en Terr SK13 9 B1
on Cl DE56 179 A3
ord Ct DE75 182 A1
bank Rd SK12 32 B3
vard St NG18 268 C4
vood St
ington S43 96 C4
sfield NG18 268 C4
vood View S43 80 B3
vood Villas 8 S43 96 C4
vorth Rd SK23 47 B3
vorth St DE22 218 B3
ert Rd NG18 268 C4
ert St SK22 33 A3
ings La NG9 223 C4
ngwood La S43 81 A3
inwood Cres S43 80 C3
eton Cl DE5 169 B1
ling Cl DE24 232 B2
ling Ct NG18 268 C4
ton Rd DE55 169 C3
La SK17 137 C4
Pl ST4 269 B2
St ST4 269 B2
s Gn S44 99 A1
La DE56 167 A3
er La S32 52 C4
ins Rd DE11 255 C3
ott Cl DE14 254 A4
Bank DE5 180 C1
Bank Rd DE15 248 A2
Cross
tington SK17 137 C3
on DE11 261 C4
Cross St 23 NG1 268 B2
Ct DE4 143 B3
Edge Dr DE56 179 C4
Edge Mews DE56 179 A3
Gr Belper DE56 179 B2
nsfield NG19 136 C1
Hazel Cl S45 131 C2
Hazel Wlk S45 131 C2
Hazels Rd S43 80 A3
Hill Rd SK22 24 B1
Holborn DE7 194 C2
Holborn Rd DE5 170 A1
La Broadbottom SK13 16 C4
loway, Dethick Common
144 C1
loway, Upper Holloway
156 B3
ymoorside S42 113 C3
ffield S12 44 C1
La Central DE7 193 C1
La E DE7 208 A4
La W DE7 193 C1
Lea Rd SK22 33 A4
Leys Rd S43 80 C1
Mdws SK13 17 A4
Meadow Cl DE5 180 B4
Pavement
per DE56 179 A2
tingham NG1 268 B1
Pk ST16 269 A3
Rd DE55 157 C2
Ridge
nsfield NG19 136 C1
tlock DE4 143 B4
Spania NG16 195 C4
St Alfreton DE55 159 A2
reton, Riddings DE55 170 B3
erknowle S18 58 A1
lborough S43 80 A4
per DE56 179 A2
sover S44 99 A1
nsall DE4 142 B1
mington S43 96 C4
nsley NG16 171 B1
xton SK17 85 A4
ver S32 72 A1
stle Donington DE74 247 A1
apel-en-le-F SK23 47 A3
esterfield S41,S43 77 B2
esterfield, Stonegravels
266 B3
y Cross S45 131 B2
wne S43 80 B2
dnor DE5 181 A4
rby DE73 233 A1
re S17 55 B4
veridge DE6 211 A1

High St *continued*
Dronfield S18 57 A1
Eckington S21 59 B2
Heanor, Loscoe DE75 181 B2
Heanor, Newlands DE75 181 C1
Ilkeston DE7 208 C4
Kilburn DE56 192 A4
Killamarsh S21 60 B3
Kimberley NG16 195 C3
Linton DE12 261 B3
Long Eaton NG10 236 C4
Longnor SK17 121 B3
Mansfield Woodhouse
NG19 136 B2
Marchington ST14 224 C1
Melbourne DE73 252 A4
Mosborough S20 59 B4
New Mills SK22 33 B4
Nottingham NG1 268 B1
Pilsley DE45 91 B2
Pleasley NG19 135 A3
Repton DE65 242 B1
Ripley DE5 169 B1
Rocester ST14 196 C2
Somercotes DE55 170 B4
South Normanton DE55 160 A3
Stapleford NG9 223 C4
Staveley S43 78 C1
Stonebroom DE55 147 A2
Stoney Middleton S32 71 C2
Swadlincote, Church Gresley
DE11 256 B2
Swadlincote, Newhall
DE11 256 A3
Swanwick DE55 169 C4
Tibshelf DE55 148 A4
Ticknall DE73 251 A2
Tideswell SK17 69 B2
Tutbury DE13 239 B3
Whitwell S80 81 C3
Woodville DE11 256 C1
High St E SK13 10 B1
High St W SK13 10 A1
High Tor* DE4 143 A2
High Tor Rd DE4 143 A1
High Trees S17 55 B4
High View Cl S41 96 B1
High View Rd DE55 160 B4
High View Sch & Tech Ctr
DE21 205 C1
High Wood Bank DE56 179 B1
High Wood Fold SK6 23 B4
Higham La Compstall SK14 15 A4
Stonebroom DE55 146 C2
Highashes La S45 113 C1
Highbank SK13 9 C4
Highbank Rd SK13 17 C4
Highbury Cl DE22 217 C3
Highbury Rd S41 95 C3
Highcliffe Ave NG20 119 B2
Highcroft Cl NG10 236 C3
Higher Albert St S41 266 B4
Higher Barn Rd SK13 9 C2
Higher Dinting SK13 10 A1
Higher Halsteads SK17 47 C2
Higher La SK12 32 C1
Higher Sq SK13 10 A4
Highfield DE45 108 C4
Highfield Ave
Chesterfield S41 95 C3
Dove Holes SK17 47 C1
Mansfield NG19 136 A1
Shirebrook NG20 119 B3
Highfield Cl
Bakewell DE45 109 B3
Heanor DE75 181 A3
Mansfield NG19 136 A1
Highfield Cotts DE21 219 C3
Highfield Ct SK14 9 A2
Highfield Dr
Bakewell DE45 109 B3
Ilkeston DE7 208 A3
Matlock DE4 143 B3
South Normanton DE55 160 A3
Highfield Gdns
Derby DE22 218 C4
Hollingworth SK14 9 B3
Highfield Hall Prim Sch
S41 95 C3
Highfield La
Chesterfield S41 95 C3
Derby DE21 219 C3
Hartington SK17 137 C3
Weston Underwood DE6 188 C3
Highfield Mews DE21 219 C3
Highfield Pl S2 43 A4
Highfield Prim Sch
NG10 223 B1
Highfield Rd
Ashbourne DE6 185 A4
Belper DE56 178 C1
Bolsover S44 99 A1
Chesterfield S41 266 A4
Derby DE22 218 C4
Derby, Littleover DE23 231 B4
Glossop SK13 17 B4
Hayfield SK22 25 B2
Hulland Ward DE6 175 C2
Kilburn DE56 191 C4
Little Eaton DE21 205 B4
Marple SK6 23 A3
Swadlincote DE11 256 A2
Swanwick DE55 169 B4
Highfield St
Long Eaton NG10 223 B1
Swadlincote DE11 256 A2
Highfield Terr
Chesterfield S41 95 C3

Highfield Terr *continued*
New Mills SK22 33 B4
Highfield View Rd S41 95 C3
Highfield Way
Mansfield NG18 268 B3
Ripley DE5 180 B4
Highfields Buxton SK17 67 A3
Codnor DE5 181 A4
Highfields Cres S18 76 A4
Highfields Dr
Holmewood S42 132 B4
Linton DE12 261 B3
Highfields Lower Sch
DE4 143 B2
Highfields Rd S18 76 A4
Highfields Sch DE4 143 C4
Highfields Way S42 132 B4
Highgate Cl S43 77 B2
Highgate Dr Dronfield S18 76 B4
Ilkeston DE7 194 B2
Highgate Gn DE22 218 A3
Highgate La S18 76 B4
Highgate Rd SK22 25 C1
Highgrove Cl
Burton u T DE13 240 B1
Heanor DE75 181 B1
Highgrove Dr DE73 232 C1
Highland Cl Buxton SK17 85 B3
Mansfield Woodhouse
NG19 136 B2
Highland Rd S43 77 B2
Highlands Dr DE15 248 A2
Highlands Pl S41 76 C1
Highlightley La S18 75 B3
Highlow Cl S40 95 B3
Highstairs La DE55 146 B4
Highstones Gdns SK13 10 C1
Highstool La SK17 106 A3
Highurst Ct 21 NG7 268 A2
Highurst St NG7 268 A2
Highview SK13 17 A4
Highway La DE6 151 C1
Highwood Ave DE56 179 B1
Highwood Cl SK13 17 A4
Highwood La S80 81 B3
Highwood Pl S21 59 B2
Higson Ave ST4 269 B2
Hilary Cl DE56 179 C3
Hilcote La DE55 148 A1
Hilcote St DE55 160 A3
Hilderstone Cl DE24 233 B3
Hill Brow DE1 267 B2
Hill Cl Derby DE21 220 C2
Stanley DE7 193 A1
Turnditch DE56 177 A1
Hill Crest Crich DE4 157 A1
Shirebrook NG20 119 B2
Hill Crest Cotts DE4 142 C4
Hill Crest Rd DE21 219 B4
Hill Cross DE45 108 C4
Hill Cross Ave DE23 231 B4
Hill Cross Dr DE23 231 A4
Hill Dr DE13 238 A2
Hill Fields DE55 160 A2
Hill Gr S43 78 A2
Hill Head S33 51 A4
Hill La S32 52 C4
Hill Nook Cl DE73 233 A1
Hill Park Cl DE23 218 A1
Hill Pond Ave SK22 24 B1
Hill Rd Ashover S45 129 C2
Eckington S21 59 C2
Heanor DE75 181 B1
Hill Rise NG9 209 B2
Hill Rise Cl DE23 231 B4
Hill Sq The DE22 205 A1
Hill St Burton u T DE15 254 C4
Clay Cross S45 131 B2
Donisthorpe DE12 262 C1
Pleasley NG19 135 A3
Ripley DE5 169 B2
Stoke-on-T ST4 269 B2
Swadlincote DE11 255 C3
Swadlincote, Church Gresley
DE11 256 B2
Hill The Derby DE22 205 A1
Glapwell S44 118 A1
Hill Top Bolsover S44 99 A1
Castle Donington DE74 247 A1
Derby DE21 205 C2
Hill Top Ave NG20 119 C2
Hill Top Inf Sch DE6 185 B4
Hill Top Rd DE55 170 B3
Hill Top Rise SK23 45 B4
Hill View Duffield DE56 190 B2
Repton DE65 242 C1
Whaley Bridge SK23 45 B4
Hill View Cl DE7 192 A4
Hill View Gr DE21 220 C3
Hill View Rd S43 96 C4
Hillary Pl DE7 208 A3
Hillberry DE5 170 A1
Hillberry Rise S40 114 C3
Hillcliff La DE56 176 C1
Hillcrest DE13 239 A3
Hillcrest Ave
Burton u T DE15 248 A2
Hulland Ward DE6 175 C2
South Normanton DE55 160 A2
Hillcrest Dr Codnor DE5 181 A4
Kilburn DE56 192 A4
Hillcrest Gr S43 78 C2
Hillcrest Rd S41 115 B4
Hillcreste Dr DE73 232 C2
Hillcroft Dr DE72 221 B2
Hillend SK14 9 A1
Hillend La SK14 9 A1
Hillfield La DE13 240 C1

Hillfield Rd NG9 209 C1
Hillfoot Rd S17 55 B3
Hillhead La SK17 85 C1
Hillhouses La S42 114 C2
Hillman Dr S43 97 B4
Hillmoor St NG19 135 B2
Hillock The S32 72 C1
Hills Croft DE6 164 A1
Hills Rd DE72 235 B4
Hills The S33 51 A3
Hillsdale Rd DE15 248 A3
Hillside Ashover S45 130 A2
Buxton SK17 85 B2
Castle Donington DE74 247 A2
Chinley SK23 47 A4
Curbar S32 72 C1
Findern DE65 230 B1
Holloway DE4 156 A3
Langley Mill NG16 182 A2
Middleton (Nr Wirksworth)
DE4 154 B2
Mosborough S20 59 B4
Tutbury DE13 239 B3
Whitwell S80 81 C3
Hillside Ave
Ashbourne DE6 173 B2
Derby DE21 220 A3
Dronfield S18 76 A4
Hillside Cl Disley SK12 32 C3
Glossop SK13 9 C2
Whitwell S80 81 C3
Hillside Cres DE21 220 C2
Hillside Ct DE73 252 C1
Hillside Dr
Chesterfield S40 95 B1
Long Eaton NG10 236 A4
Mastin Moor S43 79 B2
Hillside Gdns DE11 255 C1
Hillside Gr Marple SK6 15 A1
Sandiacre NG10 223 A3
Hillside La DE4 152 C1
Hillside Rd Derby DE21 220 C2
Linton DE12 261 B4
Hillside Rise DE56 178 C1
Hillside View SK22 33 A4
Hillsway Derby DE23 218 A1
Derby, Chellaston DE73 232 C2
Shirebrook NG20 119 B2
Hilltop DE56 168 A4
Hilltop Cl S44 118 A1
Hilltop La Belper DE56 179 C1
Thurvaston DE6 215 B3
Hilltop Rd Ashover S45 129 C3
Chesterfield S41 77 A1
Dronfield S18 76 A4
Glossop SK13 10 A2
Pinxton NG16 160 B2
Wingerworth S42 114 B2
Hilltop Way S18 76 A4
Hilltops View DE4 143 B3
Hillview Ct NG19 136 B2
Hillwood Dr SK13 17 C4
Hilton Cl Derby DE3 217 B1
Long Eaton NG10 235 C2
Swadlincote DE11 256 A4
Hilton Gdns DE72 246 A4
Hilton Park Dr DE55 170 B4
Hilton Prim Sch DE65 228 B1
Hilton Rd Disley SK12 32 A4
Egginton DE65 241 A4
Etwall DE65 229 A2
Stoke-on-T ST4 269 A2
Hincley Ct DE4 110 C1
Hind Ave DE72 235 B4
Hindersitch La DE4 156 B1
Hindscarth Cres DE3 217 C1
Hinton Gr SK14 15 A4
Hipley Cl S40 95 A3
Hipper St S40 266 B2
Hipper St S S40 266 B2
Hipper St W S40 95 C1
Hirst Ct 24 NG7 268 A2
Hixon's La DE7 208 A1
Hoades St S42 131 B4
Hoargate La DE6 200 C1
Hob Hill DE56 190 A4
Hob Hill Mdws SK13 17 B4
Hob Hurst's Ho* DE45 111 C4
Hob La Kirk Ireton DE6 176 B4
Totley S18 55 C1
Hobart Cl
Burton u T DE15 248 B1
Derby DE3 217 C1
Hobart Dr NG9 209 C1
Hobhouse Rd NG19 135 B1
Hobkirk Dr DE24 231 C1
Hobsic Cl NG16 182 B4
Hobsic La NG16 171 C4
Hobson Dr DE7 208 C3
Hobson Moor Rd SK14 9 A4
Hockerley Ave SK23 45 B4
Hockerley Cl SK23 45 B4
Hockerley La SK23 45 B4
Hockley NG1 268 B1
Hockley La Ashover S45 130 A1
Wingerworth S42 115 A2
Hockley Way DE55 159 A1
Hodder Cl DE4 156 C1
Hodge Beck Cl DE24 233 B3
Hodge Fold SK14 15 C4
Hodge La Ashover S45 128 C4
Broadbottom SK14 15 C4
Marchington ST14 224 A1
Hodmire La S44 133 C4
Hodthorpe Cl DE21 206 A1
Hodthorpe Prim Sch S80 82 B3
Hogarth Cl NG9 223 C3
Hogarth Rd SK6 23 A4

Hogarth Rise S18 75 C4
Hogarth St NG3 268 C2
Hoggbarn La DE75,NG16 181 B3
Hoggs Field NG16 182 C1
Hogshaw Villas Rd 1
SK17 85 B4
Hoillant Sq DE6 175 C2
Holbeach Dr S40 114 C4
Holbeck Ave S44 99 B1
Holbeck Cl S41 266 C4
Holbeck La S80 101 B4
Holbeck St S80 81 B1
Holbein Cl S18 75 C4
Holborn Ave NG2 268 C1
Holborn Dr DE22 218 A4
Holborn View DE5 170 A1
Holbrook Ave
Mosborough S20 59 C4
North Wingfield S42 132 A4
Holbrook CE Prim Sch
DE56 191 B4
Holbrook Centre For Autism
DE56 191 B3
Holbrook Cl
Chesterfield S40 114 B4
Pleasley NG19 135 A3
Holbrook Dr S13 44 A4
Holbrook Gn S20 60 A4
Holbrook Pl S43 97 B3
Holbrook Rd
Belper DE56 178 C1
Derby DE24 233 A3
Sheffield S13 44 A4
Holbrook St DE75 182 A1
Holbrook View DE56 192 A4
Holbrook Way S42 132 A4
Holburn Ave S18 57 A1
Holcombe St DE23 219 A1
Holden Ave DE72 246 A4
Holden Ct 28 NG7 268 A2
Holden Gdns NG9 223 C3
Holden St
Mansfield NG18 268 B3
Nottingham NG7 268 A2
Holderness Cl DE24 231 B1
Holdings The DE11 256 A1
Holdon Croft DE12 260 B3
Holestone Gate Rd S45 129 B1
Holker Ave SK17 85 B4
Holkham Cl DE7 194 B2
Holland Cl DE55 146 C3
Holland Mdw NG10 236 B3
Holland Pl 8 S2 43 A4
Holland Rd
Chesterfield S41 76 C1
Sheffield S2 43 A4
Hollens Way S40 95 A3
Hollies Cl Clifton DE6 184 C3
Dronfield S18 76 B4
Newton Solney DE15 248 C4
Hollies Cres NG7 268 A1
Hollies Dr SK6 23 A3
Hollies Farm Cl DE73 244 C2
Hollies La DE6 198 B2
Hollies Rd DE22 204 B2
Hollies The
Eastwood NG16 182 C1
Repton DE65 243 A1
Sandiacre NG10 223 A3
Hollin Cl S41 95 B4
Hollin Cross La SK13 17 B4
Hollin Dr SK23 47 A3
Hollin Hill S43 81 A2
Hollindale Dr S12 44 B3
Hollington Cl 6 DE21 219 C4
Hollingwood Cres S43 78 A1
Hollingwood Prim Sch
S43 78 A1
Hollingworth Ave NG10 223 A2
Hollingworth Prim Sch
SK14 9 B3
Hollinhey Terr SK14 9 B3
Hollins Ave SK17 85 A4
Hollins Bank SK13 9 B1
Hollins Cl SK13 9 B1
Hollins Gdns SK13 9 B1
Hollins Head S8 43 A2
Hollins Ind Pk SK13 10 A3
Hollins La Crich DE4 157 A2
Marple SK6 23 B4
Hollins Mews SK13 9 B1
Hollins Mt SK6 23 A4
Hollins Spring Ave S18 76 A4
Hollins Spring Rd S18 76 A4
Hollins St SK17 85 A4
Hollins The DE4 156 A3
Hollins Wood Cl DE4 156 A3
Hollinsclough CE Prim Sch
SK17 104 B1
Hollinsclough Rake
SK17 104 A1
Hollinsend S12 44 A2
Hollinsend Ave S12 44 B3
Hollinsend Pl S12 44 B3
Hollinsend Rd S12 44 A3
Hollinsmoor Rd SK6,SK22 24 B4
Hollinwood Rd
Disley SK12 32 B3
Marple SK6 23 A1
Hollis La Chesterfield S41 266 C2
Denstone ST14 196 A3
Hollis St DE24 233 A4
Hollow Cres DE15 248 B2
Hollow Gate S33 51 A4

Hollow La
  Burton u T DE15 . . . . .248 B2
  Mayfield DE6 . . . . .172 B1
  Mosborough S20 . . . . .59 C3
Hollow of the Moor SK17 .87 C2
Hollow Rd DE73 . . . . .252 C1
Hollow Stone NG1 . . . . .268 B1
Hollow The Bamford S33 . . . . .40 A2
  Castle Donington DE74 . . . . . . .247 A2
  Derby, Littleover DE23 . . . . . . .231 B4
  Derby, Mickleover DE3 . . . . . . .230 B4
  Holloway DE4 . . . . .156 A3
  Roston DE6 . . . . .197 C3
Holloway Rd Derby DE24 .232 C3
  Duffield DE56 . . . . .190 C2
Hollowford Rd S33 . . . . .38 A2
Hollowford Training &
  Conference Ctr S33 . . . . .38 B2
Hollowood Ave DE23 . . . . .231 B4
Hollows The N610 . . . . .237 A4
Holly Ave Breaston DE72 .222 C1
  Ripley DE5 . . . . .180 B4
Holly Bank Glossop SK13 . .17 C4
Holly Bank Ct DE4 . . . . .156 C1
Holly Brook Way DE23 . . . .230 C3
Holly Bush La DE56 . . . . . . .191 A3
Holly Cl Ashbourne DE6 . . . .185 B4
  Draycott DE72 . . . . .235 A4
  Killamarsh S21 . . . . .60 B3
Holly Ct Aston-on-T DE72 .246 A4
  Derby DE21 . . . . .217 B1
  Mansfield NG19 . . . . .136 C1
  Woodville DE11 . . . . .256 C1
Holly Gdns DE15 . . . . .254 C4
Holly Gn DE15 . . . . .254 C4
Holly Hill Rd NG16 . . . . .171 C3
Holly House Sch S41 . . . . . . .77 A2
Holly La
  Alderwasley DE56 . . . . .167 B2
  Tansley DE4 . . . . .144 A2
Holly Rd Kimberley NG16 .195 C4
  Mansfield NG19 . . . . .136 C4
  Uttoxeter ST14 . . . . .210 A1
Holly St DE15 . . . . .254 C4
Hollybank Ave S12 . . . . .44 B3
Hollybank Cl Sheffield S12 . .44 B3
  Swadlincote DE11 . . . . .256 A4
Hollybank Cres
  Sheffield S12 . . . . .44 B3
  Stoke-on-T ST4 . . . . .269 B1
Hollybank Dr S12 . . . . .44 B3
Hollybank Rd S12 . . . . .44 B3
Hollybank Way S12 . . . . .44 B3
Hollybrook Way DE23 . . . . .230 C3
Hollybush Cl DE12 . . . . .264 C4
Hollyhock Way DE14 . . . . . .253 C3
Hollyhouse Dr DE55 . . . . . .160 A3
Hollyhurst La DE6 . . . . .212 A3
Hollyhurst Row DE55 . . . . .170 C3
Hollymoor Dr DE73 . . . . . . .232 C1
Hollythorpe Cl S41 . . . . .115 B4
Hollythorpe Cres S8 . . . . . . .43 A2
Hollythorpe Rd S8 . . . . .43 A2
Hollythorpe Rise S8 . . . . . . .43 A2
Hollywell Ave DE5 . . . . .181 A4
Hollywell Prim Sch
  NG16 .195 C4
Hollywell Rd SK6 . . . . .23 C4
Holm Ave DE21 . . . . .205 A4
Holm Cl S18 . . . . .56 B1
Holm La DE55 . . . . .158 A2
Holme Bank DE6 . . . . .184 B4
Holme Cl Hatton DE65 . . . . .227 B1
  Holloway DE4 . . . . .156 A3
  Ilkeston DE7 . . . . .194 B1
Holme Croft DE7 . . . . .207 C4
Holme Farm Ave DE15 . . . .254 C4
Holme Hall Cres S40 . . . . . . .95 A3
Holme Hall Prim Sch
  S40 . . . . .95 A3
Holme Rd Bakewell DE45 .109 B4
  Derby DE21 . . . . .220 B2
Holme Park Ave S41 . . . . . . .95 B4
Holme Rd Chesterfield S41 .96 A3
  Matlock Bath DE4 . . . . .143 A1
Holme Woods La HD7 . . . . .2 C3
Holmebank Cl S40 . . . . .95 C2
Holmebank E S40 . . . . .95 C2
Holmebank View S40 . . . . . .95 B2
Holmebank W S40 . . . . .95 C2
Holmebrook View S41 . . . . .95 B3
Holmefield Cres DE7 . . . . . .209 A4
Holmefield Rd S80 . . . . .82 A3
Holmes Cl NG10 . . . . .182 A2
Holmes Ct DE11 . . . . .256 A3
Holmes Rd DE72 . . . . .235 B4
Holmes St Derby DE23 . . . .219 A1
  Heanor DE75 . . . . .181 B1
Holmesdale Cl S18 . . . . .57 B2
Holmesdale Rd S18 . . . . .57 B2
Holmesfield Cl DE4 . . . . . . .144 A3
Holmesfield Dr
  Derby DE3 . . . . .217 C1
  Shipley DE75 . . . . .194 A4
Holmesfield Rd S18 . . . . . . .56 A1
Holmewood Bsns Pk
  S42 . . . . .116 B1
Holmewood Dr NG16 . . . . . .195 A4
Holmewood Ind Est
  S42 . . . . .132 C4
Holmewood Ind Pk S42 .116 B1

Holmfield Buxton SK17 . . . . .84 C3
  Derby DE23 . . . . .231 C4
Holmgate Prim Sch
  S45 . . . . .131 A2
Holmgate Rd S42 . . . . .130 C2
Holmley Bank S18 . . . . .57 A2
Holmley La S18 . . . . .57 A2
Holmoak Cl DE21 . . . . .206 A2
Holmshaw Dr S13 . . . . .44 C4
Holmshaw Gr S13 . . . . .44 C4
Holmwood Terr 2 SK17 . . .85 B4
Holroid Ho DE24 . . . . .219 B1
Holroyd Ave NG2 . . . . .268 C1
Holt Ave DE4 . . . . .233 B3
Holt Dr DE4 . . . . .142 C4
Holt La Holloway DE4 . . . . . .156 A4
  Matlock DE4 . . . . .143 A3
Holt Rd DE4 . . . . .127 C1
Holt's La DE13 . . . . .239 A3
Holtlands Dr DE24 . . . . .232 C3
Holy Rosary RC Prim Sch
  DE4 . . . . .248 A2
Holy Trinity CE Prim Sch
  DE4 . . . . .155 A4
Holyhead Dr DE21 . . . . .206 A2
Holymoor Rd S42 . . . . .113 C4
Holyoake Ave S13 . . . . .44 C4
Holyoake Dr NG10 . . . . .236 C4
Holyrood Cl DE21 . . . . .221 A3
Holywell DE45 . . . . .109 B3
Holywell La DE45 . . . . .125 A3
Holywell Rd DE7 . . . . .194 B2
Holywell St S41 . . . . .266 B3
Home Farm Cl DE72 . . . . . .221 B3
Home Farm Ct DE11 . . . . . .255 B1
Home Farm Dr DE22 . . . . . .205 A2
Home Fm Ct NG16 . . . . .171 B3
Homecroft Dr NG16 . . . . . . .171 C4
Homefields Prim Sch
  DE73 .232 C1
Homeport Mews S41 . . . . . .266 B4
Homer Dr SK6 . . . . .23 A4
Homestead NG16 . . . . .182 A1
Homestead Rd SK12 . . . . . . .32 B3
Homestead Way S43 . . . . . . .80 B3
Honeycroft Cl DE56 . . . . . . .179 A1
Honeycroft Ct DE55 . . . . . . .160 A2
Honeyfield Dr DE5 . . . . .180 C4
Honeysuckle Cl DE11 . . . . .256 A3
Honeysuckle View
  DE15 .255 A4
Honeywall S41 . . . . .269 B2
Honeywall Mrs S14 . . . . . . .269 B2
Honeywall La DE6 . . . . .183 C2
Honingham Rd DE7 . . . . . . .194 B2
Hook La ST14 . . . . .210 A3
Hoole St S41 . . . . .115 B4
Hooley Cl NG10 . . . . .236 A3
Hooley St NG16 . . . . .171 C3
Hoon Rd DE65 . . . . .239 B4
Hoonwell La DE6 . . . . .175 C3
Hooton St NG3 . . . . .268 C2
Hop Inge The S26 . . . . .61 C3
Hope Ave DE3 . . . . .217 B1
Hope Dr NG7 . . . . .268 A1
Hope Prim Sch S33 . . . . .39 A2
Hope Rd S33 . . . . .39 B2
Hope St Chesterfield S40 . . .95 C2
  Derby DE1 . . . . .267 C2
  Glossop SK13 . . . . .10 C1
  1 Ilkeston DE7 . . . . .208 C4
  Mansfield NG18 . . . . .268 C3
  Melbourne DE73 . . . . .252 A4
  2 New Sta S33 . . . . .39 B2
  Stoke-on-T ST4 . . . . .269 A2
Hope Terr DE4 . . . . .143 A1
Hope Valley Coll S33 . . . . . . .38 C2
Hopedale Rd S12 . . . . .44 B2
Hopefield Ave S12 . . . . .44 B2
Hopeton St DE23 . . . . .219 A2
Hopewell Cl DE4 . . . . .143 B3
Hopewell Rd DE4 . . . . .143 B3
Hopewell Wlk DE7 . . . . .194 C3
Hopkins Cl NG16 . . . . .182 C2
Hopmeadow Way DE56 . . . .248 A1
Hopping Hill DE56 . . . . .190 C4
Hopping Hill Terr E
  DE56 .191 A4
Hopping Hill Terr W
  DE56 .191 A4
Hopping La DE45 . . . . .125 A2
Hopton Cl Derby DE21 . . . .206 A1
  Ripley DE5 . . . . .169 C1
Hoptonwood Cl DE4 . . . . . .154 B2
Hopwell Rd DE72 . . . . .222 A1
Horace Ave NG9 . . . . .223 B3
Hordern Cl S43 . . . . .78 C1
Horderns La SK23 . . . . .47 A3
Horderns Park Rd SK23 . . . .47 A3
Horderns Rd SK23 . . . . .47 A3
Horeston Cotts DE7 . . . . . . .192 A4
Hornbeam Cl
  Derby DE21 . . . . .205 C1
  Ilkeston DE7 . . . . .209 A4
Hornbeams The 2
  ST14 .210 A1
Hornby Row ST14 . . . . .210 A1
Horncastle Rd DE21 . . . . . .205 B1
Horner Rd 3 S7 . . . . .43 A4
Hornscroft Rd S44 . . . . .99 A1
Hornsea Rd DE21 . . . . .205 B1
Hornthorpe Rd S21 . . . . .59 B1
Horridge St DE7 . . . . .194 C2
Horse Fair Ave SK23 . . . . . . .47 A3
Horse Shoes The DE7 . . . . .247 B2
Horsecroft Cl DE7 . . . . .194 B1
Horsehead La S44 . . . . .99 B1
Horseshoe Ave S40 . . . . .95 C4
Horsewood Rd S40 . . . . .114 A4

Horsley CE Prim Sch
  DE21 .191 C3
Horsley Cl S40 . . . . .95 A3
Horsley Cres
  Holbrook DE56 . . . . .191 B4
  Langley Mill NG16 . . . . .182 A2
Horsley La DE21 . . . . .191 C3
Horsley Rd DE21 . . . . .191 C3
Horsley Woodhouse Prim Sch
  DE7 . . . . .192 B3
Horslegate La S18 . . . . .74 C4
Horsleygate Rd S17,S18 . . .74 A4
Horton Cl
  2 Mosborough S20 . . . . .59 C4
  Swanwick DE55 . . . . .169 C4
Horton Dr S20 . . . . .59 C4
Horton La DE55 . . . . .219 B1
Horwood Ave DE23 . . . . . . .218 B1
Hoselett Field Rd NG10 . . .236 C3
Hospital La DE3 . . . . .230 A4
Hoten Rd NG2 . . . . .268 C1
Houfton Cres S44 . . . . .98 C2
Houfton Rd S44 . . . . .98 C2
Houghton Ave DE7 . . . . . . .194 B2
Houghton Cl SK22 . . . . .25 B1
Houghton Ct DE21 . . . . .205 C1
Houldsworth Cres S44 . . . . .98 C1
Houldsworth Dr S41 . . . . . . .96 B3
Hoult St DE22 . . . . .218 B2
Houndkirk Rd S11 . . . . .54 B4
Hounds Gate NG7 . . . . .268 B1
Hounslow Rd DE22 . . . . . . .218 A3
Houston Cl DE21 . . . . .220 A3
Hoveton Cl DE24 . . . . .232 B2
How La S33 . . . . .38 C3
Howard Cl Glossop SK13 . . . .10 A1
  Long Eaton NG10 . . . . .223 C1
  17 NG7 . . . . .268 A2
Howard Dr
  Chesterfield S41 . . . . .77 A1
  North Wingfield S42 . . . . .131 C3
  Staveley S43 . . . . .97 B4
Howard Rd NG19 . . . . .268 A4
Howard St DE23 . . . . .218 C1
  Glossop SK13 . . . . .10 A1
  Nottingham NG1 . . . . .268 B2
Howards Mdw SK13 . . . . . . .17 A4
Howarth Cl NG10 . . . . .236 A4
Howden Cl Derby DE3 . . . . .217 B1
  Staveley S43 . . . . .78 C1
Howden Rd SK22 . . . . .24 B1
Howe St DE22 . . . . .218 B3
Howells Pl S43 . . . . .79 A2
Howitt Cres ST14 . . . . .210 A1
Howitt St Heanor DE75 . . . .181 C1
  Long Eaton NG10 . . . . .236 C4
Howth Cl DE21 . . . . .220 A2
Hoylake Ave S40 . . . . .114 B4
Hoylake Cl DE3 . . . . .217 B2
Hoylake Ct NG19 . . . . .136 C3
Hoylake Dr DE3 . . . . .217 B2
Hoyland Ct DE56 . . . . .179 C3
Hubert Shaw Cl DE24 . . . . .232 C2
Huckerby Rd DE7 . . . . .194 B1
Hucklow Ave
  Chesterfield S40 . . . . .266 A1
  North Wingfield S42 . . . . .132 A4
  Staveley S43 . . . . .97 B4
Hucklow Ct DE21 . . . . .206 A2
Hucklow Fold S SK13 . . . . . .9 B1
Hucknall Ave S40 . . . . .114 C4
Hudson Cl S26 . . . . .61 C4
Hudson Mount S44 . . . . . . .118 A4
Hudson St NG3 . . . . .268 C2
Hudson Way DE24 . . . . .219 B2
Hufton's Ct DE75 . . . . .194 A4
Hufton's Dr DE75 . . . . .194 A4
Hugh La S41 . . . . .51 A4
Hugh St SK13 . . . . .10 A1
Hulland CE Prim Sch
  DE6 . . . . .175 C2
Hulland St DE1 . . . . .267 D1
Hulland View DE22 . . . . . . .204 B1
Hulme St ST4 . . . . .269 A2
Humber Cl DE24 . . . . .233 B3
Humber Rd NG10 . . . . .223 B1
Humbleton Dr DE22 . . . . . .218 A3
Humphrey Rd S8 . . . . .56 C4
Hundall La
  Chesterfield S41 . . . . .77 A2
  Unstone S18 . . . . .77 A4
Hunger La DE6 . . . . .188 C2
Hungerhill La S45 . . . . .113 A2
Hungry La Bradwell S33 . . . .51 A3
  Hathersage S32 . . . . .53 A4
Hunloke Ave S40 . . . . .95 C1
Hunloke Cres S40 . . . . .95 C1
Hunloke Park Prim Sch
  S42 . . . . .115 A2
Hunloke Rd S42 . . . . .132 C4
Hunloke View S42 . . . . .115 A2
Hunningham Rd S21 . . . . . . .59 B2
Hunstone Ave S8 . . . . .57 A4
Hunt Ave DE75 . . . . .181 C1
Hunt La S45 . . . . .145 A4
Hunter Dr DE56 . . . . .191 C4
Hunter Rd DE56 . . . . .190 A4
Hunter's La S13 . . . . .44 B3
Hunters Croft DE23 . . . . . . .231 C1
Hunters Dr S41 . . . . .269 A1
Hunters Gn SK23 . . . . .34 C1
Hunters La S45 . . . . .145 A4
Hunters Way S14 . . . . .269 B1
Huntingdon Ave S44 . . . . . . .99 A1
Huntingdon Cl DE73 . . . . . .252 A4
Huntingdon Dr
  Castle Donington DE74 . . . . .247 A2
  Nottingham NG7 . . . . .268 A1
Huntingdon Gn DE21 . . . . .219 B3

Huntingdon Prim Sch
  NG3 . . . . .268 B2
Huntingdon Rd DE15 . . . . .254 B4
Huntingdon St NG3 . . . . . . .268 B2
Huntingdon Way 4
  NG9 . . . . .223 C1
Huntingdon Wlk 4
  NG10 .223 A3
Huntley Ave DE21 . . . . .220 C3
  Stoke-on-T ST4 . . . . .269 B1
Huntley Cl S43 . . . . .97 A4
Hunts La DE12 . . . . .264 C4
Hunts Row DE55 . . . . .157 C2
Huntsman Rd S43 . . . . .79 C1
Huntspill Rd DE65 . . . . .228 C1
Hurdlow Gn 14 SK13 . . . . . . .9 B1
Hurdlow Mews 15 SK13 . . . .9 B1
Hurds Hollow DE4 . . . . .143 A2
Hurker Rise DE4 . . . . .143 B4
Hurl Dr S12 . . . . .43 C3
Hurley Ct DE7 . . . . .207 C4
Hurlfield Ave S12 . . . . .44 A3
Hurlfield Ct S12 . . . . .44 A3
Hurlfield Dr S12 . . . . .44 A3
Hurlfield Hill S14 . . . . .43 C3
Hurlfield Rd S12 . . . . .43 C3
Hurst Dr Burton u T DE13 . .240 C1
  Stanley DE7 . . . . .207 B3
Hurst La DE55 . . . . .146 C2
Hurst Lea Rd SK22 . . . . .33 B4
Hurst Rd SK13 . . . . .10 C1
Hurst Rise DE4 . . . . .143 B3
Hurstbrook Cl SK13 . . . . . . .10 C1
Hurstclough La S32 . . . . .40 B1
Huss's La NG10 . . . . .236 C4
Hut La S21 . . . . .60 C2
Hutchings Cres S43 . . . . .80 B3
Hutchinson Gn 13 NG3 . . .268 B2
Huthwaite La DE55 . . . . . . .148 B1
Hutmoor Butts DE45 . . . . .107 A2
Hutton St Derby DE24 . . . . .232 C3
  Nottingham NG2 . . . . .268 C1
Huxley Cl DE23 . . . . .231 C4
Hyde Bank Ct SK22 . . . . .33 B4
Hyde Bank Rd SK22 . . . . . . .33 B4
Hyde Park Rd DE22 . . . . . . .218 A3
Hyde Rd SK14 . . . . .9 A2
Hydro Cl DE45 . . . . .91 C3
Hylton Cl DE14 . . . . .254 A4
Hyndley Rd S44 . . . . .98 C2

I

Ian Ave DE4 . . . . .165 C4
Ians Way S40 . . . . .95 B2
Ibbotsons Croft S32 . . . . . . .53 A4
Ibsley Cl DE24 . . . . .233 B3
Ida's Rd S21 . . . . .59 B2
Ilam Cl S43 . . . . .97 A3
Ilam Ct S43 . . . . .185 B4
Ilam Sq DE7 . . . . .194 C3
Ilford Cl DE7 . . . . .194 B2
Ilford Rd DE22 . . . . .218 A3
Ilford Wlk DE22 . . . . .218 A3
Ilion St NG19 . . . . .135 C1
Ilkeston Com Hospl
  DE7 . . . . .194 B2
Ilkeston Rd Heanor DE75 .193 C4
  Nottingham NG7 . . . . .268 A2
  Sandiacre DE7,NG10 . . . . . . .223 B4
  Smalley DE7 . . . . .192 C1
  Stanton-by-D DE7 . . . . .208 C2
  Stapleford NG9 . . . . .209 C1
  Trowell NG9 . . . . .209 B3
Ilkeston Sch DE7 . . . . .208 B4
Immingham Gr S43 . . . . .78 B1
Imperial Ct DE22 . . . . .204 B3
Imperial Rd DE4 . . . . .143 A3
Inchwood Cl 4 NG9 . . . . . .223 C1
Independent Hill DE55 . . . .158 C2
Industrial St 8 DE21 . . . . . .219 A1
Infirmary Rd S41 . . . . .266 C4
Ingestre Rd S17 . . . . .268 A3
Ingham Dr DE3 . . . . .230 B4
Ingham Rd NG10 . . . . .223 B1
Ingle Cl DE21 . . . . .220 C3
Ingle's Channel 7 DE6 .178 C2
Ingleborough Gdns 9
  NG10 .236 A4
Ingleby Ave NG3 . . . . .231 C4
Ingleby Cl
  10 Dronfield S18 . . . . .56 B1
  Swadlincote DE11 . . . . .256 A2
Ingleby La DE73 . . . . .251 A3
Ingleby Rd
  Barrow-u-T DE73 . . . . .244 B2
  Long Eaton NG10 . . . . .235 C2
Ingledew Cl DE21 . . . . .205 C1
Inglefield Rd DE7 . . . . .209 A3
Inglelton Rd S41 . . . . .115 A4
Inglewood S17 . . . . .269 A3
Inglewood Ave DE3 . . . . . . .217 B2
Inglis St S40 . . . . .269 C2
Ingliston Cl 10 DE24 . . . . .233 B3
Inkerman Rd NG16 . . . . . . .171 C3
Inkerman St NG7 . . . . .268 A2
Inkersall Dr S20 . . . . .59 C4
Inkersall Green Rd S43 . . . . .97 B4
Inkersall Prim Sch S43 . . . . .97 B4
Inkersall Rd S43 . . . . .97 C4
Inn La DE22 . . . . .204 A4
Inns La DE55 . . . . .157 C2
Institute La DE55 . . . . .159 A2
Instow Dr DE23 . . . . .231 B3
Instow Rise NG3 . . . . .268 B2
Intake Ave NG18 . . . . .268 A3

Intake Farm Fst Sch
  NG19 . . . . .268 A4
Intake La Bakewell DE45 .109 A1
  Cromford DE4 . . . . .155 A3
  Holloway DE4 . . . . .156 A4
Intake Prim Sch S12 . . . . . . .44 B3
Intake Rd S44 . . . . .98 C3
Intakes La DE56 . . . . .178 C3
Inverary Cl DE74 . . . . .247 A3
Invernia Cl DE23 . . . . .230 C3
Iona Cl Derby DE24 . . . . . . .231 C2
  Tibshelf DE55 . . . . .147 C3
Iona Dr NG9 . . . . .209 B2
Ireland Cl S43 . . . . .80 A3
Ireland Ind Est S43 . . . . .80 A3
Ireland St S43 . . . . .80 A3
Ireton St NG7 . . . . .268 A2
Iron Cliff Rd S44 . . . . .98 C3
Iron Gate DE1 . . . . .267 B3
Irongate S40 . . . . .266 B1
Ironside Cl S14 . . . . .43 C2
Ironside Pl S14 . . . . .43 C2
Ironside Rd S14 . . . . .43 C2
Ironside Wlk S14 . . . . .43 C2
Ironville & Codnor Park Prim
  Sch NG16 . . . . .170 C2
Ironwalls La DE13 . . . . .239 C3
Irvine Cl DE24 . . . . .231 C2
Irving Pl DE24 . . . . .232 C2
Isaac's La NG9 . . . . .223 C3
Isabella St NG7 . . . . .268 B1
Island The NG16 . . . . .182 A1
Islay Cl NG9 . . . . .209 B2
Islay Rd DE24 . . . . .231 C2
Isleworth Dr DE22 . . . . .217 C4
Ismay Rd DE21 . . . . .219 C3
Ivan Brook Cl 17 S18 . . . . . .56 B1
Ivanhoe Cl S42 . . . . .115 A3
Ivanhoe Ct 8 S41 . . . . .96 B3
Ivatt Dr NG2 . . . . .268 C1
Iveagh Wlk DE55 . . . . .170 C3
Ivonbrook Cl DE4 . . . . .142 A1
Ivy Cl Chesterfield S41 . . . . .266 C4
  Donisthorpe DE12 . . . . .265 B3
  Willington DE65 . . . . .242 A3
Ivy Ct Derby DE21 . . . . .221 A3
  Egginton DE65 . . . . .241 A3
  Hilton DE65 . . . . .228 C1
  Sheffield S8 . . . . .43 A3
Ivy Gr DE5 . . . . .169 C2
Ivy House Spec Sch
  DE23 .219 A1
  Elton DE4 . . . . .140 C3
Ivy Lodge Cl DE15 . . . . .255 A4
Ivy Spring Cl S42 . . . . .113 A1
Ivy Sq DE23 . . . . .219 A1
Ivybridge Cl DE21 . . . . .206 A1
Ivycroft SK13 . . . . .10 A2
Ivyside Cl S21 . . . . .60 C4
Ivyside Gdns S21 . . . . .60 C4

J

Jack Ashley Ct ST4 . . . . . . .269 B1
Jack's La ST14 . . . . .224 C4
Jackass La DE56 . . . . .167 A4
Jacklin Cl DE14 . . . . .254 A4
Jacksdale Cl DE22 . . . . .204 B2
Jacksdale Prim Sch
  NG16 .171 A2
Jackson Ave Derby DE21 .218 C4
  Ilkeston DE7 . . . . .208 B3
  Sandiacre NG10 . . . . .223 A4
  Stapleford NG9 . . . . .131 A3
Jackson Cl DE12 . . . . .262 C2
Jackson Rd
  Bramley-Vale S44 . . . . .117 C1
  Clay Cross S45 . . . . .131 B3
  Matlock DE4 . . . . .143 A3
Jackson St Derby DE22 . . . .218 C4
  Glossop SK13 . . . . .17 C4
  Glossop, Padfield SK13 . . . . . .10 C4
  Mottram in L SK14 . . . . .9 A3
Jackson Tor Rd DE4 . . . . . .143 A3
Jackson's La
  Heage DE56 . . . . .179 C1
  Ripley DE5 . . . . .169 B1
Jacksons Edge Rd SK12 . . . .32 B4
Jacksons La Belper DE56 .190 B4
  Etwall DE65 . . . . .229 B2
Jackys La S26 . . . . .61 C4
Jacobean Ct DE15 . . . . .248 B2
Jagger's La S32 . . . . .52 C3
Jaggers La DE4,S45 . . . . . . .128 C2
Jago Ave S43 . . . . .81 B3
James Andrew Cl S8 . . . . . . .56 C2
James Andrew Cres S8 . . . . .56 C2
James Andrew Croft S8 . . . .56 C2
James Ave DE55 . . . . .170 C4
James Cl DE1 . . . . .218 C2
James St Chesterfield S41 . . .96 B3
  3 Glossop SK13 . . . . .17 C4
  Kimberley NG16 . . . . .195 C4
  Somercotes DE55 . . . . .170 C4
  Stoke-on-T ST4 . . . . .269 B1
  Swadlincote DE11 . . . . .256 A3
James's La DE6 . . . . .215 A4
Jap La DE45 . . . . .110 A2
Jardine Ct DE72 . . . . .221 A2
Jardines La ST14 . . . . .210 A2
Jarnett The SK17 . . . . .120 A2
Jarvey's La DE22 . . . . .217 C2
Jarvis Ct DE24 . . . . .233 A3
Jarvis Rd DE24 . . . . .231 C1
Jasmin Cl NG20 . . . . .119 C3

CI
T DE15 ...255 A4
...21 ...220 A3
DE55 ...169 C4
Ct DE75 ...182 A1
Dr DE55 ...148 A4
La DE4 ...153 A1
ve S12 ...44 A2
t S12 ...44 A2
res S12 ...44 B2
La S12 ...44 A2
t S12 ...44 A2
lount S12 ...44 A2
d S12 ...44 A2
ew S12 ...44 B2
Way S12 ...44 A2
es Hill S40 ...115 A4
La DE73 ...252 B4
es S40 ...95 B1
a
ay DE56 ...176 C4
DE56 ...177 A4
h Ct Derby DE24 ...231 C1
am NG3 ...268 B2
an Pl DE24 ...232 C4
St S2 ...43 A3
La S33 ...51 A3
Ave DE4 ...156 C1
La DE4 ...156 C1
St NG20 ...101 A1
Cl DE23 ...230 C4
St NG18 ...268 A3
Rd S19 ...136 A1
Ct DE56 ...179 B3
rd DE14 ...254 A4
Rd S41 ...115 B4
Cl ST4 ...269 A1
Ave S12 ...44 C2
Cl S12 ...44 C2
Cres S12 ...44 C2
Dr S12 ...44 C2
Way S12 ...44 C2
are St ST16 ...269 A4
dns NG3 ...268 C2
Rd S2 ...43 A4
t DE7 ...194 C2
l S43 ...97 A3
La DE56 ...178 B4
Ave NG16 ...170 C2
Dr DE24 ...231 C1
St Codnor DE5 ...181 A4
E5 ...181 A4
Ct NG9 ...223 C3
l DE65 ...239 B4
Dr DE75 ...181 C1
l S33 ...40 B2
Ave DE56 ...179 B2
Mdw SK23 ...45 C4
Rd SK23 ...45 B4
St SK22 ...33 A4
nk La DE45 ...108 C4
rrysford Cl
...219 C3
arroll Cl NG3 ...268 C2
alton St S12 ...
avies Prim Sch
...148 C2
uncan Sch S17 ...66 A1
aton's Almshouses
...
Kennedy Gdns
...220 B3
amsteed Com Sch
...180 A1
ennedy Rd SK14 ...9 A2
ing Inf Sch NG16 ...168 B2
ing Workshop Mus*
...
ombe Dr DE1 ...219 A4
f Gaunts Way
...179 B2
ort Cl DE65 ...229 B2
ort Sch DE55 ...229 A2
t Alfreton DE55 ...159 A2
pton S43 ...97 C4
rfield S40 ...95 C2
oss S45 ...131 B2
S43 ...80 B2
tall SK6 ...15 A2
ll S80 ...81 C1
DE11 ...267 C2
ton S21 ...59 B2
p SK13 ...17 B4
r DE75 ...181 B1
t DE7 ...194 C1
SK6 ...23 A3
k DE4 ...143 A3
ngfield S42 ...131 C4
cotes DE55 ...170 B4
rd ST16 ...269 C4
incote DE11 ...255 C3
incote, Albert Village
...
incote, Lower Medway
...256 B3
urner Rd DE24 ...
Woodhead Ct
...268 A4
ygate La S18 ...75 A2
on Ave DE24 ...232 C4
on Dr DE75 ...181 C1
on La
ehay DE56 ...176 C4
sh DE45 ...107 C3
on Rd ST14 ...210 A1

Johnson St SK23 ...45 C4
Johnson Way S43 ...23 C4
Johnstone Cl S40 ...266 A1
Jones La DE73 ...175 A4
Jones St SK13 ...10 A3
Jordan Ave DE13 ...240 C1
Jordan St SK13 ...10 C1
Jordanthorpe Gn S8 ...57 B3
Jordanthorpe Parkway S8 ...57 B4
Jordanthorpe View S8 ...57 B4
Joseph Fletcher Dr S42 ...114 C1
Joseph St Belper DE56 ...178 C2
Derby DE21 ...219 A1
Eckington S21 ...59 C2
Marple SK6 ...23 A3
Joseph Wright Terr DE1 ...267 B4
Joyce Ave NG9 ...223 C2
Jubalton Cl DE24 ...232 C3
Jubilee Ave DE5 ...169 B1
Jubilee Cl DE73 ...252 A4
Jubilee Cotts S44 ...81 A2
Jubilee Cres Clowne S43 ...81 A2
Killamarsh S21 ...60 C4
Whitwell S80 ...81 C3
Jubilee Ct Belper DE56 ...179 C1
Wirksworth DE4 ...165 C4
Jubilee Gdns
New Mills SK22 ...33 B4
Whitwell S80 ...81 C3
Jubilee Pl S80 ...81 C3
Jubilee Rd
Chapel-en-le-F SK23 ...47 A3
Derby DE21 ...232 C2
Whitwell S80 ...81 C3
Jubilee Sq DE56 ...184 B4
Jubilee St
Kimberley NG16 ...195 C4
New Mills SK22 ...33 B4
Nottingham NG3 ...268 C1
Jubilee Terr DE12 ...262 C1
Judith Gr ST4 ...269 C1
Judson Ave NG9 ...223 C3
Judy Hill DE4 ...127 C1
Julia Cres DE55 ...146 C2
Julian Cl DE7 ...209 A3
Julie Ave DE75 ...182 A1
Jumble Rd S11 ...42 C1
Junction Rd NG10 ...237 A3
Junction St DE1 ...218 C2
Juniper Cl NG16 ...195 B4
Juniper Rise S21 ...60 B3
Jura Ave DE5 ...169 B1
Jury St DE1 ...267 A3

K
Katherine Dr DE24 ...223 C2
Katrine Wlk DE24 ...231 C3
Kay Dr DE11 ...255 C3
Kean Pl DE24 ...232 C4
Kearsley Rd S2 ...43 A4
Keary St ST4 ...269 B1
Keats Ave DE23 ...218 A1
Keats Cl NG10 ...236 A3
Keats Dr DE11 ...256 B3
Keats Rd Chesterfield S41 ...95 C4
Stonebroom DE55 ...146 C2
Keats Way S42 ...115 C2
Keats Wlk DE55 ...146 C2
Keble Cl Burton u T DE15 ...248 B1
Derby DE21 ...267 C1
Kedleston Cl
Burton u T DE13 ...240 B1
Chesterfield S41 ...95 B3
Derby DE22 ...204 B1
Ripley DE5 ...169 B2
Kedleston Ct
⬛ Staveley S43 ...78 C1
Tibshelf DE55 ...148 A3
Kedleston Dr DE7 ...194 B2
Kedleston Gdns DE1 ...267 A4
Kedleston Hall* DE22 ...203 C3
Kedleston Old Rd DE22 ...218 B4
Kedleston Rd Buxton SK17 ...87 A4
Quarndon DE22 ...204 A3
Weston Underwood DE22 ...203 C4
Kedleston St DE1 ...267 A4
Kedlestone C DE11 ...148 C1
Keeling La DE4 ...126 A1
Keepers La S18 ...75 C2
Kegworth Ave DE23 ...231 B3
Keilder Ct S40 ...95 A1
Kelburn Ave NG9 ...223 B3
Keldeston Cl S41 ...95 B4
Keldholme La DE24 ...233 B3
Kelgate S21 ...59 B3
Kelham La NG16 ...268 A4
Kelham Rd NG16 ...268 A4
Kelham Way NG16 ...182 C2
Kelmoor Rd DE24 ...233 A4
Kelsons Ave SK17 ...85 B3
Kelstedge La S45 ...129 B3
Kelvedon Dr DE23 ...231 B3
Kelvedon Gdns NG3 ...268 C2
Kelvin Cl NG9 ...223 B3
Kemble Pl DE24 ...232 C4
Kemp Cl S21 ...60 B3
Kempton Cl NG16 ...195 C4
Kempton Park Rd DE24 ...232 C3
Kempton Rd NG10 ...236 A3
Kendal Cl SK17 ...85 C4
Kendal Dr S18 ...56 C1
Kendal Rd S41 ...95 C4

Kendal Wlk DE21 ...205 B1
Kendon Ave DE23 ...231 C3
Kendra Cl DE56 ...179 B3
Kendricks Cl DE11 ...257 A4
Kenilworth Ave DE23 ...231 C4
Kenilworth Ct
⬛ Chesterfield S41 ...96 A3
Nottingham NG7 ...268 A1
Kenilworth Dr DE7 ...208 B3
Kenilworth Rd
Nottingham NG7 ...268 A1
Ripley DE5 ...169 C1
Kenmere Cl S45 ...131 B1
Kenmore Cl NG19 ...268 A3
Kenmore Gdns NG3 ...268 B2
Kennack Cl DE55 ...160 B3
Kennedy Ave
Long Eaton NG10 ...236 B3
Mansfield Woodhouse NG19 ...136 B2
Kennedy Cl DE21 ...220 A4
Kennedy Dr NG9 ...209 C1
Kennet Paddock NG19 ...136 B2
Kennet Vale S40 ...95 B2
Kennett Gr SK17 ...84 C3
Kenning St S45 ...131 B2
Kenninghall Cl S2 ...43 B4
Kenninghall Dr S2 ...43 B4
Kenninghall Pl S2 ...43 B4
Kenninghall Rd S2 ...43 B4
Kensal Rise DE22 ...218 A3
Kensington Ave DE75 ...181 B1
Kensington Cl NG19 ...136 C3
Kensington Gdns DE7 ...208 C4
Kensington Jun Sch DE7 ...209 A4
Kensington Rd
Burton u T DE15 ...248 A2
Sandiacre NG10 ...223 A2
Kensington St
Derby DE1 ...267 A3
Ilkeston DE7 ...208 C3
Kent Ave NG16 ...171 A2
Kent House Cl S12 ...58 C4
Kent Rd Burton u T DE15 ...254 C3
Eastwood NG16 ...195 B4
Glossop SK13 ...10 B1
Sheffield S8 ...43 A3
Kent St Chesterfield S41 ...96 A3
Derby DE21 ...219 B4
Nottingham NG1 ...268 B2
Kent's Bank Rd SK17 ...85 B3
Kentmere Cl ⬛ S18 ...56 C1
Kentwood Rd NG2 ...268 C1
Kenwell Dr S17 ...56 A3
Kenyon Rd S41 ...96 C1
Keppel Ct DE7 ...194 C2
Kepple Gate DE5 ...180 C4
Kernel Cl DE23 ...231 A4
Kerry Dr DE7 ...192 C3
Kerry St DE21 ...219 B4
Kerry's Yd DE56 ...191 C4
Kershaw St S43 ...17 B4
Kershope Dr DE21 ...206 A2
Kerwin Cl S17 ...55 B4
Kerwin Dr S17 ...55 B4
Kerwin Rd S17 ...55 B4
Kestrel Ave S13 ...256 C2
Kestrel Cl Burnaston DE3 ...230 A4
Ilkeston DE7 ...208 C2
Killamarsh S21 ...60 A4
Marple SK6 ...23 A2
Kestrel Dr S24 ...231 C1
Kestrel Dr S21 ...59 A2
Kestrel Hts S42 ...116 C1
Kestrel Way DE15 ...248 B2
Kestrels Croft DE24 ...231 C2
Keswick Ave DE23 ...231 C3
Keswick Cl Bolsover S44 ...98 C1
Keswick Cl NG10 ...223 A1
Keswick Dr S41 ...95 B4
Keswick Pl S18 ...56 B1
Keswick St NG2 ...268 C1
Ketton Ave S8 ...43 A2
Kevin Cl DE21 ...220 A4
Kew Cres Heanor DE75 ...182 A1
Sheffield S12 ...44 A1
Kew Gdns DE22 ...218 A3
Key St NG3 ...268 C2
Keyhaven Cl DE21 ...219 B4
Keynsham Cl DE24 ...232 C4
Keys Rd DE55 ...159 A1
Keys St DE1 ...267 C4
Keyworth Cl NG19 ...268 A4
Kibworth Cl
Chesterfield S41 ...115 B4
Derby DE21 ...220 A4
Kidd Rd SK13 ...17 C3
Kidsley Cl ⬛ S40 ...95 A3
Kilbourn St NG3 ...268 B2
Kilbourne Rd DE56 ...179 C3
Kilburn Dr DE7 ...194 B2
Kilburn Inf & Jun Schs DE56 ...179 C2
Kilburn La DE56 ...179 C2
Kilburn Rd S18 ...56 B1
Kilburn Toll Bar DE56 ...179 C1
Kilburn Way DE11 ...255 C1
Kilby Ho NG10 ...236 C4
Kildale Gdns S20 ...59 B4
Kildare Rd DE21 ...220 A2
Kildonan Gr S12 ...44 B2
Killamarsh Inf Sch S21 ...60 C4
Killamarsh Jun Sch S21 ...60 C4
Killamarsh La S21,S26 ...61 A2
Killingworth Ave DE21 ...231 C2
Killis La Belper DE56 ...179 B1

Killis La continued DE56 ...191 B4
Kilmory Fold SK13 ...10 C2
Kiln Bent Rd HD9 ...3 A3
Kiln Cl DE7 ...193 C1
Kiln Croft DE65 ...229 B2
Kiln Hill S18 ...57 B2
Kiln La Glossop SK13 ...10 A3
Parwich DE6 ...151 B1
Kiln Way DE11 ...256 B2
Kilnsey Ct DE23 ...230 C3
Kilverston Rd NG10 ...223 A3
Kilvington Ave S13 ...44 A4
Kilvington Cres S13 ...44 A4
Kilvington Rd S13 ...44 A4
Kimberley Cl NG16 ...195 C3
Kimberley Dr DE15 ...248 B2
Kimberley Prim Sch NG16 ...195 C3
Kimberley Rd DE72 ...221 A1
Kinder Cl S43 ...17 A4
Kinder Cres DE56 ...168 A3
Kinder Dr SK6 ...23 A3
Kinder Gr SK17 ...85 A3
Kinder Rd Hayfield SK22 ...25 C1
Staveley S43 ...97 A3
Kinder Row SK22 ...25 C1
Kinder View S22 ...33 B4
Kinder Way SK17 ...263 C1
Kinder Wlk DE22 ...218 C2
Kinderlee Way SK13 ...16 A3
King Alfred St DE22 ...267 A2
King Charles Ct S41 ...17 B4
King Charles St ⬛ S41 ...266 B3
King Ecbert Lower Sch S17 ...55 B3
King Ecbert Rd S17 ...55 C3
King Ecbert Upper Sch S17 ...55 C3
King Edward Ave S13 ...10 B1
King Edward Fst Sch NG18 ...268 A4
King Edward Gdns ⬛ NG10 ...223 A3
King Edward St
Nottingham NG1 ...268 B2
Sandiacre NG10 ...223 A3
Shirebrook NG20 ...119 C2
Wirksworth DE4 ...165 C4
King Edward VI High Sch ST17 ...269 A3
King George Ave DE7 ...208 C4
King George St
Wessington DE55 ...157 C4
Wirksworth DE4 ...165 C4
King John's Arc ⬛ NG1 ...268 B1
King St Alfreton DE55 ...158 C2
Ashbourne DE6 ...173 B1
Bakewell DE45 ...109 B3
Belper DE56 ...178 C2
Brimington S43 ...77 C1
Broadbottom SK14 ...16 A4
Burton u T DE14 ...254 B4
Clay Cross S45 ...131 B2
Clowne S43 ...80 C2
Creswell S80 ...81 C1
Creswell, Hodthorpe S80 ...82 B3
Derby DE1 ...267 B4
Duffield DE56 ...190 C2
Eastwood NG16 ...182 C1
Glossop SK13 ...17 B4
Hollingworth SK14 ...9 B3
Ilkeston DE7 ...194 C1
Long Eaton NG10 ...236 B4
Mansfield NG18 ...268 A4
Mansfield Woodhouse NG19 ...136 B1
Market Warsop NG20 ...120 B3
Middleton (Nr Wirksworth) DE4 ...154 B3
Nottingham NG1 ...268 B2
Pinxton NG16 ...160 B2
South Normanton DE55 ...159 C3
Tibshelf DE55 ...148 A4
King St S S40 ...266 B1
King William Ctr NG16 ...170 C2
King William St NG16 ...170 C2
King's Cl SK17 ...85 B4
King's Mead Cl DE22 ...267 A2
King's Mead Wlk DE22 ...267 A4
King's Newton La DE73 ...245 C3
King's Pl NG1 ...268 B1
King's Rd SK17 ...85 B4
King's Wlk ⬛ NG1 ...268 B1
Kingfisher Cl DE11 ...256 C2
Kingfisher Ct DE3 ...230 A4
Kingfisher Dr DE7 ...208 C2
Kingfisher Ho S41 ...266 C3
Kingfisher Mews SK6 ...23 A3
Kingfisher Row NG16 ...135 B1
Kingfisher Wlk DE24 ...231 C1
Kings Carsington DE4 ...164 C4
Clowne S43 ...80 C2
Creswell S80 ...81 B1
Kings Coppice S17 ...55 B3
Kings Croft DE22 ...204 C2
Kings Ct DE1 ...267 B4
Kings Dr Brinsley NG16 ...182 C4
Kings Gate DE74 ...247 C2
Kings Hill DE4 ...153 A1
Kings Mews S21 ...59 B2
Kings Rd Sandiacre NG10 ...223 A3
Swadlincote DE11 ...256 A1
Kings Way S80 ...82 B3

Kingsbury Rd DE22 ...218 A3
Kingsclere Ave DE21 ...206 A1
Kingscroft Cl S17 ...55 C4
Kingsdale Cl NG10 ...236 A3
Kingsdale Gr DE73 ...244 C4
Kingsfield Ind Est DE4 ...165 C3
Kingsfield Rd DE4 ...165 C4
Kingsgate S32 ...72 B1
Kingsland Cl DE21 ...205 C1
Kingsley Ave
Chesterfield S40 ...114 C4
Mansfield Woodhouse NG19 ...136 B3
Kingsley Cl NG19 ...136 B2
Kingsley Cres
Long Eaton NG10 ...236 A2
Stonebroom DE55 ...146 C2
Kingsley Gr NG19 ...136 B3
Kingsley Rd DE22 ...204 B2
Kingsmead Ave S42 ...231 C3
Kingsmead Ave NG9 ...209 B1
Kingsmead Hospl ST16 ...269 B4
Kingsmead Ind Est DE22 ...218 B3
Kingsmede S40 ...95 B1
Kingsmoor Fields SK13 ...10 C2
Kingsmoor Rd SK13 ...10 B1
Kingsmuir Rd DE3 ...217 B2
Kingsthorpe Cl NG19 ...136 C1
Kingston Ave
Ilkeston DE7 ...209 A2
Stafford ST16 ...269 C4
Kingston Cl DE7 ...207 B4
Kingston Rd
Burton u T DE15 ...248 B1
Mansfield NG18 ...268 C4
Kingston Row ST16 ...269 C4
Kingston St DE11 ...218 C4
Kingsway
Burton u T DE14 ...254 A4
Derby DE22 ...218 A3
Heanor DE75 ...181 B1
Ilkeston DE7 ...209 A3
Stafford ST16 ...269 A3
Stoke-on-T ST4 ...269 A3
Kingsway Cres DE56 ...192 A4
Kingsway Hospl DE3 ...218 A2
Kingsway Ind Pk DE22 ...218 B3
Kingsway Park Cl DE22 ...218 B3
Kingsway Ret Pk DE22 ...218 B3
Kingswood Ave DE56 ...179 B3
Kingswood Cl S41 ...95 B4
Kinross Ave DE21 ...219 B4
Kintyre Dr DE24 ...231 B2
Kinver Cl DE6 ...184 B4
Kinver Rd DE15 ...248 C2
Kipling Cl S18 ...76 B4
Kipling Dr DE23 ...217 B1
Kipling Rd S41 ...95 C4
Kipling St ⬛ NG18 ...268 B4
Kipps St ⬛ NG1 ...268 B2
Kirby La DE4 ...142 A4
Kirk Cl DE5 ...180 B4
Kirk Dale Ave DE21 ...220 C2
Kirk Hallam Com Tech Coll DE7 ...208 B2
Kirk Ireton CE Prim Sch DE6 ...165 A1
Kirk Langley CE Prim Sch DE6 ...202 C1
Kirk Leys Ave N DE21 ...220 C2
Kirk Leys Ave S DE21 ...220 C2
Kirk St DE1 ...219 A4
Kirk's La DE56 ...179 A2
Kirkby Ave Ilkeston DE7 ...208 C3
Sheffield S12 ...44 A2
Kirkby Dr S12 ...44 A2
Kirkby Rd S12 ...44 A2
Kirkby View S12 ...44 A2
Kirkby Way S12 ...44 A2
Kircroft Ave S21 ...60 B4
Kircroft Dr S21 ...60 B3
Kircroft La S21 ...60 B3
Kirkdale Cl S40 ...115 A4
Kirkdale Gdns NG10 ...236 A3
Kirkdale Rd NG10 ...236 A3
Kirkewhite Ave NG10 ...236 B4
Kirkewhite Ho NG10 ...236 B4
Kirkfield Dr DE72 ...235 B4
Kirkham Cl DE75 ...181 B1
Kirkham Dr NG9 ...223 C1
Kirkham La S36 ...168 A4
Kirkham Rd NG10 ...236 A3
Kirkhill S2 ...43 B4
Kirkistown Cl DE24 ...233 B3
Kirkland Ave NG18 ...268 B4
Kirkland Cl DE74 ...247 A2
Kirkland Way DE75 ...181 B2
Kirkley Dr DE75 ...181 B2
Kirkman Rd DE75 ...181 B2
Kirkstead Cl Derby DE21 ...206 A1
Pinxton NG16 ...160 B2
Kirkstead Jun Sch NG16 ...160 B2
Kirkstead Rd NG16 ...160 B2
Kirkstone Ave DE75 ...160 B2
Kirkstone Ct NG10 ...223 A1
Kirkstone Rd Buxton SK17 ...85 B4
Chesterfield S41 ...95 B4
Kirton Ave NG10 ...236 B4
Kishfield La SK23 ...45 A3
Kitchener Ave DE23 ...231 C4

Kitchener Dr NG18 ....268 C3
Kitchener Terr NG20 ....101 A1
Kitson Ave NG16 ....171 B2
Knab Rd DE4 ....127 C2
Knaphall La DE4 ....144 B3
Knapp Ave NG16 ....182 C1
Knifesmithgate S40 ....266 B3
Knight Ave ST16 ....269 C4
Knight's La Bretby DE15 ..249 A3
Repton DE15 ....249 A3
Knighton Cl S42 ....131 C3
Knighton St S42 ....131 C3
Knights Cl Beeston NG9 ...223 C1
Derby DE24 ....231 C1
Knights Ct **3** DE13 .....240 C1
Knightsbridge DE22 ....218 A3
Knightwake Rd SK22 ....33 A4
Kniveton CE Prim Sch
DE6 ....163 B1
Kniveton La DE6 ....174 B2
Kniveton Pk DE7 ....208 B4
Knob Fields DE11 ....261 C4
Knob La DE4 ....166 B3
Knoll Cl DE23 ....231 A4
Knoll St SK22 ....33 A4
Knoll The Chesterfield S40 .94 C1
Dronfield S18 ....57 B2
Mansfield NG18 ....268 A3
Shirebrook NG20 ....119 B2
Swadlincote DE11 ....256 A3
Tansley DE4 ....144 A3
Knowes Cl SK17 ....85 C4
Knowes Cres SK17 ....85 B4
Knowl Ave DE6 ....178 C3
Knowle Ave SK23 ....47 A3
Knowle Gn S17 ....55 B4
Knowle Rd S6 ....23 B3
Knowle St ST4 ....269 B2
Knowle Top S20 ....59 C4
Knowles Hill DE13 ....240 A2
Knowles Inf Est S42 ......33 B2
Knowleston Pl DE4 ....143 B2
Knutsford Dr DE21 ....205 B1
Kye La S26 ....61 C3
Kyle Gr DE21 ....206 A2
Kynance Cl Derby DE24 ...233 B3
South Normanton DE55 ....160 B3
Kynnersley Croft ST14 ...210 A1

L

Laburnam Cl S80 ....81 C1
Laburnham St S44 ....97 A2
Laburnum Ave NG20 ....119 C3
Laburnum Cl Bolsover S44 .99 B2
Darley Dale DE4 ....127 A2
Sandiacre NG10 ....223 A4
South Normanton DE55 ...160 A4
Laburnum Cres
Derby DE22 ....204 B2
Swanwick DE55 ....170 A4
Laburnum Gr
Derby DE22 ....218 A3
Killamarsh S21 ....60 B3
Mansfield Woodhouse
NG19 ....136 A2
Laburnum Rd
Burton u T DE15 ....254 C3
Swadlincote DE11 ....256 A3
Laburnum St S43 ....78 A1
Laburnum Way DE65 ......229 B2
Lace Way NG1 ....136 C2
Laceby Cl NG19 ....136 C2
Lacey Cl DE7 ....194 B2
Lacey Fields Rd DE75 ....182 A1
Ladbroke Gdns DE22 ......217 C3
Ladies Spring Dr S17 ....56 A4
Ladies Spring Gr S17 ....56 A4
Ladle End La DE12 ....253 B1
Lady Bank View S21 ......59 B2
Lady Field Rd S80 ....62 B4
Lady Grove Rd DE4 ....127 C1
Lady Lea Rd DE21/DE7 ...192 A3
Lady Ley Hill DE21 ......192 A3
Lady Manners Sch DE45 ..109 B2
Lady Mantle Cl DE73 ....232 C1
Lady Meadow CT ST14 ....196 C3
Ladybank Rd Derby DE3 ..217 B1
Mosborough S20 ....59 B3
Ladybower Cl DE11 ....256 A3
Ladybower Ct **3** S17 ...56 A3
Ladybower Dr S32 ....53 B4
Ladybower La S43 ....97 B4
Ladybower Rd DE21 ......220 C2
Ladybrook La NG18 ......268 A4
Ladybrook Pl NG19 ......268 A4
Ladycroft SK17 ....66 B1
Ladycroft Paddock
DE22 ....204 C2
Ladycross Inf Sch NG10 .223 A4
Ladyfields DE11 ....256 B3
Ladyfields Cl DE11 ......255 C3
Ladyflatts Rd DE4 ......165 C4
Ladygrove Cotts DE23 ...219 A2
Ladylea Rd NG10 ....236 A2
Ladypit Rd SK23 ....33 C2
Ladysmith Rd DE72 .....221 A1
Ladythorne Ave SK6 ....23 A3
Ladywell Cl DE13 ....240 C1
Ladywell Ct DE56 ....179 C4
Ladywood Ave DE56 .....179 A3
Ladywood Dr S41 ....95 B4
Ladywood Prim Sch
DE7 ....208 B3

Ladywood Rd DE7 ....208 B3
Lake Ave Heanor DE75 ...181 B2
Mansfield NG19 ....268 A4
Lake Dr Derby DE22 .....231 C4
Doveridge DE6 ....211 A1
Lake Lands S42 ....114 C1
Lake Side Doveridge DE6 .211 A1
Glossop SK13 ....10 A3
Lake View SK23 ....33 B2
Lakeside Ashbourne DE6 .173 B1
Bakewell DE45 ....109 A4
Wingerworth S42 ....114 C1
Lakeside Ave NG10 .....236 B2
Lakeside Cl S41 ....77 B2
Lakeside Cres NG10 ....236 B3
Lakeside Dr DE23 ......231 A4
Lakeside Inf Sch NG10 .236 B3
Lamartine Ct **7** NG3 ...268 B2
Lamartine St NG3 ......268 B2
Lamb Cres DE5 ....169 C1
Lamb Hill Cl S13 ......44 B4
Lambcroft Rd NG16 ....160 B2
Lambe Ct DE23 ....267 C2
Lambgates SK13 ....10 A3
Lambhouse La DE4 ....177 C3
Lambley Dr DE22 ......204 B1
Lambourn Ct DE22 ....205 A2
Lambourn Dr DE22 ....205 A2
Lambourne Ave DE6 ..185 B4
Lambpart La S33 .....50 B3
Lambrook Cl DE3 .....217 B1
Lambton Cl DE7 ....194 C2
Lammascote Rd ST16 .269 B4
Lamp Cl DE73 ....252 A4
Lampeter Cl DE21 ....206 A1
Lanark St DE21 ......219 C4
Lancaster Ave
Sandiacre NG10 ......223 A2
Stapleford NG9 ......223 C4
Lancaster Dr Hilton DE65 228 C1
Tutbury DE13 ....239 A3
Lancaster Rd S41 ....95 B4
Lancaster Rise DE56 .179 A3
Lancaster Sports Ctr
DE1 ....267 B4
Lancaster St S44 ....117 C1
Lancaster Wlk DE21 ..221 A3
Lancelot Cl S40 ......114 B4
Lancelot Dr DE13 ....240 C1
Lancing Rd S2 ....43 C4
Landau Forte Coll DE1 .267 C4
Lander La DE56 ......179 A2
Landmere Cl DE7 .....194 B2
Landon Cl S40 ....114 A4
Landsdown Gr NG10 ..223 C1
Landseer Cl Dronfield S18 .56 C1
Sheffield S14 ....43 B1
Landseer Dr Marple SK6 .23 B4
Sheffield S14 ....43 C1
Landseer Pl S14 .....43 C1
Landseer Wlk S14 ...43 C1
Lane Head Longnor SK17 121 A4
Stoney Middleton S32 ..71 B2
Tideswell SK17 ......69 B3
Lane Head Rd Totley SL7 .55 B2
Whaley Bridge SK23 ...45 B3
Lane The Awsworth NG16 .195 B2
Killamarsh S21 ....60 B1
Youlgreave DE4 ......126 B3
Lanes The DE4 ......145 A4
Lanesend Cotts SK23 .46 A4
Laneside Ave NG9 ...223 C1
Laneside Cl SK23 ...47 A3
Laneside Rd
New Mills SK22 .....24 C3
New Mills, Rowarth SK22 .24 C3
Laneward Cl DE7 ....194 B2
Lang Rd DE24 ......232 C3
Langdale Cl S40 ....94 C3
Langdale Dr Derby DE21 205 B1
Dronfield S18 ......57 B2
Long Eaton NG10 ...236 A3
Langdale Sq S43 ..96 B4
Langen Cl **3** NG10 ..223 A1
Langer Cl S41 .....236 C3
Langer Cl DE14 ...254 A3
Langer La
Chesterfield S40,S42 .114 C3
Wingerworth S40,S42 .114 B3
Langerfield Ave S40 .115 A4
Langford Rd Derby DE21 217 B2
Mansfield NG19 ...268 A3
Langham Pl NG18 .268 A4
Langhurst Ct S40 .95 B2
Langhurst Rd S40 .95 B2
Langley Ave Ilkeston DE7 194 C2
Somercotes DE55 ..170 B4
Langley Bsns Pk NG16 182 A1
Langley Cl
3 Chesterfield S40 ..95 A3
Mansfield NG19 ...135 C1
Langley Ct S13 ...10 A3
Langley Dr SK13 ..17 C4
Langley Inf Sch DE75 182 A1
Langley Mill CE Inf Sch
NG16 ....182 A2
Langley Mill Jun Sch
NG16 ....182 A2
Langley Mill Sta NG16 182 A2
Langley Pk NG16 ..182 A2
Langley Rd DE21 ..220 C2
Langley St DE22 ..218 B3
Langsett Ave **21** SK13 .9 B1
Langsett Dr DE73 ..233 A1
Langsett La SK13 ..9 B1
Langsett Terr **19** SK13 .9 B1
Langstone Ave S44 ..99 B1

Langton Hollow NG16 ...171 B3
Langtree Ave S41 ....77 A1
Langwith Bassett Prim Sch
NG20 ....119 C4
Langwith Dr NG20 ....100 C1
Langwith Maltings
NG20 ....100 C1
Langwith Rd
Bolsover S44 ....118 B4
Shirebrook NG20 ....119 C3
Langwith Whaley Thorns Sta
NG20 ....100 C1
Lansbury Ave
Mastin Moor S43 ....79 A2
Pilsley S45 ....132 B1
Lansbury Dr DE55 ....160 A3
Lansdale Gdns DE21 ....219 A3
Lanscombe Park Rd
DE22 ....204 C1
Lansdowne Ave S41 .....95 C3
Lansdowne Rd
Branston DE14 ....253 C4
Brimington S43 ....96 B4
Swadlincote DE11 ....256 A2
Lansing Gdns DE21 ....220 A3
Lant La DE4 ....144 A4
Lantern Gr DE21 ....217 B2
Lantern Pike View SK22 .25 A1
Lantern View SK22 ....24 A1
Lapwing Cl DE24 ....231 C1
Larch Ave Killamarsh S21 .60 B3
Mansfield Woodhouse
NG19 ....136 A3
Ripley DE5 ....169 B1
Shirebrook NG20 ....119 B2
Larch Cl DE22 ....204 B2
Larch Cres NG16 ......182 C1
Larch Dr NG10 ....223 A4
Larch Rd Eckington S21 .59 A1
Kilburn DE56 ....192 A4
Swadlincote DE11 .....255 C3
Larch Way
Chesterfield S40 ....95 B3
Glossop SK13 ....17 C4
Larchdale Cl DE55 ....160 A2
Larges St DE1 ....218 C3
Lark Cl DE23 ....231 B3
Lark Hill DE3 ....230 A4
Lark Hill Cotts SK22 .23 C4
Larkdale St NG7 .....268 A2
Larkfields Cres DE55 .169 C4
Larkhill 169 C4
Larkhill Cl DE55 ....169 C4
Larkhill Cres DE24 ..231 C2
Larkin Cl DE24 ......232 A3
Larklands Ave DE7 ..209 A4
Larklands Inf Sch DE7 209 A4
Larkspur Cl
Mansfield NG19 ......136 B1
South Normanton DE55 160 A2
Larkspur Ct DE21 ...206 A2
Larkstone La DE6 ...149 A1
Larpit Gn S80 ....82 A3
Lascelles Rd SK17 ..85 A4
Lashley Cl DE21 ....205 C1
Latham Cl DE15 ....248 B1
Lathbury Cl DE21 ..205 B1
Lathkill Dr DE55 ..159 C3
Lathkill Gr SK17 ..85 B4
Lathkill Ave Derby DE24 233 B4
Ilkeston DE7 ....194 C3
Staveley S43 ......97 B3
Lathkill Cl Sheffield S13 .44 B4
West Hallam DE7 ..207 C4
Holloway DE4 .....156 A4
Lathkill Dale National Nature
Reserve* DE45 ....124 B4
Lathkill Dr
Ashbourne DE6 ...185 C4
Ripley DE5 ....180 B3
Selston NG16 .....171 C4
Lathkill Gr
Clay Cross S45 ...131 B1
Tibshelf DE55 ....147 C3
Lathkill Rd Derby DE21 220 A4
Sheffield S13 ....44 B4
Lathkilldale Cres NG10 236 A3
Latimer Cl DE23 ..230 C4
Latimer St DE24 ..232 B3
Latrigg Cl DE3 ...217 C1
Lauder Cl DE24 ...231 C1
Launceston Rd DE24 233 A3
Laund Ave DE56 ..179 A3
Laund Cl DE56 ....179 A3
Laund Farm Mews DE56 179 B3
Laund Hill DE56 ..179 A3
Laund Nook DE56 .179 A3
Launds Ave NG16 .171 B4
Laurel Ave
Long Duckmanton S44 .97 B2
Mansfield NG18 ..268 C3
Mansfield Woodhouse
NG19 ....136 C1
Ripley DE5 ....169 B1
Laurel Cl Eckington S21 .59 B1
Shirebrook NG20 .119 B3
Swanwick DE55 ..170 A4
Laurel Cres
Brimington S43 ..78 A1
Long Eaton NG10 236 B3
Smalley DE7 .....192 C3
Laurel Dr
Aston-on-T DE72 .246 A4
Killamarsh S21 ..60 B3
Laurel Garth Cl S41 .77 A2
Laurel Gr
Burton u T DE15 .254 C3

Leawood Rd DE11 ......
Leche Croft DE56 ......
Lechlade Cl DE7 ....
Ledbury Chase DE24 ...
Ledbury Pl DE21 ......
Ledo Ave DE3 ....
Lee Cres DE7 ....
Lee Dale SK17 ....
Lee Farm Cl DE73 ....
Lee Head SK13 ....
Lee La DE75 ....
Lee Mount SK13 ......
Lee Rd S41 ....
Lee Vale Dr SK13 ....
Leebangs Rd SK14 ...
Leech Cl NG16 ....
Leedhams Croft DE12 .
Leeds Pl DE1 ....
Leeds Rd S81 ....
Leefield Rd SK23 ....
Leek Rd Buxton SK17 .
Longnor SK17 ....
Stoke-on-T ST4 .....
Leeming La NG19,NG20
Leeming La N NG19 ..
Leeming La S NG19 ..
Leeming Pk NG19 ....
Leeming St NG18 ....
Lees Brook Com Sch
DE21 ....
Lees Brook Ho S18 ..
Lees Hall Ave S8 ...
Lees Hall Pl S8 ....
Lees Hall Rd S8 ....
Lees Hill St NG2 ...
Lees House Ct S8 ...
Lees La DE55 ....
Lees Nook S8 ......
Lees Rd DE4 ....
Lees Row SK13 ....
Lees The DE72 ....
Leese St S4 ......
Leeside S33 .....
Leeswood Cl S41 .
Leeway DE21 ....
Legh Rd SK12 ...
Leicester Cl SK13
Leicester Ho **2** NG7
Leicester St
Burton u T DE14 ..
Derby DE22 ....
Long Eaton NG10 .
Leigh Rd NG9 ....
Leigh Way S42 ...
Leighton Dr Marple SK6
Leighton Rd S14 ..
Leighton St NG3 ..
Leighton View S2 .
Leisure La SK17 ..
Leman St DE22 ...
Lemont Rd S17 ...
Leniscar Ave DE75
Lennox St NG1 ...
Lens Rd DE22 ...
Lenthall Inf Sch S18
Lenton Ave Derby DE21
Nottingham NG7 ..
Lenton Rd NG7 ..
Lenton St NG10 ..
Leominster Dr DE21 .
Leonard Cheshire Cl
DE75 ....
Leonard Cl Derby DE23
Sheffield S2 ....
Leonard St DE1 ..
Leopold St Derby DE1 .
Long Eaton NG10 .
Leslie Ave NG16 ..
Leslie Cl DE23 ...
Lesser La Buxton SK17
Chapel-en-le-F SK23 .
Level La SK17 ....
Leven Cl DE24 ...
Levens Way S41 ..
Leveret Cl DE73 ..
Leverton Rd NG19 .
Lewcote La DE7 ..
Lewis Cl NG3 ....
Lewis St Derby DE23
Stoke-on-T ST4 ..
Lewiston Rd DE21 .
Lexington Rd DE21 .
Ley Ave DE55 ....
Ley Croft Hatton DE65
Mansfield Woodhouse
NG19 ....
Ley Gdns DE55 ..
Ley La
Mansfield Woodhouse
NG19 ....
Marple SK6 .....
Leyburn Cl
Chesterfield S40 .
Swadlincote DE11 .
Leycote Way DE56 .
Leyfield Rd S17 ..
Leygate View SK22 .
Leyland Cl NG9 ..
Leyland Ct DE1 ..
Leyland Gdns DE1 .
Leyland St DE1 ..
Leylands DE22 ..
Leylands La SK14 .
Leys Ct DE56 ....
Leys Field Gdns DE1 .

Entry	Ref
n Sch DE55	159 B2
DE4	154 A4
aton DE21	191 B1
acote DE11	255 C3
Ct S43	77 B2
stone Dr DE22	218 A3
d Ave DE11	256 C3
d CI NG9	223 C2
d Ct ST17	269 B3
d Dr DE24	233 A4
d Rd	
on DE13,DE14	253 B2
rfield S40	114 B4
d ST17	269 B3
d Rd S2	43 C4
nny La DE4	144 C2
E6	197 C4
t ST4	269 B1
r CI DE1	217 A1
d DE6,SK17	113 A4
lders La SK12	32 A3
not Rd ST14	210 A1
ood Ave 🖪 SK17	85 B4
rfield S21	77 C4
S40	43 C1
ood Rd	
SK17	66 A1
on S21	58 C1
ve DE22	218 A3
J Derby DE22	204 B2
wood S44	116 C1
r DE24	233 A3
r Bolsover S44	99 A3
u T DE15	254 C3
ave S44	134 A4
r DE75	181 C1
d Warsop NG20	120 C4
ook NG20	119 C3
Normanton DE55	160 A2
ews B2	204 B2
f S43	78 A1
Prime CI DE24	233 A4
nd DE55	146 A4
ton S41	95 B4
edi CI S40	114 C3
ok CI DE4	143 B3
ols The DE73	252 A4
a S17	55 B4
witch La DE65	227 C3
ve Derby DE1	267 A1
Breadsall Hilltop	
203 B1
ny Mill NG16	182 B2
s SK22	24 B1
DE5	180 A2
e S43	78 C1
CI Calow S44	97 A2
dge DE6	224 A4
n DE65	227 B1
ne NG16	160 B2
Cres Belper DE56	179 A1
et Warsop NG20	120 C4
Croft DE22	204 C2
r Ashbourne DE6	185 B4
u T DE15	254 C3
n Dale DE4	143 B2
DE21	220 A3
ott DE72	234 C4
Eaton NG10	223 A3
Normanton DE55	160 A3
sford NG9	223 B3
Grove Ave DE4	143 A3
Grove Wlk DE4	143 A3
dale La Marple SK6	23 A3
ch DE56	189 A4
La Derby DE21	206 A2
ny DE7,DE21	206 B3
Rd S21	59 A1
St Ilkeston DE7	208 C4
terr NG10	236 B4
Free Ave	
y Dale DE4	127 A2
od DE75	181 C1
ann S21	60 B3
sfield Woodhouse	
136 A3
lincote DE11	256 A4
Free Dr Derby DE3	143 B2
Free Gr	
Cross S45	131 C1
Free PI NG18	268 C3
Free Rd DE4	143 B3
t Wlk DE23	218 B1
Croft View S42	115 A2
dale Ave DE21	206 A2
kiln Fields Rd S44	99 A2
kiln Way S43	80 B3
lin The DE73	252 C1
hick Rd DE21	220 A3
dale Rd DE73	217 B1
ey Thorns NG20	101 A1
Cres NG20	119 B3
s Pk DE5	169 B2
ey The	
s in F NG11	237 C3
berley DE7	193 C2
stone Terr NG11	136 A2
ree CI S43	96 C3
cote Dr DE7	208 B3

Entry	Ref
Limetree Rise DE7	208 B3
Limmen Gdns NG3	268 C2
Limpenny St NG7	268 A2
Linacre Ave S41	95 B4
Linacre Rd S40,S42	95 A3
Linacre Resr Nature Trail*	
S42	94 B3
Linacre Way S43	17 C4
Linacres Dr DE73	233 A1
Linbery CI DE55	158 B2
Lincoln Ave Derby DE24	233 A4
Sandiacre NG10	223 A2
Lincoln Cir NG7	268 A1
Lincoln CI	
Stapleford NG9	209 C1
Tibshelf DE55	148 A3
Lincoln Dr NG19	136 B2
Lincoln Gn DE73	232 C1
Lincoln Rd DE15	254 B4
Lincoln St Alfreton DE55	158 C2
Chesterfield S40	115 A4
Nottingham NG3	268 B1
Tibshelf DE55	148 A3
Lincoln Way	
🖪 Glossop SK13	17 C4
North Wingfield DE11	131 C3
Swadlincote DE11	256 C3
Lindale Rd DE11	76 B1
Lindale Way DE73	233 A1
Linden Ave	
Chesterfield S40	95 A1
Clay Cross S45	131 B1
Stanton S43	57 A2
Linden CI DE56	192 A4
Linden Ct S41	115 B3
Linden Dr S41	115 B3
Linden Gr DE Matlock DE4	143 B3
Sandiacre NG10	223 A4
Shirebrook NG20	119 C2
Stapleford NG9	209 C1
Linden Park Gr S40	95 B2
Linden Rd S40	81 C1
Linden St	
Mansfield NG19	136 A1
Shirebrook NG20	119 C2
Linden Way SK6	32 A4
Lindford CI DE21	205 C2
Lindisfarne CI 🖪 DE24	231 B2
Lindisfarne Gr 🖪 S40	95 B1
Lindisfarne Rd S18	76 A4
Lindley St	
Mansfield NG18	268 B4
Selston NG16	171 B3
Lindon Dr DE24	233 B3
Lindrick CI Derby DE3	217 C1
Mansfield Woodhouse	
NG19	136 B3
Lindrick Gdns S40	114 B4
Lindsay CI NG18	268 B3
Lindsey CI DE21	206 C2
Lindum Gr 🖪 NG2	268 C1
Lindway La DE55	145 A1
Ling La S44	118 B2
Lingfield Rd DE14	253 C4
Lingfield Rise DE3	217 C2
Lingfoot Ave S8	57 A3
Lingfoot CI S8	57 A3
Lingfoot Cres S8	57 B3
Lingfoot Dr S8	57 B3
Lingfoot PI S8	57 B3
Lingfoot Wlk S8	57 B3
Linglongs Ave SK23	45 B3
Linglongs Rd SK23	45 B3
Lings Cres S42	132 A4
Linkmel Rd NG16	182 B2
Links CI DE24	231 C2
Links Rd	
Chapel-en-le-F SK23	46 C3
Dronfield S18	57 A1
Linley La S12	44 B3
Linnell St S12	268 C2
Linnet CI DE21	220 C3
Linnet Hill DE3	230 B4
Linnet Rd S41	77 A2
Linscott CI S41	95 B4
Linshaws Rd HD9	3 C3
Linton CI DE11	261 C3
Linton Heath DE12	261 B3
Linton Rd	
Chesterfield S40	114 B4
Linton S42	261 C4
Rosliston DE12	260 C3
Linwood Cres NG16	182 C1
Linwood Ct NG19	136 C1
Lion St S14	269 B2
Lionel St ST4	269 A1
Lipp Ave S21	60 B4
Liskeard Dr DE22	204 B2
Lismore Ct 🖪 DE24	231 B2
Lismore Gr SK17	85 A4
Lismore Rd Buxton SK17	85 A4
Sheffield S8	43 A3
Lissett Ave 🖪 DE7	208 C4
Lister CI Derby DE3	217 B1
Sheffield S12	44 A2
Lister Cres S12	44 A2
Lister Dr S12	44 A2
Lister Gate NG1	268 B1
Lister PI S12	44 A2
Lister Way S12	44 A2
Liston Dr DE22	218 C4
Litchen CI DE7	194 C1
Litchfield CI NG10	237 A4
Litchurch La DE24	219 B1

Entry	Ref
Litchurch St DE1	267 C1
Little Acre NG19	136 C3
Little Bolehill DE4	155 A1
Little Breck S40	160 A2
Little Brind Rd S40	218 C3
Little CI DE11	256 A3
Little Debdale La DE7	135 C1
Little Eaton Prim Sch	
DE21	205 B4
Little Edge S32	71 B3
Little Fen DE55	147 C3
Little Hallam Hill DE7	208 C4
Little Hallam La DE7	209 A3
Little La	
Ashford in t W DE45	89 C1
Heanor DE5	181 A2
Kimberley NG16	195 C3
Pleasley NG19	135 A3
Sheffield S12	44 A3
Shirebrook NG20	119 B2
Sutton in a NG17	148 C1
Thorpe Salvin S80	63 A3
Tideswell SK17	69 C2
Little London DE1	267 C1
Little Longstone CI DE3	217 C1
Little Lunnon NG11	237 C3
Little Meadow Rd DE7	208 C3
Little Moorside DE72	246 A4
Little Norton Rd S42,	
S45	131 A4
Little Norton Ave S8	57 A4
Little Norton Dr S8	57 A4
Little Norton La S8	57 A4
Little Norton Way S8	57 A4
Little Robins Ct NG18	268 A3
Little Thorn Ind Est	
DE11	256 C1
Little Wood Dr S12	44 A2
Little Wood Rd S12	44 A2
Little Woodbury Dr	
DE23	230 C3
Littlebrook CI DE11	206 B2
Littledale CI DE21	
Littlefield La	
Ellastone DE6	183 A1
Snelston DE6	184 A2
Littlefield Rd DE65	227 B4
Littlemoor	
Chesterfield S41	95 B4
Eckington S21	59 B4
Littlemoor Cres S41	95 C4
Littlemoor Ctr 🖪 S41	95 C4
Littlemoor La DE4	143 C1
Littlemoor Rd SK14	9 A3
Littleover Com Sch	
DE23	230 C4
Littleover Cres DE23	218 B1
Littleover La DE23	231 C4
Littleton St S16	269 C4
Littlewell La DE7	208 C1
Littleworth NG18	268 C4
Littleworth La NG19	136 A3
Litton SK13	10 A2
Litton Bank 🖪 SK13	9 E1
Litton CE Prim Sch	
SK17	69 C2
Litton Dr DE21	220 C2
Litton Gdns 🖪 SK13	9 E1
Litton Mews SK13	9 E1
Litton Rd NG19	136 C2
Liverpool Rd DE75	181 C1
Liverpool St	
🖪 Derby DE21	219 C4
Nottingham NG3	268 C2
Liversage PI DE1	267 C2
Liversage Rd DE1	267 C2
Liversage St DE1	267 C2
Livingstone Rd DE23	218 C1
Lloyds Rd S42	131 A4
Loadshead La S42	112 B4
Lochinvar CI DE21	220 C2
Lock CI DE7	208 B3
Lock La Long Eaton NG10	236 B2
Sandiacre NG10	223 A4
Locke Way S16	269 C4
Lockington CI DE73	232 C1
Lockington Rd DE74	247 B3
Locko Ct DE21	220 B3
Locko La S45	132 C2
Locko Rd DE21	220 C4
Lockford La	
Chesterfield, Stonegravels	
S41	96 A3
Chesterfield, Tapton S41	96 B3
Lockoford Rd S41	96 A3
Lockside SK6	23 A3
Locksley CI Mosb DE75	193 C4
Lockton Ave DE75	181 C1
Lockwood Rd DE22	204 B2
Locomotive Way DE24	219 B2
Lode La DE6	149 C2
Lodge Ave DE6	185 A4
Lodge Bank SK13	10 A3
Lodge CI Calow S44	97 A3
Duffield DE56	190 C2
Etwall DE65	229 B2
Lodge Ct SK14	9 A2
Lodge Dr Belper DE56	178 C3
Wingerworth S42	115 A1
Lodge Est DE55	147 C3
Lodge Farm Chase DE6	165 A1
Lodge Farm CI S40	114 B4
Lodge Hill DE13	239 C2

Entry	Ref
Lodge La Aldercar NG16	181 C4
Alstonefield DE6	149 A2
Derby DE1	267 A4
Derby, Spondon DE21	220 B2
Mackworth DE6,DE22	203 C2
Shottle DE56	177 B4
Lodge Mews DE72	246 A4
Lodge Moor Rd S10	42 C4
Lodge P1 S43	97 B3
Lodge Rd Eastwood NG16	195 A4
Long Eaton NG10	236 B3
Mapperley DE7	193 C2
Nethersea1 DE12	261 B1
Stoke-on-T ST4	269 A2
Lodge St DE72	235 A4
Lodge The Glossop SK13	17 A4
Tideswell SK17	69 B1
Lodge Way DE3	217 B1
Lodge Wlk S43	97 B3
Lohengrin Ct 🖪 DE13	240 C1
Lombard St DE22	218 C4
Lomond Ave DE24	231 C1
London CI DE24	232 B4
London Rd	
Castle Donington DE72	247 A4
Derby DE23,DE24	219 B1
Nottingham NG2	268 C1
Shardlow DE72	234 C1
Sheffield, Heeley S2	43 A3
Sheffield, Highfield S2	43 A4
Stoke-on-T ST4	269 B1
London Rd S S2	43 A4
London S S43	77 B2
Long Acre View S20	60 A4
Long Bridge La DE24	232 B4
Long Croft DE72	246 A4
Long Eaton Com Sch	
NG10	236 B4
Long Eaton Com Sch (Lower	
Site) NG10	236 B3
Long Eaton Sta NG10	236 B2
Long Field Grange S45	145 A4
Long Hill Darley Dale DE4	127 B2
Whaley Bridge SK17,SK23	65 B3
Long La Alstonefield DE6	149 A3
Ashover S42	130 A3
Broadbottom SK13	16 A3
Chapel-en-le-F SK23	47 A2
Chesterfield S21	77 B4
Holloway DE4	156 A3
Killamarsh S21	60 C3
Kirk Langley DE6	202 C1
Longford DE6	200 C1
Shipley DE75	194 C4
Shirebrook NG20	119 C2
Taddington SK17	87 C3
Thurvaston DE6	201 B1
Whaley Bridge SK23	46 B2
Long Lane CE Prim Sch	
DE6	201 C1
Long Mdw	
Great Cubley DE6	198 C3
Mansfield Woodhouse	
Long Meadow Rd DE55	158 C2
Long Rake DE45	140 B3
Long Row Belper DE56	178 C2
Nottingham NG1	268 B1
Shardlow DE72	235 A1
Long Row Prim Sch	
DE56	178 C2
Long Row W NG1	268 B1
Long Shambles S40	266 B3
Long Sleets DE55	160 B3
Long St DE15	254 C4
Longacre Rd S18	76 A4
Longacre Way S20	60 A4
Longbourne Ct NG19	136 C1
Longbow CI DE13	240 B1
Longbow Gr DE13	240 B1
Longbridge La	
Buxton SK17	67 A2
Heanor DE75	181 B1
Longcliff Wlk 🖪 S41	95 B3
Longclough Dr SK13	17 A4
Longcourse La S44	98 A1
Longcroft Ave S18	56 C1
Longcroft CI S41	266 B4
Longcroft Cres 🖪 S18	56 C1
Longcroft Rd S41	114 C4
Longcroft View S80	82 A3
Longdale NG19	136 C1
Longdale Dr SK14	9 A2
Longdale Gdns NG3	9 A2
Longdale Rise S42	209 C1
Longdendale High Sch	
SK14	9 A4
Longdon Rd DE22	220 B3
Longedge Gr S42	115 A2
Longedge La S42	114 C2
Longedge Rise S42	115 A2
Longfield Cres DE7	208 C3
Longfield La DE7	208 C3
Longfield Rd DE7	269 A2
Longford CE Prim Sch	
DE6	214 B4
Longford CI Derby DE22	204 C1
Sheffield S17	55 C3
Longford Cres S17	56 A3
Longford Dr S17	55 C3
Longford La DE6	214 C4
Longford Rd S17	56 A3
Longford Spinney S17	55 C3
Longford St DE24	218 C2
Longhedge La	
Burton u T DE13	239 C1
Pleasley NG19	134 C3

Entry	Ref
Longhurst La SK6	23 B3
Longhurst View S80	81 C3
Longlands S44	99 A1
Longlands Dr SK22	33 A4
Longlands La DE65	230 B1
Longlands Rd	
New Mills SK22	33 A4
Swadlincote DE11	256 A4
Longlands Villas DE56	167 C2
Longley La DE21	220 B3
Longload La DE4	154 C3
Longmeade Dr SK23	47 A2
Longmoor Gdns 🖪	
NG10	223 A1
Longmoor La	
Breaston DE72	222 C1
Sandiacre NG10	223 A2
Longmoor Prim Sch	
NG10	223 B2
Longmoor Rd	
Glossop SK13	17 A4
Long Eaton NG10	223 A1
Longnor Craft Ctr*	
SK17	121 B2
Longnor Gn SK13	9 B1
Longnor Mews SK13	9 B1
Longnor Way SK13	9 B1
Longreave La DE45	90 B2
Longrose La DE6	163 A1
Longshaw	
North Wingfield S42	131 C3
Staveley S43	97 B4
Longshaw Estate Ctry Pk*	
S32	54 A2
Longside Rd S43	112 C3
Longson Rd SK23	47 B3
Longster La NG20,NG19	120 B2
Longstock DE21	205 C1
Longstone CE Prim Sch	
DE45	89 C2
Longstone Cres S12	44 B2
Longstone La DE45	89 C1
Longstone Rise DE56	179 C2
Longstone Wlk DE1	267 A2
Longthorpe CI DE23	231 A4
Longwalls La DE56	178 B3
Longwood Inf Sch NG16	160 C1
Longwood Rd NG16	160 C1
Lons Inf Sch DE5	169 B1
Lonsdale Dr NG9	223 C1
Lonsdale Gr DE4	142 C4
Lonsdale PI DE22	218 B2
Lonsdale Rd	
Burton u T DE14	254 A4
Pilsley S45	132 A1
Lonsdale St ST4	269 B1
Loom CI DE56	179 B3
Loosemore Dr S12	43 C3
Lord Haddon Rd DE7	194 C1
Lord Nelson St S42	268 C1
Lord Roberts Rd S40	266 B3
Lord St Derby DE24	232 B3
Glossop SK13	10 B1
Hollingworth SK14	9 C2
Mansfield NG18	268 B3
Nottingham NG2	268 C1
Lords CI S44	99 A1
Lordship La S44	269 C2
Lordsmill St S41	266 C2
Lorien Ct ST14	269 B2
Lorne CI S18	56 B1
Lorne St DE22	218 C2
Lorraine CI DE24	232 C2
Loscoe CE Prim Sch	
DE75	181 B2
Loscoe Grange DE75	181 B2
Loscoe Rd Derby DE21	206 A1
Heanor DE75	181 B1
Loscoe-Denby La DE5,	
DE75	181 A2
Losehill Hall Study Ctr*	
S33	38 B2
Losk Cnr S44	118 B1
Losk La S44	118 B1
Lothian PI	
Castle Donington DE74	247 A3
Derby DE21	219 B4
Lothlorien CI DE24	231 A4
Loudon St DE23	218 A2
Loudoun Pl DE74	247 A2
Loughborough Ave NG2	268 C1
Loundes Rd S18	76 C3
Loundsley Ct S42	94 C2
Loundsley Green Rd S40	95 B3
Louis Cl S44	99 A1
Lousie Greaves La DE21	220 C1
Louvain Rd DE22,DE23	218 B1
Louwil Ave NG19	136 C3
Lovatt CI DE13	240 C1
Lovatt St S14	269 B2
Love La DE55	147 B2
Loveys Croft DE73	252 C1
Low CI DE7	189 A1
Low Comm S21	79 A4
Low Lea Rd SK6	23 A2
Low Leighton Rd SK22	33 B4
Low Mdw SK23	45 B4
Low Pavement	
Chesterfield S40	266 B3
🖪 Nottingham NG1	268 B1
Low's La DE7	209 A1
Lowburn Rd S13	44 B4
Lowdham St NG3	268 C2
Lowe St Derby DE24	232 C3
Stoke-on-T ST4	269 B2

Lowedges Cres S8 ...56 C3
Lowedges Dr S8 ...56 C3
Lowedges Pl S8 ...57 A3
Lowedges Prim Sch S8 ...56 C3
Lowedges Rd S8 ...56 C3
Lower Bagthorpe NG16 ...171 C2
Lower Bank S13 ...17 B4
Lower Barn Rd S43 ...9 C2
Lower Bloomsgrove Rd DE7 ...194 C1
Lower Brook St NG10 ...236 C4
Lower Burch Pl S32 ...71 C3
Lower Chapel St
 ■ Ilkeston DE7 ...194 C1
 Stonebroom DE55 ...147 A2
Lower Clara Mount Rd DE75 ...182 A1
Lower Cres ST4 ...269 A2
Lower Dale Rd DE23 ...218 C1
Lower Dr DE55 ...169 B4
Lower Gladstone St DE75 ...181 C1
Lower Gn DE65 ...230 B1
Lower Granby St DE7 ...194 C1
Lower Greenshall La S12 ...32 C3
Lower Grove Rd S40 ...266 A3
Lower Hague S32 ...32 C4
Lower Hall Cl DE56 ...191 B3
Lower Hardwick St ■ S17 ...85 A4
Lower High St DE13 ...239 B4
Lower La SK23 ...34 B1
Lower Macclesfield Rd SK23 ...45 C3
Lower Mantle Cl S45 ...131 B2
Lower Maples DE75 ...194 A4
Lower Market St SK14 ...16 A4
Lower Middleton St DE7 ...195 A1
Lower Nelson St DE75 ...181 B1
Lower Orchard St NG9 ...223 B4
Lower Park St NG9 ...223 B3
Lower Parliament St NG1 ...268 B1
Lower Rd DE22 ...217 C4
Lower Smithy La SK17 ...88 A2
Lower Somercotes DE55 ...170 C4
Lower Sq S43 ...10 A4
Lower St DE6 ...224 A4
Lower Stanton Rd DE7 ...208 C3
Lower Strines Rd SK6 ...23 A3
Lower Terr Rd SK17 ...69 A3
Lower Whitworth Rd DE7 ...208 C3
Lowerlea SK12 ...32 B3
Lowes Dr SK6 ...23 A4
Lowes Hill DE5 ...169 B2
Lowes La DE73 ...244 B4
Lowfield Ave S12 ...58 C4
Lowfield Ct 15 S2 ...43 A4
Lowfield Prim Sch S2 ...43 A4
Lowfields S43 ...79 A1
Lowgates S43 ...79 A1
Lowlands Lea DE75 ...181 C1
Lowlands Rd DE56 ...179 A2
Lowndes Cl ST4 ...269 A1
Lowry Cl SK14 ...9 A2
Lowry Dr S18 ...56 C1
Lows Ct DE73 ...233 A1
Lowside S32 ...72 A1
Lowside Cl S32 ...72 C1
Loxley Cl Chesterfield S40 ...95 A2
 Derby DE21 ...206 A1
Loxley La S80 ...82 A3
Loxton Ct DE3 ...217 B2
Loyne Cl DE24 ...231 C1
Lucas Cl DE6 ...228 C1
Lucas Rd S41 ...95 C3
Luccombe Dr DE24 ...233 B3
Lucerne Rd DE21 ...206 B2
Ludborough Wlk NG19 ...136 C2
Ludgate St DE13 ...239 B3
Ludgate Wlk DE22 ...217 C3
Ludham Cl S41 ...95 C4
Ludham Gdns S41 ...95 C4
Ludlam Ave NG16 ...195 A4
Ludlow Cl DE21 ...220 C3
Ludworth Prim Sch S41 ...23 A4
Luke La DE6 ...201 C4
Lukesland Ave S14 ...269 A1
Lullington Mews DE12 ...262 A2
Lullington Rd
 Clifton Campville B79 ...263 C2
 Overseal DE12 ...262 A2
Lulworth Cl DE23 ...231 B3
Lulworth Rise NG16 ...195 C4
Lum's Hill Rise DE4 ...143 B3
Lumb La Hazelwood DE56 ...178 B2
 Northwood DE4 ...127 A3
Lumber La DE6 ...176 B1
Lumford Cotts DE45 ...109 B4
Lumsdale Cres DE4 ...143 B3
Lumsdale Rd
 Matlock DE4 ...143 C3
 Staveley S43 ...97 B4

Luna Croft S12 ...43 C1
Lundie Cl DE24 ...231 B1
Lundy Rd S18 ...76 A4
Lune Mdw NG19 ...136 C2
Lunness Ct NG18 ...268 C3
Lupin Cl DE21 ...206 B2
Lupin Way S44 ...97 A2
Lupton Cres S8 ...56 C3
Lupton Dr S8 ...56 C3
Lupton Rd S8 ...56 C3
Lupton Wlk S8 ...57 A3
Lwr Bank Cl SK13 ...9 C2
Lychgate Cl DE21 ...205 B1
Lydden Cl S43 ...96 C4
Lydford Ave S41 ...77 A1
Lydford Rd DE55 ...159 B3
Lydgate S32 ...71 C3
Lydgate Rd DE22 ...114 C2
Lydia Gdns NG16 ...182 C1
Lydstep Cl DE21 ...206 B1
Lyle Cl NG16 ...195 C4
Lyme Park * SK12 ...32 A1
Lyme Park Ctry Pk SK12 ...32 A1
Lyme Pk SK23 ...34 C1
Lyme Rd SK12 ...32 A3
Lymefield Terr SK14 ...16 A4
Lymewood Dr S12 ...32 B3
Lynam Cl S45 ...131 C2
Lynam Rd DE55,DE56 ...168 B4
Lynam St ST4 ...269 B2
Lyncroft Ave DE5 ...169 C1
Lyndale Dr S41 ...181 A4
Lynden Ave NG10 ...236 B3
Lyndhurst Gr DE21 ...220 A3
Lyndhurst Rd NG2 ...268 C1
Lyndhurst St DE23 ...219 A1
Lyne Cl SK13 ...17 A4
Lynton Cl DE55 ...169 B2
Lynton Rd DE56 ...168 A2
Lynton St DE22 ...218 C2
Lynwood Cl
 Branston DE14 ...253 C4
 ■ Dronfield S18 ...56 B1
Lynwood Rd
 Branston DE14 ...253 C4
 Derby DE24 ...231 C2
Lytham Cl DE21 ...205 B1
Lyttelton St DE22 ...218 B3
Lytton Cl NG3 ...268 C2
Lytton St ST4 ...269 C2

M

M1 Commerce Pk S44 ...98 A2
Macaulay St DE24 ...232 A3
Macclesfield Main Rd SK17 ...84 B3
Macclesfield Old Rd SK17 ...84 B3
Macclesfield Rd
 Buxton SK17 ...85 A3
 Whaley Bridge SK23 ...45 B3
Macdonald Cl S42 ...115 C2
Macdonald Sq DE7 ...208 B3
Machins Cl S18 ...57 A1
Mackenzie St DE22 ...218 B3
Mackinley Ave NG9 ...209 C1
Macklin St DE1 ...267 B3
Mackworth Cl S14 ...256 A4
Mackworth Coll DE22 ...218 A3
Maclagan St S14 ...269 B1
Macready Pl DE24 ...232 C4
Macworth Rd DE1 ...218 C3
Maddock La DE4 ...153 A1
Madehurst Gdns S2 ...43 A4
Madehurst Rd S2 ...43 A4
Madehurst Rise S2 ...43 A4
Madehurst View S2 ...43 A4
Madeley Cl DE3 ...217 B1
Madeley St DE23 ...219 A1
Madford Ret Pk ST16 ...269 A4
Madin Dr S43 ...97 A3
Tupton S42 ...131 B4
Madison Ave DE21 ...219 C4
Madras Rd DE15 ...248 B2
Maesfield Dr ST17 ...269 A3
Mag La Creswell NG20 ...100 B3
 Idridgehay DE56 ...176 B3
Magnolia Way DE55 ...170 A4
Magson St NG3 ...268 C2
Maguire Ave SK13 ...10 A3
Maid Marian Way NG1 ...268 B1
Maiden La ■ NG1 ...268 B1
Maidstone Dr DE24 ...232 C3
Maidwell Cl DE56 ...179 B3
Main Ave Derby DE22 ...204 C3
 Totley S17 ...55 C2
Main Dr S42 ...114 C1
Main Rd Bamford S33 ...40 A2
 Bradwell S33 ...51 A3
 Brailsford DE6 ...201 C4
 Chesterfield S42 ...77 B4
 Crich DE4 ...156 B1
 Eckington S21 ...58 C2
 Elvaston DE72 ...234 A3
 Flagg SK17 ...106 C3
 Grindleford S32 ...72 B4
 Hathersage S32 ...53 A4
 Heath S44 ...117 A1
 Holmesfield S18 ...75 A4
 Old Brampton S42 ...94 C4
 Renishaw S21 ...79 A4
 Ripley DE5 ...169 A2

Main Rd continued
Ripley, Pentrich DE5 ...169 B3
Sheffield S12 ...58 C4
Shirland DE55 ...146 B1
Smalley DE7 ...192 C2
Somercotes DE55 ...170 C3
Stonebroom DE55 ...147 A3
Sudbury DE6 ...225 C3
Sudbury, Aston DE6 ...226 A2
Taddington SK17 ...88 A2
Underwood Green NG16 ...171 C1
Unstone S18 ...76 C4
Wensley DE4 ...127 B1
Westwood NG16 ...171 A2
Whaley Thorns NG20 ...101 A1
Main St Awsworth NG16 ...195 B3
 Blackfordby DE11 ...257 B1
 Bolsover S44 ...117 C4
 Branston DE14 ...253 C4
 Branston, Tatenhill DE13 ...253 A4
 Breaston DE72 ...235 B4
 Breedon on t H DE73 ...252 C1
 Brinsley NG16 ...171 B1
 Burnaston DE65 ...229 C3
 Burton u T, Stapenhill DE15 ...254 C4
 Burton u T, Stretton DE13 ...240 C1
 Caldwell DE12 ...260 C4
 Calver S32 ...72 B1
 Castle Donington DE74 ...247 B3
 Chelmorton SK17 ...106 A4
 Chapel-en-le-F SK23 ...46 C3
 Glossop SK13,SK14 ...9 C3
 Coton in t E DE12 ...260 B2
 Eastwood NG16 ...182 C1
 Egginton DE65 ...241 A3
 Elton DE4 ...140 C4
 Elvaston DE72 ...234 B3
 Etwall DE65 ...229 A2
 Findern DE65 ...230 B1
 Great Longstone DE45 ...90 A2
 Hartshorne DE11 ...257 A3
 Hilton DE65 ...228 B1
 Horsley Woodhouse DE7 ...192 B3
 Kimberley NG16 ...195 C3
 Kirk Ireton DE6 ...165 A1
 Linton DE12 ...261 B3
 Longford DE6 ...247 C3
 Long Eaton NG10 ...236 C4
 Longford DE6 ...214 B4
 Mapperley DE7 ...193 C2
 Melbourne DE73 ...245 B1
 Melbourne, Wilson DE73 ...252 C3
 Middleton (Nr Wirksworth) DE4 ...154 B1
 Moira DE11 ...256 B1
 Netherseal DE12 ...264 C4
 Newton DE55 ...148 A2
 Newton Solney DE15 ...248 C4
 Over Haddon DE45 ...109 A1
 Overseal DE12 ...262 A2
 Palterton S44 ...118 A3
 Repton DE65 ...242 B1
 Rosliston DE12 ...260 B3
 Scarcliffe S44 ...118 C3
 Shirebrook NG20 ...119 B2
 Smisby LE65 ...257 C2
 South Normanton DE55 ...160 A3
 Stanton-by-D DE7 ...222 C4
 Sutton in a NG17 ...148 C2
 Swadlincote DE11 ...255 C3
 Ticknall DE73 ...251 A2
 Ticknall, Milton DE73 ...243 A1
 Walton-on-T DE12 ...253 B1
 Weston-on-T DE72 ...245 C3
 Whaley Thorns NG20 ...101 A1
 Winster DE4 ...141 B3
Maine Dr DE21 ...220 A3
Mair Dr DE4 ...144 A3
Maize Cl DE23 ...231 A3
Makeney Rd Belper DE56 ...191 A3
 Duffield DE56 ...190 C1
 Holbrook DE56 ...191 B3
Malbon's Yd DE6 ...173 B1
Malcolm Gr DE23 ...230 C4
Malcolm St S21 ...219 A1
Malham Cl S40 ...95 B3
Malham Gdns S20 ...59 B4
Malham Rd DE23 ...230 C3
Malia Rd S41 ...96 B3
Malin Cl DE21 ...220 A3
Malinder Cl S21 ...60 B3
Malincommon La DE56 ...166 B2
Malkin St S41 ...266 C3
Mallard Cl Killamarsh S21 ...60 A4
 Derby DE23 ...218 B1
Mallard Wlk 10 DE3 ...230 B4
Mallatratt Pl NG19 ...136 A3
Mallory Cl S41 ...76 C2
Malmesbury Ave DE11 ...256 B3
Malpas Rd S41 ...143 A3
Malson Way S41 ...95 C3
Malt Mill La ST16 ...269 B4
Maltby Ave S20 ...59 C4
Maltby Cl ■ DE22 ...204 C1
Malthouse Cl
 Eastwood NG16 ...182 C1
 Wirksworth DE4 ...154 C2
Malthouse Ct DE56 ...173 B1
Malthouse La
 Ashover S45 ...129 C2
 Belper DE56 ...227 B2
 Nether Heage DE56 ...168 A1
 Stoney Middleton S32 ...72 B3
Malthouse Rd
 Ilkeston DE7 ...208 C2

Malthouse Rd continued
Whitwell S80 ...82 A3
Maltings The
 Ashbourne DE6 ...173 A1
 Burton u T DE15 ...248 A1
 Shardlow DE72 ...235 A1
Maltmill La ■ NG1 ...268 B1
Malton Pl DE21 ...205 B1
Malvern Ave DE15 ...248 A1
Malvern Cl DE21 ...217 B2
Malvern Gdns
 ■ Long Eaton NG10 ...236 A4
 Matlock DE4 ...143 A3
Malvern Rd S40 ...95 C2
Malvern Rise SK13 ...10 A3
Malvern Way DE21 ...205 B1
Malvern La DE11 ...257 B3
Manchester Rd
 Buxton SK17 ...65 C1
 Glossop SK13,SK14 ...9 C3
 Tideswell SK17 ...69 A3
Manchester St
 Derby DE22 ...218 B3
 Long Eaton NG10 ...236 B3
Manifold Ave
 Ashbourne DE6 ...173 B1
 Staveley S43 ...97 B4
Manifold Dr Derby DE24 ...233 A4
 Selston NG16 ...171 C4
Manitoba Way NG16 ...171 C4
Manknell Rd S41 ...96 A4
Manners Ave DE7 ...194 B1
Manners Cl SK23 ...34 B1
Manners Ind Est DE7 ...194 B1
Manners Rd DE7 ...194 C1
Manners St DE7 ...209 A3
Manning View DE7 ...194 C1
Mannion Cres NG10 ...236 A3
Manor Ave Brimington S43 ...96 C4
 Derby DE23 ...218 B2
 Nottingham NG2 ...268 C1
 Stapleford NG9 ...223 B4
Manor Bglws S18 ...56 C1
Manor Cl Belper DE56 ...179 A1
 Brassington DE4 ...153 A1
 Newton DE55 ...148 A2
 Swadlincote DE15 ...255 A3
Manor Cott S45 ...132 B1
Manor Coll S40 ...266 A3
Manor Comp Sch NG19 ...136 B3
Manor Court Rd S44 ...98 C2
Manor Cres S80 ...81 C3
Manor Croft
 Branston DE13 ...253 A4
 Ripley DE5 ...169 B2
Manor Ct
 Burton u T DE15 ...255 A3
 Chesterfield S40 ...95 B2
 Dronfield S18 ...56 C1
Manor Dr Brimington S43 ...96 C4
 Chesterfield S40 ...95 B2
 Long Duckmanton S44 ...98 A2
Manor Farm Rd DE72 ...246 A4
Manor Fields Dr DE7 ...208 B4
Manor Gr S43 ...80 A4
Manor House Rd NG10 ...236 C3
Manor Inf Sch S43 ...96 C3
Manor Leigh DE72 ...235 C2
Manor Park Ct S43 ...218 A2
Manor Park Rd SK13 ...10 C1
Manor Park View ...10 C1
Manor Rd Ashbourne DE6 ...173 B2
 Barlborough S43 ...80 A4
 Barton in F NG11 ...237 C3
 Belper DE56 ...178 C2
 Borrowash DE72 ...221 A1
 Calow S43 ...96 C3
 Chesterfield S40 ...95 B2
 Derby DE21 ...218 B1
 Derby, Chellaston DE73 ...232 C1
 Eastwood NG16 ...182 C1
 Harthill S26 ...61 C4
 Ilkeston DE7 ...194 C1
 Killamarsh S21 ...60 C3

Mansfield Gr NG1 ...268 B1
Mansfield Rd
 Alfreton DE55 ...159 A3
 Bramley-Vale S44 ...117 B2
 Brinsley NG16 ...182 C4
 Chesterfield S41 ...266 C4
 Clowne S43 ...80 C2
 Creswell S80 ...81 C1
 Derby DE21 ...219 C4
 Eastwood NG16 ...182 C4
 Glapwell NG19,S44 ...134 A3
 Heanor DE75 ...181 C1
 Heath S44 ...117 A1
 Holmewood S42 ...116 C1
 Killamarsh S21, S26 ...60 C2
 Mansfield Woodhouse NG19 ...136 B2
 Market Warsop NG20 ...121 A4
 Nottingham NG1 ...268 B2
 Palterton S44 ...118 A3
 Scarcliffe S44 ...118 C3
 Selston NG16 ...171 C4
 Sheffield S12 ...44 A3
 South Normanton DE55 ...160 B2
 Tibshelf DE55 ...148 A3
 Whitwell S80 ...82 A3
Mansfield St Derby DE1 ...267 B4
 Somercotes DE55 ...170 C3
Mansfield Sta NG18 ...268 B3
Mansfield Woodhouse NG19 ...136 B3
Mansfields Croft DE65 ...228 C1
Manton Cl
 ■ Burton u T DE13 ...240 C1
 Swadlincote DE11 ...255 C1
Manvers Ave DE5 ...180 C4
Manvers Rd NG20 ...120 C3
Manvers St S44 ...99 A1
Manvers St
 ■ Mansfield NG18 ...268 C3
 Mansfield Woodhouse NG19 ...136 B2
 Market Warsop NG20 ...120 C3
 Nottingham NG2 ...268 C1
 Ripley DE5 ...169 C1
Manystones La DE4 ...153 B2
Maple Ave Derby DE23 ...218 A1
 Disley SK12 ...32 C4
 Ripley DE5 ...180 B4
 Sandiacre NG10 ...223 A3
Maple Cl Doveridge DE6 ...211 A1
 Mansfield NG19 ...136 C4
Maple Ct ST17 ...269 A4
Maple Dr Ashbourne DE6 ...173 B2
 Aston-on-T DE72 ...246 A4
 Belper DE56 ...179 A1
 Creswell S80 ...81 C1
 Derby DE73 ...232 C1
 Killamarsh S21 ...60 C4
 South Normanton DE55 ...160 B4
Maple Gdns DE75 ...181 C2
Maple Gr Breaston DE72 ...235 B4
 Burton u T DE15 ...254 C3
 Glapwell S44 ...134 A4
Maple Rd DE11 ...256 A3
Maple St S44 ...99 A1
Maple View DE4 ...156 B1
Maple Way
 Branston DE14 ...253 C4
 Burton u T DE14 ...254 A4
 Selston NG16 ...171 C4
Maplebeck Ct DE1 ...267 C4
Maples The DE75 ...181 C2
Mapletoft Ave NG19 ...136 B1
Mapleton Ave DE21 ...205 C1
Mapleton Rd
 Ashbourne DE6 ...172 C2
 Draycott DE72 ...235 A4
Mapperley Ce Prim Sch DE7 ...193 C4
Mapperley La DE7 ...193 C4
Mapperley Rd 6 S18 ...56 C1
Marchington Cl DE22 ...204 C2
Marchwood Cl S41 ...115 C4
Marchwood Ct S14 ...269 B1
Marcus St S41 ...266 C4
Mardale Cl S41 ...95 C4
Maree Cl DE24 ...231 C2
Marfleet Cl DE3 ...217 C2
Margaret Ave
 Derby DE21 ...220 A2
 Ilkeston DE7 ...208 C4
 Long Eaton NG10 ...236 A4
 Sandiacre NG10 ...223 A4
Margaret St DE1 ...267 B4
Margery Cl DE6 ...173 B2
Margreave Rd DE21 ...220 A2
Marham Cl NG2 ...268 C1
Marigold Cl DE21 ...206 A2
Marigold Pl DE11 ...256 A3
Marina Dr
 Derby, Allenton DE24 ...232 C3
 Derby, Spondon DE21 ...220 C2
Marina Rd DE7 ...208 C4
Marion St SK17 ...85 B3
Maris Ct NG7 ...268 A2
Marjorie Rd DE21 ...219 C4
Marjory La DE6,DE65 ...227 C4
Mark St NG10 ...223 B1
Mark's Cl DE12 ...261 C3
Markeaton La DE22 ...217 C4
Markeaton Prim Sch DE22 ...218 A4
Markeaton St DE22 ...267 A4
Market Arc SK13 ...10 B1

et Cl
brook NG20 ....119 C2
Normanton DE55 ...160 A3
et Pl Alfreton DE55 ..158 C2
on, Riddings DE55 ...170 C3
ourne DE6 ....173 B1
r DE56 ....179 A2
ver S44 ....99 A1
uxton SK17 ....85 A4
eton S33 ....38 B1
el-en-le-F SK23 ....47 A3
erfield S40 ....266 B3
or DE5 ....181 A4
stall SK6 ....15 A1
DE4 ....156 C1
ford DE4 ....155 A3
ngton SK17 ....137 B3
ton DE7 ....208 C4
ille NG16 ....170 C2
Eaton NG10 ....236 C4
nor SK17 ....121 A3
field NG18 ....268 B4
sfield Woodhouse
 ....136 B2
ourne DE73 ....252 A4
ram in L SK14 ....9 A2
y DE5 ....169 B1
rcotes DE55 ....170 B4
Normanton DE55 ...160 A3
eley S43 ....78 C1
n in A NG17 ....148 C2
well SK17 ....69 B2
sworth DE4 ....165 C4
et Sq
tafford ST16 ....269 B4
well SK17 ....69 B2
et St Bakewell DE45 .109 B3
dbottom SK14 ....16 A4
on SK17 ....85 A4
e Donington DE74 ....247 A2
el-en-le-F SK23 ....47 A3
Cross S45 ....131 B2
y SK12 ....32 B3
cott DE72 ....235 A4
gton S21 ....59 B2
sop SK13 ....10 B1
ield SK22 ....25 B2
nor DE75 ....181 C1
ngworth SK14 ....9 B3
ston DE7 ....208 C4
ville NG16 ....170 C2
sfield NG18 ....268 B4
ram in L SK14 ....9 A2
Mills SK22 ....33 A4
ingham NG1 ....268 B1
ebrook NG20 ....119 C2
h Normanton DE55 ...160 A3
ord ST16 ....269 B4
eley S43 ....78 C1
on in A NG17 ....148 C2
dlincote DE11 ....256 A2
ley Bridge SK23 ....45 C4
kham Cres S43 ....78 C1
kham Ct Derby DE21 .205 C1
Duckmanton S44 .....98 A3
kham La S44 ....98 A2
kham Rd
sterfield S40 ....266 B2
Duckmanton S44 .....98 A3
kham Rise S45 ....131 A2
kland Ave S43 ....81 A2
kland Cres S43 ....81 A2
kland La S80,S43 ......81 A1
kland View S80 ....81 B2
borough Cres DE15 .255 A4
borough Dr DE56 ...179 B3
borough Rd
aston DE72 ....235 B4
on SK17 ....85 A4
by DE24 ....232 B4
g Eaton NG10 ....223 C1
sfield NG19 ....135 C1
borough St ST4 ....269 C1
ow Brow SK13 ....10 A2
ow Cres DE7 ....207 B4
ow Dr DE14 ....254 A4
ow St 5 Buxton SK17 .85 B4
Glossop SK13 ....10 A3
owe Ct DE23 ....231 C3
pit La Bolsover S44 ...99 B2
stone ST14 ....196 B3
stone DE6 ....183 A2
on on t H DE6 ....228 A4
pool Inf Sch DE75 ..194 A4
pool Jun Sch DE75 .182 A1
ple Rd SK13 ....16 A3
ple Sq 5 NG3 ....268 B2
ple Sta SK6 ....23 A4
ples Ave NG19 ......136 C3
quis Ct DE12 ....262 C3
quis Dr DE12 ....262 C3
riott Ave NG18 ......268 A4
rison Dr S21 ....60 B3
sden Cl DE56 ....190 C2
sden Pl 2 S40 ....95 B1
sden Row S33 ....40 A2
sden St
sterfield S40 ....266 B3
by DE24 ....232 C4
ssop SK13 ....10 A2
sh Ave Dronfield S18 ...57 A2
e S33 ....38 C2
sh Cl S20 ....59 B3
sh Green La S45 ....129 C2
sh Hall La SK23 ....46 C3
sh Hollow DE6 ......200 C3
sh La Belper DE56 ....179 A3
yfield DE6 ....183 B4

Marsh La continued
New Mills SK22,SK23 ......33 B3
Marsh Lane Cres DE56 ..179 A2
Marsh Lane Prim Sch
S21 ....58 C2
Marsh Lane Trad Est
SK22 ....33 B4
Marsh View S21 ....59 A1
Marshall Dr 1 NG9 .....223 C4
Marshall St
Alfreton DE55 ....159 A2
Heanor DE75 ....181 C1
Marsham Dr SK6 ....23 A3
Marshaw Cl DE3 ....217 C1
Marshes The S33 ....38 C2
Marshfield Gr S43 ....79 A1
Marshgreen Cl DE24 .....233 B3
Marston SK17 ....106 A4
Marston Brook DE65 ....228 C1
Marston Cl Belper DE56 ..179 B3
Derby DE23 ....231 B3
Dronfield S18 ....75 B4
Marston Cres S17 ....55 C3
Marston La
Doveridge DE6 ....211 B2
Hatton DE65 ....239 B4
Marston on D DE65 ......228 A1
Marston Montgomery Prim
Sch DE6 ....211 C4
Marston Old La DE65 ...239 B4
Marston Rd DE65 ....240 A4
Marston Rise DE15 .....254 C4
Martin Ct S21 ....59 B2
Martin Dr Derby DE21 ..220 A4
Stafford ST16 ....269 A4
Martin Rise S21 ....59 B2
Martin St ST16 ....269 B4
Martin's La DE13 ....238 A2
Martindale Ct DE56 .....179 B3
Martins La S42 ....131 A4
Martlet Ave SK12 ....32 B3
Marx Ct S45 ....131 B2
Mary Ann St S41 ....76 C2
Mary Devonshire Cotts
DE45 ....91 B1
Mary Howitt Inf Sch
DE75 ....181 B1
Mary St Eckington S21 .....59 B2
Whaley Thorns NG20 .....101 A1
Mary Swanwick Prim Sch
S41 ....77 A2
Maryfield Wlk ST4 ......269 A2
Maryland Ct
Stapleford NG9 ....209 C1
Swadlincote DE11 ....256 A4
Maryland Rd DE21 ......220 A3
Marylebone Cres DE22 ..218 A3
Masefield Ave
Derby DE23 ....231 C4
Holmewood S42 ....116 B1
Swadlincote DE11 ....256 B3
Masefield Rd S13 ....44 B4
Mason Cres S13 ....44 B4
Mason Gr S13 ....44 B4
Mason Rd DE7 ....194 B1
Mason St S80 ....81 C3
Masonic Pl NG1 ....268 A2
Masons Gr SK13 ....10 A3
Massey Gdns NG3 ....268 C2
Masson Cl S40 ....95 B3
Masson Rd DE4 ....143 A1
Masson Shopping Village
DE4 ....155 A4
Masson Wlk DE22 ....218 C2
Masterson St ST4 ....269 C1
Mastin Ave S43 ....80 B3
Mather's Way S42 ....115 B1
Matlock Ave NG18 ....268 B3
Matlock Bath Sta DE4 ...143 A1
Matlock Ct
Long Eaton NG10 ....235 C3
31 Nottingham NG1 .....268 B2
Matlock Dr S43 ....97 B3
Matlock Gdns 11 SK13 .....9 C1
Matlock Gn DE4 ....143 B2
Matlock Ho DE21 ....220 C2
Matlock Pl 12 SK13 ....9 C1
Matlock Rd
Ambergate DE56 ....167 C2
Ashover S42,S45 ....113 C2
Belper DE56 ....178 C4
Brackenfield DE55 ....145 B1
Derby DE21 ....205 C1
Holymoorside S40,S42 ...114 A4
Wessington DE55 ....157 C4
Matlock Riverside Sta*
DE4 ....143 A3
Matlock St DE45 ....109 B3
Matlock Sta DE4 ....143 A3
Matt Orch DE55 ....160 A2
Mattersey Ct NG19 ......136 A1
Matthew Cl SK13 ....9 C4
Matthew Holland Comp Sch
NG16 ....171 C4
Matthew Kirtley Mus*
DE5 ....170 A2
Matthew St DE24 ....232 C3
Matthew Way DE23 .....230 C4
Matthews Ct NG9 ....209 C1
Matthews Fold S8 ....43 B1
Matthews La S8 ....43 B1
Maude St S21 ....59 B2
Maugerhay S8 ....43 B1
Maunleigh NG19 ....136 C1
Mawfa Ave S14 ....43 B1
Mawfa Cres S14 ....43 B1
Mawfa Dr S14 ....43 B1
Mawfa Rd S14 ....43 B1

Mawfa Wlk S14 ....43 B1
Mawkin La NG16 ....160 C3
Maws La NG16 ....195 C4
Mawstone La DE45 .....125 A2
Max Rd DE21 ....219 C4
Maxey Pl S8 ....43 A3
Maxtoke Rd NG7 ....268 A1
Maxwell Ave DE22 ......218 B4
Maxwell Pl ST4 ....269 A2
Maxwell St DE72 ....235 C4
May Ave S41 ....77 B2
May S DE7 ....194 B2
May St Derby DE22 .....218 C2
Ilkeston DE7 ....194 C2
Maybank Cl SK23 ....35 A1
Mayfair DE11 ....255 C3
Mayfair Ave NG18 ......268 C3
Mayfair Cres DE22 .....217 C3
Mayfield Ave
Heanor DE75 ....181 C1
Kilburn DE56 ....192 A4
Mayfield DE6 ....184 B4
Mayfield Dr
Burton u T DE15 ....255 A4
North Wingfield S42 .....131 C3
Stapleford NG9 ....209 C1
Mayfield Gr NG10 ....223 C1
Mayfield Pl W ST4 ......269 A1
Mayfield Rd
Burton u T DE15 ....248 A2
Chesterfield S40 ....95 B1
Derby DE21 ....219 C4
Marple SK6 ....15 A1
Ringinglow S10 ....42 C4
Mayfield Terr
Hathersage S32 ....53 A4
Mayfield DE6 ....184 B3
Mayflower Ct
Sheffield S12 ....44 A3
Shirebrook NG20 ....119 C2
Mayflower Rd NG16 ....195 A4
Mayhall Ave NG19 ......136 A2
Maylands DE72 ....221 A1
Maylands Ave DE72 ....235 C4
Maynard Rd
Chesterfield S40 ....266 A1
Nether Padley S32 ....53 B1
Maynestone Rd SK23 .....34 C3
Maypole Hill DE11 ......256 A3
Maypole La DE23 ....230 C4
McAdam Cl DE15 ....248 A1
McAuley Ct DE1 ....267 B4
McGough Mews DE24 ..232 A3
McGregor's Way S40 ...115 A4
McMahon Ave S43 ....97 A3
McNeil Gr DE72 ....235 A4
Mead Cl DE24 ....231 C2
Mead Cres DE15 ....255 A3
Mead Wlk DE15 ....255 A3
Meadow Ave Buxton SK17 .67 A3
Codnor DE5 ....181 A4
Mansfield NG18 ....268 C3
Meadow Bank
Glossop SK13 ....16 C4
Hollingworth SK14 ....9 B3
Mansfield Woodhouse
NG19 ....136 C3
South Normanton DE55 ..160 A4
Meadow Brook Cl DE23 .230 C3
Meadow Cl
Barlborough S43 ....80 B3
Bolsover S44 ....118 A4
Breaston DE72 ....235 C4
Chesterfield S43 ....77 B1
Derby DE21 ....220 C2
Dove Holes SK17 ....47 C1
Draycott DE72 ....235 A4
Dronfield S18 ....57 B2
Eastwood NG16 ....182 C2
Findern DE65 ....230 B1
Horsley Woodhouse DE7 ..192 B3
Repton DE65 ....242 C1
Stoney Middleton S32 .....72 A2
Tibshelf DE55 ....148 A4
Whaley Bridge SK23 ....45 B4
Meadow Cotts NG19 ....136 B2
Meadow Cres
Castle Donington DE74 ..247 A1
Mosborough S20 ....59 A4
Meadow Croft S42 ......132 B4
Meadow Ct Belper DE56 ..178 C2
Chesterfield S43 ....77 B2
Kilburn DE56 ....192 A4
South Normanton DE55 ..159 C2
Meadow Dr S43 ....78 C1
Meadow Farm Com Prim Sch
DE21 ....220 A2
Meadow Gdns DE75 ....182 A1
Meadow Gr
Newton DE55 ....148 A2
Totley S17 ....55 C2
Meadow Grove Rd S17 ...55 B2
Meadow Head Ave S8 ....56 C4
Meadow Head Dr S8 .....56 C4
Meadow La
Burton u T DE13 ....248 A4
Derby DE1, DE21 ....267 D3
Derby, Chaddesden DE21 ..219 C3
Disley SK12 ....32 B3
Dove Holes SK17 ....47 C1
Long Eaton NG10 ....236 C4
Newton DE55 ....159 C4
Nottingham NG2 ....268 C1
Repton DE65 ....243 A2
Roston DE6 ....197 B4
Swadlincote DE11 ....256 A3
Tideswell SK17 ....69 A1

Meadow Lane Ind Est
DE55 ....159 A3
Meadow Nook DE24 ....233 B3
Meadow Rd
Awsworth NG16 ....195 B3
Clay Cross S45 ....131 A3
Derby DE1 ....267 C3
Derby, Wilmorton DE21,
DE24 ....219 C1
Ripley DE5 ....169 C1
Meadow Rise
Brassington DE4 ....153 A1
Church Broughton DE65 ..227 A4
Glossop SK13 ....16 C4
Old Brampton S42 ....94 C2
Meadow St Ilkeston DE7 .194 C1
Ironville NG16 ....170 C3
New Mills SK22 ....33 B4
Meadow Vale DE56 .....190 B2
Meadow View
Belper DE56 ....178 C2
Bolsover S43 ....80 C2
Chesterfield S40 ....114 A4
Darley Dale DE4 ....142 C4
Doveridge DE6 ....224 B4
Holmewood S42 ....132 B4
Rolleston DE13 ....240 B2
South Wingfield DE55 ....157 C3
Meadow View Cl DE21 ..206 A2
Meadow View Rd
Sheffield S8 ....56 C4
Swadlincote DE11 ....255 C3
Meadow Way
Derby DE73 ....233 A1
Swadlincote DE11 ....256 A3
Meadowbank Way
NG16 ....182 B2
Meadowbrook Ind Est
S20 ....60 A4
Meadowcroft SK14 ....9 A2
Meadowcroft Gdns S20 ..59 C4
Meadowcroft Glade S20 ..59 C4
Meadowcroft Rise S20 ...59 C4
Meadowfield SK23 ....45 B4
Meadowfield Cl SK13 ......9 C2
Meadowgrass Cl DE23 ...231 A3
Meadowhead S8 ....57 A4
Meadowhead Sch S8 ......57 A3
Meadowhead Sec Sch
S8 ....57 A4
Meadowhill Rd S41 ......115 B4
Meadowlands S44 ....99 B1
Meadowlark Gr DE21 ...206 A1
Meadows Com Sch The
S41 ....77 A2
Meadows Croft DE56 ....190 B2
Meadows Dr S43 ....97 C4
Meadows Ind Est The
DE21 ....219 B3
Meadows Prim Sch
DE56 ....190 B2
Meadows Rd SK22 ....25 B1
Meadows The
Chesterfield S42 ....94 C3
Dove Holes SK17 ....47 C1
Great Longstone DE45 .....90 A2
Heanor DE75 ....181 C1
Old Brampton S42 ....95 A3
Swanwick DE55 ....169 C4
Uttoxeter ST14 ....210 A1
Meadowside Disley SK12 ..33 A3
Mayfield DE6 ....184 B3
Whaley Bridge SK23 ....45 B4
Meadowside Cl
Shirley DE6 ....200 B4
Wingerworth S42 ....115 A2
Meads The S8 ....57 A4
Meadway Dr S17 ....55 B4
Meadway The S17 ....55 B4
Meakin St S41 ....115 B4
Meal Hill Rd HD7 ....2 C4
Meal St SK22 ....33 B4
Mear Dr DE72 ....221 A1
Mear Greaves La DE15 ..248 A2
Mease La B79 ....263 A1
Mease The DE65 ....228 C1
Measham Rd
Donisthorpe DE12 ....265 B3
Moira DE12 ....262 C2
Stretton en le F DE12 ....265 C1
Meath Ave DE21 ....220 A2
Meden Ave NG19 ....134 C4
Meden Bank NG19 ....135 A3
Meden Cl NG19 ....135 A3
Meden Rd NG19 ....136 B2
Meden Sq NG19 ....135 A3
Medina Cl DE24 ....233 B3
Medlock Cl S40 ....114 A4
Medlock Rd S40 ....114 B4
Medway Dr DE22 ....205 A3
Meerbrook Cl DE21 .....206 A1
Meerbrook Pl DE7 ....208 B3
Meersbrook Park Rd S8 ..43 A3
Meersbrook Rd S8 ....43 A3
Megaloughton La DE21 .220 B2
Megdale DE4 ....143 A3
Melandra Castle Rd SK13 ..9 B1
Melandra Ct DE22 ....218 C2
Melandra Rd SK13 ....9 C2
Melanie Cl SK13 ....17 A4
Melbourn Cl DE56 ....190 C2
Melbourne Ave
Burton u T DE15 ....248 B2
Dronfield S18 ....56 A1
Melbourne Cl
Belper DE56 ....179 A1
Derby DE22 ....204 B1
Derby, Mickleover DE3 ...217 C2

Melbourne Ct
Long Eaton NG10 ....235 C2
8 Staveley S43 ....78 C1
Melbourne Hall* DE73 ..252 A4
Melbourne Hall & Gdns*
DE73 ....252 A4
Melbourne Ho DE21 ....220 C2
Melbourne Inf Sch
DE73 ....252 A4
Melbourne Jun Sch
DE73 ....252 A4
Melbourne La
Breedon on t H DE73 ....252 C1
Ticknall DE73 ....251 B3
Melbourne Rd NG9 .....209 C1
Melbourne St Derby DE1 .267 B1
Mansfield Woodhouse
NG19 ....136 B3
Melbreak Cl DE3 ....217 C1
Melfort Cl DE24 ....231 C1
Meliden Way ST4 ....269 A1
Melling Cl S40 ....114 C4
Melling Ct S40 ....114 C4
Mellington Cl S8 ....43 B1
Mellor Dr ST14 ....210 A1
Mellor La Barlow S18 .....75 C1
Chapel-en-le-F SK23 ....47 A3
Mellor Prim Sch SK6 .....23 B3
Mellor Rd
Burton u T DE14 ....254 A4
New Mills SK6,SK22 ....24 B2
Mellor St DE24 ....232 C3
Mellor Way S40 ....115 A4
Mellor's La DE56 ....191 B3
Melrose Ave NG18 ....268 C3
Melrose Cl
Chesterfield S40 ....95 B2
Derby DE24 ....231 C1
Melrose Ct 7 S41 ....96 A3
Meltham La S41 ....96 A3
Melton Ave Derby DE23 ..231 B3
Melbourne DE73 ....252 A4
Melton Ct
Sandiacre NG10 ....223 A3
Somercotes DE55 ....170 B3
Melville Cl DE6 ....175 C2
Melville Cres S43 ....96 C2
Melville Ct DE65 ....229 A2
Melville Gdns NG3 ....268 C2
Melville St NG1 ....268 B1
Memorial Croft DE4 .....154 C2
Memorial Rd DE22 ......204 B2
Mendip Cl 1 NG10 ......223 A1
Mendip Cres S40 ....95 A2
Mendip Ct DE21 ....205 C1
Menin Rd DE22 ....204 B1
Mentmore Cl DE55 ......170 A4
Mercaston Cl S40 ....95 A3
Mercaston La
Hulland Ward DE6 ....188 A2
Mackworth DE6,DE22 ....203 A4
Mercaston Rd DE21 .....219 C4
Mercer Cres DE55 ....159 B2
Merchant Ave DE21 .....220 B2
Merchant St Derby DE22 .218 C3
Shirebrook NG20 ....120 A2
Mercia Cl
Eastwood NG16 ....195 A4
Hatton DE65 ....239 B4
Mercia Dr Dore S17 ....55 C3
Willington DE65 ....242 A3
Mercian Cl DE7 ....194 C1
Mercian Mews DE21 ....220 B2
Meredith Ct NG9 ....209 C1
Mereoak La DE11,DE73 ..257 C4
Meridian Cl DE7 ....194 C2
Merion Gr DE23 ....218 A1
Merlin Cl DE56 ....179 B3
Merlin Cres DE14 ....253 C4
Merlin Gn DE24 ....231 B2
Merlin Way
Burnaston DE3 ....230 A4
Ilkeston DE7 ....208 C2
Woodville DE11 ....256 C2
Merrial Cl DE45 ....109 B2
Merrick Cl S40 ....95 B3
Merridale Rd DE23 ......231 B4
Merrill Coll DE24 ....232 C2
Merrill Coll (Lower Site)
DE24 ....232 C3
Merrill Way DE24 ....232 B3
Merrybower Cl DE24 ...231 B2
Merrydale Rd DE15 .....255 A4
Mersey Bank Rd SK13 .....9 C2
Merthyr Ct DE21 ....206 A1
Merton Ct NG9 ....209 C1
Mervyn Rd DE15 ....248 A2
Metcalfe Cl DE24 ....233 A4
Metcalfe Way S21 ....60 B3
Meteor Ctr The DE21 ...205 B1
Methley Cl S12 ....43 C3
Metro Ave DE55 ....148 A2
Mettesford DE4 ....143 B3
Meverill Rd SK17 ....69 B3
Mevril Rd SK23 ....45 C3
Mewies Cl DE12 ....253 B1
Mews The DE73 ....252 A4
Meynell Cl
Burton u T DE15 ....248 A1
Chesterfield S40 ....95 B1
Meynell Ct DE22 ....204 B1
Meynell Rd NG10 ....236 B3
Meynell Rise DE6 ....173 B2
Meynell St Derby DE23 ..218 C1
Swadlincote DE11 ....256 A1

Meynell Way S41 ....60 B3
Meyrick Rd ST17 ....269 B3
Michael Cl S42 ....115 A3
Michael House-Rudolf
  Steiner Sch DE75 .....194 A3
Michael's La DE6 ....183 B3
Michelle Cl DE24 ....231 B2
Michigan Cl DE21 ....220 B3
Michlow Cl S33 ....51 A4
Michlow Dr S33 ....51 A4
Michlow La S33 ....51 A4
Mickleover Manor DE3 ...217 B1
Micklebring Cl DE5 ....169 B1
Micklecroft Gdns DE23 ..230 C4
Mickledon Cl ⑤ NG10 ..236 A4
Mickleover Prim Sch
  DE3 ....217 B1
Mickleross Cl DE3 ....217 B2
Mickleton Cl DE11 ......256 A1
Mickley Est DE55 ....146 B3
Mickley Inf Sch DE55 ...146 B2
Mickley La Shirland DE55 .146 B3
  Totley S17 ....55 C2
Middle Cl DE11 ....256 A2
Middle Friars ST17 ....269 B3
Middle Hay Cl S14 ....43 C2
Middle Hay Pl S14 ....43 C2
Middle Hay Rise S14 .....43 C2
Middle Hay View S14 .....43 C2
Middle Hill NG1 ....268 B2
Middle La Clay Cross S45 .131 C2
  Crich DE4 ....156 B1
Middle Ox Cl S20 ....59 C3
Middle Ox Gdns S20 ......59 C3
Middle Pavement
  Chesterfield S40 ....266 B3
  ⑤ Nottingham NG1 .....268 B1
Middle Rd S42 ....114 C1
Middle Shambles S40 ....266 B3
Middle St Bolsover S44 ...99 A1
  Bolsover, Hillstown S44 ..118 B4
Middlebeck Cl DE73 ......232 C1
Middlecroft L.Cir S43 ....97 B4
Middlecroft Rd S43 ....97 B4
Middlefield Cl S17 ....55 B4
Middlefield Croft S17 .....55 B4
Middlegate Field Dr S80 ..82 A3
Middleton Ave
  Codnor DE5 ....181 A3
  Derby DE23 ....218 B1
Middleton Dr S43 ....97 A3
Middleton La S32 ....71 B2
Middleton Prim Sch
  DE4 ....154 B2
Middleton Rd
  Ilkeston DE7 ....209 A3
  Mansfield Woodhouse
  NG19 ....136 B3
Middleton St
  Awsworth NG16 ....195 B2
  Cossall DE7 ....195 A1
  Derby DE23 ....219 A1
Middleton Top Visitor's Ctr*
  DE4 ....154 B2
Middletown Mdws S43 ....80 A3
Midhill Rd S2 ....43 A4
Midland Ave NG9 ....223 B3
Midland Cl S41 ....115 A4
Midland Pl DE1 ....267 D2
Midland Railway Ctr*
  DE5 ....169 C2
Midland Rd Derby DE1 ..267 D2
  Eastwood NG16 ....182 C1
  Heanor DE75 ....181 C1
  Swadlincote DE11 ......256 A2
Midland Road Ind Est
  DE11 ....256 A3
Midland St NG10 ....236 C4
Midland Terr
  Ambergate DE56 ....167 C2
  Barrow Hill S43 ....78 A2
  Blackwell DE55 ....147 B1
  Chesterfield S41 ....115 A4
  New Mills SK22 ....33 B4
Midland View S43 ....80 A3
Midway DE22 ....204 C1
Midway Ctr S45 ....131 B2
Midway Rd DE11 ....256 B3
Midworth St NG18 ....268 B3
Mikado Rd NG10 ....236 B3
Milbank Cl DE22 ....217 C3
Milburn Gdns DE21 .....206 A2
Milbury Cl DE21 ....205 C1
Mile Ash La DE22 ....204 C1
Milford DE45 ....109 B3
Milford Ave NG10 ....223 A2
Milford Com Prim Sch
  DE56 ....190 C4
Milford Dr DE45 ....109 B3
Milford Dr DE7 ....194 B2
Milford Dr Duffield DE56 .190 C2
  Staveley S43 ....97 B3
Milford St DE1 ....218 C4
Milken La S45 ....130 A2
Mill Acre Cl DE7 ....194 B1
Mill Brow
  Broadbottom SK14 ......16 A4
  Marple SK6 ....23 B4
Mill Cl Rd SK6 ....23 C4
Mill Cl Borrowash DE72 ..221 B1
  Findern DE65 ....230 B1
  Kilburn DE56 ....192 A4
  Newton Solney DE15 ...248 C4
  Swadlincote DE11 ......256 B3

Mill Cl continued
  Swanwick DE55 ....169 C4
Mill Cliff SK17 ....49 A4
Mill Cres Whitwell S80 ....82 A3
Mill Croft
  Ashover DE4 ....115 B2
Mill Cft DE13 ....217 B2
Mill Farm Cl S32 ....72 B1
Mill Fleam DE65 ....228 C2
Mill Gn Shardlow DE72 ..235 A1
  Staveley S43 ....78 C1
Mill Green Cl DE12 .....260 B2
Mill Hill Sch DE5 ....180 C4
Mill Hill Elvaston DE24 ..233 B2
  Long Duckmanton S44 ..117 A3
Mill Hill Dr DE15 ....169 C1
Mill Hill Dr DE15 ....248 A2
Mill Hill La
  Breaston DE72 ....222 C1
  Burton u T DE15 ....248 A2
  Derby DE1, DE23 ....267 A1
Mill Hill Rd DE23 ....267 A1
Mill Holme DE55 ....160 A2
Mill La Ashbourne DE6 ...173 C1
  Barlow S18 ....75 B2
  Belper DE56 ....179 C4
  Bolsover S44 ....99 A2
  Bolsover, Shuttlewood S44 .98 C4
  Bradbourne DE6 ....163 A3
  Castleton S33 ....38 B2
  Chesterfield S40 ....95 B1
  Clay Cross S42, S45 ....130 C3
  Codnor DE5 ....181 A4
  Cossall NG16 ....195 B1
  Derby DE3 ....217 B2
  Doveridge DE6 ....211 A1
  Dronfield S18 ....57 B4
  Ellastone DE6 ....183 A1
  Eyam S32 ....71 C3
  Grassmoor S42 ....115 B2
  Hartington SK17 ....137 B3
  Heath S44 ....117 A1
  Hilton DE65 ....228 B1
  Holloway DE4 ....156 A3
  Holmesfield S18 ....74 C3
  Holmewood S44 ....133 B4
  Pinxton NG16 ....160 B3
  Renishaw S21 ....60 A1
  Roston DE6 ....197 B4
  Sandiacre NG10 ....223 B3
  Scropton DE65 ....226 C1
  Scropton, Foston DE65 .226 B4
  Shirley DE6 ....200 B4
  Sutton in A NG17 ....148 C1
  Totley S17 ....55 C3
  Whitwell S80 ....82 A3
Mill Meadow Way DE65 .229 A2
Mill Pond DE73 ....232 C1
Mill Rd Cromford DE4 ...155 A3
  Heanor DE75 ....194 A4
  Stapleford NG9 ....223 B4
Mill Row DE21 ....220 B3
Mill St Bakewell DE45 ..109 B3
  Barlow S18 ....75 B2
  Belper DE56 ....179 A2
  Chesterfield S41 ....266 C3
  Clowne S43 ....80 C2
  Coton in t E DE12 ......260 B2
  Derby DE1 ....218 C3
  Glossop SK13 ....10 B1
  Hayfield SK22 ....25 B2
  Ilkeston DE7 ....194 C1
  Mansfield NG18 ....268 C3
  Rocester ST14 ....197 A2
  Stafford ST16 ....269 B4
  Stoney Middleton S32 ...72 A2
Mill Stream Cl S40 ....95 B1
Mill Wlk Bolsover S44 ....99 A2
  Whitwell S80 ....82 A3
Mill Yd DE55 ....170 B4
Millash La S80 ....82 A2
Millbank Heanor DE75 ..194 A4
  Stafford ST16 ....269 B4
Millbank Ave DE56 ......179 A4
Millbank Cl DE7 ....194 B2
Millbank Dr ST14 ....197 A2
Millbrook SK14 ....9 C3
Millcross La S18 ....75 C2
Milldale Ave SK17 ....84 C3
Milldale Cl
  Chesterfield S40 ....95 B3
  Ripley DE5 ....180 B3
Milldale Ct
  Ashbourne DE6 ....185 B4
  Belper DE56 ....179 A2
Milldale Rd Derby DE21 .220 C2
  Long Eaton NG10 ......236 A3
  Totley S17 ....55 C3
Milldam La DE6 ....262 C3
Millenium Ave DE12 ....262 C3
Millennium Cl DE7 ......194 C2
Millennium Way
  Chesterfield S41 ....76 C1
  Derby DE24 ....219 C2
Miller Ave S43 ....79 B2
Millers Dale Cl DE56 ...179 B3
Millers Gn DE4 ....165 C3
Millers La DE55 ....145 C1
Millersdale Ave DE7 ....194 C3
Millersdale Cl DE15 ....248 A3
Millersdale Ct S13 ......10 C1
Millersdale Way S17 ....85 A3
Millfield DE72 ....235 A4
Millfield Cl DE7 ....194 B2
Millfield Croft ⑩ DE11 .256 A4
Millfield Rd Ilkeston DE7 .209 A4
  Kimberley NG16 ....195 C4
Millfield St DE11 ....257 A1
Millhouse Ct DE72 ......235 A4

Millom Pl DE21 ....205 B1
Millpool Cl DE11 ....257 A4
Mills Cl DE72 ....235 A4
Mills Ct DE4 ....156 C1
Millstone Cl ⑤ S18 .....56 B1
Millstone La
  Ashford in t W DE45 ...108 C4
  Ripley DE5 ....169 B4
Millthorpe La S18 ....75 A3
Millthorn S43 ....10 B1
Millview Cl NG2 ....268 C1
Millway NG19 ....136 B1
Millway La DE6 ....149 C2
Milnbank Ave SK17 ......85 B4
Milner Ave Codnor DE5 .181 A4
  Draycott DE72 ....235 A4
Milner Rd NG10 ....236 B4
Milnhay Rd NG16 ....182 B1
Milton Ave Alfreton DE55 .159 B2
  Ilkeston DE7 ....194 C2
  Shirland DE55 ....146 B2
  Swadlincote DE11 ......256 B3
Milton Cres S45 ....115 A4
Milton Cl SK17 ....85 A4
Milton La S43 ....46 A3
Milton Pl S43 ....78 C1
Milton Rd Derby DE3 ...217 B2
  Ilkeston DE7 ....194 C2
  Repton DE65 ....242 B1
Milton St Derby DE22 ..218 B2
  Ilkeston DE7 ....194 C2
  Long Eaton NG10 ......236 B4
  Mansfield NG18 ....268 A4
  Nottingham NG1 ....268 B2
Milton Terr NG10 ....236 B4
Milward Rd DE75 ....181 B1
Mimosa Cres DE23 ......231 C3
Miners Hill DE4 ....153 A1
Minimum Terr S40 ......266 A2
Minshall Ct ST4 ....269 C1
Minshall St ST4 ....269 C1
Minster Rd DE21 ....205 C1
Minster Way DE55 ......169 C4
Mint Gr NG10 ....236 A4
Minton Rd DE74 ....246 C2
Minton St ST4 ....269 A2
Mires La
  Great Longstone DE45 ..90 A2
  Tideswell SK17 ....70 A2
Mires The
  Alstonefield DE6 ....149 A2
  Birchover DE4 ....142 C2
Miriam Ave S40 ....114 A4
Miry La DE65 ....227 B2
Misterton Cl DE21 ......204 C1
Misterton Ct NG19 .....136 A1
Mitcham Wlk DE22 .....218 A3
Mitchell Ave NG16 ......182 A2
Mitchell St Clowne S43 ..80 C2
  Long Eaton NG10 ......236 C4
Mitchell Terr DE7 ....209 A3
Mitchell Villas S43 ....77 C2
Mitchell Way S43 ....77 C2
Mitre Dr DE65 ....242 B1
Moat Bank DE15 ....248 B1
Moat St DE11 ....256 A1
Moat The DE74 ....247 A2
Model Village S80 ....100 C4
Model Village Prim Sch
  NG20 ....119 C2
Moffatt Rd S2 ....43 A4
Moira Cl DE21 ....220 A4
Moira Dale DE74 ....247 B2
Moira Furnace Mus*
  DE12 ....262 C2
Moira Rd
  Donisthorpe DE12 .....262 C1
  Moira DE11 ....262 C4
  Overseal DE12 ....262 A2
  Woodville DE11 ....256 C1
Moira St DE73 ....252 A4
Moisty La
  Marchington ST14 .....224 B2
  Stoney Middleton S32 ...71 A2
Molineux Ave S43 ....78 B1
Molineux St DE23 ......219 A1
Molloy Pl S8 ....43 A3
Molloy St S8 ....43 A3
Molyneaux Bsns Pk
  DE4 ....127 A2
Monarch Dr DE21 ......206 B2
Monarch Way DE75 ....181 B1
Moncreiff Dr DE21 .....241 A1
Moncrieff Cres DE21 ...220 A4
Mondello Dr DE24 .....233 B3
Monk Rd DE55 ....159 A1
Monk St Derby DE22 ...267 A2
  Tutbury DE13 ....239 B4
Monk's Rd SK13 ....17 A2
Monks Cl Derby DE24 ..231 B2
  Ilkeston DE7 ....209 A4
Monks Way S80 ....63 C4
Monks' Rd SK13 ....16 C3
Monksdale Cl SK17 ......60 A4
Monksdale La SK17 .....65 C1
Monkton Cl DE7 ....194 B2
Monkwood Rd S41 ....95 B4
Monmouth St DE21 ....219 B3
Monnies End S43 ....80 B3
Monpelier Cl DE14 .....254 A4
Monsal Ave SK17 ....85 B4
Monsal Cres Staveley S43 .97 B3
  Tibshelf DE55 ....147 C3
Monsal Dr Derby DE21 ..220 C2
  South Normanton DE55 .159 C3
Monsal Gr SK17 ....85 B4
Monsaldale Cl
  Burton u T DE15 ....248 A2

Monsaldale Cl continued
  Long Eaton NG10 ......236 A3
Monsall Ave DE7 ....194 C3
Monsdale La DE6 ....151 C1
Monsom La DE65 ....242 B2
Montagu St SK6 ....15 A1
Monteith Pl DE24 ......247 A2
Montford Mews DE24 ..247 A2
Montfort St NG7 ....268 A2
Montgomery Cl DE65 ..228 C1
Montgomery St DE23 ..218 C1
Montpelier DE22 ....204 B4
Montpelier Pl SK17 .....66 B1
Montpelier Rd DE56 ...167 C2
Montrose Cl DE24 .....231 C2
Montrose Ct NG9 ......209 C1
Montrose Pl ⑤ S18 ....56 B1
Montrose Sq NG19 .....136 A3
Monument Hill NG16 ..170 C2
Monument La NG16 ....170 C2
Monyash CE Prim Sch
  DE45 ....107 B1
Monyash Cl Derby DE21 .220 A4
  Ilkeston DE7 ....194 C2
  Staveley S43 ....97 B4
Monyash Mews ⑤ SK13 ..9 B1
Monyash Pl ⑰ SK13 ....9 B1
Monyash Rd
  Bakewell DE45 ....109 B3
  Over Haddon DE45 ....109 A1
Monyash Way DE56 .....79 A2
Moonpenny Way S18 ...57 A1
Moor Cres S20 ....59 B4
Moor Dr DE24 ....233 A3
Moor End DE21 ....220 C3
Moor End Rd SK6 ....24 A3
Moor Farm Ave S20 ....59 A4
Moor Farm Garth S20 ..59 B4
Moor Farm Rd E DE6 ..185 C4
Moor Farm Rd W DE6 ..185 C4
Moor Farm Rise S20 ....59 A4
Moor Furlong DE13 ....240 C1
Moor La Aston-on-T DE72 .246 A4
  Barrow u T DE73 ....244 A4
  Bolsover S44 ....99 A1
  Calow S44 ....142 A1
  Dale Abbey DE7 ....207 C1
  Darley Dale DE4 ....127 B2
  Derby DE24 ....232 B3
  Elton DE4 ....160 C2
  Flagg DE45 ....106 C2
  Kirk Ireton DE6 ....165 A2
  Kirk Langley DE6 ......202 C1
  Little Eaton DE21 .....191 C1
  Mansfield NG18 ....268 A4
  Ockbrook DE72 ....221 B3
  Osmaston DE6 ....185 C3
  Scarcliffe S44 ....119 A4
  Taddington SK17 ....87 C1
  Youlgreave DE45 ......125 A3
Moor Lane Fst Sch
  NG18 ....268 A3
Moor Rd Ashover S45 ..129 C2
  Breadsall DE7,DE21 ...205 C3
  Brinsley NG16 ....182 C4
  Great Longstone DE45 ..90 A2
Moor Rise DE56 ....191 B4
Moor St Derby DE21 ...220 C3
  Mansfield NG18 ....268 B3
Moor The Brinsley NG16 .182 B4
  Mansfield (Nr Wirksworth)
  DE4 ....154 B2
Moor Valley S20 ....44 C1
Moor View Rd S43 ......79 A1
Mooracre La S44 ....99 B1
Moorbridge La NG9 ....209 B1
Moorbrook La S33 ....56 C4
Moore Cl S42 ....116 B1
Moore St DE23 ....219 A2
Mooredge Dr DE4 .....143 B3
Mooredge Rd DE4 .....157 A1
Moorend DE4 ....111 B2
Moores Ave NG10 .....223 B4
Moorfield Ave DE4 ....143 B4
Moorfield Ave
  Bolsover S44 ....99 A1
  Holbrook DE56 ....191 B4
Moorfield Cres ⑤ NG10 ..223 A3
Moorfield Ct NG10 ....209 C1
Moorfield La NG20 ....100 C2
Moorfield Pct SK14 ......9 B3
Moorfield Sq S44 ....99 A1
Moorfield Terr SK14 ....9 B3
Moorfields Ave NG16 ..182 C2
Moorgate DE22 ....217 C3
Moorgate Ave NG19 ...134 C4
Moorgate Cres S18 .....76 A4
Moorgate St NG7 ......268 A2
Moorhaigh La NG19 ...135 A2
Moorhall DE45 ....109 B3
Moorhay Cl S41 ....95 A4
Moorhead Ave DE24 ..232 C3
Moorhead Prim Sch
  DE24 ....232 C3
Moorings The SK12 ....32 C3
Moorland Ave NG9 ....223 B3
Moorland Cl NG17 ....148 C4
Moorland Ct NG21 ....268 A4
Moorland Dr S44 ....116 C1
Moorland La NG16 .....268 A4
Moorland Rd Derby DE3 .217 B2
  Hathersage S32 ....53 A4
Moorland Terr DE4 ....144 A2
Moorland View
  Apperknowle S18 ....58 A1
  Sheffield S12 ....44 A1

Moorland View Rd S12 ...
Moorlands Cl NG10 .....
Moorlands Dr DE6 .....
Moorlands La
  Bonsall DE4 ....
  Stoney Middleton S32 ...
Moorlawn Ave S42 .....
Moorpark Ave S40 .....
Moorpool Cres DE56 ...
Moorside Cl
  Cromford DE4 ....
  Glossop SK13 ....
  Mosborough S20 ....
Moorside Cres DE24 ...
Moorside Gdns DE72 ...
Moorside La DE56 .....
Moorside Rd S14 ......
Moorthorpe Gdns S20 ..
Moorthorpe Gn S20 ....
Moorthorpe Way S20 ...
Moortop Rd S21 ....
Moorview Cl
  Brimington S43 ....
  Wingerworth S42 ....
Moorview Ct ⑭ S41 S17 ...
Moorway Croft DE23 ...
Moorway Ct DE23 .....
Moorway La DE23 .....
Moorways Sports Ctr
  DE24 ....
Moorwinstow Croft S17
Moorwood Ave S17 ....
Moorwoodmoor La
  DE55 ....
Moray Ct NG16 ....
Moray Pl S18 ....
Mordaunt Rd S2 ....
Morden Gn DE22 ......
Morden Rd NG16 ......
Morefern Dr DE21 .....
Moreland Cl ⑤ NG2 ...
Moreland Pl ⑤ NG2 ...
Moreland St NG2 ......
Morland Cl S14 ....
Morland Dr S14 ....
Morland Pl S14 ....
Morland Rd Hayfield SK22 .
  Sheffield S14 ....
Morledge DE1 ....
Morleston St DE23 ....
Morley Almshouses La
  DE7 ....
Morley Ave S40 ....
Morley Cl Belper DE56 .
  Dronfield S18 ....
Morley Ct NG3 ....
Morley Dr DE7 ....
Morley La
  Little Eaton DE7, DE21 ...
  Stanley DE7 ....
Morley Prim Sch DE7 ..
Morley Rd DE21 ....
Morley St Derby DE22 ..
  Glossop SK13 ....
Morleyfields Cl S18 ....
Morlich Dr DE24 ......
Morningside Cl DE24 ..
Mornington Cl NG10 ...
Mornington Cres DE22 .
Mornington Rd S42 ....
Mornington Rise DE4 ..
Morpeth Gdns DE21 ...
Morrell Wood Dr DE56 .
Morris Ave S41 ....
Morris Dr S41 ....
Mortimer St DE24 .....
Mortimer Wilson Sch
  DE55 ....
Morton Ave S45 ....
Morton Gdns S20 .....
Morton La S21 ....
Morton Mt S20 ....
Morton Prim Sch DE55 .
Morton Rd Pilsley S45 ..
  Shirland DE55 ....
Morton St NG19 ......
Morven Ave Bolsover S44 ...
  Mansfield Woodhouse
  NG19 ....
Morven St S80 ....
Mosborough Hall Farm
  S20 ....
Mosborough Moor S20 ...
Mosborough Prim Sch
  S20 ....
Mosbrough Rd S13 ....
Moscar Cross Rd S6 ...
Mosedale Cl DE24 ....
Moses La S21 ....
Moses View S81 ......
Mosley Dr ST14 ....
Mosley Rd SK17 ......
Moss Dr S21 ....
Moss Edge Rd HD9 ...
Moss La Broadbottom SK14 ...
  Hulland Ward DE6 .....
  Ripley DE5 ....
Moss Rd Ilkeston DE7 ..
  Totley S17 ....
Moss Rise Pl S21 .....
Moss St Derby DE22 ...
Hollingworth SK14 .....
Moss View Rd S43 ....
Moss Way S20 ....
Mossbank Cl SK13 ....

Nine Ladies Stone Circ* DE4 ....126 B2
Ninelands Rd S32 ....53 A4
Nix's Hill DE55 ....159 A1
No Man's Heath Rd DE12 ....264 C2
No Man's La DE7,DE27 ....222 B4
Nobel Cl S80 ....81 B1
Noble St DE11 ....267 D1
Nodder Rd S13 ....44 B4
Nodin Hill La DE56 ....168 A2
Noel St Derby DE22 ....218 C4
Mansfield NG18 ....268 B4
Noel-Baker Com Sch DE24 ....232 C2
Nook End Rd DE75 ....181 B1
Nook La S44 ....97 A2
Nook The
  Barrow u T DE73 ....244 A3
  Heanor DE75 ....181 B2
  Holbrook DE56 ....191 B4
  Shirebrook NG20 ....119 B2
  Stoney Middleton S32 ....72 A2
Nooning La DE72 ....234 C4
Norbriggs Prim Sch S43 ....79 A2
Norbriggs Rd S43 ....79 B1
Norburn Dr S21 ....60 B3
Norbury CE Prim Sch DE6 ....197 C4
Norbury Cl
  Chesterfield S40 ....95 A3
  Derby DE2 ....204 B1
  Dronfield S18 ....56 C4
  Sheffield S8 ....56 C4
Norbury Cres DE23 ....231 B3
Norbury Ct DE22 ....204 B1
Norbury Hollow DE6 ....183 B1
Norbury Way
  Belper DE56 ....179 B3
  Sandiacre NG10 ....223 A3
Norfolk Ave S42 ....115 C1
Norfolk Cl S40 ....114 A4
Norfolk Cl NG19 ....136 C3
Norfolk Dr NG18 ....268 B4
Norfolk Gdns DE22 ....218 C4
Norfolk Mid Sch S2 ....43 C4
Norfolk Prim Sch S2 ....43 C4
Norfolk Rd
  Burton u T DE15 ....254 B4
  Long Eaton NG10 ....223 C1
Norfolk Sq SK13 ....10 B1
Norfolk St Derby DE23 ....219 A1
  Glossop SK13 ....10 B1
Norfolk Wlk NG10 ....223 A3
Noregrave Way S20 ....59 C4
Norman Ave DE23 ....231 C4
Norman Cl NG3 ....268 B2
Norman Cres DE7 ....194 C2
Norman Keep DE13 ....239 B3
Norman Rd Ripley DE5 ....169 B1
  Somercotes DE55 ....170 C4
  Tutbury DE13 ....239 B3
Norman St Ilkeston DE7 ....194 C2
  Kimberley NG16 ....195 C4
Normandy Rd DE65 ....228 C1
Normanhurst Pk DE4 ....127 C1
Normanton Ave DE55 ....159 B2
Normanton Gr S13 ....44 C3
Normanton Hill S12,S13 ....44 B3
Normanton Jun Sch DE23 ....231 C4
Normanton La DE23 ....231 A4
Normanton Lodge DE23 ....231 C4
Normanton Rd DE1,DE23 ....267 B1
Normanton Spring Ct S13 ....44 C3
Normanton Spring Rd S13 ....44 C3
Normanton Village Inf Sch DE23 ....231 C4
North Ave
  Ashbourne DE6 ....173 A4
  Derby DE3 ....217 C1
  Derby, Darley Abbey DE22 ....205 A2
  Sandiacre NG10 ....223 A3
North Brook Rd SK13 ....9 C2
North Castle St ST16 ....269 A4
North Church St
  Bakewell DE45 ....109 B3
  Nottingham NG1 ....268 B2
North Circus St NG1 ....268 A1
North Cl Derby DE22 ....217 C2
  Glossop SK13 ....9 C4
  South Normanton DE55 ....159 C3
  Linstone S18 ....76 C2
  Willington DE65 ....242 A3
North Cres Killamarsh S21 ....60 C4
  Long Duckmanton S44 ....98 A3
North Derbyshire Tertiary Coll S43 ....80 C2
North Derbyshire Tertiary Coll (marklund Campus) S80 ....81 C2
North End DE4 ....154 C1
North Farm Cl S26 ....61 C4
North Gr S44 ....98 A3
North La Belper, Farnah Green DE56 ....178 B1
  Chesterfield DE56 ....190 C4
  Bralsford DE6 ....187 C2
  Old Brampton S42 ....94 B2
North Leys DE4 ....173 A1
North Moor View S43 ....96 C4

North Par Derby DE1 ....267 B4
  Matlock Bath DE4 ....143 A1
North Rd Buxton SK17 ....66 B1
  Calow S43 ....96 C2
  Clowne S43 ....80 C2
  Glossop SK13 ....10 B2
  Hayfield SK22 ....25 B2
  Long Eaton NG10 ....236 B3
  Nottingham NG7 ....268 A1
North Row DE22 ....205 A1
North Sherwood St NG1 ....268 B2
North St Alfreton DE55 ....159 A2
  Blackwell SE21 ....147 C1
  Bramley-Vale S44 ....117 B1
  Burton u T DE15 ....248 A2
  Clay Cross S45 ....131 A3
  Cromford DE4 ....155 A3
  Derby DE1 ....267 B5
  Ilkeston DE7 ....194 C1
  Langley Mill NG16 ....182 A2
  Market Warsop NG20 ....120 B2
  Melbourne DE73 ....252 A4
  North Wingfield S42 ....131 C3
  Pinxton NG16 ....160 B2
  Somercotes DE55 ....170 B3
  South Normanton DE55 ....159 C3
  Stoke-on-T ST4 ....269 B2
  Swadlincote DE11 ....256 A3
  Whaley Thorns NG20 ....101 A1
North Staffordshire Hospl Ctr (Outpatients Dept) ST4 ....269 A2
North Staffordshire Medical Inst ST4 ....269 A2
North Staffordshire Royal Infirmy ST4 ....269 A2
North Terr S41 ....115 A4
North View Crich SK13 ....168 A4
  Derby DE23 ....218 B1
North View St S44 ....98 C1
North Walls ST16 ....269 A4
North Wingfield Inf & Jun Sch S42 ....131 C4
North Wingfield Rd S42 ....115 C2
Northacre Rd DE21 ....206 A1
Northam Dr DE5 ....169 B2
Northampton St NG3 ....268 C2
Northcliffe Rd DE6 ....173 A1
Northcote Ave Sheffield S2 ....43 A3
  Stoke-on-T S14 ....269 B2
Northcote Rd S2 ....43 A3
Northcote St NG10 ....236 C4
Northern Ave S2 ....43 C4
Northern Comm S18 ....56 A1
Northern Dr NG9 ....209 B2
Northern Rd DE75 ....181 B1
Northfield Derby DE24 ....231 B2
  Kilburn DE56 ....179 C1
Northfield Ave Ilkeston DE7 ....194 C1
  Long Eaton NG10 ....236 A2
  Mansfield Woodhouse NG19 ....136 A2
  Rocester ST14 ....197 A2
Northfield Cl ST14 ....197 A2
Northfield Cres NG9 ....223 C2
Northfield Jun Sch S18 ....57 B2
Northfield La Mansfield Woodhouse NG19 ....135 C2
  Palterton S44 ....118 B3
Northfield Pk NG19 ....136 A3
Northfield Prim Sch NG19 ....136 A3
Northfield Rd NG9 ....223 C2
Northfields Clowne S80 ....80 C2
  Long Eaton NG10 ....236 A2
Northgate St DE7 ....194 C1
Northlands S26 ....61 C4
Northmead Dr DE23 ....218 C1
Northmoor Cl S43 ....96 C4
Northside S43 ....115 B1
Northumberland Cl NG3 ....268 B2
Northumberland Rd DE15 ....254 B4
Northumberland St DE23 ....218 C1
Northway Dr DE1 ....218 C3
Northwood Ave Darley Dale DE4 ....127 B2
  Derby DE21 ....219 C4
Northwood La Elkaston DE6 ....183 B2
  Darley Dale DE4 ....127 A3
Northwood Rise DE4 ....185 A4
Northwood Way NG9 ....223 B4
Norton Ave Bolsover S44 ....98 C3
  Sheffield S8,S12,S14 ....43 C1
Norton Church Glebe S8 ....43 B1
Norton Church Rd S8 ....43 B1
Norton Free Sch S8 ....43 B1
Norton Green Cl S8 ....43 B1
Norton Hall Ct S8 ....43 A1
Norton La S8 ....57 A4
Norton Lawns S8 ....43 B1
Norton Lees Cl S8 ....43 A2
Norton Lees Cres S8 ....43 A2
Norton Lees Glade S8 ....43 A2
Norton Lees La S8 ....43 A2
Norton Lees Rd S8 ....43 A2
Norton Lees Sq S8 ....43 A2

Norton Mews S8 ....43 B1
Norton Park Ave S8 ....57 A4
Norton Park Cres S8 ....57 A4
Norton Park Dr S8 ....57 A4
Norton Park Rd S8 ....57 A4
Norton Park View S8 ....57 A4
Norwell Cl NG19 ....136 A1
Norwich Cl NG19 ....136 B3
Norwich St DE21 ....219 B4
Norwood Ave S41 ....115 C3
Norwood Cl Chesterfield S41 ....115 C3
  Derby DE22 ....218 A3
Norwood Cres S21 ....60 C4
Norwood Ind Est S21 ....60 C4
Norwood Pl S21 ....60 C4
Notintone St NG2 ....268 C1
Nottingham Canal Nature Reserve The* DE7, NG16 ....195 B1
Nottingham Castle* NG7 ....268 A1
Nottingham Dr S42 ....115 A2
Nottingham High Sch NG1 ....268 A2
Nottingham High Sch for Girls NG1 ....268 A2
Nottingham La NG16 ....170 C3
Nottingham Midland Sta NG1 ....268 B1
Nottingham Rd
  Alfreton DE55 ....159 A1
  Ashby-de-la-Z LE65 ....258 C1
  Belper DE56 ....179 A2
  Borrowash DE72 ....221 B1
  Breedon on t H DE73 ....252 B1
  Codnor DE5,NG16 ....181 B4
  Derby DE1, DE21 ....267 C4
  Derby, Chaddesden DE21 ....219 C3
  Derby, Spondon DE21 ....220 C2
  Eastwood, Bailey Grove NG16 ....182 C1
  Eastwood, Gittbrook NG16 ....195 B4
  Ilkeston DE7 ....209 A3
  Long Eaton NG10 ....236 C4
  Mansfield NG18 ....268 B4
  Ripley DE5 ....169 C1
  Selston NG16 ....171 C3
  Somercotes DE55 ....159 B4
  Stapleford, Stanton Gate NG9 ....223 C4
  Tansley DE4 ....144 A2
  Trowell NG9 ....209 C3
Nottingham Sta NG1 ....268 B1
Nottingham Trent Univ NG1 ....268 A2
Nowill Ct [4] S8 ....43 A1
Nowill Pl [5] S8 ....43 A1
Nugent Gdns NG3 ....268 C2
Nun's St DE1 ....218 C3
Nunbrook Gr SK17 ....85 B3
Nunn Brook Rd NG17 ....148 C1
Nunn Brook Rise NG17 ....148 C1
Nunn Cl NG17 ....148 C1
Nunsfield Dr DE24 ....233 A4
Nunsfield Rd SK17 ....66 B1
Nursery Ave Sandiacre NG10 ....222 C3
  West Hallam DE7 ....207 C4
Nursery Cl Borrowash DE72 ....221 A1
  [6] Glossop SK13 ....17 B4
  Swadlincote DE11 ....256 A3
Nursery Croft DE4 ....165 C3
Nursery Ct NG18 ....268 C4
Nursery Dr Bolsover S44 ....98 C1
  Buxton SK17 ....66 B1
Nursery Gdns DE55 ....160 B2
Nursery Hollow DE7 ....208 C3
Nursery La SK17 ....84 C3
Nursery St Mansfield NG18 ....268 C4
  Stoke-on-T ST4 ....269 B1
Nutbrook Cres DE7 ....208 B2
Nuthall Cir DE7 ....208 B2
Nuttall Cl DE55 ....158 C2
Nuttall St DE55 ....158 C2
Nuttall Terr S44 ....117 B1
Nutwood Cl DE22 ....205 A2

O

Oadby Dr S41 ....115 B4
Oadby Rise DE23 ....231 C3
Oak Apple Cres DE7 ....208 C3
Oak Ave Aldercar NG16 ....182 A3
  Disley SK12 ....32 C3
  Mansfield NG18 ....268 C4
  Ripley DE5 ....180 B4
  Sandiacre NG10 ....223 A4
  Shirebrook NG20 ....119 B2
Oak Bank SK12 ....32 A3
Oak Bank Ave S41 ....77 A1
Oak Cl Brimington S43 ....96 B4
  Chapel-en-la-F SK23 ....47 B3
  Derby DE22 ....204 C2
  Duffield DE56 ....190 C1
  Killamarsh S21 ....60 B3
  Linton DE11 ....261 C4
  Mottram in L SK14 ....9 A2
  Ockbrook DE72 ....221 B3
  Pinxton NG16 ....160 B2
Oak Cres Ashbourne DE6 ....185 B4
  Derby DE23 ....231 B4
  Wingerworth S42 ....114 C2

Oak Dr Alfreton DE55 ....159 A2
  Derby DE3 ....217 C1
  Derby, Boulton DE24 ....233 A3
  Doveridge DE6 ....211 A1
  Eastwood NG16 ....182 C1
  Hilton DE65 ....228 B1
Oak La DE6 ....212 B2
Oak Lodge Dr NG16 ....195 C4
Oak Rd Denstone ST14 ....196 B3
  Elvaston DE72 ....233 C2
  Grassmoor S42 ....115 C2
  Matlock DE4 ....143 B3
  Sheffield S12 ....44 A1
Oak Sq DE11 ....255 C1
Oak St Brimington S43 ....78 A1
  Derby DE23 ....219 A1
  Glossop SK13 ....10 B1
  Mosborough S20 ....59 B4
  Sheffield S8 ....43 A4
  Swadlincote DE11 ....256 A1
Oak Tree Ave S44 ....134 A4
Oak Tree Cl S44 ....97 B2
Oak Tree Cotts S44 ....97 A1
Oak Tree Cres NG19 ....136 A2
Oak Tree Ct DE72 ....221 B1
Oak Tree Gdns DE4 ....144 A2
Oak Tree Rd S43 ....80 B2
Oakamoor Cl S40 ....95 A3
Oakbank Cl S17 ....55 C3
Oakdale Cl S45 ....131 C1
Oakdale Gdns DE21 ....206 A2
Oakdale Rd DE55 ....160 A2
Oakdell S18 ....57 B2
Oakerthorpe Rd DE4 ....155 A1
Oakes Cl DE55 ....170 B4
Oakes Park View S14 ....43 B1
Oakes The SK13 ....17 A4
Oakes's Row NG16 ....170 C3
Oakfield S40 ....95 A1
Oakfield Ct DE7 ....193 A1
Oakfield Dr NG10 ....223 A2
Oakfield Rd Glossop SK13 ....9 C2
  Stapleford NG9 ....223 B4
Oakfields DE13 ....238 A2
Oakham Cl DE21 ....205 B1
Oakham View DE7 ....208 C2
Oakhill Rd S18 ....57 B2
Oakhurst Cl DE56 ....178 B3
Oakland Ave Long Eaton NG10 ....236 B3
  Sutton in A NG17 ....148 C1
Oakland Cres DE55 ....170 B3
Oakland St DE55 ....159 A2
Oakland Terr NG10 ....236 B3
Oaklands Ave Derby DE23 ....231 B3
  Heanor DE75 ....182 A1
  Marple SK6 ....23 B4
Oaklands Cl DE55 ....180 B1
Oaklands Dr ST17 ....269 A3
Oaklands Rd DE65 ....228 B2
Oaklands The DE55 ....160 A2
Oaklands Way DE73 ....252 A4
Oaklea SK17 ....85 B3
Oaklea Way S42 ....131 A3
Oakleigh Ave Derby DE21 ....219 C3
  Mansfield Woodhouse NG19 ....136 C2
Oakley Ave DE23 ....218 B1
Oakley Ave S40 ....95 C2
Oakley Rd NG10 ....236 C3
Oakley's Rd NG10 ....236 B3
Oakley's Rd W NG10 ....236 B3
Oakmeadows DE55 ....160 A2
Oakover Dr DE22 ....204 B1
Oakridge DE21 ....220 A4
Oakridge Cl NG19 ....136 C1
Oaks Ave Creswell S80 ....100 B4
  Hayfield SK22 ....25 B1
Oaks Farm La S44 ....97 A1
Oaks La Ashover S45 ....129 B3
  Br Brampton S18,S42 ....94 A4
Oaks Rd DE65 ....242 A3
Oaks The DE21 ....205 B4
Oaksedge La DE4 ....144 A3
Oakside Way DE21 ....206 A2
Oakstedge La S45 ....145 A4
Oaktree Ave DE24 ....232 A4
Oaktree Cl DE55 ....170 A4
Oaktree Rd DE55 ....148 B1
Oakwell Cres DE7 ....208 C4
Oakwell Dr Crich DE4 ....156 C1
  Ilkeston DE7 ....208 C4
Oakwood St13 ....16 C4
Oakwood Cl Derby DE65 ....231 B1
  Hatton DE65 ....239 B4
Oakwood District Ctr DE21 ....206 A1
Oakwood Dr Darley Dale DE4 ....142 C4
  Derby DE21 ....206 A1
Oakwood Inf Sch DE24 ....233 A3
Oakwood Jun Sch DE24 ....233 A3
Oakwood Rd SK12 ....32 B3
Oakworth Cl S20 ....59 C3
Oakworth Dr S20 ....59 C3
Oakworth Gr S20 ....59 B3
Oakworth View S20 ....59 B3
Oakdale Rd NG18 ....268 A4
Oat Hill DE4 ....165 C4
Oats Orch S20 ....59 B3
Occupation Cl S43 ....80 A3
Occupation La
  North Wingfield S42 ....131 C4
  Sheffield S12 ....44 C2
  Woodville DE11 ....256 C1

Occupation Rd Chesterfield S41 ....
  Moira DE11 ....
  New Houghton NG19 ....
Ochbrook Ct DE7 ....
Ockbrook Sch DE72 ....
Oddfellow Terr DE4 ....
Oddfellows Cotts [7] SK17 ....
Oddfellows Row S32 ....
Oddfellows Row S32 ....
Oddfellows Terr S32 ....
Oddford La DE4 ....
Odom Ct S2 ....
Offcote Cres DE4 ....
Offerton Ave DE23 ....
Offridge Cl S43 ....
Ogden St SK14 ....
Ogdon Ct NG2 ....
Ogle Dr NG7 ....
Ogston La DE55 ....
Ogston New Rd DE55 ....
Okeover Ave DE6 ....
Oker Ave DE4 ....
Oker Dr DE4 ....
Oker La DE4 ....
Oker Rd DE4 ....
Oker Terr DE4 ....
Old Bakery Cl S41 ....
Old Bank DE6 ....
Old Barn Cl DE21 ....
Old Brick Works La S41 ....
Old Chester Rd DE1 ....
Old Church La DE22 ....
Old Coach Rd DE4 ....
Old Coalpit La SK17 ....
Old Colliery La S42 ....
Old Coppice Side DE75 ....
Old Dam La SK17 ....
Old Derby Rd
  Ashbourne DE6 ....
  Eastwood NG16 ....
Old Dr DE22 ....
Old Forge Bsns Pk [8] S2 ....
Old Forge Cl DE65 ....
Old Gate HD7 ....
Old Gate Ave DE72 ....
Old Hackney La DE4 ....
Old Hall Ave Derby DE21 ....
  Derby, Alvaston DE24 ....
  Duffield DE56 ....
  Whaley Bridge SK23 ....
Old Hall Cl Darley Dale DE4 ....
  Glossop SK13 ....
Old Hall Ct DE55 ....
Old Hall Dr DE65 ....
Old Hall Gdns
  Stoney Middleton S32 ....
  Swadlincote DE11 ....
Old Hall Jun Sch S40 ....
Old Hall La Church Broughton DE65 ....
  Marple SK6 ....
  Mottram in L SK14 ....
  Whitwell S80 ....
Old Hall Mills Bsns Pk DE21 ....
Old Hall Rd Chesterfield S40 ....
  Derby DE23 ....
Old Hall Sq [9] SK13 ....
Old Hartshay Hill DE5 ....
Old Hay Gdns S17 ....
Old Hay La S17 ....
Old Highcliff La S40 ....
Old Hill DE6 ....
Old House Mus* DE45 ....
Old House Rd S40 ....
Old Houses S41 ....
Old Lime Ct DE4 ....
Old Longhill Rd SK17 ....
Old Manor Rd NG19 ....
Old Mansfield Rd DE21 ....
Old Market Pl
  Mansfield NG18 ....
  South Normanton DE55 ....
Old Market Sq NG1 ....
Old Mill Cl Duffield DE56 ....
  Pilsley S45 ....
Old Mill Dr S40 ....
Old Mill La Calver S32 ....
  Mansfield NG19 ....
Old Park Ave S8 ....
Old Park Rd S8 ....
Old Peverel Rd S44 ....
Old Pit La DE7 ....
Old Pond The DE75 ....
Old Post Office Row S33 ....
Old Quarry Cl S43 ....
Old Rd Branston DE14 ....
  Buxton SK23 ....
  Chesterfield S40 ....
  Darley Dale DE4 ....
  Glossop SK13 ....
  Heage DE56 ....
  Mottram in L SK14 ....
  Whaley Bridge, Furness Vale SK23 ....
  Whaley Bridge, New Horwich SK23 ....
Old School Cl
  Bramley-Vale S44 ....117 B1

...chool La continued
...well SK17 ....69 B2
Orchard La
...roth NG16 ....195 B3
...erfield S44 ....96 C1
...ey La 135 A3
...chool Mews NG11 ....247 A4
...ip La S40 ....266 B3
...SK14 ....16 A4
...ation Cl
...r Dale DE4 ....126 C4
...sels S43 ....229 A2
...orth La DE55 ....160 A2
...wanwick Colliery Rd
....158 C1
...nns Cts The SK17
...ter NG19 ....134 C2
...arage Cl DE23 ....218 B1
...arage La DE2 ....204 B3
...arage Sch The
....205 A2
...hieldon NG14 ....269 C1
...hittington La S18 ....76 C3
...r DE11 ....256 B3
...d La
...on DE65 ....241 A4
...aston DE6 ....164 C1
...ton DE6 ....164 C1
...on De6 ....184 A2
...ey DE4 ....142 A4
...y Cl S17 ....55 B3
...ote La DE15 ....248 C2
...ow Rd SK6 ....23 A3
...t St S14 ....17 A4
...age Cl S40 ....95 A1
...h Cl S17 ....55 B2
...d NG3 ....268 C2
...Ave
...Eaton NG10 ....223 C1
...rook NG20 ....119 B3
...Gr DE21 ....219 C3
...Grove Rd S2 ....43 A4
...Rd S20 ....59 B4
...St DE22 ....218 C1
...err SK14 ....16 A4
...r Cl Heanor DE75 ....182 A1
...ngham NG7 ....268 A2
...Lodge Ho S14 ....269 B2
...on Rd Ilkeston DE7 ....208 B3
...on S14 ....269 A2
...St NG7 ....268 A2
...Rd S8 ....43 A2
...nett Ave S8 ....219 A1
...nett La SK22 ....24 C1
...Rd DE3 ....217 B2
...w Rd DE3 ....217 C2
...Cotts SK17 ....85 B4
...Cl DE21 ....206 A1
...erne NG16 ....170 C2
...wood Rd DE56 ....179 C2
...woodgate DE56 ....179 B2
...ge Cl NG20 ....119 C3
...ge St DE55 ....159 A2
...Cl NG3 ....268 C2
...rd Ave
...e Donington DE74 ....247 A2
...ey Bridge SK23 ....45 B4
...ard Bsns Pk
...rd Cl 194 B1
...erre NG10 ....223 B3
...ard Cl
...borough S43 ....80 A4
...er DE56 ....191 A4
...rer S44 ....99 A1
...ston DE72 ....235 C4
...ne S43 ....80 C2
...ch DE23 ....231 B4
...aston DE24 ....233 B2
...n DE55 ....159 A2
...Crook DE72 ....221 B2
...y DE5 ....181 A4
...rbrook NG20 ....119 C3
...bury DE6 ....225 C3
...rker ST14 ....210 A1
...on-on-T DE12 ....253 B1
...Hallam DE7 ....207 C4
...ngton DE65 ....242 A3
...ard Com Prim Sch
....247 A2
...rd Cres
...well S43 ....134 A4
...wick DE55 ....169 B4
...ard Ct Derby DE21 ....220 C4
...ston DE24 ....211 A1
...ley Mill NG16 ....182 A2
...r Normanton DE55 ....159 C2
...ard Dr Creswell S80 ....81 C1
...easley SK13 ....9 C1
...ard La DE6 ....185 B1
...ard Lee S26 ....61 C3
...ard Pl S21 ....60 B3
...ard Rd Compstall SK6 ....15 A1
...ley Dale DE4 ....142 C4
...lock Bath DE4 ....143 A1
...arcotes DE55 ....170 B3
...ey Bridge SK23 ....45 B4
...ard Rise DE75 ....181 C1
...ard Sq ⊞ S18 ....56 B1
...ard St Derby DE1 ....267 A4
...y, Mickleover DE3 ....217 B1
...on DE7 ....208 C4

Orchard St continued
Kimberley NG16 ....195 C3
Langley Mill NG16 ....182 A2
Long Eaton NG10 ....236 C4
Mansfield NG19 ....136 A1
Stafford ST17 ....269 B3
Stapleford NG9 ....223 B4
Swadlincote DE11 ....255 C3
Orchard The
Belper DE56 ....179 A2
Codnor DE5 ....170 A1
Disley SK12 ....32 B3
Horsley Woodhouse DE7 ......192 B3
Stanton-by-D DE7 ....222 C4
Uttoxeter ST14 ....210 A2
Youlgreave DE45 ....125 B3
Orchard View
Bolsover S44 ....117 C4
Mansfield Woodhouse
NG19 ....136 C3
Orchard View Rd S40 ....95 B2
Orchard Way
Derby DE73 ....232 C1
Sandiacre NG10 ....223 A4
Orchards The
Derby DE22 ....204 B2
Westwood NG16 ....171 A2
Orchards Way S40 ....95 B1
Orchid Cl
Burton u T DE15 ....255 A4
Calow S44 ....97 A2
Orchid Way NG20 ....119 B2
Ordish Ave DE21 ....219 C3
Ordley La DE6 ....183 C4
Oregon Way DE21 ....220 B3
Orford St S14 ....32 B3
Organ Way SK14 ....9 B3
Oriel Cl ST4 ....267 C1
Oriel St ST4 ....269 B2
Orkney Cl DE24 ....231 B2
Orly Ave DE74 ....247 A1
Ormesby Cl S18 ....56 B1
Ormond Cl
Chesterfield S40 ....114 A4
Sheffield S8 ....57 A3
Ormond Rd S8 ....57 A3
Ormond St S8 ....57 A4
Ormonde St NG16 ....182 A2
Ormonde Terr NG16 ....182 A2
Ormsby Rd S41 ....95 C4
Ormskirk Rise DE21 ....220 C2
Orpen Way NG9 ....223 C1
Orpen St S14 ....43 C1
Orton Way DE56 ....179 A4
Orwins Cl S41 ....95 B4
Osborne Cl
Long Eaton NG10 ....236 B4
Mansfield Woodhouse
NG19 ....136 B1
Osborne Croft S26 ....61 C3
Osborne Pl S43 ....10 A3
Osborne Rd Derby DE21 ......219 B2
Stoke-on-T ST4 ....269 A2
Osborne St DE15 ....248 A2
Osmaston CE Prim Sch
DE6 ....185 C2
Osmaston Park Ind Est
DE24 ....232 C4
Osmaston Park Rd
DE23,DE24 ....232 B4
Osmaston Rd DE23,DE24 ...219 A1
Osmaston Pk Ind Est
DE24 ....219 B3
Osmond Rd S21 ....59 B2
Osprey Cl
Burton u T DE15 ....248 B2
Derby DE24 ....231 C1
Ossington Cl NG1 ....268 B2
Osterly Gn DE21 ....218 A3
Ostrich La DE6 ....163 A1
Oswestry Cl DE21 ....206 A2
Otter St DE1 ....219 A4
Otterburn Dr DE22 ....204 A1
Oulton Cl DE24 ....232 B2
Oundle Dr Ilkeston DE7 ......209 A4
Mansfield NG19 ....135 B1
Our Lady's RC Prim Sch
S14 ....43 C1
Ousley La DE6 ....183 B3
Out La S42,S44 ....132 C3
Outfield Rd DE15 ....254 C4
Outgang La
Mansfield Woodhouse
NG19 ....136 B2
Pleasley NG19 ....135 B3
Outram Ct DE5 ....169 C1
Outram Dr DE11 ....256 B2
Outram Rd S41 ....95 C3
Outram St DE5 ....169 C1
Outram Way DE24 ....231 C1
Outseats Dr DE55 ....159 A2
Oval Cl DE23 ....231 B4
Oval The ST17 ....269 B3
Over Haddon Craft Ctr*
DE45 ....109 A1
Over Hill Rd SK22,SK23 ....34 A3
Over La Baslow DE45 ....91 C3
Hazelwood DE56 ....178 A1
Over Rd DE45 ....91 C3
Overcroft Rise S17 ....55 B2
Overdale
Glossop SK13 ....10 A2
Overdale Ave SK17 ....85 B4
Overdale Cl NG10 ....236 A3
Overdale Gdns S17 ....55 B3
Overdale Rd Derby DE23 ....218 C1

Overdale Rd continued
New Mills SK12 ....32 C3
Overdale Rise S17 ....55 B3
Overend Cl S14 ....43 B2
Overend Dr S14 ....43 B2
Overend Rd S14 ....43 B2
Overend Way S14 ....43 B2
Overlees S18 ....78 C2
Overmoor View DE55 ....148 A4
Overseal Manor Sch
DE12 ....262 A2
Overseal Prim Sch
DE12 ....262 A2
Oversetts Ct DE11 ....255 C3
Oversetts Rd DE11 ....255 C3
Overstone Cl DE56 ....168 B4
Overton Cl S43 ....78 C2
Owen Ave NG10 ....237 A4
Ower Bar Rd S17 ....54 A2
Owers La DE56 ....166 C4
Owlcotes View S44 ....118 A3
Owler Car La S18 ....57 C3
Owlers La DE23 ....218 B1
Owlston Cl NG16 ....182 C2
Owlswick Cl DE23 ....231 A4
Owlthorpe Ave S20 ....59 A4
Owlthorpe Cl S20 ....59 A4
Owlthorpe Gr S20 ....59 A4
Owlthorpe Gr S20 ....59 A4
Owlthorpe La S20 ....59 A4
Owlthorpe Rise S20 ....59 A4
Ox Cl S45 ....131 B2
Ox Close Ave S17 ....56 A3
Ox Hill S20 ....59 A4
Oxbury Rd NG16 ....195 C4
Oxclose La
Alsop en le D DE6 ....150 B1
Dronfield S18 ....57 A3
Mansfield NG19 ....135 B2
Mansfield Woodhouse
NG19 ....136 A2
Oxclose Park Rd S20 ....59 C3
Oxclose Park Rd N S20 ....59 C3
Oxcroft East S44 ....99 B4
Oxcroft La Bolsover S44 ....99 A3
Elmton S44 ....99 C4
Oxcroft Way S43 ....80 A3
Oxenhope Cl DE23 ....230 C4
Oxford Cl NG19 ....136 C4
Oxford Cres ST4 ....269 B2
Oxford St Blackwell DE55 ....147 C1
Bramley-Vale S44 ....117 C1
Derby DE1 ....267 C1
Derby, Spondon DE21 ....220 C3
Eastwood NG16 ....182 C1
⊞ Ilkeston DE7 ....208 C4
Long Eaton NG10 ....236 B4
Mansfield NG19 ....136 B1
Nottingham NG1 ....268 B1
Ripley DE5 ....169 B1
Stoke-on-T ST4 ....269 B2
Swadlincote DE11 ....256 A1
Oxley Rd DE15 ....248 A2
Oxmead DE6 ....184 B4
Oxpasture La NG20 ....100 A3
Oxton Cl NG19 ....136 A4
Oxton Rake Rd S18 ....94 A4
Oxwich Cl DE21 ....206 A1
Ozier Holt NG10 ....236 B3

P

Pack Horse Rd DE73 ....252 A2
Packenham Bvd DE65 ....227 A2
Packer's Row S40 ....266 B3
Packman La S26 ....62 B3
Paddock Cl
Castle Donington DE74 ....246 C2
Wingerworth S42 ....114 C2
Paddock Cres S2 ....43 C3
Paddock Croft DE21 ....205 C1
Paddock La S43 ....79 A4
Paddock The
Blackwell DE55 ....147 C1
Bolsover S44 ....99 A1
Burton u T DE15 ....248 A2
Buxton SK17 ....84 C4
Elvaston DE72 ....233 B2
Glossop SK13 ....9 C3
Holbrook DE56 ....191 B3
Hollingworth SK14 ....9 C2
Ockbrook DE72 ....221 B2
Pleasley NG19 ....135 A3
Rolleston DE13 ....240 A2
Swadlincote DE11 ....255 C3
Paddocks The
Mansfield Woodhouse
NG19 ....136 C3
Pilsley S45 ....132 B1
Sandiacre NG10 ....223 A3
Staveley S43 ....79 B2
Sutton in a NG17 ....148 C1
Swadlincote DE11 ....255 C3
Paddocks Way NG19 ....236 A4
Padfield Com Prim Sch
SK13 ....10 A3
Padfield Gate SK13 ....17 B4
Padfield Main Rd SK13 ....10 B3
Padget High Sch DE14 ....254 A4
Padley Cl Derby DE22 ....205 A3
Ripley DE5 ....169 B2
Padley Hill
Mansfield NG18 ....268 B3

Padley Hill continued
Nether Padley S32 ....53 C1
Padley Rd S32 ....53 B1
Padley Way S42 ....131 C3
Padley Wood La S45 ....147 A4
Padley Wood Rd S45 ....118 A1
Padstow Cl DE24 ....231 B2
Padstow Rd DE24 ....233 B3
Painter's La DE6 ....186 A3
Painters Way
Darley Dale DE4 ....127 B1
Winster DE4 ....141 B3
Paisley Cl S43 ....97 B4
Palace La DE56 ....166 B1
Palace Rd SK17 ....85 A4
Palatine Gr DE23 ....230 C4
Palatine St NG7 ....268 A1
Palerow La DE56 ....166 C2
Palissy Cl DE11 ....256 B2
Pall Mall DE21 ....205 C2
Palladium Dr DE23 ....231 A3
Palm Cl DE23 ....218 A1
Palmbourne Ind Pk
ST16 ....269 A4
Palmer Cl
Burton u T DE14 ....254 A4
Stafford ST16 ....269 C4
Palmer Cres S18 ....57 A1
Palmer Dr
Stapleford NG9 ....223 B3
Swanwick DE55 ....169 C4
Palmersgate S40 ....266 B3
Palmerston Cl DE7 ....194 C3
Palmerston Gdns NG3 ....268 B2
Palmerston St
Derby DE23 ....218 C1
Westwood NG16 ....171 C1
Westwood NG16 ....171 B2
Palterton La S44 ....117 B3
Palterton Prim Sch S44 ......117 B3
Pankhurst Pl S45 ....131 B2
Panton Cl ST16 ....266 C4
Parade The S18 ....57 B1
Paradise St SK13 ....10 A3
Parcel Terr DE22 ....218 B3
Pares Way DE72 ....221 B3
Pargate Cl DE5 ....180 B3
Park Ave Ashbourne DE6 ....173 B1
Awsworth NG16 ....195 A3
Castle Donington DE74 ....246 C2
Darley Dale DE4 ....127 B2
Dronfield S18 ....57 A1
Glapwell S44 ....118 B1
Holmesfield S18 ....75 A4
Ilkeston DE7 ....208 C4
Mansfield NG18 ....268 C4
Mansfield Woodhouse
NG19 ....136 B2
New Mills SK22 ....33 B4
Nottingham NG7 ....268 A1
Over Haddon DE45 ....110 B3
Ripley DE5 ....169 B1
Shirebrook NG20 ....119 C3
Stapleford NG9 ....223 C4
Swadlincote, Church Gresley
DE11 ....256 B1
Swadlincote DE11 ....255 B3
Park Ave continued
Eckington S21 ....59 C2
Park Hill Cl SK22 ....24 B1
Park Hill Dr DE23 ....231 C4
Park Ho DE56 ....179 A2
Park House Prim Sch
S45 ....132 A2
Park Jun & Inf Schs The
NG20 ....119 C3
Park La Hayfield SK22 ....25 B3
Castle Donington DE74 ....246 C2
Chesterfield S41 ....95 C4
Derby, Allestree DE22 ....205 A1
Derby, Normanton Park
DE23 ....218 B1
Heage DE56 ....179 C4
Holbeck NG20,S80 ....101 B3
Mansfield NG18 ....268 B3
Over Haddon DE45,DE4 ....110 B3
Pinxton NG16 ....160 B1
Ripley DE5 ....169 A4
Shirland DE55 ....158 C4
Shirley DE6 ....200 B4
South Wingfield DE55 ....157 B1
Tutbury DE13 ....239 A3
Weston-on-T DE72 ....245 C2
Youlgreave DE45 ....126 B3
Park Leys Ct DE22 ....220 C2
Park Mews
Mansfield Woodhouse
NG19 ....136 B2
Somercotes DE55 ....159 B4
Park Rd S8 ....159 B4
Park Pale The DE13 ....239 B3
Park Ravine NG7 ....268 A1
Park Rd Ashbourne DE6 ......173 B1
Bakewell DE45 ....109 B3
Belper DE56 ....179 A4
Buxton SK17 ....85 A4
Chapel-en-le-F SK23 ....47 A3
Chesterfield S40 ....266 B2
Chesterfield, Queen's Park
S40 ....266 A1
Derby DE3 ....217 B1
Derby, Spondon DE21 ....220 C3
Donisthorpe DE12 ....262 C1
Duffield DE56 ....190 B2
Glossop SK13 ....10 A2
Heage DE56 ....179 C4
High Lane SK12 ....32 A3
Holmewood S42 ....116 C1
Ilkeston DE7 ....208 C4
Linton DE12 ....262 A3
Mansfield Woodhouse
NG19 ....136 A2
New Mills SK22 ....33 B4
Nottingham NG7 ....268 A1
Over Haddon DE45 ....110 B3
Ripley DE5 ....169 C1
Shirebrook NG20 ....119 C3
Stapleford NG9 ....223 C4
Swadlincote DE11,DE15 ....255 B3
Swadlincote, Church Gresley
DE11 ....256 B1
Tupton S42 ....131 B4
Whaley Bridge SK23 ....45 B3
Park Rise S18 ....75 A4
Park Row Clay Cross S45 ....131 B2
Nottingham NG1 ....268 A1
Park Side Belper DE56 ....179 A2
Somercotes DE55 ....170 B4
Park Spring Cl S2 ....43 B4
Park Spring Dr S2 ....43 B4
Park Spring Gr S2 ....43 B4
Park Spring Pl S2 ....43 B4
Park Spring Way S2 ....43 B4
Park St Alfreton DE55 ....158 C3
Barlborough S43 ....80 A4
Breaston DE72 ....235 B4
Chesterfield S41 ....115 A4
Derby DE1 ....267 D2
Derby DE75 ....181 B1
Heanor DE75 ....181 B1
Long Eaton NG10 ....223 B1
Mansfield Woodhouse
NG19 ....136 A1
Ripley DE5 ....169 C1
Stafford ST17 ....269 B3
Stapleford NG9 ....223 C4
Swadlincote DE11 ....256 A3
Uttoxeter ST14 ....210 A1
Wessington DE55 ....157 C4
Park Terr Northwood DE4 ....127 A3
Nottingham NG1 ....268 A1
Park The Darley Dale DE4 ....127 B2
Ironville NG16 ....170 C2
Mansfield NG18 ....268 C4
Mayfield DE6 ....184 B4
Park Valley NG7 ....268 A1
Park View
Aston-on-T DE72 ....246 A4
Bakewell DE45 ....109 B3
Barlborough S43 ....80 A4
Chesterfield S41 ....115 B4
Clowne S43 ....80 C3
Heanor DE75 ....181 B1
Mansfield NG19 ....135 A3
Somercotes DE55 ....170 B3
Whaley Thorns NG20 ....109 C4
Park View Ave S20 ....59 C4
Park View Cl DE23 ....218 B2
Park View Ct
⊞ Nottingham NG3 ....268 B2
Sheffield S8 ....43 A1
Park View Dr SK23 ....47 A3

Park View Ho DE21 ....219 B3
Park View Rise SK22 ....24 B1
Park View Way NG18 ....268 C2
Park Way DE65 ....229 B2
Park Wharf NG7 ....268 A1
Parker Ave S44 ....96 C2
Parker Cl DE21 ....267 A4
Parker Ctr DE21 ....219 A4
Parker Gdns NG9 ....223 C4
Parker St DE1 ....218 C4
Parker's Croft Rd ST17 ....269 B3
Parker's La NG19 ....136 B2
Parkers Cl DE11 ....256 C3
Parkers La S17 ....55 B4
Parkfield Cl S2 ....43 A4
Parkfield Cres DE12 ....265 C1
Parkfield Croft SK17 ....85 A4
Parkfield La DE6 ....184 B2
Parkfields DE22 ....218 C4
Parkfields View DE56 ....179 C4
Parkgate Cl S20 ....59 A4
Parkgate Croft S20 ....59 A4
Parkgate Dr S20 ....59 A4
Parkgate La S21,S43 ....77 C3
Parkham Rd NG16 ....195 C4
Parkhill S21 ....60 B1
Parkhouse Cl S45 ....131 A2
Parkhouse Dr DE55 ....159 C2
Parkhouse Rd S45 ....132 A2
Parkin St DE55 ....159 A2
Parkland Ave SK22 ....24 B1
Parkland Dr S42 ....115 A1
Parklands Dr DE73 ....245 A4
Parklands Inf Sch NG10 ....223 A1
Parks Ave DE55 ....157 C2
Parkside Ave NG10 ....236 A4
    Chesterfield S41 ....96 A4
    Heage DE56 ....179 C4
Parkside Ave NG10 ....236 A4
Parkside Cl NG16 ....170 C2
Parkside Com Jun Sch
    DE6 ....173 B1
Parkside Com Sch S40 ....266 A2
Parkside Dr
    Ironville NG16 ....170 C2
    Long Eaton NG10 ....236 A4
Parkside La S46 ....23 B3
Parkside Rd DE21 ....220 A3
Parkside Sh Ctr S21 ....60 B4
Parkside View S40 ....95 A3
Parkstone Ct DE3 ....217 B1
Parkstone Delph S12 ....44 A1
Parkview DE21 ....205 B4
Parkview Prim Sch
    DE21 ....206 A1
Parkville Cl SK17 ....85 B3
Parkway DE73 ....232 C1
    New Mills SK22 ....24 B1
    Whitwell S80 ....82 A3
Parkway Ct S8 ....56 C4
Parkway The DE4 ....127 B2
Parkwood Sch DE55 ....158 C2
Parliament Cl DE22 ....218 C2
Parliament Rd NG19 ....268 A4
Parliament St
    Derby DE22 ....218 C2
    Swadlincote DE11 ....255 C3
Parr Ct 12 NG7 ....268 A2
Parson's Wlk DE72 ....221 C3
Parsonage Cl S20 ....59 B4
Parsonage Croft DE45 ....109 B3
Parsonage Gdns SK6 ....23 A2
Parsons Cl
    Hartington SK17 ....137 B3
    Swadlincote DE11 ....256 A1
Parsons Gate S33 ....40 A3
Parsons Gr DE55 ....180 B1
Parsons La S33 ....39 B2
Parthenon Cl NG19 ....134 C3
Partington Ct S43 ....10 C1
Partington Pk SK13 ....10 B2
Partridge Cl DE21 ....59 A2
Partridge Dr DE11 ....256 C2
Partridge Way DE24 ....218 A2
Parture Gr S21 ....59 B2
Parwich Cl S40 ....95 A3
Parwich La DE4 ....151 C4
Parwich Prim Sch S42 ....151 B1
Parwich Rd S42 ....131 C3
Pasteur Ave DE21 ....169 B1
Pasture La
    Brassington DE4,DE6 ....152 B1
    Flagg SK17 ....106 B3
    Hilcote DE55 ....148 B1
    Long Eaton NG10 ....237 A3
    Stoneroom DE55 ....147 A2
Pasture Rd NG19 ....209 B1
Pastures Ave DE23 ....230 C4
Pastures Hill DE23 ....231 A4
Pastures The
    Duffield DE56 ....190 C2
    Eastwood NG16 ....195 A4
    Mansfield Woodhouse
        NG19 ....136 C3
    Repton DE65 ....242 A1
    Swadlincote DE11 ....255 C3
    Weston-on-T DE72 ....245 C3
Patchwork Row NG20 ....119 C2
Paterson Ave DE21 ....220 A3
Patmore Sq DE23 ....231 A1
Paton Gr S43 ....96 B4
Patrick Cl DE12 ....261 B3
Patten Ct DE24 ....232 A3
Patterdale Cl 3 S18 ....56 C1
Patterson Pl NG18 ....206 A1

Pattison St S44 ....98 C3
Paulet High Sch DE15 ....254 C4
Paulson's Dr NG18 ....268 B4
Pavilion Cl S43 ....80 C1
Pavilion Gdns*
    Buxton SK17 ....85 A4
    New Houghton NG19 ....134 C4
Pavilion Rd Derby DE23 ....231 B4
    Ilkeston DE7 ....194 C3
Pavilion Workshops
    S42 ....116 B1
Paxton Cl Derby DE3 ....217 B1
    Matlock DE4 ....143 A3
Paxton Ct S14 ....43 C2
Paxton Gdns NG3 ....268 C2
Paxton Rd S41 ....96 A3
Payler Cl S2 ....44 A4
Payne St DE22 ....218 B3
Peach Ave Selston NG16 ....171 C3
    South Normanton DE55 ....160 A4
Peach St Derby DE22 ....218 B3
    Heanor DE75 ....181 B1
Peachey St NG1 ....268 B3
Peacock Cl Glossop SK13 ....9 C2
    Killamarsh S21 ....60 B3
Peacock Dr DE23 ....231 A3
Peacock Pl DE7 ....194 B2
Peacock St NG18 ....268 B3
Peacock Way DE55 ....169 C4
Peacroft Cl DE65 ....228 B1
Peacroft La DE65 ....228 B1
Peafield La NG19 ....136 C2
Peafield Lane Prim Sch
    NG19 ....136 C2
Peak Ave DE55 ....170 A3
Peak Cavern* S33 ....38 A1
Peak Cl S45 ....132 A2
Peak Dale Prim Sch
    SK17 ....67 A3
Peak District Mus of
    Mining* DE4 ....143 A1
Peak Dr DE23,DE24 ....232 A4
Peak Forest CE Prim Sch
    SK17 ....49 A2
Peak Ho SK13 ....10 A3
Peak Pl S43 ....97 B4
Peak Rd SK22 ....33 B4
Peak Rly* DE4 ....143 A3
Peak The NG20 ....119 C3
Peak View Clowne S43 ....80 B3
    South Normanton DE55 ....159 C3
Peak View Dr DE6 ....173 B3
Peak View Rd S40 ....95 B3
Peakdale Cl
    Long Eaton NG10 ....236 A3
    Ripley DE5 ....180 B3
Peakdale Cres S12 ....44 C2
Peakdale Rd Glossop SK13 ....9 C2
    Marple SK6 ....23 A2
Peakland View DE4 ....127 A2
Peaknaze Cl SK13 ....17 A4
Pear Tree Ave
    Ripley DE5 ....180 B4
    Swadlincote DE11 ....255 C4
    Wingerworth S42 ....114 C2
Pear Tree Cl
    Brimington S43 ....97 A4
    Glossop SK13 ....9 C2
    Hartshorne DE11 ....257 A4
    Killamarsh S21 ....60 B3
    Marple SK6 ....23 A2
Pear Tree Com Jun Sch
    DE23 ....219 A1
Pear Tree Cres DE23 ....232 A4
Pear Tree Dr
    Linton DE12 ....261 B3
    Shirebrook NG20 ....119 C3
Pear Tree Rd S45 ....132 B1
Pear Tree St DE23 ....219 A1
Pearce La S42 ....114 B2
Pearl Bank DE6 ....211 C4
Pearl Cl DE21 ....206 A4
Pearl Way SK14 ....9 A1
Pearson Croft S41 ....95 B3
Peartree Cl DE74 ....247 A2
Peartree Ct DE21 ....205 B1
Peartree La NG17 ....134 A4
Peartree Sta DE23 ....232 A4
Peas Hill Rd NG3 ....268 B2
Pease Cl DE55 ....159 A2
Pease Hill DE55 ....159 A2
Peasehill DE5 ....180 C4
Peasehill Rd DE5 ....180 C4
Peasunhurst La S45 ....113 A1
Peat La DE4,DE56 ....166 B2
Peatburn Ave DE75 ....181 B1
Peatfield Ct NG9 ....209 B1
Peatfield Rd
    Killamarsh S21 ....60 C4
    Stapleford NG9 ....209 B1
Peats Cl DE6 ....165 A1
Peckham Gdns DE22 ....218 A3
Pedley Ave 11 S20 ....59 C4
Pedley Dr 2 S20 ....59 C4
Pedley St DE7 ....208 C4
Peebles Cl DE24 ....231 C1
Peel Cres NG19 ....135 B1
Peel Gdns S18 ....56 C1
Peel Rd NG19 ....268 A4
Peel St Derby DE22 ....218 B3
    Glossop SK13 ....10 B3
    Langley Mill NG16 ....182 A2
    Long Eaton NG10 ....236 B4
    Nottingham NG1 ....268 A2
    South Normanton DE55 ....160 A3
    Stafford ST16 ....269 A4
Peers Cl DE21 ....206 A1

Peet St DE22 ....218 C2
Pegasus Sch DE12 ....260 C4
Pegasus Way DE65 ....228 C1
Peggars Cl S43 ....80 A3
Peggs Wlk DE21 ....206 A1
Pegwell Cl DE21 ....231 B4
Pelham Ave DE7 ....194 C1
Pelham Cres NG7 ....268 A1
Pelham St Derby DE22 ....218 C2
    Ilkeston DE7 ....194 C1
    Mansfield NG18 ....268 C4
    15 Nottingham NG1 ....268 B1
Pemberton St NG1 ....268 B1
Pemberton The DE55 ....160 A2
Pembleton Dr NG19 ....135 B1
Pembrey Cl NG9 ....209 B1
Pembroke Cl 7 S40 ....95 B1
Pembroke Ct 6 S41 ....95 C4
Pembroke Rd
    Dronfield S18 ....76 A4
    Shireoaks S81 ....63 C4
Pembroke St DE21 ....219 B4
Pen Cl DE55 ....148 A2
Penalton Cl DE24 ....232 C3
Pencroft Gr DE23 ....231 B3
Pendean Cl DE55 ....147 C2
Pendennis Cl DE24 ....233 A3
Pendine Cl DE55 ....160 B3
Pendlebury Dr DE7 ....217 C1
Pendleside Way DE23 ....230 C4
Pendleton La DE56 ....166 C4
Penfold Way S45 ....147 A3
Penge Rd DE22 ....218 A4
Penhaligan's Cl DE73 ....232 C1
Penine View DE56 ....179 C4
Peniston Rise DE73 ....232 C1
Penistone Gdns S45 ....131 B1
Penkhull Inf Sch ST4 ....269 B2
Penkhull New Rd ST4 ....269 B1
Penkhull St ST4 ....269 B1
Penkridge St ST4 ....269 B1
Penmore Cl S41 ....115 B4
Penmore Gdns S41 ....96 B1
Penmore La S41 ....115 B4
Penn La DE73 ....252 A4
Penn Moor Cl NG10 ....236 A3
Penn St NG3 ....179 A2
Penncroft Dr S45 ....131 B1
Penncroft La S45 ....131 B2
Pennine Cl NG10 ....236 B2
Penniment La NG16 ....135 A1
Pennine Cl DE55 ....170 B4
Pennine Cl
    Long Eaton NG10 ....223 A1
    Mansfield Woodhouse
        NG19 ....136 B2
    Newton DE55 ....148 A2
    Sutton in a NG17 ....148 C2
    Tibshelf DE55 ....147 C3
Pennine Dr Selston NG16 ....171 C4
    South Normanton DE55 ....159 C2
Pennine Rd SK13 ....17 A4
Pennine View S44 ....118 A3
Pennine Way
    Chesterfield S40 ....95 B3
    Grassmoor S42 ....115 C2
    Swadlincote DE11 ....256 A2
Pennine Way Jun Sch
    DE11 ....256 A1
Penns Rd S2 ....43 B3
Penny Engine La S21 ....59 C2
Penny Gn S80 ....82 A3
Penny La S17 ....55 B3
Penny Long La DE22 ....218 C4
Pennycress Cl DE23 ....231 A4
Pennycroft La ST14 ....210 A1
Pennycroft Rd ST14 ....210 A1
Pennycrofts ST16 ....269 B4
Pennycrofts Ct ST16 ....269 B4
Pennyfields Bvd NG10 ....236 A4
Pennyfoot St NG1 ....268 C1
Pennytown Ct DE55 ....159 B1
Pennyunk La DE45 ....89 C1
Pennywell Dr S42 ....114 B3
Penrhyn Ave DE23 ....218 B1
Penrhyn Cl NG3 ....268 B2
Penrith Pl DE21 ....205 B1
Penrose Cres S44 ....97 B2
Penryn Cl DE55 ....160 B3
Pentagon The DE21 ....219 B3
Pentewen Cl DE21 ....204 C1
Penthorpe Cl S12 ....44 A3
Pentland Cl
    5 Chesterfield S40 ....95 B3
    Derby DE21 ....206 A1
Pentland Gdns NG10 ....223 A1
Pentland Rd S18 ....56 B1
Pentrich Rd Ripley DE5 ....169 B1
    Swanwick DE55 ....169 B4
Pentridge Dr DE7 ....194 B2
Penzance Rd DE24 ....233 A3
People's Coll The
    Nottingham, Castle Lock
        NG1 ....268 C2
    Nottingham, Sneinton NG3 ....268 C2
Pepper La DE7 ....208 C1
Pepper St NG1 ....268 B1
Percy St Derby DE22 ....218 C2
    Ilkeston DE7 ....208 C4
Percy Wood Cl DE55 ....228 B1
Peregrine Cl
    Burton u T DE15 ....248 B2
    3 Derby DE24 ....231 B2
Peregrine Way S26 ....61 C3

Perlethorpe Ave
    Mansfield NG19 ....136 A1
    Nottingham NG2 ....268 C1
Perrymount Ct S14 ....269 A1
Pershore Dr DE24 ....231 A2
Perth Cl Burton u T DE15 ....248 B1
    Derby DE3 ....217 C2
    Mansfield Woodhouse
        NG19 ....136 B3
Perth Dr NG9 ....209 C1
Perth St Derby DE21 ....205 B1
    Nottingham NG1 ....268 B2
Peter Baines Ind Est
    DE22 ....267 A1
Peter More Hill S80 ....81 C2
Peter St Ashbourne DE6 ....173 B1
    Glossop SK13 ....10 A3
Peterborough St DE21 ....219 C4
Peterdale Cl S43 ....96 C4
Peterdale Rd S43 ....96 C4
Peterhouse Terr 2
    DE23 ....219 A1
Peterlee Pl DE24 ....233 A3
Peters Ave S45 ....131 A2
Peters Ct DE65 ....227 B1
Petersgate NG10 ....223 A1
Petersgate Cl NG10 ....223 A1
Petersham Ct 5 NG10 ....223 A1
Petersham Dr DE24 ....233 B3
Petersham Rd NG10 ....223 A1
Peterway DE55 ....170 A3
Pettifor Terr DE55 ....147 B1
Petty Close La DE6 ....202 B1
Pettyclose La S41,S43 ....96 B3
Petworth Ave NG9 ....223 C2
Pevensey Ave S41 ....95 C3
Pevensey Ct S41 ....95 C4
Peveril Ave
    Borrowash DE72 ....221 B1
    New Mills SK22 ....24 B1
Peveril Castle* S33 ....38 B1
Peveril Cl Castleton S33 ....38 B1
    Darley Dale DE4 ....127 B2
    Somercotes DE55 ....170 B3
Peveril Cres
    Long Eaton NG10 ....235 C3
    West Hallam DE7 ....207 C4
Peveril Ct
    1 Glossop SK13 ....17 C4
    Ripley DE5 ....169 B1
Peveril Dr Ilkeston DE7 ....194 B1
    Nottingham NG7 ....268 A1
    Somercotes DE55 ....170 B3
Peveril Gdns SK12 ....33 A3
Peveril Mews S41 ....33 A3
Peveril Rd Buxton SK17 ....85 B4
    Castleton S33 ....38 B1
    Chesterfield S41 ....95 C4
    Eckington S21 ....59 C2
    Tibshelf DE55 ....147 C3
Peveril St DE24 ....232 B3
Peveril Rd S44 ....98 C2
Pewit Cl S42 ....132 B4
Pewit La Pilsley DE55 ....147 B3
    Tibshelf DE55 ....147 B3
Pheasant Field Dr DE21 ....221 A3
Pheasant Hill NG19 ....136 A2
Philip Howard Rd SK13 ....17 B4
Philips Croft DE56 ....190 C2
Philipway DE55 ....170 B4
Phoenix Cl S12 ....44 C1
Phoenix Rd S12 ....44 C1
Phoenix St DE1 ....267 B4
Phyllis Gr NG10 ....236 C4
Pic Tor La DE4 ....143 A2
Piccadilly La DE6 ....172 B1
Piccadilly Rd S41 ....96 B2
Pickard La DE56 ....168 B2
Pickburns Gdns DE56 ....191 C4
Pickering Ave NG16 ....182 C1
Pickering Rise DE21 ....205 B1
Pickford Pl SK23 ....47 A3
Pickleys La DE6 ....224 B4
Pickton Cl S40 ....95 B1
Pictor Cl SK17 ....85 B4
Pictor Rd SK17 ....85 B4
Piddocks Rd DE15 ....255 A3
Pig La DE4 ....111 A2
Pighills La S18 ....75 A2
Pike Cl S40 ....95 A3
Pike View Cl SK23 ....34 C1
Pike's La SK13 ....17 A4
Pilcher Gate NG1 ....268 B1
Pilgrim Cl S81 ....63 C4
Pilgrim Pl S16 ....269 B3
Pilgrim St S16 ....269 B3
Pilgrims Way DE24 ....231 B2
Pilhough La DE4 ....126 B3
Pilhough Rd DE4 ....126 B3
Pilkington's Yd S21 ....59 C2
Pillar Butts DE4 ....165 C4
Pilsley CE Prim Sch
    DE45 ....91 B3
Pilsley Cl DE56 ....179 B3
Pilsley Prim Sch S45 ....132 B1
Pilsley Rd Clay Cross S45 ....131 C2
    Stonebroom DE55 ....147 A3
Pimlico Derby DE22 ....218 A3
    Ilkeston DE7 ....208 B3
Pimm's Rd DE6 ....217 A4
Pinch The DE6 ....150 A1
Pinchom's Hill Rd DE56 ....179 A2
Pincot Rd SK22 ....33 B4
Pindale Ave S43 ....97 B4
Pindale Rd S33 ....38 C1
Pinder St NG1 ....268 B1
Pine Ave NG16 ....182 A2
Pine Cl Burton u T DE14 ....254 A4

Pine Cl continued
    Creswell S80 ....
    Derby DE21 ....
    Etwall DE65 ....
    Killamarsh S21 ....
    Mansfield Woodhouse
        NG19 ....
    Ripley DE5 ....
    Shirebrook NG20 ....
    Smalley DE7 ....
Pine Croft DE6 ....
Pine Gr DE11 ....
Pine St S43 ....
Pine Tree Wlk NG16 ....
Pine View Chesterfield S40 ....
    Clay Cross S45 ....
Pine Wlk DE11 ....
Pinecroft Ct DE21 ....
Pinegreaves Dr DE73 ....
Pines The DE72 ....
Pinewood Ct DE55 ....
Pinewood Cl DE55 ....
Pinewood Rd
    Belper DE56 ....
    Burton u T DE15 ....
    Matlock DE4 ....
Pinfold S43 ....
    Holymoorside S42 ....
    Repton DE65 ....
    Tutbury DE13 ....
Pinfold Cres SK17 ....
Pinfold Hill S32 ....
Pinfold La Bradley DE6 ....
    Repton DE65 ....
    Stapleford NG9 ....
Pinfold Rd SK17 ....
Pinfold St S21 ....
Pinfold The Belper DE56 ....
    Elvaston DE72 ....
    Glapwell S44 ....
    Middleton DE45 ....
Pinfold View DE45 ....
Pingle
    Pingle Cres DE56 ....
    Pingle Farm Rd DE11 ....
    Pingle Grange S43 ....
Pingle La Belper DE56 ....
    Carsington DE4 ....
Pingle Rd S21 ....
Pingle Sch DE11 ....
Pingle The Derby DE21 ....
    Long Eaton NG10 ....
    Melbourne DE73 ....
Pinglehill Way DE73 ....
Pingott La SK13 ....
Pintail Dr DE24 ....
Pinxton Gn NG16 ....
Pinxton La
    Kirby-in-A NG17 ....
    South Normanton DE55 ....
Piper Ave S45 ....
Piper La S45 ....
Pipeyard La S21 ....
Pippenwell Rd SK17 ....
Pippin Hill DE5 ....
Pipworth La S21 ....
Pit Close La DE7 ....
Pit La Codnor DE5 ....
    Crich DE4,DE55 ....
    Ripley DE5 ....
    Sheffield S2 ....
    Shipley DE75 ....
    Shirland DE55 ....
Pitch Cl S43 ....
Pitt Hill NG20 ....
Pitt St S21 ....
Pittar St DE22 ....
Pittlemere La SK17 ....
Pittywood Rd DE4 ....
Placket La DE11 ....
Plackett Cl
    Breaston DE72 ....
    Stapleford NG9 ....
Plain The DE6 ....
Plains La DE56 ....
Plainspot Rd NG16 ....
Plaistow Green Rd DE4 ....
Plant La NG10 ....
Plantagenet Ct 10 NG3 ....
Plantagenet St NG3 ....
Plantain Gdns DE23 ....
Plantation Cl S80 ....
Plantation Rd S8 ....
Plantations The 9
    NG10 ....
Plantin Rise S20 ....
Plantin The S20 ....
Platt St Glossop SK13 ....
    Pinxton NG16 ....
Platts Ave DE75 ....
Pleasant Ave S44 ....
Pleasant Cl DE11 ....
Pleasant Pl S41 ....
Pleasant Rd S12 ....
Pleasant View SK6 ....
Plimsoll St DE22 ....
Plough Gate DE22 ....
Plough La NG1 ....
Ploughfield Cl DE23 ....
Plover Ave DE11 ....
Plover Ct DE3 ....
Plover Way S44 ....
Plowman Ct NG9 ....
Plowright Cl S14 ....
Plowright Dr S14 ....
Plowright Mount S14 ....

ight Way S14 . . . . . .43 B3
sbridge Rd SK6 . . . . .23 A2
bley Hall Mews S20 . .59 B3
bley Hall Rd S20 . . . .59 B3
bley La S20 . . . . .59 A3
her Rd DE11 . . . . . . .256 A3
otre CI NG16 . . . . . . .182 C1
otre Pl NG1 . . . . . . .268 B1
otre Sq NG1 . . . . . . .268 B1
otre St S43 . . . . .77 B4
otre Way NG16 . . . . .182 C1
tre Rd NG16 . . . . . . .182 A3
outh Ave NG16 . . . . .160 C1
hedge La S42 . . . . . .113 B4
La Marple S42 . . . . . .24 A2
Mills SK22,S6 . . . . . .24 A2
s Rd DE6 . . . . .217 A4
rd's Rd NG18 . . . . . .268 C4
rds Oaks DE72 . . . . .221 B1
Froggat La S32 . . . . .72 A1
ields La S44 . . . . . . .118 A4
La Tupton S42 . . . . . .131 B4
erworth S42 . . . . .114 C2
Rd DE56 . . . . .191 B4
St S40 . . . . .266 B2
well Cnr S43 . . . . . . .96 C4
well Dr S43 . . . . .96 C4
enby Terr DE1 . . . . . .218 C3
efract St DE24 . . . . . .232 B4
ypool CI DE21 . . . . . .206 A1
CI Elvaston DE24 . . . .233 B2
ley NG16 . . . . .160 B1
Rd DE73 . . . . .252 B3
St DE11 . . . . .256 B1
s La S21 . . . . .77 B4
ar Terr NG16 . . . . . . .171 C3
e St DE24 . . . . .232 C3
e's Cavern* SK17 . . . .85 A3
s Brook Ctry Pk* 79 A1
sbrook Ave S43 . . . . .98 A4
sbrook Country Pk* 97 C4
sbrook Cres S43 . . . .98 A4
sbrook Prim Sch 98 A4
sbrook Rd S43 . . . . . .98 A3
sbrook Sq S43 . . . . . .98 A4
sbrook View S43 . . . .98 A4
e Carr Rd DE4 . . . . . .143 B3
ham St NG1 . . . . . . .268 B1
ar Ave
esterfield S40 . . . . . .95 A1
oy DE21 . . . . .220 C3
Dr DE21 . . . . .262 C1
w Mills SK22 . . . . . . .24 B1
ey DE5 . . . . .180 B4
diacre NG10 . . . . . . .223 A4
dlincote DE11 . . . . . .256 A3
ar CI Derby DE24 . . . .233 A4
nfield S18 . . . . .78 B4
amarsh S21 . . . . .60 B3
ar Cres DE6 . . . . . . .185 B4
ar Dr
esterfield S42 . . . . . .115 B1
swell S44 . . . . .134 A4
ington NG3 . . . . .135 A2
ar Nook DE22 . . . . . .204 C2
ar Rd Breaston DE22 . .235 C4
ington S21 . . . . .59 B1
h Normanton DE55 . . .160 A4
ar Row DE22 . . . . . . .205 A1
ar St
nsfield Woodhouse
e 136 B2
tingham NG1 . . . . . . .268 C1
lar Terr S43 . . . . .47 A4
lar Way High Lane SK6 . .32 A4
or DE5 . . . . .180 B3
lars The Derby DE21 . . .204 C2
well S80 . . . . .82 A3
py CI NG20 . . . . . . .119 B2
py Gdns DE55 . . . . . .148 A4
lock CI 3 NG10 . . . .236 A4
Rock CI DE21 . . . . . .206 A1
t Way DE21,DE56 . . . .191 B3
teous CI DE4 . . . . . . .127 B2
ter La DE4 . . . . .154 C2
ter Rd DE23 . . . . . . .218 C1
ter St S43 . . . . .78 B1
ter's La Derby DE21 . . .205 C2
adern DE65 . . . . .230 B1
terhouse Rd DE5 . . . .169 C1
ters Farm CI S14 . . . .224 C1
tincavl Pl DE21 . . . . . .206 B1
tico Rd DE23 . . . . . . .231 A3
rtland Ave Bolsover S44 . .99 A1
on-T DE14 . . . . .254 A4
eswell S80 . . . . .81 C1
rtland CI DE3 . . . . . .217 B1
rtland Cres
slsover S44 . . . . .99 A1
nsfield Woodhouse
e 136 B2
apleford NG9 . . . . . . .223 C3
rtland Ct Mews DE21 . .136 B2
rtland Gr SK23 . . . . . .34 C1
rtland Rd
eston NG9 . . . . .223 C1
astwood NG16 . . . . . .195 A4
reston DE7 . . . . .194 C2
ang Eaton NG10 . . . . .236 A2
w Mills SK22 . . . . . . .24 B1
ottingham NG7 . . . . . .268 A2
elper DE56 . . . . .119 C2
haley Thorns NG20 . . .101 A1
rtland Ret Pk NG18 . . .268 B3
rtland Sq DE45 . . . . .109 B3

Portland St Clowne S43 . . .81 A2
Derby DE23 . . . . .232 A4
Etwall DE65 . . . . .229 A2
Mansfield NG18 . . . . .268 B3
Mansfield Woodhouse
NG19 . . . . .136 B2
New Houghton NG19 . . . .135 A4
Whitwell S80 . . . . .81 C3
Portland Terr NG20 . . . . .101 A1
Portman Chase DE24 . . . .231 B1
Portreath Dr DE22 . . . . . .204 C2
Portway CI DE22 . . . . . . .205 A2
Portway Dr DE13 . . . . . . .239 63
Portway Inf Sch DE22 . . . .204 C2
Portway Jun Sch DE22 . . .204 C2
Post St SK13 . . . . .10 A3
Postern St 4 NG1 . . . . . .268 A1
Postmans La S42 . . . . . . .116 B2
Posy La DE72 . . . . .246 A4
Potato Pit Hill DE7 . . . . . .208 A1
Potlocks The DE65 . . . . . .242 B3
Potter Rd SK13 . . . . .9 C2
Potter St Derby DE21 . . . .220 B2
Melbourne DE73 . . . . . . .252 A4
Potters CI S41 . . . . .77 B1
Potters Croft
Clifton Campville B79 . . . .263 C1
Swadlincote DE11 . . . . . .256 A3
Potters La DE4,DE65 . . . .157 A3
Potters Nook S81 . . . . . . .63 C4
Pottery La DE5 . . . . .209 A4
Pottery La CI DE56 . . . . . .179 B3
Pottery La DE5 . . . . .180 B2
Pottery La E S41 . . . . . . .96 A4
Pottery La W S41 . . . . . . .96 A4
Pottery Prim Sch DE56 . . .179 B2
Poulson St S14 . . . . .269 B2
Poulter Ctry Pk NG20 . . . .100 C1
Poulter St NG20 . . . . . . .100 C1
Poulton Dr NG2 . . . . .268 B1
Poultry N41 . . . . .268 B1
Powell Dr S21 . . . . .60 B3
Powell St DE23 . . . . .218 C1
Pown St SK17 . . . . .137 A3
Powtrell Pl DE7 . . . . .209 A3
Poynter CI DE75 . . . . . . .181 B1
Poynton Wood Cres S17 . .56 A3
Poynton Wood Glade
S17 . . . . .56 A3
Poyser Ave DE21 . . . . . . .220 A4
Poyser La DE6 . . . . .203 A1
Pratt CI NG19 . . . . .135 B1
Pratthall La DE4 . . . . . . .166 A3
Premier Ave DE6 . . . . . . .185 A4
Prescot CI DE3 . . . . .217 B1
Prescott Ave SK16 . . . . . .269 C2
Press La S42 . . . . .130 B3
Prestbury CI DE21 . . . . . .206 A1
Preston Ave DE55 . . . . . .159 A2
Preston St 10 S8 . . . . . . .43 A4
Prestwold Way S41 . . . . . .115 B4
Prestwood CI S17 . . . . . .269 B3
Prestwood La S14 . . . . . .196 C4
Prestwood Park Dr
DE11 . . . . .256 B3
Pretoria St S44 . . . . .98 C3
Previn Gdns NG3 . . . . . . .268 C2
Pride Park Stad (Derby FC)
DE24 . . . . .219 C2
Pride Parkway DE21,DE21 .219 B2
Priestcliffe Rd SK17 . . . . .87 C2
Priestfield Gdns S41 . . . . .95 A4
Priestland Ave DE21 . . . . .220 B2
Priestley Ave DE5 . . . . . .146 B3
Primary CI DE56 . . . . . . .179 A2
Prime Ind Est DE23 . . . . .219 B1
Prime Ind Pk DE23 . . . . .219 B1
Prime Parkway DE1 . . . . .267 C5
Primrose Ave NG16 . . . . .171 C1
Primrose CI Derby DE21 . .205 C2
Killamarsh S21 . . . . .60 C4
South Normanton DE55 . . .160 A4
Primrose Cotts DE72 . . . .222 B2
Primrose Cres 8 S13 . . .17 A4
Primrose CI SK22 . . . . . .25 B2
Primrose Dr
Burton u T DE14 . . . . . . .254 A4
Morley DE7 . . . . .206 B4
Primrose Hill
Blackwell DE55 . . . . .147 C1
Glossop SK13 . . . . .17 A4
Killamarsh S21 . . . . .60 C4
Marple SK6 . . . . .24 A2
Primrose Mdw DE11 . . . . .256 A4
Primrose Rise NG16 . . . . .195 A4
Primrose St DE7 . . . . . . .194 C2
Primrose Terr 8 SK13 . . .17 A4
Primrose Way NG20 . . . . .119 C3
Primula CI NG20 . . . . . . .119 B2
Primula Way DE23 . . . . . .231 B2
Prince Charles Ave
DE22 . . . . .218 A3
Prince Edward Prim Sch
S2 . . . . .44 A4
Prince of Wales Rd S2 . . .44 A4
Prince St Ilkeston DE7 . . .194 C1
Long Eaton NG10 . . . . . .236 B4
Prince's Rd SK17 . . . . . . .85 B4
Princes Dr DE23 . . . . . . .218 A1
Princes Rd Chinley SK23 . .34 C1
Stoke-on-T ST4 . . . . .269 A1
Mansfield NG18 . . . . . . .268 B3
4 Stafford ST16 . . . . . . .269 B4
Princess Ave
Linton DE12 . . . . .261 B3

Princess Ave continued
South Normanton DE55 . . .160 A3
Princess CI Heanor DE75 . .181 B1
Woodville DE11 . . . . .256 C1
Princess Ct S2 . . . . .44 A4
Princess Dr
Borrowash DE72 . . . . . . .221 A1
Sandiacre NG10 . . . . . . .223 A2
Princess PI S45 . . . . .131 B1
Princess Rd Dronfield S18 .57 A1
Uttoxeter ST14 . . . . .210 A1
Princess St
Brimington S43 . . . . .96 C4
Chesterfield S40 . . . . . . .266 A4
Eastwood NG16 . . . . . . .182 C2
Glossop SK13 . . . . .17 B4
Long Eaton NG10 . . . . . .236 B4
Swadlincote DE11 . . . . . .256 A1
Princess Way DE13 . . . . .240 C1
Printers Fold SK14 . . . . . .9 B3
Printers Pk SK14 . . . . . . .9 C3
Priors Barn CI DE72 . . . . .221 B1
Priorway Ave DE72 . . . . . .221 B1
Priorway Gdns DE72 . . . . .221 B1
Priory Cl Derby DE73 . . . .245 A4
Ilkeston DE7 . . . . .208 B3
Swadlincote DE11 . . . . . .256 A3
Tutbury DE13 . . . . .239 A3
Yeaveley DE6 . . . . .199 B3
Priory CI S26 . . . . .61 C3
Priory Gdns Derby DE21 . .205 C2
Swanwick DE55 . . . . . . .170 A4
Priory Lands DE11 . . . . . .240 C1
Priory Rd Alfreton DE55 . .159 A3
Eastwood NG16 . . . . . . .182 C1
Mansfield Woodhouse
NG19 . . . . .136 A2
Priory Sq NG19 . . . . .136 A2
Pritchard Dr NG9 . . . . . . .223 C3
Pritchett Dr DE23 . . . . . .230 C4
Private Dr S43 . . . . .78 A1
Progress CI DE65 . . . . . .109 B3
Promenade 21 NG2 . . . . .268 B2
Prospect Ave DE55 . . . . .159 C3
Prospect Ct
10 Sheffield S17 . . . . . .56 A3
Sutton in A NG17 . . . . . .148 C1
Prospect Dr Belper DE56 . .178 C1
Matlock DE4 . . . . .143 A3
Sheffield S17 . . . . .56 A3
Shirebrook NG20 . . . . . .119 C2
Prospect Gdns DE55 . . . .169 C4
Prospect PI 5 S17 . . . . . .56 A3
Prospect Rd
Chesterfield S40 . . . . . . .76 C1
Denby DE5 . . . . .180 A1
Dronfield S18 . . . . .57 B2
Heanor DE75 . . . . .194 A4
Pilsley DE5 . . . . .132 B1
Sheffield, Lowfield S2 . . . .43 A4
Sheffield, Tinsley Rise S17 .56 A3
Stafford ST16 . . . . .269 B4
Prospect St
Alfreton DE55 . . . . .159 A2
Mansfield NG18 . . . . . . .268 C3
Prospect Terr
Chesterfield S40 . . . . . . .95 C2
Crich DE4 . . . . .168 A4
Providence Ct DE11 . . . . .256 C1
Providence PI
Alfreton DE55 . . . . .158 C2
8 Ilkeston DE7 . . . . . . .194 C1
Providence Rd NG16 . . . .171 A2
Providence St DE5 . . . . . .180 C4
Provident St 9 DE23 . . . .219 A1
Pryor Mede S26 . . . . .61 C3
Pudding Bag La S45 . . . . .129 C2
Pulborough Gdns DE23 . . .231 A3
Pullman CI S43 . . . . .78 C2
Pullman Rd Derby DE24 . . .219 C2
Nottingham NG2 . . . . . . .268 C1
Pump CI DE4 . . . . .143 B2
Pump La DE6 . . . . .224 A4
Pump St ST4 . . . . .269 B2
Purbeck Ave S40 . . . . . . .95 B2
Purbeck CI
Long Eaton NG10 . . . . . .236 A4
Mansfield Woodhouse
NG19 . . . . .136 B3
Purchase Ave DE75 . . . . .181 B1
Purdy Mdw NG10 . . . . . .235 C3
Purseglove Dr SK17 . . . . .69 B2
Purseglove Rd SK17 . . . . .69 B2
Putney CI DE22 . . . . .217 C3
Pybus St DE23 . . . . .218 B3
Pye Bridge Ind Est
DE55 . . . . .170 C3
Pye Hill Rd NG16 . . . . . .171 A2
Pygreave Rd SK13 . . . . . .10 C1
Pyegrove SK13 . . . . .10 C1
Pykestone CI DE21 . . . . . .205 C1
Pym Leys NG10 . . . . . . .235 A3
Pym St NG3 . . . . .268 C2
Pym Wlk NG3 . . . . .268 C2
Pynot St S41 . . . . .77 A1
Pytchley CI DE56 . . . . . . .179 B2

Q

Quadrant The
Buxton SK17 . . . . .85 A4
Totley S17 . . . . .55 C3
Quaker CI DE73 . . . . . . .252 A4
Quaker La NG18 . . . . . . .268 B3
Quaker Way NG18 . . . . . .268 B4
Quantock CI DE24 . . . . . .231 B1
Quantock Rd NG10 . . . . .223 A1

Quantock Way S40 . . . . . .95 A3
Quarn Gdns DE1 . . . . . . .218 C4
Quarn St DE1 . . . . .218 C4
Quarn Way DE1 . . . . . . .218 C4
Quarndon Hts DE22 . . . . .204 B2
Quarndon View DE22 . . . .204 B1
Quarry Ave S14 . . . . .269 A2
Quarry Bank DE4 . . . . . .143 A4
Quarry Bank Rd S41 . . . . .96 B1
Quarry Berry La DE12 . . . .264 C1
Quarry CI SK13 . . . . .10 B1
Quarry Hill Eckington S21 . .58 C1
Mosborough S20 . . . . . . .59 A4
Stanton-by-D DE7 . . . . . .223 A4
Quarry Hill Ind Est DE7 . . .209 A2
Quarry Hill Ind Pk DE7 . . .208 C3
Quarry Hill Rd DE7 . . . . .208 C3
Quarry La Alton S42 . . . . .130 B3
Brackenfield DE55 . . . . . .145 B3
Chesterfield S40 . . . . . . .95 B1
Mansfield NG18 . . . . . . .268 B3
Matlock DE4 . . . . .143 C4
Stoneybroom DE55 . . . . .146 C2
Quarry Rd
Apperknowle S18 . . . . . . .58 A1
Belper DE56 . . . . .178 C1
Bolsover S44 . . . . .99 A2
Hayfield SK22 . . . . .25 C1
Kilamarsh S21 . . . . .60 B4
Morley DE7 . . . . .192 A1
New Mills SK22 . . . . .33 B4
Somercotes DE55 . . . . . .170 B4
Stoke-on-T ST4 . . . . .269 A2
Quarry Vale Gr S12 . . . . . .44 B2
Quarry Vale Rd S12 . . . . . .44 B2
Queen Anne St S14 . . . . .269 B2
Queen Elizabeth CE Comp
Sch NG19 . . . . .136 A1
Queen Elizabeth Ct DE6 . .173 A1
Queen Elizabeth Way
DE7 . . . . .208 B3
Queen Elizabeth's Gram Sch
DE6 . . . . .173 B2
Queen Elizabeth's Lower Sch
Department DE1 . . . . . . .185 B3
Queen Mary Cres S2 . . . . .44 A4
Queen Mary Cres S2 . . . . .44 A4
Queen Mary Ct DE1 . . . . .218 C4
Queen Mary Gr S2 . . . . . .43 C4
Queen Mary Mews S2 . . . .44 A4
Queen Mary Rd
Chesterfield S40 . . . . . . .95 A1
Sheffield S2 . . . . .44 A4
Queen St Belper DE56 . . .179 A2
Brimington S43 . . . . .77 C1
Chesterfield S40 . . . . . . .266 A4
Clay Cross S45 . . . . .131 B2
Creswell S80 . . . . .81 C1
Derby DE1 . . . . .267 B4
Eckington S21 . . . . .59 C2
Glossop SK13 . . . . .17 A4
Ilkeston DE7 . . . . .208 C4
Ironville NG16 . . . . .170 C2
Langley Mill NG16 . . . . . .182 B2
Long Eaton NG10 . . . . . .236 C4
Longnor SK17 . . . . .121 A3
Mansfield NG18 . . . . . . .268 B4
Marple SK6 . . . . .23 A3
Middleton (nr Wirksworth)
DE4 . . . . .154 B3
Mosborough S20 . . . . . . .59 B4
22 Nottingham NG1 . . . . .268 B2
Pilsley S45 . . . . .132 C1
Pinxton NG16 . . . . .160 B2
Ripley DE5 . . . . .181 A4
Somercotes DE55 . . . . . .170 B4
South Normanton DE55 . . .159 C3
Staveley S43 . . . . .78 B2
Swadlincote DE11 . . . . . .256 A1
Tideswell SK17 . . . . .69 B2
Queen St N S41 . . . . .96 A4
Queen Victoria Rd
Totley S17 . . . . .55 C3
New Tupton S42 . . . . . . .115 B1
Queen's Ave S41 . . . . . . .266 A4
Queen's CI S41 . . . . .266 A4
Queen's Dr Belper DE56 . .178 C1
Derby DE23 . . . . .218 B1
Ilkeston DE7 . . . . .208 C4
Swadlincote DE11 . . . . . .256 A3
Queen's Park Sports Ctr
S40 . . . . .266 A2
Queen's Rd N17 . . . . . . .85 B4
Nottingham NG2 . . . . . . .268 B1
Stoke-on-T ST4 . . . . .269 A2
Queen's Sq NG16 . . . . . .182 C1
Queen's Way Sch S42 . . . .115 B1
Queen's Wlk Sutton S42 . .115 B1
Whaley Thorns NG20 . . . .101 A1
Queens Ave Heanor DE75 .181 B1
Ilkeston DE7 . . . . .209 A3
Stanley DE7 . . . . .207 B3
Sutton S80 . . . . .82 B3
Queens Ct
Burton u T DE14 . . . . . . .254 A4
Creswell S80 . . . . .81 C1
Draycott DE72 . . . . .235 A4
Derby DE22 . . . . .218 B3
Queens Dr Brinsley NG16 .182 C4
Derby DE23 . . . . .218 B1
Sandiacre NG10 . . . . . . .223 A2
Queens Gr NG2 . . . . .268 B1
Queens L Ctr DE1 . . . . . .267 B4
Queens Rd Creswell S80 . .82 B3

Queens Rd continued
Sheffield S2 . . . . .43 A4
Queens Rd N NG16 . . . . .182 C1
Queens Rd S NG16 . . . . .182 C1
Queens Rd Pk S2 . . . . . . .43 A4
Queens Rise DE13 . . . . . .239 B3
Queens Wlk S42 . . . . . . .115 B1
Queensbury Chase
DE23 . . . . .231 A3
Queensgate Gdns DE24 . .232 C2
Queensgate Dr DE73 . . . .244 C4
Queensland CI DE3 . . . . .217 C2
Queensland Cres DE55 . . .248 B1
Queensview Dr DE5 . . . . .181 A4
Queensville Ave ST17 . . . .269 C3
Queensville Bridge
ST17 . . . . .269 C3
Queensway
Castle Donington DE74 . . .246 C2
Derby DE22 . . . . .204 C1
Holmewood S42 . . . . . . .116 C1
Melbourne DE73 . . . . . . .252 A4
Pilsley S45 . . . . .132 B1
Stafford ST16 . . . . .269 B4
Stoke-on-T ST4 . . . . .269 C1
Somercotes DE55 . . . . . .146 C2
Queenville S17 . . . . .269 C3
Quenby La DE55 . . . . . . .169 C1
Quentin Rd SK23 . . . . . . .47 B3
Quick CI DE73 . . . . .252 A4
Quick Hill Rd DE24 . . . . .231 B1
Quillings Way DE72 . . . . .221 B1
Quilow La DE6 . . . . .185 C2
Quixhill Bank ST14 . . . . . .196 C4
Quixhill CI DE6 . . . . .185 A4
Quixhill La ST14 . . . . . . .196 B4
Quoit Gn S18 . . . . .57 A1
Quorn CI DE15 . . . . .248 A1
Quorn Dr S40 . . . . .95 A3
Quorn Rise DE23 . . . . . . .231 C3
Quorndon Cres NG10 . . . .236 B3

R

Rabown Ave DE23 . . . . . .231 B4
Racecourse Ind Est
DE21 . . . . .219 B4
Racecourse Mount S41 . . .95 C4
Racecourse Rd S41 . . . . .95 C4
Racester Way S42 . . . . . .131 C2
Rad Mdws NG10 . . . . . . .236 B3
Radbourne Gate DE3 . . . .217 B3
Radbourne La DE22 . . . . .217 C3
Radbourne Rd NG2 . . . . .268 C1
Radbourne St
Derby DE22 . . . . .218 B3
Mansfield Woodhouse
NG19 . . . . .136 C2
Radburn Ct NG9 . . . . . . .209 C1
Radcliffe Ave DE21 . . . . . .219 C4
Radcliffe Dr DE22 . . . . . .218 B2
Radford Rd DE7 . . . . .192 C3
Radford St Derby DE24 . . .232 C4
1 Mansfield NG18 . . . . .268 B3
Radmanthwaite Rd
NG19 . . . . .135 B2
Radnor PI NG19 . . . . . . .135 B2
Radnor St DE21 . . . . . . .219 B4
Radstock Gdns DE21 . . . .205 C1
Radstone CI DE21 . . . . . .206 A1
Raeburn CI S14 . . . . .43 C2
Raeburn Dr Beeston NG9 .223 C1
Marple SK6 . . . . .23 A4
Raeburn PI S14 . . . . .43 C2
Raeburn Way S14 . . . . . . .43 C2
Raglan Ave DE22 . . . . . . .218 B3
Raglan St Alfreton DE55 . .159 A2
Fenton ST4 . . . . .269 C1
Raglan Wlk DE7 . . . . . . .269 C1
Railway Ave S80 . . . . . . .100 B4
Railway Cotts
Derby DE23 . . . . .243 A4
Eggington DE65 . . . . . . .241 A4
Holmewood S42 . . . . . . .116 C1
Kimberley NG16 . . . . . . .195 C4
Railway Row NG16 . . . . . .170 C2
Railway Side DE11 . . . . . .256 A1
Railway St Glossop SK13 . .10 B1
Glossop, Hadfield SK13 . . .10 A3
Stafford ST16 . . . . .269 A4
Railway Terr Buxton SK17 . .85 B4
Chesterfield S41 . . . . . . .115 A4
Derby DE1 . . . . .267 D2
Disley SK12 . . . . .32 B3
Rain's La DE4 . . . . .154 B2
Rainham Gdns DE24 . . . .233 A3
Rainier Dr DE21 . . . . . . .220 A3
Rake Head Rd HD7 . . . . . .2 C4
Rake La DE45 . . . . .124 B2
Rake The DE45 . . . . .123 A3
Rakes La DE6 . . . . .162 B4
Rakes Rd DE45 . . . . .107 B1
Raleigh CI DE7 . . . . .194 C2
Raleigh Rd
Mansfield NG18 . . . . . . .268 A4
Sheffield S2 . . . . .43 A3
Raleigh Sq 18 NG7 . . . . .268 A2
Raleigh St Derby DE22 . . .218 B3
Nottingham NG7 . . . . . . .268 A2
Ralph Dr DE55 . . . . .170 B4
Ralph Rd S43 . . . . .79 A1
Ralston Croft S20 . . . . . . .59 C3
Ralston Ct S20 . . . . .59 B3

Ralston Gr S20 . . . . .59 B3
Ralston Pl S20 . . . . .59 B3
Rambler Cl DE11 . . . . . .256 A3
Ramblers Dr DE21 . . . . .206 B2
Ramper Ave S43 . . . . . . .80 C1
Ramscliff Ave DE12 . . . .265 C4
Ramsdean Cl DE21 . . . .219 B4
Ramsden Cl SK13 . . . . . . .10 B1
Ramsden La HD9 . . . . .3 A4
Ramsden Rd HD9 . . . . .3 A4
Ramsey Ave S40 . . . . . . .95 B1
Ramsey Cl NG9 . . . . . . .209 C1
Ramsey St ST4 . . . . . . .269 A2
Ramshaw Cl 6 S41 . . . .95 B4
Ramshaw Rd S18 . . . . . . .76 C3
Ramshaw Way DE22 . . .218 C2
Ranby Wlk NG3 . . . . . . .268 A2
Randall Dr DE11 . . . . . .256 A2
Randall Pl S2 . . . . .43 A4
Randall St S21 . . . . .59 A1
Randolph Rd DE23 . . . . .231 C4
Ranelagh Gdns DE21 . . .205 A4
Raneld Mount S40 . . . . .114 B4
Rangemoor La DE6 . . . .183 B3
Rangemore Cl DE4 . . . .217 C2
Ranmoor Cl S41 . . . . . . .115 B4
Ranmoor Hill S32 . . . . . . .52 C4
Ranmoor La S32 . . . . . . .52 C4
Rannoch Cl Derby DE22 . .204 C2
 Derby, Spondon DE21 . . . .220 C3
Rannoch Dr NG19 . . . . .268 A3
Ratcliffe Ave DE24 . . . . .232 B2
Ratcliffe Cl DE4 . . . . . . .254 A4
Ratcliffe Gate NG18 . . .268 C3
Ratcliffe St NG16 . . . . . .182 C1
Rauche Cl DE23 . . . . . . .267 C1
Raven Ave DE55 . . . . . . .147 C3
Raven Cl DE55 . . . . .170 B3
Raven Oak Cl DE56 . . . .179 A2
Raven St DE22 . . . . .218 C2
Ravencar Rd S21 . . . . . . .59 A2
Ravenscourt Rd DE22 . . .218 B3
Ravenscroft Ave S13 . . . .44 C4
Ravenscroft Cl S13 . . . . .44 C4
Ravenscroft Cres S13 . . .44 C4
Ravenscroft Ct S13 . . . . .44 C4
Ravenscroft Dr
 Derby DE21 . . . . .219 C3
 Sheffield S13 . . . . .44 C4
Ravenscroft Oval S13 . . .44 C4
Ravenscroft Pl S13 . . . . .44 C4
Ravenscroft Rd S13 . . . . .44 C4
Ravenscroft Way S13 . . .44 C4
Ravensdale Ave
 Long Eaton NG10 . . . . . . .223 A1
 Mansfield NG18 . . . . .268 C4
Ravensdale Cl S43 . . . . . .97 B3
Ravensdale Inf & Jun Schs
 DE3 . . . . .217 C2
Ravensdale Rd
 Derby DE22 . . . . .204 B2
 Dronfield S18 . . . . .56 B1
 Mansfield NG18 . . . . .268 C4
Ravenside Ret Pk S40 . . .266 B2
Ravenstor Rd DE4 . . . . . .143 A1
Ravenswood Rd S40 . . . .95 A3
Rawdon Cl DE74 . . . . . . .247 A2
Rawdon Rd DE12 . . . . . .262 C3
Rawdon Side DE11 . . . . .256 B2
Rawdon St DE23 . . . . . . .218 C1
Rawlins Ct S18 . . . . .57 B2
Rawlinson Ave DE23 . . . .232 A4
Rawson Gn DE56 . . . . . .179 C1
Ray's Ave DE75 . . . . .181 C1
Rayleigh Ave S43 . . . . . . .96 B4
Raynald Rd S2 . . . . .44 A4
Rayneham Rd DE7 . . . . .194 B2
Raynesway DE21 . . . . . .220 A1
Raynesway Park Dr
 DE21 . . . . .220 A1
Reader St DE21 . . . . . . .220 C3
Rebecca St ST4 . . . . . . .269 B2
Recreation Cl
 Blackwell DE55 . . . . .147 C1
 Clowne S43 . . . . .80 C2
Recreation Dr NG20 . . . .119 C1
Recreation Gd (Chesterfield
 FC) The S40 . . . . .266 A4
Recreation Rd Calow S43 . .96 C3
 New Houghton NG19 . . . . .134 C4
 Sandiacre NG10 . . . . .223 A3
 Shirebrook NG20 . . . . . . .119 C2
 Tideswell SK17 . . . . .69 B2
 Wirksworth DE4 . . . . .165 C4
Recreation St
 Long Eaton NG10 . . . . . . .236 C4
 Mansfield NG18 . . . . .268 C4
Recreation Terr NG9 . . . .223 B3
Recreation View NG20 . . .119 C3
Rectory Farm Mews
 DE72 . . . . .245 C2
Rectory Gdns
 Aston-on-T DE72 . . . . . . .246 A4
 Hartshill S26 . . . . .61 C3
 Killamarsh S21 . . . . .60 B3
Rectory La
 Breadsall DE21 . . . . .205 B3
 Kirk Ireton DE6 . . . . .165 A1
 Stretton en le F DE12 . . . .265 C1

Rectory Mews DE65 . . . .241 A2
Rectory Pl NG11 . . . . . . .237 C3
Rectory Rd
 Breaston DE72 . . . . .235 C4
 Clowne S43 . . . . .80 C2
 Killamarsh S21 . . . . .60 B3
 Long Duckmanton S44 . . . .98 A3
 Staveley S43 . . . . .78 C1
Reculver Cl DE23 . . . . . .231 B4
Red Barn Cl DE55 . . . . .148 A2
Red Hill DE4 . . . . .144 B2
Red Hill La DE4 . . . . . . .144 B2
Red La Belper DE56 . . . . .191 A3
 Brinsley NG16 . . . . .171 C1
 Disley SK12 . . . . .32 B3
 South Normanton DE55 . . .159 C2
Red Lion Hill DE4 . . . . . .153 A1
Red Lion Sq DE75 . . . . . .181 C1
Red Lion St ST16 . . . . . .269 B4
Redacre Cl S44 . . . . .99 B1
Redbarn La DE55 . . . . . .148 A2
Redbrook Ave S41 . . . . . .115 A4
Redbury Cl DE1 . . . . .218 C2
Redcar Gdns DE21 . . . . .205 B1
Redcliffe Rd NG18 . . . . .268 B3
Reddish Ave S43 . . . . . . .45 B3
Reddish La SK13 . . . . . . .45 B3
Reddish Rd SK23 . . . . . . .45 B3
Redens The NG10 . . . . . .236 A2
Redfern Ave DE55 . . . . . .169 C3
Redfern Cl SK13 . . . . .10 A3
Redfern Rd ST14 . . . . . . .210 A1
Redfern St S42 . . . . .131 B4
Redgap La SK17 . . . . .86 A4
Redgate SK13 . . . . .10 B2
Redgate Cl NG19 . . . . . .268 A4
Redgate Sch NG19 . . . . .268 A4
Redgate St
 Mansfield NG19 . . . . .268 A4
 Pinxton NG16 . . . . .160 B2
Redgrave Dr ST16 . . . . . .269 A3
Redgrove Way S40 . . . . .114 B4
Redhill Ct DE56 . . . . . . .179 A1
Redhill La DE13 . . . . .9 A3
Redhill Lodge Rd 6
 DE11 . . . . .256 A4
Redhill Prim Sch DE72 . .221 B3
Redhouse Cl S43 . . . . . . .77 B2
Redhouse La S43 . . . . . . .77 B2
Redhouse Stables Working
 Carriage Mus* DE4 . . . .127 B1
Redland Cl Derby DE24 . .231 C2
 Ilkeston DE7 . . . . .194 C2
Redmires Dr DE13 . . . . . .233 A1
Redmires Rd S10 . . . . . . .42 A4
Redmoor Cl
 Burton u T DE15 . . . . . . .248 A2
 Codnor DE5 . . . . .170 A1
Redmoor La Disley SK12 . .33 A2
 New Mills SK22 . . . . .33 A3
Rednall Cl S40 . . . . .95 B3
Redruth Pl DE24 . . . . . . .233 B3
Redshaw St DE1 . . . . . . .218 C4
Redstart Cl DE21 . . . . . .220 C3
Redthorn Rd S13 . . . . . . .44 C4
Redvers Buller Rd S40 . . .266 B1
Redway Croft DE73 . . . . .252 A4
Redwing Croft DE23 . . . .231 B4
Redwood Cl S43 . . . . .97 A4
Redwood Dr DE15 . . . . . .255 A4
Redwood Inf Sch DE24 . .231 C2
Redwood Jun Sch DE24 . .231 C2
Redwood Rd DE24 . . . . . .231 C2
Reedman Rd NG10 . . . . .236 A2
Reeves Ave S45 . . . . . . .132 B1
Reeves Rd DE23 . . . . . . .219 A1
Regal Gate DE73 . . . . . . .244 C4
Regency Cl Derby DE23 . .231 B4
 Glossop SK13 . . . . .10 B1
Regent Ct Ironville NG16 . .170 C2
 Swadlincote DE11 . . . . . .256 A1
Regent St Clowne S43 . . . .80 C2
 Derby DE1 . . . . .267 C1
 Glossop SK13 . . . . .10 B1
 Glossop, Padfield SK13 . . . .10 A3
 Ilkeston DE7 . . . . .208 C4
 Kimberley NG16 . . . . .195 C3
 Langley Mill NG16 . . . . . .182 A2
 Long Eaton NG10 . . . . . . .236 B4
 Mansfield NG18 . . . . .268 B4
 Nottingham NG1 . . . . .268 A1
 Stapleford NG9 . . . . .223 B3
 Stoke-on-T ST4 . . . . .269 B1
 Swadlincote DE11 . . . . . .256 A1
Reginald Rd N DE21 . . . .219 C4
Reginald Rd S DE21 . . . .219 C3
Reginald St DE21 . . . . . .219 A1
Regis Cl DE21 . . . . .206 A1
Registry St ST4 . . . . .269 B2
Reigate Dr DE22 . . . . . . .218 A4
Reigate Prim Sch DE22 . .217 C4
Rembrandt Dr S18 . . . . . .56 C1
Rempstone Dr S41 . . . . .115 B4
Renals St DE23 . . . . .267 B1
Reney Ave S8 . . . . .56 B3
Reney Cres S8 . . . . .56 B3
Reney Dr S8 . . . . .56 B3
Reney Rd S8 . . . . .56 B3
Reney Wlk S8 . . . . .56 B3
Renfrew Ct NG19 . . . . . . .268 A3
Renfrew St DE21 . . . . . . .219 C4
Renishaw Hall Mus & Craft
 **Ctr* S21 . . . . .79 C1
Renishaw Prim Sch S21 . .79 A4
Renishaw Rd S43 . . . . . . .79 B2
Renshaw Dr DE11 . . . . . .255 C3
Rent Cl S41 . . . . .95 C3

Repton Ave DE23 . . . . . .218 B1
Repton Cl S40 . . . . .95 A3
Repton Ct NG19 . . . . . . .136 C2
Repton Dr DE7 . . . . .209 A4
Repton Prep Sch DE65 . .243 B1
Repton Prim Sch DE65 . .242 C1
Repton Rd
 Hartshorne DE11 . . . . . . .256 C4
 Newton Solney DE15 . . . . .248 C4
 Willington DE65 . . . . .242 A3
Repton Sch DE65 . . . . . .242 B2
Reservoir Hill DE12 . . . . .262 B3
Reservoir Rd SK23 . . . . . .45 B4
Reservoir Terr S40 . . . . . .95 C2
Resthaven DE11 . . . . . . .256 A3
Retford Cl DE21 . . . . . . .205 B1
Revill Cl DE7 . . . . .194 B1
Revill Cres NG9 . . . . .223 C4
Revolution House Mus The*
 S41 . . . . .77 A1
Reynard Cres S21 . . . . . . .79 A4
Reynards La SK17 . . . . . .137 C2
Reynolds Ave DE5 . . . . . .169 C1
Reynolds Cl S18 . . . . .76 C4
Reynolds Dr SK6 . . . . .23 A4
Rhodes Ave S41 . . . . .95 C3
Rhodes Cotts S43 . . . . . . .80 C2
Rhodes Ho DE15 . . . . . . .248 B2
Rhodes St SK13 . . . . .10 A3
Rhodes Wlk NG18 . . . . . .268 A3
Rhodesia Rd S40 . . . . . . .95 B1
Rhodeswood Dr SK13 . . . .10 A3
Rhuddlan Pl SK23 . . . . . . .34 B1
Ribbledale Cl DE22 . . . . .204 B1
Ribbledale Dr S12 . . . . . . .59 A4
Ribbledale Rd NG10 . . . .236 A3
Riber Ave DE55 . . . . .170 B4
Riber Bank 17 SK13 . . . . . .9 C1
Riber Cl Long Eaton NG10 . .236 B3
 Staveley S43 . . . . .97 B3
 West Hallam DE7 . . . . . . .207 C4
Riber Cres S42 . . . . .131 A3
Riber Fold SK13 . . . . .9 C1
Riber St SK13 . . . . .9 C1
Riber Rd Holloway DE4 . . .156 A4
 Matlock DE4 . . . . .143 B1
Riber Terr S40 . . . . .266 A2
Riber View Cl DE4 . . . . . .144 A3
Richard La S45 . . . . .132 B1
Richard Wakefield CE Prim
 Sch DE13 . . . . .239 B3
Richards Ave ST16 . . . . . .269 C4
Richards Rd S2 . . . . .43 A4
Richardson St DE22 . . . . .218 B3
Richardson Endowed Prim
 Sch DE7 . . . . .192 C3
Richardson St DE22 . . . . .218 B3
Richmond Ave
 Derby DE23 . . . . .231 B4
 Ilkeston DE7 . . . . .194 C2
 Long Eaton DE72 . . . . . . .236 A4
 Sandiacre NG10 . . . . .223 A2
 Sheffield S13 . . . . .44 C4
Richmond Cl
 Chesterfield S40 . . . . . . .114 C4
 Derby DE23 . . . . .231 A4
 Glossop SK13 . . . . .10 A3
 West Hallam DE7 . . . . . . .207 B4
Richmond Ct
 Repton DE65 . . . . .242 B1
 Sheffield S13 . . . . .44 B4
Richmond Dr
 Duffield DE56 . . . . .190 B3
 Mansfield Woodhouse
 NG19 . . . . .136 B1
Richmond Gr S13 . . . . . . .44 C4
Richmond Hall Ave S13 . .44 B4
Richmond Hall Cres S13 . .44 B4
Richmond Hall Dr S13 . . .44 B4
Richmond Hall Rd S13 . . .44 B4
Richmond Hall Way S13 . .44 C4
Richmond Hill Rd S13 . . .44 B4
Richmond Park Rd S13 . .44 C4
Richmond Pl S13 . . . . .44 B4
Richmond Rd
 Derby, Chaddesden DE21 . .219 C3
 Derby, Rose Hill DE23 . . . .219 A1
 Sheffield S13 . . . . .44 B4
 Sheffield S13 . . . . .269 B2
 Wirksworth Rd S13 . . . . . .44 C4
Rick St NG1 . . . . .268 B2
Ricroft Rd SK6 . . . . .15 A2
Ridd Way S42 . . . . .115 A2
Riddings Cl DE22 . . . . . .204 C2
Riddings Cl S2 . . . . .44 A4
Riddings Croft S41 . . . . . .95 B4
Riddings Inf Sch DE55 . . .170 B3
Riddings Jun Sch DE55 . .170 B3
Riddings La S32 . . . . .72 A2
Riddings St DE22 . . . . . . .218 C2
Riddle St DE4 . . . . .126 B3
Ridge Ave SK6 . . . . .23 A2
Ridge Cl SK13 . . . . .9 C2
Ridge End Fold SK6 . . . . .23 A1
Ridge La
 Chapel-en-le-F SK23 . . . .65 B4
 Chapel-en-le-F, Combs
 SK23 . . . . .46 C1
Ridge Rd Eckington S21 . .58 C1
 Marple SK6 . . . . .23 A2
Ridge The
 Blackwell DE55 . . . . .147 C1

Ridge The continued
 Marple SK6 . . . . .23 A2
Ridge Top La SK22 . . . . . .25 B1
Ridgedale Rd S44 . . . . . .118 A4
Ridgedale View DE55 . . .169 B1
Ridgehill Ave S12 . . . . . . .44 A3
Ridgehill Gr S12 . . . . .44 A3
Ridgeway Derby DE23 . . .245 A4
 Dronfield S18 . . . . .57 B2
 Heanor DE75 . . . . .193 C4
Ridgeway Ave
 Bolsover S44 . . . . .99 B1
 Derby DE23 . . . . .231 B3
Ridgeway Craft Ctr*
 S18 . . . . .58 C4
Ridgeway Cres S12 . . . . .44 A3
Ridgeway Dr
 Ilkeston DE7 . . . . .208 A3
 Sheffield S12 . . . . .44 A3
Ridgeway Inf Sch DE23 . .231 B3
Ridgeway La DE56 . . . . . .168 B2
Ridgeway Moor S12 . . . . .58 C3
Ridgeway Prim Sch S12 . .58 C4
Ridgeway Rd
 Burton u T DE15 . . . . . . .254 C4
 Sheffield S12 . . . . .44 A2
Ridgeway St NG3 . . . . . .268 C2
Ridgeway The SK12 . . . . .32 B3
Ridgeways The S12 . . . . . .25 B1
Ridgewood Ct DE21 . . . .205 C1
Ridgewood Dr DE4 . . . . .155 B3
Riding Bank DE73 . . . . . .251 C3
Ridings Rd S13 . . . . .9 C3
Ridings The
 Mansfield NG19 . . . . .136 C1
 Ockbrook DE72 . . . . .221 B3
Ridley St ST4 . . . . .269 C1
Ridley Wlk ST4 . . . . .269 C1
Rigga La NG16 . . . . .191 A1
Riggotts Way S42 . . . . . . .94 C4
Riggs La DE6 . . . . .212 A4
Ripley Ave DE 10 DE7 . . .194 C1
Rigsby Ct DE7 . . . . .217 B2
Riley Ave DE55 . . . . .157 B4
Riley Back La S32 . . . . . . .71 C3
Riley La DE5 . . . . .169 A1
Rimsdale Cl DE24 . . . . . .231 C2
Ring-o-Bells La SK12 . . . .32 B3
Ringer La S43 . . . . .80 C2
Ringer Way S43 . . . . .80 C2
Ringinglow Rd S10,S11 . .42 C2
Ringstone Way S43 . . . . . .45 B4
Ringwood Ave
 Chesterfield S41 . . . . .95 C4
 Compstall SK14 . . . . .15 A4
 Staveley S43 . . . . .97 B4
Ringwood Cl 4 DE7 . . . . .194 C1
Ringwood Rd S43 . . . . . . .96 C4
Ringwood View 14 S43 . . .96 C4
Rink Dr DE7 . . . . .256 A2
Ripley Ho DE21 . . . . .220 C2
Ripley Hospl DE5 . . . . . .169 B1
Ripley Inf Sch DE5 . . . . .180 B4
Ripley Jun Sch DE5 . . . . .180 B4
Ripley Rd DE56 . . . . .168 B3
Ripon Cres DE21 . . . . . . .219 C4
Ripon Dr S41 . . . . .85 B3
Risborrow Cl DE65 . . . . .229 B2
Rise The Derby DE22 . . . .204 C1
 Swadlincote DE11 . . . . . .255 C3
 Whaley Bridge SK23 . . . . .45 B3
Rises The SK13 . . . . .9 B3
Risley Ct DE7 . . . . .194 C2
Risley La DE72 . . . . .222 B1
Risley Lower Gram CE Prim
 Sch DE72 . . . . .222 C2
Ritson Cl NG3 . . . . .268 B2
Rivenhall Cl DE23 . . . . . .230 C4
River St DE1 . . . . .267 B4
River View
 Aldercar DE55 . . . . .171 A3
 Belper DE56 . . . . .190 C4
 Chesterfield S40 . . . . . . .115 B4
 Longnor SK17 . . . . .88 B4
 Tideswell SK17 . . . . .88 B4
Riverbank DE4 . . . . .110 C1
Riverbank Way DE65 . . . .242 A3
Riverbank Way SK13 . . . .17 C4
Rivercroft Cl ST14 . . . . . .197 A2
Riverdale S32 . . . . .72 B4
Riverdale Cl DE15 . . . . . .248 A3
Rivermead Ho DE1 . . . . .267 B5
Riversdale DE56 . . . . . . .168 A2
Riversfield Dr ST14 . . . . .196 C2
Riverside Baslow DE45 . . .91 B3
 Walton-on-T DE12 . . . . . .253 B1
Riverside Cl Calver S32 . . .72 B1
 Glossop SK13 . . . . .10 B1
Riverside Cres S40 . . . . .113 C4
Riverside Croft S32 . . . . . .72 B1
Riverside Ct
 Ambergate DE56 . . . . . . .167 C2
 Baslow DE45 . . . . .91 C3
 Derby DE24 . . . . .219 B2
Riverside Dr
 Branston DE14 . . . . .253 C4
 Calver S32 . . . . .72 B1
 Riverside L S14 ST16 . . . .269 B4
Riverside Rd DE21 . . . . . .219 B2
Riverside Way
 Bolsover S44 . . . . .98 C1
 Mansfield Woodhouse
 NG19 . . . . .136 B3
Riverview Cotts 5 SK13 . .17 B4
Riverway ST16,ST17 . . . .269 B3
Rivington Rd 8 NG9 . . . .223 C1

Roadmeadow Cl DE6 . . . . . .
Robert Ave DE4 . . . .
Robert Cl S18 . . . .
Robert Rd S8 . . . .
Robert St DE1 . . . .
Robert Sutton RC High Sc
Roberts Ave NG17 . . . .
Roberts Dr DE55 . . . .
Roberts St Ilkeston DE7 . . . .
 Nottingham NG2 . . . .
Robertson Rd SK17 . . . .
Robertson's Ave S44 . . . .
Robey Dr NG16 . . . .
Robian Way DE11 . . . .
Robin Croft S40 . . . .
Robin Croft Rd DE22 . . . . . .
Robin Hood Chase NG3 . . . .
Robin Hood Cl NG16 . . . .
Robin Hood Ind Est 1
 NG3 . . . .
Robin Hood Prim Sch
 NG19 . . . .
Robin Hood Rd S43,NG7 . . . .
Robin Hood Terr 20
 NG3 . . . .
Robin Rd DE1 . . . .
Robin's Cross La DE65 . . . . .
Robina Dr NG16 . . . .
Robincroft Rd S42 . . . .
Robinettes La NG16 . . . .
Robinlands La S33 . . . .
Robins Cl 16 DE72 . . . .
Robinscross DE72 . . . .
Robinson Ind Est DE23 . . . . .
Robinson Rd DE1 . . . .
Robinson Way S21 . . . .
Robinson's Hill DE73 . . . . . .
Robinwood Lodge 18
 SK13 . . . .
Robridding Rd S45 . . . .
Robson Cl DE24 . . . .
Roby Lea DE74 . . . .
Roche 17 S20 . . . .
Rochester Cl
 Derby DE24 . . . .
 Long Eaton NG10 . . . .
Rochley Cl DE21 . . . .
Rock Bank Buxton SK17 . . . .
 Whaley Bridge SK23 . . . .
Rock Cres S45 . . . .
Rock Ct NG18 . . . .
Rock Dr NG7 . . . .
Rock Hill NG18 . . . .
Rock Ho DE56 . . . .
Rock House Cl DE55 . . . .
Rock La S44 . . . .
Rock Mill Bsns Pk S32 . . . . .
Rock Side NG16 . . . .
Rock St Mansfield NG18 . . . .
 New Mills SK22 . . . .
Rock Terr Bakewell DE45 . . .
 Buxton SK17 . . . .
Rock Valley NG18 . . . .
Rock View SK17 . . . .
Rockbourne Cl DE24 . . . . . .
Rockcliffe Cl DE11 . . . .
Rockeries The DE56 . . . .
Rockfield Rd SK17 . . . .
Rockford St NG9 . . . .
Rockhall Terr SK22 . . . .
Rockhouse Rd DE24 . . . .
Rockingham Cl 7 S20 . . . . .
Rockingham Cl
 Chesterfield S40 . . . .
 Derby DE22 . . . .
 4 Dronfield S18 . . . .
Rocklands The NG20 . . . . . .
Rockley Cl S40 . . . .
Rockley Way NG20 . . . .
Rocks The DE4 . . . .
Rockside Stps DE4 . . . .
Rockside View DE4 . . . .
Rockvale Terr DE4 . . . .
Rockvale Villas DE4 . . . .
Rod Moor Rd S18 . . . .
Roden St NG3 . . . .
Rodge Croft S41 . . . .
Rodger's La DE55 . . . .
Rodknoll La S42 . . . .
Rodney Cl DE65 . . . .
Rodney Dr NG2 . . . .
Rodney Wlk DE23 . . . .
Rodsley Cl S40 . . . .
Rodsley Cres DE23 . . . .
Rodsley La Rodsley DE6 . . . .
 Yeaveley DE6 . . . .
Roebuck Ave S43 . . . .
 Roe Cross Ind Est S14 . . . . .
Roe Cross Rd SK14 . . . .
Roe Farm La DE21 . . . .
Roe Farm Prim Sch
 DE21 . . . .
Roe Wlk DE23 . . . .
Roe's La DE4 . . . .
Roebuck Pl SK23 . . . .
Roebuck St ST4 . . . .
Roehampton Dr
 Derby DE22 . . . .
 Stapleford NG9 . . . .
Rogers Ave S80 . . . .
Rogers Ct DE65 . . . .
Rogerstone Ave ST4 . . . .
Rolaine Cl NG19 . . . .

ton Cres NG16 ...195 C4
con Dr NG16 ...195 A4
ton La DE13 ...239 B3
s La SK6 ...15 A1
1 Bank NG19 ...136 B2
y Rd DE7 ...219 A4
l Way DE21 ...221 B1
ey Cres S43 ...80 B2
rd Way S43 ...78 A2
ey Cl DE11 ...256 B3
ey Dr S18 ...53 A3
ey Gdns S7 ...43 A3
antin Pl NG10 ...236 C4
ey Cl DE7 ...217 B2
Cl Derby DE24 ...231 C2
ield NG18 ...268 A3
d Cl DE23 ...230 C4
La Clowne S43 ...80 C2
ehay DE7 ...176 C3
ry The NG18 ...268 A1
velt Ave
  DE21 ...220 A3
Eaton NG10 ...236 B3
t NG18 ...268 B3
d DE4 ...165 C4
r Ave DE75 ...193 C4
walk Ct 65 NG16 ...268 A2
walk Ind Ctr DE7 ...195 A1
walk The
  DE75 ...193 C4
ton DE7 ...195 A1
ngham NG1 ...268 A1
  DE7 ...193 A1
mond Ave S17 ...56 A3
mond Cl S17 ...56 A3
mond Cl S17 ...56 A3
mond Glade S17 ...56 A3
mond Pl S17 ...56 A3
mond's Ride DE23 ...231 B4
Ave
owash DE72 ...221 B1
ur t DE13 ...241 A1
n S44 ...97 A2
e S43 ...81 A3
ton DE7 ...194 C1
Bank Cl SK14 ...9 B3
Cottage Dr NG17 ...148 C1
Cotts S41 ...96 B1
Cres S43 ...79 B2
Ct Clay Cross S45 ...131 A2
Eaton NG10 ...223 A1
End Ave DE4 ...143 B2
Hill Chesterfield S40 ...266 B3
borough S20 ...59 A4
ford ST16 ...269 A4
dlincote DE11 ...256 C2
Hill Ave S20 ...59 A4
Hill Cl S20 ...59 A4
Hill Dr S20 ...59 A4
Hill E S40 ...266 B3
Hill Mews S40 ...59 A4
Hill S DE23 ...219 A1
Hill W S40 ...266 A3
La
sfield Woodhouse
  ...136 B2
all DE73 ...251 A2
Tree La DE11 ...255 C4
Valley DE11 ...256 A3
S21 ...60 B3
Wood Cl S41 ...95 A4
berry Ct DE21 ...206 A1
bery Hill NG18 ...268 C3
croft Gdns DE11 ...256 B2
dale Ave
sterfield S40 ...115 A4
ley DE24 ...233 A3
dale Cl NG10 ...236 A3
dale View S40 ...114 A4
ale Way NG10 ...136 C1
garth Cl S41 ...96 B1
heath Cl DE21 ...231 C3
ill cl DE7 ...99 A1
hill Int Sch DE23 ...219 A2
hill Sch NG3 ...268 C2
leigh Cres DE11 ...255 C3
mary Ave NG18 ...268 B4
mary Dr DE24 ...233 A3
mary St NG18,NG19 ...268 A1
mor La DE21 ...206 A1
mount Ct DE21 ...204 B2
engrave St DE1 ...267 B2
atte Cl DE21 ...206 B2
ewood Cl
  DE7 ...233 B4
n Normanton DE55 ...160 A4
ewood Cres DE75 ...182 A1
ewood Rd DE15 ...254 C3
per Cres DE55 ...170 A4
ing Way S44 ...97 B1
iston CE Prim Sch
  ...260 B3
iston Forestry Ctr*
  ...260 B3
on u T DE15 ...254 C4
dlincote DE15 ...254 B2
ton-on-T DE12 ...254 C3
iston Rd S DE15 ...254 C3
yn Cres S32 ...53 A4
yn Rd S32 ...53 A4
s Wlk DE21 ...205 C1
sell Dr NG9 ...223 C3
sendale Cl DE4 ...194 C2
sendale St S41 ...114 C4
ser Ave S21 ...43 C1

Rossington Dr DE23 ...230 C3
Rossington Rd NG2 ...268 C2
Rosslyn Gdns DE24 ...233 A3
Roston Cl 10 S18 ...56 B1
Rothay Cl S18 ...75 C4
Rothbourne Croft DE6 ...151 B1
Rothbury Ave S40 ...209 B1
Rothbury Pl DE21 ...205 C1
Rother Ave S43 ...78 A2
Rother Cl DE11 ...256 B3
Rother Croft S42 ...131 B4
Rother Jun Sch S40 ...115 A4
Rother St S41 ...132 B1
Rother Valley Way S20 ...60 A4
Rother Way S41 ...96 A3
Rotherham Cl S21 ...60 C4
Rotherham Rd
Barlborough S43 ...61 B1
Bolsover S44 ...99 C1
Clowne S43 ...80 C3
Killamarsh S21 ...60 B4
Mosborough S20 ...59 C3
New Houghton NG19 ...134 C4
Scarcliffe S44 ...118 A4
Shirebrook S44 ...118 B2
Rotherham Rd N S20 ...59 C2
Rotherside Rd S21 ...59 C2
Rothervale Rd S40 ...115 A4
Rotherwood Dr S17 ...269 A4
Rotherwood Gdns ST16 ...269 A4
Rothesay Cl DE24 ...231 C2
Rothey Gr S40 ...94 C3
Rothley Ave NG3 ...268 C2
Rothwell La DE56 ...179 A2
Rothwell Rd DE3 ...217 B2
Rothwell St S4 ...268 C1
Rough Heanor Rd DE3 ...218 A1
Rough La DE6 ...186 B3
Roughpiece La DE4 ...166 B3
Roughton Cl DE23 ...230 B4
Round Hill Cl S43 ...77 A2
Round Way SK22 ...33 B4
Roundhouse Rd DE24 ...219 B2
Rouse Cl ST16 ...269 A3
Rouse St S45 ...132 B1
Routh Ave DE74 ...247 A4
Row The DE4 ...156 A4
Rowan Ave Ripley DE5 ...180 B4
Stapleford NG9 ...209 C1
Rowan Cl Creswell S80 ...81 C1
Darley Dale DE4 ...127 A2
Derby, Cherrytree Hill
  DE21 ...220 A3
Derby, Sinfin DE24 ...231 B2
Ilkeston DE7 ...208 C3
Mansfield NG18 ...136 B1
Rowan Croft NG17 ...148 C3
Rowan Dr Kilburn DE56 ...192 A4
Selston NG16 ...171 B4
Shirebrook NG20 ...119 B3
Shirland DE55 ...146 B1
Rowan Park Cl DE23 ...231 A4
Rowan Sch The S17 ...55 C3
Rowan Tree Cl
Ashbourne DE6 ...185 B4
Killamarsh S21 ...60 B3
Rowan Tree Dell S17 ...55 C2
Rowan Tree Rd S21 ...60 A3
Rowan Wlk S13 ...9 C2
Rowarth Ave 7 SK13 ...9 B1
Rowarth Fold 8 SK13 ...9 B1
Rowbury Dr DE15 ...248 A1
Rowdale Cres S12 ...44 B3
Rowditch Ave DE22 ...218 B2
Rowditch Cotts DE1 ...218 B2
Rowditch Pl DE22 ...218 B2
Rowena Cl DE24 ...232 C4
Rowland Cl DE55 ...158 C2
Rowland Rd 1 S2 ...43 A4
Rowland St
Alfreton DE55 ...159 A2
Derby DE24 ...232 C3
Rowley Ave S17 ...269 A4
Rowley Cl DE11 ...256 A2
Rowley Gdns DE23 ...231 B4
Rowley Hall Dr S17 ...269 A4
Rowley La DE23 ...231 B4
Rowley Rise Derby DE23 ...231 B4
Long Eaton NG10 ...236 A3
Rowsley CE Prim Sch
  DE4 ...126 C4
Rowsley Cres S43 ...97 B4
Rowsley Gr S43 ...9 C1
Rowsley Mews S13 ...9 C1
Rowsley South Sta*
  DE4 ...127 A3
Rowthorne Ave DE55 ...170 A4
Rowthorne La
Ault Hucknall S44 ...134 A4
Glapwell S44 ...134 A4
Rowton Grange Rd SK23 ...47 A3
Roxburgh Ave DE21 ...219 C4
Roxton Ave S8 ...56 C4
Roxton Ct S8 ...56 C4
Royal Albert Ct 5 NG7 ...268 A2
Royal App DE73 ...244 C4
Royal Cl DE72 ...221 A1
Royal Croft Dr DE15 ...91 C3
Royal Crown Derby Visitor
  Ctr* DE23 ...267 C1
Royal Gate DE56 ...179 B2
Royal Gr DE21 ...206 B2
Royal Hill Rd DE21 ...220 B3
Royal Oak Pl DE45 ...109 B3

Royal Rd SK12 ...32 B3
Royal Sch for the Deaf
  DE22 ...218 B3
Royal Standard Ho NG1 ...268 A1
Royale Cl S21 ...59 C2
Roydon Cl DE3 ...217 B2
Royle Ave SK13 ...10 A1
Royston Cl
Ashbourne DE6 ...185 B4
Chesterfield S40 ...114 A4
Royston Dr DE56 ...179 B3
Rubens Cl Dronfield S18 ...56 C1
Marple SK6 ...23 A4
Ruby Paddocks NG16 ...195 C3
Rudyard Ave DE21 ...220 C2
Rufford Ave NG18 ...268 C4
Rufford Cl S40 ...95 C1
Rufford Dr NG19 ...136 C2
Rufford Rd NG10 ...236 A2
Ruffstone Cl DE56 ...191 B4
Rugby Ave DE55 ...159 B2
Rugby Cl DE24 ...254 B4
Rugby St DE24 ...219 C1
Rugeley Ave NG10 ...237 A4
Ruislip Cl NG16 ...195 C4
Runnymede Cl 11 NG7 ...268 A2
Rupert Rd Ilkeston DE7 ...195 A1
Pilsley S45 ...132 A2
Rupert St S13 ...43 C4
Rush Leys NG10 ...236 B3
Rushcliffe Ave NG19 ...136 C1
Rushcliffe Gdns DE21 ...219 C3
Rushdale Ave
Derby DE23 ...231 B3
Sheffield S8 ...43 A3
Rushdale Mount S8 ...43 A3
Rushdale Rd S8 ...43 A3
Rushdale Terr S8 ...43 A3
Rushen Mount S40 ...114 C3
Rushes The Glossop SK13 ...9 C2
Mansfield Woodhouse
  NG19 ...136 B3
Rushleigh Ct S17 ...55 B4
Rushley Ave S17 ...55 B4
Rushley Cl S17 ...55 B4
Rushley Dr S17 ...55 B4
Rushley Rd S17 ...55 B4
Rushpool Ave NG19 ...136 C1
Rushton Cl NG19 ...136 C1
Rushton Dr SK6 ...23 A3
Rushup Ave NG19 ...136 C1
Rushup La NG10,DE72 ...222 C3
Rushycroft SK14 ...9 A2
Ruskin Ave NG10 ...236 B4
Ruskin Rd Derby DE1 ...218 C4
Mansfield NG19 ...135 B1
Ruskin Sq S8 ...43 A4
Russell St S16 ...269 B3
Russell gdns S42 ...131 A3
Russell Pl NG1 ...268 A2
Russet St Compstall SK6 ...15 A2
Derby DE21 ...219 B3
Long Eaton NG10 ...223 B1
Nottingham NG1 ...268 A2
Swadlincote DE11 ...256 B2
Russet Ct DE21 ...206 A1
Russett Cl Chesterfield S40 ...95 A3
Swadlincote DE11 ...256 A2
Tutbury DE13 ...239 B3
Rutherford Dr DE21 ...205 C1
Rutherford Pl ST4 ...269 A2
Ruthyn Ave S43 ...77 B3
Rutland Ave Bolsover S44 ...99 A1
Borrowash DE72 ...221 B1
Matlock DE4 ...143 B3
Ripley DE5 ...181 A4
Rutland Cl Ilkeston DE7 ...209 A3
Rutland Dr DE3 ...217 C2
Rutland Gr NG10 ...223 B3
Rutland Pl DE56 ...168 A3
Rutland Rd
Chesterfield S40 ...266 A3
Westwood NG16 ...171 B2
Rutland Sq DE45 ...109 B3
Rutland St
Chesterfield S41 ...77 A1
Derby DE23 ...219 A1
Ilkeston DE7 ...194 C1
Mansfield NG18 ...268 C3
Matlock DE4 ...143 B3
6 Nottingham NG1 ...268 B3
Rutland Terr Barlow S18 ...75 C2
Ilkeston DE7 ...194 C1
Rutland Way SK23 ...34 B1
Ryal Cl DE72 ...221 B3
Ryan Cl DE24 ...231 C2
Rycroft Cle Mid Sch
  ST14 ...196 C2
Rycroft Rd DE74 ...247 B3
Rydal Ave NG10 ...223 A1
Rydal Cl Derby DE22 ...204 C1
Dronfield S18 ...56 B1
Rydal Cres S41 ...95 C4
Rydal Rd SK16 ...269 B4
Rydal Way S45 ...131 A2
Ryder Cl DE11 ...255 C3
Rye Butts DE73 ...232 C1
Rye Cl DE21 ...205 C2
Rye Cres S45 ...131 B2
Rye Flatt La S40 ...95 B1

Rye Flatts La DE65 ...227 B1
Ryecroft DE4 ...127 B1
Ryecroft Glen Rd S17 ...56 A4
Ryecroft St NG9 ...223 C4
Ryecroft Way S17 ...55 B4
Ryedale Gdns DE23 ...231 B3
Ryegrass Cl DE56 ...179 B2
Ryegrass Rd DE21 ...206 B1
Ryehill Ave S40 ...95 A1
Ryemere Cl NG16 ...182 C1
Ryemere Ct NG16 ...182 C1
Rykneld Cl DE23 ...230 C3
Rykneld Ct S45 ...131 B2
Rykneld Dr DE23 ...230 C4
Rykneld Rd DE23 ...230 C4
Rykneld Rise Birch DE14 ...253 C4
Rykneld Sq S40 ...266 B3
Rykneld St DE55 ...180 A1
Rykneld Way DE23 ...230 C4
Rylah Hill S44 ...118 A3
Rymill Dr DE21 ...205 C1
Ryton Way DE65 ...240 B4

S

Sabine St S17 ...269 B3
Sacheveral La S45 ...140 C2
Sacheverall Ave NG16 ...160 B2
Sacheverel St DE1 ...267 B2
Sackerville Terr S21 ...60 A4
Sackville Cl S40 ...114 A4
Sackville St S40 ...231 C4
Saddlers Cl NG19 ...136 C1
Saddleworth Wlk DE24 ...232 C2
Sadler Gate DE1 ...267 B3
Sadler St NG19 ...268 A4
Saffron Dr DE21 ...206 A1
Sage Dr DE21 ...256 C2
Saint Philip Howard Comp
  Sch SK13 ...10 A1
St Agnes Ave DE22 ...204 B2
St Aidan's Ave S2 ...43 B4
St Aidan's Dr S2 ...43 B4
St Aidan's Pl S2 ...43 C4
St Aidan's Rd S2 ...43 C4
St Aidan's Way S2 ...43 C4
St Alban's RC Prim Sch
  DE21 ...219 C3
St Albans Cl
Holmewood S42 ...132 C4
Long Eaton NG10 ...236 C3
St Albans Pl SK22 ...33 B4
St Albans Rd DE22 ...218 B2
St Albans St S42 ...131 A3
St Alkmund's Cl DE56 ...190 C2
St Alkmund's Way DE1 ...267 B4
St Alkmunds Rd DE56 ...190 C2
St Andrew's CE Jun Sch
  SK13 ...9 C2
St Andrew's CE Prim Sch
Dronfield S18 ...56 B1
Stanley DE7 ...207 A3
St Andrew's CE Sch
  B79 ...263 C1
St Andrew's Dr
Ilkeston DE7 ...208 C4
Swanwick DE55 ...169 C4
St Andrews Cl DE55 ...170 A4
St Andrews Cl SK13 ...10 A2
St Andrews Rise SK13 ...9 C2
St Andrews Spec Sch
  DE21 ...205 C1
St Andrews View DE21 ...205 C1
St Ann's Cl SK22 ...33 B4
St Ann's Hill Rd S41 ...46 C3
St Ann's St NG1 ...268 B3
St Ann's Valley NG3 ...268 C2
St Ann's Way NG3 ...268 B3
St Ann's Well Rd NG3 ...268 B2
St Anne's CE Prim Sch
  DE55 ...91 C3
St Anne's Cl Baslow S42 ...91 C3
Derby DE1 ...218 C3
St Anne's RC Prim Sch
  SK17 ...66 A1
St Anne's Well (Micrarium)*
  ...85 A4
St Annes St SK14 ...16 A4
St Anselm's Sch DE45 ...109 B3
St Augustine St DE23 ...218 C1
St Augustines Ave S43 ...114 A4
St Augustines Cres S43 ...114 A4
St Augustines Dr S40 ...266 B1
St Augustines Mount
  S40 ...266 B1
St Augustines Rise S40 ...114 A4
St Austin's RC Prim Sch
  ST17 ...269 A3
St Barnabas Ho 6 S2 ...43 A4
St Barnabas La S2 ...43 A4
St Barnabas Rd S2 ...43 A4
St Barnabas Cath NG1 ...268 A1
St Bartholomew's CE Prim
  Sch SK17 ...121 A4
St Benedict Sch DE22 ...204 B1
St Benedicts Cl S2 ...43 A4
St Bride's Wlk DE22 ...218 A3
St Catherine St NG18 ...268 C3
St Catherine's Rd DE11 ...255 C3

St Catherines Prep Sch
  SK6 ...23 A4
St Cecilia Gdns NG3 ...268 B2
St Chad's CE Inf Sch
  DE23 ...218 C2
St Chad's Cl
Denstone ST14 ...196 B3
Draycott DE72 ...235 A4
St Chad's Pl 12 ST16 ...269 B4
St Chad's Rd Derby DE23 ...218 C1
Nottingham NG3 ...268 C2
St Charles St SK13 ...9 C3
St Charles RC Prim Sch
  ...9 C3
St Christopher Ave ST4 ...269 A1
St Christopher St S2 ...268 C1
St Clare's Cl DE22 ...218 B1
St Clare's Specl Sch
  DE3 ...218 A1
St Cuthbert's Rd
Derby DE22 ...218 B2
Nottingham NG3 ...268 C2
St David's Cl DE22 ...218 B2
St David's Rise S40 ...114 B4
St Davids Rd B79 ...263 C1
St Dominics Jun Sch
  ST4 ...269 A2
St Edmund's Ave NG19 ...136 B2
St Edmund's Cl DE22 ...204 C2
St Edmunds CE Prim Sch
  NG19 ...136 B2
St Edward's Prim CE Sch
  DE74 ...247 A2
St Edward's Rd DE74 ...247 A1
St Edwards St DE11 ...261 C1
St Edwards Ct S12 ...255 C3
St Elizabeth Cl S2 ...43 A4
St Elizabeth's RC Prim Sch
  DE56 ...178 C3
St Elphin's Sch DE4 ...127 C1
St Francis Ley Ind Pk
  DE23 ...219 A1
St George's CE Prim Sch
  DE11 ...256 A1
St George's Pl 6 DE56 ...178 C2
St George's RC Prim Sch
  DE23 ...231 B4
St Georges Dr S17 ...269 A4
St Georges Dr NG9 ...223 C1
St Georges Hospl ST16 ...269 B4
St Georges Rd SK22 ...33 B4
St Giles CE Prim Sch
  DE4 ...143 B2
St Giles CE Sch S21 ...60 B3
St Giles Cl S40 ...115 A4
St Giles Rd DE23 ...218 C1
St Giles Specl Sch DE21 ...205 B1
St Giles Wlk DE4 ...143 B2
St Helen's Cl
Chesterfield S41 ...266 B4
Darley Dale DE4 ...127 A2
Grindleford S32 ...72 B4
St Helen's Cres NG9 ...209 B2
St Helen's Dr NG16 ...171 B4
St Helen's La DE4 ...126 A4
St Helen's St
Chesterfield S41 ...266 B4
Derby DE1 ...267 A4
Nottingham NG7 ...268 A2
St Helens Ave NG16 ...160 B2
St Hugh's Cl DE21 ...205 A1
St James Ave DE7 ...209 A4
St James Cl
Chesterfield S41 ...266 B3
Derby DE23 ...267 C1
St James' CE Inf Sch
  DE23 ...267 C1
St James' Dr NG16 ...182 B4
St James' Sq SK22 ...33 B4
St James' St
5 Buxton SK17 ...85 A4
Derby DE1 ...267 B3
Derby, Rose Hill DE23 ...219 A1
St James' Terr SK17 ...85 A4
Nottingham NG1 ...268 A1
St James's St
Stapleford NG9 ...223 B3
5 Nottingham NG1 ...268 A1
St James's Terr
Stapleford NG9 ...223 B3
St John Fisher RC Prim Sch
  DE24 ...233 B4
St John Houghton RC Sch
  DE7 ...208 B3
St John St Hayfield SK22 ...25 B1
Mansfield NG18 ...268 B4
St John's CE Mid Sch
  NG18 ...268 B4
St John's CE Prim Sch
Belper DE56 ...179 A3

St John's CE Prim Sch
continued
Ripley DE5 .....169 C1
Stafford ST16 .....269 C4
Stapleford NG9 .....223 C4
St John's Cl
Brinsley NG16 .....171 B1
Derby DE22 .....204 B2
St John's Dr Derby DE21 .220 A3
Kilburn DE56 .....192 A4
Swadlincote DE11 .....255 C3
St John's Mount S41 .....95 C4
St John's Pl NG18 .....268 B4
St John's Rd
Belper DE56 .....179 A2
Buxton SK17 .....85 A4
Chesterfield S41 .....95 C4
Dronfield S18 .....76 C4
Ilkeston DE7 .....209 A4
Matlock Bath DE4 .....143 A2
Smalley DE7 .....192 C3
Stafford ST17 .....269 B3
Tideswell SK17 .....69 B2
St John's St
Ashbourne DE6 .....173 B1
Long Eaton NG10 .....236 B4
Wirksworth DE4 .....165 C4
St John's Terr DE1 .....218 C3
St John's Wlk NG16 .....171 A2
St Johns Cl Bamford S33 .....40 A2
Chesterfield S40 .....114 A4
Ripley DE5 .....169 C1
St Johns Pl S43 .....78 B1
St Johns Rd S43 .....78 B1
St Johns Road Bsns Ctr
S41 .....95 C3
St John's Cres S43 .....80 C2
St Joseph's Convent Day
Sch S41 .....266 A4
St Joseph's Prep Sch
NG1 .....268 A2
St Joseph's RC Prim Sch
Derby DE23 .....267 A1
Matlock DE4 .....143 B3
Shirebrook NG20 .....119 C3
Staveley S43 .....97 B4
St Joseph's St DE4 .....143 B3
St Katherine's La DE4 .....110 C1
St Laurence CE Prim Sch
NG10 .....236 C3
St Laurence Ct NG10 .....236 C3
St Lawrence Ave S44 .....118 B4
St Lawrence Cl DE75 .....181 C1
St Lawrence Rd S42 .....131 C3
St Lawrence View S80 .....81 C3
St Leonard's Ave ST17 .....269 C3
St Leonard's Prim Sch
ST17 .....269 C3
St Leonards Dr S41 .....96 B1
St Leonards Pl DE55 .....146 C1
St Luke's CE Prim Sch
SK13 .....10 B1
St Luke's Sch S81 .....63 C4
St Luke's St NG3 .....268 C2
St Lukes Ct 7 S41 .....95 C4
St Margaret St NG18 .....268 C3
St Margaret's Dr S40 .....266 A3
St Margaret's RC Prim Sch
SK13 .....16 B4
St Mark's Cl DE4 .....155 A3
St Mark's Rd
Chesterfield S40 .....95 C2
Derby DE21 .....219 B3
St Marks St S41,NG3 .....268 B2
St Martin's Cl S41 .....95 C3
St Martin's La ST16 .....269 B3
St Martin's Rd S4x 23 A3
St Martin's Specl Sch
DE24 .....232 C4
St Martin's Wlk S80 .....82 B3
St Martins Ct DE55 .....158 C2
St Mary & All Saints Church
(Crooked Spire)* S40 .266 B3
St Mary St DE7 .....208 C4
St Mary's Ave DE72 .....235 A4
St Mary's CE Fst Sch
ST14 .....210 A1
St Mary's Cl Derby DE24 .233 A3
Newton Solney DE15 .....248 C4
St Mary's Cres ST14 .....210 A1
St Mary's Ct DE1 .....267 B4
St Mary's Dr DE13 .....240 C1
St Mary's Gate
Chesterfield S41 .....266 C3
Derby DE1 .....267 B3
Nottingham NG1 .....268 B1
St Mary's Pl ST16 .....269 B4
Wirksworth DE4 .....165 C4
St Mary's Gr 6 ST16 .....269 B4
St Mary's Pl
Chesterfield S41 .....266 C3
Nottingham NG1 .....268 B1
St Mary's Pl B ST16 .....269 B4
St Mary's RC High Sch
S41 .....95 B4
St Mary's RC Prim Sch
Chesterfield S40 .....266 A4
Derby DE1 .....267 B4
Glossop SK13 .....17 B4
Marple SK6 .....23 A4
New Mills SK22 .....33 A4
St Mary's Rd Disley SK12 .32 B3
Glossop SK13 .....17 B4
New Mills SK22 .....33 A4
St Mary's Wlk NG16 .....171 A2

St Marys Wharf Rd DE1 .219 A4
St Matthew's Cl S43 .....96 B2
St Matthew's Wlk 4
DE22 .....204 C1
St Matthias Rd NG3 .....268 C3
St Mawes Cl DE22 .....204 B2
St Mellion Cl DE3 .....217 C1
St Michael's CE Prim Sch
S32 .....53 A4
St Michael's Cl
Holbrook DE56 .....191 B3
Shirley DE6 .....200 B4
Willington DE65 .....242 A3
St Michael's Dr
South Normanton DE55 .160 A4
Stretton en le F DE12 .....265 C1
St Michael's La DE1 .....267 B4
St Michaels Cl Crich DE4 .156 C1
Derby DE24 .....233 B4
St Michaels View
Derby DE24 .....233 B4
Selston NG16 .....171 C3
St Nicholas Cl DE22 .....204 B1
St Nicholas Pl DE1 .....267 A5
St Nicholas St NG1 .....268 B1
St Norbert Dr DE7 .....208 B2
St Oswald Cres DE6 .....173 B1
St Oswald's CE Inf Sch
DE6 .....173 A1
St Oswald's Hospl DE6 .173 A1
St Pancras Way DE1 .....267 C5
St Patrick's Pl 1 ST16 .269 B4
St Patrick's St DE1 .....269 B4
St Paul's CE Prim Sch
ST17 .....269 B3
St Paul's Rd DE1 .....219 A4
St Pauls Ave S41 .....115 B3
St Pauls Ct NG16 .....195 C3
St Peter & St Paul Sch
S41 .....115 B4
St Peter & St Paul's Sch
S41 .....96 B2
St Peter's CE Fst Sch
ST14 .....224 C1
St Peter's CE High Sch
ST4 .....269 A2
St Peter's CE Jun Sch
DE23 .....218 B1
St Peter's CE Prim Sch
DE12 .....264 C3
St Peter's Churchyard
DE1 .....267 B3
St Peter's Cl DE56 .....179 A2
St Peter's Gate NG1 .....268 B1
St Peter's Rd Buxton SK17 .66 B1
Derby DE21 .....233 A1
Thorpe Salvin S80 .....62 C4
St Peter's Sq NG1 .....268 B1
St Peter's St DE1 .....267 B3
St Peter's Way NG18 .....268 C3
St Peters Cl
Long Duckmanton S44 .....98 A2
Stoke-on-T ST4 .....269 B2
St Peters Croft DE56 .....179 A2
St Philip Howard RC Sch
SK13 .....17 A4
St Philip Neri's RC Prim Sch
NG18 .....268 B4
St Philip's Dr S41 .....115 A4
St Philomena's Convent Prim
Sch DE1 .....267 B4
St Quentin Cl
Derby DE22 .....218 B2
St Quentin Dr S17 .....56 A3
St Quentin Mount S17 .....56 A3
St Quentin Rise S17 .....56 A3
St Quentin View S17 .....56 A3
St Ronan's Ave DE56 .....190 C2
St Stephen's Ave 5
NG2 .....268 C1
St Stephen's Cl DE23 .....231 B3
St Stephen's Cl DE11 .....256 C2
St Stephen's Rd NG2 .....268 C1
St Stephens Ct DE7 .....221 A1
St Swithin's Cl DE22 .....218 B2
St Theresa's RC Prim Sch
S2 .....44 A4
St Thomas Aquinas RC Prim
Sch ST14 .....269 A2
St Thomas Cl DE55 .....147 C3
St Thomas More RC Sch
SK17 .....85 A4
St Thomas of Canterbury
Prim Sch S8 .....56 C4
St Thomas RC Prim Sch
DE7 .....208 C3
St Thomas Rd DE23 .....219 A1
St Thomas St S16 .....269 C4
St Thomas' St DE1 .....267 C3
St Vincent Cl NG10 .....236 C3
St Werburgh's CE Prim Sch
Derby DE21 .....220 B3
Hanbury DE13 .....238 A2
St Werburgh's View
DE21 .....220 B3
St Wilfrid's Rd
Sheffield S2 .....43 A4
West Hallam DE7 .....207 C4
St Wystan's Rd DE22 .....218 B2
St Wystans Sch DE65 .....242 B1
Salcey Cl DE55 .....169 C4
Salcey Dr NG9 .....209 B1
Salcey Sq 9 S40 .....95 B1
Salcombe Rd DE55 .....159 B3
Sale & Davys CE Sch
DE73 .....244 A3

Sale St DE23 .....219 A1
Sales Ave S42 .....131 B4
Sales La DE15 .....248 B2
Salford Gdns NG3 .....268 B2
Salisbury Ave
Burton u T DE15 .....248 B2
Chesterfield S41 .....95 C4
Dronfield S18 .....76 A4
Salisbury Cl NG19 .....136 B2
Salisbury Cres S41 .....95 C4
Salisbury Dr Belper DE56 .179 B3
Stafford ST16 .....269 C4
Swadlincote DE11 .....256 C3
Salisbury La DE73 .....252 A4
Salisbury Rd Dronfield S18 .76 A4
Mansfield NG19 .....268 A4
Stafford ST16 .....269 C4
St Michaels Dr Swy DE23 .267 B3
Glossop SK13 .....10 A3
Long Eaton NG10 .....236 C4
Sallyfield La DE6 .....183 C4
Sallywood Cl DE24 .....231 B1
Salmond Ave ST16 .....269 B3
Salt Ave ST17 .....269 B3
Salt Rd ST17 .....269 B3
Saltburn Cl DE21 .....205 B1
Salter Cl DE74 .....246 C2
Salter St S116 .....269 B4
Saltergate S40 .....266 B3
Saltergate La S30 .....40 B1
Salters La DE4 .....142 C2
Salvin Cres S43 .....80 C2
Samantha Ct DE21 .....206 A1
Sampson's La NG19 .....135 A2
Samuel Bruns Way
NG18 .....268 C4
Samuel Cl
Mansfield NG19 .....268 A4
Sheffield S2 .....43 A4
Samuel Ct DE55 .....180 B4
Samuel Dr S2 .....43 A4
Samuel Pl S2 .....43 A4
Samuel Rd S2 .....43 A4
Samuel St SK14 .....9 B2
Sand La DE6 .....211 A1
Sandalwood Cl DE24 .....233 B4
Sandalwood Rd DE15 .....254 C3
Sandbach Cl DE21 .....206 A1
Sandbed La DE56 .....179 B1
Sandby Cl S14 .....43 C1
Sandby Ct S14 .....43 C1
Sandby Dr Marple SK6 .....43 C1
Sheffield S14 .....43 C1
Sandcliffe Pk DE11 .....256 B4
Sandcliffe Rd DE11 .....256 B3
Sandcroft Cl DE11 .....256 B3
Sandcroft Rd DE21 .....220 C3
Sanderling Heath DE3 .....230 A4
Sanders Cl DE7 .....194 B1
Sanderson Rd DE21 .....220 C3
Sandfield Cl DE21 .....220 A4
Sandfield Rd 10 NG9 .....223 C1
Sandford Ave NG10 .....236 C4
Sandford Brook DE55 .....228 C1
Sandgate Ave NG19 .....136 B2
Sandgate Cl DE24 .....233 A3
Sandgate Rd NG19 .....136 B2
Sandhall La DE56 .....166 C3
Sandham La DE56 .....169 B1
Sandhill La
Broadbottom SK6 .....16 A1
Marple SK6 .....15 C1
Sandhills Rd S44 .....99 B1
Sandiacre Rd NG9 .....223 B3
Sandiway
Chesterfield S40 .....114 B4
Glossop SK13 .....17 C4
Sandlands The DE11 .....256 B3
Sandlands Way NG19 .....136 C1
Sandown Ave DE7 .....217 B2
Sandown Cl
Burton u T DE14 .....254 A4
Eckington S21 .....59 A2
Sandown Rd
Beeston NG9 .....223 C1
Derby DE24 .....232 C4
Sandringham Ave DE55 .248 A1
Sandringham Cl
Buxton SK17 .....85 A4
Mansfield Woodhouse
NG19 .....136 A3
Sandringham Dr
Derby DE21 .....220 C3
Heanor DE75 .....181 B1
Mansfield Woodhouse
NG19 .....136 A3
Sandringham Ho DE21 .219 B1
Sandringham Rd DE7 .....208 B3
Sandringham Rd
Calow S44 .....97 A2
Derby DE21 .....205 C1
Mansfield Woodhouse
NG19 .....136 B2
Nottingham NG2 .....268 C1
Sandiacre NG10 .....223 A2
Sands Cl S14 .....43 C2
Sandstone Ave S40 .....114 A4
Sandwell Cl NG10 .....236 A3
Sandwood Cl DE55 .....148 A2
Sandy Cl S80 .....81 C3
Sandy La
Broadbottom SK13 .....16 A2
Caldwell DE12 .....261 A4
Crich DE4 .....167 C4
Horsley DE21,DE7 .....192 A2
Mansfield NG18 .....268 C4
Matlock DE4 .....143 B4

Sandybank Cl SK13 .....9 C2
Sandybrook Cl DE6 .....173 B2
Sandycliffe Cl NG19 .....136 C1
Sandyford Cl ST16 .....269 B4
Sandyford La DE56 .....166 C2
Sandyhill Cl DE73 .....233 A1
Sandypits La DE65 .....229 B2
Sanforth St S41 .....96 A3
Sankey Dr DE11 .....256 B1
Santolina Dr DE21 .....205 C1
Sapperton Cl DE23 .....231 B3
Sapperton La DE65 .....213 C1
Sappertonfield La DE6,
DE65 .....213 B2
Sapphire Dr DE1 .....180 A1
Sarah Cl DE55 .....170 B4
Sargent Gdns NG3 .....268 C2
Sark Rd 8 S2 .....43 A4
Sash St ST16 .....269 B4
Saundby Ave NG10 .....236 C4
Saundersfoot Way DE21 .206 B1
Savage La S17 .....55 B4
Saville Cl NG9 .....223 C4
Saville House Sch NG19 .136 B2
Saw Pit Ind Est DE55 .....146 B3
Saw Pit La DE55 .....148 A3
Sawley Jun & Inf Schs
NG10 .....236 A3
Sawley Rd
Breaston DE72 .....235 C3
Draycott DE72 .....235 A4
Sawmand Cl NG10 .....236 B3
Sawmills Ind Pk DE56 .....181 B2
Sawpit La DE65 .....227 B1
Saxon Cl
Breedon on t H DE73 .....252 C1
Burton u T DE15 .....254 C4
Saxon Croft DE55 .....242 B2
Saxon Gr DE65 .....242 A3
Saxon Rd S8 .....43 A4
Saxon St SE3 .....254 C4
Saxondale Ave DE7 .....217 B2
Saxton Ave DE75 .....181 C1
Scalby Cl NG16 .....182 B1
Scalcid Cl SK22 .....33 A4
Scalpcliffe Rd DE15 .....248 A1
Scarborough Ave DE7 .208 C4
Scarborough Rise DE21 .205 B1
Scarborough St NG3 .....268 B2
Scarcliffe Cl DE24 .....232 C2
Scarcliffe La NG20 .....119 B4
Scarcliffe St
S44 .....118 C3
Scarcliffe Terr NG20 .....101 A1
Scargill CE Prim Sch
DE7 .....207 B4
Scargill Rd DE7 .....207 C4
Scargill Wlk NG16 .....182 C2
Scarsdale Ave
Derby, Allestree DE22 .....204 B2
Derby, Littleover DE23 .....218 B1
Scarsdale Cl S18 .....76 A4
Scarsdale Cres S43 .....96 B4
Scarsdale Cross S18 .....57 A1
Scarsdale Hospl S40 .....266 B4
Scarsdale Pl 5 S43 .....85 A4
Scarsdale Rd
Chesterfield S41 .....96 A4
Dronfield S18 .....57 A1
Duffield DE56 .....190 C2
Scarsdale St S44 .....117 C4
Scarthin DE4 .....155 A3
Schofield Cl DE4 .....110 C1
School Ave S20 .....59 C4
School Board La S40 .....95 C2
School Cl Blackwell DE55 .147 B1
Darley Dale DE4 .....127 B2
Fenny Bentley DE6 .....162 A1
Moira DE11 .....256 B1
Newton DE55 .....148 A2
Shirland DE55 .....146 B1
Stonebroom DE55 .....146 C2
School Croft DE55 .....170 B3
School House Hill DE56 .168 B1
School La Ashbourne DE6 .173 A1
Baslow DE45 .....91 C3
Beeley DE4 .....111 A2
Brackenfield DE55 .....145 B1
Castle Donington DE74 .....247 A2
Compstall SK6 .....15 B2
Crich DE4 .....157 A1
Darley Dale DE4 .....126 C4
Derby DE73 .....233 A1
Dronfield S18 .....57 A1
Eckington S21 .....59 C1
Hassop DE45 .....90 C3
Hathersage S32 .....53 A4
Heage DE56 .....168 B1
Long Duckmanton S44 .....97 B2
Mansfield Woodhouse
NG19 .....136 B2
Old Brampton S42 .....93 C2
Ripley DE5 .....169 B1
Rolleston DE13 .....240 A2
Sheffield, Greenhill S8 .....56 C4
Sheffield, Norton S8 .....57 B4
South Normanton DE55 .160 A2
Stanton-by-D DE7,NG10 .222 C4
Sudbury DE6 .....225 C2
Taddington SK17 .....87 C2
Youlgreave DE4 .....126 B2

School Sq DE7 2
School St Eckington S21 2
Moira DE12 2
Mosborough S20 2
Swadlincote DE11 2
Schoolpiece La DE65 2
Scotches The DE56 2
Scotia Cl S2 2
Scotia Dr S2 2
Scotland St S80 2
Scotswood Rd NG19 2
Scott Cl S42 2
Scott Cres DE55 2
Scott Dr Belper DE56 2
Marple SK6 2
Somercotes DE55 2
Scott St Derby DE23 2
Whaley Thorns NG20 2
Scotts The DE11 2
Scowerdons Cl S12 2
Scowerdons Dr S12 2
Scratta La S80 2
Screetham La S80 2
Scropton Old Rd DE65 2
Scropton Rd DE65 2
Scropton Wlk DE24 2
Sea Breeze Terr S13 2
Seaburn Rd NG9 2
Seaford Way DE7 2
Seagrave Ave S12 2
Seagrave Cl DE21 2
Seagrave Cres S12 2
Seagrave Dr
Chesterfield S43 2
Sheffield S12 2
Seagrave Rd S12 2
Seal View DE12 2
Seale St DE1 2
Sealey Cl DE65 2
Seals Rd DE12 2
Sealwood La
Linton DE12 2
Overseal DE12 2
Seamer Rd NG16 2
Seanor La S45 2
Searl St DE1 2
Searle Ave ST16 2
Searson Ave S44 2
Searston Ave S42 2
Seascale Cl DE21 2
Seaton Cl DE3 2
Sebastion Cl SK6 2
Second Ave
Branston DE14 2
Derby DE73 2
Risley DE72 2
Sedbergh Cres S41 2
Sedgebrook Cl DE21 2
Sedgebrook St NG19 2
Sedgefield Gn DE3 2
Sedgefield Rd
Branston DE14 2
Burton u T DE14 2
Sedgemoor Cl S40 2
Sedgemoor Rd NG10 2
Sedgley Ave DE23 2
Sedgley Cl NG2 2
Sedgwick Cl NG11 2
Sedgwick St
Langley Mill NG16 1
Westwood NG16 1
Seely Rd NG7 2
Sefton Ave NG9 2
Sefton Cl DE15 2
Sefton Rd DE21 2
Sefton Way S42 2
Selborne St DE24 2
Selby Cl Beeston NG9 2
Chesterfield S40 1
Selhurst Rd S41 2
Selina Cl DE74 2
Selina St DE73 2
Selkirk St DE21 2
Selly Oak Gr S8 2
Selly Oak Rd S8 2
Selmer Ct S43 2
Selston CE Inf Sch
NG16 1
Selston Rd NG16 1
Selworthy Cl DE21 1
Selwyn St Bolsover S44 1
Derby DE22 2
Stoke-on-T ST4 2
Senners La DE17 2
Serina Ave DE23 2
Serlby Dr S26 C
Serlby La S26 2
Serlby Rise NG2 26
Serpentine Wlk S8 5
Setcup La S21 2
Sett Cl SK22 2
Settlement The DE72 2
Setts Way S42 1
Seven Acres Way ST4 2
Seven Oaks Rd DE22 2
Sevenoaks Ave DE22 2
Severals NG20 2
Severn Cl DE13 2
Severn Cres S42 1
Severn Sq DE55 15
Severn St DE24 2
Severnale Cl DE22 2
Sewell Rd S20 5
Sexton St SK13 1
Seymour Cl DE21 2
Seymour La NG7 26
Seymour St
Seymour La S43 2

aur Rd NG16 ....182 C1
aur St NG3 ....268 C2
eecross CI DE72 ....221 B1
Gr DE65 ....228 B1
CI DE65 ....228 C1
esbury Ave
 erfield S40 ....95 B2
 Eaton NG10 ....236 A2
 field NG19 ....135 C1
 acre NG10 ....135 C1
esbury Cres DE23 ....219 A1
esbury St 219 A1
esbury St S DE23 ....219 A1
on CI S45 ....131 C2
on Wlk S45 ....131 C2
espeare Ave
 nell S80 ....81 B1
 field Woodhouse
 ....136 A2
 and DE55 ....146 B2
espeare CI
 Cross S42 ....131 A3
 on DE65 ....242 B1
 lincote DE11 ....256 B3
espeare Cres S18 ....76 B4
leet Dr DE21 ....233 B3
cross Ave SK23 ....45 C2
cross Cres DE23 ....45 C2
cross Rd SK23 ....45 C2
nbles The S40 ....266 B3
rock Pl S43 ....79 B4
rock St DE23 ....218 C1
dwick Ct DE24 ....231 B2
klin Dr NG9 ....223 B4
non CI DE23 ....231 B3
non Sq DE21 ....220 A2
CI ■ S40 ....95 B3
llow Prim Sch
 ....234 C1
dlow Rd
 on-on-T DE72 ....246 A4
 y DE24/DE73 ....233 B3
man CI
 knowle S18 ....58 A1
 e-on-T S14 ....269 A2
man Wlk S18 ....58 A1
o CI Ilkeston DE7 ....208 B3
y Eaton NG10 ....236 B3
pe Ave S8 ....56 C4
pswood Manor
 ....256 C2
rard CI S12 ....44 A3
rard Dr S12 ....44 A3
rard Gr S12 ....44 A3
rard Rd S12 ....44 A3
ton La S32,S33 ....51 C4
e La Belper SE56 ....191 A4
sop SK13 ....9 C2
oway DE4 ....156 B4
aston Montgomery DE6 ....198 A1
y St Chesterfield S41 ....96 A4
y DE22 ....218 C3
field S18 ....57 B2
sop SK13 ....17 B4
newood S42 ....116 B1
tram in L SK14 ....9 A2
ecries DE55 ....170 B3
w St DE7 ....209 A3
n St DE7 ....209 A3
n Wood View DE55 ....157 C2
n's Row S40 ....95 B1
n's Yd DE56 ....191 C4
ncroft DE6 ....173 B1
ncroft Ave DE55 ....170 B3
yfield Rd SK13 ....9 C2
ws Gn DE22 ....218 C3
ws Hill DE4 ....156 B1
nf Bank S2 ....43 A4
urdhall Ave SK12 ....32 C3
ards CI ■ S18 ....56 C1
ards Dr ■ S18 ....56 C1
ards Way S18 ....56 C1
arsby Dr NG19 ....136 C1
arwater CI DE23 ....231 B4
mbridge La
 esterfield S41 ....76 C1
field NG18 ....268 A3
epcote Rd S21 ....60 B3
phill Rd S21 ....42 C1
eplea La S45 ....129 C4
epwash La S45 ....145 A4
et Stones Ind Est
40 ....236 B3
ffield Coll Norton Ctr
 ....57 A4

Sheffield Rd continued
Sheffield S12 ....44 C1
Unstone S18,S41 ....76 C2
Shelburne St ST4 ....269 B1
Shelden CI S43 ....9 B1
Shelden Fold SK13 ....9 B1
Shelden PI SK13 ....9 B1
Shelden CI NG10 ....223 A2
Shelden Ct DE24 ....232 C2
Sheldon Ave S44 ....116 C2
Sheldon Gdns DE4 ....156 C1
Sheldon Mews SK13 ....9 B1
Sheldon Rd
 Chesterfield S40 ....95 A1
 Heanor DE75 ....181 B3
Shelford CI DE7 ....217 B2
Shelford Hill NG19 ....268 A3
Shelford La DE4 ....156 A4
Shelley Ave NG19 ....136 A2
Shelley Dr Derby DE24 ....232 A3
 Dronfield S18 ....76 B4
Shelley Gr DE55 ....159 C2
Shelley St S42 ....116 B1
Shelly Rd DE11 ....256 B3
Shelmory CI DE24 ....232 C3
Shelton CI NG19 ....135 C1
Shelton Dr DE24 ....232 C2
Shelton Jun & Inf Sch
 DE24 ....232 B2
Shelton Old Rd DE24 ....269 B2
Shelton St NG3 ....268 B2
Shenington Way DE21 ....206 A1
Shepherd St DE11 ....218 B1
Shepherd's La DE73 ....251 B3
Shepherd's Row S18 ....77 A4
Shepley St
 Chesterfield S40 ....95 B1
 Glossop SK13 ....10 C1
 Glossop, Hadfield SK13 ....9 C2
Shepley's Yd S40 ....266 B3
Sheppard St S4 ....269 B1
Shepston CI DE7 ....194 B2
Sheraton Way S41 ....66 A1
Sherbourne Ave S41 ....95 C4
Sherbourne Dr
 Belper DE56 ....179 B3
 Burton u T DE14 ....254 A4
Sherbrook Gr SK17 ....85 B3
Sherbrook Lodge (Youth
 Hostel)* S41 ....85 B3
Sherbrooke Rd SK12 ....32 B3
Sheridan Ct NG9 ....209 C1
Sheridan Ctr ST16 ....74 B4
Sheridan St Derby DE24 ....231 C3
 Stafford ST16 ....269 C4
Sheriff Dr DE4 ....143 A3
Sheriffs Way NG2 ....268 B1
Sheringham Dr NG18 ....268 C3
Sherriff CI DE55 ....228 C1
Sherriff's Lea NG9 ....223 C1
Sherston CI DE21 ....206 A1
Sherwin CI NG3 ....268 B2
Sherwin Rd NG9 ....209 C1
Sherwin St DE22 ....218 C4
Sherwin Wlk ■ NG3 ....268 B2
Sherwood Ave
 Borrowash DE72 ....221 B1
 Creswell S80 ....81 B1
 Derby, Chaddesden DE21 ....219 C4
 Derby, Littleover DE23 ....231 B3
 Hope S33 ....39 A2
 Pinxton NG16 ....160 B2
 Shirebrook NG20 ....119 C2
Sherwood Chase S17 ....55 C3
Sherwood Copse S17 ....69 B2
Sherwood CI NG19 ....136 A1
Sherwood Dr NG20 ....119 C2
Sherwood Fold S33 ....16 B4
Sherwood Foresters
 Regiment Meml* DE4 ....156 C2
Sherwood Hall L Ctr
 DE4 ....143 B2
Sherwood PI ■ SK18 ....56 B1
Sherwood Rd Buxton SK17 ....85 B3
 Dronfield S18 ....60 C4
 Matlock DE4 ....143 B2
 Tideswell SK17 ....69 B2
Sherwood Rise
 Eastwood NG16 ....182 C1
 Mansfield Woodhouse
 NG19 ....136 C2
Sherwood St
 Bolsover S44 ....117 C4
 Chesterfield S40 ....266 C1
 Derby DE22 ....218 C2
 Mansfield NG18 ....268 B3
 Mansfield Woodhouse
 NG19 ....136 A1
 Newton DE55 ....148 B3
 Shirland DE55 ....146 B3
 Somercotes DE55 ....170 B4
 Sutton in A NG17 ....148 C2
Shetland CI Derby DE21 ....219 B4
 Mansfield NG19 ....136 A1
Shetland Rd Dronfield S18 ....76 A4
 Tibshelf DE55 ....147 C3
Shields Cres DE74 ....246 C2
Shieling The DE65 ....227 B1
Shilling Way NG10 ....236 A4
Shiloh Rd SK22, SK6 ....24 A3
Shilton CI S14 ....269 A1
Shining Cliffe YH*
 DE56 ....167 B3
Shinwell Ave S43 ....97 A4
Shipley CI DE14 ....254 A4
Shipley Common La
 DE7 ....194 B2

Shipley Country Park Visitor
 Ctr* DE75 ....193 C3
Shipley Ctry Pk* DE7 ....194 A2
Shipley La DE7/DE75 ....193 C3
Shipley Wlk DE24 ....232 C2
Shipman Ct S20 ....59 B4
Shirburn Ave NG18 ....268 C4
Shire Hill Hospl SK13 ....10 C2
Shire La S44 ....116 C2
Shire Way SK13 ....10 C2
Shirebrook Bsns Pk
 NG20 ....119 B3
Shirebrook Com Sch
 NG20 ....119 B3
Shirebrook Ctry Pk* S8 ....17 C4
Shirebrook Rd S8 ....43 A3
Shirebrook Sta NG20 ....120 A2
Shiregate Gdns DE23 ....231 A3
Shireoaks DE56 ....178 B3
Shireoaks CI DE23 ....231 B4
Shireoaks Comm S81 ....63 C4
Shireoaks Row S81 ....63 C4
Shireoaks Sta S81 ....63 C4
Shires The NG19 ....136 C1
Shirland Prim Sch DE55 ....146 B1
Shirland St 266 B4
Shirley CI
 Castle Donington DE74 ....247 A2
 Chesterfield S40 ....95 A2
 Hope S33 ....39 A2
Shirley Cres DE74 ....235 B4
Shirley La DE6 ....200 A3
Shirley Park Rd DE23 ....231 C2
Shirley Rd Derby DE21 ....205 C1
 Ripley DE5 ....169 B1
 Swanwick DE55 ....169 C4
Shirley St NG10 ....236 A2
Shop La DE56 ....168 B1
Shop Stones DE7 ....221 B3
Shoreham St S2 ....43 A4
Short Ave DE22 ....204 C1
Short Brook Prim Sch
 S20 ....59 C4
Short CI S42 ....113 B4
Short Hill
 Breedon on t H DE73 ....252 C3
 Nottingham NG1 ....268 B1
Short La DE74 ....246 C2
Short Lands DE56 ....179 A2
Short Row ■ DE56 ....179 A2
Short St Belper DE56 ....179 A2
 Burton u T DE15 ....254 C4
Short Street Com Inf Sch
 DE15 ....254 C4
Shortbrook Bank ■ S20 ....59 C4
Shortbrook CI ■ S20 ....59 C4
Shortbrook Croft ■ S20 ....59 C4
Shortbrook Dr ■ S20 ....59 C4
Shortbrook Rd S20 ....59 C4
Shortbrook Way ■ S20 ....59 C4
Shortbrook Wlk ■ S20 ....59 C4
Shortheath DE12 ....262 B2
Shortheath Rd DE12 ....262 C2
Shortlands The DE4 ....143 A2
Shucks La S17 ....55 A3
Shortwood CI NG1 ....268 B1
Shorwell Gdns 233 B3
Shottle Wlk DE24 ....232 C3
Shotwood CI DE13 ....240 A2
Shotwoodhill La DE13 ....240 A3
Shrewsbury CI DE21 ....206 B1
Shrewsbury Rd
 Burton u T DE13 ....240 C1
 Stafford ST17 ....269 B3
Shrewsbury St SK13 ....10 B1
Shropshire Ave
 Derby DE21 ....219 C4
 Westwood NG16 ....171 B2
Shropshire Dr SK13 ....17 C4
Shrubbery The DE7 ....257 A1
Shuckstone La DE4 ....156 C3
Shudehill CI SK22 ....25 B2
Shunters Drift S43 ....80 A3
Shuttlewood Rd S44 ....99 A2
Shute La DE45 ....109 B2
Sibthorpe St NG18 ....268 B3
Sicklebrook La S18 ....57 C2
Sickleholme S33 ....40 A1
Siddals La DE22 ....204 B1
Siddals Rd DE1 ....267 C2
Siddals St DE11 ....248 A2
Siddons La DE6 ....203 A1
Side End La SK23 ....45 A1
Sidings The S43 ....80 A4
Sidings The Derby DE21 ....220 A2
Sidlaw CI ■ DE21 ....206 A1
Sidmouth CI DE24 ....233 B4
Sidney CI DE3 ....217 C2
Sidney St Derby DE1 ....267 C1
 Kimberley NG16 ....195 C3
Siemens Rd ST17 ....269 B3
Silk Hill SK23 ....45 C4
Silk Mill La DE13 ....239 B3
Silk St S15 ....10 C1
Silken Holme DE55 ....160 A2
Silkstone CI Sheffield S12 ....44 C2
 Swadlincote DE11 ....256 A1
Silkstone Cres S12 ....44 C2
Silkstone PI S12 ....44 C2
Silkstone Rd S12 ....44 C2

Sillito PI ST4 ....269 B1
Silver Birch Cres DE55 ....159 B4
Silver Hill Rd DE23 ....219 A1
Silver La Elvaston DE72 ....234 A3
 Marchington ST14 ....224 C1
Silver Mill Rd S2 ....43 A4
Silverburn Dr DE21 ....206 A1
Silverdale NG9 ....223 A3
Silverdale Ave NG19 ....136 A2
Silverdale CI
 Chesterfield S41 ....76 C1
 Derby DE73 ....233 A1
Silverhill CI DE11 ....240 B1
Silverhill La NG17 ....148 C4
Silverhill Prim Sch DE7 ....217 B2
Silverhill Rd DE21 ....220 C2
Silverlands SK17 ....85 B4
Silverlands CI SK17 ....85 B4
Silverlands Pk SK17 ....85 B4
Silverton Dr DE24 ....231 B1
Silvey Gr DE21 ....220 B2
Simcoe Leys DE73 ....233 A1
Simcrest Ave S21 ....60 B3
Simmondley Gr SK13 ....17 A4
Simmondley La SK13 ....17 A4
Simmondley New Rd
 SK13 ....17 A4
Simmondley Prim Sch
 SK13 ....17 A4
Simon Fields CI DE7 ....194 B1
Simonburn Ave ST4 ....269 A2
Simon Wlk SK13 ....17 A4
Simpson St DE24 ....232 C3
Sims Ave DE1 ....218 C3
Sims Croft S41 ....77 B2
Sinclair Ct Derby DE22 ....231 C2
 Heanor DE75 ....193 B4
Sinder Ave DE11 ....256 A3
Sinfin Ave DE24 ....232 B2
Sinfin Com Sch DE24 ....231 C2
Sinfin Fields Cres DE24 ....232 B3
Sinfin La
 Barrow u T DE73 ....244 A3
 Derby DE23,DE24 ....232 C2
Sinfin Moor La DE73 ....231 C1
Sinfin Moor Prim Sch DE24 ....231 C3
Sir Frank Whittle Rd
 DE21 ....219 B4
Sir Harold Jackson Prim
 Sch S17 ....56 A3
Sir Henry's La DE73 ....252 A2
Sir Joseph's La DE4 ....127 A2
Sir William Hill Rd S32 ....71 B4
Sir William Terr 72 B4
Siskin CI DE3 ....230 A2
Siskin Dr DE24 ....231 B3
Sisley Ave NG9 ....223 C3
Sister's La DE72 ....221 B3
Kirk Ireton DE4 ....165 A2
Sitch Rd DE4 ....142 B4
Sitwell ■ S20 ....59 C4
Sitwell Ave S40 ....266 A1
Sitwell CI DE21 ....205 C4
Sitwell Dr DE56 ....192 A4
Sitwell Grange La
 Pilsley S45 ....147 B4
 Tibshelf S45 ....147 B4
Sitwell St Derby DE1 ....267 B2
 Derby, Spondon DE21 ....220 C2
Sitwell Villas DE55 ....146 C3
Skaddi Ct ■ NG2 ....268 C1
Skeavington's La DE7 ....194 C3
Skegby La NG18, NG19 ....268 A3
Skegby Mount NG18 ....268 A3
Skeldale Dr S40 ....115 A4
Skelton Rd S8 ....43 A3
Skelwith CI S41 ....95 B4
Sketchley St NG3 ....268 C2
Ski 2000 Ilkeston NG16 ....195 A4
Skiddaw CI ■ S40 ....95 B3
Skiddaw Dr DE3 ....217 C1
Skinner St NG3 ....81 B1
Skinners Way DE11 ....256 B3
Skipton CI DE7 ....194 B4
Skipton Gn DE21 ....205 B1
Skye Gdns DE55 ....147 C3
Skylark Way DE24 ....231 B2
Slack La Ashover S45 ....129 B1
 Brailsford DE6 ....187 B4
 Chesterfield S40 ....95 A2
 Derby, Allestree DE22 ....204 C1
 Derby, New Zealand DE22 ....218 B3
 Hartshorne DE11 ....257 A3
 Mayfield DE6 ....184 B4
 Nether Heage DE56 ....168 B3
 Ripley DE5 ....169 B1
 Shipley DE75 ....193 C4
 Somercotes DE55 ....170 A3
 Wessington DE55 ....158 B4
Slack Rd DE7 ....193 C2
Slacks La S45 ....132 B1
Slackey La DE12 ....262 B2
Slacks Cott DE7 ....84 C3
Slacks La S22 ....25 B3
Slade CI Etwall DE65 ....229 B2
 Ilkeston DE7 ....209 A3
 South Normanton DE55 ....160 A2
Slade Fields ST14 ....210 A1
Slade Hollow La DE6 ....201 A2
Slade La DE6 ....202 C4
Slade St S43 ....77 B3
Slaidburn CI DE7 ....217 C1
Slaley La DE4 ....154 B4
Slaley View Rd S43 ....80 A3
Slaney CI DE24 ....232 C4

Slant CI SK13 ....17 C4
Slant La NG19 ....136 A2
Slant The NG20 ....119 B2
Slate St S2 ....43 A4
Slatelands Ave SK13 ....17 A4
Slatelands Rd SK13 ....17 A4
Slatepit La S18,S42 ....93 B4
Slater Ave DE22 ....218 C3
Slater Cres DE4 ....165 C4
Slater St S45 ....131 B2
Slayley Hill S43 ....80 B2
Slayley View S43 ....80 B3
Slaypit La S80 ....62 B3
Sledgegate La DE4 ....156 A4
Sledmere CI DE24 ....233 B4
Sleepy La DE73 ....245 B1
Slessor CI DE55 ....170 A4
Slessor Rd S16 ....269 C4
Slindon Croft DE24 ....233 B3
Slipperlow La S45 ....87 C1
Sloade La S12 ....58 C3
Sloane Rd DE22 ....218 A3
Small Gate NG19 ....136 C3
Small Knowle End SK17 ....67 B3
Small Meer CI DE73 ....232 C1
Small Thorn PI DE11 ....256 A1
Smalldale Cotts SK17 ....67 B4
Smalldale Head Rd S33 ....50 C4
Smalldale Rd Buxton SK17 ....67 B4
 Sheffield S12 ....44 B2
Smalley Dr DE21 ....206 A2
Smalley Mill Rd DE21 ....192 A2
Smallman St ST16 ....269 B4
Smeath Rd NG16 ....171 C1
Smeckley Wood CI S41 ....76 B2
Smedley Ave
 Ilkeston DE7 ....209 A4
 Somercotes DE55 ....159 B1
Smedley CI DE65 ....241 A3
Smedley PI SK13 ....10 A2
Smedley St DE4 ....143 A3
Smedley St W DE4 ....143 A4
Smedley's Ave NG10 ....223 A3
Smeeton St DE75 ....182 A1
Smelter Wood Ave S13 ....44 C4
Smelter Wood CI S13 ....44 C4
Smelter Wood Cres S13 ....44 C4
Smelter Wood Ct S13 ....44 C4
Smelter Wood Dr S13 ....44 C4
Smelter Wood La S13 ....44 C4
Smelter Wood PI S13 ....44 C4
Smelter Wood Rd S13 ....44 C4
Smelter Wood Rise S13 ....44 C4
Smelter Wood Way S13 ....44 C4
Smeltinghouse La DE4 ....75 C2
Smisby Rd LE65 ....258 A1
Smisby Way DE24 ....232 C2
Smith Ave Codnor DE5 ....170 A1
 Melbourne DE73 ....245 A1
 Staveley S43 ....78 C4
Smith Cres S41 ....96 B1
Smith Dr NG16 ....182 A2
Smith Rd DE4 ....143 A3
Smith-Hall La DE6 ....188 A4
Smithbrook CI SK23 ....47 B3
Smithfield Ave
 Chesterfield S41 ....115 B4
 Trowell NG9 ....209 B2
Smithfield Rd S12 ....44 A2
Smithpool Rd S14 ....269 A4
Smithson Ave S44 ....99 A1
Smithurst Rd NG16 ....195 A4
Smithy Ave S45 ....131 B2
Smithy Brook Rd S21 ....79 B4
Smithy CI Glossop SK13 ....9 C1
 Parwich DE6 ....151 B1
Smithy Croft S18 ....56 B1
Smithy Fold SK13 ....10 B1
Smithy Hill S41 ....51 A4
Smithy Knoll Rd S32 ....72 B1
Smithy La
 Clifton Campville B79 ....263 C1
 Marple SK6 ....15 C1
 Taddington SK17 ....88 A2
Smithy Mdws S32 ....53 A4
Smithy PI S42 ....113 C3
Smithy Row NG1 ....268 B1
Smuse La DE4 ....143 C2
Snake La DE56 ....190 C2
Snake Rd S33 ....28 B4
Snake Woodland Forest
 Walk* S33 ....19 C2
Snape Hill S18 ....57 A1
Snape Hill CI S18 ....57 A2
Snape Hill La S18 ....57 A2
Snapehill CI S18 ....57 A2
Snapehill Cres S18 ....57 A2
Snelsmoor La DE73 ....233 A1
Snelston CI S18 ....56 B1
Snelston Cres DE23 ....218 B1
Snipe CI S42 ....113 B4
Snipesmoor La DE6 ....185 C4
Snitterton Rd DE4 ....143 A3

Snow Hill ST16 .... 269 B4
Snowberry Ave DE56 ...179 A2
Snowdon La S21 .... 58 A2
Snowdrop Valley DE ...168 A4
Snowfield View DE4 ...165 C3
Snows Yd ST16 ....269 A4
Soaper La S18 .... 57 A1
Soarbank Cl NG16 ....195 C4
Society Pl DE23 ....219 A1
Soft Water La S33 .... 51 A4
Solney Cl DE11 ....255 C2
Soloman Pk NG16 ....195 A1
Soloman Rd DE7 ....195 A1
Solomons View S42 .... 83 B4
Solway Cl DE21 ....206 A1
Solway Rise S18 .... 56 B1
Somerby Way DE21 ....205 C1
Somercotes Hill DE55 ..170 B4
Somercotes Inf Sch
  DE55 ....170 A3
Somercotes Rd S12 ....44 B3
Somerlea Park Jun Sch
  DE55 ....170 B4
Somerleyton Dr DE7 .....209 A2
Somersall Cl DE24 ....232 C2
Somersall Cl S40 .... 95 A1
Somersall La S40 .... 95 A1
Somersall Park Rd S40 .. 95 A1
Somersall St NG19 ....268 A4
Somersall Willows S40 .. 95 A1
Somersby Ave S40 ....114 A4
Somerset Cl Buxton SK17 . 85 C2
  Long Eaton NG10 ....237 A4
Somerset St S41 .... 97 A4
Somerset Rd DE15 ....254 B3
Somerset St DE21 ....219 B4
Somme Rd DE22 ....204 A2
Sookholme Cl NG20 ......119 C2
Sookholme La NG20,
  NG19 ....120 C3
Sookholme Rd
  Market Warsop NG20 ...120 C2
  Shirebrook NG20 ....119 C2
Soresby St S40 ....266 B3
Sorrel Dr DE11 ....256 C2
Sough La Bolehill DE4 ...155 A1
  Taddington SK17 .... 87 B1
  Wirksworth DE4 ....154 C1
Sough Rd DE55 ....160 A4
Soughley La S10 .... 42 B4
South Ave Buxton SK17 ... 85 A4
  Derby DE23 ....218 B1
  Derby, Chellaston DE24 .232 C2
  Derby, Darley Abbey DE22 205 A2
  Derby, Spondon DE21 ...220 C2
  Shirebrook NG20 ....119 C2
South Brae Cl DE23 ......231 B4
South Broadway St
  DE14 ....254 B4
South Church St DE45 ...109 B3
South Cl Glossop SK13 ... 9 C4
  Unstone S18 .... 76 C3
South Cres Bolsover S44 .. 99 A1
  Killamarsh S21 .... 60 C4
  Long Duckmanton S44 ... 98 A3
South Ct S17 .... 55 C4
South Darley CE Prim Sch
  DE4 ....142 A4
South Dr
  Derby, Chellaston DE73 .232 C2
  Derby, Cherrytree Hill
  DE21 ....220 A3
  Derby, Littleover DE23 ..218 A1
  Derby, Little Chester DE1 .218 C4
  Swadlincote DE11 ....255 C3
South East Derbyshire Coll
  Heanor DE75 ....181 C1
  Ilkeston DE7 ....208 C3
South Farm Ave S26 ..... 61 C3
South Hill Rolleston DE13 240 B2
  Shirland DE55 ....145 C4
South Hill La DE55 ....145 C3
South Lodge Ct S40 ...... 95 A2
South Marlow St SK13 ... 10 A2
South Oak St DE14 ....254 A4
South Par
  Matlock Bath DE4 ....143 A1
  3 Nottingham NG1 ....268 B1
South Park Ave DE4 ......127 B2
South Pl
  Chesterfield, Boythorpe S40 .95 B1
  Chesterfield, Stonegravels
  S40 ....266 B2
  Ripley DE5 ....169 B1
South Rd NG7 ....268 A1
South Sherwood St
  NG1 ....268 B2
South St Ashbourne DE6 .173 B1
  Blackwell DE55 ....147 C1
  Buxton SK17 .... 85 A4
  Chesterfield S40 ....266 B2
  Derby DE1 ....218 C3
  Draycott DE72 ....235 A4
  Eastwood, Bailey Grove
  NG16 ....182 C1
  Eastwood, Giltbrook NG16 195 B4
  Ilkeston DE7 ....208 C4
  Long Eaton NG10 ....236 C4
  Melbourne DE73 ....252 A4
  Mosborough S20 .... 59 B3
  Pilsley S45 ....132 B1
  Somercotes DE55 ....170 B3
  South Normanton DE55 .160 A3
  Stafford ST16 ....269 A4

South St continued
  Swanwick DE55 ....169 C4
  Woodville DE11 ....257 A1
South St N S43 .... 77 B2
South Terr ST14 ....269 B1
South Uxbridge St
  DE14 ....254 A4
South View Bamford S33 .. 40 A2
  Derby DE23 ....218 B1
  Mayfield DE6 ....184 B3
  Mosborough S20 .... 60 A4
  New Mills SK22 .... 33 A4
  Pilsley DE45 .... 91 B3
  Whitwell S80 .... 81 C3
South View Rd S43 .... 17 C4
South View Wlk ST14 ....196 C2
South Walls ST16 ....269 B4
South Wingfield Prim Sch
  DE55 ....157 C2
South Wolf St ST4 ....269 B2
Southampton St NG3 .....268 C2
Southard's La S80 .... 62 C3
Southbourne Cl S17 ..... 55 B3
Southbrook Cl SK13 .... 9 C2
Southcote Dr S18 .... 56 B1
Southcroft Alfreton DE55 .159 A2
  Buxton SK17 .... 85 A4
Southdene DE21 ....205 A3
Southdown Ave S40 .... 95 B3
Southdown Cl DE24 ......231 B1
Southend S42 ....115 C1
Southend St NG7 ....268 A2
Southfield Ave S41 ....115 B3
Southfield Cl S80 .... 81 C3
Southfield Dr
  Dronfield S18 .... 76 B4
  Mansfield Woodhouse
  NG19 ....136 C3
  Southfield Ind Side S80 .. 82 A2
Southfield La S80 .... 82 A2
Southfield Mount S18 ... 76 B4
Southfields Clowne S43 .. 80 C2
  Long Eaton NG10 ....236 C4
Southfields Ave NG16 ...195 A4
Southgate S21 .... 59 C2
Southgate Cl DE3 ....217 B2
Southgate Cres S40 ...... 80 C3
Southgate Ct S21 .... 59 C2
Southgate Inf Sch DE22 .218 A2
Southgate Way S43 ...... 78 A2
Southmead Way DE3 .....218 A2
Southmoor Cl S43 .... 96 C2
Southwark Cl DE22 ......218 A3
Southwell Rd NG1 ....268 B1
Southwell Rise NG16 ....195 A4
Southwood Ave S18 ...... 76 A4
Southwood Dr S20 .... 80 C2
Southwood St DE24 .....232 C4
Southworth Rd DE72 ....252 C1
Sovereign Gr NG10 ......236 A4
Sovereign Dr DE14 ....254 A4
Sovereign Way
  Derby DE21 ....206 B2
  Heanor DE75 ....181 B1
Sowbrook Brook DE7 ....208 C2
Sowbrook La DE7 ....208 C2
Sowter Rd DE1 ....267 B4
Sowters Row S40 ....266 B3
Spa Brook Cl S12 .... 44 C2
Spa Brook Dr S12 .... 44 C2
Spa Croft DE55 ....147 C3
Spa La
  Chesterfield, Hady S41 ..266 C3
  Chesterfield, Stonegravels
  S41 ....266 C2
  Derby DE1 ....267 A1
Spa View Ave S12 .... 44 C2
Spa View Dr S12 .... 44 C2
Spa View Pl S12 .... 44 C2
Spa View Rd S12 .... 44 C2
Spa View Terr S12 .... 44 C2
Spa View Way S12 .... 44 C2
Spalden Ave DE6 ....173 B2
Spalding Rd NG3 ....268 C2
Spang La NG17 ....148 C2
Spaniel Row **4** NG1 ...268 B1
Spanker La DE56 ....168 A1
Spanker Terr DE56 ....168 B1
Spark St ST4 ....269 B2
Spark Terr ST4 ....269 B2
Sparrow Cl Derby DE24 .231 B2
  Ilkeston DE7 ....209 A3
Sparrowbusk Cl S43 ..... 80 A3
Speedwell SK13 .... 9 C4
Speedwell Cl
  Derby DE21 ....206 B2
  Glossop SK13 .... 9 C4
  Woodville DE11 ....256 C2
Speedwell Ind Est S43 .. 78 C1
Speedwell Inf Sch S43 .. 78 C1
Speedwell La NG16 ......195 C3
Speetley View S43 .... 80 A4
Speighthill Cres S42 ....114 C2
Spenbeck Dr DE22 ....205 A3
Spencer Ave
  Belper DE56 ....179 A2
  Derby DE24 ....232 B2
  Sandiacre NG10 ....223 A3
  Staveley S43 .... 79 A1
Spencer Cl
  Ashbourne DE6 ....185 B4
  Burton u T DE13 ....240 B1
Spencer Cres NG9 ....223 C4
Spencer Dr DE55 ....170 B4
Spencer Rd Belper DE56 .179 A2
  Buxton SK17 .... 85 A3
  Chapel-en-le-F SK23 .... 46 C3
  Sheffield S2 ....43 A4

Spencer Rd continued
  Stoke-on-T S4 ....269 C2
Spencer St Bolsover S44 .117 C4
  Chesterfield S40 ....266 B4
  Derby DE24 ....233 A4
  Mansfield NG18 ....268 B3
  Stanley DE7 ....193 A1
Spend La DE6 ....161 A1
Sperry Cl NG16 ....171 C3
Spilsbury Cl DE65 ....242 B3
Spindletree Dr DE21 .....205 C1
Spinkhill Ave S13 .... 44 B4
Spinkhill Dr S13 .... 44 B4
Spinkhill Immaculate
  Conception Prim Sch
  S21 .... 60 B1
Spinkhill La S21 .... 60 A1
Spinkhill Rd
  Killamarsh S21 .... 60 C2
  Sheffield S13 .... 44 B4
Spinnerbottom SK22 ..... 24 C1
Spinners Way DE56 ......179 B3
Spinney Cl Derby DE22 ..205 A1
  Glossop SK13 .... 10 B1
  Mansfield Woodhouse
  NG19 ....136 C3
Spinney Cres NG9 ....223 C2
Spinney Dr NG10 ....223 B1
Spinney Hill DE73 ....252 A4
Spinney Lodge
  Repton DE65 ....242 B1
  Tutbury DE13 ....238 C3
Spinney Rd
  Branston DE14 ....253 C4
  Derby DE22 ....218 C2
  Derby, Chaddesden DE21 .219 C4
  Ilkeston DE7 ....208 C3
  Long Eaton NG10 ....223 B1
Spinney Rise NG9 ....223 C2
Spinney The
  Belper DE56 ....179 A3
  Borrowash DE72 ....221 B1
  Brailsford DE6 ....201 C4
  Castle Donington DE74 ..247 A2
  Derby DE65 ....247 C4
  Spital Gdns S41 .... 96 B1
  Spital La S41 .... 96 B1
  Spitalbrook Cl S41 ...... 96 B1
  Spiterwinter La S18,S42 .93 B4
  Spittal Cl DE74 ....247 A2
  Spittal Gn S44 ....118 A4
  Spittal Hill DE74 ....247 A2
  Spode St S43 ....269 B1
  Spondon Sta DE21 ......220 B2
  Spooner Dr S21 .... 60 B3
  Spooner La S32 .... 72 B3
  Spoonley Wood Ct
  DE23 ....230 C4
  Sporton Cl DE55 ....160 A4
  Sporton La DE55 ....160 A4
  Spotswood Cl S14 .... 43 C2
  Spotswood Dr S14 ...... 43 C2
  Spotswood Mount S14 .. 43 C2
  Spotswood Pl S14 .... 43 B2
  Spotswood Rd S14 ...... 43 B2
  Spout La Spout DE56 ...166 B2
  Tansley DE4 ....144 A2
  Spridgeon Cl **13** NG10 .223 A1
  Spring Bank Buxton SK17 .67 B2
  Great Longstone DE45 ... 90 A2
  Spring Bank Rd
  Chesterfield S40 ....266 A3
  New Mills SK22 .... 33 B4
Spring Cl Belper DE56 ...178 C3
  Bradwell S33 .... 51 A4
  Breaston DE72 ....235 B4
  Renishaw S21 .... 79 B4
  Swadlincote DE11 ....256 A1
  Wirksworth DE4 ....154 C1
Spring Cl Belt S14 .... 43 C2
Spring Cl Mount S14 .... 43 C2
Spring Cl View S14 ...... 43 C2
Spring Cottage Rd
  DE12 ....262 B3
Spring Ct Mews SK14 .... 9 C4
Spring Dale Gdns NG9 ..209 B2
Spring Garden Terr
  DE7 ....194 C1
Spring Gardens Ctr The
  SK17 .... 85 A4
Spring Gdns Buxton SK17 .85 A4
  Derby DE21 ....219 C4
  Glossop SK13 .... 10 A1
Spring Hill
  Kimberley NG16 ....195 C3
  Mansfield Woodhouse
  NG19 ....136 A2
  Whitwell S80 .... 82 A3
Spring Hollow DE56 .....190 B4
Spring House Ct S42 .... 94 C3
Spring La Elmton S80 ...159 C2
  Heanor DE75 ....181 C1
  Sheffield S2 .... 43 C4
  Sheffield S2 .... 43 C4
  Shireoaks S80,S81 .... 63 C3
  Mansfield SK22 .... 33 B4
Spring Rd S40 ....266 B3
Spring Rd DE55 ....170 C3
Spring Rise S13 .... 16 C4
Spring St
  Broadbottom SK14 ...... 16 A4
  Derby DE22 ....218 C2
  Glossop SK13 .... 10 A1

Spring St continued
  Hollingworth SK14 .... 9 B3
  Swadlincote DE11 ....262 A4
  Whitwell S80 .... 82 A3
Spring The NG10 ....236 B3
Spring Vale Rd
  Brimington S43 .... 96 C4
  Hayfield SK22 .... 25 C1
Spring Water Dr SK13 ... 9 C2
Spring Wood Cl S41 ..... 95 B4
Springbank S43 .... 9 C3
Springdale Ct DE21 .....217 C1
Springfarm Rd DE15 ....248 A1
Springfield
  Broadbottom SK13 ...... 16 B3
  Derby DE23 ....218 A1
Springfield Ave
  Ashbourne DE6 ....185 B4
  Chesterfield S40 .... 95 B2
  Heanor DE75 ....181 A3
  Long Eaton NG10 ....236 C4
  Sandiacre NG10 ....223 A2
  Shirebrook NG20 ....119 C3
Springfield Cl Clowne S43 .80 B2
  Crich DE4 ....157 A1
  Eckington S21 .... 59 B2
  Glossop SK13 .... 9 C2
  Swadlincote DE11 ....256 A3
Springfield Cres
  Bolsover S44 .... 98 C2
  Somercotes DE55 ....170 B4
Springfield Ct NG10 .....209 C1
Springfield Dr DE56 .....190 B2
Springfield Gdn DE7 ....194 C1
Springfield Jun Sch
  DE11 ....256 B3
Springfield Prim Sch
  Derby DE23 ....220 B3
  Stoke-on-T S4 ....269 A1
Springfield Rd Barlow S18 .75 B2
  Bradwell S33 .... 51 A4
  Derby, Chellaston DE73 .232 C1
  Derby, Cherrytree Hill
  DE21 ....220 A3
  Etwall DE65 ....229 A2
  Holmewood S42 ....132 C4
  Repton DE65 ....242 B1
  Swadlincote DE11 ....256 A3
Springfield Rise DE4 ....143 B3
Springfield Terr
  Burton u T DE15 ....248 A1
  Hayfield SK22 .... 25 B1
  Ripley DE5 ....169 C1
Springfields Rd S14 .....269 B1
Springhill DE11 ....257 A4
Springhill Way DE5 .....181 A4
Springmeadow DE13 .... 16 B4
Springvale Cl S45 ....131 B1
Springvale Rd S45 ....131 B1
Springwell Com Sch S43 .97 B4
Springwell Hill S21 .... 77 C3
Springwell Park Dr S43 .97 B4
Springwell St NG17 .....148 C1
Springwood S13 .... 16 C4
Springwood Cl S43 ...... 80 C2
Springwood Dr DE21 ....206 A1
Springwood Farm Rd
  DE11 ....256 A4
Springwood Gdns DE56 .179 A2
Springwood Rd S8 .... 43 A3
Springwood St S42 ....116 A2
Sprinkswoods La DE6 ...184 C3
Spruce Ave NG16 ....171 B3
Spruce Rise S21 .... 60 B3
Spurr St S2 .... 43 A4
Square The Bretby DE15 .249 A2
  Buxton SK17 .... 85 A4
  Clay Cross S45 ....131 C2
  Derby DE3 ....217 B1
  Derby, Darley Abbey DE22 205 A1
  Eyam S32 .... 71 C3
  Marchington ST14 ....224 C1
  Monyash DE45 ....107 B1
  Squires La DE73 .... 38 B2
  Squires View S14 ....269 C2
  Squires Way S14 ....231 A4
  Squirrel La DE73 ....252 C2
  Squirrel Wlk DE12 ......262 A2
  Stable Cl DE4 ....156 A3
  Stable La DE6 ....149 A1
  Stable Mews DE11 ......256 C1
  Stables Ct S44 .... 99 B1
  Stables St DE22 ....218 B3
Stacey Rd NG19 ....135 B1
  Staden Bsns Pk SK17 ... 85 C3
  Staden La S17 .... 85 C2
  Stadium Ind Pk NG10 ..236 C4
  Stadium View DE24 .....219 C2
  Stadmoor Ct DE73 ......232 C1
  Staffa Dr DE55 ....147 C3
Stafford Cl
  1 Dronfield S18 .... 56 B1
  6 Glossop SK13 .... 17 C4
  Smalley DE7 ....192 C3
  Stafford Coll ST16 ......266 B4
  Stafford Coll (The Oval
  Annexe) ST17 ....269 B3
Stafford Cres DE4 ....165 C4
Stafford St Derby DE1 ...267 A3
  Long Eaton NG10 ....236 C4
  Mansfield NG18 ....268 B3
  New Mills S42 .... 24 B1
  Stafford ST16 ....269 B4
  Stafford Sta ST16 ....269 A3
Staffordshire General Hospl
  ST16 ....269 C4

Staffordshire Univ Stoke
  Campus) ST4 ....
Staines Cl ST4 ....
Stainforth St NG19 ....
Stainsbor La DE4,DE6 ..... .
Stainsby Ave
  Heanor DE75 ....
  Horsley Woodhouse DE7 . .
Stainsby Cl S42 ....
Stainsby Gr NG17 ....
Stainsby Mill* S44 ....
Staithes Wlk DE21 ....
Staker La DE3 ....
Stalybridge Ctry Pk*
  SK15 ....
Stalybridge Rd SK14 ..... .
Stamer St S13 ....
Stamford Cl NG10 ....
Stamford St
  Awsworth NG16 ....
  Derby DE24 ....
  Heanor DE75 ....
  8 Ilkeston DE7 ....
Stamps Cl DE15 ....
Stanage Gn DE12 ....
Stanage Rise S12 ....
Stanage Way S40 ....
Stancliffe Ave DE4 ....
Stancliffe Hall Sch DE4 .. .
Stancliffe View DE4 ....
Stand Park Ind Est S41 .. .
Stand Rd S41 ....
Standard Hill **7** NG1 .. .
Standard St ST4 ....
Standing Butts Cl DE12 .. .
Standlow La DE6 ....
Stanedge Rd DE45 ....
Stanford Rd S18 ....
Stanford St NG1 ....
Stanford Way S40 ....
Stanhope Glade DE15 ... .
Stanhope Rd Derby DE3 .. .
  Sheffield S12 ....
  Swadlincote DE11 ....
Stanhope St
  Bramley-Vale S44 ....
  Burton u T DE15 ....
  Derby DE23 ....
  Ilkeston DE7 ....
  Long Eaton NG10 ....
  Nottingham NG1 ....
  Stanton-by-D NG10 ....
Stanier Way Derby DE21 . .
  Renishaw S21 ....
Staniforth Ave S21 ....
Stanleigh Gdns DE12 .... .
Stanleigh Rd DE12 ....
Stanley Ave Ripley DE5 .. .
  Staveley S43 ....
Stanley Cl Derby DE21 .. .
  Ilkeston DE7 ....
  Nethersseal DE12 ....
  Woodville DE11 ....
Stanley Comm Prim Sch
  DE7 ....
Stanley Cres ST14 ....
Stanley Ct NG16 ....
Stanley Dr NG9 ....
Stanley Hall La SK12 .... .
Stanley La S44,NG17 .... .
Stanley Matthews Sports Ctr
  ST4 ....
Stanley Pl NG1 ....
Stanley Rd
  Derby, Allenton DE24 .... .
  Derby, Cherrytree Hill
  DE21 ....
  Sheffield S8 ....
  Stoke-on-T ST4 ....
Stanley St Chesterfield S41 . .
  Derby DE72 ....
  Ilkeston DE7 ....
  Killamarsh S21 ....
  Long Eaton NG10 ....
  Somercotes DE55 ....
Stanshope La DE6 ....
Stanstead Rd S12 ....
Stanton Ave DE56 ....
Stanton Cl DE4 ....
Stanton Cres S12 ....
Stanton Gate DE7 ....
Stanton Hill DE73 ....
Stanton La DE6 ....
Stanton Moor View
  DE4 ....
Stanton Pl
  Mansfield NG18 ....
  New Houghton NG19 .... .
Stanton Prim Sch DE15 .. .
Stanton Rd
  Ashbourne DE6 ....
  Burton u T DE15 ....
  Ilkeston DE7 ....
  Sandiacre NG10 ....
Stanton St Derby DE23 .. .
  New Houghton NG19 .... .
Stanton Vale Spec Sch
  DE7 ....
Stanton View DE4 ....
Stanton-in-Peak CE Prim
  Sch DE4 ....
Stantonhall La DE4 ....
Stanwood Dr S40 ....
Stanyforth St SK13 ....
Stapleford La NG9 ....
Stapleford Rd
  Stapleford NG9 ....

NG9 ....209 B2
on Rd DE7 ......194 C2
.. La NG10 ....223 B4
ss Ct DE3 ....217 B2
imes Rd DE4 ....143 B1
. Ave DE4 ....246 C2
. La SK23 ....45 A4
.e La DE4 ....144 A2
.. Bank DE75 ....181 C1
n Ave S42 ......131 B4
.n St DE22 ......218 C4
.. App
.gate DE56 ......167 C2
...........85 A4
DE1 ....267 C2
t DE56 ....190 C2
sage S32 ....53 A4
.. Back La S41 ...266 C3
. Cl DE73 ......232 C1
Cotts NG19 .....135 A3
. Ct 10 DE7 .....194 C1
.. DE12 ....262 C2
Hill NG19 ....136 A2
La

.nowle S18 ....58 A1
.rfield S41,S43 .....177 B1
...........181 A3
ill S33 ....40 A1
..on-T DE12 ......232 C3
. La End Est S41 ...77 A1
New Rd S42 .....131 B4
Rd

.rne DE6 ....173 A1
.rth NG16 ....195 B3
.rth DE45 ....109 C3
.ed S33 ....40 A1
.. Hill S43 ....78 A2
.. Ave S44 ....98 C1
.vash DE72 ......221 A1
.all DE21 ....205 C2
.gton S40 ....96 B4

.u T DE13 ....35 A3
SK17 ....85 B4
.Donington DE74 ..247 A3
. Doninmton DE74 ..247 A3
..-en-le-F SK23 ...47 A3
..-en-le-Frith SK23 ..47 A1
. .West La S44 ....266 C3
.rfield, Old Whittington

.r SK23 ....34 B1
. S43 ....84 B3
.. Dale DE4 ......127 B1
DE3 ....180 A2
DE3 ....217 B2
. Chellaston DE23 ...232 C1
. Spondon DE21 ....220 B2
.r SK17 ....47 C1
.tt DE72 ....65 C3
.of DE56 ....190 C2
.ton S21 ....59 C2
.p SK13 ....10 A3
.Longstone DE45 ...89 C2
.. Sage

.DE65 ....239 B4
DE22 ....25 B1
.ld, Birch Vale SK22 ..25 A3
.S33 ....39 A2

.n DE7 ....194 C1
.e NG16 ....170 C2
.arsh S21 ....60 A3
.arsh, Spinkhill S21 ...60 B1
.rley NG16 ....195 C3
.ry Mill NG16 .....182 A1
.aton DE21 ....205 B4
.Eaton NG10 ......236 C4
.ld NG18 ....268 B3
.t SK6 ....23 A4
.. Stirres SK6,SK22 ...25 B1
.urne DE73 ....252 B4
.rough S20 ....59 C4
.ills SK22 ....33 A4
.S21 ....33 A4
.Wingfield S42 ....131 C3
.S45 ....148 C3
.ton DE13 ....242 B2
.cre NG10 ....223 B3
.iffe S44 ....118 C3
.ne NG16 ....160 C1
.roog NG20 ......119 C3
.rd DE76 ....269 A3
.r DE7 ....207 B3
..-nT ST4 ....269 B2
.room DE55 ......147 A3
.diff DE55 ....147 C3
.DE7 ....207 B4
. By Bridge SK23 ...33 B2
.rell S80 ....82 A3
. Hill DE11 ......256 C1

.n St
.aurne DE6 ....173 A1
.n DE7 ....195 A1
.op SK13 ....10 B1
.Eaton NG10 ......236 C4
.ld NG18 ....268 B3
.eld Woodhouse

.gham NG2 ....268 B1
.incote DE11 .....261 C4
.n View NG20 ....119 C2
. N Wlk SK17 .....85 B4
.ton Ave DE23 ....231 C4
.ton Cl DE74 .....247 A2
.ton Harold Resr Visitor

.DE73 ....251 C3
.ton La DE73 .....251 A1

Staveley Cl DE24 ....232 C2
Staveley Jun Sch S43 ...78 F1
Staveley La
  Barrow Hill S21,S43 ....78 A3
  Eckington S21 ....59 C1
Staveley Rd
  Chesterfield S43 ....77 C2
  Long Duckmanton S44 ..97 C2
  Poolsbrook S43 ....98 A4
  Sheffield S8 ....43 A4
Staverton Dr DE3 ....217 B2
Stead Mews S21 ....59 B2
Stead St S21 ....59 B2
Steam Mill La DE5 ......181 A4
Steel La S44 ....99 A1
Steel St DE4 ....269 A2
Steel's La S44 ....118 A3
Steele Ave S43 ....85 A4
Steele Ct SK17 ....85 A4
Steep La S42 ....114 A2
Steep Turnpike DE4 .....143 B3
Steeping Cl S43 ....96 C4
Steeple Cl DE21 ....205 C1
Steeple End Fold S32 ....27 B2
Steeple Grange DE4 ....154 C2
Steeple Light Rly*
  DE4 ....154 C2
Steeplegate S40 ....266 B3
Steetley La S80 ....63 C2
Stella St NG18 ....268 B3
Stenson Ave DE23 ......231 C3
Stenson Ct DE5 ....169 C1
Stenson Fields Prim Com Sch
  DE24 ....231 B1
Stenson Rd DE23,DE24 ..231 B2
Stenton Rd S8 ....56 C4
Stephens Rd DE14 ......254 A4
Stephenson Pl
  Chesterfield S40 ......266 B3
  Clay Cross S45 ....131 C2
Stephenson Rd S43 .....78 C1
Stephensons Way DE21 ..220 C2
Stepping Cl DE22 ......218 C3
Stepping La DE22 ......218 C3
Sterland St S40 ....95 C2
Sterndale Cl SK17 ......69 C2
Sterndale La SK17 ......69 C2
Sterndale Moor SK17 ...105 C3
Sterndale Rd NG10 .....235 A3
Sterry Cl S43 ....80 C1
Steven Cl NG9 ....223 C2
Stevenage Cl DE24 .....232 C3
Stevens La DE72 ....235 A4
Stevens Rd NG10 ....223 A3
Stevenson Ave DE72 ....235 A4
Stevenson Jun Sch
  NG9 ....223 C4
Stevenson Pl DE23 .....231 A4
Stevenson Rd DE6 ......224 A4
Stewart Cl
  Burton u T DE14 .....254 A3
  Derby DE21 ....220 C3
Stewart St Fenton S14 ..269 B2
  Somercotes DE55 .....170 B3
Stile Croft DE4 ....154 B3
Stiles Cl SK13 ....9 C3
Stiles Rd DE24 ....233 A4
Stillman Cl S41 ....115 B4
Stinting La
  Mansfield NG19 ......136 C1
  Shirebrook NG20 .....119 B1
Stirland St DE5 ....170 A1
Stirling Cl NG19 ....268 A3
Stirling Cl DE21 ....205 A1
Stirling Gr NG16 ....195 C4
Stock La ST14 ....224 B1
Stockbrook Rd DE22 ....218 B2
Stockbrook St DE22 ....218 C2
Stockdove Cl DE24 .....233 B2
Stocker Ave DE24 ......233 B2
Stockley La S44 ....117 C1
Stockley View S44 .....118 A3
Stockport Rd SK6 ....23 A3
Stocks Brow SK13 ......10 A3
Stocks Green Cl S17 ....55 B2
Stocks Green Dr S17 ....55 B2
Stocks Rd NG16 ....195 C2
Stocks The SK13 ....10 A4
Stockton Dr SK23 ....34 C1
Stockwell Ct
  Chesterfield S40 .....114 C4
  Mansfield NG18 .....268 B3
Stockwell Gate NG18 ...268 B3
Stoddard Dr DE75 ......181 C1
Stodhart La S42,S44 ....269 B1
Stoke Cl DE56 ....179 C3
Stoke Rd DE24 ....233 A4
Stoke Recn Ctr ST4 ....269 B1
Stoke-on-Trent Sta

Stollard St S45 ....131 B2
Stone Bench Way SK17 ..85 C4
Stone Bridge Rd NG3 ...268 C2
Stone Cl Derby DE21 ....57 B2
  Dronfield S18 ....57 B2
Stone Cres DE6 ....173 A1
Stone Cross Cl NG18 ....268 B3
Stone Cross La NG18 ...268 B3
Stone Furlong Rd DE45 ..91 C3
Stone Hill Rd DE23 .....231 C3
Stone La S43 ....77 B2
Stone Mdws NG10 .....236 C3
Stone Rd S18 ....57 B2
Stone Row
  Chesterfield S40 ......95 B1
  Marple SK6 ....23 A3

Stone St Mosborough S20 ..59 B4
  Stoke-on-T ST4 ......269 B2
Stonebench La S41 .....106 B2
Stonebridge La End Est
  NG3 ....268 A2
Stonebridge La NG20 ...120 C2
Stonebridge La DE55 ...147 A3
Stonebroom Prim Sch
  DE55 ....147 A2
Stonebroom Wlk DE24 ..232 C2
Stonechat Cl DE21 .....218 A2
Stonecliff Terr S41 ......85 B4
Stonecroft Rd S17 ......55 B2
Stonedale Cl S20 ....59 B4
Stonegravels Croft S20 ..59 C4
Stonegravels La S41 .....96 A3
Stonegravels Way S20 ...59 C3
Stoneheads S45 ....45 B4
Stonehill DE74 ....247 A1
Stoneholes Dr S45 .....131 C1
Stoneleigh St 20 NG10 ..268 C3
Stoneleigh Way DE55 ...169 C4
Stoneley Cl S12 ....44 A1
Stoneley Cres S12 ......44 A1
Stoneley Dell S12 ....44 A1
Stoneley Dr S12 ....44 A1
Stonelow Cres S18 ......57 A1
Stonelow Jun Sch S18 ...57 B1
Stonelow Rd S18 ....57 B1
Stonepit La DE6 ....164 A2
Stoneridge S9 ....9 C3
Stonerows La S45 ......145 C3
Stones Cl S33 ....38 A1
Stonesby Cl DE21 .....205 C1
Stonesdale Ct 11 DE24 ..233 A4
Stonewell La S17 ....137 B3
Stoney Cl DE45 ....109 B2
Stoney Cross DE21 .....220 C2
Stoney Flatts Cres
  DE21 ....231 A4
Stoney Gate Rd DE21 ...220 B2
Stoney Hollow S18 ......57 A1
Stoney La Ashover S42 ..130 B2
  Brinsley NG16 ....182 B3
  Derby DE6 ....220 C3
  Hognaston DE6 ....164 A1
  Selston NG16 ....171 C4
  Stretton en le F DE12 ..262 C1
  Trowell NG9 ....209 A3
Stoney Middleton CE Prim
  Sch S32 ....71 C2
Stoney St NG1 ....268 B1
Stoney Way S42 ....143 B2
Stoney Wood Dr DE4 ...156 B1
Stoneycroft La S42 .....114 A3
Stoneydale Cl DE11 ....255 C3
Stoneyfield Bank DE56 ..179 B3
Stoneyland Dr SK22 .....33 A4
Stoney La DE56 ....191 B3
Stony Ridge Rd S17 .....54 B3
Stonyhurst Ct DE24 ....232 C2
Stoodley Pike Gdns
  DE22 ....204 C1
Stoops Cl S40 ....95 B3
Stoppard Cl DE7 ....194 B1
Storer La DE4 ....166 A2
Stores Rd DE21 ....219 A4
Storforth La S41 ....115 A4
Storforth Lane Terr S41 ..115 A4
Storforth Lane Trad Est
  S40 ....115 A4
Stormont Cl DE55 .....160 A2
Stornoway Cl 11 DE7 ...194 C1
Storrs Rd S40 ....95 A1
Stort Sq NG19 ....136 B3
Storth Bank SK13 ....16 C4
Storth La DE55 ....159 C3
Storth Meadow Rd SK13 ..16 C4
Storthfield Way DE55 ...160 A2
Stour Cl Brimington S43 ..96 C4
  Hilton DE65 ....240 C4
Stourdale Cl NG10 .....236 A3
Stourport Dr DE73 .....233 A2
Stow Ct NG19 ....136 C2
Stowmarket Dr DE21 ...219 B4
Stradbroke Ave S13 .....44 C4
Stradbroke Cres S13 ....44 C4
Stradbroke Dr S13 ......44 C4
Stradbroke Pl S13 ......44 C4
Stradbroke Prim Sch
  S13 ....44 B4
Stradbroke Rd S13 .....44 B4
Stradbroke Rise S40 ....114 B4
Stradbroke Way S13 ....44 B4
Strand DE1 ....267 B3
Strand Arc DE1 ....267 B3
Stranfaer Cl DE55 .....170 A4
Stranraer Cl NG19 .....136 C3
Stratford Cl DE65 ......242 B1
Stratford Rd DE21 .....205 C1
Strathallan Cl DE14 ....127 B2
Strathaven Ct DE21 ....205 C1
Strathglen Cl NG16 ....195 C4
Strathmore Ave DE24 ..233 A3
Stratton Rd S44 ....99 A1
Straw La DE55 ....146 C2
Strawberry Bank NG17 ..148 C2
Strawberry La
  Blackfordby DE11 ....257 A1
  Rosliston DE12 ......260 B3
Strawberry Lee La S17 ...55 C1
Streatham Rd DE22 ....218 A3
Street Farm Cl S26 ......61 C2

Street Forest Walks The*
  SK17 ....64 C2
Street La DE5 ....180 A3
Street Lane Prim Sch
  DE5 ....180 A3
Street The SK10,SK41 ...64 B3
Streetfield Cres S20 .....59 B3
Streetfield La S20 ....59 C3
Streetfields S20 ....59 C3
Strelley Ave DE5 ....180 B4
Stretfield Rd S33 ....39 A1
Stretta La DE55 ....146 B1
Stretton Brook Sch
  DE13 ....240 B1
Stretton Cl DE3 ....217 B1
Stretton Handley CE Prim
  Sch DE55 ....145 B4
Stretton Rd
  Clay Cross S45 ......131 B1
  Shirland DE55 ......146 B4
  Stonebroom DE55 ...146 C3
Stretton View DE12 ....265 C3
Striding Edge Cl 8
  NG10 ....223 A1
Strines Rd Marple SK6 ...23 A2
  New Mills SK6 ....32 B4
Strines Sta SK6 ....23 B1
Stroma Cl DE24 ....233 C3
Strutt St Belper DE56 ...178 C2
  Derby DE23 ....219 A1
Stuart Cl S41 ....96 B3
Stuart St DE1 ....267 C3
Stubben Edge La S45 ...130 B1
Stubbin Wood Sch
  NG20 ....119 C3
Stubbing Rd S40 ....114 C4
Stubbins La S43 ....34 B1
Stubbins Wood NG20 ...119 C3
Stubbins Wood La
  NG20 ....119 C3
Stubley Cl S18 ....56 C2
Stubley Croft S18 ......56 C1
Stubley Dr S18 ....56 C1
Stubley Hollow S18 ....56 C2
Stubley La S18 ....56 C1
Stubley Pl S18 ....56 C1
Stubwood Hollow ST14 ..196 B3
Stubwood La ST14 .....196 B2
Studbrook Cl DE74 .....247 A1
Studfarm Cl DE73 .....252 C1
Studland Cl NG19 ......136 B3
Sturge Croft S2 ....43 A3
Sturges La DE72 ....233 C2
Sturgess St ST4 ....269 B1
Sturston Rd DE6 ......173 A3
Stychfields S17 ....269 B3
Sudbury Ave
  Chesterfield S40 ......95 A3
  Derby DE1 ....218 C3
Sudbury Cl
  Chesterfield S40 ......95 A3
  Derby DE1 ....218 C3
Sudbury Dr NG10 .....235 C2
Sudbury Dr NG17 ......148 C1
Sudbury Hall & Mus of
  Childhood* DE6 .....225 B3
Sudbury Mews NG16 ...182 C1
Sudbury Pk DE6 ....225 B3
Sudbury Prim Sch DE6 ..225 C2
Sudbury St DE1 ....218 C3
Sudhall Cl S41 ....95 B4
Suff La NG16 ....160 B2
Suffolk Ave DE21 .....219 C4
Suffolk Rd DE15 ......254 B4
Sugworth Rd S6 ....31 C3
Sulley Field Cl DE22 ...204 B4
Summer Cross SK17 ....64 A2
Summer Dr DE4 ....165 C4
Summer La Totley S17 ...55 B2
  Wirksworth DE4 .....165 C4
Summer Leys La NG2 ...268 B1
Summer St DE22 ......218 B2
Summer Wood Dr DE23 ..231 B4
Summerbottom SK14 ...16 A4
Summercroft Cl DE22 ...218 C2
Summerfield Cres S43 ...96 C4
Summerfield Rd
  Chesterfield S40 ......266 A1
  Dronfield S18 ....57 A2
Summerfields Way DE7 ..194 B2
Summerfields Way S
  DE7 ....194 B1
Summerley Lower Rd
  S18 ....57 A1
Summerley Rd S18 .....57 A1
Summerskill Gn S43 ....97 B4
Summerwood La S18 ...56 C2
Summerwood Pl 8 S18 ..57 A1
Summit Dr NG20 ......119 C2
Sumner St DE23 ....17 A4
Sumners Pl S43 ....96 A3
Sun La DE4 ....156 C1
Sun St Derby DE22 ....267 A2
  Woodville DE11 .....256 C1
Sunart Cl DE21 ....231 C1
Sundew Cl DE21 ......205 C1
Sundown Ave DE23 ....231 B3
Sundown Cl SK22 ......33 A4
Sunflower Cl NG20 ....119 B2
Sunningdale Cl DE13 ...240 B1
Sunlaws St SK13 ....17 A4
Sunlea Cres NG9 ......223 C3
Sunningdale Ave
  Derby DE22 ....220 B3
  Heanor DE75 ....193 C4

Sunningdale Cl S40 .....114 C4
Sunningdale Dr
  Glossop SK13 ....10 C1
  Ilkeston DE7 ....208 A3
Sunningdale Rise S40 ...114 B4
Sunninghill Cl DE7 .....207 B4
Sunny Bank
  Great Longstone DE45 ..90 A2
  Mayfield DE6 ....184 B4
  Tibshelf DE55 ....147 C3
Sunny Bank Gdns DE55 ..178 C1
Sunny Bank La S17 .....69 B2
Sunny Banks 3 SK13 ...17 A4
Sunny Brook Cl S43 ....80 C2
Sunny Gr DE21 ....220 A3
Sunny Hill DE56 ....190 C4
Sunny Springs S41 .....266 B4
Sunnybank DE4 ....110 C1
Sunnyfield SK17 ....85 C1
Sunnyhill Ave DE23 ....231 C3
Sunnyhill Inf Sch DE23 ..231 C4
Sunnyside
  Swadlincote DE11 ....255 C4
  Whitwell S80 ....82 A3
Sunnyside Rd ST14 ....210 A1
Sunnyvale Ave S17 .....55 B2
Sunnyvale Rd S17 ......55 B2
Surbiton Cl DE22 ......218 A3
Surbiton Ct DE7 ....207 B4
Surgery La DE4 ....157 A1
Surrey Dr NG19 ....268 A4
Surrey St Derby DE22 ...218 B3
  Glossop SK13 ....10 B1
Sussex Cir DE21 ....219 C4
Sussex Cl NG16 ....195 A4
Sussex Rd DE15 ....254 C3
Sussex Way NG10 .....223 A3
Sutherland Rd DE23 ...219 A1
Sutherland St ST4 .....269 C1
Sutton Ave DE73 ......232 C2
Sutton Cl DE22 ....218 B3
Sutton Cres S43 ....97 B4
Sutton Ct NG16 ....182 C1
Sutton Dr Derby DE24 ..231 A1
  Stoke-on-T ST4 .....269 A1
Sutton Hall Rd S44 ....117 C4
Sutton La Etwall DE65 ..229 A3
  Hatton DE65 ....227 C2
  Hilton DE65 ....228 B2
  Long Duckmanton S44 ..116 C4
Sutton Rd
  Church Broughton DE65 ..227 B4
  Mansfield NG18 .....268 A3
  Sutton in a N NG17 ...148 B4
Sutton Road Fst Sch
  NG18 ....268 A3
Sutton Scarsdale Hall*
  S44 ....117 A3
Sutton View S44 ....118 A4
Sutton Way SK13 ......10 A3
Suttons La SK6 ....23 A3
Swaddale Ave S41 ......96 A3
Swaddale Cl S41 ....96 A3
Swadlincote La DE11 ...256 C2
Swadlincote Rd DE11 ...256 C2
Swadlincote Ski Ctr
  DE11 ....256 B2
Swaines Mdw DE7 .....165 B4
Swalebank Cl S40 ......114 C4
Swaledale Cl 2 DE24 ...233 B3
Swallow Cl DE7 ....194 B1
Swallow House Cres
  SK22 ....25 B2
Swallow House La SK22 ..25 B2
Swallow Rd DE11 ......256 C2
Swallowdale Rd DE24 ...231 B2
Swan La SK116 ....269 A3
Swan La DE72 ....136 A2
Swan St S14 ....269 B2
Swanbourne Cl DE73 ...96 B1
Swanmore Rd DE23 ....231 A4
Swann Yd NG17 ....148 C2
Swanson Ave NG17 ....148 C2
Swanwick Ave NG20 ...119 C2
Swanwick Gdns DE21 ..206 A1
Swanwick Hall Sch
  DE55 ....169 C4
Swanwick Hill DE55 ...169 C4
Swanwick Junc Sta
  DE55 ....170 A3
Swanwick Prim Sch
  DE55 ....169 B3
Swanwick Rd DE55 ....170 A4
Swanwick St S41 ....77 A1
Swarkestone Dr DE23 ..231 B3
Swarkestone Rd
  Barrow u T DE73 ....244 A3
  Derby DE73 ....244 C4
Swathwick Cl S42 ......114 C2
Swathwick La S42 .....114 B2
Swayfield Cl DE3 ......217 B2
Sweetbriar Cl DE4 .....233 A3
Swift Cl Derby DE22 ...218 A2
  Woodville DE11 .....256 C2
Swift Ct NG16 ....182 C1
Swinburne St Derby DE1 ..268 C2
  Nottingham NG3 .....268 C2
Swinderby Dr DE21 ....206 B1
Swindon Cl NG16 .....195 B4
Swiney Way NG9 .....223 C1
Swinger La S45 ....129 B4
Swinney Bank DE56 ...179 A3
Swinney La DE56 .....179 A3
Swinscoe Hill DE6 ....172 A1
Swinscoe Way S40 .....95 A3

Swinson Cl ST14 . . . . .197 A2
Swithland Cl S41 . . . . .115 B4

Sycamore Ave
Chesterfield S40 . . . . .95 C1
Creswell S80 . . . . .81 C1
Derby DE72 . . . . .204 B2
Dronfield S18 . . . . .57 A2
Findern DE65 . . . . .230 C1
Glapwell S44 . . . . .134 A4
Ripley DE5 . . . . .180 B4
Swadlincote DE11 . . . . .256 A4
Sycamore Cl Bolsover S44 . .99 B1
Burton u T DE15 . . . . .254 C3
Buxton SK17 . . . . .66 A1
Etwall DE65 . . . . .229 B2
Linton DE12 . . . . .261 B3
Mapperley DE7 . . . . .193 C2
New Mills SK22 . . . . .24 C1
Pinxton NG16 . . . . .160 B2
Selston NG16 . . . . .171 B4
Shirland DE55 . . . . .146 B2
Sycamore Cotts DE6 . . . . . .151 B1
Sycamore Cres NG10 . . . . .223 B4
Sycamore Ct Derby DE21 . .220 C3
Willington DE65 . . . . .242 A3
Sycamore Dr Calow S44 . . .96 C2
Ilkeston DE7 . . . . .209 A4
Killamarsh S21 . . . . .60 B3
Sycamore Jun & Inf Schs
NG3 . . . . .268 B2
Sycamore La
Barlborough S43 . . . . .80 A3
Brimington S43 . . . . .78 A1
Sycamore Rd
Awsworth NG16 . . . . .195 B3
Brimington S43 . . . . .78 A1
Burton u T DE15 . . . . .254 C3
Castle Donington DE74 . . . .247 A3
Chapel-en-le-F SK23 . . . . . .47 A2
Hayfield SK22 . . . . .24 C1
Long Eaton NG10 . . . . .236 B3
Mansfield Woodhouse
NG19 . . . . .136 B3
Matlock DE4 . . . . .143 A3
Mayfield DE6 . . . . .184 B4
Sycamore St
Market Warsop NG20 . . . . .120 C3
Mosborough S20 . . . . .59 B4
Sycamore Terr SK22 . . . . . .25 B2
Sycamores The
Eastwood NG16 . . . . .182 C1
Glossop SK13 . . . . .9 C2
South Normanton DE55 . . .160 A3
Syda La S42 . . . . .93 C1
Sydenham Rd DE22 . . . . . .218 A4
Sydney Cl NG19 . . . . .136 B3
Sydney St Chesterfield S40 .95 C2
Draycott DE72 . . . . .235 A4
Sydnope Hill DE4 . . . . .128 A3
Syerscote La NG9 . . . . .263 A1
Sylvan Cl S41 . . . . .266 C1
Sylvan Cliff SK17 . . . . .85 B4
Sylvan Dr S42 . . . . .131 A3
Sylvan Pk SK17 . . . . .85 B4
Sylvester St NG18 . . . . .268 A3
Sylvia Rd S18 . . . . .76 B3
Sywell Cl DE55 . . . . .169 C4

T

Tabley Gdns SK6 . . . . .23 A2
Taddington & Priestcliffe CE
Sch SK17 . . . . .87 C2
Taddington Cl **8** DE21 . .219 C4
Taddington Rd
Chesterfield S40 . . . . .95 A3
Derby DE21 . . . . .205 C1
Taft Ave NG10 . . . . .223 A3
Tagg La DE45 . . . . .107 A1
Taggs Knoll S33 . . . . .40 A2
Taghole La DE6 . . . . .188 C1
Tailby Dr DE65 . . . . .242 A3
Talbot Cres S41 . . . . .115 B4
Talbot Dr NG9 . . . . .209 B1
Talbot Pl DE12 . . . . .265 C4
Talbot Rd Glossop SK13 . . .10 B1
Stafford ST17 . . . . .269 B3
Talbot St
Chesterfield S41 . . . . .115 B4
Derby DE1 . . . . .218 C3
Glossop SK13 . . . . .10 B1
Nottingham NG1 . . . . .268 A2
Pinxton NG16 . . . . .160 B1
Swadlincote DE11 . . . . .256 A1
Talgarth Cl DE21 . . . . .206 B1
Tamar Ave DE22 . . . . .204 B2
Tamworth Rd
Castle Donington DE72,
NG10 . . . . .235 C1
Long Eaton NG10 . . . . .236 B3
Stretton en le F DE12 . . . . .265 C1
Tamworth St DE56 . . . . . . .190 C2
Tamworth Terr DE56 . . . . . .190 C2
Tanner's La DE65 . . . . .242 B2
Tansley Ave DE7 . . . . .193 A1
Tansley Dr S40 . . . . .95 A4
Tansley House Gdns
DE4 . . . . .144 A2
Tansley Prim Sch DE4 . . . .144 A2
Tansley Rd S42 . . . . .131 C3
Tansley Rise DE21 . . . . .205 C1
Tansley Way S43 . . . . .97 B3
Tants Mdw DE56 . . . . .191 C3

Tantum Ave DE75 . . . . .181 B2
Tanyard Cl DE74 . . . . .247 A2
Tap La S40 . . . . .266 A3
Taplow Cl DE23 . . . . .217 B1
Tapton La S41 . . . . .266 C3
Tapton Lock Hill S41 . . . . . .96 A3
Tapton Terr S41 . . . . .266 C4
Tapton Vale S41 . . . . .96 B3
Tapton View Rd S41 . . . . . .95 C3
Tapton Way S44 . . . . .96 C2
Tarina Cl DE73 . . . . .233 A1
Tarnside Fold **6** SK13 . . .17 A4
Tarporley Gr S14 . . . . .269 A1
Tasman Cl DE3 . . . . .217 C2
Tatenhill La
Branston DE14 . . . . .253 B4
Branston, Tatenhill DE13 . .253 A4
Tatham's La DE7 . . . . . . .194 C1
Tattersall Wlk NG19 . . . . . .136 C2
Tattershall Dr NG7 . . . . . . .268 A1
Tattle Hill DE7 . . . . .207 C1
Taunton Cl DE24 . . . . .233 B4
Tavern Rd SK13 . . . . .9 C2
Taverners Cres DE23 . . . . . .231 B4
Tavistock Ave DE5 . . . . .169 B1
Tavistock Cl DE24 . . . . .231 B2
Tavistock Sq DE55 . . . . .159 A3
Tawney Croft DE4 . . . . .144 A2
Tawny Way DE23 . . . . .231 A4
Taxal & Fernilee CE Prim Sch
SK23 . . . . .45 B3
Taxal Ctr The S43 . . . . .45 B3
Taxal Dr Derby DE24 . . . . . .231 B1
Taxal Moor Rd SK23 . . . . . .45 B2
Tay Cl Derby DE24 . . . . .231 B1
Dronfield S18 . . . . .56 B1
Tay Wlk DE22 . . . . .204 C2
Taylor Cres
Chesterfield S41 . . . . .96 B1
Stapleford NG9 . . . . .223 C4
Taylor La DE75 . . . . .181 B2
Taylor St Derby DE21 . . . . . .219 C1
Hollingworth SK14 . . . . .9 B1
Ilkeston DE7 . . . . .194 C1
Taylor's La Spout DE4 . . . . .166 A2
Trusley DE6 . . . . .215 C3
Taylors La ST14 . . . . .196 B2
Tayside Cl DE24 . . . . .231 B2
Teal Cl NG20 . . . . .119 B2
Tealby Wlk NG19 . . . . .136 C2
Tean Cl DE15 . . . . .248 A1
Teasel Dr DE11 . . . . .256 C2
Tedder Ave S41 . . . . .85 B2
Tedgness Rd S32 . . . . .53 C1
Tedworth Ave DE24 . . . . . . .231 B1
Teesdale Rd
Long Eaton NG10 . . . . .236 A3
Mosborough S20 . . . . .58 C4
Telegraph St ST17 . . . . .269 B3
Telford Cl DE3 . . . . .217 C1
Telford Cres S43 . . . . .78 C1
Telford Rd SK6 . . . . .23 A2
Telmah Cl DE13 . . . . .240 B1
Temperance Hill DE55 . . . .145 C4
Temperance Sq SK14 . . . . . .9 A2
Temperance St S14 . . . . . . .16 A4
Temple Cl DE24 . . . . .231 B2
Temple Ave SK13 . . . . .10 B3
Temple Ct S41 . . . . .85 A3
Temple Normanton Bsns Pk
S41 .116 A2
Temple Normanton Prim Sch
S42 .116 B2
Temple Rd Buxton SK17 . . .85 A3
Matlock Bath DE4 . . . . .143 A1
Temple St Derby DE23 . . . .219 A2
Fenton ST4 . . . . .269 C1
Glossop SK13 . . . . .10 B3
Temple View SK17 . . . . .85 A4
Temple Wlk DE4 . . . . .143 A1
Templebell Cl DE23 . . . . . . .231 A3
Ten Foot Cl SK13 . . . . .10 A1
Tenant St DE1 . . . . .267 B3
Tenby Dr DE21 . . . . .206 B1
Tennessee Rd DE21 . . . . . . .220 A4
Tennis Dr NG7 . . . . .268 A1
Tennyson Ave
Chesterfield S40 . . . . .266 A3
Mansfield Woodhouse
NG19 . . . . .136 B1
Swadlincote DE11 . . . . .256 B3
Tennyson Rd S80 . . . . .81 B1
Tennyson Sq NG16 . . . . . . .171 B4
Tennyson St Derby DE24 . .232 B4
Holmewood S42 . . . . .116 B1
7 Mansfield NG18 . . . . .268 B4
Nottingham NG7 . . . . .268 A2
Shirland DE55 . . . . .146 B3
Tennyson Way S42 . . . . .115 C2
Tenter Cl NG10 . . . . .236 B3
Tenter La Heage DE56 . . . .168 B1
Mansfield NG18 . . . . .268 C4
Tenterbanks S18 . . . . .269 A4
Tern Ave DE11 . . . . .256 C2
Terr The DE21 . . . . .219 C4
Terrace La NG19 . . . . .134 C3
Terrace Rd Buxton SK17 . . .85 A4
Chapel-en-le-F SK23 . . . . . .47 A3
Mansfield NG18 . . . . .268 C4
Tideswell SK17 . . . . .69 B2
Terrace The DE4 . . . . .143 C4
Terret Gr SK17 . . . . .84 B3
Terrey Rd S17 . . . . .55 C3
Terry Pl DE24 . . . . .232 C4
Tetford Wlk NG19 . . . . .136 C2
Teversal Ave NG7 . . . . .268 A1
Tevery Cl NG9 . . . . .223 C4
Teviot Pl DE21 . . . . .206 A1

Tewkesbury Ave NG19 . . . .136 B2
Tewkesbury Cres DE21 . . . .219 B4
Tewkesbury Dr NG16 . . . . .195 C4
Tewkesbury Rd NG10 . . . . .236 C3
Thackeray Rd DE55 . . . . . . .146 C2
Thackeray St DE24 . . . . .232 A3
Thanet Dr DE24 . . . . .233 A3
Thanet St S45 . . . . .131 B2
Thatch Cl DE21 . . . . .204 C1
Thatchers La DE4 . . . . .144 A2
Theatre La S41 . . . . .266 C3
Theatre Sq NG1 . . . . .268 B2
Theatre Yd S40 . . . . .266 B3
Thickley Cl NG20 . . . . .119 C2
Thirlmere Ave DE22 . . . . . .204 C2
Thirlmere Cl **9** DE21 . . . .223 A1
Thirlmere Rd
Chesterfield S41 . . . . .95 B4
Long Eaton NG10 . . . . .223 A1
Thirsk Pl DE24 . . . . .232 B4
Thirteen Row S44 . . . . .118 A2
Thistle Cl NG16 . . . . .195 A4
Thistle Green Cl DE75 . . . .182 A1
Thistle Dr DE7 . . . . .209 A2
Thistledown Cl DE22 . . . . . .205 A1
Thistley Hough S14 . . . . . . .269 A1
Thistley Hough High Sch
ST4 .269 A1
Thomas Cl NG3 . . . . .268 B2
Thomas Cookson Cl DE3 . .252 A4
Thomas St Compstall SK6 . .15 A1
Glossop SK13 . . . . .10 C1
Thompson Cl S41 . . . . .96 A4
Thompson St
Langley Mill NG16 . . . . .182 A2
Thomson Dr DE5 . . . . .181 A4
Thoresby Ave
Nottingham NG2 . . . . .268 C1
Shirebrook NG20 . . . . .119 C2
Thoresby Cl Derby DE21 . .206 A1
Ripley DE5 . . . . .169 C1
Thoresby Cres DE7 . . . . . . .234 C4
Thoresby Pl S43 . . . . .97 B3
Thoresby Rd
Long Eaton NG10 . . . . .236 B3
Mansfield Woodhouse
NG19 . . . . .136 A2
Thoresby St NG18 . . . . .268 B4
Thoresey Ave S45 . . . . .81 A2
Thorn Ave NG19 . . . . .135 C1
Thorn Cl Buxton SK17 . . . . .85 C4
Derby DE22 . . . . .204 B2
Thorn Dr NG16 . . . . .195 A4
Thorn St Derby DE23 . . . . .218 C1
Woodville DE11 . . . . .256 C1
Thorn Street Mews
DE11 . . . . .255 C4
Thorn Tree Gdns DE5 . . . .182 C2
Thorn Tree La DE11,
DE15 . . . . .255 C4
Thornborough Cl S2 . . . . . .43 B4
Thornborough Pl S2 . . . . . .43 B4
Thornborough Rd S2 . . . . . .43 B4
Thornbridge Ave S12 . . . . . .44 B2
Thornbridge Cl S12 . . . . . . .44 B2
Thornbridge Cres
Chesterfield S40 . . . . .115 A3
Sheffield S12 . . . . .44 C2
Thornbridge Dr S12 . . . . . . .44 B2
Thornbridge Education Ctr
DE45 . . . . .89 C1
Thornbridge Gr S12 . . . . . . .44 B2
Thornbridge La S12 . . . . . . .44 B2
Thornbridge Pl S12 . . . . . . .44 B2
Thornbridge Rise S12 . . . . .44 C2
Thornbridge Way S12 . . . . .44 C2
Thornbrook Cl SK23 . . . . . . .47 B3
Thornbrook Rd SK23 . . . . . .47 B3
Thornburrow Dr ST4 . . . . . .269 A2
Thorncliffe Ave DE4 . . . . . .127 A3
Thorncliffe Rd SK13 . . . . . . .9 C2
Thorndene Cl S41 . . . . .96 A3
Thorndike Ave DE24 . . . . . .233 A4
Thorntree Cl DE3 . . . . .230 B4
Thorntree Cotts DE4 . . . . . .154 C1
Thorntree Ct S40 . . . . .114 C4
Thorntree La DE1 . . . . .267 B3
Thornway SK6 . . . . .32 A4
Thornwood Ct SK17 . . . . . . .85 A4

Thoroton St **7** NG7 . . . . . .268 A2
Thorp Cl S2 . . . . .43 A4
Thorpe Ave Dronfield S18 . .57 B2
Whitwell S80 . . . . .81 C3
Thorpe Cl
Burton u T DE15 . . . . .248 B1
10 Chesterfield S41 . . . . .95 C4
Stapleford NG9 . . . . .223 B4
Thorpe Croft DE4 . . . . .156 A3
Thorpe Downs Rd DE11 . .256 A1
Thorpe Dr DE21 . . . . .217 C2
Thorpe Hill Dr DE75 . . . . . .193 C4
Thorpe House Ave S8 . . . . .43 A2
Thorpe House La S8 . . . . . .43 A2
Thorpe House Rise S8 . . . . .43 A2
Thorpe La S80,S81 . . . . .63 B3
Thorpe Leys NG10 . . . . . . .236 B3
Thorpe Rd
Eastwood NG16 . . . . .182 C2
Harthill S26 . . . . .62 A4
Thorpe St Glossop SK13 . . .10 C1
Ilkeston DE7 . . . . .194 C2
Thorpe Way DE56 . . . . .179 A3
Thorpe's Rd
Heanor DE75 . . . . .181 B1
Shipley DE75 . . . . .193 B4
Thorpelands Ave NG19 . . .136 A2
Thorpelands Dr DE22 . . . . .204 C1
Thorpleigh Rd S43 . . . . .79 A1
Three Gates DE56 . . . . .178 C1
Thrift Rd DE14 . . . . .254 A4
Throstle Nest Way DE6 . . .201 C4
Thrumpton Ave NG10 . . . .237 A4
Thrumpton Hall* NG11 . . .237 A2
Thrushton Cl DE65 . . . . . . .242 A3
Thruxton Cl DE24 . . . . .233 B3
Thunderpit La S32 . . . . .71 A2
Thurcaton Way DE55 . . . . .148 A2
Thurcroft Cl DE22 . . . . .218 B1
Thurgarton Ct DE6 . . . . . . .173 B1
Thurgarton St NG2 . . . . . . .268 C1
Thurland St **16** NG1 . . . . .268 B1
Thurlby Ct NG19 . . . . .136 C2
Thurlow Ct DE21 . . . . .206 A1
Thurman St DE7 . . . . .209 A3
Thurrows Way DE73 . . . . . .233 A1
Thurstan Ave S8 . . . . .56 C4
Thurston Ave DE55 . . . . . . .170 B4
Thurstone Furlong
DE73 . . . . .232 C1
Thurvaston Rd DE6 . . . . . . .197 C1
Thyme Cl DE21 . . . . .231 B2
Tiber Cl **17** DE24 . . . . . . .233 B3
Tibshelf Inf Sch DE55 . . . . .148 A4
Tibshelf Rd
Blackwell DE55 . . . . .147 B1
Holmewood S42 . . . . .132 C4
Tibshelf Sch DE55 . . . . .148 A4
Tickham Ave DE24 . . . . .231 B1
Ticknall La
Denby DE5,DE56 . . . . .180 A1
Hartshorne DE11 . . . . .257 A4
Ticknall Wlk DE23 . . . . .231 C3
Tideswell Bank 14 SK13 . .9 C1
Tideswell Cl S43 . . . . .97 B3
Tideswell Ct NG18 . . . . .268 C4
Tideswell Gn DE11 . . . . . . .255 C3
Tideswell La S22 . . . . .71 A3
Tideswell Rd DE21 . . . . .205 C1
Tiger Yd DE6 . . . . .173 A1
Tilbury Pl DE24 . . . . .233 A3
Tilford Gdns NG9 . . . . .223 C3
Tiller Cl DE23 . . . . .231 A3
Tillotson Cl S8 . . . . .43 A3
Tillotson Rise S8 . . . . .43 A3
Tilson Ave S14 . . . . .269 A2
Tilton Gr DE7 . . . . .208 B3
Timber La S45 . . . . .132 C3
Timberfields Rd ST16 . . . . .269 A4
Timbersbrook Cl DE21 . . . .206 A1
Timsbury Ct DE21 . . . . .205 C1
Tinderbox La DE65 . . . . . . .229 B3
Tinker Croft DE7 . . . . .208 C4
Tinkerley La DE6 . . . . .165 B1
Tinkley La S42 . . . . .130 B2
Tinsell Brook DE65 . . . . . . .228 C1
Tinsley Rd DE75,NG16 . . . .182 C1
Tintagel Cl
Burton u T DE13 . . . . .240 C1
5 Derby DE23 . . . . .219 A1
Tintwistle CE Prim Sch
Glossop SK13 . . . . .10 A4
Tip Tree Cl NG16 . . . . .195 C4
Tipnall Rd DE74 . . . . .247 A2
Tipper's La DE65 . . . . .227 A4
Tippett Ct NG3 . . . . .268 C2
Tippett Ave DE21 . . . . .220 B3
Tirebuck Way S43 . . . . .78 C1
Tirnic Cl Derby DE24 . . . . .231 C2
Stapleford NG9 . . . . .209 B1
Tishbelf DE55 . . . . .147 C3
Tissington Cl S40 . . . . .95 A3
Tissington Dr DE21 . . . . . . .206 A2
Tissington Terr **15** SK13 . .9 B1
Titchfield Ave NG19 . . . . . .136 B2
Titchfield St Creswell S80 . .81 C2
Mansfield NG18 . . . . .268 B4
Whitwell S80 . . . . .81 C3
Tithe Barn Cl SK17 . . . . .69 B2
Tithe Barn Rd ST16 . . . . . . .269 C4
Tithe Barn Rd ST16 . . . . . . .269 C4
Tithebarn La DE6 . . . . .215 B3
Tithes La S41 . . . . .77 A3
Tiverton Cl S31 . . . . .269 C1
Tiverton Cl DE3 . . . . .217 C2
Tivoli Gdns DE1 . . . . .218 C4
Tixall Rd ST16 . . . . .269 C4
Toadmoor La DE56 . . . . . . .167 C2
Tobermory Way DE24 . . . . .231 B2

Todbrook Cl SK23 . . . . .45 B4
Todd St S41 . . . .
Tolkien Way ST4 . . . .
Toll Bar Ave S12 . . . .
Toll Bar Cl S12 . . . .
Toll Bar Dr S12 . . . .
Toll Bar Rd S12 . . . .
Toll House Mead S20 . . . . .
Tollbridge Rd S43 . . . .
Tollemache Cl SK14 . . . . . .
Tollemache Rd SK14 . . . . .
Tollgate Cotts DE6 . . . .
Tollhouse Hill **8** NG1 . . .
Tom Brads Croft SK23 . . . .
Tom La
Chapel-en-le-F DE6 . . . .
Staveley S44 . . . .
Tomlinson Ct DE24 . . . .
Tomlinson Ind Est DE21 . .
Tomlinsons Cotts DE21 . . .
Tomwood Rise S43 . . . .
Tonbridge Dr DE24 . . . .
Tonge La DE73 . . . .
Tongue La DE6 . . . .
Tongue La Ind Est SK17 . .
Tontine Rd S40 . . . .
Top Farm Ct DE56 . . . .
Top Fingle Cl S43 . . . .
Top Hag La DE56 . . . .
Top La Crich DE4 . . . .
Mansfield NG19 . . . .
Old Brampton S42 . . . .
Shottle DE56 . . . .
Top Lons DE6 . . . .
Top Manor Cl DE72 . . . . . .
Top Mdw DE11 . . . .
Top Rd Calow S44 . . . .
Wingerworth S42 . . . .
Top Row NG16 . . . .
Tophill La DE4 . . . .
Tophole Rd S33 . . . .
Topley Gdns DE21 . . . .
Toppham Dr S8 . . . .
Toppham Rd S8 . . . .
Toppham Way S8 . . . .
Topshill La DE6 . . . .
Tor Ave DE55 . . . .
Tor Cl DE4 . . . .
Tor Rise DE4 . . . .
Tor View Rise DE4 . . . .
Torksey Wlk NG19 . . . .
Torr St SK17 . . . .
Torr Top St S22 . . . .
Torrance Cl DE14 . . . .
Torrani Way S42 . . . .
Torridon Cl DE24 . . . .
Torrs Valley SK22 . . . .
Torrvale Rd SK22 . . . .
Tors The DE4 . . . .
Torside Way S43 . . . .
Torwood Dr S8 . . . .
Totley All Saints CE Prim
S17 . . . .
Totley Brook Cl S17 . . . . . .
Totley Brook Croft S17 . . .
Totley Brook Glen S17 . . .
Totley Brook Gr S17 . . . . . .
Totley Brook Rd S17 . . . . .
Totley Brook Way S17 . . . .
Totley Cl S13 . . . .
Totley Gdns S13 . . . .
Totley Gn **21** SK13 . . . . .
Totley Grange Cl S17 . . . . .
Totley Grange Dr S17 . . . .
Totley Grange Rd S17 . . . .
Totley Hall Croft S17 . . . . .
Totley Hall Dr S17 . . . .
Totley Hall La S17 . . . .
Totley Hall Mead S17 . . . .
Totley La S17 . . . .
Totley Laurels **22** SK13 . .
Totley Mews S43 . . . .
Totley Mnt S43 . . . .
Totley Pl SK13 . . . .
Totley Prim Sch S17 . . . . . .
Toton Banks Road Inf Sch
NG9 . . . .
Toton Bispham Drive Jun
. . . .
Toton La NG9 . . . .
Toulmin Dr DE11 . . . .
Tower Bsns Pk S45 . . . .
Tower Cl Sheffield S2 . . . . .
Somercotes DE55 . . . .
Tower Cres S44 . . . .
Tower Dr S2 . . . .
Tower Rd
Burton u T DE15 . . . .
Hartshorne DE11 . . . .
Tower St DE24 . . . .
Tower View Prim Sch
DE15 . . . .
Towers La S42 . . . .
Towle Cl DE72 . . . .
Towle St NG10 . . . .
Towles Pastures DE74 . . . .
Town End
Apperknowle S18 . . . .
Bolsover S44 . . . .
Buxton SK17 . . . .
Shirland DE55 . . . .
Town End dun Sch
. . . .
Town End Rd DE72 . . . .
Town Fold SK6 . . . .
Town Gate S33 . . . .

Hall Yd DE6 ....173 B1
Head DE6 ....173 B1
La Bradwell S33 ....51 A4
Bottom SK13 ....16 B3
otton S41 ....148 A2
..St Brassington DE4 ..153 A1
l DE56 ....190 C2
ook DE56 ....191 B3
s SK6 ....23 A4
n NG16 ....160 C2
acre NG16 ....223 A3
ne Dr 205 B4
view NG16 ....195 C4
held La S33 ....39 C1
esan S32 ....71 B3
head La S33 ....33 A3
head La S33 ....78 B1
ad Rd S17 ....55 B4
cliffe La SK6 ....23 A3
end Gr DE73 ....231 A1
ide Cl NG10 ....182 B1
on Ave NG16 ....182 B1
t St ST4 ....92 C1
gar Rd
Eaton NG10 ....236 B3
on-T ST4 ....269 A2
gar Sq NG10 ....236 C4
gar Terr NG10 ....236 C4
t St Derby DE1 ....267 C2
ngham NG2 ....268 A1
s Terr
w Hill S43 ....78 A2
erfield S41 ....115 A4
erd Way DE23 ....231 B4
were S45 ....131 B2
aal Terr S44 ....118 A3
rs Ct S14 ....269 C1
rs Rd NG10 ....223 A3
d Rd S2 ....44 A4
Cliff Cavern * S33 ...37 C2
roft St S43 ....17 A4
gar Dr DE21 ....206 A1
euk Cl S40 ....95 A2
l Ct DE23 ....231 A4
ron Cl DE21 ....206 B1
ny Way DE24 ....231 B2
rney Rd S45 ....131 B2
hard Ave S16 ....269 C4
hard Dr SK17 ....85 B2
Ave Buxton SK17 ....85 B2
end DE25 ....242 B3
Bridge Ct DE23 ....231 B4
Cl Derby DE65 ....231 B1
on DE65 ....242 B3
Coll NG10 ....236 B4
Cl DE23 ....231 B3
Dr Alfreton DE55 .....159 A1
field S18 ....57 A2
Ho NG10 ....236 A2
La
le Donington DE74 ...247 A3
Eaton NG10 ....236 C3
ourne DE73 ....231 B1
ourne DE73 ....245 B1
on Solney DE15 ....248 C4
ngham NG2 ....268 C1
on-on-T DE7 ....245 C2
Lane Ind Est
.....................247 A3
Rd Ilkeston DE7 ......208 B2
ngham NG2 ....268 C1
l Rise DE21 ....220 C2
St Derby DE24 ....233 A4
n Eaton NG10 ....236 C4
ngham NG1,NG2 ....268 B1
t Valley Rd ST4 ......269 A1
. WIk NG19 ....136 C2
tton NG10 ....237 A4
ton Gn DE21 ....220 A3
ton Green Dr DE21 ....220 A3
llian Cl DE22 ....204 C1
ssall Cl DE7 ....209 A4
elyn Cl DE15 ....248 B1
eris Cl DE21 ....220 C2
one Ave NG9 ....223 C3
ose Cl S40 ....114 B4
gle The DE7 ....209 A3
kett Cl S33 ....38 B2
La
sterfield S40 ....266 A4
ston DE7 ....194 C2
ty Cl S41 ....266 B4
ty Ct DE11 ....256 A2
ty Mews S41 ....266 A4
ty Sq NG1 ....268 B2
ty St DE1 ....267 C2
ty View NG10 ....236 C4
ty WIk Rd NG1 ....268 B2
key La S32 ....72 A2
ram Cr DE11 ....240 C1
en Cl Burton u T DE3 .240 B1
sterfield S40 ....114 B4
by DE23 ....231 A4
rberley NG16 ....195 C4
La S17 ....70 A3
agh La NG16 ....195 C4
abrook Hill S43 ......97 A4
atbeck Gr DE43 ....78 A1
atbeck Gr DE23 ......231 A4
bridge Cl DE21 ....205 C1
vell Ave DE7 ....209 A3
vell CE Prim Sch
.....................209 B2
vell Gr
g Eaton NG10 ....223 B1
pleford NG9 ....209 B2
vell Park Dr NG9 .....209 B1
vell Rd NG9 ....209 B1
vels La DE22 ....218 B2
eman St DE7 ....194 C2

Truman St Cossall DE7 ..195 A1
Truman St
Kimberley NG16 ....195 B4
Truro Cl DE11 ....256 C3
Truro Cres DE21 ......219 C4
Trusley Gdns DE23 ....231 B3
Trusley WIk NG19 ....136 C2
Trustley CI NG19 ....126 A4
Tuckers La NG18,NG21 .268 A4
Tudor Cl
Long Eaton NG10 .....223 C1
Stoke-on-T ST4 ......269 B1
Tudor Ct Derby DE22 ..204 C2
Tudor Dr Mansfield NG ..268 A2
Tudor Falls DE75 ....181 C2
Tudor Field Cl DE73 ..233 A1
Tudor Pl DE7 ....208 B3
Tudor Rd DE21 ....220 A3
Tudor Rise B79 ....263 C1
Tudor St S43 ....78 B1
Tudor Way DE11 ....256 A3
Tudorhouse Cl DE11 ..256 A4
Tuffolds Cl S2 ....44 A4
Tufnell Gdns DE22 ...218 A4
Tulip Rd NG16 ....195 A3
Tulla Cl DE24 ....231 C1
Tullis Cl ST16 ....168 C1
Tumbling Hill DE56 ..168 C1
Tuncliffe Ct DE11 ...256 B2
Tunnel Rd NG7 ....268 A1
Tunnel Yd DE6 ....173 A1
Tunstall Gn S40 ......114 B4
Tunstall Way S40 .....95 B1
Tuphall Cl DE73 .....233 A1
Tupton Hall Sch S42 .131 B4
Tupton Moor Cl S42 ..115 B1
Tupton Prim Sch S42 .115 B1
Tupton Rd S41 ....115 B4
Turf Lea Rd SK6 ......23 A1
Turf Lea Rd SK6 ......23 A1
Turlowfields La DE6 .175 B4
Turnberry Cl
Chesterfield S40 ....114 B4
Ilkeston DE7 ....194 B1
Turnbull Cl S40 ......266 A1
Turnbury Cl DE14 ....254 A4
Turncliffe Cl SK17 ...84 C3
Turnditch CE Prim Sch
DE56 ....177 A1
Turner Ave NG16 .....182 A2
Turner Cl ◆ Dronfield S18 56 C1
Stapleford NG9 ......223 C3
Turner Dr
Eastwood NG16 ......195 A4
Staveley S43 ....97 A4
Turner Rd NG10 ......236 B2
Turner St DE24 ....232 C3
Turners La DE55 .....170 A4
Turnlee Cl SK13 ....17 B4
Turnlee Dr SK13 ....17 B4
Turnlee Rd SK13 ......17 B4
Turnley Rd DE55 .....160 B3
Turnoaks Bsns Pk S40 .115 A3
Turnoaks La S40 .....115 A4
Turnpike Cl
Alfreton DE55 ....158 C1
Matlock DE4 ....143 B3
Turton Cl NG10 ......182 A2
Tutbury & Hatton Sta
DE65 ....239 B4
Tutbury Castle* DE13 239 A4
Tutbury Rd DE13 .....240 A1
Tuxford Cl DE21 .....206 A1
Tuxford WIk DE22 ...268 C2
Twayblade DE14 .....254 A4
Twentylands DE13 ...240 B2
Twentywell Dr S17 ...56 A3
Twentywell La S17 ...56 A3
Twentywell Rd S17 ...56 A3
Twentywell Rise S17 .56 A3
Twentywell View S17 .56 A3
Twickenham Cl S20 ..59 C3
Twickenham Cres S20 59 C3
Twickenham Dr DE22 218 A4
Twickenham Gdns S20 .59 C3
Twickenham Glen S20 59 C3
Twickenham Gr S20 ..59 C3
Twiggs Row DE4 .....143 A4
Twin Oaks Cl DE23 ..230 A3
Twisses Bank DE6 ...213 A1
Twyford CE Inf Sch
Swadlincote DE11 ...255 C1
West Hallam DE7 ....207 B4
Willington DE65 ......242 B3
Twyford Rd
Barrow u T DE73 .....244 A3
Long Eaton NG10 ....235 C2
Willington DE65 ......242 A3
Twyford St DE23 .....267 B1
Tylney Rd S40 ....114 B4
Tynedale Chase DE24 231 B1
Tyndall Pl S14 ....269 A2
Tynedale Cl NG10 ...236 A3
Tynefield Ct DE65 ...229 A1
Tynefield Mews DE65 229 A1
Tynsel Parkes CE Fst Sch
ST14 ....210 A1
Tythe The DE11 ......256 A4

Ullswater Cl continued
Dronfield S18 ....56 C1
Mosborough S20 ......59 C3
Ullswater Dr Derby DE21 220 C3
Dronfield S18 ....56 C1
Ullswater Pk ◆ S18 ..56 C1
Ullswater PI S18 ......56 C1
Ulster Terr S14 ......269 B1
Ulverston Rd S41 .....95 B4
Underhall DE4 ....127 B1
Underhill Ave DE23 ..231 C4
Underhill Cl DE23 ...231 C3
Underhill Rd S43 .....80 A3
Underpass The DE1 ..267 C4
Undertown La DE6 ...175 A1
Underwood CE Prim Sch
NG16 ....171 C1
Underwood Terr DE4 143 A4
Union Rd Ilkeston DE7 208 C4
New Mills SK22 ....33 B4
Nottingham NG3 .....268 B2
Swadlincote DE11 ...256 A3
Union St Ashbourne DE6 173 A1
Glossop SK13 ....10 B1
Harthill S26 ....61 C3
Long Eaton NG10 ....236 C4
Mansfield NG18 ......268 B4
Melbourne DE73 .....252 A4
South Normanton DE55 159 C3
Unity Cl DE11 ....256 A3
Unity Prim Sch NG7 268 A2
Univ of Derby DE22 .204 B1
Univ of Derby (Buxton
Campus) SK17 ....85 B2
Univ of Derby (Sch of Art &
Design) DE1 ....267 B2
Univ of Sheffield S41 115 A4
Univ of Sheffield (Research
Labs) SK17 ....4 B2
Unstone Dronfield By-Pass
S18 ....76 C4
Unstone Hill S18 .....76 B4
Unstone Jun Sch S18 .76 C4
Unstone Rd S18 ....76 C2
Unstone St Mary's Inf Sch
DE56 ....76 C4
Unthank La S18 ....76 A1
Upchurch Cl DE3 ....217 B2
Upland Rise S40 ......95 B1
Uplands Ave DE23 ...231 B3
Uplands Gdns DE23 .218 C1
Uplands Way S45 ....131 B4
Vancouver Ave DE22 220 B2
Compstall SK14 ....15 A3
Upper Albert Rd S8 ..43 A3
Upper Bainbridge St
DE23 ....219 A2
Upper Barn Cl S43 ...181 C1
Upper Blindlow La
SK17 ....106 A3
Upper Boundary Rd
DE22 ....218 C2
Upper College St ◆
NG1 ....268 A2
Upper Cres ST4 ......269 A2
Upper Croft
Clay Cross S45 ......131 C2
Upper Croft S43 ......96 C4
Upper Dale Rd DE23 218 C1
Upper Dunstead Rd
NG16 ....182 A2
Upper Eldon St NG2 268 C1
Upper End Rd SK17 ..67 B2
Upper Furlong St S20 269 C1
Upper Greenhill Gdns
DE4 ....143 B3
Upper Hall Cl DE56 .191 B3
Upper Hollow DE21 .218 B1
Upper King St S43 ...77 C1
Upper La ST4 ....175 C2
Upper Mantle Cl S45 131 B2
Upper Marehay Rd DE5 180 B3
Upper Moor St S45 ...95 A1
Upper Nelson St DE75 181 B1
Upper Newbold Cl S40 95 A4
Upper Orchard St ◆
NG9 ....223 C4
Upper Parliament St
NG1 ....268 B2
Upper School La S18 76 A4
Upper Town La DE4 ..126 A1
Upper Valley Rd S8 ..43 A3
Upper Wellington St
NG16 ....223 B1
Upper Yeld Rd DE45 109 B2
Uppermoor Rd DE24 232 C3
Upperthorpe Rd S21 60 B3
Upperthorpe Villas S21 60 B3
Uppertown La DE4 ...142 B1
Upperwood Rd DE4 143 A1
Upton Cl DE75 ....182 A1
Upton Mount NG19 ..135 C1
Upwoods Rd DE6 .....151 A3
Upwoods Rd DE6 .....211 A1
Utah Cl DE65 ....228 C1
Uttoxeter New Rd DE22 218 B2
Uttoxeter Old Rd DE22 218 B2
Uttoxeter Rd Derby DE3 217 C1
Hatton DE65 ....227 A1
Hilton DE65 ....228 B1
Scropton, Foston DE65 226 C2
Scropton, HM Detention Ctr
DE65 ....226 B2
Uxbridge St DE14 ...254 B4

Vale Cl Bolsover S44 ..99 A1
Dronfield S18 ....57 A1
Vale Dr NG20 ....119 C3
Vale House Dr SK13 ..10 A3
Vale Mills DE22 .....218 C2
Vale Rd Hartshorne DE11 257 A2
Mansfield Woodhouse
NG19 ....136 A2
Swadlincote DE11 ...256 A3
Vale St ST4 ....269 B2
Vale The DE7 ....194 C2
Valemount S41 ....114 B4
Valentine Ave NG16 171 C4
Valerian Cl SK17 .....85 B4
Valerie Rd DE72 .....246 A4
Vallance St NG19 ...136 A2
Valley Cl S45 ....132 A2
Valley Dr
Chapel-en-le-F SK23 ..47 B3
Killamarsh S21 ....60 B4
Valley Gdns SK14 ....15 C4
Valley Ho Ho7 ....75 B2
Valley Rd Barlow S18 ..75 C4
Bolsover S44 ....118 A4
Broadbottom S14 ...15 C4
Chesterfield S41 ......96 B1
Clay Cross S45 ......131 A2
Derby DE23 ....218 B1
Derby, Cherrytree Hill
DE21 ....220 A3
Glossop SK13 ....16 C4
Hayfield SK22 ....25 C1
Ilkeston DE7 ....208 C3
Killamarsh S21 ....60 B4
Kimberley NG16 .....195 B4
Mastin Moor S43 ....79 B2
Overseal DE12 ......262 A2
Sheffield S8 ....43 A3
Shirebrook NG20 ....119 C3
Valley Rise Barlow S18 75 B2
Swadlincote DE11 ...256 A3
Valley View Belper DE56 179 B1
Ilkeston DE7 ....208 C3
Valley View
Chesterfield S41 ....115 C4
Eckington S21 ....59 B1
Valley View Dr DE7 ..193 A1
Valley View Rd DE55 197 B2
Valley WIk S14 ......197 A2
Vanbrugh Rd NG10 .236 A4
Vanguard Trad Est S40 115 A4
Vaughan St S24 ......232 B3
Vaughan Pl NG20 ...119 C3
Vaughan Rd SK23 .....45 C3
Vaughan Way ST17 ..269 A3
Vauxhall Ave DE7 ...224 B1
Ventura Ct S42 ....28 B1
Venture Cres DE55 ..159 A1
Venture Way S41 .....76 C1
Verbena Dr DE23 ...231 B2
Vere Cl DE65 ....242 A3
Vermont Dr DE21 ....220 B3
Verney St NG19 .....134 C4
Verney Way NG19 ...134 C4
Vernon Cotts DE4 ...154 C1
Vernon St Bakewell DE45 109 B3
Derby DE1 ....267 A4
NG16 ....182 A2
Vernon Dr
Bakewell DE45 ....109 A4
Derby DE21 ....205 C4
Vernon Gn DE45 ....109 A4
Vernon Rd
Chesterfield S40 ......95 B2
Dore S17 ....55 C3
Stoke-on-T ST4 ......269 B2
Vernon Rise S42 .....115 C1
Vernon St Derby DE1 218 C3
Derby DE1 ....194 C2
Nottingham NG1 ....268 A2
Shirebrook NG20 ...120 A2
Vernongate DE1 .....218 C3
Veronica Dr NG16 ...195 B4
Vestry Rd DE21 ......205 C2
Vetchfield Cl DE24 ..231 C1
Via Gellia Rd DE4 ...154 B4
Vicar La Chesterfield S40 266 B3
Tibshelf DE55 ....148 A3
Vicarage Ave
DE23 ....218 C1
Ilkeston DE7 ....194 B2
Vicarage Cl Belper DE56 179 A2
Burton u T DE15 .....248 A2
Heath S44 ....148 B4
Holmesfield S18 ......75 A4
Nottingham NG3 ....268 B2
Shirebrook NG20 ...119 C2
Smalley DE7 ....192 B4
Swanwick DE55 .....169 C4
Vicarage Ct DE3 ....217 B1
Vicarage Dr DE72 ...220 A4
Uttoxeter ST14 ....210 A2

Vicarage Gdns
Clay Cross S45 ......131 B1
Swanwick DE55 .....169 C4
Swadlincote DE11 ...256 B2
Vicarage La
Ashford in t W DE45 108 C4
Darley Dale DE4 .....143 C1
Derby DE22 ....55 B4
Duffield DE56 ....190 C2
Hayfield SK22 ....25 B1
Ironville NG16 ....170 C2
Little Eaton DE21 ...205 B4

Vicarage Mews DE55 ..170 C3
Vicarage Rd Belper DE56 190 C4
Derby DE3 ....217 B1
Derby, Chellaston DE73 232 C1
Stoke-on-T ST4 ......269 A2
Swadlincote DE11 ...256 B2
Woodville DE11 .....256 C1
Vicarage St DE7 .....194 B2
Vicarage Way ST17 .269 A3
Vicarage WIk DE12 ..260 B3
Vicarwood Ave
Derby DE22 ....204 C1
Holbrook DE56 ......191 B4
Victor Ave DE22 ....218 C4
Victor Cres NG10 ...223 B2
Victor Rd S17 ....55 C4
Victoria Ave
Borrowash DE72 ....221 A1
⑦ Buxton SK17 ......85 B4
Draycott DE72 ......235 A4
Glossop SK13 ....10 A3
Nottingham NG2 ....268 C1
Staveley S43 ....79 A2
Victoria Cl DE3 ......217 C2
Victoria Cotts DE55 159 B1
Victoria Cres NG16 170 C2
Victoria Cl Ilkeston DE7 194 C1
Long Eaton NG10 ...236 B4
Mansfield NG18 ....268 B3
Matlock DE4 ....143 B3
Victoria Ctr NG1 ....268 B2
Victoria Ct DE55 ....147 C1
Victoria Gr S43 ....80 C1
Victoria Hall Gdns DE4 143 B3
Victoria Ho S80 .....81 C1
Victoria Park Rd
Buxton SK17 ....85 B4
Calow S41 ....96 C3
Victoria Rd Bamford S33 40 A2
Draycott DE72 ......235 A4
Pinxton NG16 ....160 B2
Ripley DE5 ....169 B3
Sandiacre NG10 ....223 A3
Selston NG16 ....171 C3
Stafford ST16 ....269 A4
Victoria Sq St Alfreton DE55 159 A2
Bolsover S44 ....118 A4
Brimington S43 ....77 C1
Castle Donington DE74 247 A3
Chesterfield S41 ....266 B4
Clay Cross S45 ......131 B2
Cresswell S80 ....81 C1
Derby DE1 ....267 A4
Dronfield S18 ....56 C1
Glossop SK13 ....17 B4
Ilkeston DE7 ....194 C2
Ironville NG16 ......170 C2
Langley Mill NG16 ..182 B2
Long Eaton NG10 ...236 A3
Melbourne DE73 ....252 A4
New Mills SK22 ....33 A3
Nottingham NG1 ....268 A1
Ripley DE5 ....169 C2
Shirebrook NG20 ...119 C2
Somercotes DE55 ..170 B4
South Normanton DE55 159 B4
Stafford ST16 ....269 B4
Stapleford NG9 ......223 B4
Victoria St N S41 .....76 C1
Victoria St W S40 .....95 B1
Victoria Terr
Great Longstone DE45 ..89 C1
Tibshelf DE55 ....148 A4
Victory WIk S42 .....115 C1
Victory Gr S45 ....169 C1
Victory Cl NG10 ....169 C1
Victory Dr NG19 ....136 C1
Victory Rd DE24 ....232 A3
View Rd S2 ....43 A4
Viewdales Cl DE6 ...175 C1
Viking Bsns Ctr DE11 256 C2
Vikinglea Cl S2 ....44 A4
Vikinglea Dr S2 ....44 A4
Villa St Draycott DE72 235 A4
Villa The SK14 ....269 B1
Village Ct DE56 .....190 C2
Village St DE23 ......231 C4
Village The
Dale Abbey DE7 .....207 C4
West Hallam DE7 ....207 C4
Villas Rd Bolsover S44 98 B2
Toadmoor DE56 ....167 C2
Villas The Bolsover S44 99 A1
Whaley Thorns NG20 101 A2
Villiers Cl S2 ....43 C3
Villiers Dr S2 ....43 C3
Vincent Ave Derby DE21 220 C2
Ilkeston DE7 ....208 C4
Vincent Cl DE56 .....192 A4
Vincent Cres S40 ....95 A1
Vincent La S40 ....95 A1
Vincent St DE23 ....218 C1
Vine Cl DE23 ....231 A4
Vine Cres NG10 .....223 A3
Vine Farm Cl DE7 ...192 B4
Vine St S41 ....269 B1
Vineyard Terr DE4 ..127 B2
Viola Cl DE22 ....206 B2
Violet Ave NG16 ....195 A4

Violet Cl
Donisthorpe DE12 ....**262** C1
Shirebrook NG20 ....**119** B2
Violet La DE15 ....**254** C4
Violet Lane Inf Sch
DE15 ....**254** C4
Violet St DE23 ....**218** C1
Violet Way DE15 ....**255** B4
Virginsalley La DE6 ....**184** B1
Vista The NG9 ....**223** C3
Vivian St Bolsover S44 ....**98** C3
Derby DE1 ....**219** A4
Vulcan St DE23 ....**219** A1
Vyse Dr NG10 ....**236** B3

W

Wade Ave Derby DE23 .....**218** B1
Ilkeston DE7 ....**209** A4
Wade Dr DE3 ....**217** C1
Wade St DE23 ....**218** B1
Wadebridge Gr DE24 ....**233** B3
Wadham St ST4 ....**269** B2
Wadhurst Gdns NG3 ....**268** B2
Wadsworth Ave S12 ....**44** B3
Wadsworth Cl S12 ....**44** B3
Wadsworth Dr S12 ....**44** B3
Wadsworth Rd
Sheffield S12 ....**44** B3
Stapleford NG9 ....**223** C4
Wagstaff La NG16 ....**171** B3
Wagtail Cl DE24 ....**231** B2
Wain Ave S42 ....**132** A4
Wain Dr S14 ....**269** A1
Wain Way S42 ....**132** A4
Wainfleet Cl DE7 ....**194** B2
Waingroves Prim Sch
DE5 ....**181** A4
Waingroves Rd
Codnor DE5 ....**181** A3
Ripley DE5 ....**181** A3
Wainhouse Brow SK22 ....**25** B2
Wainman Cl S41 ....**47** C1
Wainwood Rise S14 ....**269** A1
Wainwright Ave S13 ....**44** B4
Wainwright Cres S13 ......**44** B4
Wakami Cres DE23 ....**233** A2
Wakefield Ave DE13 ....**239** A3
Wakefield Croft DE7 ....**194** B2
Wakefield Ct DE7 ....**247** B2
Wakelyn Cl DE72 ....**234** C1
Walbrook Rd DE23 ....**218** C1
Walcote Cl DE56 ....**179** B3
Walden Rd S2 ....**44** A4
Waldene Dr DE24 ....**233** A3
Waldley La DE6 ....**211** B4
Waldorf Ave DE24 ....**233** A4
Waldorf Cl DE24 ....**233** A4
Walford Rd Killamarsh S21 ..**60** A2
Rolleston DE13 ....**240** B2
Walgrave Cl DE56 ....**179** A3
Walgrove Ave S40 ....**95** C1
Walgrove Rd S40 ....**95** B1
Walk Cl DE72 ....**235** A4
Walk Mill Rd S42 ....**25** B1
Walk The DE56 ....**192** A4
Walkdale Brow SK13 ....**17** A4
Walkden St NG18 ....**268** B4
Walker Ave S45 ....**169** C1
Walker Brow SK17 ....**47** C1
Walker Cl DE7 ....**209** A2
Walker Gr NG9 ....**223** C3
Walker La DE1 ....**267** A4
Walker St Glossop SK13 ...**10** A2
Nottingham NG3 ....**268** C1
Walkers Ave NG16 ....**182** C3
Walkers La S21 ....**60** B3
Wall Ditch DE6 ....**149** A1
Wall Rd DE14 ....**254** A4
Wall St Burton u T DE7 ....**85** B4
Ripley DE5 ....**169** B1
Wallace Gdns [9] NG9 ....**223** C1
Wallace St DE22 ....**218** B3
Wallfields Cl DE65 ....**230** B1
Wallis Cl DE72 ....**235** A4
Wallis Rd NG18 ....**268** C4
Walls La S80 ....**81** A4
Walnut Ave Derby DE24 ...**233** A4
Shireoaks S81 ....**63** C4
Walnut Cl
Aston-on-T DE72 ....**246** A4
Barrow u T DE73 ....**244** A3
Burnaston DE65 ....**229** C3
Derby DE73 ....**245** A4
Ilkeston DE7 ....**209** A4
Repton DE65 ....**243** A1
Swadlincote DE11 ....**256** A3
Walnut Dr S21 ....**60** B3
Walnut Rd DE14 ....**179** A2
Walnut St DE24 ....**232** B4
Walpole St DE21 ....**219** B3
Walseker La S26 ....**61** B4
Walsham Ct DE21 ....**205** B1
Walter Evans CE Prim Sch
DE22 ....**204** C1
Walter St Derby DE1 ....**218** B4
Draycott DE72 ....**234** C4
Nottingham NG7 ....**268** A2
Walters Cres NG16 ....**171** B3
Waltham Ave DE24 ....**231** C2
Walthamstow Dr DE22 .....**218** A3
Waltheof Rd S2 ....**44** A4
Walton Ave Derby DE24 ....**232** C2
Nottingham NG3 ....**268** C2

Walton Back La
Chesterfield S40 ....**114** A4
Holymoorside S42 ....**113** C4
Walton Cl
Chesterfield S40 ....**114** A4
Dronfield S18 ....**56** B1
Swadlincote DE11 ....**256** A2
Walton Cres
Ashbourne DE6 ....**173** B1
Sheffield S40 ....**95** C1
Fenton S14 ....**269** C1
Walton Ct Sheffield S8 ......**56** C4
West Hallam DE7 ....**207** B4
Walton Dr
Chesterfield S40 ....**95** C1
Derby DE23 ....**231** C4
Walton Drive Ct S40 ....**95** C1
Walton Fields Rd S40 ....**95** B1
Walton Hill DE74 ....**247** A2
Walton Holymoorside Prim
Sch S42 ....**113** B4
Walton Hospl S40 ....**114** C4
Walton Rd
Chesterfield S40 ....**95** B1
Derby DE21 ....**219** C3
Swadlincote DE15 ....**254** B3
Walton St S40 ....**96** A3
Walton Way S42 ....**114** C2
Walton Wlk S40 ....**96** A3
Walton-on-Trent CE Prim
Sch DE12 ....**259** B4
Wanboat Cl Rd [2] NG7 ....**268** A2
Wansfell Ct DE3 ....**217** C1
Wapentake La DE6 ....**165** B1
Warburton Cl S2 ....**43** B4
Warburton Gdns S2 ....**43** B4
Ward Dr DE55 ....**170** B4
Ward La Barlborough S43 ..**80** A4
Disley SK12 ....**32** C2
Ward Pl Mansfield NG18 ...**268** A3
Ward St Derby DE22 ....**218** C2
Tupton S42 ....**131** B4
Ward's La Breaston DE72 ...**235** B4
King's Newton DE73 ....**245** A1
Melbourne DE73 ....**244** C2
Wardgate Way S40 ....**95** A3
Wardlow Ave NG3 ....**268** C1
Wardlow Cl S40 ....**114** C4
Wardlow Fold [2] SK13 ....**9** B1
Wardlow Mews SK13 ....**9** B1
Wardlow Rd
Ilkeston DE7 ....**194** C2
Sheffield S12 ....**44** B3
Wardlow Wlk [22] SK13 ....**9** B1
Warwick DE7 ....**268** B3
Warehouse La S33 ....**51** C2
Warhurst Fold [4] SK13 ....**10** A2
Warmbrook DE4 ....**165** C4
Warmbrook Jun Sch
SK23 ....**47** B3
Warmbrook Rd SK23 ....**47** B3
Warminster Cl S8 ....**43** A2
Warminster Cres S8 ....**43** A2
Warminster Dr S8 ....**43** A2
Warminster Gdns S8 ....**43** A2
Warminster Pl S8 ....**43** A2
Warminster Rd S8 ....**43** A2
Warmwells La DE5 ....**180** B3
Warner St
Chesterfield S41 ....**266** C1
Derby, Mickleover DE3 ....**217** B2
Derby, St Luke's DE22 ....**218** C2
Warney Rd DE4 ....**127** B1
Warren Ave NG9 ....**223** B4
Warren Ave Extension
NG9 ....**223** B4
Warren Cl
Burton u T DE13 ....**240** C1
Pilsley S45 ....**132** B1
Warren Cres S21 ....**58** C1
Warren La S21 ....**58** C1
Warren Rise S18 ....**57** B2
Warren St DE24 ....**232** C4
Warren Wlk S21 ....**58** C1
Warrendale Ct DE73 ....**233** A1
Warser Gate NG1 ....**268** B1
Warsop Rd NG19 ....**136** B2
Warwick Ave DE23 ....**218** B3
Warwick Cl
Branston DE14 ....**253** C4
Glossop SK13 ....**17** C4
Swadlincote DE11 ....**256** C3
Warwick Dr DE7 ....**194** B2
Warwick Gdns DE56 ....**179** B3
Warwick Rd
Long Eaton NG10 ....**237** A4
Somercotes DE55 ....**159** B3
Warwick St
Chesterfield S40 ....**115** A4
Derby DE21 ....**219** B1
Wasdale Ave S20 ....**59** C3
Wash Gn DE56, DE4 ....**166** A4
Wash Hills Cl DE4 ....**153** A1
Wash House La S40 ....**95** B1
Washbrook La DE6 ....**161** C2
Washford Rd DE65 ....**240** C4
Washhouse Bottom SK17 ....**69** C4
Washington Ave DE24 .....**220** A3
Washington Cl DE73 ....**252** A4

Washington Cotts DE72 ...**221** B1
Washington Dr NG9 ....**209** C1
Wasnidge Cl NG3 ....**268** B2
Wasnidge Wlk [6] NG3 ....**268** B2
Watburn Rd SK22 ....**24** B1
Watchorn Cl DE1 ....**256** B3
Watchorn Cotts DE55 ......**158** C2
Watchorn La DE55 ....**158** C1
Water La Bakewell DE45 ...**109** B3
Bamford S33 ....**40** A2
Bolsover S44 ....**117** C4
Cromford DE4 ....**155** A3
Eyam S32 ....**71** C3
Hollingworth SK14 ....**9** B3
Mansfield NG19 ....**135** A2
Middleton (Nr Wirksworth)
DE4 ....**154** B3
Shirebrook NG19 ....**118** C1
South Normanton DE55 ....**160** A3
Tideswell SK17 ....**68** C3
Wirksworth DE4 ....**165** C4
Water Mdws The DE73 .....**244** B3
Water Meadow La S40 ......**95** A4
Water Orton Cl NG9 ....**223** C2
Water St Bakewell DE45 ...**109** B3
Buxton SK17 ....**85** A4
Glossop SK13 ....**10** C1
Stafford ST16 ....**269** B4
Stoke-on-T ST4 ....**269** B1
Watercress La S45 ....**131** B1
Waterdown Cl NG19 ....**136** B3
Waterfoot Cotts SK14 ......**9** A2
Waterfoot La SK23 ....**45** B3
Waterford Dr DE21 ....**220** A2
Watergo La S43 ....**230** C4
Watering La DE56 ....**191** B3
Wateringbury Gr [9] S43 ..**78** C1
Waterloo Cl DE55 ....**160** B4
Waterloo Ct NG1 ....**268** A2
Waterloo Ct DE1 ....**267** C5
Waterloo La NG9 ....**209** C3
Waterloo Pl DE11 ....**256** A2
Waterloo Prom NG7 ....**268** A2
Waterloo Rd
Matlock Bath DE4 ....**143** A1
Nottingham NG7 ....**268** A2
Waterloo St
Bramley-Vale S44 ....**117** C1
Clay Cross S45 ....**131** B3
Stoke-on-T ST4 ....**269** A1
Watermede S21 ....**59** A1
Watermeadow Rd DE24 ....**233** A3
Watermeadows The
NG10 ....**236** A4
Waterpark Rd DE6 ....**224** A4
Waters Edge La S43 ....**23** A4
Waters Edge [4] SK13 .....**47** B3
Waterside
Burton u T DE15 ....**254** C4
Glossop SK13 ....**10** A3
Ironville NG16 ....**170** C2
Marple SK6 ....**23** A3
Waterside Bsns Pk SK13 .....**9** C3
Waterside
Derby DE22 ....**205** A1
Sandiacre NG10 ....**223** A2
Waterside Com Jun Sch
DE15 ....**254** C4
Waterside Rd
Burton u T DE15 ....**254** B4
Disley SK12,SK22 ....**32** C4
Waterswallows La SK17 ....**66** C1
Waterswallows Mews
SK17 ....**66** C1
Waterswallows Rd SK17 ...**66** C1
Waterthorpe Cl S20 ....**59** C4
Waterthorpe Cres S20 .....**59** C4
Waterthorpe Gdns [6]
S20 ....**59** C4
Waterthorpe Glade S20 ...**59** C4
Waterthorpe Glen [6]
S20 ....**59** C4
Waterthorpe Rise [7] S20 ..**59** C4
Waterway The NG10 ....**223** B2
Watery La Bretby DE15 .....**249** B2
Clifton DE6 ....**184** C4
Ellastone DE6 ....**183** A2
Scropton DE65 ....**226** C1
Swadlincote DE11 ....**255** B3
Thurvaston DE6 ....**215** B4
Watford Bridge Ind Est
SK22 ....**24** B1
Watford Bridge Rd SK22 ..**24** B1
Watford La SK22 ....**24** B1
Watford Rd Buxton SK17 ...**84** C4
New Mills SK22 ....**24** B1
Watford St ST4 ....**269** C2
Watkin Ave SK13 ....**9** C2
Watkin St Fenton ST4 ......**269** C1
Nottingham NG1,NG3 ....**268** B2
Watnall Cres NG18 ....**181** B1
Watnall Cres NG19 ....**268** A4
Watson Ave
Heanor DE75 ....**181** C1
Mansfield NG18 ....**268** C4
Watson La S42 ....**114** B2
Watson Rd DE7 ....**194** B1
Watson St Derby DE1 ....**218** C3
Derby, Markeaton DE3 ....**218** C4
Stoke-on-T ST4 ....**269** B2
Watten Cl DE24 ....**231** C1
Watts Dri DE45 ....**108** C4
Waveney Cl DE22 ....**205** A3
Waverley Cl S41 ....**96** A3
Waverley Ct [2] S41 ....**96** A3
Waverley House Sch
NG7 ....**268** A2
Waverley St Long Eaton NG10 ..**236** C4
Nottingham NG7 ....**268** A2

Waverley St continued
Tibshelf DE55 ....**148** A4
Wayfaring Rd DE21 ....**206** A1
Wayford Ave S41 ....**266** C1
Wayside S43 ....**96** B4
Wayside Cl S42 ....**132** A4
Wayside Ct S43 ....**96** B4
Wayside Dr DE21 ....**219** B3
Weaddow La DE45 ....**124** C1
Weakland Cl S12 ....**44** C2
Weakland Cres S12 ....**44** C2
Weakland Dr S12 ....**44** C2
Weakland Way S12 ....**44** C2
Weaver Cl
Ashbourne DE6 ....**185** B4
Crich DE4 ....**156** C1
Weaver Rd ST14 ....**210** A1
Weavers Cl Belper DE56 ...**179** B3
Borrowash DE72 ....**221** B1
Weavers Croft DE5 ....**180** C4
Weavers Ct SK14 ....**9** A2
Weavers St S18 ....**217** B1
Weavers The ST14 ....**196** B3
Weaving Ave S33 ....**38** B1
Webbs Orch SK23 ....**45** B4
Webster Ave NG16 ....**182** C1
Webster Croft S41 ....**77** A1
Webster Ct S40 ....**95** C3
Webster St DE1 ....**267** A2
Webster's Terr DE4 ....**143** B2
Wedgewood Cl DE15 ....**248** A1
Wednesbough SK14 ....**9** B3
Weekday Cross NG1 ....**268** B1
Weighbridge Rd NG18 .....**268** C3
Weightman Dr NG16 ....**195** A4
Weir Bank DE15 ....**254** C4
Weirfield Rd DE22 ....**205** A1
Weirside DE6 ....**184** B4
Welbeck Ave Buxton SK17 ..**85** A3
Ilkeston DE7 ....**208** B3
Welbeck Cl
[20] Dronfield S18 ....**56** B1
Nottingham NG3 ....**268** B2
Staveley S43 ....**97** B3
Welbeck Ct Clowne S43 ....**80** C2
[7] Staveley S43 ....**78** C1
Welbeck Dr S42 ....**114** C2
Welbeck Gdns NG9 ....**223** C2
Welbeck Gr DE22 ....**204** B2
Welbeck Rd Bolsover S44 ..**99** A1
Long Eaton NG10 ....**223** B2
Mansfield Woodhouse
NG19 ....**136** B2
Welbeck St Creswell S80 ..**81** C1
Mansfield NG18 ....**268** B4
Whitwell S80 ....**82** A3
Welbeck Wlk [3] NG3 ......**268** B2
Welbeck Workshops [6]
NG3 ....**268** B2
Welbury Gdns S20 ....**59** C3
Welby St S4 ....**269** C1
Welch Ave NG9 ....**223** C4
Welch St S14 ....**269** B2
Welfare Ave S40 ....**95** B2
Welfare Cl NG20 ....**119** C2
Welfitt Gr NG20 ....**101** A1
Well Banks DE6 ....**165** A1
Well Cl DE6 ....**175** C2
Well Gate SK13 ....**10** C1
Well La Belper DE56 ....**190** C4
Blackfordby DE11 ....**257** A1
Holymoorside S42 ....**112** C4
Repton DE65 ....**242** B1
Shirland DE55 ....**146** B2
Well Rd S8 ....**43** A3
Well Row SK14 ....**16** A4
Well Spring Cl [11] S43 ....**96** C4
Well St Brassington DE4 ...**152** C1
Derby DE1 ....**267** B5
Elton DE4 ....**140** C4
New Mills SK22 ....**33** A4
Ripley DE5 ....**169** B1
Well Yd Belper DE56 ....**179** A3
Welland Cl
Burton u T DE15 ....**248** A3
Derby DE24 ....**217** B2
Welland Ct NG3 ....**268** C2
Welland Rd DE65 ....**228** B1
Wellcarr Rd S8 ....**43** A3
Wellcroft Cl DE24 ....**231** A1
Wellcroft St NG18 ....**268** A3
Welldon St NG3 ....**181** A2
Wellesley Ave DE23 ....**231** B4
Wellfield DE4 ....**143** B3
Wellfield Cl S12 ....**44** C1
Wellfield Rd DE4 ....**143** B3
Wellfield St DE75 ....**181** B3
Wellhead Rd [5] S8 ....**43** A3
Wellington Cir [4] NG1 ....**268** A1
Wellington Cl DE65 ....**143** B4
Wellington Cres DE1 ....**267** C2
Wellington St [5] DE56 ....**178** C2
Wellington Mews DE55 ....**146** B1
Wellington Pk NG5 ....**146** B1
Wellington Pl NG16 ....**182** C1
Wellington Rd DE14 ....**253** C4
Wellington Sq [32] NG7 ...**268** A2
Wellington St
Chesterfield S43 ....**77** B2
Derby DE1 ....**267** D2
Eastwood NG16 ....**182** C2
Heanor DE75 ....**181** B2
Long Eaton NG10 ....**223** B1
Matlock DE4 ....**143** B3

Wellington St continued
Nottingham NG3 ....
Ripley DE5 ....
Stapleford NG9 ....
Wellington Terr [5] NG7
Wellington Villas [28]
NG7 ....
Wells Cl NG19 ....
Wells Ct DE23 ....
Wells Rd DE23 ....
Wells St S44 ....
Wellspring Cl
Barlborough S43 ....
Wingerworth S42 ....
Wellspring Dale NG9 ......
Wellwood Rd DE11 ....
Wellwyn Ct S12 ....
Welney Cl DE3 ....
Welshpool Pl S40 ....
Welshpool Rd DE24 ....
Welton Ave DE56 ....
Welwyn Ave Derby DE22 ..
Derby, Allenton DE24 ....
Mansfield Woodhouse
Welwyn Cl
Chesterfield S40 ....
Sheffield S12 ....
Welwyn Rd S12 ....
Wembley Gdns DE22 ....
Wendover Cl DE3 ....
Wenham La NG17 ....
Wenlock Cl
Chesterfield S40 ....
Derby DE3 ....
Eastwood NG16 ....
Wenlock Cres S40 ....
Wenlock Dr S42 ....
Wensley Dr DE21 ....
Wensley Rd
North Wingfield S42 ....
Winster DE4 ....
Wensley Way S43 ....
Wensleydale Cl NG10 .....
Wensleydale Rd NG10 .....
Wensleydale Wlk DE24 ....
Wentworth Ave S40 ....
Wentworth Cl Derby DE3 ..
Mansfield NG19 ....
Wentworth Croft DE75 ....
Wentworth Ct NG16 ....
Wentworth Cres DE75 .....
Wentworth Dr S41 ....
Wentworth Rd S18 ....
Wentworth St DE7 ....
Werburgh Cl DE21 ....
Werburgh St DE22 ....
Werneth Low Ctry Pk
SK14 ....
Werneth Low Rd SK14 ....
Werneth Rd SK13 ....
Wesley Ct S43 ....
Wesley La DE72 ....
Wesley Pl NG9 ....
Wesley Rd
Ambergate DE56 ....
Derby DE24 ....
Stonebroom DE55 ....
Wesley St Glossop SK13 .....
Glossop, Hadfield SK13 ....
Ilkeston DE7 ....
Langley Mill NG16 ....
Wesleyan Chapel La
SK17 ....
Wesleyan Chapel Wlk
NG9 ....
Wessex Dr NG16 ....
Wessex Gdns S17 ....
Wessington Bank [1] SK13
Wessington Dr S43 ....
Wessington Gn [2] SK13 ..
Wessington La DE55 ....
Wessington Mews
Derby DE22 ....
Gamesley SK13 ....
Wessington Prim Sch
DE55 ....
West Ave Derby DE1 ....
Derby, Chellaston DE73 ....
Draycott DE72 ....
Hilton DE65 ....
Ripley DE5 ....
Sandiacre NG10 ....
Stapleford NG9 ....
Stoke-on-T ST4 ....
West Bank
Matlock Bath DE4 ....
Stoke-on-T ST4 ....
T: adnoor DE4 ....
Winster DE4 ....
West Bank Ave
Crich DE4 ....
Derby DE22 ....
Mansfield NG18, NG19 ....
West Bank Cl DE22 ....
West Bank Lea NG19 ......
West Bank Link NG19 ......
West Bank Rd DE22 ....
West Bank Wynd NG18 ....
West Bars S40 ....
West Cl Derby DE22 ....
Stafford ST16 ....
West Cres
Long Acdmonton S44 ....
Matlock DE4 ....
West Croft Ave DE23 ....
West Croft Cl DE45 ....
West Croft Ct S43 ....
West Croft Dr S43 ....

Dr Derby DE3 ....217 B1
ridge DE6 ....211 A1
op SK13 ....9 C4
Edge Cl S45 ....129 B2
End Alfreton DE55 ....159 A2
borough S43 ....80 A4
wood S43 ....152 C1
ddbottom SK14 ....15 C4
Rise 140 C3
on NG16 ....160 B2
sworth DE4 ....165 C4
End Cl DE7 ....159 A2
End Cres DE7 ....208 B4
End Dr
ton DE7 ....208 B4
dlow DE72 ....234 C1
End St NG9 ....223 B3
End View S43 ....59 B1
Gate Holme HD9 ....9 C4
ng Eaton NG10 ....236 C4
sfield NG18 ....268 B4
sfield NG18 ....268 B4
Gr DE21 ....232 B3
Hill Codnor DE5 ....181 A4
sfield NG18 ....268 B4
Hill Ave NG18 ....268 B4
Hill Dr NG18 ....268 B4
Hill Pk NG18 ....136 A2
Hill Rise NG18 ....268 B4
Hill Way NG18 ....268 B1
Lawn DE65 ....230 B1
Lea Barborough S43 ...98 B2
sterfield S40 ....95 A1
st Lea Cotts S43 ......80 A4
st Lees Rd S33 ....40 A2
st Nottinghamshire Coll
.........................268 B4
st Par ST14 ....269 C1
st Park Rd DE22 ....218 C4
Barlow SK17 ....85 A3
rby DE21 ....220 B3
st Row DE22 ....205 A1
st Service Rd DE21 ...117 B1
st St Bramley-Vale S44
ton u T DE15 ....248 A2
sterfield S40 ....95 A1
y Cross S45 ....131 A2
swine S43 ....81 A3
eswell S80 ....81 B1
onfield S18 ....59 B1
End Dr7 ....95 B4
ossop SK13 ....9 C4
aron DE75 ....181 B1
angley Mill NG16 .....182 A2
arket Warsop NG20 ...120 B2
Nottingham NG2 ......268 C1
omercotes DE55 ....170 B3
outh Normanton DE55 ..159 C3
tonebroom DE55 ....146 C2
wadlincote DE11 ....256 A2
haley Thorns NG20 ...101 A2
est Terr B DE7 ....194 C1
est View
arlborough S43 ....80 A3
reen DE4 ....118 A4
ayfield DE6 ....184 B3
cester ST14 ....197 A2
staveley S43 ....78 B1
est View Ave S18 .....231 A4
est View Cl S17 ....55 C3
est View La S17 ....55 C3
est View Rd S17 ......95 C3
est Way
omercotes DE55 ......159 B1
tafford ST17 ....269 A3
est Way Gn ST17 .....269 A3
estacre Dr DE11 ......255 C1
estbank Cl S18 ....57 A2
estbank Ct S18 ....57 A2
estbourne Ave DE55 ..147 A2
estbourne Cl S10 .....136 C2
estbourne Gr S40 .....95 A2
estbourne Pk DE22 ...217 A4
estbridge Rd S43 .....80 A4
Westdale Rd
Mansfield NG19 ....136 A1
Westwood NG16 ....171 B2
Westdene Ave DE24 ...232 B3
Westerlands NG9 .....223 C3
Western Ave NG16 ....169 B4
Western Dr DE75 .....193 C4
Western La DE45 ....46 A4
Western Rd Derby DE3 ..217 C1
Derby, Rose Hill DE23 ..219 A1
Western St B NG1 ...268 B2
Western Terr NG7 ....268 A1
Western View DE4 ....90 A2
Western Villas DE45 ...167 C2
Westfield Ave
Chesterfield S40 ....95 A1
Heanor DE75 ....181 C1

Westfield Bank S43 ....80 A4
Westfield Cl
Chesterfield S40 ....95 A1
Ilkeston DE7 ....208 B3
Mansfield NG18 ....268 A4
Westfield Cres S20 ....59 C4
Westfield Ctr S20 .....59 C4
Westfield Dr
Blackwell DE55 ....147 C1
Ilkeston DE7 ....194 B1
Mansfield NG19 ....268 A4
Westfield Gdns S40 ....95 A1
Westfield Inf Sch S40 ..95 A1
Westfield La
Barlborough S43 ....79 C4
Chesterfield S21 ....95 A1
Mansfield NG18 ....268 A4
Westfield Northway S20 ..59 C4
Westfield Rd
Dronfield S18 ....76 B4
Killamarsh S21 ....60 B3
Swadlincote DE11 ....256 A3
Westfield Sch S20 .....59 B4
Westfield Southway S20 ..59 C4
Westgate St NG3 .....268 C2
Westgreen Ave DE24 ..232 B3
Westhall Rd DE3 ......217 B1
Westhead Ave ST16 ...269 C4
Westhill La S42 ....115 C2
Westhorpe Ave NG2 ...268 C2
Westhorpe Dr NG10 ...236 B4
Westhouses Prim Sch
DE55 ....147 B1
Westland Dr NG16 ....160 B2
Westland Gdns S20 ...59 B4
Westland Gr B S20 ..59 C4
Westland Rd S20 .....59 C4
Westlands The ST14 ...196 B3
Westlea View S43 .....80 B2
Westleigh NG19 ....136 B3
Westleigh Ave DE24 ...231 C2
Westleigh Cl S20 .....95 C3
Westley Cres DE21 ...191 B1
Westminster Ave NG10 ..223 B3
Westminster St DE24 ..232 C4
Westmoor Rd S43 .....96 C2
Westmorland Cl DE21 ..219 B3
Westmorland Way
NG16 ....171 A2
Weston Bank S18 .....197 C1
Weston Cl S40 ....95 A2
Weston Cres S12 .....235 C2
Weston Ct DE72 ....245 C2
Weston Park Ave DE24 ..232 C2
Weston Park Gdns
DE24 ....232 B2
Weston Rd
Aston-on-T DE72 ......246 A4
Stafford ST16 ....269 C4
Weston-on-T DE72 ...245 C3
Weston Rise DE72 ....245 A4
Weston Spot Cl DE5 ...180 B4
Weston St Heanor DE75 ..194 A4
Swadlincote DE11 ....256 A3
Westthorpe Fields Rd
S21 ....60 B2
Westthorpe Rd S21 ....60 B3
Westward Cl ST14 ....210 A1
Westwell Pl S20 ......59 C4
Westwick Cres S8 ....56 C4
Westwick Gr S8 ......56 C4
Westwick La S40 ......95 C1
Westwick Rd S8 ......56 C4
Westwood DE7 ....209 A3
Westwood Ave S43 ...97 B3
Westwood Dr
Derby DE24 ....232 C4
Staveley S43 ....97 A3
Westwood Dr Gdns S43 ..97 A3
Westwood La S43 .....96 C2
Westwood Pk DE11 ...255 C3
Westwood Rd Calow S44 ..97 A2
Nottingham NG2 .....268 C1
Wetherby Cl NG10 ...195 C4
Wetherby Ct DE21 ...253 C4
Wetherby Rd DE24 ...232 C4
Wetherel Rd DE15 ....248 A4
Wetlands La S43,S44 ...96 C2
Weyacres DE72 ....207 B4
Weybridge Cl DE7 ....194 C3
Whaley Bridge Prim Sch
SK23 ....45 C4
Whaley Bridge Sta SK23 ..45 C4
Whaley Comm S44 ...100 B2
Whaley Rd NG20 .....100 C3
Whaley Thorns Heritage
Ctr⁕ NG20 ....101 A2
Whaley Thorns Prim Sch
NG20 ....101 A2
Whaley Ave S14 .....269 A1
Wharf Cl St23 ....253 A1
Wharf Hos DE13 .....253 A1
Wharf La
Chesterfield S41 .....266 B4
Chesterfield S41 ....78 C2
Wharf Pl S14 ....97 A4
Wharf Rd
Nottingham NG7 .....268 A1
Pinxton NG16 ....160 B1
Whaley Bridge SK23 ..45 C4
Wharf The DE72 ......235 A1
Wharfdale Rd NG10 ...236 A3

Wharfedale Cl DE22 ...205 A2
Wharmby Ave NG19 ...135 B2
Wharncliffe Cl S43 ....9 C2
Wharncliffe Rd DE7 ...156 B1
Whatstandwell Sta DE4 ..167 A2
Wheal La SK17 ....107 B4
Wheatbridge Rd DE4 ..266 A3
Wheatbridge Ret Pk
.........................266 A3
Wheatcroft SK13 ......9 C2
Wheatcroft
Clay Cross S45 ....131 B1
Wingerworth S42 .....115 A2
Wheatcroft La DE4 ...115 A2
Wheatcroft Way DE21 ..205 B1
Wheatcroft La S45 ...136 C3
Wheatfield Way S42 ...94 C3
Wheatfields S43 ......47 B4
Wheathill Cl Calow S44 ..96 C2
Chesterfield S42 ....94 C3
Wheathill Gr DE23 ...231 A3
Wheathill La S41 .....96 B2
Wheatland Cl DE21 ...231 B1
Wheatlands DE11 ....256 A4
Wheatlands La DE45 ..91 B3
Wheatlands Rd
Burton u T DE15 .....254 C4
Wingerworth S42 .....114 C2
Wheatley Ave
Somercotes DE55 ....159 B1
Stoke-on-T ST4 ....269 A1
Wheatley Cl NG19 ...136 C1
Wheatley Gdns DE21 ..127 B1
Wheatley La DE15 ...248 B2
Wheatley Rd DE4 ....127 B1
Wheatsheaf Cl DE21 ..206 B1
Wheatsheaf La DE4 ...156 C1
Wheatsheaf Rd SK23 ..45 C3
Wheeldon Ave
Belper DE56 ....179 A2
Derby DE22 ....218 C4
Wheeldon Cres S44 ...96 B4
Wheeldon Way DE6 ...175 C2
Wheeler Gate NG1 ...268 B1
Wheelwright Way DE7 ..194 C1
Whenby Cl DE21 .....217 B1
Whernside Cl DE23 ...231 B3
Wheston Bank DE4 ...156 A3
Whetmorhurst Rd SK6 ..23 C2
Whieldon Cres S44 ...99 B4
Whieldon Rd St4 ....269 C1
Whilton Ct DE7 ......207 B4
Whilton Ct DE56 .....179 B2
Whinacre Cl S8 ....57 A3
Whinacre Pl S8 ....57 A3
Whinacre Wlk S8 ....57 A3
Whinbush Ave DE24 ..232 C3
Whinney Bank NG19 ..136 B2
Whinney Hill NG19 ...136 B2
Whistlestop Cl DE7 ...217 B2
Whiston St DE23 .....219 A1
Whitaker Gdns DE23 ..218 C1
Whitaker Mews ST14 ..196 C2
Whitaker Rd DE23 ....218 C1
Whitaker St DE23 ....219 A1
Whitburn Rd NG9 ....223 C2
Whitby Ave DE7 .....169 B1
White Edge Cl S40 ...95 B3
White Edge Dr DE45 ..91 C3
White Gate Rd HD9 ...3 A3
White Gates S45 .....131 A4
White Hart St NG18 ..268 B4
White Hart Yd NG16 ..191 C4
White Horse La DE55
.........................145 B4
White Knowle Cl SK17 ..85 B3
White Knowle Pk SK17 ..85 B3
White Knowle Rd SK17 ..85 B3
White La Sheffield S12 ..44 A2
Sheffield S12 ....44 C2
Shottle DE56 ....177 B2
Shottle S12 ....177 B2
White Leas Ave S42 ..132 A4
White Lion Sq DE7 ...207 B3
White Lion St S17 ....269 B3
White Lodge La DE45 ..91 C3
White Rd New Mills SK22 ..24 B1
Staveley S43 ....79 B2
White St DE22 ....218 C3
White Thorns Cl S8 ...57 A3
White Thorns Dr S8 ..57 A3
White Thorns View S8 ..57 A3
White Tor Rd DE4 ...143 B1
White's La DE55 .....170 A4
Whitebank Cl S41 ....266 C1
Whitecar La DE55,S45 ..145 B3
Whitecotes Cl S40 ...114 C4
Whitecotes La S40 ...114 C4
Whitecotes Prim Sch
S40 ....114 C4
Whitecotes S40 ......114 C4
Whitecross Rd SK6 ...23 B1
Whitecross Ave S42 ..69 B2
Whitecross Gdns DE24 ..218 C4
Whitecross St SK17 ..114 C4
Whitefield La
Ashover S45 ....129 A3
Chelmorton SK17 ....108 B4
Whitegates Way NG17 ..148 C1
Whitehall Terr SK23 ..34 B1
Whitehaven Cl DE7 ...194 B1
Whitehead Cl DE7 ...194 A1
Whitehead Dr NG16 ..182 B4
Whitehead St E S43 ..78 C1
Whitehough Head La
SK23 ....46 C4

Whitehouse Cl DE24 ..232 B2
Whitehouse Rise DE56 ..178 C3
Whitehouses S41 .....266 C1
Whitehurst St DE24 ...232 B4
Whitelea La DE4 .....144 A3
Whiteleas Rd SK23 ...45 B3
Whiteley Rd DE5 .....180 C4
Whiteley La
Dore S17 ....55 A4
DE4 ....153 C4
Whitely Cl ⬛ DE21 ..205 C4
Whitemoor Hall DE56 ..179 B3
Whitemoor La DE56 ...179 B3
Whites Cl DE55 ......179 A3
Whites Croft View S43 ..80 A3
Whitesmead Cl SK12 ..32 B3
Whiteway DE22 ......218 A3
Whitewell Gdns DE24 ..233 B3
Whitewells La DE56 ...178 A1
Whitewells Rd DE56 ...167 C1
Whitewood Way DE4 ..143 A2
Whitfield Ave SK13 ...17 B4
Whitfield Cross SK13 ..17 B4
Whitfield La DE45 ...124 C1
Whitfield Pk SK13 ...17 B4
Whiting Ave B NG9 ..223 C1
Whiting St S8 ....43 A3
Whitle Bank Rd SK22 ..24 A1
Whitle Rd SK22 ......24 A1
Whitley Way DE4 ....115 C1
Whitmore Ave S42 ...114 A4
Whitmore Rd DE21 ...219 C3
Whitstable Cl DE23 ..231 B4
Whittaker La DE21 ...191 B1
Whitting Mews S41 ...76 C1
Whitting Valley Rd S41 ..77 A1
Whittington Hill S41 ...77 A1
Whittington La S18 ...76 C3
Whittington Rd S40 ...77 C2
Whittington Way S41 ..77 A1
Whittlebury Dr DE23 ..230 C4
Whitwell Cl ❸ SK13 ..9 B1
Whitwell Fold ❶ SK13 ..9 B1
Whitwell Gn ❷ SK13 ..9 B1
Whitwell Prim Sch S80 ..82 A3
Whitwell Rd S80 .....63 A2
Whitwell Sta S80 ....82 A3
Whitworth Ave DE4 ...127 B2
Whitworth Hospl DE4 ..142 C4
Whitworth Rd
Chesterfield S41 ......96 A3
Darley Dale DE4 .....127 A2
Ilkeston DE7 ....208 C3
Northwood DE4 .....127 A2
Whysall St DE75 .....181 C1
Whyteleafe Gr DE21 ..206 A1
Wickersley Cl ❶ DE22 ..204 C1
Wickets The DE5 ....254 C4
Wickfield Cl S12 .....44 C3
Wickfield Dr S12 .....44 C2
Wickfield Gr S12 .....44 C2
Wickfield Rd S12 .....44 C3
Wickfield S12 ....44 C3
Wickins Pl S42 ....79 A2
Wicksteed Ct DE56 ...179 B3
Widdop Cl S13 ....44 B4
Widdop Croft S13 ....44 B4
Widdybank Cl DE22 ..204 B1
Wideshaft DE11 ......256 B2
Widmerpool St NG16 ..160 C2
Wigley Cl NG3 ....268 C2
Wigley Prim Sch S42 ..93 C2
Wigley Rd DE55 ......147 A3
Wigmore Cl DE3 .....217 B2
Wilberforce Rd NG19 ..135 B1
Wilbury Dr S12 ......44 A3
Wilcox Ave NG19 ...136 A3
Wilcox Rd DE7 ......219 B3
Wild Hill NG17 ......148 C4
Wild La DE55,S45 ...158 B2
Wild St DE1 ....218 B3
Wildaygreen La S18 ..75 A1
Wilderbrook La DE56 ..178 B1
Wilders Lea Ct DE56 ..179 A1
Wildersley Rd DE56 ..179 A1
Wildhay La DE6 .....183 B4
Wildpark La NG7 ....268 A2
Wildsmith St DE24 ..233 A4
Wilford Rd NG2 .....268 B1
Wilford St NG2 ......268 B1
Wilfred St ST4 ....269 A2
Wilhallow La NG16 ...171 C1
Wilkin Hill S18 ....75 C1
Wilkins Dr DE24 ....232 C4
Wilkinson Cl
Chesterfield S40 .....115 A3
Pleasley NG19 ....135 A3
Wilkinson Dr S43 ....97 A4
Will Shore's La NG16 ..181 B4
Willcock Rd DE7 ....194 A4
Willersley Cl ❸ S41 ..95 B4
Willersley Ho DE21 ..236 A3
Willersley La
Matlock DE4 ....155 B4
Matlock Bath DE4 ...155 B4
Willesden Ave DE22 ..217 C4
Willetts Rd DE21 ....220 A4
William Allitt Sch DE11 ..255 C2
William Ave NG16 ...182 C1
William Booth Inf Sch
NG2 ....268 C1
William Cres S43 ....59 B3
William Gilbert Endowed
Prim Sch DE56 ......190 C2

William Howitt Jun Sch
DE75 ....181 B1
William Levick Prim Sch
S18 ....56 B1
William Nadin Way
DE11 ....255 C2
William Newton Cl
DE11 ....241 A3
William Rd NG9 ......223 B4
William Rhodes Prim Sch
S40 ....266 C1
William Shrewsbury Prim
Sch DE13 ....240 C1
William St Belper DE56 ..178 C2
Chesterfield S41 ......96 A3
Derby DE1 ....218 C3
Eckington S21 ....59 B2
Long Eaton NG10 ...223 B1
William St N S41 .....76 C1
Williams Cl DE55 ...170 B3
Williamson Ave SK17 ..66 B1
Williamson Cres S43 ..45 B4
Williamson Rd S43 ...45 B4
Williamson St SK17 ..268 A4
Williamthorpe Cl S42 ..132 A4
Williamthorpe Ind Pk
S42 ....116 B1
Williamthorpe Rd S42 ..132 A4
Willington Prim Sch
DE65 ....242 A3
Willington Rd
Etwall DE65 ....229 B2
Findern DE65 ....242 B4
Repton DE65 ....242 A2
Willington Sta DE65 ..242 A3
Willn St DE23 ....218 C1
Willoughby Ave NG10 ..223 B2
Willoughby Cl DE72 ..235 C4
Willoughby Ct DE21 ..222 B2
Willoughby Ho DE7 ..256 B2
Willoughby St NG9 ...195 A1
Willow Ave
Long Eaton NG10 ...223 B1
Ripley DE5 ....180 B4
Shirebrook NG20 ....119 B3
Stapleford NG9 .....223 B3
Willow Brook Cl S18 ..228 B1
Willow Cl Alfreton DE55 ..159 A3
Aston-on-T DE72 ....246 A4
Creswell S80 ....81 C1
Derby DE72 ....204 C1
Heanor DE75 ....182 A2
Pilsley S45 ....132 B1
South Normanton DE55 ..160 A3
Stanley DE7 ....193 A1
Willow Croft DE24 ...233 B2
Willow Ct Ashbourne DE6 ..185 B4
Calow S44 ....97 A2
Swadlincote DE11 ...256 B2
Willow Dr
Chapel-en-le-F SK23 ..47 A3
Mastin Moor S43 ....79 B2
Swadlincote DE11 ...255 C4
Willow Farm Bsns Pk
DE74 ....247 A3
Willow Farm Ct DE55 ..230 B1
Willow Garth Rd S41 ..95 B4
Willow Gr Belper DE56 ..179 A1
Willington DE65 ......242 B3
Willow Ho DE21 ......219 B3
Willow Meadow Rd DE6 ..185 B4
Willow Park Way DE72 ..246 A4
Willow Pl DE71 ......254 C4
Willow Rd
Castle Donington DE74 ..247 A3
Kilamarsh S21 ......60 B3
Willow Rise DE21 ...223 B3
Willow Row DE1 .....267 A4
Willow St DE55 ......146 B1
Willow Tree La S18 ..57 A1
Willow Way DE4 ....142 C3
Willowbath La DE4 ...165 C4
Willowbrook Grange
DE73 ....233 A1
Willowcroft Rd DE21 ..220 C2
Willowdale Ave ST4 ..269 C1
Willowfields DE65 ...243 C1
Willowherb Cl DE24 ..231 C1
Willowpit La DE65 ...229 A3
Willows Ave DE55 ...159 B3
Willows Ct DE55 .....169 B1
Willows The
Hulland Ward DE6 ...175 C2
Pleasley NG19 ....135 A3
Willowsend Cl DE65 ..230 B1
Willridding La DE6 ...183 B4
Wilson Ave DE23 ....231 B4
Wilson Ave DE4 .....231 B4
Wilmans Wlk SK13 ...10 A4
Wilmington Ave DE24 ..233 A4
Wilmore Rd DE24 ...232 A3
Wilmorton Com Prim Sch
DE24 ....219 C1
Wilmorton Tertiary Coll
DE24 ....219 C1
Wilmot Ave Chellaston DE73 ..233 A1
Aston-on-T DE72 ....245 C3
Wilmot Dr DE7 ......192 C3
Wilmot Rd NG10 ....223 B2
Wilmot Rd Belper DE56 ..179 A2
Swadlincote DE11 ...256 A3
Wilmot St Derby DE1 ..267 B2
Heanor DE75 ....181 C1

Wilmot St *continued*
Ilkeston DE7 .....194 C1
Long Eaton NG10 .....236 A3
Matlock DE4 .....143 A3
Wilmslow Dr DE21 .....206 A1
Wilne Ave NG10 .....236 A2
Wilne Cl NG10 .....235 C2
Wilne La Breaston DE72 .....235 B2
Shardlow DE72 .....235 A1
Wilne Rd Draycott DE72 .....235 B3
Long Eaton NG10 .....235 C2
Wilshaw Cl S43 .....47 B3
Wilson Ave
Blackwell DE55 .....147 C1
Clowne S43 .....80 C3
Heanor DE75 .....181 A2
Wilson Cl Burnaston DE3 .....230 B4
Clay Cross S45 .....131 B1
Wilson Dr DE55 .....170 B4
Wilson La S44 .....117 A1
Wilson Pl S8 .....43 A4
Wilson Rd Derby DE21 .....219 C4
Dronfield S18 .....57 B2
Eastwood NG16 .....182 C1
Wilson Rise DE73 .....252 C3
Wilson St Alfreton DE55 .....159 A2
Derby DE1 .....267 B2
Dronfield S18 .....76 A4
Heanor NG16 .....135 B1
Pinxton NG16 .....160 B2
Wilson's Terr SK13 .....17 A4
Wilsthorpe Com Sch
NG10 .....223 A1
Wilsthorpe Rd
Breaston DE72 .....235 C4
Derby DE21 .....220 A4
Long Eaton NG10 .....236 A3
Wilton Cl DE24 .....231 B1
Wilton Pl DE7 .....194 C1
Wilton St DE7 .....194 C1
Wiltshire Ave NG16 .....171 A2
Wiltshire Dr S43 .....17 C4
Wiltshire Rd DE21 .....219 C4
Wimbledon Rd DE22 .....218 A4
Wimborne Cl S41 .....95 C4
Wimborne Ct DE73 .....233 A1
Wimpole Gdns DE22 .....218 A3
Wimsey Way DE55 .....159 A1
Wincanton Cl DE24 .....219 B1
Winchcombe Dr DE15 .....248 A1
Winchcombe Way DE21 .....205 C2
Winchester Cl S42 .....131 C3
Winchester Cres DE7 .....209 A4
Winchester Dr
Burton u T DE14 .....254 B4
Linton DE12 .....261 B3
Mansfield Woodhouse
NG19 .....136 B2
Swadlincote DE11 .....256 B3
Winchester Rd S41 .....95 C4
Windermere Ave
Dronfield S18 .....56 C1
Ilkeston DE7 .....208 B3
Windermere Cres DE22 .....204 C2
Windermere Dr DE21 .....220 C3
Windermere Gdns
NG10 .....223 A1
Windermere Ho ST16 .....269 B4
Windermere Rd
Chesterfield S41 .....95 B4
Clay Cross S45 .....131 A2
Long Eaton NG10 .....223 A1
Winders Cnr S43 .....80 A3
Windlea Rd DE55 .....170 B3
Windley Cres DE22 .....204 C1
Windley Dr DE7 .....194 B2
Windley La
Idridgehay DE56 .....176 C3
Turnditch DE56 .....177 A1
Windley DE56 .....189 C4
Windley DE56 .....192 B4
Windmill Cl Bolsover S44 .....99 A2
Castle Donington DE74 .....247 A1
Elvaston DE24 .....233 B2
Nottingham NG3 .....268 C2
Ockbrook DE72 .....221 B3
Uttoxeter ST14 .....210 A1
Windmill Dr ST14 .....224 C2
Windmill Greenway S20 .....59 B2
Windmill Hill La DE22 .....218 B3
Windmill La
Aldwarkley DE56 .....166 C3
Ashbourne DE6 .....173 B2
Belper DE56 .....179 A2
Eyam S32 .....71 B3
Mansfield NG18 .....268 C4
Nottingham NG2,NG3 .....268 C2
Snelston DE6 .....184 C1
Unstone S18 .....77 A3
Windmill Rd DE65 .....229 A2
Windmill Rise
Belper DE56 .....179 A3
Somercotes DE55 .....170 B4
South Normanton DE55 .....159 C3
Windmill St DE11 .....256 A1
Windmill View DE56 .....179 C4
Windrush Cl DE22 .....205 A3
Windrush Cl S43 .....96 C4
Windses S12 .....53 B1
Windsmoor Rd NG16 .....182 B4
Windsor Ave Derby DE23 .....231 A4
Melbourne DE73 .....252 A4
Windsor Cl
Ashbourne DE6 .....173 B2

Windsor Cl *continued*
Borrowash DE72 .....221 B1
Windsor Pl Derby DE22 .....218 A3
 4 Chesterfield S40 .....95 B1
Heanor DE75 .....181 C2
Swadlincote DE11 .....256 A3
Swanwick DE55 .....170 A4
Trowell NG9 .....209 A3
Windsor Cres
Ilkeston DE7 .....208 C2
Stapleford NG9 .....223 C4
Windsor Ct Derby DE3 .....217 B1
Long Eaton NG10 .....236 C4
Sandiacre NG10 .....223 A2
West Hallam DE7 .....207 B4
Windsor Dr Derby DE21 .....221 A3
Dronfield S18 .....56 B1
Windsor Gn NG18 .....268 A3
Windsor Park Rd SK17 .....85 B4
Windsor Rd Buxton SK17 .....85 B4
Linton DE12 .....261 B3
Mansfield NG18 .....268 C3
Uttoxeter ST14 .....210 A1
Windsor St NG9 .....223 C4
Windsor Wlk S41 .....96 A3
Windy Fields Rd S42 .....113 B4
Windy House La S12 .....44 A4
Windy La DE21 .....191 B1
Windyridge SK17 .....121 A3
Winfield Gr SK6 .....15 A1
Wingerworth Ave S8 .....56 B4
Wingerworth Cotts S42 .....115 C2
Wingerworth Park Rd
DE21 .....220 C3
Wingerworth St S42 .....115 C2
Wingfield Cl S18 .....56 B1
Wingfield Cres S12 .....44 B3
Wingfield Dr Derby DE21 .....205 C1
Ilkeston DE7 .....194 B2
Wingfield Gr SK13 .....17 C4
Wingfield Rd
Alfreton DE55 .....158 C2
Tupton S42 .....131 B4
Wingfield View S45 .....131 C2
Winhill Rd SK22 .....24 B1
Winkburn Rd NG18 .....
Winn La DE6 .....174 C4
Winnat Pl S43 .....97 B4
Winnats S33 .....37 C1
Winnats Cl
Chesterfield S40 .....95 B3
Glossop SK13 .....17 C4
Winney Hill S26 .....61 C2
Winney La S26 .....61 C2
Winnington Rd SK6 .....23 A4
Winshill Inf Sch DE15 .....248 A2
Winslow Ave SK14 .....9 A1
Winster Ave Derby DE21 .....220 B3
Winster CE Prim Sch
DE4 .....141 B3
Winster Cl Belper DE56 .....179 A3
Clay Cross S42 .....131 A3
Winster Ct S41 .....96 A3
Winster Gn DE11 .....255 C3
Winster Gr SK17 .....85 C4
Winster La DE4 .....140 C4
Winster Market Ho*
DE4 .....141 B3
Winster Mews SK13 .....17 C4
Winster Rd Derby DE21 .....205 C1
Staveley S43 .....97 B4
Winster Sq SK17 .....85 C4
Winster Way NG10 .....235 C3
Winston Cl NG9 .....223 C3
Winter Closes NG16 .....171 C1
Winterbourne Dr NG9 .....209 C1
Wintercroft La DE6 .....161 C1
Winterbourne Dr DE73 .....230 C3
Winton Sq S14 .....269 C2
Wintonfield St S14 .....269 C2
Wire La S55 .....148 A2
Wirksmoor Rd SK22 .....33 A4
Wirksworth CE Inf Sch
DE4 .....165 C4
Wirksworth Hall Gdns
DE4 .....165 C4
Wirksworth Ind Ctr DE4 .....154 C2
Wirksworth Inf Sch
DE4 .....154 C1
Wirksworth Jun Sch
DE4 .....155 A1
Wirksworth Rd
Duffield DE56 .....190 A2
Holloway DE4 .....156 A1
Idridgehay DE56 .....176 C3
Ilkeston DE7 .....208 B2
Kirk Ireton DE6 .....165 A1
Shottle DE56 .....177 B2
Wisbech Cl S40 .....114 C4
Wisgreaves Rd DE24 .....232 C4
Wishing Stone Way
DE4 .....143 C3
Witham Cl
Chesterfield S41 .....96 B3
Hilton DE65 .....228 C1
Witham St S41 .....95 B2
Witham Dr DE23 .....231 B3
Witney Cl DE24 .....232 B4
Witney St S8 .....43 A4
Wittering Cl NG10 .....236 C3
Witton Cl DE24 .....231 B2
Woburn Cl
Blackwell DE55 .....147 C1
Swanwick DE55 .....169 C4
Woburn Cotts DE4 .....143 A4
Woburn Croft NG10 .....223 A2
Woburn Ct DE55 .....147 C1

Woburn La NG19 .....135 B2
Woburn Pl Derby DE22 .....218 A3
Mansfield NG19 .....135 B2
Woburn Rd NG19 .....135 B2
Wolds Rd DE4 .....143 B3
Wolds Rise DE4 .....143 B4
Wolfa St DE22 .....218 C2
Wolfcote Cl S45 .....131 B1
Wolfe Cl S40 .....95 B1
Wolfe St S14 .....221 A4
Wolfscote Dale DE11 .....255 C1
Wollaton Ave S17 .....56 A3
Wollaton Dr S7 .....56 A3
Wollaton Rd DE21 .....219 C4
Sheffield S17 .....56 A3
Wollaton Rd S DE21 .....205 C1
Wollaton St NG1 .....268 A2
Wollen Cl S80 .....81 C1
Wolseley Rd S8 .....43 A4
Wolverhampton Rd
ST17 .....269 B3
Wolverley Grange DE24 .....233 B3
Wood Ave Creswell S80 .....81 B1
Sandiacre NG10 .....223 A3
Wood Cl S42 .....114 B2
Wood Croft DE23 .....231 B4
Wood End DE4 .....156 A3
Wood End Rd DE4 .....181 C1
Wood Farm La DE11 .....256 C2
Wood Gdns SK22 .....25 B2
Wood La Belper DE56 .....190 C4
Creswell S80 .....100 B4
Hanbury DE13 .....238 A2
Hayfield SK22 .....25 B2
Holloway DE4 .....144 A1
Horsley Woodhouse DE7 .....192 B3
Ible DE4 .....153 C3
Idridgehay DE6,DE56 .....176 C4
Kniveton DE6 .....163 A1
Market Warsop NG20 .....120 C4
Pleasley NG20 .....119 C1
Ripley DE5 .....169 A2
Scarcliffe S44 .....118 C3
Shirebrook NG20 .....119 C1
Swadlincote DE11 .....256 A4
Wood Nook Cl NG16 .....171 C3
Wood Rd
Derby, Chaddesden DE21 .....220 A4
Derby, Oakwood DE21 .....205 C1
Derby, Spondon DE21 .....220 A3
Wood St Alfreton DE55 .....159 B3
Codnor DE5 .....181 A4
Derby DE1 .....267 C4
Eastwood NG16 .....182 C2
Glossop SK13 .....17 B4
Hollingworth SK14 .....9 B3
Ilkeston DE7 .....194 C1
Mansfield NG18 .....268 B4
New Mills SK22 .....33 A4
Nottingham NG7 .....268 A2
Ripley DE5 .....169 B1
Somercotes DE55 .....170 B4
Swadlincote DE11 .....256 A1
Wirksworth DE4 .....154 C1
Wood St N S45 .....131 B3
Wood View S21 .....79 A4
Woodale Cl DE23 .....230 C3
Woodall La S26 .....61 B3
Woodall Rd S21 .....
Woodbeck Ct DE7 .....206 A1
Woodberry Ave ST4 .....269 A1
Woodberry Cl ST4 .....269 A1
Woodbine Terr SK23 .....47 A3
Woodbine Villas DE4 .....253 C3
Woodborough Rd
Mansfield NG19 .....135 C1
Nottingham NG3 .....268 B2
Woodbourne Rd SK22 .....33 A3
Woodbridge Cl DE73 .....232 C1
Woodbridge Jun Sch
DE55 .....159 A2
Woodbridge Rise DE55 .....114 A4
Woodbrook S23 .....45 C4
Woodchester Dr DE24 .....233 B3
Woodcock Gr SK13 .....10 C1
Woodcock Rd S43 .....11 A1
Woodcock Sq DE3 .....230 B4
Woodcote Way DE23 .....231 A4
Woodfall La DE6 .....189 C2
Woodfield Cl S43 .....9 C3
Woodfield Dr Ripley DE5 .....181 A4
Swadlincote DE11 .....256 B3
Woodfield Rd
Pinxton NG16 .....160 B2
South Normanton DE55 .....159 C2
Woodford Rd DE22 .....218 A4
Woodford Way S42 .....78 A2
Woodgate Ct S42 .....268 C2
Woodgate Dr DE73 .....233 A1
Woodhall Dr DE23 .....230 C4
Woodhead La S45 .....130 B1
Woodhead Rd
Glossop SK13 .....10 B3
Glossop, Tintwistle SK13 .....10 A4
Holme HD7 .....C3
Sheffield S2 .....43 A4
Woodhouse Ct NG19 .....136 B1
Woodhouse La
Barlborough S43 .....79 C3
Bolsover S44 .....98 C2
Darley Dale DE4 .....126 C4
Mastin Moor S43 .....79 B3
Scropton DE6 .....226 C4
South Normanton DE55 .....159 C3
Winster DE4 .....141 B3

Woodhouse Rd
Kilburn DE56,DE21 .....192 A4
Mansfield NG18 .....268 B4
Sheffield S12 .....44 A3
Woodhouse St
Nottingham NG3 .....268 C2
Stoke-on-T ST4 .....269 B1
Swadlincote DE11 .....256 B2
Woodhouse West Prim Sch
S13 .....44 C4
Woodhurst Cl DE21 .....219 B4
Woodland Ave
Borrowash DE72 .....221 B1
Ilkeston DE7 .....194 B2
Sutton in a NG17 .....148 C2
Woodland Dr
Scropton DE6 .....226 B2
Sheffield S12 .....44 A1
Woodland Gr
Barlborough S43 .....80 A3
Clowne S43 .....81 A2
Mansfield Woodhouse
NG19 .....136 B2
Woodland Pl S17 .....55 C3
Woodland Rd
Derby DE22 .....218 C4
Sheffield S8 .....43 A2
Swadlincote DE15 .....255 A2
Woodland View Dore S17 .....56 A4
Sheffield S12 .....44 A1
Whaley Bridge SK23 .....45 C1
Whaley Thorns NG20 .....101 A2
Woodland Views S41 .....224 C1
Woodland Way
Clay Cross S42 .....131 A3
Eastwood NG16 .....182 C1
Woodland Wlk S40 .....94 C3
Woodlands Brimington S43 .....96 B4
Great Longstone DE45 .....89 C2
Wirksworth DE4 .....165 C4
Woodlands Ave
Breaston DE72 .....235 C4
Derby DE24 .....232 C2
Woodlands Brow DE56 .....173 B2
Woodlands Cl
Glossop SK13 .....9 C3
Little Eaton DE21 .....205 A4
Melbourne DE73 .....252 A4
Thorpe DE6 .....161 B1
Woodlands Com Sch
DE22 .....204 B2
Woodlands Dr DE21 .....262 A2
Woodlands Gr S42 .....131 A3
Woodlands La
Derby DE73 .....245 A4
Quarndon DE22 .....204 B3
Woodlands Rd
Chapel-en-le-F SK23 .....47 A2
Derby DE22 .....204 C3
High Lane SK12 .....32 A3
New Mills SK22 .....33 A4
Overseal DE12 .....262 A2
Woodlands The
Branston DE13 .....253 A4
Mansfield NG19 .....136 A1
Melbourne DE73 .....252 A4
Whaley Thorns NG20 .....101 A2
Woodlands Yd DE73 .....245 A4
Woodlea Gr DE21 .....205 B4
Woodlea Rd S43 .....17 A4
Woodleigh Cl S40 .....95 A2
Woodmans Croft DE65 .....227 B1
Woodmere Dr S41 .....77 B2
Woodminton Dr DE73 .....232 C2
Woodnook Cl S42 .....95 A2
Woodnook La S42 .....94 C2
Woodnook Way S42 .....94 C2
Woodpecker Hill DE7 .....208 A1
Woodrising Cl DE21 .....206 A2
Woodroffe Wlk DE23 .....231 C4
Woodrove Ave S13 .....44 A4
Woodrove Cl S13 .....44 A4
Woods La
Burton u T, Stapenhill
DE15 .....254 C4
Burton u T, Stapenhill
DE15 .....254 C4
Derby DE22 .....267 A1
Woods Mdw DE72 .....233 B3
Woodseats La S18 .....16 A3
Woodseats La S13 .....C4
Woodside Buxton SK17 .....85 B4
Eastwood NG16 .....182 C2
Horsley DE7 .....192 B2
Woodside Ave
Holmesfield S18 .....75 A4
Killamarsh S21 .....60 C4
Ripley DE5 .....180 B4
Woodside Cl
Bakewell DE45 .....109 B3
Chesterfield S40 .....95 A2
Woodside Cres
Ilkeston DE7 .....194 B3
Long Eaton NG10 .....236 A4
Woodside Dr
Bakewell DE45 .....109 B3
Derby DE22 .....205 A2
Shirland DE5 .....146 B4
Woodside Rd
Sandiacre NG10 .....223 A3
Shirebrook NG20 .....119 C3
Woodside St SK22 .....33 A3
Woodside View S45 .....75 A4
Woodsome Pk S42 .....116 B1
Woodsorrel Dr DE21 .....206 A2
Woodstock Cl DE22 .....204 B3

Woodstock Ct 5 S41 .....
Woodstock Dr S41 .....
Woodstock Rd NG9 .....
Woodstock Rise S41 .....
Woodthorpe Ave
Clay Cross S45 .....
Derby, Allenton DE24 .....
Derby, Chaddesden DE21 .....
Woodthorpe CE Prim Sch
S43 .....
Woodthorpe Cl
Bolsover S44 .....
Sheffield S44 .....
Woodthorpe Com Prim Sch
S13 .....
Woodthorpe Cres S13 .....
Woodthorpe Rd
Bolsover S44 .....
Sheffield S13 .....
Woodvale Cl S40 .....
Woodview Cl S42 .....
Woodview Rd DE11 .....
Woodville CE Jun Sch
DE11 .....
Woodville Rd
Hartshorne DE11 .....
Overseal DE12 .....
Woodward Way DE11 .....
Woodward's PH DE11 .....
Woodwards Cl DE72 .....
Woodyard La DE65 .....
Woolaton La S17 .....
Wooley Cl S42 .....
Woolscroft Cl DE7 .....
Wooley Bridge Rd SK13 .....
Woolley Cl SK14 .....
Wooley La SK14 .....
Woolley Mill La SK13 .....
Woolley Rd DE4 .....
Woolley Yd DE4 .....
Woolpack La NG1 .....
Woolrych St DE23 .....
Woolsthorpe Cres S20 .....
Woosnam Cl DE14 .....
Worcester Ave NG19 .....
Worcester Cres DE21 .....
Worcester Gr SK13 .....
Worcester Mews DE7 .....
Worcester Rd DE15 .....
Wordsworth Ave
Derby DE24 .....
Mansfield Woodhouse
NG19 .....
Swadlincote DE11 .....
Wordsworth Dr DE24 .....
Wordsworth Pl S18 .....
Wordsworth Rd
Awsworth NG16 195
Chesterfield S41 95
Works La S43 97
Worksop Rd S43 78
Worksop Sch
Mastin Moor S43 79
Nottingham NG3 268
Thorpe Salvin S80 62
Whitwell S80 .....
Worrall Ave NG16 223
Worthington La DE73 252
Wortley Ave NG9 209
Wortley Cl DE7 209
Wortley Ct S33 .....
Wragley Way DE24 231
Wray Cl NG3 268
Wreakes La S18 56
Wren Cl DE11 256
Wren Nest Rd SK13 10
Wren Nest Terr SK13 10
Wren Park Cl
Belper DE56 178
Chesterfield S40 114
Finders DE65 230
Sheffield S12 58
Wren Park Prim Sch
DE3 218
Wren Way DE3 230
Wrenpark Rd S42 114
Wretham Cl DE3 230
Wright Ave DE5 169
Wright St DE5 181
Wrexham Cl DE24 232
Wulfric Cl S2 43
Wulfric Pl S2 43
Wulfric Rd Eckington S21 59
Sheffield, Deep Pit S2 43
Sheffield, Manor Estate S2 44
Wyaston Cl DE22 204
Wyaston Gdns DE6 185
Wyaston Rd DE6 185
Wyatts Way DE5 169
Wybersley Rd SK6 32
Wychwood Dr NG9 209
Wycliffe Rd DE55 159
Wycombe Grange NG19 136
Wye Bank DE45 109
Wye Bank Gr DE45 109
Wye Croft Ct DE45 109
Wye Dale DE11 255
Wye Gr SK17 85
Wye Head Cl SK17 84
Wye St Buxton SK17 85
Wye Terr DE4 223
Wyedale Cl
Bakewell DE45 109
Buxton SK17 85
Wyedale Cres DE45 109

...ale Ct **S** S41 ....95 C4
...ale Dr DE45 ....109 C2
...ale View DE45 ....109 C2
...ands Ci SK17 ....84 C4
...ing Brook Dr S10 ....42 A4
...l The S21 ....79 B4
...ale Dr DE7 ....208 B3
...tham Cres DE15 ....248 B2
...tham St DE24 ....233 A4
...on Ave DE24 ....232 C4
...tor Ave DE4 ....141 B3
...ward Cl DE7 ....194 B2
...ll Cl NG19 ....135 C1
...an Ct DE65 ....242 B1
...on Brook DE65 ....228 B1
...burn Rd S41 ....95 B4
...er La DE56 ....178 C3
...ern Ave NG10 ....236 B3
...ern Cl
...ern Bsns Pk DE21 ....220 A2
...rn Cl
...wood NG16 ....195 A4
...lock DE4 ....143 A3
...ern Gdns S17 ....55 C3
...ern Way DE21 ....220 A2
...ernside DE21 ....219 C2

Y

Yard Cl DE11 ....256 A2
Yardley Cl DE55 ....169 C4
Yardley Way DE56 ....179 B2
Yarncliff Cl S40 ....95 B3
Yarrow Cl DE24 ....231 C1
Yarwell Cl DE21 ....205 B1
Yates Ave DE72 ....246 A4
Yates Rd SK22 ....33 B4
Yates St DE23 ....219 A1
Yeaman St ST4 ....269 B1
Yeardsley Ave SK23 ....33 B2
Yeardsley Gn SK23 ....45 B4
Yeardsley La SK23 ....33 B2
Yeld Cl DE45 ....109 B2
Yeld Rd DE45 ....109 B3
Yeld The DE45 ....109 B3
Yeldersley Cl S40 ....95 A3
Yeldersley La
  Brailsford DE6 ....187 A1
  Osmaston DE6 ....186 C3
Yelt La DE6 ....224 B4
Yeoman Park Specl Sch
  NG19 ....136 B2

Yeoman St DE4 ....142 B1
Yeovil Cl DE24 ....233 B4
Yerley Hill DE6 ....172 B3
Yew Tree Ave DE72 ....221 B3
Yew Tree Cl Ashover S45 ....129 C2
  Darley Dale DE4 ....127 A2
Yew Tree Cotts DE72 ....222 C2
Yew Tree Dr
  Chesterfield S40 ....114 A4
  Clay Cross S42 ....131 A3
  Killamarsh S21 ....60 B3
  Shirebrook NG20 ....119 B3
  Sutton in A NG17 ....148 C1
Yew Tree Gdns DE12 ....260 B3
Yew Tree Hill DE4 ....156 A3
Yew Tree La Bradley DE6 ....186 C4
  Elvaston DE72 ....233 C2
Yew Tree Rd
  Hatton DE65 ....227 B1
  Rosliston DE12 ....260 B3
  Swadlincote DE11 ....255 C4
Yewdale Gr DE21 ....206 B2
Yews Cl DE73 ....233 A1
Yewtree Cl DE24 ....233 B4
Yewtree Cres DE15 ....254 C4
Yokecliffe Ave DE4 ....165 C4

Yokecliffe Cres DE4 ....165 C4
Yokecliffe Dr DE4 ....165 C4
Yokecliffe Hill DE4 ....165 C4
York Ave Sandiacre NG10 ....223 A3
  Westwood NG16 ....171 A2
York Cl DE11 ....256 B3
York Cres S44 ....117 C1
York Pl
  North Wingfield S42 ....132 A4
  Shireaks S81 ....63 C4
York Rd Derby DE21 ....219 C4
  Long Eaton NG10 ....223 B1
  Shirebrook NG20 ....119 C2
  Swadlincote DE11 ....256 A1
York St Chesterfield S41 ....115 B4
  Derby DE1 ....218 C3
  Glossop SK13 ....10 C1
  Mansfield NG18 ....268 B3
  Nottingham NG1 ....268 B2
York Terr Glossop SK13 ....17 B4
  Pinxton NG16 ....160 B1
Yorke St NG19 ....136 A1
Yorkshire Way SK13 ....17 C4
Youlgreave Cl DE21 ....205 C1
Youlgreave Cres SK13 ....9 B1
Youlgreave Dr S12 ....44 B3

Youlgreave YH* DE45 ....125 B3
Young St DE23 ....218 C1
Younger St ST4 ....269 C1
Yoxall Ave ST4 ....269 A2
Ypres Rd DE22 ....204 B1

Z

Zetland Cres DE24 ....231 B1

NH	NJ	NK
NN	NO	NP
NS	NT	NU
NX	NY	NZ
SC	SD	SE	TA
SH	SJ	SK	TF	TG
SN	SO	SP	TL	TM
SS	ST	SU	TQ	TR
SX	SY	SZ	TV

Any feature in this atlas can be given a unique reference to help you find the same feature on other Ordnance Survey maps of the area, or to help someone else locate you if they do not have a Street Atlas.

The grid squares in this atlas match the Ordnance Survey National Grid and are at 1 kilometre intervals. The small figures at the bottom and sides of every other grid line are the National Grid kilometre values (**00** to **99** km) and are repeated across the country every 100 km (see left).

To give a unique National Grid reference you need to locate where in the country you are. The country is divided into 100 km squares with each square given a unique two-letter reference. Use the administrative map to determine in which 100 km square a particular page of this atlas falls.

The bold letters and numbers between each grid line (**A** to **C**, **1** to **4**) are for use within a specific Street Atlas only, and when used with the page number, are a convenient way of referencing these grid squares.

Example *The railway bridge over DARLEY GREEN RD in grid square A1*

Step 1: Identify the two-letter reference, in this example the page is in **SP**

Step 2: Identify the 1 km square in which the railway bridge falls. Use the figures in the southwest corner of this square: Eastings **17**, Northings **74**. This gives a unique reference: **SP 17 74**, accurate to 1 km.

Step 3: To give a more precise reference accurate to 100 m you need to estimate how many tenths along and how many tenths up this 1 km square the feature is. This makes the bridge about **8** tenths along and about **1** tenth up from the southwest corner.

This gives a unique reference: **SP 178 741**, accurate to 100 m.

Eastings (read from left to right along the bottom) come before Northings (read from bottom to top). If you have trouble remembering say to yourself "Along the hall, THEN up the stairs"!

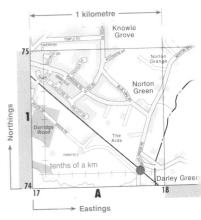

me and Address	Telephone	Page	Grid reference

Addresses

Name and Address	Telephone	Page	Grid reference

Addresses

ame and Address	Telephone	Page	Grid reference

Street Atlases from Philip's

Philip's publish an extensive range of regional a
local street atlases which are ideal for motoring,
business and leisure use. They are widely used b
the emergency services and local authorities
throughout Britain.

Key features include:

◆ Superb county-wide mapping at an extra-large scale of
3½ inches to 1 mile, or 2½ inches to 1 mile in pocket edit

◆ Complete urban and rural coverage, detailing every nam
street in town and country

◆ Each atlas available in two handy sizes – standard spiral
and pocket paperback

'The mapping is very clear... great in scope and value'

★★★★ BEST BUY   AUTO EXPRESS

1 Bedfordshire
2 Berkshire
3 Birmingham and
  West Midlands
4 Bristol and Bath
5 Buckinghamshire
6 Cambridgeshire
7 Cardiff, Swansea
  and The Valleys
8 Cheshire
9 Cornwall
10 Derbyshire
11 Devon
12 Dorset
13 County Durham
  and Teesside
14 Edinburgh and East
  Central Scotland

15 North Essex
16 South Essex
17 Glasgow and
  Central Scotlo
18 Gloucestershi
19 North Hamps
20 South Hampsh
21 Hertfordshire
22 East Kent
23 West Kent
24 Lancashire
25 Leicestershire
  and Rutland
26 Lincolnshire
27 London
28 Greater Manc
29 Merseyside
30 Norfolk
31 Northamptons
32 Nottinghamsh
33 Oxfordshire
34 Shropshire
35 Somerset
36 Staffordshire
37 Suffolk
38 Surrey
39 East Sussex
40 West Sussex
41 Tyne and Wec
  Northumberla
42 Warwickshire
43 Worcestershire
44 Wiltshire and S
45 East Yorkshire
  and Northern
  Lincolnshire
46 North Yorkshi
47 South Yorkshir
48 West Yorkshire

How to order

The Philip's range of street atlases is
available from good retailers or
directly from the publisher by phoning
01903 828503